UNITED STATES 1840-1850

///////// DISPUTED TERRITORY
/////////// DIVISION BETWEEN SLAVE AND FREE STATES

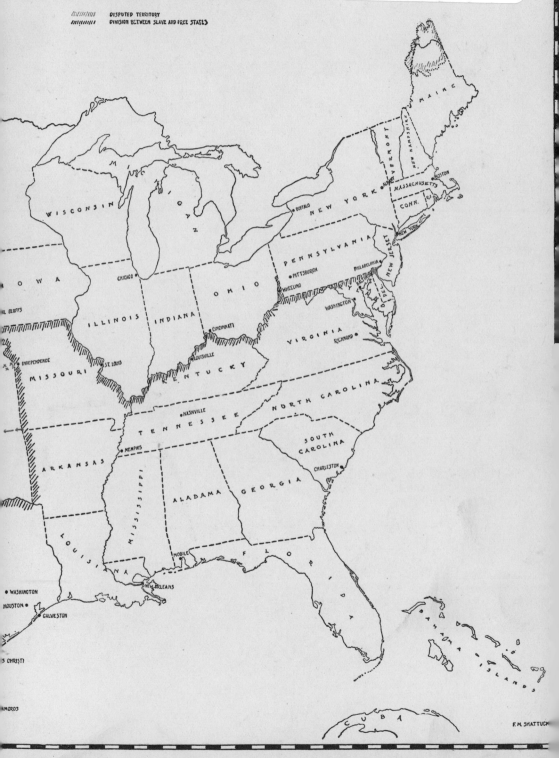

F.M. SHATTUCK

JOHN C. CALHOUN
Sectionalist, 1840-1850

JOHN C. CALHOUN, ABOUT 1848

JOHN C. CALHOUN

SECTIONALIST, 1840-1850

by

Charles M. Wiltse

THE BOBBS-MERRILL COMPANY, INC.

Publishers

INDIANAPOLIS   NEW YORK

First Edition

TABLE OF CONTENTS

TABLE OF CONTENTS—*Continued*

LIST OF ILLUSTRATIONS

LIST OF ILLUSTRATIONS—*Continued*

JOHN C. CALHOUN
Sectionalist, 1840-1850

CHAPTER I

THE CAMPAIGN OF 1840

1

BALTIMORE was in the grip of sheer madness, but it was madness shared with two thirds of the United States. In the Maryland metropolis a hundred thousand people—equivalent to the entire population of the city—lined the streets, cheering, singing, waving handkerchiefs and banners, stamping and jostling as an endless line of marchers moved slowly toward the Canton race track on the edge of town. Every state in the Union had a place in the procession, with separate displays for counties and Congressional districts. Each group had its own particular form of lunacy, but a common theme united them all: log cabins, from tiny birdhouse size mounted on poles to huge full-scale affairs drawn by teams of horses. With the cabins went barrels of hard cider, real or symbolic, a coonskin or two nailed to the rough bark-covered walls, and a latch string ostentatiously out. Each delegation carried identifying banners, and others conspicuously displaying the names of Harrison and Tyler.[1]

The date was the fourth of May 1840 and the occasion was a national convention of Whig young men, called to ratify the party nominations of five months earlier. For President of the United States the Whigs had chosen not the brilliant, ambitious, loved and hated Henry Clay, but General William Henry Harrison of Ohio, veteran of the War of 1812 and now gray, placid, and uncommitted at sixty-seven. On the ticket for the second office was lanky, sandy-haired John Tyler who had served in the Senate as a State Rights Democrat from Virginia until Jackson's uncompromising nationalism drove him to the opposition in 1832. At fifty he was a State Rights Democrat still, and it was because rather than in spite of that fact that his name was now coupled with that of the victor of Tippecanoe in the most famous of all American campaign slogans.[2]

The young Whigs had chosen the place and time of their meeting with audacity and skill. At noon the following day the Democrats

11

were scheduled to gather in the same city to endorse the hapless Martin Van Buren for another four years in the White House. Torn by a decade of internal strife, with public confidence impaired by their failure to make headway against a depression already three years old, the Democrats were in no position to match the enthusiasm of their rivals.

The Whig contingent was led by Clay and heavy-set, beetle-browed Daniel Webster, tacitly recognized as rivals for control of the administration, should Harrison be successful, and as competitors for the succession after four years. In point of fame, services, and real ability Clay was the natural leader of his party, but even the adulation of the crowd, as necessary to his well-being as water or air, was hardly enough to console him for the desertion of his followers in the nominating convention. Webster was the accepted spokesman for the industrial and financial interests that expected to rise with the Whigs, and he expected them in turn to remember their champion. The two undeclared rivals rode in open carriages at the head of the great Whig parade, submerged for the moment in a popular frenzy that had nothing to do with them.

After the parade there was an orgy of speechmaking that lasted on into the night and was resumed the next day. Clay and Webster each took a turn on the platform. There was thunderous applause for young Caleb Cushing of Massachusetts, for eloquent and volatile William C. Preston of South Carolina, for Clay's Senate colleague and personal spokesman, John J. Crittenden of Kentucky, and for fiery young Henry A. Wise of Virginia in whose Accomac district both Harrison and Tyler had first drawn breath. There were men like Senator Samuel Southard of New Jersey and Representative John Sergeant of Pennsylvania, whose careers went back to the less turbulent times of James Monroe; and others who would inherit the future like Buffalo's able Congressman, Millard Fillmore. The speeches varied as widely as the men who made them, but the theme was always the same: the days of Democratic "tyranny" and "misrule" were numbered, the country needed a change, it was time that honest men filled public office, hurrah for Tip and Ty!

The Whigs were still whooping in the streets and drinking in the taverns when the Democratic national convention met in the Music Hall at noon on May 5. There was no matching the exuberant confidence of the Whig young men, but it might in part be neutralized by dignity, order, and intelligent discussion of public issues. The procedure was as deliberate and precise as a meeting of the Senate and far less less exciting, for there was no room for argument here and no shadow of doubt as to the outcome. When the preliminaries were out of the way Martin Van Buren would be nominated unanimously for re-election as President of the United States. Even those delegates who most disliked the soft-spoken little New Yorker would go along with the majority. The party could not repudiate its President without disavowing his program, and it was Van Buren's program alone that had brought if not harmony at least a cessation of hostilities among warring Democratic factions. A positive platform that looked toward economic recovery and sectional peace was all they had to offer to an electorate that would rather sing and march and drink hard cider than wrestle with the crucial problems of the day.[3]

Yet beneath the surface the old cleavage was still there. Virginia and South Carolina sent no delegates; but the most conspicuous figure in the whole affair was the tall, angular person of John Caldwell Calhoun, senior Senator from the latter state, who was not present either in spirit or in flesh.

2

Calhoun's position in national affairs was unique and powerful. A man of tremendous energy, strong and original mind, magnetic personality, and utter sincerity, he had run the political gamut over the past dozen years and had emerged seemingly the stronger for it. The ambition for the Presidency that had first flamed in him two decades earlier was now tempered and controlled, subordinated to a political program which was itself derived from a carefully thought-out philosophy of government.

Though Vice President of the United States at the time, he had gone into opposition when convinced that Andrew Jackson did not share his political faith, and he had risked his political life—perhaps his mortal life as well—in the ensuing battle. Throughout Jackson's second term and the first years of Van Buren's regime Calhoun had stood alone, voting now with one party, now with the other, as individual measures met or failed the test of his own principles. Gradually a small but talented party had formed around him and at the end of 1839, with Congress almost evenly balanced between Whigs and Democrats, a Calhoun partisan was chosen Speaker of the House. Van Buren, in his third annual message, made the Calhoun program his own, and on New Year's Day 1840, for the first time in ten years, the South Carolina Senator attended a White House levee. A few days later he assumed as if by right the leadership of the administration forces, and privately advised his friends to support the Van Buren ticket.

The Democracy had been driven almost inevitably to Calhoun's intellectual position by the nature of the Whig program and by the necessities inherent in the geographical distribution of its own strength. The Whigs by 1840 were recognized, even among themselves, as the party of property, of business, of economic stability. Their leaders still vehemently denied any kinship with the Federalists of Hamilton's time, but in fundamental beliefs the lineage was direct. Like the Hamiltonians of half a century earlier, the Whigs of 1840 believed in fostering enterprise and in binding to the support of the government through positive economic benefits the propertied and the well-to-do. They believed, therefore, in tariffs, in central banking, in public works, which is to say they believed that industry should be subsidized, that the credit of the government should be at the disposal of the business community, and that such indispensable aids to commerce as highways, canals, railroads, lighthouses and harbor improvements should be constructed at the public expense. They required accordingly a central government strong enough to do all these things, and as a necessary corollary an interpretation of the Constitution that would give them such a government. Webster, building on the foundations provided by John Marshall, had set forth just such a Constitutional theory in his famous debate with Hayne in 1830; and Jackson, who by training, affiliations, and professed beliefs should have been on the other side, confirmed the theory in his Proclamation against the Nullifiers in 1832.

It was then that Calhoun and many other Southern leaders had left the Jackson party. The livelihood of those they represented was made by agriculture, and that in itself would have been enough. But they produced a crop that depended on a foreign market and produced it with a system of labor disapproved by a growing body of their fellow citizens. They believed with a sincerity equal to that of their Whig opponents that to concede such an interpretation of the

Constitution as Webster and Jackson had laid down would be to destroy them utterly. To subsidize industry was to force down the price of cotton; but to concede to the general government the power to subsidize industry was to concede also the power to emancipate the slaves. So Calhoun and his followers clung tenaciously and with spectacular skill to a constitutional theory that rested the actual sovereignty with the states and yielded to the Federal Government only such powers as had been specifically delegated to it.

Jackson had courted both sides, sustaining the tariff and the power to pass a tariff for the nationalists, and overthrowing in the interest of state sovereignty the concept of federally financed public works. At the same time he destroyed the national bank for the small farmers of the growing West who fancied, as Western farmers have always fancied, that inflation was to their advantage. Jackson's intention was probably only to bind the West to himself and to use it as a political buffer between the two older sections, but he succeeded in splitting the Democratic party from top to bottom. For the basic question, and in the end that on which all others rested, was the question of power. The general government either did or did not possess what would amount to sovereign powers. The Whigs took the affirmative and so the Democrats were compelled to disagree, but the logic of their own denial forced them into the State Rights camp.

Van Buren came unwillingly, and the most potent of his partisans did not come at all. Senator Thomas Hart Benton of Missouri had never deviated from the Jacksonian, or Locofoco, wing of the party, while Calhoun as leading dogmatizer of the Nullifiers or extreme State Rights men had stood in opposition most of the time. Many believed, and Benton was probably among them, that Jackson himself had designated the robust Missourian for the succession after Van Buren; yet Calhoun had not only steered the party to his own political beliefs, he had maneuvered himself into what appeared to be the preferred position for 1844. So Benton also stayed away from Baltimore while the Democratic members of Congress more or less openly took sides between the two.

3

In normal times only the professional politicians and the spokesmen for special interests weigh election choices in terms of tangible gains to themselves. In times of economic collapse the process is extended down to the most humble in the land. For those who are jobless and penniless want above all else the wherewithal for food and shelter and they consider candidates for office in terms of their willingness to promise these necessities of existence. In 1840 the times were hard and the whole fabric of society was shifting uneasily as family after family started the long westward trek already so much a part of the American scene, while others, less adventurous, stirred the cauldron of discontent in the eastern centers of population.

In statistical terms the gross value of imports had dropped from $190 million in 1836 to $107 million in 1840, and the government revenues, which had been just short of $51 million in 1836, declined to less than half that figure. In the same period the average price of cotton, which accounted for the bulk of the country's export trade, dropped on the Charleston market from 16.8 to 8.4 cents a pound. In human terms these figures meant widespread unemployment in the industrial cities of the North and East, bankruptcy and business stagnation in the commercial and financial centers, and in the agricultural regions of the South and West only such living as the soil itself afforded.[4]

Jackson's personal vendetta against the Bank of the United States had destroyed the only effective legal control over the circulation and value of the currency, without supplying a substitute, and this had opened the way for the spiraling inflation of 1834-1836 with its accompanying fever of speculation and its inevitable aftermath of panic. Jackson had bequeathed the deluge along with his square-cut mantle to Martin Van Buren, who had struggled manfully but generally without success against the tide of popular reaction. In the sphere of internal improvements Democratic policy had again been a contributing factor. The South, with its deeply rooted fear of the centralization of power in Washington, had opposed the building of roads and canals by the Federal Government for a score of years, and Jackson had confirmed that view with his crushing veto of the Maysville Road Bill in 1830. So the states undertook such construction for themselves, and by 1840 had issued bonds for canals, railroads, and turnpikes to the tune of $120 million, with $50 million more to finance banking institutions. Only a small fraction of these ventures had reached the point of yielding a return before the depression left the states concerned unable to redeem their bonds, or even to pay interest on them.[5]

The tariff compromise of 1833 had specifically abandoned the policy of subsidizing American manufactures by prohibitively taxing competing articles made abroad. It had also provided for the progressive lowering of import duties over a ten-year period until a uniform level of 20 percent, deemed adequate for revenue purposes, should be reached. The depression, however, had served to reopen the whole tariff question. It was understandably easy for the manufacturers of New England and Pennsylvania to convince unemployed industrial workers that their misfortunes were directly attributable to the destruction of the protective system.

The depression also gave new impetus to a standing controversy over the price and administration of the public lands, which constituted both a source of revenue and a means of relief for the impoverished. And, perhaps most significant of all, the panic and its aftermath gave a new and explosive twist to the slavery controversy. Northern capital had been freely lent to the South for the expansion and improvement of the plantation system, slavery and all, because the North shared through its control of the carrying trade in the profits of that system. Again the depression made these loans impossible to repay and so Northern distress was aggravated by Southern losses. On this slender basis, with but the most imperfect knowledge of the economics of the relationship, the publicists of abolition reasoned that the very existence of slavery was a threat to free labor. Because of her slaves, so the argument ran, the South was bankrupt, and industrial workers in the North were jobless because the money that would have paid their wages in productive enterprise had been sacrificed to Southern inefficiency. The point was underscored when the abolitionist movement entered the sphere of political action in 1840 with the creation of the Liberty party and the nomination of precise, bearded James G. Birney of Kentucky for the Presidency.[6]

4

For all its lighthearted antics and thoughtless gaiety, the campaign of 1840 was thus overshadowed by the specters of hunger, of poverty, of human distress. The prevailing mood was one of disillusion with all that had been done in the past and of naïve faith that any change would necessarily be for the better. The individual voter persisted in thinking only in terms of work for himself and subsistence for his family, while the real issues arising out of alternative solutions to economic problems were ignored or hopelessly confused. Party lines and personal loyalties were inextricably tangled, and the democratic process was exhibited at its unintelligent worst.

General Harrison had supplanted Clay at the Whig convention of December 1839 because he was thought to be pliable, and because he had no recent political record against which men could vote. To be sure he had been Territorial Governor of Indiana early in the century, and had served undistinguished terms in both houses of Congress, but for a decade he had been out of public life and he was identified with no policy or program. He lived on a farm, which made it relatively easy to overlook his aristocratic ancestry and represent him as a man of humble origins and pursuits. His military background, though uninspired, was adequate for the creation of a legend. Above all he had no enemies. Tyler on the other hand was a man whose active career as Representative in Congress, as Governor of Virginia, and as Senator, had been outspoken and sometimes spectacular. His had been the only vote against the Force Bill in the Senate in 1833, which gave him special distinction as an opponent of centralized power. He had opposed the Bank of the United States as vigorously as had Jackson, but had equally opposed Jackson's arbitrary assumption of power in the removal of the government deposits from the Bank. He was a firm opponent of abolitionism in any form. In all these things he stood with Calhoun and the South Carolina Nullifiers, and his presence on the ticket was specifically to allay the fears of the South.

So the Whigs could argue from their partisan record or on the basis of their candidates that they were on either side of every important question of the day. They preferred, however, not to argue at all but merely to sing and to cheer, to wave banners, hold mammoth open-air feasts, coin slogans, and fill the papers with clichés and platitudes, while their political managers organized Tippecanoe clubs at the local grass roots and made lavish promises of office in their candidate's name.

In a negative sort of way the Democrats were in a very similar position. Though they now embraced Calhoun and the State Rights party of the South, they were also responsible for the centralization of Jackson's time. Though they now proclaimed as immutable dogma the separation of government and banks, they had in Jackson's day created government banks at will. Though they now denied that the government could legitimately subsidize one interest to the injury of another, they had themselves been largely responsible for the tariffs of 1828 and 1832. There had been defalcations and mismanagement of funds; and worst of all there had been the greatest financial panic in the nation's history while the Democrats were in power. Inescapably their record put them on the defensive, while the Whigs could promise everything or nothing as the circumstances might require.

Individuals were as badly scrambled as doctrines. In the Whig camp were such ill-assorted characters as William Cabell Rives of Virginia who had once sacrificed his seat in the Senate to the defense of Andrew Jackson; James A. Hamilton of New York who had once been a political lieutenant of Martin Van Buren; Duff Green of Baltimore who had been Calhoun's editor and close associate through the whole critical time of nullification; and Judge Joseph Story of Massachusetts on whose shoulders had fallen the intellectual mantle of John Marshall. On the Democratic side were Silas Wright of New York who had drafted the tariff of 1828 and John C. Calhoun of South Carolina who had nullified it; George McDuffie who had led the fight to recharter the Bank of the United States, and Thomas Hart Benton who next to Jackson himself had done most to destroy the Bank; Joel R. Poinsett who had prepared to sustain the Force Act in arms, and Littleton Waller Tazewell who believed that act foreshadowed the end of the Union.[7]

5

The economic issues of the campaign were clarified by the party spokesmen in Congress during the winter and spring of 1840. Save for the long disputed Independent Treasury no significant legislation was passed, but Whig proposals to distribute among the states the revenue from the public lands and to assume the state debts offered sounding boards for widely publicized speeches. Clay and Webster spoke for the Whigs, Benton and Calhoun for the Democrats, with Calhoun on every point going back to underlying premises. To him the choice was clearly between antagonistic theories of government, historically identified with the names of Jefferson and Hamilton, but forming in fact the core of the political problem in the nineteenth century: a choice between a national government limited only by its own sense of restraint, and a government so decentralized that its power could not be abused. The one might advance immeasurably the welfare of the people, but it might also deprive them at discretion of their property and their liberties. The other would force upon the individual the major responsibility for his own welfare but it would also leave him free within generous limits to determine his own course.[8]

There were few who cared to substitute the cold logic of political theory for the catch phrases and public entertainments so popular with the masses, and hardly more who saw any virtue in reasoned arguments as against the sly insinuations of propaganda. So the campaign was ended as it began, in a blaze of enthusiasm for men who represented what each individual voter most desired. The newspapers on both sides attacked character and consistency with complete abandon while party managers concentrated on organizing and delivering the vote.[9]

Led by the *Globe* of Francis Preston Blair, the administration press proclaimed the relationship between Whig and Federalist parties, and demonstrated to the satisfaction of Southern Democrats that Harrison was an abolitionist. But the tactics were wrong, because Harrison did not have to reply. The Northern Whig managers knew very well that without support from men who disapproved of slavery they would have difficulty in carrying a single free state, but if the support were not too open they might still run strongly in the South. So they let the *Globe* make a case for them with the antislavery voters and in the South they relied on John Tyler and on Harrison's own Virginia birth.[10]

The Whig press, with the *National Intelligencer* showing the way, concentrated its fire on the all too vulnerable record of the Democracy, particularly on the abuse of patronage and on the financial irresponsibility of Jacksonian days. There was also a conscious effort to split the Nullifiers and the Locofocos, an effort in which Calhoun bore more than his share of the abuse. The *Madisonian*, representing the self-styled "Democratic Whigs," even sought to show that Harrison was the true State Rights leader, and there were enough old Nullifiers in the Whig ranks to make the argument plausible.

As the summer advanced the dilemma of the Nullifiers became increasingly difficult to escape, for though Calhoun had argued in his Senate speeches that Harrison's election would mean the restoration of the Bank and the tariff, Van Buren under Northern pressure had begun to hedge on the slavery issue, and the little New Yorker's support of Jackson's centralism was still too fresh to inspire the confidence of cotton planters. Late in June Robert M. T. Hunter of Virginia, Speaker of the House of Representatives, informed his constituents that he could not support either party. Others, like George McDuffie of South Carolina, accepted the Democracy only as the lesser of two evils and specifically not as Van Buren partisans.[11]

Calhoun worked conscientiously for the Democratic cause, and carried with him many of his Southern supporters, despite his own grave reservations. Before the end of July, however, he was convinced that Harrison had taken the lead in a canvass "discreditibly low on both sides." August saw the returns of state and local elections begin to come in, and they were sweeping victories for hard cider. Calhoun consoled himself with the argument that Harrison's following was too heterogeneous to hold together when the time came to divide the spoils, and by September he was reasoning that whichever party won, the administration would be weak and that his own principles would thereby be advanced.[12]

But the truth was that the Democratic party was as badly split as the Whigs. The defeat of Van Buren would emphasize that split and would precipitate a struggle for control within the ranks of the Democracy. Calhoun's followers were uncertain how either the defeat or the victory of the party could be used to advance their own leader; yet his ultimate elevation to the Presidency they regarded as essential to vindicate the principles for which he stood—the only principles, so they believed, on which the planting states could continue their free existence in an enduring Union.[13]

Blair announced the results of the election on November 9 with a bad grace that could perhaps be explained by the fact that he would shortly lose his lucrative post as public printer. "Gen. Harrison," wrote the *Globe's* redoubtable editor, "the standard bearer of the Federal and Abolition parties, has been elected, if the process by which this result has been brought about can be called an election." The Charleston *Courier*, Whiggish in sympathy throughout the campaign, had the news two days after the *Globe*, but there was no rejoicing to match the annoyance of Van Buren's editor. "For weal or for woe, for better or for worse," announced the *Courier,* "the people have . . . overthrown the present administration, and we have only to say God grant that it may be for the welfare of our beloved country." [14]

Calhoun had accurately forecast the result before the election took place, and he was careful once again to explain his position to his followers. South Carolina remained the only state in the Union to cast her Presidential vote through her legislature, but her action early in December would not alter the result. The temptation was strong to throw away her ballots on some doctrinaire who was not actually in the field, just as she had done in 1832 and again in 1836. But Calhoun was firm that it was a point of honor as well as of expediency to vote for Van Buren. It would strengthen the opposition to the incoming administration, and it would absolve South Carolina's leaders of any charge that they had joined the Van Buren cause only to share in the plunder. For the Vice Presidency he recommended his old friend Littleton W. Tazewell of Virginia, and so it was done.[15] At the same time he advised his followers to join the opposition—meaning his late Locofoco allies—only if it were based on the old Jeffersonian principles of 1798. Should any other ground be taken by the Democratic minority, the Nullifiers were once more to draw apart and to treat each separate measure on its individual merits.[16]

Calhoun had become by 1840 a man with one fixed idea about which all else revolved. He would save the Union if he could, but first of all he would save the South: from exploitation for the economic gain of others, and from the bloody and fanatical horrors of an interracial war of extermination. For it was this and only this that he and thousands of his fellow planters believed must be the inevitable sequel to abolition. Save only for the precarious balance she enjoyed in the Senate as a result of the Missouri Compromise, the South was already in a permanent minority, and her only hope lay, as Calhoun conceived it, in enforcing a constitutional theory under which she could protect herself. He had arrived at the State Rights position slowly and painfully, over a long period of time, but he was now there to stay; for there and only there could his prophetic vision see safety for the South he loved, or permanence for the Union he loved equally well. So he bade his partisans pursue still the narrow State Rights road; so he saw in Van Buren's defeat the inevitable consequence of departure from that path.

"I regard the fall of those in power," he wrote to his eldest son soon after the election, "as the result of a deep principle of retributive justice. All the old sins of Jackson's time have come back on them; and, although I deplore the mode, in which they have been put down, and the immediate grounds on which it was done, I am not prepared to say, but what it will, in the end, contribute to a more thorough reform than could have been effected by the opposite result." [17] It was, in short, a political catharsis which he hoped would enable the party to move forward with new strength and vigor, now that the base metal had been purged and purified. To his tenacious Scotch mind there was only one direction in which the party could now go—the direction in which he himself had been moving for the past decade and a half. And who could better lead a reoriented Democracy to the promised land than the prophet who had looked upon Canaan from the mountaintop?

CHAPTER II

RESTORATION OF THE BOURBONS

1

As Whig factions scrambled for the spoils the rival segments of the defeated party battled for leadership of the opposition. Within a month of Harrison's election Benton called on the Democracy to unite once more behind Van Buren while the *Globe* declared that the Bourbons had been restored and the people betrayed. Jackson, from his retirement at the Hermitage, enlarged on the theme of political corruption and bank influence and followed with a ringing declaration in favor of Van Buren's re-election in 1844. But the real target was Calhoun and the stake was the future policy of the party. Benton's prospects were premised on the backing of Jackson and Van Buren, and so he was bound to yield the next round to the New Yorker. Calhoun was under no obligation to step aside, and indeed could not do so unless he wanted to see the full power of the Democratic machine directed over the next eight years to the service of his Missouri rival. So the Carolinian marked time and bade his followers be guided by principles alone—those State Rights principles that he knew Benton could never accept.[1]

Among the victorious Whigs the factions were more numerous, with Southern and Northern partisans, old Federalists and Democratic bolters, Clay men and Webster men, each calling on the President-elect for his reward. Harrison's personal acquaintances among public men were limited and his opportunities to judge the qualities of potential officeholders had been few indeed. Along with a high sense of personal responsibility he had an understandable reluctance to face the hungry devotees of a party twelve years out of power. Least of all did he relish the prospect of being bullied by the domineering, ambitious, nimble-witted Clay who was already being called the "President-maker" and the power behind the throne. Yet he realized that he must seek the advice and rely on the judgment of politicians more experienced and more closely in touch with affairs than he.

As soon as he was sure of his election Harrison wrote to Charles A. Wickliffe whom he felt he knew well enough to trust. Wickliffe had served several terms in Congress and more in the Kentucky Legislature and only within the past two months had retired as Governor of that state. Harrison explained that he was on the way to Frankfort, where he wanted Wickliffe to meet him. Then with a political innocence incredible in one who had just gone through a Presidential campaign, he informed Clay of his plans and told the Kentucky Senator bluntly to stay away. The old General professed to believe that a personal interview would cause too much speculation, that even letters would be unwise, and suggested that Clay name an intermediary through whom they might communicate.[2]

Clay hastened instead to Frankfort and had it out. He found Harrison "much broken" but with a mind that retained "all its strength and vigor," and he quickly convinced himself that no slight had been intended by the invitation to Wickliffe and the rebuff to himself. Harrison did not even know that there were factions among Kentucky Whigs. To clear the air, Clay removed himself as a possibility for appointive office, and left for Washington and the December session of Congress sure that his own interests would be represented in the Cabinet. He knew also, however, that Webster would be consulted and would probably be offered a place.[3]

Harrison did indeed invite the Massachusetts Senator to a Cabinet seat almost immediately after Clay left him, suggesting the Treasury but leaving the final choice to Webster himself. The New England champion considered the proposal only briefly, passed up the Treasury, and took the State Department. By the middle of December it was also known that John J. Crittenden, Kentucky Senator and lifelong friend of Clay, would be Attorney General. It was anticipated that equal representation would be given to free and slave states, but beyond that all was speculation.[4]

It was on the morning of February 9, 1841, that the President-elect, cheerful and seemingly untroubled, entered the Capital he was so soon and so briefly to rule. Snow and cold did not deter the Whigs from staging a celebration oddly out of keeping with the informality of the campaign, and the Democratic papers made the most of it; but the old General remained good-humored and unruffled.[5]

The office seekers were there before him, and they continued to fill up the city as the time of the incumbents grew short. Harrison saw everyone, promised everything, and went serenely about his business, a conquering hero not quite aware that his army meant to loot where he meant only to govern.

Calhoun called on him shortly after his arrival, and was received as callers invariably were "with all familiarity, as if we had been old cronies." The same indifference to partisan divisions was revealed again on February 15 when Harrison visited the Senate unannounced, passed up his own followers, and approached Calhoun with a friendly tap on the shoulder. The South Carolina Senator felt the situation to be awkward for both, and quickly led the President-elect into the lobby where Harrison "immediately began the most familiar kind of conversation, as to the course he intended to take." Calhoun thought him "as unconscious as a child of his difficulties and those of his country," pleased in a personal sort of way at his elevation, but with "neither physical nor mental powers equal to the task." [6]

Within three or four days of Harrison's arrival the Cabinet rumors were in agreement and on February 15 the list of advisers was official. Webster was to be Secretary of State, Thomas Ewing of Ohio was given the Treasury post, John Bell of Tennessee was the new Secretary of War, and Crittenden would be Attorney General. The Navy Department went to George E. Badger, a relative unknown from North Carolina without national political experience. The Post Office, with its extensive patronage, was confided to Francis Granger of New York, currently a member of the House of Representatives, who had contested unsuccessfully for the governorship of his state on the old National Republican ticket, and had failed to win the Vice Presidency as a Whig in 1836. It was a Cabinet whose majority was probably loyal to Clay, which gave rise to a general belief that the Kentuckian was to have a clear field for 1844; but the dominant figure was Webster, who had other ideas.

2

In the Senate, meanwhile, Clay had taken things into his own capable hands, and was seeking to commit the party in advance to his personal program. With the bland audacity that had so often turned the political tides in his favor, he assumed that Harrison's victory meant popular approval of the course proposed by Henry Clay. As a preliminary step he introduced near the beginning of the session a resolution calling for repeal of the act of the previous winter establishing the Independent Treasury.[7]

When the matter came up for discussion on December 15 Silas Wright, who was personally and politically closer to Van Buren than was any other man in public life, welcomed the issue but denied that the late election had expressed the popular will in any particular save that General Harrison was to be President. Indeed, if it proved anything, it was that "they were to take down the splendid edifice in which he then stood, and erect a log cabin in its place." Clay parried the thrust, and Calhoun took the floor to disagree with both the Senators who had spoken. He regretted that Clay had seen fit to keep the old controversies alive and to fashion from them a program for the incoming President to adopt. He would prefer to give the people time to think things over, and to let Harrison advance his own measures when the Congress elected with him and dominated by his partisans would be in position to carry them out. As to himself, he would reserve his judgment and support the next administration whenever its policies were such as he could approve. He wanted to be sure, however, that they were the policies of the party and not merely the whims of the Senator from Kentucky.[8]

Clay ignored his critics, proceeding as though he already led a majority and spoke for a party in power. On December 30 his friend and colleague, Senator Crittenden, introduced the same bankruptcy bill that had failed of passage at the previous session. Then on January 8, 1841, came the core of the Kentuckian's legislative program. On that day Crittenden moved that Benton's familiar and often argued bill to grant pre-emption to actual settlers on the public lands be recommitted, with instructions to include in the same bill the distribution of land revenues among the states. A week later Clay called on the Secretary of the Treasury to lay before the Senate a plan for the revision of the tariff system; and just before the end of January Senator Albert S. White of Indiana created an opportunity to advocate the re-establishment of a national bank.[9]

Clay did not, of course, expect that any of his favorite measures would be enacted, since the Democrats still controlled both houses of Congress. His purpose was rather to force his own program upon the incoming administration by making Whig preferences a matter of record in advance of any declaration by Harrison. To Calhoun it all meant that the central government was to be immeasurably strengthened and the states weakened in proportion. It meant that the protective tariff, so injurious to the cotton planters of the South, was to be re-established, and with it a constitutional doctrine under which slavery could endure only at the sufferance of the majority. He knew that he could count on no help from Northern Democrats, but he seized the first opportunity that offered to appeal to Harrison directly.

The opening came late in January in the course of debate on Clay's distribution scheme. Calhoun's argument was one already long familiar to his fellow Senators: that distribution of the proceeds from the sale of public lands was meant to impoverish the Treasury and so force a substantial increase in the tariff to keep the government solvent. He traced the consequences of this policy as they had been experienced in the past and forecast disaster should it now be revived. "Much—very much will depend on the President elect. If he should rest his policy on the broad and solid principles maintained by his native State, in her purest and proudest days, his name will go down to posterity as one of the distinguished benefactors of the country; but, on the contrary, if he should adopt the policy . . . advocated by his prominent supporters in this Chamber, and attempt to erect anew the fallen temple of consolidation, *his overthrow, or that of his country, must be the inevitable consequence.*" [10]

Webster answered immediately, accepting the issue as Calhoun had defined it and resting his case squarely on an interpretation of the Constitution that gave pre-eminence to national power. It was the same constitutional theory he had first advanced in pleading the Dartmouth College case before the Supreme Court in 1819, and had amplified in his replies to Hayne in 1830, and in his debates with Calhoun in 1833 and in 1838—a theory under which the Federal Government might legislate in the interest of a class or section, might raise tariff walls to prohibitive heights, and might if the majority saw fit emancipate the Southern slaves.[11]

Calhoun rejoined a few days later, confining his argument to the single point that distribution was unconstitutional; but his text was from Burke, and it was one that Webster had also used upon occasion. The great Irish statesman had declared that the revenue is the state. Calhoun added that to distribute the revenue among the members of a confederacy would be to destroy the federal relationship. For the ultimate sovereignty must lie in the hands that hold the purse strings, and to make the states of the Union financially dependent on the Federal Government would be in the end to reduce them to the level of mere administrative units in a consolidated whole. The real difference between Webster and Calhoun, like that between Hamilton and Jefferson in an earlier day, was that one desired while the other feared this outcome.[12]

3

"The Harrison leaders in the Senate," wrote Calhoun to his nephew in the midst of the foregoing debate, "seem determined that his administration should commence before his inauguration." [13] There was some disagreement, however, as to just who the Harrison leaders were. In addition to the rivalry between Clay and Webster for the Presidential succession there were numerous lesser cleavages along sectional and economic lines. The Virginia Whigs, for whom Henry A. Wise was chief spokesman, were unalterably opposed both to a national bank and to the assumption of state debts, yet it was to this group that Vice President-elect John Tyler belonged. The Democratic "seceders" of 1836, now calling themselves "Conservatives," were also lukewarm on leading Whig measures, with Senators Rives of Virginia and Tallmadge of New York, the dominant spirits of the group, identified with the system of state banks as opposed to the national bank desired by Clay and Webster. There were Southern Whigs like Waddy Thompson and William C. Preston of South Carolina, John M. Botts of Virginia, Senator-elect John Macpherson Berrien of Georgia, and Willie P. Mangum of North Carolina, who were willing to accept the bank and if need be the tariff, but wanted no agitation of the slavery question. And there were Northern Whigs, like the acid-tongued John Quincy Adams and the more aggressive William Slade of Vermont and Joshua R. Giddings of Ohio, who were frankly abolitionist. Slade, Giddings, and their following in particular supported the Whig program, bank, tariff, and all, for precisely the reason that Calhoun opposed these measures: because they would strengthen the North, drive the South into irreconcilable opposition, and eventually make slavery a political issue.[14]

It was something of a personal triumph when Clay got the warring factions together in a caucus of Whig Senators on the evening of January 30, 1841. Webster was in the chair with Crittenden acting as secretary, but the meeting was Clay's and Clay's was the business at hand. The Kentucky strategist had whipped his cohorts up to fever pitch, but he knew that innumerable local issues and sectional jealousies would intervene and that his forces would begin to fall away if he allowed his program to cool until the next December. So, although Webster and the veteran Senator Southard dissented, the caucus agreed that Harrison should call a special session of Congress. Even so the division on the bank question would be exceedingly close, and all of Clay's persuasiveness would be needed to see it through.[15]

The arrival of the President-elect early in February and the subsequent announcement of the Cabinet gave new impetus to the factional struggle for control of the patronage. More important even than the Cabinet seats themselves was the collectorship of the port of New York, a prize that carried more influence and secondary patronage than any other in the government except the Post Office. The New York collectorship had formed the bone and sinew of Van Buren's political machine, and in the hands of an adroit politician could well be the deciding factor in any New York state election. There were two candidates for the job: Edward Curtis, friend and political supporter of Daniel Webster, who had actively opposed Clay's nomination at Harrisburg in December 1839; and R. C. Wetmore, who was in Clay's camp. Governor William H. Seward and the powerful Thurlow Weed of the Albany *Journal* both favored Curtis, and Clay's New York supporters soon found themselves being smilingly frozen out.[16]

4

For Harrison's inauguration Washington swarmed with visitors as it had not done since Jackson's time, but the fates did not smile on the Hero of Tippecanoe as they had always smiled on the Hero of New Orleans. The day was bitterly cold with a damp, penetrating wind from the northeast and leaden skies. As befitted a military man, Harrison, mounted on a "mean-looking white horse," led the inaugural procession to the Capitol. There were bands and banners and colorful costumes in abundance, with the ever-present log cabin in

JOHN TYLER IN 1841
by Hart

THOMAS HART BENTON
probably by Bingham

the midst of smartly uniformed troops, but the President-elect was simply clad in black frock coat and top hat. It was said that nearly a hundred thousand cheered along his route, though Washington itself boasted less than twenty-five thousand souls all told.[17]

The Senate, gathered in extra session, had already witnessed the swearing-in of Vice President John Tyler and those of its own members who were new or newly re-elected. In the former category were Levi Woodbury of New Hampshire, Van Buren's Secretary of the Treasury; John Macpherson Berrien of Georgia who had been Jackson's first Attorney General but was now a Whig; and James T. Morehead, former Whig Governor of Kentucky and now successor to the able and polished John J. Crittenden. Webster's successor, Rufus Choate, whose exploits at the bar were already being woven and embellished into legend, had taken the oath on March 2. In the group of re-elected members were such veterans as William R. King of Alabama, Willie P. Mangum of North Carolina, Robert J. Walker of Mississippi, and Calhoun himself.[18]

Harrison was received in the Senate chamber shortly before noon, and was escorted to the eastern portico of the Capitol by the customary entourage of Senators, Supreme Court Justices, diplomats, and miscellaneous functionaries. There, facing into the wind, his thinning gray hair blowing, while the crowd in front shivered in overcoats, he read his inaugural address in a voice firm, clear, and unemotional. For an hour and a half the old man delivered himself of platitudes and evaded issues, but his audience cheered him to the echo. In his virtual renunciation of the veto power and his assurance that he regarded the manner of raising and managing the revenue as strictly up to Congress, he nodded in Clay's direction; but the speech as a whole showed the editorial hand of Webster. The Whig press was as noncommittal as the address itself, but the Charleston *Mercury* aptly quoted the *Merchant of Venice:* "Gratiano speaks an infinite deal of nothing." [19]

Later in the day there was the usual reception at the White House, and in the evening the inaugural ball. There was also a quiet, informal gathering at the home of Henry D. Gilpin, the retiring Attorney General, in honor of Martin Van Buren. Members of the old Cabinet were there: lanky, side-whiskered John Forsyth of Georgia, who had held the State Department since 1834; Levi Woodbury whose speculative eyes and courtly manner concealed unvoiced ambitions of his own; handsome and romantic Joel R. Poinsett who held the War Department in reward for his services to Jackson during the nullification crisis; the host, loyal but detached, ambitious only for literary success; James K. Paulding to whom literary fame had long since come and who had found in the Navy Department an inexhaustible source of material for his racing pen; and devious John M. Niles of Connecticut, "father Niles" to the inner circle, who had dispensed the party patronage through the Post Office since Amos Kendall's resignation in the spring of 1840. Senators Calhoun and Benton, recognized aspirants for the party leadership, were there, outwardly friendly and confident; and Van Buren, though suffering from a cold, was ever his suave and cordial self. "It was a meeting of the friends of an overthrown dynasty; yet there was no grumbling nor despondency, but general cheerfulness & an excellent spirit." [20]

There must have been tension, nonetheless, and deep undercurrents of feeling. Forsyth had been directly responsible for the historic quarrel between Calhoun and Jackson in 1830, but it had not won him the leadership of the South as he had hoped. Benton had already placed Van Buren in the field for 1844, with himself in reserve for the succession thereafter; and Calhoun was not indifferent to movements being made in his own behalf. Woodbury, even while in Jackson's Cabinet, had maintained his personal friendship for the South Carolinian, and would soon be openly supporting Calhoun against the field. Poinsett lived only to see Calhoun's power in South Carolina broken in his own favor; and Niles remained aloof, weighing the chances before he attached himself to the winning side.

If the internal rivalries among the Democrats were for the moment put aside, those in the Whig fold were ready to erupt in violence. Within three or four days of the inauguration Clay let it be known that a special session of Congress would be called, to meet on or before the first of June. Harrison ignored the matter and Clay brought to bear the personal pressure he knew so well how to apply. He pressed also with all his skill and address for the appointment of his own partisan as collector of customs in New York. The aged President knew himself no match in argument for the imperious Kentucky Senator, and retreated behind the stocky figure of his Secretary of State, directing Clay to communicate with him in future in writing rather than in person. Clay, furious and frustrated, threatened to retire from public life, and leave the factions to fight their Senate battles without him. The proclamation calling Congress to meet in extraordinary session on May 31, 1841, to cope with "sundry important and weighty matters, principally growing out of the revenue and finances of the country" was finally issued on March 17, but not before Edward Curtis, henchman of Seward and Weed and partisan of Webster, was confirmed for the prized New York collectorship. Clay packed his bags and set out for Kentucky, not sure that he would ever return, while Webster quietly directed the distribution of offices in his own interest.[21]

5

Harrison seemed to share none of the factional bitterness of which he was in part himself a victim. Subordinate offices were filled without his knowledge, and removals were made which he did not sanction nor approve. He treated his opponents as he treated his partisans, assuming they were all his personal friends and united with him, at least in seeking the public good. On March 13, shortly before the Senate finished its work, the President gave a dinner at which the guests included Van Buren's Cabinet along with his own, Vice President Tyler and ex-Vice President Richard M. Johnson, Senators Calhoun and Clay, Rives and Tallmadge, and ex-President John Quincy Adams. It was a heterogeneous and ill-assorted group, but Harrison saw no incongruity in it. Indeed, the old man called Van Buren too his friend, though he sent a wry message to his predecessor that he had left no bed of roses. Even as the *Globe* and its partisan satellites screamed "proscription" and published long lists of men removed from public office, Harrison regretted that he had not retained Van Buren's Cabinet, at least until they had taught his own appointees the details of their various departments.[22]

Harrison had always lived a simple and unpretentious life, and he insisted on living it still. Shopping himself at the Center Market, walking the streets of Washington too often coatless, calling on friends and acquaintances without thought of political affiliations, careless of the hours he kept, he exposed himself needlessly and drew too heavily on the reserves of strength in which he took such pride. After an early morning visit to the market on March 27 he was seized with a chill. Rumor spread quickly over Washington that the President was ill, but officially there was only silence. The Democratic *Globe* was first with the news on March 29 and the *Madisonian* had it the next day. On March 31 the *National Intelligencer,* official Whig organ, took its first notice of the situation, but only to pronounce the President "decidedly better."

For the next three days both *Intelligencer* and *Madisonian* kept up the pretense that improvement was steady, while the *Globe* continued to call the illness "serious" and "critical." But those who had the entree to the White House knew by April 1 that the case was hopeless. Specialists were summoned from Baltimore and Philadelphia, but there was nothing medical science could do. Harrison lingered on until the very early morning of April 4 before he yielded up the high office he had filled indifferently for exactly one month.[23]

The world of furious political conflict which Harrison left was one of which he had never really been a part, and he had not yet breathed his last before his erstwhile partisans were busy planning the division of his power. The Democrats, with nothing at stake, could be more charitable, if it was charity to say out loud that Harrison had died most fortunately for his own fame and perhaps also for his country's good—died in the hour of his greatest glory, before his own weakness and the rival ambitions of those around him could send him down to degradation and defeat.[24]

In reverent but speculative silence the Capital waited for the arrival of John Tyler, hastily summoned from his Williamsburg home to be President of the United States.

CHAPTER III

HIS ACCIDENCY

1

JOHN TYLER was back in Washington before dawn on April 6, 1841. He rested briefly, then called Harrison's Cabinet to meet with him and asked each man to remain at his post. Later, in their presence, he took the oath as President of the United States.[1]

The occasion was historic, immediate in its impact, and far-reaching in its consequences. For many believed, among them learned and strait-laced old John Quincy Adams, that the true meaning of the Constitution was very different. It was not the office, they contended, but only the "powers and duties" of the office that were meant to devolve on the Vice President in such a case, and Tyler was therefore only acting President for the next four years. "His Accidency," they came tartly to call him before many weeks were out.[2]

Even before he reached the city Tyler's probable course was a matter for lively speculation. Whig politicians wrote hopefully to one another that he was a good man and surely would not let them down, but it was clear that they would feel happier when he had pledged himself not to veto a national bank. The Whig press quoted comforting passages out of context from past Tyler speeches and assured its readers that the new President would now support the same measures he had opposed when a member of the Senate. The New York *Herald*, with that prince of opportunists, James Gordon Bennett, in its editorial chair, hinted at another term if Tyler would only be true to himself and shake off all partisan shackles. The *Globe*, in its role of house organ to the Democracy, invited the wayward Virginian back to the party of his youth, pledging Democratic support from North and South alike if he would remain steadfast in his known opposition to bank, tariff, and public debt.[3]

The reaction of the State Rights wing of the Democracy was much the same as Blair's own, but they carried the analysis further than Jackson's editor was interested in carrying it. On his record and all

35

past associations John Tyler belonged in the same ideological fold as Calhoun and should have returned to the Democratic ranks when the great Nullifier returned. They were ready to receive him now if he would stand once more where he stood in 1833, even though it might mean giving Tyler another term and postponing Calhoun's aspirations until 1848.[4] For Calhoun had imbued his followers with something of his own intellectual obsession. The personal elevation of any individual was unimportant when weighed against the economic freedom of the South. What counted, in their eyes, was the triumph of the political philosophy in terms of which they had learned to defend their institutions.

Tyler himself realized only too well the difficulties of his position, and it is perhaps no wonder that in the welter of gratuitous advice showered on him from all sides he became confused. He was a proud man, obstinate and independent, but very far from being the weakling that some of his friends and many of his enemies thought him. He was not likely to respond to Clay's imperious approach, nor yet to the blandishments of Blair, but he had enough ambition of his own to be flattered by Bennett's hint of future greatness. Those who knew him well must have anticipated that very thing, for on his progress through Virginia Tazewell had persuaded him that he must publicly renounce any desire to be his own successor. Perhaps if someone as able as Tazewell had come on to Washington with him he might have acted other than he did, but he had little time to seek or listen to advice. His party, the opposition, the country as a whole, demanded to know where he stood and what he meant to do. The pressure was too great to withstand and he temporized.

On April 9, 1841, Tyler issued a carefully prepared address to the people of the United States—his "inaugural address" the papers called it. It was prepared with considerable skill, and it was probably entirely his own. In addition to Tazewell he had talked briefly with a handful of Virginia intellectuals, including Judge Beverley Tucker and probably President Thomas R. Dew of William and Mary College, before he left for the Capital; and Duff Green and Henry A. Wise soon joined him there. Green was responsible for dropping a paragraph already written disclaiming any future political ambition; but Wise's advice to drop the Cabinet and form a new one of his own was disregarded. There is no evidence, internal or otherwise, that the address was influenced by anyone, though it was probably read by members of the Cabinet before being released.[5]

Tyler paid tribute to his predecessor and acknowledged briefly the uniqueness of his own position, then plunged directly into an exposition of his own views. With Jackson's regime in mind he called for a clear divorce between the Executive and the Treasury, and for an end to proscription except where public officers had interfered with elections. He aligned himself with the State Rights school in his demands for strict economy, no public debt in peacetime, and a rigid adherence to the separation of powers between state and federal governments. On the all-important question of bank or no bank he said both yes and no. He promised to approve "any constitutional measure which, originating in Congress, shall have for its object the restoration of a sound circulating medium"; but he would first "resort to the fathers of the great republican school for advice and instruction."

No mention of state debts, of distribution, of the tariff! He would sanction a national bank if, after communing with the writings of the founding fathers, he thought it compatible with the Constitution. In all matters he would adhere strictly to the constitutional division of powers. In terms of Clay's announced program Tyler's views could be interpreted either way, and were. He had made no bid for the support of any group or faction but had tried to leave an opening for them all. As usually happens in such cases, they were all soon baying at his heels.

2

Over the next six weeks the first indications of new partisan alignments were briefly visible. In the matter of appointments to office, Tyler tried bravely to live up to his precepts: that there would be no proscription for party's sake but that all who had abused the powers of office to influence elections would be removed. The removals were extensive enough to turn Blair and the Locofoco Democrats to bitter opposition, but they were far short of the demands of the office-hungry Whigs, who complained as bitterly as did the *Globe*. Duff Green continued to exercise considerable influence in determining appointments, and Green for all he had become a Whig remained personally close to Calhoun. Wise gradually achieved the status of a personal counselor to the President. Major William B. Lewis, self-styled President-maker of Jackson's time, cast in his lot with the Conservatives and pledged to Tyler the "cordial and zealous" support of Senator Rives. By May the *Madisonian,* originally founded in the interest of the Conservatives, appeared to be supplanting the *National Intelligencer* as the administration paper, and Rives too began to exercise some influence in patronage matters.[6]

In Tyler's official family there was outward harmony but inner turmoil. All of the Cabinet except Webster and possibly Granger represented the Clay interest, and devoted themselves to furthering the Clay program. Webster did what the circumstances forced him to do: he took sides, though not yet overtly, with Tyler. There was still no open split, and Ewing was probably honest though amazingly obtuse when he wrote Clay early in May that the Cabinet and the President himself would support the program. But the time for the special session was approaching, when politicians of all faiths would have to show their colors by their deeds.[7]

Tyler's message to Congress, delivered on June 1, 1841, was almost as equivocal on the controversial issues as his inaugural had been. Though the Treasury showed a deficit he gave grudging assent to Clay's distribution scheme, providing that it did not force a departure from the tariff compromise of 1833. He pronounced the assumption of state debts to be unconstitutional; and he conceded the necessity for some kind of "fiscal agent, capable of adding increased facilities in the collection and disbursement of the public revenues." The details he left to Congress, reserving the right to reject the result if he deemed it at odds with the Constitution. But the "fiscal agent" as explained by the Secretary of the Treasury looked very much like a bank, and Clay was explicit that a national bank was what the President would get.[8]

The Senate was quickly organized with Clay in full control. Each of the Whig factions was represented on the nine-man Select Committee which would have the major business of the session in charge, but Clay himself was chairman and his would be the guiding hand. The only concessions to Tyler's following were the selection of Rives to be chairman of the Committee on Foreign Relations and the choice of Thomas Allen of the *Madisonian* to be Senate printer.[9]

In the House of Representatives the net result was much the same. John White of Kentucky, a Clay partisan, was elected Speaker on the first ballot, and the key committees went to men of similar views: Ways and Means to Millard Fillmore of New York and the Select Committee on the Currency to John Sergeant of Pennsylvania. The House did not get down to work, however, until a bitter two-week wrangle over the gag rule had momentarily obliterated all party lines save only that between North and South. At the bottom of it was old John Quincy Adams, short, rotund, bald, shaking slightly with the weight of his crowded seventy-four years but still quick, alert, forceful, and relentless in pursuit of his ends. Before it was over Southern Whigs who had scoffed at the fears of the Nullifiers caught in their own nostrils the acrid smell of brimstone. They drew closer to their fellow slaveholders across the chamber, while the President, who was also a Southern Whig, reconsidered his position.[10]

3

Clay's program consisted of five specific measures: repeal of the Independent Treasury Act; incorporation of a national bank; authorization of a substantial Treasury loan; enactment of a tariff to increase the revenues; and distribution of the proceeds from the sale of the public lands. In part as a *quid pro quo* for the votes necessary to pass the last-named measure, the establishment of a uniform system of bankruptcy was added.[11]

First came repeal of the subtreasury, introduced on June 4 and passed five days later in the Senate. It was in vain that Calhoun pointed out to the Whigs the inconsistency of their own action; for repeal, without the provision of a substitute, would force the Secretary of the Treasury to keep the government funds in those very state banks they had themselves pronounced illegal as depositories. Clay meant to provide a substitute in due time and the need would make it easier. The only shadow of a Democratic triumph was to force the sitting well on into the evening of June 9. "We intend, they shall not get their victory so cheap as they expected," wrote Levi Woodbury from the Senate chamber shortly before the vote. "It shall cost them their dinners at least." [12]

On June 7, with subtreasury repeal still pending, the Senate majority called upon the Secretary of the Treasury to communicate a plan for a bank or fiscal agent; and on June 10 Clay brought in the distribution bill. On the same day John Henderson of Mississippi reintroduced the bankruptcy bill of the previous Congress. June 12 saw Secretary Ewing's bank plan laid before the Senate, and on June 21 Clay introduced the key measure of the whole program: a bill to incorporate the subscribers of a Fiscal Bank of the United States.[13] Since it was the bank rather than the program as a whole that ultimately broke the party, that issue will be reserved for separate treatment.

The whole chain of measures to which Clay had committed his party continued to be forged link by link in both houses of Congress; and Calhoun, in the role of spokesman and floor leader for the Democrats, continued to direct his fire at the whole chain rather than at any given link. As each item in the total reached the Senate floor the tall, intense South Carolinian went back again over all the ground. National debt, distribution, national bank, tariff—these things were but expressions of a theory of government. It was a theory that would concentrate power at the center, destroy the only effective instrument through which it could be restrained, and open the way for a form of absolutism worse in its effects than that against which the colonies had rebelled in 1776.[14]

By the latter part of June, when the Senate turned most of its energies to the bank question, the House of Representatives was sufficiently calm and orderly to resume consideration of the public business. The distribution bill was offered in the lower chamber by W. Cost Johnson of Maryland in a form more comprehensive than the Senate bill, for which it was presently substituted. This was followed on June 24 by a bill to authorize a twelve-million-dollar loan, introduced by Fillmore from the Committee on Ways and Means. The last of the measures comprising Clay's program was a tariff bill, also sponsored by Fillmore, which was presented on July 14. Even Clay would not risk openly junking the compromise of 1833 in view of Tyler's stated opinions, so the bill avoided raising duties above 20 percent. Instead imposts of that amount were levied on articles previously on the free list. The parliamentary device of the previous question was used by the party leaders with ruthless efficiency, and although their majority was reduced by the defection of Southern Whigs like Wise, Hunter, and Thomas W. Gilmer, they kept it rigidly in line. The distribution bill passed on July 6 by the close margin of 116 to 108, and the loan bill was carried by a larger majority a week later.[15]

In the Senate Clay drove the loan bill through on July 19 by a slim three-vote margin. It was not accomplished, however, without drawing another broadside from Calhoun, again aimed at the consolidating tendency and nationalistic purpose of the whole Whig program, and concluding with a pointed appeal to those State Rights men who had supported Harrison in expectation of reform. He looked searchingly around the Senate chamber and no doubt his somber, deep-set eyes came to rest on his old friends Willie P. Mangum and John M. Berrien as he uttered words that were meant also for John Tyler. Where were they now, he asked, those State Rights men who had placed their hopes in Harrison? He found them in "the ranks of the bitter and determined opponents of all they ever professed and contended for—doomed, unless they speedily separate from faithless allies, to loss of caste and endless disgrace." [16]

An explosion was approaching rapidly now. The bank bill passed the Senate on July 28, and the House on August 6, but the Constitution gave the President ten days in which to act and he used all ten. In the interim the tariff bill and the repeal of the subtreasury were driven through the House. But the session was lengthening out toward autumn. As Democratic spirits remained high the Whigs grew sullen and uncertain, and did not hesitate to blame their troubles on "the indecision of the President." [17]

4

Just why Tyler chose in his message to be cryptic in his reference to a "Fiscal Agent" is not clear, unless it was a deliberate lure in hopes that Clay would overreach himself. The scheme the President had in mind was already worked out and had been discussed with various official and unofficial advisers before the session began. In the latter group were Duff Green and Henry A. Wise, and in the former the Secretary of the Treasury. Ewing probably lost no time in letting Clay know privately the nature of the plan, and being thus forewarned the Kentuckian was forearmed. The nature of the Fiscal Agent became public property on June 12 when Ewing's report, with a draft of a bill, was laid before the Senate. The project was long and complicated, but the significant features were that the Fiscal Bank of the United States was to be located in the District of Columbia, where the power of Congress to issue a charter could not be disputed; and it was to be empowered to set up branches only with the consent of the states in which they were to be located.[18]

As so often happens with patchwork products designed to pander to many tastes, the Fiscal Bank really satisfied no one, not even Tyler. Save only on the score of location and branching power it was open to all the objections the Jacksonians had hurled against Biddle's Monster of Chestnut Street, and yet those very exceptions weakened its power to perform adequately the functions of a central bank. It was an ungainly hybrid between the true national bank desired by the Clay group and the league of state banks for which Rives had stood sponsor since 1836, with a hard-money clause tossed in Benton's direction and the elimination of commercial operations put in to placate Calhoun and the other subtreasury advocates.[19]

When Clay made his report to the Senate on June 21 he paid tribute to the Treasury plan, and noted that his committee had incorporated certain of its features in their own draft. Beyond a location in the District of Columbia, however, there was little resemblance between the two schemes. Clay's project was a thoroughgoing national bank in the most comprehensive sense. As Ewing had done before him, he used the charter of the Second Bank of the United States as a basis, but the Treasury modifications tended to weaken while Clay's tended to increase the power of the institution.[20]

Clay's bill was taken on both sides of the chamber to be a declaration of war against Tyler, and few doubted that the President would veto the bill if he dared. The Kentuckian became "more imperious and arrogant" than ever, but his control of the Senate never wavered, and the passage of the bill was assumed to be sure. The break came when Rives sought to include by way of amendment the provision from Ewing's draft that required assent of the states for the establishment of branches. The next day Rufus Choate supported Rives and declared that without the amendment there would be no bank at all. Clay challenged the Massachusetts Senator's authority for such a statement and Choate declined to reveal it, all of which made it plain that he was giving the Senate an ultimatum from the President and that the adherents of the Secretary of State were no longer to be relied on. Rives' amendment was defeated roundly on July 6, but Whig votes on Tyler's side included the Senators from Massachusetts and Vermont who were regarded as Webster's men.[21]

For the next three weeks the Senate spent most of its time on the bank bill with Democrats proposing one crippling amendment after another, debating each, and forcing each to a vote. The assembled talent and expertness among the opposition Senators was great indeed and Clay was pushed back again and again, to be saved from disaster only by cracking the party whip when the votes were taken, and never sure that Isaac C. Bates and Choate of Massachusetts or Rives of Virginia would go along to insure his minimum majority of three. The assault was led by Calhoun, who had drafted the charter of the Second Bank of the United States a quarter century before and had then let the bank die in Jackson's time; by Levi Woodbury, who had served almost seven years through prosperity and panic as Secretary of the Treasury; by Silas Wright, whose financial genius had made him a private adviser to two Presidents and had given him undisputed pre-eminence on such matters within his party. Benton, Buchanan, King, all veterans of the Senate and powerful in debate, stood ready to spell the leaders whenever they could get the floor.

As the long contest neared its end, Clay changed his tactics and in a last-minute attempt to make the bill acceptable to Tyler allowed and himself moved one significant alteration. The amendment he proposed on July 27 was a watered-down version of Rives' earlier proposal: the assent of a state to the establishment of a branch office of the bank was to be assumed unless the legislature at its first session following the passage of the act should specifically reject it. The modification passed by a single vote. It was probably suggested by Ewing who thought thus to circumvent his chief, but Ewing both underestimated Tyler's intelligence and misjudged his own influence.[22]

Tyler's ten-day delay before sending in the anticipated rejection was probably in part to prepare public opinion for what he meant to do, and partly in the hope that the bankruptcy bill might pass the House and the distribution bill the Senate before the veto raised havoc with party organization. Clay must have had some hopes as late as August 13, for on that day he quelled a revolt among his followers who were bent on ending the session and going home. Calhoun seems to have had no doubts, writing categorically to his son that there would be a veto. He pledged the Nullifiers to support the President to that extent, "and, if he goes through with their principles

& policy, throughout"; and he assumed that the Cabinet would resign. Others went further, predicting that Calhoun himself would be offered a portfolio when the blowup came.[23]

The veto message was almost an anticlimax, so keyed up was Congress in anticipation of it, by the time it finally arrived on August 16. The Cabinet, with even Webster joining in the plea, had urged the President to sign the bill; but Webster at least knew that he would not and anyone who took the trouble to examine Tyler's public career must have agreed. For Tyler prided himself more than anything else on his consistency and his pride would never have let him yield in the face of threats of political reprisal. The message was brief and pointed, recalling in pithy phrases a record of twenty-five years of public statements that he believed a national bank to be unconstitutional, beginning in the Virginia Legislature, and most recently in the course of the 1840 campaign. His party, he said bluntly, knew where he stood before they elected him Vice President, and he would not forswear his oath to "preserve, protect, and defend the Constitution" as he understood it. There was a short review of bank history, a few tart paragraphs devoted to exposing the sophistry of Clay's last-minute amendment, and he was through. The Whigs screamed bloody murder and denounced him for an apostate and a tyrant, but the Nullifiers welcomed him back to the fold, and the *Globe* ranked Tyler's bank veto along with that of Jackson, "as a great deliverance from that fatal system of corruption which in the course of time could not fail to make dollars, and not votes, sovereign in this country." [24]

5

In the course of the next few days the Whigs spent much time in caucus and the State Rights wing of the Democracy made pointed overtures to the President. Berrien, Sergeant, and Webster served as liaison between the Capitol and the White House, seeking without success to find out what kind of bank bill Tyler would sign. The *Madisonian,* now official in name as well as in fact, called upon the Cabinet to resign if its members could not sustain their chief. Consideration of the veto was delayed in the hope that an understanding could be reached, and Webster appealed eloquently for peace between the Executive and the Congress.[25]

The truce ended abruptly on August 19 when Clay denounced the President with savage thoroughness. He was answered in kind by Rives and in the subsequent exchange between the two Clay referred contemptuously to those professing to be the President's special friends. A "cabal" he branded them, dedicated to the overthrow of the Cabinet, but one that "did not amount to enough to make a corporal's guard." The phrase stuck and Tyler's personal adherents, particularly those in the House, were thenceforward called the corporal's guard. Clay did not name them even when pressed to do so, but they were not hard to identify: Wise, Gilmer, and Dr. Frank Mallory of Virginia; W. W. Irwin of Pennsylvania; George H. Proffit of Indiana; and, a host within himself, pugnacious Caleb Cushing of Massachusetts. In the Senate only Rives could properly be counted, but from that day forward it was Rives and not Clay who was recognized by the administration as its Senate floor leader.[26]

It was probably on that same day that Webster showed the President a draft of a substitute bank bill from Sergeant's committee in the House. Tyler made sundry alterations but neither inserted nor questioned the absence of the disputed provision requiring the consent of the states to the establishment of branches within their limits. Either late that day or early the next morning Webster passed the changes on to Sergeant, but in such fashion as to leave the President still wholly uncommitted. On August 20 Sergeant introduced the scheme in the House, in the form of an amendment to a bill earlier reported but dropped in favor of the Senate's version. Proffit asked if the assent of the states was to be required but was shouted down without an answer.[27]

It was also on August 20 that Tyler saw the Botts "Coffee House Letter." It should be explained that John Minor Botts was one member of the Virginia Congressional delegation who most emphatically did not belong to the corporal's guard. If possible he abhorred the President even more wholeheartedly than did Clay. There was in Richmond a certain Coffee House where politically minded Virginians were wont to gather, and various public men had formed a habit of writing news letters for the edification and instruction of these gentlemen. Addressed simply to the Coffee House, the letters were left, opened, on a table for all to read. Botts wrote—and signed—such a letter on August 16. The theme was the bank veto, and the letter insinuated that through personal ambition Tyler was deliberately seeking a break with his party. "Our Captain Tyler," wrote Botts, "is making a desperate effort to set himself up with the *loco-focos;* but he'll be headed yet, and, I regret to say, it will end badly for him. . . . He has refused to listen to the admonition and entreaties of his best friends, and looked only to the whisperings of ambitious and designing mischief makers who have collected around him." A friend of the President saw the letter in Richmond, hastily copied it, and sent it to Thomas Allen, the editor of the *Madisonian*. It arrived in Washington on the twentieth, was shown at once to Tyler, and the next day appeared with appropriate comment in the administration paper.

Tyler was already smarting under Clay's attack in the Senate of the day before, and the Botts letter destroyed any lingering hope that might have remained for reconciliation with the Whigs. Webster listened for an hour to the President's woes and abandoned the second bank bill then and there. To be sure Tyler sent Wise to explain to Sergeant that the pending bill did not overcome his constitutional scruples, but by that time it probably would not have made much difference what the bill contained. Shortly thereafter he sent Webster on another fruitless errand to the Capitol, this time to ask that the whole thing be dropped until the regular session in December.[28]

For the moment the bank was put aside while the Senate took up the distribution bill, already passed by the House. The State Rights Democrats, with the aid of an occasional Southern Whig, had sought persistently to restrict the terms so that distribution could not be used as an instrument for raising the tariff, and Clay was compelled at last to yield the point to keep his own Southern followers in line. An amendment stopping the distribution whenever import duties rose over 20 percent was prepared by Berrien, and passed on August 23. Four days later the amended bill was carried by a five-vote margin, although Calhoun denounced it as a gross violation of the Constitution and reminded the Southern Whigs once more that their way of life could not survive under the kind of government to which such measures would lead.[29]

The second bank bill, meanwhile, had passed the House where the President was caustically denounced by Botts as a traitor to his party. Tyler told his Cabinet he would not sign it, and the Whigs held another caucus on September 1. Two days later the bill passed the Senate without alteration, and the seventh saw the tariff also passed. Except for the bank Clay came very close to getting all he wanted out of the special session.[30]

6

Tyler's second veto message was read in the House of Representatives on September 9, 1841. He could not, the President declared, reconcile the provisions of the bill with his honest understanding of the Constitution, and he was therefore compelled by his oath of office to return it without his signature. But the tone of the whole message was conciliatory, and there was a forthright plea for harmony and understanding. Tyler was willing to yield much to the legislative will, and as anxious as Congress to settle the question at issue. In a few months the regular session would be held and he promised to recommend then such measures as he deemed appropriate.[31]

The Clay Whigs were in no mood to accept conciliation, and they did not accept it. On the evening of September 9, after the veto message had been read, the Cabinet held a rump session with Webster absent, and Secretaries Ewing, Bell, Badger, and Crittenden agreed to resign. Webster was informed the next day, and made it plain that he would follow his own course. That night he met with the Massachusetts Congressional delegation, laid his cards on the table (as if they did not know already what he held), and expressed the conviction that the international negotiations in which he was then engaged would justify his remaining at his post. The delegation, with Cushing of the corporal's guard the most aggressive spirit, gave Webster their blessing, but even then he solicited other opinions before he finally settled on his course. Granger also put the issue up to the Congressional delegation from his own state, and on their advice cast in his lot with the rebels.[32]

The breakup of the Cabinet was known all over Washington almost as soon as the decision was made, or perhaps a little ahead of that; and between 12:30 and 5 P.M. on September 11, 1841, the entire group with the exception of the Secretary of State stepped out. Congress had already agreed to end the session on September 13, so the President had less than two days, and one of them a Sunday, to fill the vacancies.[33]

On the day of the Cabinet resignations a Whig caucus resolved to issue an address to the public, and set up a committee of Senators and Representatives to report such an address. They met again on the evening of September 13, a few hours after Congress had adjourned, and adopted unanimously the document that had been prepared for them. The test of Whiggery was attendance at the caucus. The address was an elaborate review of aims, accomplishments, and failures, and its purpose was to read out of the party John Tyler and all who came to his defense.[34]

That Tyler was able to rebuild his Cabinet in the matter of hours left to him to get Senate confirmation of his appointees would probably be sufficient evidence in itself that he had already anticipated the necessity. The truth seems to be, however, that he not only anticipated the dissolution of the Cabinet but intended to dissolve it himself as soon as the adjournment should leave him a free hand.[35] He had his list ready when the time came and all were confirmed by the Senate, but again no single group or faction was appeased. Secretary of the Treasury was Walter Forward of Pennsylvania, a former Democrat who was then serving as first comptroller of the Treasury on Harrison's appointment. The War Department went to Judge John McLean, and on his refusal was filled in the recess by John C. Spencer, then Secretary of State for New York, who had achieved prominence as prosecutor of the Morgan abductors in the notorious scandal of a decade earlier. He was a protégé of Seward, and like Seward himself had come into the party by way of Antimasonry. The new Attorney General was Hugh Swinton Legaré of South Carolina, a very able lawyer but one whose affiliations were not likely to endear him to the Calhoun group. The Navy Department went to a State Rights Virginian who was entirely in accord with Calhoun on doctrine, Judge Abel P. Upshur; and for Postmaster General Tyler selected the anti-Clay Whig leader in Kentucky, Charles A. Wickliffe.[36]

It was indeed, as the *National Intelligencer* pointed out, a new administration, having small connection with the victorious party of 1840. Though all the new Cabinet officers had been active in the Harrison campaign, all had been Jackson men in the 1820's. Again Tyler had temporized and again he was to suffer the penalty; for though he had left the Whigs proper and had broken irrevocably with Clay, he had not seen fit to cast in his lot with the Democracy, nor even to return unreservedly to the State Rights group. He was therefore compelled to fall back on advisers who could not aid in the one particular he needed most—congressional support.[37]

Tyler's discomfiture was in fact but a further evidence of the wisdom of Calhoun's consistent attitude toward the Whigs. For Calhoun had recognized from the very beginning the fundamental antagonism of principle between the State Rights, or Southern, position, and the political ideology to which the Whigs were, and inevitably must be, committed. Drawing its main support as it did from the manufacturing states, the Whig party had no choice but to follow the philosophy of consolidation, which could only mean, in time, the extinction of slavery. To those who upheld and defended the slave system there was only one real alternative—an interpretation of the Constitution that would render the Federal Government impotent to interfere with Southern institutions. Calhoun had made this distinction clear from the time he first acted with the Whigs against Jackson's absolutism in 1834 until he finally dissolved the coalition three years later. By the early 1840's it should have been clear to those State Rights men who had joined the Whigs with Calhoun in Jackson's time that they had only two choices: to get out or to compromise their beliefs. Tyler eventually got out, Mangum compromised, Rives temporized for another decade. But Calhoun never doubted, never faltered, never wavered in his course. He was dedicated to the defense of an institution that civilized men have long since condemned, but his belief in it was wholly sincere and the logic of his position, given his premise, was unassailable. It was this logical realism that made him the giant figure he was, towering over most of his contemporaries as his native mountains towered above the coastal plain.

CHAPTER IV

SOUTH CAROLINA SNEEZES

1

IN ANY SOCIETY whose economy rests on hand labor no threat can be so dangerous as a threat to the labor supply. The slave states of the 1840's presented such a society; one that was, moreover, already sensitive to the point of rebellion over a discriminatory tax policy. A further complication was the fact that the laborer was of another race and culture, in the first instance forcibly and brutally taken from his native land. Denied the advantages of civilization as his masters understood it, he had preserved various primitive customs from his tribal past. Might he not also have handed down to his descendants an atavistic lust for vengeance against the whole race of his captors? Would he not celebrate his freedom with bloody sacrifice and strive to be master where he had once been slave? Southern planters very generally believed just that. Calhoun had stated the argument for them all in his report on incendiary publications in 1835, but it had been advanced many times before and would be offered many times again. The literature of social reform through the first half of the nineteenth century makes it evident that the Negro slave in the United States worked under conditions that did not differ greatly from those suffered by his fellow workers of other races the world over; but he was a black man and in his aborignal state had been a savage. The memory of Indian massacres and slave revolts was still green and provided an element of dread to confirm the reasoning.

Rational or merely emotional or compounded of a thousand shades of each, that was the mental attitude of Calhoun's generation. The overwhelming preponderance of opinion in the South held, first, that the Southern economy without the slave would collapse, consigning the people of that fair region, some seven million of them by 1840 in an area of more than 600,000 square miles, to utter and irretrievable ruin; and second, that to grant freedom to the slave without removing him physically from the face of the land would be to precipitate a bitter and bloody struggle between black and white that could end only in the extermination of one or the other. An appreciation of this state of mind is necessary if we would understand John C. Calhoun, or the nature of the power he wielded in South Carolina and in the South as a whole between 1840 and 1850.

If South Carolina sneezed when Calhoun took snuff it was because he always seemed to know the precise moment when a sneeze was necessary to clear the head. During the long controversy between South Carolina and the general government over the tariff, finally settled by the compromise of 1833, Calhoun had pursued a middle course. The nullification formula was meant to be, and by Calhoun and his aides was always regarded as, a compromise between withdrawal from the Union and submission to the will of the stronger power. Withdrawal, to Calhoun's generation, was the last extremity; submission was to concede that the sovereignty did indeed rest with the numerical majority and that the slaveholding minority had rights by sufferance only. Out of that controversy had come two distinct parties: the State Rights and Free Trade party, or Nullifiers, dominated by moderates but including also young fire-eaters who would have gone further still had they not been held rigidly in check; and the State Rights and Union party, made up largely of conservatives who liked the tariff no better than their opponents but who admitted the right of the Federal Government to impose it and saw no remedy but the ballot box. For a few years the bitterness remained, but as the rising tide of antislavery agitation became more threatening to the security of the South there was a strong disposition on both sides to make up old differences.

The tendency of controversial national issues to split the state once more into factions, in the face of the danger represented by the whole attack on slavery, seemed to Calhoun to be little less than a prelude to inevitable disaster, and he dedicated himself to the cause of unity in the state and in the South. It had been toward the end of 1839, about the same date as his own reconciliation with Van Buren, that Calhoun's partisans moved to wipe out the last vestiges of the old split between Unionist and Nullifier, and to turn both wholeheartedly to the defense of the *status quo*. Isaac E. Holmes, a thoroughgoing Nullifier, had been elected to Congress from the Charleston district in 1838 with Unionist support, and now an old Unionist was to be elected Governor by the votes of Calhoun men.

The scheme was engineered by the Rhett-Elmore machine, already powerful in South Carolina affairs and destined to be more powerful still. Robert Barnwell Rhett was a veteran in South Carolina politics when he entered Congress in the panic year at the age of thirty-seven. Bombastic and master of all the arts of the demagogue when bombast would serve his turn, or silky and smooth as mellowed honey when persuasiveness was needed, Rhett had been a radical since he first entered public life in 1826. He did not share the reverence of Calhoun's generation for the founding fathers, and could contemplate without fear and without regret the possibility of a separate nation south of the Potomac. He went with Calhoun when the great Nullifier happened to be going in the same direction, and on more than one occasion his aid had been decisive. But he was too independent to be a good lieutenant and too powerful to risk turning into a foe.

Franklin H. Elmore, only a year older than Rhett, had served a term and a half in Congress before becoming president of the State Bank in 1839. Thin-faced and full-lipped, and frail in appearance beside the robust Rhett, Elmore was a man of widely varied interests, business and political. Calmly persuasive and of great personal charm, he enjoyed power for its own sake but cared little for the honors that adorned it.

Back of these two, with their personal combination of political and financial power, were extensive and talented family connections. Ben Elmore was potent in state affairs until his untimely death in the fall of 1841, and Benjamin Rhett was a director in Elmore's bank. Albert Rhett, as brilliant as his "Brother B" and probably more so, was the most influential single member of the legislature despite a degree of arrogance that made him personally distasteful to many who should have been his friends. Two more Rhett brothers, James and Edmund, were being groomed for political positions. The Charleston *Mercury,* edited by John A. Stuart, a brother-in-law of the Rhetts, was both the propaganda vehicle for the machine and upon occasion a semiofficial spokesman for Calhoun. A further tie to the national political scene and those who acted on it was through Dixon H. Lewis, the mountainous member of Congress from Alabama, whose wife was a sister of the Elmores. And to complete the picture, another Elmore sister was married to Albert Rhett.

Early in 1840 Robert Barnwell Rhett, who shared Calhoun's mess

during the first session of the Twenty-sixth Congress, made a flying trip to Charleston, and immediately thereafter the *Mercury* announced that the "Democratic-State Rights-Subtreasury" candidate
for Governor of South Carolina was Colonel John P. Richardson,
lately a member of Congress and in the internal struggle of an earlier
day a prominent Unionist. Backed by the Nullifiers, Richardson's
election was finally to heal the breach and unite all factions in South
Carolina. In early February the *Courier* brought out another old
Unionist, Judge David Johnson, as a rival candidate. The *Mercury*
promptly branded Johnson as a Whig, but there was no real local
issue between the two and the election of either would have the same
effect—the restoration of the old anti-Calhoun faction to a share in
the state government.[1]

2

Just as the process of reconciliation seemed sure of success, a new
and potentially more dangerous rift appeared in the too-smooth surface of South Carolina politics. It had been in the making for two
months, but without Calhoun's knowledge, when it was abruptly
publicized with the announcement in mid-February that James H.
Hammond was a candidate for Governor, running as a Nullifier.[2]

The trouble went back to the Democratic caucus of December 1839
in Washington where Calhoun's cousin and protégé, Francis W.
Pickens, was withdrawn without his knowledge as a candidate for
Speaker of the House. Those who withdrew him were Lewis and
Rhett, and Lewis promptly became a candidate himself, only to lose
out in the balloting. Pickens was ambitious beyond his powers, of
a moody and jealous temper, and inordinately vain of a political success that he owed in fact almost entirely to his kinship with Calhoun.
He concluded at once that he had been made the first victim of a
political plot, probably aimed ultimately at the Senator, and because
of the personalities involved he not unnaturally laid his grievances
at the door of the Rhett-Elmore junto. Among the consequences he
envisioned was that Rhett rather than himself would be promoted
to the Senatorship whenever Preston could be got out of the way.
He did not, however, take his suspicions to Calhoun, who would have
disposed of them readily enough. He let them fester for a month, by
the end of which time he had convinced himself that the thing to do

was to destroy the power of his South Carolina rivals by frontal attack.[3]

Pickens apparently did not understand or did not approve the strategy behind Richardson's campaign for Governor, but again he did not discuss the problem with Calhoun. He sounded out, instead, the other Representatives from his state and found in Sampson H. Butler a kindred spirit. Between them they concluded that the Richardson nomination was meant simply to consolidate the power of the Rhett-Elmore cabal by combination with the old Unionists; that the purpose of the cabal was to overthrow Calhoun; that if Calhoun understood it as they did he would be against it; and that Hammond, because of his past services as party editor and Congressman, would certainly be Calhoun's choice over Richardson. The next step was to plant the seed in Hammond's mind, and that was almost ridiculously easy.[4]

Hammond assumed, naturally enough, that overtures from Pickens had Calhoun's approval, and that he would therefore be running as Calhoun's candidate. The idea appealed to him and after consulting a few close friends he allowed his name to be put up along with those of Richardson and Johnson. It must be remembered that Calhoun, Pickens, and Rhett were all in Washington while this was going on. Calhoun was deeply involved with the problems created by his reconciliation with Van Buren and probably gave very little thought to South Carolina affairs, relying on Rhett who lived in the same house to keep him informed. Rhett was probably also his primary contact for the moment with the rest of the South Carolina Congressional delegation, not because he had lost confidence in Pickens but because he was too busy to seek out one man when another equally satisfactory for his purposes was already at his elbow. He did not seem to realize, or perhaps chose to ignore, the fact that Rhett and Pickens were potential rivals for his own mantle of leadership, and that both were indecently eager for his retirement. In the circumstances they were hardly likely to be close, and since Pickens' failure in the Democratic caucus of December they had not in fact been on speaking terms.

Had Hammond been a different type of man there need still have been no difficulty, but he was proud and hypersensitive, sure of his merits and supremely confident of his own powers. He was a man of great ability with a mind probably second only to Calhoun's. But he was deeply introspective, preoccupied with his own future greatness, suspicious of all who crossed his path. His letters, and especially his diary, give the impression of a man who sought public office not to establish any principle or to accomplish any given end but solely to gratify his own vanity. He had been of immeasurable service to the nullification cause in 1830-1831 as editor of the *Southern Times,* but he had suddenly wearied of it and had withdrawn to the seclusion of his Savannah River Plantation. He had come out of retirement in 1835 to accept a seat in the House of Representatives, where he distinguished himself as the ablest of Calhoun's partisans in the fight against reception of abolition petitions; but again he retired after a few months, this time because of illness. His seat had gone to Elmore, and Calhoun had tried to persuade him to return to it when Elmore withdrew in 1839, but Hammond was no longer interested. He fancied the governorship for a term, the Senate for a year or two, perhaps a foreign mission if the grade were sufficiently high; and he would have accepted graciously the role of patriot-founder of a new nation.

He was, in short, like Calhoun himself, a man who could not follow. But, unlike Calhoun, he would not fight and drive and argue his way to leadership. He would accept leadership as his right if the sphere of action were to his liking, and if it carried a sufficient recognition of his own particular worth, but he wanted none but himself to select the spot where his talents were to be put into play. It was inevitable that despite the similarity of their thought processes, Calhoun and Hammond would sooner or later clash, and that Hammond would come off second best.

When the *Mercury* received Hammond's candidacy coldly and chided him for threatening the harmonious reunion of Nullifiers and Unionists which the election of Richardson was designed to bring about, he was only the more fully persuaded that it was his destiny to rescue South Carolina from the corrupt clutches of the Rhetts and Elmores. Nor did he doubt that Calhoun, with whom he was in friendly correspondence, would ultimately back him up.

The first Calhoun heard of it was when he read the story in the *Mercury,* including the charge that Hammond's candidacy was against his interest. He did not need to see Preston's jubilant reaction to realize that this new situation threatened to divide the state once more into warring factions. He knew also that if he himself took sides it would only make things worse. So he reproved the *Mercury* for bringing his name into its article, and succeeded in impressing on those around him in Washington the importance of internal unity.

To Hammond he wrote cordially but without enthusiasm. He professed ignorance that the gubernatorial question had been raised, or that he had known until he saw the formal announcements that either Hammond or Richardson desired the place. He would personally be "well pleased" with either, and so his own position in the contest must be one of strict neutrality. "I trust," he added, "you will place a just estimate on my motives in taking the course I have prescribed to myself on the occasion. My strength here depends on the union at home, as far as I am concerned, and my usefulness, while I remain, depends on my strength." He must have anticipated, for he forestalled, moves already in the making to commit Pickens publicly to Hammond; and he was probably behind the sudden explanations and reconciliation between Pickens, Elmore, and Rhett. For the moment he could do no more.[5]

Although a governor would not actually be elected until the legislature met in late November the campaign gained momentum and intensity through the spring and summer. Contrary to expectations Judge Johnson did not withdraw, but instead of the old Union men being split between Richardson and Johnson as Hammond's supporters confidently predicted, it began to look as though the Calhoun vote would divide between Hammond and Richardson. James Hamilton, another veteran of the nullification days, joined the Hammond cause and undertook to explain to Calhoun why he must publicly support his former editor. Hammond argued in his own behalf that the whole policy of reconciliation with the Unionists, a party guilty not alone of treason to the state but of inviting a "foreign enemy to our shore," was wrong. Pickens, seeking a way out for himself, tried alternately to get Hammond to withdraw and Calhoun to change his mind. Newspapers claimed Calhoun's support for each contestant and letter writers tried to tie the contest to the Harrison-Van Buren struggle then moving toward its climax. But Calhoun resisted every pressure, continuing to appeal for unity and peace.

As his supporters began slowly to drop away, Hammond indicated to Calhoun that he might be guided by the Senator's advice. Calhoun answered as he had always answered before. He wished Hammond well, and had every confidence in him, but he could not take sides without weakening his own position as spokesman for the state in national affairs. The important thing was to avoid any acrimonious quarrel at home that might lend color to Whig charges that his views were not those of the South. But he told Pickens frankly that Hammond could not win and that "an honest & honorable withdrawal" would give him "a very high position in the state in future." [6]

Pickens passed the hint along to Hammond, as it was doubtless intended that he should, but Hammond simply was not built that way. Recalling how preponderant the strength of the Nullifiers had always been, he insisted that no Unionist could beat him with Union votes alone. He would stick to his guns and if he lost he would at least know where he stood. He would know, in short, that Calhoun had tipped the scales against him. The state was seething as it had not been for years by the time Calhoun returned from Washington near the end of July and put a stop to it.

3

There is no evidence as to what was said or done after Calhoun resumed his residence at Fort Hill about the first of August, but the gubernatorial campaign seemed suddenly to lose its sharpness. The political letters appeared less frequently, and began to turn more on the personal records of the candidates than on their former party affiliations. Hammond continued to be almost morbidly sensitive but he became less quarrelsome. For a time he probably contemplated a Senate seat as solace for the lost governorship, if Preston could be forced out; but that would have meant more friction and bitterness with rival claimants, particularly Rhett and Pickens. Early in October this possibility, too, was put at rest, by the "authorized" announcement that should Preston give up his seat, George McDuffie would be a candidate. Once more the hand of Calhoun was in evidence behind the scenes; for he and McDuffie were as close as brothers, and McDuffie's services to South Carolina were so great that his prior claim to any office in her gift could not be challenged.[7]

As the national election approached, with its forecast of Democratic defeat, the South Carolina contest faded into the background. The legislature met the last week in November and the gubernatorial election was held on December 9. Calhoun had apparently made no further effort to get Hammond to withdraw, a restraint that indicated a thorough understanding of the younger man's psychology; for Hammond would ever after have believed he could have won, and his usefulness to the party would have been still further impaired. At the last minute Johnson withdrew and Richardson was chosen by 104 votes to 47 for Hammond.

Hammond continued to insist for some time that he had been beaten because he refused to compromise with those who had betrayed nullification. But he was also aware that Calhoun viewed the matter in a quite different light, and he was quick to inquire of Pickens how Calhoun now felt toward him.[8] Calhoun was deeply engaged in the Senate in those early months of 1841, seeking to show how the economic program that Clay had laid down for the Whigs must result in a dangerous concentration of political power. For the time being the Democrats agreed, but the South Carolina Senator knew that his reasoning of the previous spring was now more than ever true. His power in national affairs depended on his political support, and that in turn depended on a united front, in South Carolina and the South. He could risk no continuation of old squabbles in his native state, and his course was probably already determined before he received Hammond's overture.

Whether Calhoun was directly behind it or not, he certainly knew of it and approved when Albert Rhett sought out one of Hammond's close friends early in February 1841. The message was direct, and seemingly straightforward. Hammond's friend was to say "that the opposition to you by gentlemen in the lower Districts was not personal, but they desired to elect Col. Richardson as a compliment to the old Union party, believing that his election would go far to heal old party differences, and that now they would be pleased to have you for the next governor." By way of inducement Rhett suggested that the governor elected in 1842 ought to be a Nullifier because he would probably have to cope with difficult problems of federal-state relations created by the incoming Whig administration; and he hinted that, if Hammond agreed to be their candidate, they could gain him the compliment of a unanimous election.[9]

In private correspondence, and in his diary, Hammond bridled at the thought of accepting the governorship at the hands of the same "Regency" he had previously denounced as unprincipled and corrupt, but though he raised questions and objections he was careful not to close the door. Negotiations continued through the summer, with Hammond alternately blowing hot and cold, but again Calhoun's influence was brought to bear when he returned to the state after the special session, and an understanding was ultimately reached.[10]

4

By the time the South Carolina Legislature met late in November 1841 everything was under control. Calhoun's "instructions" were carried to Columbia by Armistead Burt, member of the Assembly from Abbeville. Burt's wife was the daughter of William Calhoun, the Senator's older brother. Like so many Calhoun connections, Burt was being groomed for future political service, starting where Calhoun himself had started, in the state legislature. The letter he carried with him expressed the wish that the distribution act of the special session of Congress should be condemned, and that the position taken by Virginia in her then pending quarrel with New York over the printing and dissemination of abolition literature should be endorsed. The question of the next governorship, still a year distant, was not pressed, presumably because that matter was in the capable hands of Albert Rhett.[11]

The legislature did as Calhoun suggested. The Virginia position was upheld and the distribution act was condemned to the extent of refusing to accept any money under it. Then a private caucus of party leaders was held at which Hammond was endorsed as the candidate for governor in 1842, though no announcement to that effect was made for more than a month after the adjournment. For this delay Albert Rhett took full responsibility, and Hammond professed himself entirely satisfied. There remained undercurrents of jealousy and suspicion but outwardly at least South Carolina was of but one opinion. That opinion was John C. Calhoun's.[12]

CHAPTER V

SLAVERY AND ANGLO-AMERICAN RELATIONS

1

SHORTLY after the resignation of Clay's supporters from the Cabinet, Tyler sent Duff Green to England as his personal representative. Green's instructions were not made public, nor even confided to Congress when word of his activities filtered back to Washington, but they were in fact to explore the possibilities for a commercial treaty with Great Britain. The mission was Tyler's way of approaching a bafflingly complex tangle of international relations, transatlantic economic interests, and domestic differences on both sides of the water that had brought the two nations to the verge of war.[1]

Stimulated by a panic-inspired wave of migration, Western grain harvests since 1838 had been more than adequate for local needs, with surpluses mounting as continued depression drove prices down. At the same time a succession of poor harvests in Europe had left Britain in desperate straits, with breadstuffs in short supply and prices beyond the reach of the masses. Yet the Corn Laws, which imposed a heavy tax on all imported grain, made it economically impossible to market the overabundance of the Northwestern states where it was so badly needed.[2]

In the light of this situation the Anti-Corn Law League was organized in Manchester early in 1839 and achieved in both countries publicity spectacular for that day. The long tariff controversy in the United States had educated the public to a general understanding of the reciprocal nature of trade. It was assumed that repeal of the British Corn Laws, should the League be successful, would involve tariff concessions in the United States. By 1840 the question was being forced into politics on both sides of the water, and early in that year Calhoun made another bid for an antitariff alliance between South and West, offering in return to cede the public lands to the states in which they lay. For wheat as well as for cotton there would be an unrestricted British market. The domestic institutions of the South would be secured by Western votes while the public-land states would at last have.tangible assets to pledge for the repayment of their debts.[3]

The state debts themselves constituted another factor in the economics of Anglo-American relations, with the bulk of the indebtedness—perhaps $150 million—being held in England. By 1840 the possibility of payment looked almost hopeless, and in consequence America had no financial standing anywhere in Europe. Britain began to press for payment by the Federal Government and the assumption of state debts became a plank in the campaign platform of the Whigs, who counted among their numbers a preponderance of the bankers, merchants, and businessmen generally who suffered by the curtailment of credit abroad. On the Democratic side there were responsible men who frankly favored war with England to justify repudiation.[4]

A further source of irritation was the long-disputed boundary between Maine and New Brunswick which had flared up in the "Aroostook war" between rival logging interests early in 1839. Armed militia of both parties remained in the embattled area, while Congress voted $10 million and authorized the President to call for 50,000 volunteers.[5] More serious still as a potential cause of immediate hostilities was the whole train of events arising out of American interference in the abortive Canadian rebellion of 1837-1838; and from the long-range point of view the most stubborn of all obstacles in the way of friendly relations was the persistent antislavery sentiment that colored British policy in the Western Hemisphere.

2

Great Britain in the nineteenth century had the most advanced form of industrial capitalism so far developed anywhere in the world. It was not therefore surprising that she should be the first to feel the economic disadvantages of the slave system. She abolished the slave trade in 1807 and emancipated her own West Indian slaves in 1833, but though humanitarians like Wilberforce and Clarkson were vocal and persuasive, the real basis of British antislavery policy was economic, and was so recognized when the issues were debated in Parliament. The economic function of the slave was to supply cheap, abundant, but relatively unskilled labor for those forms of production in which labor represented the major item of expense. He fitted easily into the plantation economy but he was producer rather than consumer. Under the industrial system as it was developing in Britain in the early decades of the century a market for manufactured goods was more important than a supply of cheap labor. The necessary conditions could be found only in a society in which the worker was free to buy and had money to spend. It was to create markets for British manufactures that slavery was abolished in the West Indies and that the South African colonial settlement was deliberately confined to free men. Similar reasoning lay behind the British interest in wiping out the slave trade, and British antagonism toward slavery in Texas and in the United States was motivated at least in part by a desire to gain a competitive advantage for the products of labor no less enslaved in India.[6]

The British and Foreign Anti-Slavery Society was organized almost simultaneously with the Anti-Corn Law League, and there was a significant duplication of membership. The parallelism was also clear to American antislavery leaders, who turned their activities into political channels in 1839. Their long-term hope for success lay in the Northwestern states, where slavery had been excluded from the beginning and where people of New England stock were predisposed to accept their teaching. A relaxation of the Corn Laws would build up the economic strength of this grain-growing region, and would enhance in consequence its political power. Only the existing party alignments stood in the way. The Whigs leaned toward abolition but were against free trade. The Democrats were inclined toward free trade but their Southern ties made them wary of antislavery agitation. The Northwestern wheat grower who wanted both abolition and free trade was thus faced with a choice of political evils until the Liberty party came to his rescue. It was as much in the interest of Corn Law repeal as of world-wide abolition that James G. Birney, already the nominee of the Liberty party for President of the United States, attended the World Antislavery Convention in London in the summer of 1840.[7]

3

British official policy toward slavery in the Western Hemisphere was operating meanwhile to bring closer a crisis in Anglo-American relations. It was not uncommon for American vessels to be driven by stress of weather to British soil in the West Indies, and occasionally these were coasting vessels carrying slaves from one United States port to another. Such were the *Comet* (1830) and the *Encomium* (1834), both wrecked upon the Bahama keys; and such was the *Enterprise*, which took refuge in the harbor of Port Hamilton in 1835. In each case British authorities liberated the slaves, the owners demanded compensation, and the matter was eventually referred to Whitehall, where it encountered interminable delay. Under almost continuous pressure from the State Department and the American Minister, a settlement covering the *Comet* and *Encomium* was reached in 1839. Lord Palmerston in the Foreign Office then blandly denied responsibility in the case of the *Enterprise*, on the ground that the incident had occurred after emancipation had become effective in the British West Indies, and that the slaves could not therefore have been legally held.[8]

The South, always morbidly sensitive on any question touching her peculiar institution, saw in all this only further evidence of a British "plot" to abolish slavery, and her spokesmen in Congress, of whom Calhoun was foremost, began to apply pressure. Clearly a principle of major importance was at stake, for if the distinction Palmerston had drawn between the cases of the *Comet* and *Encomium* and that of the *Enterprise* were allowed to stand, then British municipal law was paramount to the law of nations and American commerce would move upon the oceans of the world on British sufferance or it would not move at all. Yet Van Buren's acceptance of the settlement in the earlier cases seemed to imply a concurrence with the explanation in the last. Calhoun responded by committing the Senate to an unequivocal endorsement of the long established international rule that goods follow the flag. Resolutions to that effect were offered early in March 1840 and Calhoun spoke to them on the thirteenth of that month.[9]

He had little difficulty in showing how irrelevant was the British claim that slaves could not legally be held on British soil, for the *Enterprise* was the "soil" of the United States. He attributed Palmerston's current attitude to local politics, which had put enormous pressure on the existing Whig ministry in behalf of world-wide abolition; but whatever the reason for it the position was untenable. Calhoun argued, correctly, that Britain could justify her refusal to compensate for the *Enterprise* slaves on only one of two alternative grounds : "either that her municipal laws are paramount to the law of nations, when they come in conflict; or that slavery—the right to hold property in man—is against the law of nations." The latter alternative had already been abandoned by the payment of damages in the earlier cases. The former would result in the destruction of all international law, with incalculable consequences for international trade. The rest of Calhoun's speech was devoted to a biting exposure of conditions in Ireland and India which could not fail to make British antislavery professions seem in Southern eyes the most barefaced hypocrisy. Circulated abroad in pamphlet form the speech became another weapon in the diplomatic arsenal.[10]

Closely related to the slave cases discussed above, both in its purposes and in the American reaction to it, was Great Britain's war against the slave trade. It was a trade long outlawed by all civilized countries but the profits were so great that it was still being extensively carried on, primarily for Brazilian and Cuban markets. There is no doubt that the American flag was illegally used by slavers more frequently than that of any other nation. The United States Government was of course aware of the abuse, and kept naval units continuously cruising the African coast in an effort to stop it.

The approach of Great Britain to the problem was more thoroughgoing. In 1838 she began actively seeking the co-operation of the other great powers of Europe in a joint arrangement whereby each would concede to the others a right of visit and search. A suspicious vessel flying the flag of any of the nations concerned might be stopped and searched by the naval forces of any of the others, and if the ship proved to be a slaver she could be detained. A quintuple agreement to this effect was ultimately reached with France, Russia, Prussia, and Austria late in 1841, and was signed in London on December 20 of that year, two months being allowed thereafter for ratification.[11]

From the start of the negotiations two things were obvious : that Britain alone had a naval force adequate to do the policing, and that the whole enterprise would fail unless the right of search were extended to vessels flying the American flag. The United States was invited to join in the agreement, but the official reply was always a cold assurance that slavers violating American law would be dealt with by American authorities. The British insisted nonetheless on a right to visit ships flying American colors to satisfy themselves that they were in fact of United States registry. As in the Bahama slave cases the municipal laws of England were held in effect to transcend and to modify the accepted international code. It was a pretension that no commercial nation could accept, and Tyler reaffirmed the traditional American stand in vigorous language in his first annual message to Congress, December 7, 1841.[12]

4

The crisis in Canadian-American relations over the burning of the *Caroline* and the trial of Alexander McLeod also reached its high point in the fall of 1841, and it too bore on vexed domestic problems as well as on the issue of peace or war with England.

It was in the late months of 1837 that a rebellion broke out in Lower Canada, and unemployed Americans along the border from Maine to Michigan hastened to join it. William L. Mackenzie, the rebel leader, openly set up headquarters in Buffalo early in December of that year and there on American soil he organized a "patriot army" of Canadians and Americans. In a very few days the rebels took up an advance position on Navy Island on the Canadian side of the Niagara River a short distance above the falls. The American-owned steamer *Caroline* was acquired as a supply ship and was cut out of the ice at her dock in Schlosser on the New York side of the river on December 28. The next day the Canadian military commander ordered the ship to be destroyed wherever she might be found. She was found that night, not at Navy Island but at her berth in Schlosser. The Canadians nevertheless carried out their orders to the letter. The ship was boarded and captured after a brief struggle in the course of which one American was killed. She was then set afire and towed into the current where she sank.[13]

President Van Buren quickly intervened to withdraw the Americans and the rebellion was effectively crushed, leaving the aftermath to the diplomats. There were minor irritations and sporadic border forays as negotiations dragged out, but there was no major incident until November 12, 1840. On that date Alexander McLeod was arrested in Lockport, New York, where he was charged with arson and murder in connection with the destruction of the *Caroline*. A former Canadian deputy, McLeod was a familiar figure in Western New York where he had often gone in search of evidence against border raiders. He had been arrested twice before on suspicion of complicity in the *Caroline* affair, but had been released for lack of evidence. This time the local citizenry mobbed the jail and threatened to lynch him if he were turned loose. The New York authorities had no alternative but to hold him for trial.[14]

The British Minister in Washington demanded McLeod's release but Secretary Forsyth, a Georgian thoroughly imbued with the Southern interpretation of the fundamental law, waved the demand politely aside. McLeod was charged with an offense against the state of New York and the Federal Government had no jurisdiction in the case. By this time the election had been held and Congress was again in session. Millard Fillmore, representing the district in which the affair had occurred, called for the correspondence which was referred to the House Committee on Foreign Affairs. Francis W. Pickens, the committee's chairman, reported in February 1841 and he was probably reflecting Calhoun's views. J. Q. Adams, ranking Whig on the same committee, called it "an inflammatory invective against the British Government," and in many respects it was. It served, however, to clear the air by bringing to a focus the outstanding differences with Great Britain: the Northeastern boundary, Oregon, the right of search, the West Indian slave cases, and the *Caroline*.[15]

Pickens followed Forsyth in upholding the jurisdiction of New York in the McLeod case, but Daniel Webster, who became Secretary of State three weeks later, took a different view. In the interval McLeod was indicted for murder and the British Government sharpened its tone. Webster had been only a few days in office when he received a blunt demand for McLeod's release, with an unequivocal avowal from London of official responsibility for the *Caroline*. There was also a very plain threat that if anything happened to the prisoner war would follow. News of McLeod's indictment reached London at the same time as Pickens' report and public opinion in England was roused to fever pitch. Webster sent Attorney General John J. Crittenden to Lockport to look after McLeod's interest, and in his answer to the British note he agreed that the official character of the act in dispute rendered all individuals concerned immune from personal liability.[16]

This reversal of Forsyth's position was ignored by the New York Supreme Court, which upheld the jurisdiction, and by Governor William H. Seward, who ordered the trial to proceed. Before that event occurred Congress had met in special session and the President and his party had gone their separate ways. The McLeod case was debated in both houses during the summer, but as long as New York held firm there was nothing the Federal Government could do about it, short of sending troops to seize the prisoner. Tyler was not ready to follow in Jackson's footsteps, and so the matter was allowed to ride.

The net effect of the debate was to make the McLeod case itself a political issue between Whigs and Democrats, with the latter upholding the State Rights position of the Van Buren administration, and the former, in the language of their opponents, "truckling to Great Britain." It was unfortunate for Whig solidarity that Seward saw fit to disagree with his party, and perhaps fortunate for the Democrats that McLeod had an ironclad alibi for the night of December 29, 1837. At all events the Canadian ex-sheriff was acquitted on October 12, 1841, and the tension eased enough to make such negotiations as those contemplated in Green's instructions appear within the realm of possibility.[17]

Another and perhaps still more important factor in improving the situation was the collapse of the Whig Ministry at the beginning of September. Sir Robert Peel succeeded Lord Melbourne, and the combative Palmerston turned over the keys of the Foreign Office to the more conciliatory Lord Aberdeen.

5

Duff Green arrived in London near the beginning of December 1841, and within a month or so was firmly intrenched. He wrote letters home, to Tyler, to Webster, to Calhoun; he wrote letters to the papers and quarreled with the *Times:* he made contact with Edward Everett, newly appointed American Minister; he got in touch with the banking house of Baring and eventually also with a wide cross section of business, political, and financial leaders. He was actively digging behind the British political and economic scene when the Quintuple Treaty was signed on December 20, and he was still in London when a day or two after Christmas Aberdeen indicated to Everett his intention to send a special minister to the United States

"with full powers to make a final settlement of all matters in dispute."
It quickly became a matter of public knowledge that this special minister was to be Alexander Baring, Lord Ashburton.[18]

Early in January 1842 Green went over to Paris at the invitation
of Lewis Cass, who had been American Minister to France since
the fall of 1836. Also in Paris at the same time was the scholarly and
accomplished Henry Wheaton, already a recognized authority on
international law, who was ostensibly vacationing from his own post
as Minister to Prussia. Everett too had been in Paris just before he
assumed his official duties at the Court of St. James's, and had discussed outstanding diplomatic questions with Cass and Wheaton.
The real purpose behind this convergence of American diplomats at
this particular time was Cass's belief that British claims to a right of
search could be most effectively attacked by blocking French ratification of the Quintuple Treaty, and that such an outcome would
strengthen the American position in all pending negotiations with
Britain.[19]

Cass and his coadjutors took full advantage of an already existing
undercurrent of hostility to Britain and all things British on the
part of the French people, who liked no better than Americans the
idea of allowing the arrogant mistress of the seas to search their
merchant ships. The question came up about the middle of January
in the French Chambers where the opposition promptly took ground
against the treaty. Wheaton attended the debates and talked freely
to members of both parties, while Cass attacked the whole British
contention in a widely circulated pamphlet. When he thought the
time was ripe, Cass addressed a formal protest against ratification to
the French Foreign Minister. He acted without instruction and so
informed Guizot, but at the same time he wrote to Webster threatening to resign if he were not upheld.[20]

Guizot was not bound to clear the treaty with the Chambers before
ratification, but he preferred to do so, and was shrewd enough to
capitalize on the assistance gratuitously given him by the Americans.
France did not ratify and the Quintuple Alliance died stillborn. For
this result Aberdeen blamed American interference, and again war
seemed threatening. In fact, however, the crisis was past, for events
in France had shown that if the United States must fight once more
to uphold the freedom of the seas she probably would not have to
fight alone. Ashburton's departure had been delayed pending news

from across the Channel, and he assumed his mission with the full knowledge that in the McLeod trial and in the failure of the Quintuple Treaty the Americans had already won two victories.

6

Another and more irritating slave case had meanwhile arisen, to complicate yet further the course of Anglo-American relations and to drive still deeper the wedge between North and South. Late in October 1841 the brig *Creole*, Virginia-owned with some 135 slaves aboard, cleared Hampton Roads bound for New Orleans. The slaves rose in mutiny, killed a passenger, and took possession of the ship which they directed to Nassau in the Bahamas. The British authorities arrested the ringleaders for murder but refused to turn them over to the United States consul. They refused also to detain the remaining slaves, most of whom quietly slipped away to freedom under the British flag.

The news did not reach Washington in time to be included in the President's message at the opening of Congress, but when it was received Calhoun immediately called for the documents. He saw the case, as he now saw every public issue, in the long perspective of the economic and political interests of his section. "If we may not safely sail on our own coast, with our slave property on board, because Great Britain may choose to deny our right to hold property in slaves," he asked his fellow Senators, "may she not, with equal propriety, extend the same rule to our cotton and other staples? If we have no right to those whose labor produced them, what better right have we to the product of their labor?" Yet he restrained his followers from raising the same question in the House lest it touch off another of those long, acrimonious debates on slavery that already crowded the journals session after session.[21]

For that very reason the militant abolitionists seized upon it, and wove it into the sweeping indictment of the whole slave system then being formulated with increasing aggressiveness in the lower chamber. Early in 1842 some of the leading publicists of the abolition movement congregated in Washington, including Theodore Weld, Joshua Leavitt of the *Emancipator,* and Lord Morpeth of the British and Foreign Anti-Slavery Society, and they were often closeted with Adams, Giddings, and other antislavery Congressmen. They were waiting for the petitions they had "planted" to reach the capital, at which time, so Weld intimated to his wife, "you may expect some southern developments." [22]

They had not long to wait. On January 21 John Quincy Adams— that "mischievous bad old man" as Calhoun now called his erstwhile friend—offered a petition from Georgia praying for his own removal as chairman of the Committee on Foreign Affairs. When Wise raised the eternal question of reception Adams cried "Privilege" and used the right to speak that thus became his due for an attack on slavery more direct and forthright than any yet made in Congress. He was eventually silenced, but he still held the floor for the presentation of petitions. His next offering was from citizens of Haverhill, Massachusetts, praying for a peaceable dissolution of the Union. Gilmer moved a vote of censure which once more made it a question of privilege and again gave the irascible old ex-President an opportunity to speak in his own behalf. [23]

Giddings, in the role of floor manager for the abolitionists, assigned Weld and Leavitt to help Adams prepare his defense and for days they plied the battle-scarred Massachusetts Congressman with documents and statistics. For two weeks the struggle continued, with Adams intermittently holding the floor and proving himself more than a match for all his foes together. It was during this interval that the *Creole* case came up in the Senate. Already split into Clay and Tyler factions, the Whigs broke down into Northern and Southern wings. As their party disintegrated the Whig leaders called off the fight and the case against Adams was tabled.

Public opinion in the stronger and more populous portion of the Union was slowly hardening, and it would soon be impossible for Northern and Southern men to understand one another. Six weeks later Giddings presented resolutions that made of the *Creole* case a point of departure for roundly condemning the labor system of the South. The overwhelming majority saw in them a deliberate and unjustified attempt to make trouble, and the next day the aggressive crusader from the Western Reserve district of Ohio received the censure Adams had been powerful enough to avoid. Giddings immediately resigned his seat, but he was back in a matter of weeks after a special election in which his constituents all but unanimously approved his course. For both North and South, it was a portent of things to come. [24]

By the time Lord Ashburton arrived in Washington early in April 1842 the Northern and Southern states seemed farther apart than England and America.

7

Ashburton had often been in the United States in the course of his sixty-seven years. His wife was an American, and he had numerous business and personal friends in the country to which he had been accredited, not least among them being Daniel Webster. A minister more acceptable personally or more likely to succeed could not have been chosen. Despite the seriousness of the problems at issue, the negotiation was conducted with complete informality. In the give-and-take of uninhibited discussion, without audience or written record, the two men thrashed out the points of controversy one after another, only resorting to the formal exchange of diplomatic notes after the ground had been covered and an understanding reached.[25]

Ashburton sought information wherever he could find it, and was careful to investigate every point of view. His discussions with Calhoun were many, dating almost from his arrival, and we know that he also talked with men representing such divergent views as Clay, Adams, Preston, Rives, Choate, and Legaré.[26] Webster was equally anxious to rub no salt into domestic wounds in the process of dressing those of an international nature. Over a period of some four months, most of it in the sticky heat of a Washington summer, the negotiations continued, but mutual good will and persistence found ways at last around enough of the outstanding points of friction to make a treaty.

The major item settled was the Northeastern boundary, a feat the more difficult because the states of Maine and Massachusetts also had to be satisfied with the settlement. The disputed territory was divided by a conventional line, with the states concerned each receiving a cash settlement for territorial losses. The line between the United States and Canada was carried west to the Rocky Mountains, settling all questions of jurisdiction over lakes, rivers, and islands, and in every instance allowing both countries free navigation of all channels lying in border waters. The division of the Oregon country, under joint occupancy since 1818, offered such difficulties that negotiations on that problem were put off until some later occasion; and Ashburton's instructions forbade him even to mention the subject of impressment. There was, however, an article on the slave trade by which each power agreed to maintain a minimum naval force in African waters and to police its own merchant ships. The whole explosive issue of search was quietly dropped, and the *Caroline* case was passed over, Webster pressing no claims and Ashburton expressing his "regret" that the incident had occurred. The *Creole* case offered difficulties that seemed at times insurmountable, but Webster accepted at last a provision for mutual extradition, and Ashburton gave personal assurances that there would be no further incidents of the type.

The actual terms of the treaty had not yet been made public when the Washington *Globe,* representing the Van Buren-Benton interest in the Democratic party, began attacking it. The Democracy, briefly united for the election of 1840, was breaking down once more into Northern and Southern elements. The Benton bloc was preparing to base its claims to power on expansion in Oregon, and saw in a squabble with Great Britain a convenient road to Western votes through repudiation of state debts. The Calhoun bloc was also bidding for Western support, offering instead of debt repudiation a British market for grain and cheaper manufactures. This was to be achieved by patching up all differences between the two countries preliminary to a reciprocal elimination of trade barriers.

These underlying considerations made it almost a certainty that the Democrats would divide on the treaty, with Benton in opposition and Calhoun in favor of ratification. Webster took the precaution, however, to sound out the South Carolinian before the treaty was submitted to the Senate, and received assurances of full support.[27] William Cabell Rives, spokesman for the Tyler administration, reported the treaty favorably on August 15, and the seventeenth was fixed for debate in executive session. Rives led off with an explanation and justification of the terms, and Benton opened the attack along the lines laid down by Blair in the *Globe:* The treaty was a dishonorable surrender of territory in the matter of the Maine boundary, and a pusillanimous sacrifice of national interests in its failure to deal with Oregon, the *Creole* case, and impressment. There were various other speeches, but it was Calhoun who convinced the doubters and insured the margin of victory with a speech on August 19. So clear and cogent is his argument that the effect could hardly have been other than what it was.[28]

His thesis was that they could not reject the treaty simply because it did not settle every point at issue, for to do so would be to lose the real gains arising from the points it did settle. The omissions could always be made good later. "It is not whether all has been done which it was desirable should be done;—not whether we have gained all we could desire, but whether we shall retain what we have gained. To decide this as it ought to be, it is our duty to weigh, calmly and fairly, the reasons for and against ratification, and to decide in favor of the side which preponderates." Like Webster and Tyler, he was willing to accept as a diplomatic victory Ashburton's assurance that American ships would not in future be molested in British ports; but even without that assurance he thought the gains preponderant.

When Calhoun had finished speaking almost the entire Senate gathered around him while members individually offered their congratulations. A few, like Preston, who would not speak to him personally, rushed over to the other house to tell their friends that Calhoun had "covered himself with a mantle of glory." There was no audience in the galleries and no reporters so that all accounts of the speech came from the Senators themselves. On such authority the *Madisonian* pronounced it the "greatest effort" of its author's life, which had "swept every opposing obstacle away"; and Daniel Webster expressed privately a very similar opinion. Whether it was due to Calhoun's speech or not, the Treaty of Washington was ratified by the Senate on August 20, 1842, by a count of 39 to 9—seven votes more than the necessary two thirds.[29]

Back of Calhoun's mighty effort in behalf of the Webster-Ashburton Treaty lay his conviction that peace was better than war, and that commerce was the great promoter of peace. He had no doubt that all outstanding difficulties between Great Britain and the United States could be adjusted on the basis of free trade between the two nations, even their conflicting attitudes toward slavery. Free trade and mutual tolerance would permit the two economies to complement each other—would save the West, rescue the South, and benefit even the manufacturing North by speeding the flow of goods and cheapening raw materials. Throughout the period of negotiation Calhoun was in direct correspondence with Duff Green and other Americans abroad, and with British capitalists in both countries, who confirmed his views and strengthened his belief that salvation for the South lay not in war but in *rapprochement* with Britain.[30]

CHAPTER VI

THE "BLACK TARIFF"

1

As THE PANIC of 1837 receded into the past without noticeable improvement in economic conditions, agitation increased for a return of the protective tariff.[1] The compromise of 1833 was presently being represented in the manufacturing states as one of the causes of the long depression. The legislative program Clay sought to force upon his party after the election of 1840 was calculated to bring about a restoration of high duties by indirection, and after the bank vetoes of the special session the enactment of a new protective tariff became the primary objective of the Clay Whigs.

The choice of this issue automatically made Calhoun the leader of the opposition, and brought to his side not only the whole cotton-growing South but also substantial interests in the great commercial cities like Boston, New York, and Philadelphia, and potentially the grain states of the West. It was an issue, however, that left President Tyler in a position even more awkward, if possible, than that in which Clay's bank fight left him. For Tyler's own record in Congress had been as consistently antitariff as it had been antibank, yet his Secretaries of State and Treasury were high-tariff men and the leader of the party in the Senate was the very originator of the American System—a system that had once designed to spend freely on federally sponsored public works in order to justify large revenues from protective duties, and now proposed to accomplish the same result by paying off state debts.

Again Tyler was faced with a choice between capitulation at the cost of his own consistency, or reliance for support upon the Democrats, but this time the choice was harder to make. To defeat the tariff would almost certainly be to restore the Democrats to power, not in his own person but most probably in the person of John C. Calhoun. To accept the tariff would be to abdicate in favor of Henry Clay all but the ephemeral trappings of his Presidential office.

The President thought he discerned a third alternative in the creation of a party of his own with a program designed to split both Democrats and Whigs. With the executive patronage in his hands, with his personal leaning toward the views of the Southern Democrats, and with New England, New York, and Pennsylvania represented in his Cabinet, the prospect was not without hope. Tyler continued to receive encouragement from the powerful New York *Herald,* and by the time Congress met in December 1841 the *Madisonian* had been converted into a daily under the editorial direction of youthful but hard-hitting John B. Jones.[2]

The core of Tyler's program was to be a scheme for managing the finances of the government, distinct alike from national bank and independent treasury, which could be offered in redemption of the pledge in his final bank veto. Before the end of October both reconstituted Cabinet and unofficial advisers were at work on the problem. Judge Tucker submitted a plan, and Tazewell offered criticisms and suggestions. So, presumably, did Rives, and probably others. But the plan that finally emerged, for a Board of Exchequer to function under the Secretary of the Treasury but with various independent powers to manage the currency and to employ banks and other institutions as agents, was forged in the Cabinet. Tyler himself was probably the guiding spirit, but John C. Spencer, the Secretary of War, had the most profound knowledge of finance. Upshur, Legaré, and Forward each contributed, while Webster wrote the detailed report explaining the plan to Congress and to the public.[3]

In his first annual message sent to Congress December 7, 1841, the President in effect laid down his platform and invited members from both camps to enlist under his banner. In the matter of foreign relations the message, with its challenge to British policy, was almost truculent, but on the domestic side the President was tactful and soft-spoken. The finances were in a sorry state, with requirements greater than income; there was a noncommittal paragraph on the tariff; but a third of the document extolled the merits of the Board of Exchequer.[4]

It was something of a literary triumph that both Thurlow Weed and Andrew Jackson should find the message satisfactory, but politically it probably meant only that each saw in it evidence of surrender to his side.[5] In fact Tyler had closed the door to compromise. He had parted from the Whigs without joining forces with the Democ-

the whole into the broad concept of government that had guided his own actions for more than a dozen years.[10]

He began by challenging the whole philosophy that he conceived to lie behind the Whig attack on the Presidential veto. "The Senator from Kentucky . . . maintained that the people of these States constitute a nation; that the nation has a will of its own; that the numerical majority of the whole was the appropriate organ of its voice; and that whatever derogated from it, to that extent departed from the genius of the Government, and set up the will of the minority against the majority." It was not difficult to show that these propositions were far removed from the purposes of the Constitution.

The President was not chosen by a numerical majority of the whole, but by states. Seven of the twenty-six states then in the Union had a majority of the population by a million and a half, but the other nineteen had a majority of one in the electoral college. The Senate, certainly, did not represent the numerical majority, for Senators from fourteen states whose aggregate population was barely four million could outvote those from states whose combined population was nearly three times that figure. In the judiciary the numerical majority played no part at all, for the judges were appointed by the President who might be elected by a minority, and were confirmed by the Senate a majority of whose members represented a minority of the population; yet the Supreme Court might override laws made by the only branch of the government that was based on the numerical majority, the House of Representatives.

There were other and equally cogent arguments. The Constitution itself had been neither made nor ratified by numerical majorities, and the process by which it could be amended was the complete negation of mere majority will. It would have been possible in 1842 for twenty states with less than half the total population to amend the fundamental law, while seven states with scarcely more than 10 percent of the whole population could prevent amendment. Decidedly the government of the United States was not and was never intended to be one of the numerical majority, and the veto accorded the President against anything less than two thirds of both houses of Congress was but another evidence of it.

Calhoun went on to expound the theory of the government as he conceived the founders had meant it, arguing as he was to argue throughout the rest of his life that it was precisely in its departure from the principle of the numerical majority that its great strength lay. From the very beginning of the government there had been "a deep conflict of interests, real or supposed, between the different portions of the community, on subjects of the first magnitude." If the government had in fact been one of the numerical majority, what could the result have been "but to give the dominant interest, or combination of interests, an unlimited and despotic control over all others? What, but to vest it with the power to administer the Government for its exclusive benefit?"

He granted that rule by a minority would be even less just, but there was a solution. It lay, according to the South Carolina Senator, in the doctrine of the concurrent majority, which he had already discussed at large in his public papers of the nullification days, and now restated in the present context. The ends of government, "justice and security, within and without," could be achieved "by a judicious and wise division and organization of the Government and community, with reference to its different and conflicting interests,—and by taking the sense of each part separately, and the concurrence of all as the voice of the whole." It was such a government he believed to have been intended by the Constitution of the United States.

As he neared the end of his speech Calhoun returned to the point of Whig attack. If, he argued, the President's power had been increased beyond the limits originally contemplated, it was because Congress had placed that power in his hands. To withdraw or modify his veto would not change it, for that was neither cause nor symbol of his strength. "Is it not clear that, so far from the veto being the cause of the increase of his power, it would have acted as a limitation on it, if it had been more freely and frequently used? If the President had vetoed the original bank, the connection with the banking system, the tariffs of 1824 and 1828, and the numerous acts appropriating money for roads, canals, harbors, and a long list of other measures not less unconstitutional,—would his power have been half as great as it is now? He has grown great and powerful, not because *he used* his veto, but because *he abstained* from using it."

When he was through the Senators crowded around to congratulate him and to shake his hand, and there were no party lines observed in the general approval bestowed on him. That, at least, was the opinion of the reporter for the *Congressional Globe,* and of Calhoun himself. The speech received unprecedented circulation, with some

46,000 pamphlet copies going out from Washington alone in the next three weeks, along with complete texts in papers all over the land. It was indeed an extraordinary thing that while professed nationalists like Clay and Adams were busy agitating the most sharply sectional issues on the respective floors of Senate and House, the high priest of the Nullifiers could make so calm, restrained, and generally unanswerable an analysis of the political process: an analysis, moreover, that put in proper proportions the sectional conflict of interest, and showed it to be not irreconcilable within the constitutional framework. As a campaign document it was well worth the circulation it received, though it came up, as Calhoun himself noted, "almost to nullification." [11]

3

For another three months the Whig factions fought each other while the Democrats nursed their strength before the real issue of the session was directly debated. Clay's policy resolutions came up in March and Calhoun seized the occasion to produce another campaign document. In a speech unusually long for him he reviewed once more the tariff and revenue history that had led to the compromise of 1833, and produced elaborate statistical tables to demonstrate the benefits of that act. Clay's success in maintaining his control of the party against Tyler made him virtually certain of the Whig Presidential nomination for 1844, and Calhoun had therefore a specific platform in contrast to which he could build his own. Adroitly he argued that the whole structure of Clay's political edifice was built on the tariff, and in his own criticisms of the protective system he made his appeal to all who stood to profit by free trade; not the South alone, but the West and the commercial interest of the Northern cities. [12]

The Treasury meanwhile was again exhausted. The note issue authorized in January had proved inadequate and a mounting deficit loomed ahead. The partisan majority in Congress still ignored the revenue question, and as the financial crisis deepened Tyler himself was forced at last to capitulate to Clay. Late in March he sent in a special message reluctantly recommending that tariff duties be raised above the 20 percent level as the only way to provide funds needed for operating the government. At the same time, however, he expressed his disapproval of the Distribution Act of the previous session, and recalled with satisfaction that under its own terms the disbursement of land proceeds among the states would cease with the proposed increase in tariff duties.[13]

Clay was now sure both of his control over his party and of the success of his program. On March 31, 1842, he surrendered his Senate seat to John J. Crittenden and retired to private life, thereby freeing his hands for the coming Presidential campaign. In a brief and moving speech the brilliant Kentuckian bade farewell to all those with whom he had worked and quarreled, and asked that harsh words uttered in the heat of contest be forgotten and forgiven. For the moment, under the magic spell of Clay's personality, they were, and all crowded around to shake his hand as he took his leave. Among them was Calhoun, who had probably already determined on his own retirement at the end of the Congress, and who at that date fully expected to be the Democratic candidate who would oppose Clay and the whole program of government subsidies and centralized power for which he stood.[14]

A few days later Calhoun again underscored the relationship of banks, tariffs, loans, expenditures, and the consolidation of governmental power when he spoke against a new loan bill on April 12. He argued as he had in January that the government was impoverished because the expenses were too heavy, and that expenses had been made deliberately burdensome for the specific purpose of overriding the tariff schedules fixed in the Compromise Act. The automatic termination of distribution whenever duties rose above 20 percent was not compatible with Whig policy as Calhoun expounded it, and he predicted that before the session ended the pledge to that effect would be repudiated.[15]

Clay's withdrawal seemed only to intensify the bitterness between Tyler and the Whigs. To Clay's supporters the Tyler men were "Palace slaves," and under the growing pressure of party organization the number of the President's adherents dwindled to almost nothing. In the Senate Rives, Tallmadge, Preston, already renegades from the Democratic ranks, found it increasingly difficult to maintain an independent position, and in the House Wise and Cushing led an all but nonexistent party. Whig strength grew with evidences of returning unity, and with it boldness in their war against the President. The *Madisonian* lost the Senate printing and party leaders boasted openly that they would do precisely as Calhoun had forecast they would—repeal the restrictive clause in the Distribution Act and pass a high protective tariff.[16]

The campaign to "head" the President showed every evidence of careful planning. The periodical agitation in Congress, the flood of petitions and memorials demanding higher duties, the prominence given to popular suffering and distress, all were elements in the battle for protection. So was Clay's perfectly timed attack on the veto power, and the resolutions that were to commit the Senate. But the most potent weapon in the Whig armory was the empty Treasury. Public officers were not paid and public obligations were not met, yet the months dragged on with no move on the part of the Whig leaders either to raise the revenue or to reduce the expenditures. Even the appropriation bills for current expenses were held up until after Tyler's message of March 25 had committed him to higher duties. The Whig press called on the President to resign and lost no opportunity to taunt and torment the unhappy man whose thin sandy hair was already turning white under the strain of his office.

Through April and May the stalemate lasted, with June 30 the fateful day on which the country would be left with no revenue at all. The time was dangerously short, but the shorter it became the greater was the pressure on the President and the more difficult it would be for him to reject any measure that would bring money into the Treasury. Congress had been in session for six months before Fillmore on June 3 at last brought in his version of a revenue bill from the Committee on Ways and Means. It was a document of fifty pages, filled with tariff schedules on which no member could hope to pass an intelligent judgment in the bare three weeks that remained for the existing law to run.[17]

For a few days the President was allowed to squirm as he studied the schedules. Then on June 7 Fillmore offered a new and shorter bill: a mere twelve lines of print extending until August 1 all revenue laws in force on the first of June, "Provided, That nothing herein contained shall suspend the distribution of the proceeds of the public lands." Though the Compromise Act expired with the last reduction of duties, it provided a moral obligation that the imposts were not thereafter to be increased. On June 1, however, the last reduction had not yet taken place, so that the new bill would in effect keep the duties at a level higher than 20 percent after June 30. This in itself was a roundabout violation of the compromise, and the proviso made it also a violation of the Distribution Act. In a week's time the "Little Tariff," as it came to be called, was pushed through the House, and on June 24 it passed the Senate, going to the President the following day.[18]

Tyler's dilemma was as vicious as any President had yet faced. After almost seven months of stalling, the Whig majority in Congress had now given its Chief Magistrate exactly five days in which to choose between leaving the country entirely without revenue, or repudiating the compromise of 1833 which was in part his own work and accepting at the same time the distribution which he had already publicly condemned. To his eternal credit be it said that John Tyler did not need five days. On June 29 he returned one of the most stinging vetoes to which any Congress has been forced to listen, and assured the lawmakers that in default of other legislation he would collect duties at the rate of 20 percent ad valorem as laid down in the compromise.[19]

4

Calhoun returned to Washington on July 6 from a hurried four-weeks trip to the South. He had gone to investigate a sensational gold strike on his own Georgia property, of which we shall have more to say in another chapter. He found the House at work on the Fillmore bill, the "Big Tariff" which had been temporarily side-tracked in favor of the measure Tyler had vetoed. This bill too included a clause to keep the distribution in effect in spite of sharply increased duties, but it was forced through the House in ten legislative days, with debate so curtailed as to be a travesty, and a majority for the party policy that sometimes dropped as low as four votes. The process of bargaining and trading between representatives of different interests—call it lawmaking, logrolling, backscratching, or what you will, but do not call it statesmanship—by which this slender majority was secured was obvious and open, and went on until a matter of hours before the final passage. The margin of victory for protection-with-distribution was 116 to 112.[20]

Although no one doubted that the Big Tariff would meet at the President's hands the same fate as its predecessor, the farce was

A week later Adams offered a report which was read and immediately forced to a vote, receiving the approval of 100 members to 80 in opposition. The document, couched in the trenchant and caustic prose of which Adams was past master, had little enough to do with the veto message which was its excuse for being. It went back instead to the special session of 1841 and condemned the President at every point where he had disagreed with Congress. Even so had Andrew Jackson been condemned in his time, and John Tyler had voted "Aye." But Jackson at least had been accused of violating the law, whereas Tyler was charged with no more than disagreeing with his party.[26]

Perhaps Tyler thought grimly of his fiery predecessor and the protest the old General had returned without avail as he penned his own fruitless protest, which was laid before the House on August 30. In vain he quoted the fundamental charter on the Presidential power, and denied the right of Congress to censure him for doing his constitutional duty as he saw it. Even as the Senate of Tyler's day had treated Jackson the House now treated Tyler. The protest was not entered on the *Journal* and on Botts's motion three resolutions condemning the President's action were passed.[27]

6

For a week or more following the veto the House verged on dissolution, with Western Whigs refusing to pass any revenue bill at all rather than surrender the distribution of the land proceeds. The manufacturing interests of New England and Pennsylvania whipped them into line, however, by threatening to abandon Clay, and an agreement was reached on August 21. The next day the Fillmore bill without the distribution clause was reintroduced, and under the pitiless operation of the previous question was driven through to passage before the House rose. In the process the bill was twice killed by the Speaker's casting vote, but was reconsidered and ultimately carried by 104 to 103.[28]

The bill went immediately to the Senate, was reported back from the Committee on Finance with a minimum of delay, and for two days was debated in Committee of the Whole. Sundry amendments were adopted but none to alter the real character of the bill, which came up for final passage on August 27. Before the vote was taken there were various speeches of explanation, most important of them by James Buchanan and Silas Wright. So far the Democratic party had been united against every Whig move to re-establish the protective policy, but now these two key Senators, from the two most populous states, announced their purpose to vote for the bill before them. Both put it on the ground that chaos would result should the government be left without revenue, and both held out the promise that this return to a policy repudiated by their own party was a temporary expedient, forced by necessity. When the Democrats returned to power, which they expected to do at the next congressional election, the law, they promised, would be modified.[29]

Calhoun took the floor just ahead of the vote. With great gentleness but obvious disappointment he expressed his regret at this defection from the Democratic ranks. He branded the bill in terms similar to those he had used three weeks earlier as worse than the tariff of 1828—a bill calculated to yield the maximum protection to industry with the minimum of revenue and the greatest hardship upon the agricultural states. The needs of the government, he warned, would not grow less, nor would the demands of the manufacturers abate as they prospered under this law, and he prophesied that even the return of the Democracy to power would not be permitted to affect the protective policy once re-established. Then the vote was taken and the bill passed by 24 to 23. Wright and Buchanan voted with the majority but three Southern Whigs—Berrien, Graham, and Mangum—cast their ballots against the policy.[30]

Since Tyler had grounded his previous veto on the coupling of tariff and distribution he had no alternative but to sign the modified bill, though his signature on it went far to destroy the good will that had been growing between President and Southern Democrats. It was largely because Tyler yielded on this crucial point that Calhoun declined to enter the Cabinet as Secretary of State, and Jackson's nephew, A. J. Donelson, refused the Treasury.[31] The tariff also created a new rift in the Democratic phalanx, or rather it reopened the deep chasm of Jackson's time. The desertion of Buchanan and Wright was to Calhoun a matter of the greatest significance and portent, both for his Presidential aspirations and for the ultimate success of the economic policy he held essential to the prosperity of the

South. For Wright's vote, in part with an eye to his own re-election, was also in part to smooth Van Buren's path in Pennsylvania. Back in South Carolina after the adjournment Calhoun was able to quell an angry move to nullify this new "black tariff" then and there only because his followers expected him to be elected President in two years' time.[32]

CHAPTER VII

AGAIN THE GLITTERING CROWN

1

THE PRESIDENCY had been in Calhoun's thoughts at least since the winter of 1839-1840, when his personal differences with Van Buren had been patched up and the Democracy had come over almost without reservation to his political position. At the close of the special session of 1841, with the Whigs split into warring factions and the Democrats united as they had not been for decades, he decided the time for action had come. Rhett brought the word to South Carolina where the powerful state machine was readied to play its part in the coming contest.[1]

As soon as he returned to Fort Hill in September Calhoun began writing to friendly Democratic leaders in various parts of the country. In these letters he analyzed the political situation as he saw it, and stated his conclusion that the next Presidential election would turn on the issue "between Republicanism and Federalism; State Rights and Consolidation; Democracy and an artificial moneyed aristocracy engendered and fostered by the Government." He expressed his own principles as they had been embodied in his speeches during the past two sessions of Congress, and suggested that the next Democratic nominee should be from the South. The reader was expected to fill in the name for himself.[2]

At the same time the men of the inner circle—Francis W. Pickens; Dixon H. Lewis, the 400-pound Congressman from Alabama; Robert M. T. Hunter, the Virginian who had lately been Speaker of the House; Rhett; Elmore—these and their associates wrote in more forthright vein to the same politicians and to others elsewhere, upholding the case for Calhoun's nomination by the Democracy. He himself probably suggested many of the men to be approached in this fashion, and he undoubtedly indicated the tone he wanted the Charleston *Mercury* and the Columbia *South Carolinian* to take. By mid-October cautiously worded feelers were going out to selected

89

party leaders over the nation, and out of the responses local Calhoun organizations would presently be built up. The method of approach is well illustrated in a letter from Pickens to Levi Woodbury, written at Calhoun's suggestion.

"It is not to be disguised," Pickens explained, after a preliminary paragraph on local prospects, "that the friends of Mr. Calhoun in Va N. Ca. Geo. Ala Ill: and Penn: are very anxious to put up his name immediately, but so far as I have written it has been to discourage any movement yet a while. He has enthusiastic friends, and there can be no doubt but that he could carry every Southern State except Lou: and Tenn:" These enthusiastic friends, however, did not want to move without consulting prominent members of the party throughout the country. Though they felt the merits of their candidate to be incontrovertible, they wanted the forthright backing of the whole party. "But," Pickens went on, "I need not dwell on these points to one of your sagacity & experience. I write you candidly & freely, and would be glad to hear from you in the same spirit. If we can act together, as far as I am concerned . . . I should rejoice to go into the great contest with N. H. & So Ca side by side. Our States have been more united and unshaken than any in the confederacy, and our feelings are decidedly that two of their eminent citizens like yourself & Mr. Calhoun shall head our ticket in our next contest. It would be a fine moral lesson to the Confederacy, to see the Rep: Party rallying on two citizens from two of the smaller states of the Union." [3]

It was adroitly done, for Woodbury knew that Calhoun had always commanded a following in New England and in Pennsylvania in spite of his antitariff views. He could see the returns coming in showing Whig defeats in states where Calhoun was admittedly strong; and the Vice Presidency so circumspectly held out to him was not yet the niche for nonentities that it later became.

As optimistic reports came in Calhoun's own excitement rose, and by November 1841 he was sure that the fruit was his for the plucking. Even among his intimates, however, he still maintained the aloof detachment that propriety required and displayed all the traditional reluctance to undertake the heavy responsibilities of the Presidency. His words were calm and dispassionate but under the surface he was seething. "Many of my friends think the time has arrived when my name ought to be presented for the next presidency. It is my own impression, that, if it is ever intended, now is the time. . . . Personally, I feel little solicitude on the subject. If I know myself I would not accept the place, if proffered by the people, except from a sense of duty. At my time of life it has few charms for me; but if it should be thought, that I can best restore the constitution and reform the Government, I would not shrink from the responsibility." [4]

His friends were equally sanguine but were in disagreement as to how far they should go or where they should strike. There was danger that a Democratic victory in the New York elections might precipitate a formal Van Buren nomination in that state, and there was a distinct advantage in being first in the field, always providing the right kind of endorsement could be secured in the right quarters. All agreed that Calhoun should not be brought forward initially by the legislature of his own state, but beyond that each followed his own bent. Among those who regarded themselves as his managers there were some who wanted the first nomination of the South Carolinian to come from Pennsylvania or New York or Ohio: almost anywhere except the South. Others thought the South to be preferred as long as it was not South Carolina. Guarded letters from the North indicated a general willingness to support him if the party manifested a preference in that direction. Only Van Buren was seriously spoken of as a competitor, and no one had yet placed the ex-President in formal nomination except Benton. Friends in Georgia thought their state would do it for Calhoun, and presently convinced him that a nomination there, in view of his ancient and bitter quarrel with William H. Crawford, would be a special sort of triumph. [5]

With that incredibly buoyant temperament of his, Calhoun never for a moment doubted the unanimity of his support in South Carolina. The old internal wounds must be healed for he himself had applied the salve. So he wrote to Governor Richardson, whom he seemed to regard as now a creature of his own, to inform him that a nomination would shortly be made in Georgia and probably also in one of the Western states. He apparently expected that the Governor would then see to it that South Carolina properly acknowledged these outside tributes to her favorite son. Richardson told the story to Poinsett, who promptly passed the word along to Van Buren. [6] The Georgia gesture quickly bogged down in the dismal swamp of internal politics, and who is to say that some forewarned Van Burenite was not responsible?

Neither man was nominated that winter, and when Calhoun reached Washington for the regular session he found the consensus against any premature agitation of the Presidential question. In this he saw nothing to shake his faith in his own ultimate success, nor was he disturbed to find that James Buchanan was also busily campaigning. Indeed, as the session progressed and the leading issues raised by the Clay Whigs continued to be those with which Calhoun was most closely identified, he felt that he had "never been stronger." [7]

His managers gradually widened the range of their operations, and by the spring of 1842 they were dangling the Vice Presidency before a not unreceptive Silas Wright as well as Woodbury. There were even elliptical overtures to Van Buren designed to convince him that while he could not win himself, a Calhoun-Wright ticket was a certainty if only he would endorse it. As Buchanan's prospects faded the Calhoun managers added him also to their list of Vice Presidents presumptive, while they sought strength in another doubtful state by trying to wean Tennessee's James K. Polk away from his New York allegiance. Calhoun limited his own activities for the time being to formulating policy and advancing a political program on the Senate floor.[8]

2

Circumstances and adroit political management combined during the first six months of 1842 to underline the ideological differences between State Rights and Locofoco wings of the Democracy as well as to point up the issues separating Democrats from Whigs. Reference has already been made to Clay's antiveto resolutions, and to Calhoun's brilliant performance in defense of government by the concurrent majority. What Clay was actually trying to do, in addition to annoying John Tyler, was to take advantage of the rising power of the common man. He was appealing, in a way he knew to be perfectly safe, to the doctrine of unvarnished majority rule, and Calhoun answered him on that ground: that government by the numerical majority alone was tyranny in its worst form, was never contemplated by the founding fathers, and could never be put into practice without destroying all that was unique and valuable in the structure of the American government. But in taking this position Calhoun was putting himself in opposition only incidentally to Clay. The real egalitarians were the Locofocos.

The background of the equal-rights movement need not concern us here, save only that it stemmed from the industrial revolution and in one form or another extended throughout the Western world. Most of the familiar isms of the 1840's—abolitionism, socialism, Fourierism, Chartism, communism, and the rest—had common roots. The factory system had created a class of urban workers, no longer tied to the soil, and for that very reason without the political power that traditionally belonged to the yeoman farmer. Yet the profits of the capitalistic system, potentially and actually far greater than those under any previous form of economic organization, were clearly gravitating into the hands of a relatively small group. The remedy seemed to lie in the more equitable distribution of wealth through political action, which required in turn the extension of the franchise and ultimately the control of the numerical majority.

None of this was explicit in the theorizing of the politicians, but Jefferson had demonstrated long ago how easily one might ride to power on the basis of mass appeal. The party system itself had forced the gradual liberalization of voting qualifications, and Van Buren's New York machine, handed down from Burr and Clinton, rested on the organization of the masses. The power of the Crawford Radicals of the 1820's had been similarly based, and when these two machines had merged in the Jackson movement they had carried over the same methods. It was not an idealistic belief in the worth and dignity of man (though the movement attracted many idealists to its ranks); it was simply good politics. The party that secured to each new segment of the population the privilege of voting might legitimately expect to receive its reward at the ballot box. The party that promised to improve the condition of the working man would be inept indeed if it could not secure the working man's vote in consequence. By the 1840's that vote, in the more highly industrialized states like Pennsylvania and New York, had become worth bidding for.

The issue was rudely injected into politics early in 1842. Rhode Island, where the factory system first took root on American soil, was still governed under a colonial charter with the franchise narrowly confined to a small group of freeholders. Agitation over a period of years resulted in a constitutional convention, unsanctioned by law and unblessed by authority, in the fall of 1841, and the constitution so drafted was ratified by a popular, but still illegal, vote that included majorities both of the adult males and of the freeholders. The authorities tried to recapture the situation with a convention and a new constitution of their own, which was submitted to the voters and rejected early in March 1842. Despite an unofficial opinion of the state Supreme Court that the "People's Constitution" had no legal validity, and in defiance of an act of the legislature imposing criminal penalties against those who ran for office under it, an election was held in April and a roster of state officers headed by Thomas Wilson Dorr was elected.[9]

The legal Governor of Rhode Island appealed to President Tyler to back him up, and Tyler had no alternative but to pledge the full support of the Federal Government should actual rebellion occur. The Washington *Globe* declaimed volubly of oppression and violated faith and by May the official paper of the Democratic party was openly espousing the cause of the rebels. The New York Democracy pledged men and money to the popular side and under Blair's prompting the aged Hero of New Orleans sent his personal blessing from the Hermitage. The Whig press defended the President and the *status quo,* but the terms of the defense were those of Calhoun's concurrent majority, and the Calhoun managers were quickly convinced that the whole affair was being used for a covert attack on the South Carolina Senator.[10]

Encouraged by the enthusiasm of the Locofocos, Dorr prepared to invade Rhode Island with volunteers from other states and take over by force the power that had been voted illegally into his hands. At this point Tyler sent the Secretary of War to the scene and moved troops to strategic points. The volunteers vanished forthwith, and the movement collapsed without bloodshed in June 1842, leaving Dorr and his followers to face charges of treason against the state. The episode was over but it had served to align the Van Buren-Benton-Blair wing of the Democracy on the side of popular sovereignty in opposition to the conservative balance of interests that alone represented security to the South.[11]

The same conflict of principle also ran through the debates over reapportionment which were carried on almost simultaneously with the Dorr uprising, from the latter part of April until early June 1842. The crucial point was a proposal offered in the House by John Campbell of South Carolina. After each previous census Congress had done no more than determine the ratio of inhabitants to Representatives in the lower chamber, leaving the manner of their selection exclusively to the states. In most cases the members were chosen from specific geographical areas or districts, but in a few instances, including Georgia, Alabama, New Hampshire, New Jersey, and parts of New York and Pennsylvania, elections were by general ticket only. It was obvious that in these states the party that held the majority, however narrow the margin might be, would elect all the Representatives. Yet it was highly unlikely, even with the aid of the iniquitous gerrymander, that Congressional districts of approximately equal population would all show the same partisan majority in any relatively evenly balanced state, and in fact they did not. The district system, in short, offered the minority party a chance to be represented, and divided the total representation more nearly in proportion to actual party strength. Campbell's amendment made the district system mandatory, and it so passed the House.[12]

Calhoun's partisans were divided on the question, and his own position was awkward. The State Rights philosophy certainly could not condone interference by the Federal Government in a matter left by the Constitution to the states; yet the doctrine of the concurrent majority would be better served by the district system, and Calhoun himself, although he said little on the subject, favored that arrangement.

In the Senate the apportionment bill went to the Judiciary Committee of which Berrien of Georgia was chairman, and when it reached the floor toward the middle of May the disputed provision had been rendered harmless. It was promptly restored to its original form, and the principle behind it was expounded by Jabez W. Huntington of Connecticut in language that might have been borrowed from Calhoun. Benton and the Van Buren group defended the general ticket for the same reason that they supported Dorr: the unlimited right of the majority to rule was the basis of their power. The district system passed the Senate as it had the House, and though he had grave misgivings the President signed it.[13]

3

From the very beginning of his campaign Calhoun had too many managers with not enough sound political understanding. Instead of keeping all the threads firmly in his own hands, or delegating the whole direction of the campaign to one able individual, he allowed his partisans to do more or less as they pleased. He thought it undignified to work directly in his own behalf and steadfastly refused to talk of anything but principles or to ask anything except victory for the Democracy. He would not suppress his views nor guard his speech, and he would not make promises that he could not redeem. He would sooner have renounced forever the high office he so deeply desired than admit even to his intimates that he really wanted it. He was too inflexible for campaign purposes, and so those who most ardently desired his election did not always tell him what they meant to do, nor warn him of breakers ahead.

Perhaps none of them foresaw Wright's vote to re-establish the protective system, but practical politicians aware of the economic forces by which men were moved should have been prepared for such an outcome. During the months of the tariff fight the signs were there, but with even the Washington *Globe* praising him as one of the great men of the Democracy Calhoun never doubted that all was going well. Yet Blair and Wright and Benton were alert to every shift of the political breeze and aware of every change in the public pulse, and when the time was ripe they did as they were bound by their own sectional ties to do. In his August 5 attack on the tariff Calhoun called the pending bill worse than that of 1828 on which he blamed many—doubtless too many—of the financial and political evils of the past decade and a half. He said nothing of it on this occasion, but in times past he had freely taunted Benton and Van Buren and Wright for their part in the passage of that earlier "bill of abominations," and Benton now chose to regard Calhoun's remarks as directed at himself and his friends.[14]

Three weeks later Wright voted for the tariff on its final passage in the Senate. Calhoun knew then that the Northern Democracy had made peace with the manufacturers and would in time make peace with the abolitionists. There would be no more talk of Silas Wright for

[PRIVATE.]

I enclose you a Prospectus of a Newspaper, which the friends of Mr. Calhoun have selected to be the Central Organ of the Calhoun portion of the Democratic Party. The Spectator will continue to be published Weekly, as

account to him for the same, at two prices named in the Prospectus, as I have informed him of the number of receipts that I send you.

Calling your early attention to the subject, which is important,

I remain, with respect, &c.

Your obedient servant,

Prospectus of the *Spectator*, 1843

VIRGIL MAXCY   ROBERT M. T. HUNTER

ABEL P. UPSHUR   ROBERT BARNWELL RHETT

JAMES H. HAMMOND   DIXON H. LEWIS

Vice President, and the rift between Calhoun and Van Buren would never again be healed.

The tariff of 1842 served only to re-emphasize the deep sectional cleavage underlying the political currents of the time. Southern Democrat and Southern Whig, Northern Democrat, Northern Whig, Liberty man, Native American—in a few more years there would be only North and South. It would not be so because Calhoun opposed the tariff and defended slavery, nor because John Quincy Adams attached himself to the abolitionist crusade, nor because the North lived on a higher moral plane than the South. It would be so because of the nature of man, because of the character and quality of the nineteenth century, because of history itself. It would be so because men are forever opening Pandora's boxes that they have not skill nor strength nor will to close; because human ingenuity is forever turning loose amoral forces whose tendencies human wisdom is inadequate to foresee and whose power the political process is impotent to control. Already partisan differences were being overshadowed by sectional community of interest. The slave question was being deliberately agitated in order to create precisely that Northern solidarity which made tariffs possible, and that Southern unity which made resistance sure.

4

By the time Congress adjourned on the last day of August 1842 both the organization and the tactics of Calhoun's campaign had been worked out. The over-all direction was in the hands of a Central Committee in Washington of which Hunter was chairman and Lewis and Pickens members. Subordinate committees were established as rapidly as possible at the state level, where they secured control of newspaper outlets and served as the inspirational sources for local groups on down the line. Through these committees passed a furious exchange of letters, news stories, and advice. It was the same pattern Calhoun had followed in his first Presidential campaign twenty years before, and many among his older counselors had been with him then.[15]

In spite of the sectional cleavage on the tariff issue, the prospects on the whole were favorable as of the fall of 1842. Woodbury was now openly committed, and it was generally agreed that Calhoun was at that date the choice of a majority of the Democratic Senators, perhaps also of the members of the House. His outspoken championship of the Webster-Ashburton Treaty had strengthened him in the North where a growing free-trade interest was already backing him, and there was nothing really against him except his defense of slavery and an afterimage of emotionalism going back to the nullification days.[16]

In North Carolina, Virginia, Massachusetts, New York, the Calhoun organizations were active, turning local issues to their own uses and enlisting local politicians in their ranks. In North Carolina they succeeded in blocking the election of a Van Buren partisan to the United States Senate, even though they had not strength to elect their own man, Romulus M. Saunders. The choice fell on William Haywood, who had expressed no preference between the South Carolinian and the New Yorker.[17] The abolition and tariff questions were turned by his Virginia followers to Calhoun's advantage, and every effort was made to enlist the support of Thomas Ritchie and his powerful Richmond *Enquirer*. Hunter directed the Virginia campaign, but Pickens and Rhett both found occasion to call on Ritchie during the fall, and Calhoun himself spent a day in Richmond in December.[18] In Massachusetts David Henshaw emerged from political retirement and began building a Calhoun party to contest the Democratic leadership of George Bancroft and Marcus Morton. He was aided by Woodbury's influence which reached out from New Hampshire into most of New England, and presently Charles Greene brought the influential Boston *Post* to Calhoun's support.[19]

It was in Van Buren's own stronghold of New York that the greatest challenge lay, but it was there that the divided counsels of the Calhoun managers told most heavily against their cause. The New York Democracy, out of power since 1840, was split into two major factions. One group stood for financial stability and opposed any extension of the costly and graft-ridden canal system. These came to be known as "Barnburners," charged by their foes with wanting to burn the barn to get rid of the rats; but they were for the most part Locofocos who had espoused the popular side in the Dorr rebellion and acknowledged Martin Van Buren as their leader. Those who sought to extend the canal system even though it must be done with borrowed funds were "Hunkers" whose primary object was said to be a large "hunk" of the spoils of office. Among the

Hunkers the most important figure was former Governor William L. Marcy.[20]

The original issue between the two factions was soon submerged in a forthright battle for political power, which threatened to come to a head in 1842. Controlled by Van Buren, the state Democratic convention which met at Syracuse early in September brought about a temporary reconciliation. William C. Bouck, one of the Canal Commissioners, was nominated for Governor, but was pledged to a platform opposing any increase in the state debt. At the same time, however, with an eye on Calhoun's New York organization, resolutions were passed commending Wright's vote in favor of the tariff of 1842.[21]

The Calhoun campaign was in the hands of a small but articulate group in New York City, of which Joseph A. Scoville was the moving spirit. A journalist by profession, Scoville was well versed in the intricacies of New York politics, was a man of abundant energy and infectious enthusiasm, and had a literary flair that led him later to become a novelist. There was no question of his devotion to Calhoun, nor of the disinterestedness of his considerable labors in the Carolinian's cause, but he was indiscreet in his confidences, and his performance often fell below his intentions. Rhett, Elmore, and Thomas D. Sumter of the South Carolina Congressional delegation, who visited New York in the fall, thought Scoville not to be trusted, but they nevertheless accepted uncritically his interpretation of Bouck's election as a Calhoun triumph.[22]

5

Calhoun had probably decided early in the year to retire from the Senate at the end of the current Congress, and although his advisers were divided on that question, as they were on most others, he prepared to submit his resignation when the South Carolina Legislature met in late November 1842. On all of the major issues of the day he was fully committed and had made lucid speeches that could be handed around in answer to the inevitable questions. If he continued on the firing line any or all of these matters might be reopened, and he might be forced under pressure from his opponents to go further than would be politically expedient. It was suspected, moreover, that a deliberate attempt to embarrass him might be made, either by a full-scale debate on the Rhode Island controversy or by allowing R. H. Bayard's standing effort to repeal the expunging resolution of 1836 to come to the floor. Either of these maneuvers would have the effect of embroiling Calhoun once more with the Locofoco Democrats, with all those who held that Andrew Jackson could not be wrong, and ultimately with Jackson himself, at the very time that Calhoun's managers were trying by fair means or foul to win the old Hero over to their side.[23]

Calhoun's letter of resignation was dated November 26, 1842. On Monday November 28 the *Mercury* proclaimed him a candidate for President (as though it had not been treating him as such for two years already!) and placed at the head of its editorial column the "Democratic Banner" set forth in Calhoun's antitariff speech of August 5: "Free Trade; Low Duties; No Debt; Separation from Banks; Economy; Retrenchment; and a strict adherence to the Constitution."

The following day William C. Preston, now that his term had only a few more months to run, tendered his own resignation, effective immediately. Because he was present in Columbia at the time while Calhoun was still at Fort Hill, Preston's resignation was received first, and on December 2, by unanimous vote, George McDuffie was chosen to fill both the unexpired term and the full term of six years from March 4, 1843.[24]

Calhoun's resignation was laid before the legislature on December 3, and precipitated an immediate furor. It had been widely advertised beforehand, giving ample time for rival Senatorial candidates to build organizations. Not Barnwell Rhett and Pickens alone, but Daniel E. Huger and William F. Davie, both old Unionists, appeared as aspirants. Rhett and Pickens were both in Washington for the session of Congress, but each had left his affairs in competent hands. Rhett's manager was his brother Albert, while Pickens seems to have confided his own prospects to Hammond.[25]

Consideration of Calhoun's resignation was postponed until after the gubernatorial election, which took place on December 8. Hammond won out according to plan, but by the slimmest of margins. The virtually unanimous election to which he had looked forward for more than a year vanished suddenly when the last unreconstructed remnants of the old Union party put up the popular and much respected R. F. W. Allston to run against him. The final count was 83 for Hammond, 76 for Allston, and two scattered. In the background was a degree of personal distaste for Hammond, resentment against the Rhett-Elmore clique, and a stubborn battle over the re-districting of the state, which lost two seats in the House under the reapportionment act of 1842.[26]

Following Hammond's election, the legislature returned to Calhoun's resignation. Christopher G. Memminger, outspoken Unionist of a decade before and one day to be Secretary of the Treasury in the Confederacy, had been named chairman of a joint committee to consider the question. Memminger reported a series of resolutions commending Calhoun's services in extravagant terms, and concluding that South Carolina would regard his withdrawal with deep regret, "were it not for the expectation that they are about to yield up their separate claim upon his services, to share them in common with the whole Union." It quickly developed, however, that a substantial segment of opinion opposed accepting the resignation at all, while another group favored accepting it but immediately re-electing Calhoun to the vacancy. These were younger men, less concerned about Calhoun's Presidential prospects than about South Carolina's destiny. As one of them frankly put it in debate, their great champion's services might yet be needed in the Senate, for South Carolina "had *nullified* a tariff law, not so bad as the one now in force, and her spirit was no less now than then." Truly Calhoun had sown the wind and the whirlwind was already visible, a tiny cloud on the horizon. The debate was warm, but the House finally passed the resolutions on December 13, and the Senate the following day.[27]

The battle over a successor was then fought out on December 15. On the first ballot Huger polled 56, Rhett 46, Pickens 30, and Davie 29. The second ballot added five to Huger's total and ten to Rhett's, but on the third ballot Pickens was withdrawn and his strength thrown to Huger. At least that is what Albert Rhett was sure had happened when Huger won out by 82 to Rhett's 71 with a handful scattered. The younger Rhett thereafter blamed Pickens for his brother's defeat, but the real responsibility lay elsewhere. Calhoun had long been bent on wiping out the old rift between Unionist and Nullifier. Two Senate seats were vacated at once, and to one of them George McDuffie, outstanding among the nullification leaders, had been unanimously elected. A former Nullifier had also been chosen Governor, and both fairness and politics dictated that the other Senate seat should go to a Unionist. Rhett, moreover, had spoken and written too openly of secession to make him acceptable to Calhoun. No, it was not Pickens but undoubtedly Calhoun himself who threw the election to Huger, even though he thereby brought into conflict with one another men who should have been united behind his own campaign.[28]

The legislature closed its session by passing unanimously a joint resolution nominating John Caldwell Calhoun for the Presidency of the United States.

CHAPTER VIII

CANDIDATE ONCE MORE

1

CALHOUN took his seat in the Senate on December 15, 1842, supremely confident that it would be his last session as a member of that body. Though he was nearing the end of his sixtieth year and had long suffered from an undue susceptibility to bronchial and lung infections, he was this winter in excellent health and humor. There was about him a sort of exaltation as though already he transcended in spirit the station he occupied and dwelt on that he hoped to attain. On January 1, 1843—a mild, springlike day such as Washington now and again produces in midwinter—the tall, spare Carolinian dominated the largest Presidential levee ever held up to that date. One did not have to guess at his thoughts as he stood smiling in the center of the East Room of the White House surrounded by lovely women and distinguished men, the social, political, and business leaders of the day.[1]

There were other Democratic aspirants, of course, and their pretensions could not be overlooked, but as of the beginning of 1843 Calhoun appeared the favorite. It was true that a nomination by the Georgia Legislature, following that in South Carolina, had been achieved only with considerable difficulty; but one had only to watch the confident way he moved about the Senate chamber, the easy assurance of his partisans in both houses, the deference of Democrats of all persuasions, to be sure that he was indeed, as his managers claimed, the choice of the party's legislators. Van Buren was conceded to be the most dangerous rival still, and there were those who claimed for him an outright ascendency, but the claim was premature.[2]

The campaign was gaining momentum on all fronts. Big, heavy-jowled Lewis Cass stopped off in Boston and New York on his way home from France, and talked with many people before he reached Washington, where he arrived just in time to show himself at the

103

New Year's levee. His platform was opposition to the British treaty, which was the declared reason for his resignation, but his organization had been quietly at work for months. Among his backers he already counted Major William B. Lewis, Senator Rives of Virginia, and Governor David Porter of Pennsylvania, and in New York he was openly bidding for the support of Marcy and the Hunkers. A campaign biography, devoting much space to Cass's services as Secretary of War during the nullification crisis, was in the mill, and the Pennsylvania Legislature was expected to declare itself in his favor.[3] Richard M. Johnson, Vice President under Van Buren and last available hero of the war of 1812, also had a following though as yet no boom.

A new and potentially greater threat to Calhoun's chances appeared early in January when the New York *Union* placed at its masthead the names of John Tyler for President and Governor William C. Bouck for Vice President, meaning as it apparently did that Tyler had made up his mind to seek the Democratic nomination for himself. Similiar Tyler banners appeared in other places, and the Van Buren men began to take alarm. The *Madisonian* suddenly became a Democratic sheet, and the *Globe's* pretense of neutrality between Van Buren and the field wore very thin. Yet Tyler was ideologically much closer to Calhoun than to any other candidate. Was he not, perhaps, merely a stalking horse for the gaunt South Carolinian?[4]

2

The Calhoun managers met each new challenge by extending their own activities and intensifying their efforts from Washington down to the local grassroots. They were men familiar with the political process and they enlisted in their cause practical politicians at all levels of government. They knew, or thought they knew, how Van Buren had secured his own election in 1836, and the two victories for Jackson that preceded it, and they prepared to fight the little Dutchman on his own ground, with his own weapons. How far Calhoun himself was aware of the activities of Hunter, Lewis, and their local henchmen cannot be certainly determined, but perhaps he privately agreed that the less he knew about it the better.

The most potent political engine on a nationwide scale was the Post Office. The Treasury, through the patronage of the various collectors of customs, was powerful in the seaboard states and especially so in New York. The State Department, through its contracts for printing the laws and other public notices, was in position to subsidize partially or wholly at least one newspaper in each state. The control of these avenues of access to the public will had formed the backbone of the Democratic machine since Crawford's day, and the subsequent growth in population, in national wealth, and in the cost of government only added to their potency.

It was these earthy tools of politics that Calhoun's managers sought to secure in the interest of their candidate. With local postmasters as agents a staggering volume of campaign publicity could be distributed without cost for postage to voters in every village and hamlet in the land, and as Scoville cynically noted, "Mr. Calhoun need not appear in it, nor Tyler either." They felt the same way about the customhouses, and especially that in New York City where Collector Edward Curtis, originally a Webster partisan, was now presumably working in Tyler's interest. There was already an infiltration of Calhoun men in that office, and should rumor prove true that Curtis was to be removed, they counted on Woodbury and other friendly Senators to see that none but a Calhoun man was confirmed to replace him.[5]

Another of the New York group wrote to Hunter with even greater frankness about the methods they hoped to employ. "The Post office department properly managed," he explained, "can be used as one of the most powerful engines in getting Mr. Calhoun nominated." He wanted the control of it at once, and seemed to regard the Postmaster General as the only obstacle to that end. "I hope," he continued, "Mr. Calhoun will not hesitate in so important a matter in having a satisfactory personal interview with Mr. W—— and hand him a carte blanche for his own use when Mr. C—— comes in—providing Wickliffe will do right." In the thirteen free states alone he counted 8,440 Post Offices: "8440 active politicians" with the franking privilege.[6]

There is no evidence that Hunter ever passed on to Calhoun this blunt proposal that Wickliffe be suitably suborned, and it is hardly likely that he did. It is quite possible, however, that Lewis, or Rhett, or Hunter himself had a quiet talk with the Postmaster General. These men who had Calhoun's campaign in charge were of a different generation from their leader. They were born in Jefferson's time and bred to politics in the days when the first national machine was coming into its own. In their experience the only methods that had elected Presidents were those they now proposed to use, and they would not risk having their candidate interfere with their plans. Not that Calhoun would fail to appreciate the importance of the Post Office in the political scheme of things: it would simply have been impossible for him to give Wickliffe a blank check on future office. He would, instead, have called on that potent functionary, talked long and brilliantly of the need for tariff reform, for curbing the abolitionists, and for all the other items of his creed; and he would have come away persuaded by his own eloquence that Wickliffe agreed with him and would therefore be on his side.

The Calhoun organization was no doubt responsible for the laudatory sketch of the South Carolinian in the January 1843 number of the *Democratic Review,* with an unusually good steel engraving from Blanchard's miniature for frontispiece. Since its founding in the fall of 1837 the *Review* had been an official party organ, but it had been as undeviating as the *Globe* in its adherence to Van Buren. Now it seemed almost captured for the service of the ex-President's most formidable rival. Calhoun was boldly called "the great Nullifier" and was hailed as belonging to "that foremost few from whom the Democratic Party is at this moment hesitating in its choice of its next candidate for the Presidency." [7]

The enthusiasm of Calhoun's partisans could not be doubted, but the success of their activities was dubious. Though they understood the methods of the machine politician well enough, they were singularly inept in carrying them out; either that, or the quality of their candidate was too great a handicap. For the political machine is amoral and completely indifferent to the finer points of political theory. Its job is to deliver votes in return for offices, contracts, and legislation favorable to the interests of those who cast the ballots or supply the campaign funds, and a man who pursued a principle without regard to party over a score of years was a questionable risk. The Calhoun newspapers, led by the *Mercury,* reported steady gains, and local workers up and down the land thought every move they made in behalf of the South Carolina Senator a sure success. Yet the personnel of Post Offices and customhouses changed but little, and the incumbents seemed very slow to alter allegiances already held. Van Buren, whose henchmen advised him of every move that Hunter and his agents made, was content for the time being to wait.[8]

3

The friends of the various candidates juggled issues at will to serve their purposes. Tyler stated his own case in his second annual message, again playing up the Board of Exchequer and suggesting that the tariff, "somewhat hastily and hurriedly passed near the close of the late session of Congress," might well be revised. He also made much of the Webster-Ashburton Treaty and expressed the hope that the Oregon boundary might be similarly settled at an early date.[9]

The Oregon question also appealed to the Locofocos, though for a different reason. Blair was still condemning the Ashburton Treaty in the *Globe* when Senator Lewis F. Linn of Missouri introduced a bill for the occupation and settlement of Oregon. A major controversy was soon in progress, with the Locofocos and Western men of all parties supporting Linn. It was a question Calhoun's managers would have preferred to avoid, but it was one on which he had decided views and he proclaimed them. So did George McDuffie, who took his seat on January 9 as junior Senator from South Carolina. The position of the two Carolinians was simply that international obligations were sacred. The United States occupied Oregon jointly with Great Britain under a treaty first made in 1818 and renewed in 1827. Either nation might end the arrangement by giving one year's notice. To conservatives like Calhoun and McDuffie, Linn's bill, which provided for fortifications and grants of land, was a plain violation of the joint occupancy agreement. If the United States wished to fortify Oregon and distribute the land among her citizens, the treaty must first be denounced in due form and the required year allowed to elapse.

McDuffie's speech on January 25 was his first in the Senate. So great was his reputation that the House, where he had served a thirteen-year apprenticeship, was all but deserted while the members crowded the floor and galleries of the Senate chamber to hear him. Calhoun followed six days later, with another of those definitive speeches of his, so complete that there was nothing more to add, so compact that nothing could be omitted without destroying the logical unity of the whole. It was on this occasion that he pronounced the true American policy toward Oregon to be "a wise and masterly inactivity." The United States was weaker than Britain in the Northwest, both on land and on the ocean, but settlers by the thousands were disgorging year by year into the fertile valleys of the Columbia and the Willamette. In a few short years the issue would be dead and Oregon fully peopled by the hardy pioneer stock that had in a single generation pushed from the Mississippi to the Pacific.[10]

Even the Washington *Globe* praised the speech as unanswerable if one accepted the premise that the treaty of joint occupancy would be violated by the proposed policy. But of course Blair believed no such thing, and in his subtle way he insinuated that anyone who did believe it was no true friend of the West. In truth, as Webster explained in a private letter to the American Minister in London, "This new outbreak of interest and zeal for Oregon has its origin in motives and objects this side the Rocky Mountains. . . . Mr. Benton, as leader of the Van Buren party . . . is disposed to make war upon everything which Mr. Calhoun supports." With his eyes wide open Calhoun had walked boldly into the trap he knew was there. Though his Oregon speech was sound and statesmanlike and courageous, it cost him more strength in the West than he could afford to lose.[11]

4

All this was a deliberate muddying of the waters to divert attention. The real issue between Calhoun and Van Buren, or more properly between the Southern and Northern wings of the Democracy, was a basic economic question, strictly sectional in its bearings. When Silas Wright voted for the tariff of 1842 he did so with a full understanding of the situation. Over a period of years the protection of domestic industry had become in Northern eyes the indispensable condition of prosperity, just as free trade and the retention of the slave system seemed to Southerners to lie at the very foundation of their economy. Van Buren and his partisans were aware of the free-trade sentiment in the commercial cities but they realized that it was bound in the end to be submerged in the stronger interest. So Van Buren, who had won the Presidency in 1836 as the Northern man with Southern principles, was ready in 1842 to accept the tariff, and by 1844 he would also accept the antislavery position. The cleavage within the party was a clear sectional line based on divergence of economic interest, with the West holding the balance of power. The Van Buren group made its bid for Western support on the basis of territorial expansion and distrust of Great Britain. The Calhoun group held out to Western grain growers the prospect of lush British markets under a system of free trade.[12]

Though all states had not yet voted, the off-year elections showed so strong a Democratic trend that control of both houses in the Twenty-eighth Congress was assured. The policy to be followed by that Congress thus became itself an issue in the contest for the Democratic Presidential nomination. In the South resentment against the tariff of 1842, both in itself and for the manner of its passage, overshadowed all other considerations. Calhoun had been able to hold his more radical followers in check only by assurances that the tariff would be reformed, but this time they were not content with promises. They insisted that the desired legislation be enacted before they nominated a candidate for President, and so they demanded that the party convention be held no earlier than May 1844. Let Van Buren's followers vote first to restore the compromise of 1833 and they would accept him if they must, but not before.[13]

Just to make doubly sure of the ascendency of their policy, Calhoun's partisans asked also for a convention whose members were elected by Congressional districts and voted as individuals. They were in this adapting the same arguments they had used in support of the district system for electing Representatives under the reapportionment following the 1840 census. On the face of it the procedure was democratic and would give full expression to the popular will; but in practice it meant that no protectionist could be nominated. Free-trade sentiment was strong enough in the commercial cities to split the vote of New York, Pennsylvania, Massachusetts; and the grain regions of the West would be similarly split. The South, with its greater economic unity, would be solidly for a free-trade candidate. In short, Van Buren could control the convention if delegates were chosen by general ticket because he had small majorities in enough states to give him a preponderance of the total. By districts Calhoun would be as strong because he could command virtually unanimous support in some states and strong minorities in most of the others.

The burden of proof was on Calhoun because he was advocating a departure from the customary practice, so it was his partisans who launched the convention as an issue. On January 25, 1843, the Charleston *Mercury* published a pointed "Appeal to the Democratic Party, on the Principles of a National Convention for the nomination of President and Vice President of the United States." It was issued simultaneously in pamphlet form and franked in quantity up and down the land. It was also published in full in Bennett's New York *Herald,* where it carried the signature of Robert Barnwell Rhett. The substance of the appeal was that true democracy and the national welfare alike would best be served by postponing the convention until May or June of 1844 and by using the district system in the choice of delegates.[14]

The Van Buren managers had anticipated the issue, and were vigorously pressing for a convention date not later than November 1843, conveniently ahead of the meeting of Congress. As a countermeasure they charged that Calhoun's followers were merely seeking an excuse to reject the convention nominee if it happened to be someone not to their taste. All state and local nominations of Van Buren were made specifically "subject to the decision of a Democratic Convention," and the Locofocos demanded similar assurances of good faith from the State Rights men. The familiar questions always asked of candidates began to include one as to the willingness of the aspirant to abide by the convention choice, but Calhoun refused to be trapped. His name, he answered, had been presented for the Presidency not by himself but by his friends, and it was up to them to decide what course they would pursue. He professed, however, "no reason to doubt, but that they will cheerfully abide by the decision of a convention, fairly called, and fairly constituted; that would allow ample time for the full development of public opinion, and would represent fully, equally, and fairly, the voice of the majority of the people." Thus qualified, the assurance could be given, and the *Mercury* added the line under Calhoun's name at the head of its editorial column on February 8.[15]

5

The Calhoun managers emphasized principles rather than personalities, but they believed their candidate to be so completely identified with the doctrines they designed to establish that a victory for one would automatically be a triumph for the other. It was very important nevertheless to reiterate at every opportunity the nature and scope of the South Carolinian's views. To the average citizen of the North and West, thanks largely to the skillful propaganda job turned out by Francis Preston Blair a dozen years earlier, nullification and treason were still synonymous. Since that time the tall, shaggy-headed Scot had become something of a hero to the Democracy, even in the free states, and it was worth considerable effort so to clarify his career as to eliminate the lingering prejudice. The obvious way was to publish a carefully prepared biography and a volume of well-chosen speeches.

There were various memoirs in newspaper and pamphlet form already in existence, going back to Calhoun's first campaign in 1822, but there had been nothing of a comprehensive nature since Virgil Maxcy's sketch in the *United States' Telegraph* in 1831. Scoville, with whom the project seems to have originated, began pressing Calhoun directly, and indirectly through Hunter, for the materials necessary to bring the story up to date. Calhoun responded on September 30, 1842, in characteristic fashion. He thought it important that both a biographical sketch and a collection of his "speeches, reports and communications, at least on the subjects that may bear on the coming contest" should be published, but to him it seemed "much more important, that it should be well done, than speedily done." The volume of speeches he promised to prepare himself, in such leisure as his correspondence afforded. As for the sketch, he promised that with the materials he had at hand he would "get a friend next week to commence preparing" it.[16]

The manuscript was probably in final form by the end of 1842. On the twenty-third of January 1843 Scoville signed a contract with Harper and Brothers covering both the biography and the speeches, and within a day or so the proof sheets of the former were in his hands. Maxcy, who had just returned from his tour of duty as United States chargé in Brussels, witnessed the contract. Harpers announced the work at the same time and it was ready for distribution about the middle of February 1843. The price was 12½ cents, but there was a quantity rate of $80 per thousand.[17]

In its final form the volume was about fifty thousand words in length, was unsigned, and bore the impressive and not altogether inaccurate title: *Life of John C. Calhoun, Presenting a Condensed History of Political Events from 1811 to 1843*. The only direct contemporary evidence as to authorship comes from Calhoun himself, who told his daughter early in February that Hunter had "rewritten" most of it; "so much so as fairly to be entitled to the authorship." When he mailed a copy from Washington to his brother-in-law later that month he referred to it as having been "prepared by some of my friends here"; and early in the following year, in a letter to Hunter, he speaks of "my life, prepared by yourself." [18] The first half of the work is in fact only an expansion of Maxcy's 1831 sketch, retaining much of the original language. The last two pages of the *Life*, in particular, are taken without any alteration from the conclusion of the Maxcy sketch. There is stylistic evidence of more than one hand in the composition, but there seems no valid reason to doubt Calhoun's statement that Hunter was responsible for the final version.[19]

As such things go the *Life* was a very creditable job, which evaded neither Calhoun's early championship of the Second Bank of the United States, nor the touchy nullification issue. The distribution, however, was mishandled almost from the start. The volume of speeches that was supposed to accompany it did not appear until more than three months later, and even then the title page was incorrect because no one bothered to give the correct one to the printer, or to revise the proofs. For these failures the Calhoun organization was to blame, but Scoville most of all. No one made firm arrangements with local dealers; no one provided funds to purchase copies for free distribution. Somewhere along the line Scoville gave up the contract simply by turning a blank assignment over to Maxcy, but he neglected to inform the Harpers, who were frantically trying to get him to correct proofs of the volume of speeches. Eventually Maxcy and Hunter moved in and straightened out the tangle as best they could, but valuable time had been lost. There were no more than eighteen thousand copies of the *Life* in circulation by June, and these included the stocks of local dealers, while the *Speeches* did not appear at all until the end of May.[20]

6

Scoville had not really lost interest in the *Life* and the *Speeches;* he had simply carried the business as far as he thought necessary, and had moved on to the next project, leaving others to clean up the old one. The new project was a Calhoun newspaper in Washington. The decision was made by the Central Committee before Calhoun left the city at the close of the session, and the arrangements undoubtedly had his approval. It was the Washington group that should have had full control, but the ebullient Scoville lost no time in making the whole venture, so far as might be, his own. It was only the steady hand of Virgil Maxcy in the background that prevented something like catastrophe.

The paper acquired was the *Spectator,* a weekly, Democratic in politics, with a slight preference for Buchanan and more debts than either its assets or its circulation justified. The paper had been started sometime in 1842 by Dr. J. L. Martin, who had associated with him John Heart from the staff of Blair's *Globe.* Around the first of March 1843 Martin agreed to withdraw for no more solid consideration than that of being relieved of all responsibility for the paper's debts. It appears to have been Lewis, Maxcy, and Scoville who made the deal. Heart remained as proprietor, but Maxcy was the real directing force behind the scenes, and until another could be found, Scoville was the editor. [21]

The formal shift of ownership was effected on March 18, 1843, and in a signed editorial Heart pledged that his paper would thenceforth "zealously urge upon the country" the claims of John C. Calhoun of South Carolina to the Presidency. As long as it remained in existence the *Spectator* continued to be an undeviating personal organ for the great Nullifier, upholding the district system and the late convention date, attacking the tariff, abolition, Henry Clay, and Martin Van Buren. The hands were variously those of Scoville, Maxcy, Hunter, and Rhett, but the voice was unmistakably Calhoun's.[22]

7

During the last frantic days of the Twenty-seventh Congress Tyler undertook to reward those who had served him well. Prominent among his last-minute appointments were those of Henry A. Wise to succeed Lewis Cass as Minister to France, and Caleb Cushing to be Secretary of the Treasury in place of Walter Forward whose tariff views made him no longer acceptable. Both were rejected by the Senate, but Tyler sent both names in again on March 3. Again they were rejected, by larger margins; but still the President persisted. The pair was before the Senate still a third time that same evening, and as the final minutes ticked away both were turned down by an almost unanimous vote. A few days earlier Cushing had sustained the South on one of the ever more frequent sectional issues before the House, and Adams had coined for his colleague the epithet of "doughface." In these votes on confirmation the South reciprocated, with Calhoun and McDuffie sustaining the nominations against both Whigs and Democrats.[23]

The decision Tyler had been so long evading, whether to run himself or to cast in his lot with Calhoun, was thus forced upon him, and a tentative coalition was hammered out. Already in New York the Tyler forces were said to be working in Calhoun's interest, using Mordecai Noah's *Union* for that purpose; and it was widely believed in Washington that a bargain had been struck. Tyler was to have his chance, with the support of the Calhoun organization, but if he did not show strength the roles were to be reversed.[24]

The subsequent events lent some show of color to the supposition. As soon as Congress had defiantly adjourned around midnight of March 3, 1843, Washington began to empty of its dignitaries and the scene shifted to New York. A few days later the *Herald* announced the formal launching of the Tyler campaign, with Governor Bouck as running mate. There was to be a monster meeting on the evening of March 15 at the great Broadway Tabernacle, where Wise and Cushing would be among the principal speakers, and if all went well the self-styled Napoleon of the press would himself become the President's champion. At the same time the *Madisonian* stoutly defended the "generous and noble Carolinian" from what its editor termed the "despicable" attacks of the *Globe*. Samuel Gouverneur, a veteran of Calhoun's first Presidential campaign, made a hurried trip to New York a few days before the meeting, and at least one observer thought he was to muster the Calhoun forces for the Tyler demonstration.[25]

The meeting was held as planned, with as much publicity as the popular *Herald* could give it; but the demonstration was so dismal a failure that Bennett promptly declared Tyler out of the running. The sensational New York editor had already begun to give space to Calhoun meetings, and by the time the *Spectator* made its appearance in Washington as a Calhoun sheet he had begun to wonder editorially if the Carolinian would not now command the backing of the administration. The *Madisonian*, to be sure, insisted that the New York meeting had been a great success, and on the strength of it ran up the Tyler banner complete with a statement of principles. Thereafter it carried at the masthead the names of John Tyler and William C. Bouck, but the principles that followed were indistinguishable from those that adorned the editorial column of the *Spectator*.[26]

CHAPTER IX

RETIREMENT

1

WHILE Calhoun's political lieutenants headed for New York and the great Tyler meeting that was to force the President to support their candidate, the gaunt South Carolina Senator himself was hurrying home. He was already in Charleston on March 9, 1843, when the meeting was announced in the New York *Herald,* and well before the event itself he had resumed the life he loved above all others. For the first time since his election to the state legislature in 1808 John C. Calhoun was a private citizen, responsible only for his plantation and its people. For months he had been anticipating his retirement with mounting eagerness, and now at last he was free to pursue his own inclinations and interests.[1]

Preoccupied though he often seemed with politics and with his own intellectual variations on political themes, Calhoun's world centered around the beautiful patchwork of woods and fields that he always called his "farm." From its broad bottom lands along the turbulent Seneca River the Fort Hill tract rose steeply through wooded ravines and carefully cultivated slopes to the two-hundred-foot elevation on which the large, comfortable-looking house was forever in process of remodeling. The gleaming white pillars of the eastern portico caught the early morning sun as it filtered through the sheltering branches of oak and cedar, and outlined obliquely the larger and more imposing columns of the north portico. A stone's throw south of the house stood the square white building that served Calhoun as library and office, detached, uncompromising, and unadorned, as befitted the qualities of the man who worked there, often by candlelight or oil lamp before the sun was up.

Early in 1842 the size of the place had been doubled by the fortunate purchase of 552 acres of upland adjoining the original property on the north. The acquisition included land Calhoun had coveted since he had first made Fort Hill his permanent home, but it had been unavailable until the death of its owner in 1840. Thus enlarged to 1100 acres the farm, already self-sufficing, might reasonably be expected to supply a moderate living for its owner and the hundred or so persons, including perhaps eighty Negro slaves, who were entirely dependent on it now Calhoun had removed himself from the public pay roll.[2]

At sixty-one Calhoun was the undisputed chieftain of a large but scattered clan, all three of his own brothers having died since 1840.[3] Those of the next generation were striking out for themselves, through South Carolina and the South, and on to the remote corners of the globe. Yet Fort Hill, because Calhoun lived there, remained the heart and center of a family to which he was, affectionately and with all proper respect, "the old man."

By and large it was Calhoun's own character and way of life that made his home the attractive and restful place it was, for all of its constant buzzing of activity. Always he fought hard and ingeniously for what he believed, but he never rebelled against defeat or suffering, and never lost faith in the ultimate rightness of the Divine Plan. Mary Boykin Chesnut tells how, some years after his death, she heard a distinguished group of Southerners exhalting his hospitality. "He allowed everybody to stay all night who chose to stop at his house. An ill-mannered person, on one occasion, refused to attend family prayers. Mr. Calhoun said to the servant, 'Saddle that man's horse and let him go.'" "I believe in Mr. Calhoun's hospitality," commented Mrs. Chesnut, "but not in his family prayers. Mr. Calhoun's piety was of the most philosophical type, from all accounts." Philosophical it was, but none the less deep or sincere for that. To Calhoun the universe itself, moving inscrutably according to discoverable laws, was sufficient proof of order and purpose beyond the comprehension of men. He did not, therefore, question either the good or the evil that he found in the world or in his own life. "I look with perfect composure on the advance of time," he wrote when he was nearing sixty to an old college friend, "knowing that it is in the order of Providence and that it is our highest duty to acquiesce in his decrees. My confidence in his wisdom & goodness is without limits, and has been the support, which has sustained me through all the vicissitudes of life."[4]

So friends and strangers alike found him calm, unruffled, imperturbable, at once austere and friendly, reserved and approachable. His manners were graceful and without guile, his interests cultured, his personal habits temperate. Worth repeating, even though it is probably not wholly true, is the story of a visit to a distinguished Alabaman between sessions of Congress in the spring of 1841. The visit was well publicized in advance, and the home of his host was crowded with local dignitaries who had come from miles around to meet the famous Senator. In due time the guests were invited to another room to have something to drink. Calhoun did not rise, and soon found himself alone with an elderly gentleman who had brought his two sons with him. Pressed for an explanation, Calhoun remarked, "I never drink." "I would vote for him," the old gentleman is quoted as saying, "if for no other reason but for the sake of such an example to the young men of the country." [5]

The story was told, of course, as a bit of campaign propaganda, but it was characteristic of the man. He would, moreover, have declined so graciously that neither his host nor his fellow guests would have felt any embarrassment for their own indulgence. He was not prudish or puritanical. He simply believed that temperance in food and drink was better for body and mind than indulgence. He did not extend his abstinence to wine, which was usually served with dinner at Fort Hill.[6]

2

Floride Calhoun was her husband's first cousin once removed. Ten years his junior, she was in temperament and interests at the opposite pole. Rather short and inclined to be stout in these latter years, she contrasted physically with the tall, lanky Senator as strikingly as she did in her qualities of mind. Gracious and charming, renowned as a hostess, convivial and gregarious most of the time, Floride was yet of a suspicious temper, meting out personal blame for all that went wrong and for many things that were wrong only in her imagination. She cared nothing at all for politics, or the intellectual pursuits that occupied her husband's time. Neither was she interested in agriculture. But her home was beautifully kept and her house servants excellently trained. She was devoted to her children, but she could quarrel with them in thoroughgoing fashion. Only with Calhoun she did not quarrel, because he recognized her faults of temperament, made allowances for them, and accepted them with Calvinistic fatalism as part of life.[7]

Calhoun preferred family life to all others, as his nostalgic letters from Washington reveal again and again. He liked to have Floride with him when he attended sessions of Congress, though she seldom found it possible to go; and as the children grew up he always felt happiest when one or more of them shared his periodic exiles in the Capital. To Floride he wrote regularly when they were separated, chafed when letters went astray or when for some reason she did not write to him as often as he wished. "Say to your Mother," runs a typical passage in a letter to one of his daughters, "I will write her in a few days; and that I have not received a single line from her in return to the letters, which I have written since I left home." Yet that was in the special session of 1841, and he had been away only a month.[8]

He was always picking up oddments for the family and the farm, and was eternally responding to requests from home to buy this or attend to that. Perhaps it was "plumb stones" of some special variety that he slipped into a parcel of magazines so they might be planted at Fort Hill; or gloves for Floride to try, with a promise that if the family approved them, he would get similar ones for the others. There were many things one could not buy in Pendleton village, and so letters from home would contain such passages as this from Anna: "While I think of it mother sends love & desires me to say she forgot to tell you she wished two pair of buckskin & one pair of velvet shoes the size of her measure. She also wishes you to get her a dozen ivory rings for table napkins. You can get them ready made & numbered at the jewellers." [9]

In the summer of 1842, when questions so vital to him as the tariff and the British treaty were before the Senate, Calhoun prepared to rush home on learning that Floride had been attacked by "giddiness" that might be apoplectic. He was dissuaded only when his wife's ever reliable brother, James Edward Calhoun, who had been hastily summoned to Fort Hill wrote that there was no danger. Even then he remained uneasy until he heard from Floride herself. [10]

3

Calhoun gave generously of his time and affection to his children. Andrew Pickens Calhoun, in his thirty-second year at the time of his father's retirement, was a planter in his own right on the rich bottom lands of the Tombigbee River in Alabama. There he lived with his wife, the former Margaret Green, and his small son, Duff Green Calhoun; but there would be many others in Andrew's family. Next in order came Anna Clemson, not yet twenty-six, who with her husband and two infants was still at Fort Hill, though they too would shortly leave for a place of their own. The two Clemson children were and remained the favorites of their maternal grandparents, for whom they were named: John Calhoun Clemson, born in July of 1841; and Floride Elizabeth Clemson who appeared on the scene just two days before the end of 1842.

The other Calhoun children were unmarried, and four of them were still in school. The exception was Patrick—Lieutenant Patrick Calhoun of the United States Army, then twenty-two and stationed, to his disgust, at a frontier post in the Southwest. After Patrick came John Caldwell, Jr., two years younger than his military brother; and the partially crippled Martha Cornelia, who celebrated her nineteenth birthday shortly after her father's return home in the spring of 1843. James Edward, also called "junior" to distinguish him from the uncle for whom he was named, followed Cornelia after a two-year lapse; and the baby of the family was William Lowndes Calhoun, who was a mere thirteen in that same spring of 1843.

Of them all, Calhoun was closest to Anna. She alone had inherited his quick and penetrating mind, and shared the great range of his interests. The deep affection between father and daughter was apparent even through the wall of reserve behind which Calhoun habitually sheltered his personal life.

Anna suffered a long period of illness in 1840 and 1841, but even though she was frequently flat on her back, she wrote cheerful and gossipy letters to her father. Clemson was "out early & late" attending to the business of the farm. The boys were taking dancing lessons in the village. Floride was "as busy as ever, & paddles in & out, in cold & wet, & I scold her for doing it but can make no impression or change." Cornelia was having trouble with her eyes, and the family conspired to occupy her time, so that she would not read too much. Often the house would be full of guests, and Anna would write of the young cousins who took up the carpet in the great entrance hall of Fort Hill every Friday and Saturday night to "dance very happily," even though she herself was not well enough to join them. "It seems to me," she complained almost loverwise to her father, "instead of being accustomed to being separated from you, I feel it more & more I suppose because I have so few pleasures, that, like a miser, I wish to hoard them closer." [11]

Calhoun responded with long letters in which political discourses were enlivened by comments on people and events. After Christmas dinner at the White House in 1841 he noted for Anna's benefit that Mrs. Robert Tyler was an accomplished hostess, "sensible and very well behaved," while Elizabeth Tyler was "really quite hansome." A few months later he passed on his impressions of Charles Dickens who visited Washington in March 1842. He found the famous novelist "rather good looking; but not strikingly so; young, fair complexion and a pleasant countenace, with easy simple manners. Not very marked for anything, that I could see, but nothing in the slightest degree offensive. . . . His lady is quite homely and somewhat countrified in her manners, but I would say amiable and sensible, of which I think she gave proof by continuing at her needle all the time, when I visited them in the morning, except when she took part in the conversation." [12]

There was never a hint in these letters that the writer was an active candidate for President of the United States, and calmly confident that he would be elected to that office. The correspondence between Calhoun and Anna Clemson revealed only an unusually close father-and-daughter relationship between two highly gifted people.

4

If Anna was her father's greatest comfort, Patrick was his greatest trial. The "little Irishman" of twenty years earlier was now the dashing officer of dragoons, adept at all that enticed the gay young blade of the 1840's. More than once while he was still at West Point there had been sudden revelations of gambling debts, of substantial sums hastily borrowed from friends or relatives, of questionable com-

panions. But his father never reproached or berated him, accepting
Pat's extravagance as he accepted Floride's temper, with complete
composure and no diminution of his own affection.

The young lieutenant was in Charleston in January of 1842, commissioned but not yet assigned, and finding ways no doubt to entertain himself in what was then and is today one of America's most
fascinating cities. He was already talking of resigning his commission, though without much idea what he would do then. Calhoun
wrote, by way of Anna, that he would offer no objection to Pat's
leaving the army, provided he would settle down in a good business,
or alternatively, marry a girl with enough money to support him.
Calhoun did not put it quite that bluntly, to be sure, but that was the
point.[13] Anna, who loved the genial, good-looking, devil-may-care
Pat almost as much as she loved her father, passed on the paternal
wishes with embellishments of her own. Pat was in no hurry either
to settle down or to marry, even for money, and so he stayed in the
army.

At the post to which he was shortly assigned Pat picked up
acquaintances with his customary ease and uncriticalness, lent money
to one of them, and lost it. Calhoun learned of the misadventure
by accident. Typically, Pat poured out his troubles to Anna, but the
letter was delivered to his father in Washington, having arrived
there, no doubt, with military dispatches; and Calhoun read it before
he sent it on. He was quite willing that Anna should be the one to
put salve on the young officer's wounds, but he suggested that she
also warn him that men who borrowed money and vanished were not
the only adventurers. There were also unscrupulous women seeking
husbands, and for one of these Pat would be an easy conquest.[14]

As late as the winter of 1842-1843 the evidences of Patrick's
past good times in the fleshpots of the East were still coming in.
His father, the Presidential candidate whose name was as widely
known as that of any man in the country and whose personal honor
and integrity were above reproach, paid off his son's debts as they
came to his notice, but he did not blame or criticize. He accepted
Pat's word that the bills he took up in Boston and New York were
the last outstanding, and contented himself with a warning that he
would be financially unable to extend further aid. "I hope," Calhoun
wrote of the transactions to Anna, "throwing him on his pay, will
teach him the importance of prudence & economy. His expense, from

the time he graduated till he returned home, was enormous; not less than $700 or 800 for a few months." [15]

5

The younger boys, Johnny and Jimmy and Willie, went to school in Pendleton village, but they showed little inclination toward scholarship. They dallied and frittered away the time, while their father urged application, asked them to write to him of their progress, and finally wondered if the curriculum itself were not at fault. Johnny should have been ready for college in 1841, but he was not. Calhoun decided that the boy's studies had not followed his bent, and so he wrote to Clemson to have a talk with the teacher. Clearly Johnny had no taste for Latin or Greek. "I wish him to cease their study, and direct his studies to arithmetick, Geometry, English Grammer, if not already familiar with it, writing, including spelling and composition, till I return," and Clemson was to urge on the errant scholar "the importance of exerting himself." If all went well, John was then to be entered at the University of Virginia, where he would enjoy greater freedom in the choice of studies than most colleges then allowed.[16]

It was actually not until March of 1843 that John directed his steps toward Charlottesville, where he went first of all to call upon Henry St. George Tucker, Professor of Law at the University. Tucker had served with Calhoun in the House of Representatives many years before, and had lately resigned as Chief Justice of the Virginia Supreme Court of Appeals to accept the position he now held. For old friendship's sake Tucker at once undertook to supply a father's place while Johnny was at Virginia, and Calhoun was pleased and flattered. The Judge agreed as to the boy's potentialities and advised a strictly scientific course.[17]

During the same period the girls of the Calhoun household— Cornelia, Eugenia who was the daughter of Calhoun's brother William, undoubtedly another cousin or two—and probably the daughters of some of the Fort Hill neighbors went to school to Miss Mary Bates. Miss Bates was the accomplished New England girl who dwelt in the Calhoun home for several years as virtually one of the family while she taught French and music and letters and such other accomplishments as well-bred young ladies of the 1840's were supposed to possess—the same Mary Bates who has left us such an intimate picture of Calhoun's home life. Tuition was $100 a year for each pupil, and we have it on Calhoun's authority that there was "no better school in the State." [18]

Also members of the Calhoun household in 1843 were James Rion and his mother. After her illness in 1842 Floride felt the need of help in managing her overflowing household, and her choice fell on Mrs. Rion, who had served competently for a year or so as housekeeper at the Old Pendleton Hotel. Just who first suggested the installation of Mrs. Rion in a similar capacity at Fort Hill is not clear, but Dave Sloan later took the credit for it, and it may indeed have been his doing. For Dave, the son of Calhoun's old friend and neighbor Colonel William Sloan, was about the age of Willie Calhoun. Mrs. Rion's own son, Jim, was of the same age, and ever since he had entered Pendleton school the three boys had been inseparable. It no doubt seemed an excellent thing in their eyes that Jim should be established at Fort Hill instead of four miles away in Pendleton village. And an excellent thing it was, for Mrs. Rion quickly made herself indispensable, and James Rion, with Calhoun's patronage, went on to college and became one of South Carolina's most distinguished lawyers. [19]

6

Between the fall of 1840 and Calhoun's retirement in the spring of 1843 Fort Hill was managed by Thomas G. Clemson, the tall, energetic, imaginative young mining engineer who had married Anna Maria Calhoun in 1838. Though he was Pennsylvania-born and trained in Europe, Clemson adjusted easily to the Southern way of life. The one thing he could not adjust to was the character of his brother-in-law, Andrew Calhoun. The original cause of friction between the two was money, but even had there been no financial dealings it would probably have arisen anyway, from purely temperamental differences.

Andrew had little of his father's intellectual grasp and had no particular concern for politics save as public policy might increase his private profit. He was concerned primarily with material success, in an age not overscrupulous in its economic morality. Had he been reared in the North he might well have become an industrial promoter and perhaps a power in business. As it was he planted cotton and ever more cotton, on lands bought with borrowed funds, with field hands many of whom were taken from Fort Hill; and year after year he reinvested such profits as there were in further expansion. The twenty thousand dollars with which his Alabama lands were bought came originally from Thomas Clemson, who, as a member of the family, should not be too concerned about repayment.[20]

Clemson did not see it that way. In mind and character he resembled his father-in-law more closely than any of Calhoun's own children except his beloved Anna; but his interests ran to exact science, pure and applied, rather than to politics. He was a pioneer in the application of chemistry to agriculture, in which he first became interested through his association with Calhoun. Like his father-in-law he was a competent man of business, and enough of a moralist and logician to believe that contracts should be fulfilled, whether they were constitutional guarantees or notes of hand. Both Andrew and Clemson inclined to truculence, and so with the contracting currency and expanding horizons of the early 1840's all the elements for a family quarrel were at hand.

Calhoun's persistent but veiled attempts to smooth things out were ignored by Andrew and were taken by Clemson to imply censure of himself. In his reserved and ever so proper way, the older man was trying to be strictly impartial in a quarrel of which he tried to appear ignorant. But he was hurt by the very existence of the difficulty, and distressed that Clemson should think him dissatisfied. "I deeply regret," he wrote to Anna in the spring of 1840, "that there should be any alienation of feelings between him [Clemson] and Andrew. I could not but see it last fall, but, of course, propriety forbid me from seeming to see it, or to make any enquiry into the cause." [21]

Somehow things were patched up, probably by Anna's mediation, and Clemson's energies were presently absorbed in the management of the Fort Hill plantation. Andrew, meanwhile, had contracted other family debts, this time to his Uncle James Edward, and again Calhoun felt compelled to intervene. He visited Cane Brake, as Andrew's place was called, shortly before he left for the special session of 1841, and was impressed as he never failed to be by the scope and magnificent promise of his son's undertaking. There were 620 acres in all, 400 of them in cotton, which he was sure would produce not less than 400 clean pounds to the acre. So Calhoun passed along to his brother-in-law his son's regrets "that he has not been able to pay you owing to the difficulty of collecting his debts in Alabama & the heavy expenses he has been subjected [to] in the settlement of a new place," but added Andrew's assurances "that he would certainly pay you out of the coming crop unless it should fall greatly below his calculations." [22]

Despite the excellence of his crop Andrew's debts were not paid in 1841. James Edward could be relied on to wait with tolerant patience; and Clemson found a new interest about harvest time that absorbed his attention for the next several months. With Fort Hill back on its feet the young scientist agreed to make a mineral survey of the island of Cuba for a private firm. Calhoun dropped a note to Daniel Webster, the Secretary of State, about passports and necessary clearances with Spanish authorities, and in January 1842 Clemson set off, taking Anna and their small son along. Willie Calhoun went too, "for his health" he said, but really no doubt for a lark, and his father agreed, providing Anna would send him back in the spring. In Charleston before sailing they picked up Patrick also, just commissioned but still unassigned, and he too went along for a brief holiday. Pat was off to his army post in the spring, and Willie, Anna, and the child were back at Fort Hill in time to escape the damp heat of the Caribbean summer. Clemson himself followed in June, his return hastened by a sensational gold discovery on one of Calhoun's Georgia properties.[23]

7

Calhoun was already conspicuous throughout the country on account of his Presidential prospects and for his outspoken advocacy of free trade when in the summer of 1842 he became the central figure in a widely publicized gold strike. He had been interested in the gold-producing lands around Dahlonega, Georgia, since about 1830, and had been owner of the O'Bar mine since 1833, but had concentrated his capital and such Negroes as he could spare in developing another tract near by.[24] The venture had never much more than paid expenses, and Calhoun had turned his attention once more to cotton, getting deeper and deeper in debt as Andrew invested larger and larger sums in his Alabama lands.

Then somewhere past the middle of May 1842, with tariff, slavery, and British relations all critically at issue in Congress, came word of a fabulously rich gold strike at the O'Bar mine. The property was being operated on a profit-sharing basis and friends in Georgia wrote hurriedly that Calhoun must come at once to look after his own interests. Calhoun was not one to leave his post of duty lightly at a critical time, and he had seen too many rich strikes in the Georgia fields turn out to be isolated pockets soon exhausted to take the news too seriously. He did, however, write at once to Clemson, who was finishing up his Cuban survey, asking him to look over the O'Bar mine as soon as he returned to the states; and he also asked his old friend and onetime mining associate, John R. Matthews, who was on the ground, to assess the situation for him.[25]

The dispassionate evaluation was almost as fantastic as the rumor. He was told that with only eight workmen and no machinery $8,000 worth of gold had been taken from the mine in two weeks, not counting ore still unrefined. The vein, moreover, was growing richer. The only limiting factor seemed to be the size of the working force, and ordinarily sober men talked glibly of returns perhaps running into the millions. Calhoun waited another three weeks until a suitable lull in the legislative program was reached. Then on June 10, 1842, he left Washington and four days later was at Dahlonega. He discounted the wild speculations of his friends but he was too badly in need of funds to risk losing even a moderate sum by his own indifference.[26]

Calhoun was almost immediately joined by Clemson, who directed operations from that time on with a technical skill and scientific knowledge theretofore unknown in the Georgia gold fields. The Senator himself stayed only a few days before going on to Fort Hill to visit briefly with his family. He left on June 28 by the overland route, through Greenville and Raleigh, and was back in his seat when the Fourth of July recess was over.[27]

For the next two months Calhoun's losing battle against the tariff was punctuated by frequent letters from Clemson, running the gamut from riches to poverty and back again. On the day Calhoun left Fort Hill to return to Washington Clemson was unrestrained: "Some of the pans give, not including the rock specimens I think I may safely say from forty to fifty pennyweight, of loose gold—I have seen a good deal in the way of mining but this specimen of the capability of the mine passes every thing I have heard of—& if it continues as I think it will . . . you may really say that money is no object." He found it too expensive to crush the ore by hand, and drew plans for a mill. At the same time he wrote Anna at Fort Hill to send two more hands. Anna herself arrived on July 9, with such Negroes as could be spared from the farm; but was called back to Fort Hill almost immediately by the illness of her mother. Clemson pushed ahead with the new workmen. The vein, he wrote ecstatically later that month, "continued to be rich beyond what I have seen anywhere else. It would excite you to see it & really if it continues there is no telling to what extent it may yield." Then abruptly the gold vanished and for three days the mine yielded nothing at all, only to resume once more as rich as ever but with the character of the rock completely altered.[28]

That was really the end of the bonanza, though the mine continued to yield erratically for some years. Clemson made a hurried trip to Fort Hill at the beginning of August, and with James Edward, Sr., saw Floride off to Glenn Springs, a popular health resort near Spartanburg. When he returned to Georgia he brought Anna and her infant son with him—"a most fatiguing journey over the worst of roads." The gold-bearing vein, meanwhile, had "become very small, the rock very hard," and the tunnel flooded. There was another promising vein, but Clemson wanted Calhoun to look over the ground before he started a new digging, which would involve considerable capital outlay. For the six weeks or so that Clemson had been in charge Calhoun had received in toll $281 from the previous operations and $385 from Clemson's first deposit at the Dahlonega mint. Another 507 pennyweights had since been deposited, and 244 more were ready to be turned in for coinage. In short, it was profitable enough as a small operation, but it was a far cry from the original claims made for it as well as from Clemson's own first enthusiasm.[29]

Calhoun visited the mine again when he returned from Washington in September 1842, but the excitement was gone. It no longer represented a potential fortune, but merely a routine business venture involving considerable risk. The mill came into operation sometime in December and was crushing about 150 bushels of ore a day by the middle of January, but the quality was poor. When Calhoun was able once more to look over the ground in the spring of 1843 the accessible ore was visibly petering out and he faced the necessity for extensive tunneling and draining. His real interests lay elsewhere, and early in 1844 he leased the property to Benjamin M. Milner, for one quarter

NORTH PORTICO OF FORT HILL

MRS. JOHN C. CALHOUN
by James A. Bogle

of the profits and the privilege of engaging in independent operations on the tract if he chose.[30]

8

Shortly after he took over the O'Bar mine in the summer of 1842 Clemson bought a quarter interest in the Habersham Iron Works and Manufacturing Company at near-by Clarksville, Georgia. The deal was apparently a good one, with Clemson paying only $807 for his share of a property that included some hundreds of acres of land, a forge furnace, mills and sundry improvements, and 10,000 pounds of pig iron. The plan seems to have been for Clemson to run the establishment, for which purpose he estimated that he needed at least $10,000 of working capital. To get it he reopened the old financial issue with his father-in-law. He wanted "our Alabama affairs arranged & should like that you would arrange with Mr. Andrew Calhoun so that the papers be in readiness at as early a period after your return as you can make convenient—as it is not only important for every one to put his affairs in order, but particularly so for me at this time in order to make every thing suit my future plans & disbursements." [31]

Again some sort of adjustment was made, but again it was only a temporary expedient. There were, moreover, additions to the total indebtedness, which Calhoun himself assumed. The iron works did not prove any more successful than had the gold mine, probably because there was no suitable source of iron ore near by, and Clemson was left once more with an excess of energy to be absorbed. He surrendered the management of Fort Hill to its rightful proprietor on Calhoun's retirement from the Senate, and started looking for a plantation of his own. A satisfactory location was found near Edgefield, unfortunately called, like Andrew's place, "Cane Brake" or "Canebrake," as both were alternatively spelled. The place had been owned by Eldred Simkins, another of Calhoun's old friends, who had died in 1831. Since that time the property had been managed for the estate, among the heirs being Eliza, wife of Francis Pickens, and Maria, wife of James Edward Calhoun. A distribution of the estate was ordered in 1841, which required the sale of the property. The matter was still hanging fire in the summer of 1842 when Eliza Pickens died, bringing still further delay. The Clemsons finally acquired the plantation sometime in the spring of 1843, though they did not take up residence there at once.[32]

The purchase of Canebrake meant that Clemson was again in need of capital, for which he turned once more to his father-in-law. This time Calhoun did not press Andrew for funds, or seek to make an "arrangement." He undertook to borrow the necessary sum, or as much of it as he could, on his own personal credit. John S. Barbour, one of his Virginia political friends, undertook to lend him $18,000 out of a large estate recently inherited by Mrs. Barbour from her father, and Clemson went to Virginia late in April to close the deal. In the meantime he had arranged to buy thirty Negroes from John Ewing Calhoun, Floride's older brother whose extravagance had forced him to this last humiliation. The price of the slaves was $6,500, which Calhoun undertook to pay, borrowing $4,500 from Elmore's State Bank and giving his brother-in-law a short-term note for the rest. The bank loan was also to be arranged by Clemson, who went via Charleston for that purpose on his way to Virginia. The whole sum was to be credited against the joint indebtedness of Andrew and his father to Clemson.[33]

Calhoun's financial hopes were soon blasted by events beyond his personal control. The bulk of Mrs. Barbour's inheritance was in trust for her children, and when Barbour sought appointment as administrator the court ruled that he could not lend any part of the money for which he would be responsible outside Virginia except on the security of real estate. Calhoun's landholdings, including Fort Hill, were already mortgaged, and so the deal fell through, or rather was trimmed to $5,000 at a later date.[34]

What with one delay and another, it was October of 1843 before Clemson and the Calhouns finally had an accounting. A statement drawn up at Fort Hill at that time, and signed by Clemson, Andrew P. Calhoun, and John C. Calhoun, indicated that the two Calhouns jointly owed Clemson at that time the sum of $31,925. This sum included interest, but was reduced to $24,114 by credits to John C. Calhoun, mostly for the purchase of the Negroes from John Ewing. To liquidate the debt, Clemson was given a due bill for $7,114, payable on demand, and two promissory notes for $8,500 each, one due in March 1845 and the other one year later. Clemson collected the due bill at once from Matthews and Bonneau, the Calhoun factors in Charleston, and Andrew pledged himself to deliver to them 100,000

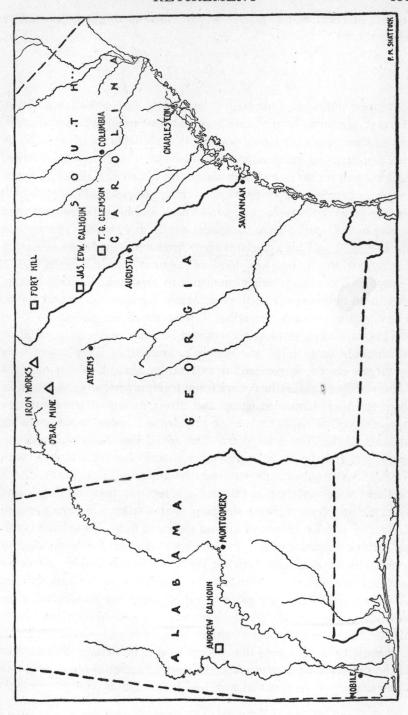

P. M. SHATTUCK

pounds of clean cotton and as much more as might be needed to redeem it.[35]

9

Andrew anticipated his largest harvest so far in the fall of 1843. His plantation had by that date been enlarged to eight hundred acres, and neither he nor his father doubted that all debts could presently be paid and financial independence established.[36] Ever since 1839, when Andrew had set up as a cotton planter on his own, Calhoun's imagination had conjured up bigger and ever bigger yields of cotton, which were to give comfortable livings to himself and his children, and were to give to the South almost boundless wealth and power. Throughout the 1840's he and his associates seem fired with the dream of empire that created the "cotton kingdom" of the next decade. Cotton was to be produced in ever-growing quantities to supply the limitless market opened up by improved textile machinery, by faster ships and trains, by exploiting hitherto "uncivilized" portions of the globe.

This expanding production required large amounts of hand labor, which could be supplied, in the firm conviction of the planters, only by Negro slaves; it required a vast outlet abroad, which meant a corresponding market in America for foreign products; and both of these together demanded cheap and direct means of transportation from the cotton fields to Europe and from Europe to the growing markets of the American West. Out of all this came renewed emphasis on free trade, a stiffening opposition to interference with slavery in any form, a demand for the annexation of Texas, and a new and wider interest in railroad connections between South and West to complement direct shipping routes from Southern ports to Liverpool and Le Havre. Calhoun's eternal fight against the tariff, his stubborn defense of slavery, his repeated efforts to bring about a working political alliance between West and South, and his insistence on peaceful settlement of outstanding differences with Great Britain, all were parts of a single pattern and all were but reflections of the same drive that led the great Nullifier to dedicate his retirement to increasing his own output of cotton.

It must be remembered that we are now approaching the midpoint of the nineteenth century, when the vast impersonal forces let loose by mechanical invention and world-wide revolution were just gathering momentum. In New York and Pennsylvania and the New England states the surplus wealth concentrated by tariff-fostered industry and by the financial vagaries of the Jackson era was about to become the working capital of the early tycoons, whose gains, once constitutional restraints were removed by the Civil War, would become in turn the springboard for the age of big business. The same impulses to expansion and power were at work in the South, with less pliable materials and inferior resources, but with enthusiasm and drive and ruthlessness the equal of any to be found elsewhere.

CHAPTER X

THE MACHINE TRIUMPHS

1

THE FIRST real test of strength between Calhoun and the Van Buren machine came in Virginia in the spring of 1843. On the second day of March the state Democratic convention met in Richmond, where it was called to order by sharp-featured and rapier-tongued old Thomas Ritchie, headman of the Richmond Junto and for a quarter century the undisputed master of Virginia politics. Ritchie's preference was for Van Buren but Andrew Stevenson, who succeeded him as presiding officer, was less firmly committed and two of the three vice presidents, William Fitzhugh Gordon of Albemarle and William P. Taylor of Caroline, were Calhoun men.[1]

The resolutions committee was headed by George C. Dromgoole, Van Buren's spokesman, but it was dominated by twenty-eight-year-old James A. Seddon, who would one day sit briefly as Secretary of War in the Cabinet of Jefferson Davis. Under Seddon's persuasion the committee recommended the whole Calhoun platform: a national convention to be held not earlier than May 1844, with delegates elected by Congressional districts and voting as individuals. The triumph was short-lived as it was spectacular. With Dromgoole commanding a disciplined majority on the floor the report of his own committee was voted down, and the delegation, however it might be selected, was pledged to vote under the unit rule. Just before adjournment on the evening of March 4 two resolutions were adopted without a division. The first read out of the party in advance "any individual, however eminent" who refused to support the nominee of the national convention; the second recommended that the convention be held in late November.[2]

It was a clear political defeat for the Calhoun forces, but the South Carolinian himself looked deeper and saw farther than either his partisans or his foes. In the kind of national convention to which the Richmond action pointed he saw the ultimate destruction of the

134

South. A body so constituted would always be dominated by the sentiment of the majority in the more populous states, and the North would sway the Presidency as it already wielded the Congress. "It would place permanently the control of the ballot box, the patronage of the Government and the veto in the same hands, and those the least safe of any, in which they could be placed." So he warned his Virginia followers that the election was not an end in itself. It was only a means of combating the trend toward centralization that meant disaster for the section they represented.[3]

Immediately after the meeting of the Virginia Democratic convention the state legislature, controlled by the same machine and made up in part of the same men, redivided the state into fifteen Congressional districts to absorb the loss of six seats in the House under the 1840 census. The job was done in the best interests of the Richmond Junto and the Locofoco wing of the Democracy.

As soon as the lines were fixed the campaign to elect new Representatives began. Through March and April Ritchie appealed for party unity and warned Virginians that the horrible consequence of division would be Whig ascendancy. The Calhoun group fought a game but losing battle. Hunter, Seddon, Gordon, and the others charged that the state had been skillfully gerrymandered in Van Buren's interest. They spoke and wrote letters and requisitioned newspapers. They tried to bring Rives and his conservative followers over to their side. To the best of their considerable ability they exposed the issue in terms of sectional survival as Calhoun had taught them. But their best efforts were of no avail against the power of the machine. On April 27 Virginians went to the polls with Ritchie's exhortations still ringing in their ears, and the result was overwhelming.[4]

Hunter himself was beaten in a district made dominantly Whig by gerrymandering; and in the dominantly Democratic districts the Calhoun men were beaten by Locofocos. The final count showed the election of three Whigs; two Tyler partisans, Wise and Gilmer, whose party designation was in doubt; and ten Van Buren Democrats.[5]

The South Carolina convention, meeting in Columbia late in May, took Virginia's action as its point of departure and tried to reestablish the tariff as the major issue. In a well-contrived "Address to the Democratic Republican Party of the United States" the free-

trade argument was followed by another exposition of the merits of
the district system for choosing delegates, who were to vote as individuals. The case rested on minority representation and the protection of the small states, even as the Constitution itself protected
them; but the truth was that Pickens, Elmore, and the Rhett brothers
who controlled the proceedings still believed that free-trade sentiment
was too widely distributed over the United States to permit the
nomination of a protectionist by a convention constituted as they proposed. As to the date of meeting, the "Address" adroitly took the
ground that the last Monday in May 1844 was already agreed upon,
since only Virginia, New York, Tennessee, and Missouri had expressed preference for an earlier time. Calhoun was offered as a
suitable candidate for President, but a pledge to support the party
nominee, whoever he might be, was pointedly omitted.[6]

2

Back in Washington the Van Buren forces concentrated their attacks against the *Spectator,* whose part-time editors were no match
for the veteran Blair. The *Globe* had the further advantage of being
a daily and so could keep its weekly rival constantly in arrears in the
battle of epithets. The circulation of the *Spectator* increased, but it
was immediately obvious that it would never be really effective until
it could be issued every day. Money was an indispensable prereq-
uisite, and Maxcy spent far more time than should have been necessary in appeals for funds.[7]

His task was made immeasurably more difficult by internal dissension. Heart and Scoville were quickly at loggerheads, and there
was rising friction between Scoville and the members of the Calhoun
Central Committee, for which he was now acting as secretary. Disagreements as to procedure and policy reached crisis proportions late
in April. On the first of that month the *Mercury* had placed Woodbury's name at its masthead as candidate for Vice President. Shortly
thereafter Scoville got out a printed circular on the letterhead of the
Central Committee, but signed only by himself, calling on all Calhoun
papers to do likewise. When the circular reached South Carolina
Elmore exploded. "It is out of the question," he wrote Maxcy, "to
put ourselves & our cause in hands irresponsible—indiscreet—and
assuming so much for us. There must be a clear settlement of this

matter before our party here can be brought to act anything decidedly for the Spectator." [8]

It was not that there was any objection to Woodbury. He was undoubtedly the first choice of most of Calhoun's supporters for the second office. But it was one of the fundamental tenets of the game that the Central Committee, assumed to speak for the candidate him-self, should back no individual for Vice President. That was a pre-rogative left to the local groups, each of which was to be free to in-sert the name of its own favorite son, and gain thereby such political strength as it might for the head of the ticket. The *Mercury's* action had been dictated by an apparent indecision on Woodbury's part, but for that very reason there could be no unanimity on the question until the New Hampshire Senator demonstrated his own willingness to deliver effective political strength. Neither could the Calhoun par-tisans afford to unite on any candidate for Vice President as long as Van Buren's managers were uncommitted.

It was pretty clear that the incident was less a disaster in itself than simply the latest and worst in a long series of blunders. Maxcy spoke sharply to Scoville, who apologized and protested his own great loy-alty to Calhoun. He insisted that he had merely followed Wood-bury's own wishes and those of New England generally, and he could not see that any real harm had been done. In his own defense he pointed out that the chairman of the Central Committee was no longer in Washington, and that he was therefore compelled to make for himself decisions that should have been made by Hunter, all of which was true enough.[9]

The correspondence of the Central Committee was thereafter routed through Hunter at his Virginia home, but friction over the operations and policy of the *Spectator* continued as before. By the end of May Hunter, Maxcy, Lewis, Elmore, Henshaw, and others of the inner circle agreed that Scoville must have no further connec-tion with the paper. An amicable arrangement was somehow made, but it left the *Spectator* without an editor. Hunter was free now that his re-election had been lost, and the job might easily have been com-bined with his chairmanship of the Central Committee so as to bring him an income and enable him to live in Washington. He would not undertake it, however, for fear of losing caste in Virginia. Maxcy wanted Richard K. Crallé who had served competently as a Calhoun editor at intervals since 1830, but he was not available. All agreed that a paper in Washington was of the first importance, but potential backers wanted to know who the editor was to be before they risked their money.[10]

3

The tempo of the campaign was stepped up when Daniel Webster resigned the State Department early in May. His departure could mean only that the President had finally decided to return to his old Democratic allegiance, and if circumstances warranted to seek the party nomination for himself. Webster could not accept this decision and remain a Whig, nor could he avoid accepting it and remain in the Cabinet. Another factor was the orientation of administration policy toward the annexation of Texas, with its involvement in the slavery controversy, but this will be discussed in more detail in the next chapter.[11]

Webster's resignation had been rumored for many months, and the decision was actually made before Congress adjourned in March. He agreed to remain a month or so longer, however, apparently to give Tyler time for the selection of a successor. There is some evidence that the State Department was again offered to Calhoun at this time. The South Carolinian had already refused it in September of 1842, and toward the end of that year he had also declined to go on a special mission to England. He now refused once more to serve the Tyler administration, but before leaving Washington he advised his friend Abel P. Upshur, the Secretary of the Navy, to take the first place in the Cabinet, should it be offered. Upshur was still hesitating two months later when Webster resigned, and so for the time being the Attorney General, Hugh Swinton Legaré of South Carolina, became Secretary of State *ad interim*.[12]

The Treasury, following Cushing's rejection by the Senate, had meanwhile been filled by promoting John C. Spencer of New York, the Secretary of War. James M. Porter, brother of Governor David Porter of Pennsylvania and a conservative, anti-Van Buren Democrat, was then named to the War Department.

A month after Webster's retirement the President and his Cabinet went to Boston for the dedication of the Bunker Hill monument, in what was widely regarded as a flamboyant bit of electioneering. There were the usual receptions along the route, ostentatiously boycotted by Whigs and attended without enthusiasm by Democrats. The dedication took place on June 17, and Webster, at his magnificent best, scored one of his greatest oratorical triumphs. That night there was a dinner in Tyler's honor at Faneuil Hall, with toasts and responses by members of the company and the Cabinet. All were there but the scholarly Legaré, who had been taken suddenly ill. Three days later he died, and Tyler had two Cabinet posts to fill.[13]

The Presidential party was back in Washington on June 23, and the next day Upshur assumed the duties of Secretary of State *ad interim*. July 1 saw the appointment of John Nelson, a Maryland Democrat, as Attorney General, and on the twenty-fourth of that month the Cabinet was again full. Upshur was officially elevated to the Department of State and his place as Secretary of the Navy was taken by David Henshaw, the Calhoun leader in Massachusetts. With Upshur and Spencer also favorably disposed, the Calhoun managers were soon dispensing federal patronage as though it were their own, and there seemed to be ample ground for the belief of many that Tyler was in fact backing the South Carolinian.[14]

4

The contest between Calhoun and Van Buren reached its maximum intensity during the summer of 1843, or roughly between the meeting of the South Carolina convention late in May and the meeting of the New York convention early in September. There were a thousand battlegrounds, and each of them was the field that must be won, for the real campaign was waged on the local hustings where the supporters of each candidate carried the case down to the individual voter. The Calhoun forces continued to emphasize the issue of tariff reform and to argue for a late convention, organized on the district plan. Yet all their arguments came to nothing because they were trapped by their own logic. When the pressure became too great, Van Buren yielded on the convention date, but the State Rights philosophy forced even the *Mercury* to concede before the end of July the right of each state to determine for itself how its delegates were to be chosen. In August the *Madisonian* came out as champion of the district system and per capita voting, but the battle was already lost. It was a defeat fatal to Calhoun's chances, just as postponement of the convention until May was probably fatal to Van Buren's.[15]

Calhoun's chances were slim enough, despite gains in New England and his control of much of the South, even had he won both the points at issue. He was fighting with an improvised and not always cohesive organization against an intrenched political machine that had held power uninterruptedly for a dozen years, and the federal patronage placed at his disposal by the Tyler administration came too late to affect the outcome materially. He was, moreover, a candidate peculiarly unmalleable from the point of view of practical politics. He would yield nothing of principle for the sake of votes. He would not travel or show himself to the people, though few men could win friends by personal contact as readily as he. He held the Presidency an office too high and responsible to be "the object of personal solicitude, or sought by personal canvass, or even to be accepted on any other ground than that of duty." [16]

He was equally candid and stiff-necked about the evolution of his views on government. Late in June, after a delay of three months, the volume of speeches that was to have accompanied the campaign biography finally appeared. As the *Mercury* commented, it would indeed have been "difficult to make a volume better deserving the deep and thoughtful study of every political reader." But the *National Intelligencer,* still official organ of the Clay Whigs, was quick to point out the omission of those ringing nationalistic speeches of Calhoun's Congressional days of 1811-1817. The editors hinted at deliberate suppression, and proceeded to make good the loss by republishing in their own columns the South Carolinian's great Bank speech of 1816. Others followed in succeeding issues: speeches on the direct tax, the tariff, internal improvements, in which the young Calhoun pleaded with energy and skill and something of genius for measures long since repudiated by Calhoun, the elder statesman.[17]

The *Spectator* sprang to the defense of its candidate, but clearly had not consulted him as to the line to take. It was the period, too, after Scoville's ejection, when there was no regular editor. The defense was therefore weak. The early speeches had been omitted, no doubt, explained the *Spectator's* leading editorial for July 15, because of the difficulty of obtaining authentic texts (though the *Intelligencer* had found it easy enough) ; but it didn't really matter because the speeches were immature. The *Globe* took it up and explained away in similar terms Calhoun's early advocacy of a national bank; but in Blair's hands the discussion served by the sort of innuendo he handled so skillfully to hold up the Carolinian as a renegade bank man, and as such probably dangerous to the party.[18]

Harper and Brothers entered the discussion a few days later with a letter to the editors of the *Intelligencer* in which they took full blame on themselves. The title of the volume, which actually read "Selections from Mr. Calhoun's Speeches . . . from 1811 to the Present Time," should have included the words "referred to in his Life." Calhoun, meanwhile, was in blissful ignorance of the controversy raging around him. He had not even seen the volume, but he had observed the erroneous title in an advertisement, and had written immediately to have it corrected. He was too late for the first edition, but later printings carried his version of the title: "A Selection from the Speeches, Reports, and other writings of Mr. Calhoun, subsequent to his election as Vice President of the United States, including his leading speech on the late war delivered in 1811." The Harper correction would not do, as he himself noted, because the earlier speeches were referred to in the *Life;* the volume, moreover, was not confined to speeches.

It was near the end of July when two issues of the *Intelligencer* were placed in Calhoun's hands, and he wrote at once to the editors. He flatly denied, of course, the allegation of willful misrepresentation, and explained the inaccurate title as noted above. He then took full personal responsibility for the selection. The volume had been published because his friends had held him up as a candidate for President. It was due to the people and to himself to "afford them the means of ascertaining the opinions and sentiments I entertain on all political subjects, particularly on those which have agitated the country of late, and on which the presidential election will probably in a great measure turn." It was, in effect, his substitute for personal electioneering. Clearly for this purpose it was his present views that were required, and for that reason the selection covered the period it did. "It is the period in which my speeches and other publications contain my mature and settled opinions on the principles and policy of the government; adopted after long experience and much reflection; which have modified, or changed, if you prefer, in many particulars, my earlier and less mature expressions." [19]

What could be franker? He was by no means ashamed of his earlier speeches, and professed gratitude to the *Intelligencer* for reprinting them as he had no copies in his own files. On rereading them, he thought they spoke a lofty patriotism of which he remained proud and of which he believed no American could complain. It was true that he had altered many of the views therein expressed, but "should I be ashamed to acknowledge that I have lived to improve, and have had the sense to see, and the firmness to correct early errors?" Gales and Seaton made a bid for the last word when they reprinted, a few days after publishing Calhoun's letter, another speech omitted from the volume: the Carolinian's castigation of Andrew Jackson, called forth by the President's protest against the censure of the Senate in the Bank war. It was probably a deliberate attempt to inflame the old Jacksonians, and to renew the internal strife among the Democrats. But Calhoun had included better anti-Jackson speeches, and he wisely let the matter drop.[20]

5

Another serious disadvantage encountered by the Calhoun managers was the inadequacy of the newspapers at their disposal. The *Mercury* was well edited and effective, but it was no substitute for aggressive dailies in Washington and New York. From March 1843 on the *Madisonian* treated Calhoun as a co-partisan of Tyler, but the assistance derived from that source was conditional and for the most part negative. The *Spectator,* without a regular editor and largely in the hands of an absentee board of strategy, was not inaptly characterized by Blair as "a sort of weekly tender to the avowed administration organ." [21] In New York the *Journal of Commerce* was friendly, Mordecai Noah's *Aurora and Union* slanted more toward Calhoun than toward Tyler, and occasional very substantial help was rendered by the *Herald;* but there was no paper really controlled by the Calhoun group. It was absolutely necessary that such expertly edited and widely circulated Van Buren papers as the Washington *Globe* and the New York *Evening Post* be met on something like equal terms, and the Calhoun Central Committee set itself to raise the requisite funds.

A circular, with text in the form of an urgently worded letter from Maxcy to Elmore, was issued by the Central Committee in August 1843, but the work was already well under way. It was not easy. "I have been disgusted beyond expression," Elmore wrote bitterly. "I have appealed, entreated & urged our friends until I actually felt humiliated at their indifference, no not that, but their apparant insensibility to the calls of duty & honor." He had nevertheless secured in Charleston pledges totaling $5,000, and felt assured of actually getting double that amount. And so he did, but the base was too small; too many of the contributors of substantial sums were the active party workers like Elmore himself, Rhett, James Edward Calhoun, Ker Boyce, George McDuffie, Francis Pickens.[22]

At the end of August Robert Barnwell Rhett left for Washington with "ample funds" in his pocket and a blanket commission from the Central Committee to put the *Spectator* "in fighting trim," after which he was to go on to New York and procure a paper there, with local funds if possible, but if not, with those already at his command. The *Spectator* was to be made a daily in time to contest with the *Globe* for the printing of the already elected Democratic Congress, and until a suitable editor was found, Rhett undertook to handle the paper himself.[23]

The best man for the job would have been John A. Stuart of the *Mercury,* but Stuart's services, even at home, had already been lost through illness. He was then at Saratoga Springs convalescing, while Albert Rhett looked after editorial affairs in Charleston. Second choice was Hunter, but he once more declined the place, as did Dr. J. L. Martin from whom the *Spectator* had originally been secured. Negotiations were then opened with Washington Greenhow of the Petersburg *Republican,* and Rhett made a special trip to the Virginia city in an effort to close the deal. He found that Seddon and the others of the Richmond Calhoun Committee would not consent to any move that might cost them the services of the paper Greenhow then edited. The best they would agree to was that the young editor should move to the Capital as soon as a suitable replacement for him in Petersburg could be found, but that time never came.[24]

Through September and well on into October Rhett divided his time between Washington, where he edited the *Spectator,* and New York, where he sought to buy or establish a Calhoun daily. For a time it was thought that the *Journal of Commerce* might be secured, but Rhett soon convinced himself that a wholly new sheet would be required. The cost would be a minimum of $10,000, but $20,000 would be better. He found enthusiastic and co-operative friends, but none with the kind of money he needed to start from the beginning. So he did the best he could, and toward the end of October the defunct

New York *Gazette* was revived in Calhoun's interest. Rhett then left for South Carolina to enjoy a brief respite before Congress convened, but he reached home only in time to attend the deathbed of his young and brilliant brother Albert.[25]

6

In the arts of practical politics the Calhoun men, like their leader himself, seem in retrospect to have been singularly ineffective. It was only in the intellectual sphere that they were at their best. If they could not win votes they could at least present convincing arguments. That was essentially all they did by way of preparation for the New York convention, held at Syracuse on September 5, 1843. Van Buren won the New York City delegation after a spirited fight in mid-August, and the Calhoun partisans were reduced at once to their ultimate weapon—pamphlets. Two of these appeared just before the convention, one an excellent "Address" by Orestes Brownson, the other a definitive statement of the case for the district system from the pen of Virgil Maxcy. They were simply ignored by the machine, and the convention rolled on to its predetermined end.[26]

The only Calhoun victory at Syracuse was effected by a small but vocal band of rebels who refused to adhere to the unit rule for voting county delegations and thus prevented unanimity for Van Buren's program. The ex-President's lieutenants managed as they had the previous year to gloss over the Hunker-Barnburner feud, making Marcy the convention president and endorsing Governor Bouck's administration along with Van Buren's. The fourth Monday in May 1844 was approved as the date for the national convention and full support was pledged to the convention nominee. A tariff "founded on revenue principles and wisely discriminating for the encouragement of labor in agriculture, commerce, and manufactures" was declared to be the true Democratic policy. Then by a vote of 103 to 19 it was agreed to select delegates to the national convention by general ticket, and a complete slate of Van Buren partisans was chosen. At this point the Calhoun leader read into the record a short but pithy protest and walked out.[27]

On September 13, a week after the adjournment of the Syracuse convention, Massachusetts Democrats met at Worcester, and, adroitly manipulated by George Bancroft, followed the same pattern.

Governor Marcus Morton, who shared with Bancroft the leadership of the Van Buren forces, was endorsed for re-election, and Bancroft himself headed the delegation chosen by general ticket to go to Baltimore in May. It was a delegation of eleven reliable Van Buren men and one who would "not dare to avow his secret preference for Calhoun." [28] At Syracuse the Van Buren forces had bowed once more to the protectionist sentiment of the North. At Worcester they went still farther down the sectional road, invoking the slavery question as an argument against Calhoun. The disparate elements of the Northern Democracy, like those that composed the democracy of the South were beginning to coalesce under the impact of economic pressure.

The Syracuse and Worcester conventions marked the turning point of the campaign. By October enough states had indicated their preferences to reveal the futility of further argument for the district system. The Calhoun partisans, however, did not relax but rather intensified their efforts. Many, perhaps most, of those close to the South Carolina Senator no longer believed his nomination possible, and Calhoun himself probably agreed; but the choice of Van Buren could still be prevented, and this they intended to do. For Van Buren now stood more clearly than ever before for concessions on both the tariff and slavery, and on those questions the South could yield nothing without ultimately yielding all.

So the attacks on Van Buren's record, the elaboration of the convention theme, and the incessant hammering on the Southern version of true Democratic policy were kept up until December. Calhoun meetings continued to be held at strategic centers, and a "Central Committee of Correspondence" in New York undertook to agitate at the local level against convention delegates already chosen by general tickets. [29] A "Calhoun Text Book," containing pertinent excerpts from the press, was issued in pamphlet form from the office of the New York *Herald;* and a much condensed version of the "Life and Character of the Hon. John C. Calhoun" played heavily on popular taste with tales of the heroic exploits of Calhouns and Caldwells in the American Revolution. There were crude woodcut illustrations of the type Bennett was then introducing into the *Herald.* It was at about the same period that the New York *Gazette* was exhumed for a brief career of a month or so; and the *Spectator,* still without the services of a full-time editor, became a daily with its issue of November 28. The means were thus at hand for exerting considerable pressure upon the Democratic majority when the new Congress met.

There were many in the South who were beginning to see the problem as Calhoun saw it, and to realize that it was their own way of life that hung in the balance. Upshur privately indicated to one of the backers of General Cass that Calhoun's following would support any Democrat except Van Buren; and one by one the Democratic seceders of 1836 prepared to return to their old allegiance, having tardily discovered the meaning of Calhoun's Edgefield letter of 1837. In the confusion Webster made his peace with Clay, and with the Whigs thus strengthened the *Globe* pleaded, cajoled, and threatened in the interest of Democratic unity. But unity, to Blair, meant support of Van Buren and all he stood for. The principles at stake between the warring factions were irreconcilable in the eyes of most of those who dwelt below the Potomac, and Calhoun already knew before Congress met that he could never allow his name to go before a convention constituted as it was certain by December that it would be.[30]

7

The victorious Democrats, who would hold a decisive majority in the Twenty-eighth Congress, began streaming back to Washington toward the end of November 1843, and held their first caucus on December 2. Rhett proposed that Calhoun's partisans stay away, and arranged a deal with the Pennsylvania delegation whereby they would support Judge William Wilkins of that state for Speaker against the caucus candidate. Buchanan and Charles J. Ingersoll intervened to dissuade the Pennsylvanians, however, and the scheme was dropped. The alternative strategy was devised by Dixon H. Lewis, who herded the Calhoun men into the caucus and demanded that the nominations be made only by two-thirds vote of those present. He seemed to think he could command enough more than a third of the votes to force the Locofocos to compromise, but he was badly in error. Van Buren's supporters agreed readily, and on the first ballot John W. Jones of Virginia was selected as the party's candidate for Speaker with 78 votes against only 36 for the combined total of six other aspirants. There was no longer any room for doubt. Van Buren still controlled the Democracy.[31]

With a quorum present on the first day of the session the Democrats presented a completely united front, and elected Jones to the Speakership by 128 to 59 for the Whig candidate, John White of Kentucky, and one for Wilkins. Then on the evening of the fifth the caucus met again, and again by two-thirds majorities disposed of the other party offices. A clerk and a sergeant-at-arms were chosen; Blair was returned to the lucrative printing assignment; and an agreement was presumably reached on the personnel of the committees. The Van Buren men were jubilant, as well they might be. So efficiently had the old party machine done its work over the past year that of the 129 Democrats who appeared in their seats in the House on the opening day of the session, Calhoun could count on no more than twenty-five, Buchanan half that number, Richard M. Johnson perhaps three or four, and Cass not a single one. The rest were all Van Buren men.[32]

Calhoun had no alternative but to withdraw, and he did so as soon as he learned the extent of his defeat in the organization of the House. His "Address to his Political Friends and Supporters," dated from Fort Hill, December 21, 1843, was just such a document as those who knew him might have anticipated. He thanked his friends for the confidence that had led them to offer him as a candidate for President, but he could not allow his name to go before a nominating convention constituted in the manner already determined for that scheduled to meet in Baltimore in May. He presented his objections at length, with full analysis of each point, but the upshot was that the mode of choosing delegates, the number of delegates chosen, and the way they were to vote, all tended to give undue weight to the large Eastern states, and to give the final voice in those states to the controlling political machine. He then moved on to the tariff and pulled no punches, recalling enough of tariff history to make clear his reasons for distrusting the Democratic leadership of those very states that would, under the system adopted, control the convention and name the candidate.[33]

One copy of the letter he sent to the Charleston Committee and another to the South Carolina Senators in Washington, so that his supporters could work out their own future course of action in the light of his. He left it to the Charleston Committee to publish when they saw fit, asking only that there should be no unnecessary delay. The Calhoun managers, long accustomed to disagreeing among themselves, held it up for almost six weeks. In Charleston the document was read by Elmore, Gourdin, Alexander Mazyck, Boyce, J. B. I'On, Hamilton, and others. In Washington the critics included Upshur, Maxcy, Duff Green who was just back from England, Lewis, McDuffie, Rhett, and the entire South Carolina Congressional delegation. They agreed fairly generally that the passages on the tariff should be modified. Other than that there were all shades of opinion from those who wanted it made stronger than it was to those who wanted nothing published at all lest Calhoun again be isolated from the Democratic party as he had been in Jackson's time. The consensus was that the door should not be fully closed, and so the more caustic references to the tariff and all allusions personal to Van Buren were deleted. On January 27, 1844, the Charleston *Mercury* dropped the names of Calhoun and Woodbury from its masthead, and two days later published the "Address" itself, as emasculated by the party managers. Even in its watered-down form, however, the document still managed to be explicit on the vexed sectional issues of the day.[34]

There were those among Van Buren's partisans who saw only "petulance and an over weening confidence" in the Carolinian's stand, but the more thoughtful among them realized that the ex-President's way lay over a very rugged road if he could not now conciliate Calhoun; and the Calhoun partisans were even more emphatic in private than their leader had been in public as to what conciliation meant. Unless the Democratic majority in Congress saw fit to reform the tariff and put down the antislavery agitation with a minimum of delay, Calhoun would be run as an independent, with the expectation of throwing the election into the House and cutting the relative weight of New York and Pennsylvania down to scale.[35]

Calhoun's "Address" appeared in Richmond on January 31, 1844, where the Democracy of the Old Dominion was already gathered for a party convention scheduled to open the following day. The South Carolinian's Virginia followers, with Hunter at their head, went immediately into caucus, then met with leaders of the Van Buren faction and offered terms. Next day, by prearrangement, Hunter, William Fitzhugh Gordon, and John S. Barbour informed the convention that they were prepared to support the party nominee in return for pledges as to principles. Ritchie himself replied, and as the hall rang with cheers the hatchet was buried, this time for good and all. The Virginia delegates were pledged to Van Buren, but they were also pledged to a platform on which Van Buren could not stand.[36]

It would not be Calhoun but Van Buren who would, in another Presidential term, be read out of the party.

CHAPTER XI

TEXAS

1

SHORTLY before Calhoun's withdrawal the Texas question was tossed like a flaming faggot into the tinderbox of Presidential politics. It was not done, as Benton insisted, in an attempt to force Calhoun into the White House; nor was it, as Adams professed to believe, a deliberate move to destroy the Union.[1] It was simply an inevitable outgrowth of all that had gone before; a by-product of the Missouri Compromise, and a forward step in the development of the characteristic economy of industrialism.

The question of Texas and her relation to the United States had never been fully closed since the birth of the Lone Star Republic in 1836. Save for sporadic hostilities between Texas and Mexico, however, and strained diplomatic relations between Mexico and the United States, the matter was temporarily shelved when the Texan request for annexation was withdrawn in 1838. Then in January 1842 John Quincy Adams presented the Haverhill petition for a dissolution of the Union, and sectional animosity rose to a new peak. In the course of the ensuing debate Henry A. Wise spoke at length on the grievances of the South, and one of those grievances was that the organized abolitionists of the Northern states and their closely co-operating brethren in England had secured the defeat of Texas annexation. He recalled the Missouri Compromise and pointed to the vast territory to the Northwest that would one day clamor for statehood, with no slave territory left to maintain the balance. For a brief moment the deep-rooted fear of the South lay quivering and exposed: that her one remaining safeguard, the Constitution, would be taken from her by the amending process, and she would lose at once her means of livelihood and her way of life.[2]

Duff Green, it will be remembered, was in England at that time, remaining through most of 1842 and going back again in the following year. Among those with whom he associated himself were Ashbel Smith who represented the Texas Republic at London and Paris; and General James Hamilton, formerly of South Carolina, who had preceded Smith as Texan envoy, but remained in Europe until September 1842. In the summer of that year Sir Robert Peel, the Prime Minister, admitted in the House of Commons that the British Indies, since the emancipation of 1833, could not compete with areas in which slavery still existed, and intimated that British policy required the abolition of slavery in the rest of the Western Hemisphere to restore the balance. Abolition in Texas would be a long step in that direction, and it could be brought about either by the restoration of Mexican sovereignty, or by independence under British hegemony so long as Her Majesty's Government was willing to put up the money to compensate the slaveholders.[3]

There was nothing secret or undercover about any of this. Duff Green explained it almost frantically to Calhoun and Tyler and Everett in private letters, and publicly in letters to the press. Ashbel Smith explained it coldly to the government of Texas in a long series of official dispatches. He wrote also to Isaac Van Zandt, the Texan chargé in Washington, who showed the letters to Tyler and probably to others; and Anson Jones, the Texan Secretary of State, was in correspondence with both Webster and Calhoun. Add to all this the long-standing grievances of the South against Great Britain in the *Enterprise* and *Creole* cases, the bitterly contested right of search, the near-war with Canada over the *Caroline* and its aftermath, the Maine boundary, and Oregon, and it is perhaps not too difficult to see why Southern slaveholders wanted Texas annexed to the United States before Britain made it a hostile colony of her own.[4]

It was clearly best, in view of all the circumstances, to do nothing about the Texas question until after the Webster-Ashburton negotiations had been concluded, but once the ratifications were exchanged in October 1842 it was possible to consider a course of action. By that time the Presidential campaign was getting under way in earnest, and sectional issues were already deeply involved. By signing the "black tariff" of 1842 Tyler had made a gesture toward Northern interests; the annexation of Texas would be a compensating gesture toward the South. The appropriate feeler was put out in January 1843 in the form of a letter from Thomas W. Gilmer, Virginia Congressman and close friend of the President.

Gilmer's argument was simply that Texas must inevitably become a part of the United States or must fall a prey to British cupidity. The Prime Minister himself had avowed a desire to abolish slavery in Texas and in the United States, for the admitted purpose of raising the cost of production and thereby giving a competitive advantage to British colonies. The only way to prevent this scheme from being carried out was to acquire Texas before Great Britain did. The letter appeared in the *Madisonian* for January 23, 1843, in the midst of the Senate debate on the occupation and settlement of Oregon, and the contrast served once more to recall the balance of sectional power set up under the Missouri Compromise.

On the day it appeared the paper containing Gilmer's letter was forwarded to Andrew Jackson by Aaron V. Brown, Nashville Congressman, together with a request for comment. From the old General came an answer by return mail. He agreed entirely with Gilmer, and added further reasons of his own. One was his long-cherished notion that Texas had in fact been included in the Louisiana Purchase, but that title to it had been illegally surrendered by the Florida Treaty of 1819. Another was military necessity; for Texas could be used by an unfriendly power—and Great Britain was generally placed in that category in the 1840's—as a base both for making war upon the United States and for inciting the slaves of the South to revolt. Jackson's letter was not published at the time, but was held in reserve to be used when it would do the most good.[5]

The Gilmer letter instantly aroused the suspicions of old John Quincy Adams, who bided his time until the end of the session. Then on March 3, 1843—the day on which Calhoun's resignation from the Senate became effective—Adams and a dozen other abolitionist Congressmen, including Gates, Slade, and Giddings, issued a circular. They reviewed the history of relations with Texas, including Wise's speech of January 1842 and Gilmer's letter. They went back to 1837 to quote Daniel Webster against annexation in any form. They identified as the only real issue involved the extension or extinction of slavery; and they concluded with an unequivocal declaration that "annexation effected by any act or proceeding of the federal government . . . would be identical with dissolution" of the Union.[6]

It was at this time that Webster determined to leave the Cabinet, which he did early in May.

2

In the summer of 1843 a World Convention of abolitionists met in London, with full representation from the United States. A committee of delegates called on Lord Aberdeen, who assured them that "Her Majesty's Government would employ all legitimate means to attain so great and desirable an object as the abolition of Slavery in Texas." The statement was quickly public property, and Ashbel Smith called on Aberdeen for an explanation. He learned no more than he already knew, but the high source whence it now came increased its impact. According to the Foreign Minister, the British Government was indeed considering ways of compensating Texas slaveholders in the event of emancipation, and had let it be known that in such circumstances Britain stood ready to offer effective mediation between Texas and Mexico. Smith was under no illusions as to what was going on, or why. "The abolition of slavery in Texas by itself considered," he reported to his own government, "is not regarded in England as of any great importance, but it is ardently desired as preliminary to its abolition in the United States. . . . Besides motives of philanthropy, the British people wish the abolition of slavery in America in reference to the culture of sugar and cotton, in which there exists a rivalry with their colonies, and in reference to the advantages which the production of cotton in America gives to its manufacturers and the employment which these staples afford to American shipping." [7]

In an earlier day Ashbel Smith, despite his New England origins, had edited a nullification paper in North Carolina. He was personally known to Calhoun, and had a fairly clear understanding of what the South Carolinian was trying to do. It is not surprising, therefore, that there should have been a correspondence between the two men at this time. Calhoun stood pre-eminently as the great champion of the Southern way of life, based as it was on Negro slavery and free trade, and Texans who shared his views turned to him as a matter of course. So it was that Ashbel Smith's account of the abolitionist meetings in London, and of the official and unofficial British reaction to pressure for emancipation in Texas, presently found its way into Calhoun's hands, and was forwarded by him to Upshur who had just become Secretary of State. Upshur had already received much the same information from other sources, including Edward Everett in London; Isaac Van Zandt, the Texan chargé in Washington; and W. S. Murphy, United States representative in Texas. He had already made up his mind what course he ought to take, and had instructed Murphy to do all in his power to block the British designs.[8]

Upshur had also discussed the whole question of Texas annexation with Southern leaders, including Virgil Maxcy who promised to get Calhoun's opinion. Events were moving too rapidly for the roundabout approach, and when Calhoun forwarded a letter from Ashbel Smith, the Secretary of State seized the opportunity to lay the problem directly before the South Carolinian. "My own mind," he wrote in mid-August, "is very much disturbed on the subject of Texas, and I shall be much gratified to know from you, either that my apprehensions are well founded, so that I may act on them boldly, or that they are unfounded, so that I may no longer feel them." His reasoning, as he continued, was just such as Calhoun himself might have applied to the same question.

"There can be no doubt, I think, that England is determined to abolish slavery throughout the American continent and islands if she can. It is worse than childish to suppose that she meditates this great movement, simply from the impulse of philanthropy. . . . I can find no other motive than a desire to find or create markets for her surplus manufactures, and to destroy all competition with the laborers of her colonies. . . . The present attempt upon Texas is the beginning of her operations upon us." Upshur went on to analyze the effects of commercial rivalry with a Texas under British dominance, both on the Southern planter and on the Northern manufacturer. In both cases the advantage lay all with England. Yet the Secretary could not contemplate the condition of Texas "without being convinced that she is under an absolute necessity to throw herself upon the protection of some stronger power. That power must be either England or the U. States." He concluded that Texas must be admitted as a slave state into the Union. "To admit Texas as a non-slave holding State, or permit her to remain an independent and sovereign non-slave holding state, will be fatal to the Union, and ruinous to the whole country." He realized that the North would oppose, but in the end he was sure the manufacturers would be the chief gainers. "To the South, it is a question of *safety;* to the North, it is one of the interest. *We* should introduce rivals of our most productive industry, and should be, so far, losers; *they* would profit by that very rivalry. I have never known the North to refuse to do what their interest required." Calhoun's reply was an endorsement of all that Upshur said.[9]

Duff Green, meanwhile, was back in England partly because Tyler knew that the sympathies of Edward Everett, the American Minister, lay wholly with the abolitionists; and partly because the broader objectives of the administration's foreign policy were not such as could be satisfactorily promoted through official channels. More and more, as he aligned himself with the Southern Democrats, the President regretted his own agency in procuring the tariff of 1842, and he sought now a reciprocal basis for free trade. While Everett dealt with the British Government, Green dickered with the Whig opposition, especially with Palmerston and Lord John Russell. He found the Whigs more interested in American grain than in American slavery, undisposed to fight with the United States over Texas or anything else, and strong enough to produce a Cabinet crisis almost at will.[10]

Thus when Tyler and his Secretary of State decided to go ahead with negotiations looking toward the annexation of Texas to the United States, it was with full knowledge of the factors favoring as well as those against their cause. They knew that the American abolitionists and the people of the North generally would be bitterly hostile to the acquisition of more slave territory, but they believed that economic interest would bring the manufacturers around. They knew that the British Government would like to interfere to keep Texas out of the Union, but they knew also that the party in power was not strong enough to risk war on such an issue. As for domestic politics, the Texas question, in Upshur's phrase, had nothing to do with "whiggism and democracy." It was the safety of the South and ultimately the perpetuation of the Union that were at stake, and these they would not endanger by making it a partisan matter.

3

Even from the confusion of available documents it now seems clear that Calhoun himself had nothing to do with the decision of the Tyler administration to annex Texas. He had followed the tangled relations of Great Britain, Texas, and Mexico as closely as he could since the beginning of 1842, and because his information came largely from the same sources relied on by Tyler and Upshur, he arrived at much the same conclusions. But he did not offer advice or counsel until after annexation had been decided on, and then only when asked to do so. He was undoubtedly kept fully informed, however, as to the progress of negotiations, through both official and unofficial channels.[11]

In September 1843 James G. Birney was again nominated by the Liberty party on a platform forthrightly abolitionist and antiannexationist, and Birney's ties to the British antislavery movement merely called attention to the international aspects of the question. At the same time Sam Houston, serving his second term as President of Texas, was busily engaged in playing England, Mexico, and the United States off against one another, permitting just enough publicity to intensify the fears of the South. Houston was also in correspondence with Andrew Jackson, who still insisted that Texas rightfully belonged to the United States and must be regained at any cost; and Jackson kept in touch with the administration through William B. Lewis, who was on familiar terms with Upshur.[12]

The forces making for and against annexation of Texas, in short, were compounded of economic interest, political ambition, sectional and international rivalry, personal prestige, and moral zeal, with overtones of saber rattling and intrigue. But the antislavery crusade had already gained such momentum that no Northern man could take a public stand in favor of annexation, and it is not surprising that Calhoun's followers saw in this an opportunity to eliminate Van Buren. Rhett and Hunter discussed the possibilities with Upshur early in October, but by that time Tyler had seen possibilities in it for himself. When the Van Buren forces took the offensive in Virginia later in the same month, Henry A. Wise brought the whole business into the open.[13]

Thereafter until the meeting of Congress early in December, the *Madisonian* devoted more and more of its space to the Texas question, publishing statements of Brougham and Aberdeen in Parliament, emphasizing British designs in Texas, and playing up the angle of national defense. Upshur continued to solicit and to act on Calhoun's advice, but the views of the two men were so nearly identical that it was no more than a gesture.[14]

4

Such was the situation at the time the Twenty-eighth Congress met to place offices and committees in the hands of Van Buren partisans by solid two-thirds majorities of the Democratic vote. This caucus action meant that Calhoun was out of the Presidential race; it meant that the tariff would not be adjusted by that Congress; and it meant, or seemed to mean, that the administration could not count on Democratic votes from the Northern states to annex Texas. It was there that Jackson's letter of February came in, for the old General's endorsement would justify Van Buren Democrats in voting for annexation even though Van Buren himself, because of his sectional ties, might have to take a stand against that measure.

In his message of December 5, 1843, Tyler took note of Mexican threats against the United States, should Texas be annexed, and spurned them with suitable vigor. He scored the hostilities still existing between Mexico and Texas, and declared that the interest of the United States required that they be ended. He referred to the close proximity and common origin of Texans and Americans; he spoke in generalities of the throwing off of shackles by colonial settlers; and he intimated that should any collision occur, it would be owing to the bad behavior of Mexico. He did not actually ask for the annexation of Texas to the United States, but he stated so strongly the case for severing the ties between Texas and Mexico, and stressed so cogently the mutual interests of Texas and the United States, the inference was unmistakable.[15]

The Van Buren managers, and particularly Benton who still hoped to succeed the New Yorker in the White House, saw in the raising of the Texas issue at this time only another move in the Presidential chess game, and they used their control of Congress, as we have seen, to force Calhoun out of the contest. They also engineered the rejection of the interim Cabinet appointments, Henshaw and Porter, and refused to confirm Spencer for a vacant seat on the Supreme Court. After Calhoun's withdrawal had been published and the Virginia Democrats had reunited, Wise was confirmed as Minister to Brazil and two other members of the House, William Wilkins of Pennsylvania and Thomas W. Gilmer of Virginia, were confirmed for the vacant War and Navy posts.[16]

Upshur and Van Zandt, meanwhile, had agreed on the terms of a treaty of annexation, and Tyler's supporters, working primarily with Democrats and Southern Whigs, sought to prepare the ground for its ratification. By mid-January 1844 Upshur was assured that the treaty would command the necessary two-thirds majority in the Senate.[17] Both sides continued to argue the question in the press, however, and annexation was soon one of the topics included when local committees asked prominent men where they stood. Webster answered such a request late in January, stating the case against Texas on constitutional and frankly antislavery ground, but held up its publication until March. The definitive case for annexation was offered by Senator Robert J. Walker of Mississippi in a very long letter appearing in the *Globe* on February 3, 1844.[18]

Walker's letter occupied three full newspaper pages, and appeared simultaneously in pamphlet form. The Mississippi Senator incorporated in one document every variety of argument for annexation. He reasoned skillfully that Texas had been and still was part of the United States. He showed that Adams and Clay and Jackson and Van Buren had each tried to acquire the territory. He proved to his own satisfaction that annexation could be brought about constitutionally by treaty, by simple act of Congress, or by action of the adjoining states to extend their limits. He stated the case for strategic necessity in terms of national defense; and the case for economic necessity in the light of British designs. He painted in glowing hues the Texas market for Northern manufactures, and in somber tones the destruction of American commerce that would follow if Texas became a British dependency. He even appealed to the antislavery sentiment in the free states with the contention that slavery could ultimately be eliminated only if it were diffused over a wider area. He argued finally that the Union itself could not long survive the failure to annex Texas, because that failure would throw the Lone Star Republic into the arms of Britain. British ports would then be closed to American cotton, and the Southern and Southwestern states would be forced into the orbit of Texas to market their staples, leaving Britain supreme on the continent.

Only the sudden coyness of Sam Houston appeared to stand in the way. It is quite probable that Houston really desired to maintain the independence of Texas, which with boundaries extended westward to the Pacific would have been an imperial domain, and might in time have come to dominate the hemisphere. But he was under tremendous pressure, from Jackson, from the United States, from the Texans themselves; and he was not in position, financially or militarily, to ignore the dangers implicit in his relations with Mexico and with Great Britain. When Upshur offered annexation, with assurance that a treaty would be ratified, and asked that the Texan representative in Washington be given full powers to negotiate, Houston could do nothing but yield. He dispatched a second commissioner, J. Pinckney Henderson, with the requisite powers. At the same time, however, he wrote Jackson, in light and bantering tone but stating clearly that this time annexation must go through or it would be forever too late, and Texas would work out her own destiny in her own way. His stipulation was that during the negotiations and pending the ratification of a treaty by the two Senates, the United States must agree to protect Texas against any possible aggression from Mexico, and there is little doubt that Houston believed this stipulation would not be met.[19]

While the official letters were passing back and forth, Upshur and Van Zandt continued to discuss the terms of the treaty of annexation, and toward the latter part of February 1844 all the major points had been agreed on, subject to the receipt of final instructions from Texas being brought by Henderson. "Had instructions arrived to authorize me to consumate it," Van Zandt wrote, "the treaty could have been concluded in a day." [20]

5

It was at this point that the most spectacular accident of the time occurred, forcing further delay, giving Whigs and Northern Democrats time to organize for battle, perhaps altering the shape of things to come, and certainly changing the career of John C. Calhoun.

The President, members of his Cabinet, Senators and Representatives, prominent men and women of Washington and other cities, all were guests of Commodore Stockton of the Navy aboard the newly commissioned battleship *Princeton*. She was the last word in fighting ships, steam-powered with screw propellers, and with huge fore and aft guns that hurled a ball weighing 225 pounds. Everything had been thoroughly tested long before the President and his party went aboard the morning of February 28, 1844. Through a day of cruising on the Potomac, during which the various guns were fired more than once, all went smoothly, and no one was more pleased than Thomas W. Gilmer, Secretary of the Navy for a bare ten days.

The ship was returning to Washington late in the afternoon when the great gun "Peacemaker" was fired one more time. This time the gun burst, hurling huge fragments of ragged metal into the assembled spectators. Tyler had stepped back into the dining room to answer a lady's question, and so was spared; but among the dead were Upshur, Gilmer, and Virgil Maxcy. Also killed were Captain Beverley Kennon of the Navy; and David Gardiner of New York, Yale classmate of Calhoun's and father of Julia Gardiner who would in a few months become the second Mrs. John Tyler. The rugged and durable Thomas Hart Benton was picked up, white and shaken but uninjured, from the welter of blood on the deck, and there were many other escapes so close as to seem providential to the survivors.[21]

Among those spared was Isaac E. Holmes, Charleston Congressman, who was aboard as guest of the Secretary of the Navy. During the day he had been much with Upshur, Maxcy, and Gilmer, "talking about Calhoun, for they were all his friends." They were indeed, but Maxcy was too close for such trite phrases. It was more than a week before news of the tragedy reached Fort Hill, and Calhoun wrote, in script not quite as firm as usual, to Mrs. Maxcy: "The stroke which deprived you of the kindest & best of husbands deprived me of the most faithful of friends, and whose place I can never hope to supply. . . . I loved him, as a brother."[22]

The same mail brought him news that he would almost certainly be nominated for Secretary of State, and this time he knew that he could not refuse.

CHAPTER XII

THE STATE DEPARTMENT

1

ON MARCH 6, 1844, just a week after the *Princeton* disaster, Tyler sent to the Senate the name of John C. Calhoun of South Carolina to be Secretary of State. The appointment was considered immediately, and without hearing or reference to committee was unanimously confirmed, Benton having stalked ostentatiously from the chamber before the vote was taken.

Behind that simple sequence of events lies an interesting study in historical plausibility. In his reminiscences, published in 1872, Henry A. Wise takes full credit for the appointment to himself, and historians have generally been content to let him have it.[1] As he tells it, Wise made up his mind as soon as Upshur was killed that Calhoun must have the place. Early on the morning of February 29 he called on McDuffie, whom he found not yet dressed, to ask if Calhoun could be persuaded to accept the State Department. McDuffie was doubtful but agreed to write and urge it on him, on Wise's assurance that the South Carolinian's name would probably be sent to the Senate at once. Wise did not say he came from Tyler, but he allowed McDuffie to infer it. He then went to the President and urged that Calhoun be appointed, but Tyler refused until Wise confessed he had already asked McDuffie to intercede for Calhoun's acceptance.

It makes a good story, but it is most unlikely that Wise consulted McDuffie without Tyler's knowledge, or that he found at the White House any such reluctance as he depicts. The contemporary record seems to indicate that the great Nullifier was the immediate choice of the President, whose only problem was whether a man who had twice refused the same office at his hands would accept it now. Wise brought him a promise that McDuffie's influence would be used to that end, but Tyler did not stop there. He sounded out the whole South Carolina Congressional delegation and as many of Calhoun's

161

friends from other states as he could reach. The President himself talked to McDuffie and to Isaac Holmes, while various intermediaries consulted others in position to guess at the South Carolinian's reaction or to influence his decision. The consensus seemed to be that Calhoun would take it, if he could be convinced that it was a matter of patriotic duty.[2]

If the circumstances had actually been as Wise relates them, there would have been no necessity for the lapse of a week, during which these various consultations were going on, before Calhoun's name was sent to the Senate. There was immediate newspaper speculation, of course, as to who would fill the key Cabinet vacancy, and the names of Daniel Webster, Littleton W. Tazewell, and William C. Rives were among those mentioned. The most common choice of the editors, however, was Senator Robert J. Walker of Mississippi whose recent pamphlet on Texas annexation had given him sudden prominence. Then on March 5 the New York *Herald*, whose pipe line to the White House was a standing grievance to other editors, pronounced Calhoun to be the obvious and ideal man for the place.[3]

On that same day, in Washington, McDuffie had an interview with Tyler at Wise's urging. "The President," he wrote immediately afterward to Calhoun, "is very anxious that you should accept and come on immediately, as the Texas negociation admits of no delay, and requested me to say so to you. The moment you communicate your willingness to do so, your name will be sent in to the Senate, and I, therefore, wish you to write to me immediately. I now repeat the opinion I expressed in my last, that it is my decided opinion and that of your friends here that your acceptance would be regarded by the country as a magnanimous offering at the shrine of patriotism, and that you ought not to hesitate. I mention to you in confidence that the Texas question is in such a state, that in ten days after your arrival the Treaty of annexation would be signed, and from poor Upshur's count 40 senators would vote for it. The President says he has hopes of the acquiesence of Mexico. It is a great occasion involving the peace of the country and the salvation of the South, and your friends here have ventured to say for you, that no party or personal considerations would prevent you from meeting the crisis." [4]

Far from being fixed against the elevation of Calhoun to the first office in the Cabinet, Tyler appears to have been singularly eager to bring that event to pass, with the reluctance all on the other side. The President still hoped that he himself could capture the Democratic nomination, and department heads are supposed to endorse the ambitions of their chief. Webster had left the Cabinet in part at least because he could not get on the Tyler band wagon, and for similar reasons Calhoun had twice refused to enter the charmed circle. But Calhoun had now withdrawn his own name, without endorsing anyone else. He had in fact made it very clear that he could not support anyone who favored, or whose friends favored, a protective tariff or agitation of the slave question. That eliminated both Van Buren and Clay, but if Tyler could explain away his own signature on the tariff of 1842, why should Calhoun not support him? The mere presence of the Carolinian in the official family would give prestige and power to the President, even if there were no overt support. Certainly one of the considerations weighed by Calhoun's friends was whether he could accept the place without committing himself to Tyler. They believed that he could, but Tyler would hardly look at it that way.[5]

Although McDuffie and other friends of Calhoun promised to write and urge upon him the propriety and indispensable necessity of his acceptance of the State Department, Tyler was still not sure of the issue. It was then that he played his trump card, sending the Carolinian's name immediately to the Senate without waiting for a reply to McDuffie's query, and doing it so promptly that news of the confirmation would arrive at Fort Hill as soon as the offer itself. That was what happened, and was probably what turned the balance in favor of acceptance. "Thus it is, Dr Sir," wrote Tyler in the gracious prose he handled so well, "that the country unites with me in the call which I have made upon you. I may leave the rest to the promptings of your own patriotic feelings."[6]

2

Calhoun received the news of the *Princeton* disaster and of the probability of his own appointment in Upshur's place on March 9, 1844.[7] He had no wish to return to political office, and he still hoped it could be avoided. With great explicitness he tried to make his position clear in a letter presumably intended for McDuffie. When he retired it was with the firm intention of never returning to public life unless by popular election to the Presidency. He had given his best years to his country's service and he had earned his rest. Only a few days earlier he had refused to go back to the Senate, and there was even less inducement to go into the Cabinet. He conceded that the job to be done—the annexation of Texas and the settlement of the Oregon dispute—was of the first importance, but it had not been demonstrated that he alone could do it. Only a conviction of duty could lead him to give up the retirement he found so pleasant, but so far as his information went, the case for duty had not been established.[8]

March 9 was a Saturday, so that it would have been Monday March 11, or even later before Calhoun's unenthusiastic letter was posted at Pendleton. On the fifteenth he wrote his daughter, explaining his great reluctance to accept the State Department, and his earnest hope that it would not be necessary. He expected "to hear the result in 12 or 13 days." That same day, March 15, 1844, he received Tyler's two letters of March 6, the first informing him of his appointment, the second of his unanimous confirmation by the Senate. With the President's letters were twenty or thirty more, all urging on him the duty of accepting, and they were by no means all from his own political friends, or even from members of his own party. The impression they uniformly gave of urgency, of confidence, of bipartisan support from every section of the country, would have moved a man of less vanity than Calhoun possessed. He recognized and bowed to the call of duty, with the proviso that he might retire when the Texas and Oregon questions were settled.[9]

Calhoun's motive for returning to public life at this time was undoubtedly disinterested and patriotic, and his linking of Texas and Oregon was the key. The South, without distinction as to party, wanted Texas; the North, with unanimity almost equally bipartisan, did not want Texas. Each side thought the Union would be destroyed if its own views were not met to the letter, and holding the balance between them were the expansionists of the West: men who wanted all of Oregon, the Bay of San Francisco, and a British market for their grain. If the President, the Congress, and the country would sustain him, Calhoun thought he might join the interest of the West in Oregon to the interest of the South in Texas, and in the process reforge the alliance of South and West for which he had worked so long: the alliance that would at last produce enough votes in the

House and Senate to repeal all traces of the protective system and open wide the markets of England and America to reciprocal trade with each other.[10]

There were a few seasoned politicians who saw deep political motives behind the appointment, and far-reaching political consequences to follow from it, but they did not agree on the nature of the one or the character of the other. The newspaper press for the most part sustained it, and the country at large heaved an almost audible sigh of relief when it became generally known that Calhoun would accept. Cities along his route prepared to honor him as he traveled on his way to the Capital, and his friends with difficulty prevented a noisy public welcome at the steamboat wharf in Washington. He arrived on March 29, six days from Fort Hill, had a two-hour interview with Tyler the following morning, and entered on the duties of his office on Monday, April 1, 1844.[11]

3

It was an essential part of Calhoun's nature to throw himself wholly into whatever he undertook, and to approach everything he did with order and system and logical method. His first task in the State Department was to familiarize himself with the current situation, particularly with respect to Texas. His second act, no less important for the effective conduct of diplomatic business, was to establish close and harmonious relations with the Senate Committee on Foreign Relations and with the House Committee on Foreign Affairs. Chairman of the Senate group was William S. Archer of Virginia, while the House committee was under Charles J. Ingersoll of Pennsylvania. With both of these Calhoun's intercourse was full and unreserved. They knew exactly what was going on, where negotiations stood at any given moment, what was intended and what it was sought to avoid. Both felt free to make suggestions based on the probable reaction of the bodies they respectively represented; and both kept the secrets of the department inviolate. When Silas Wright paid a courtesy call a few days after Calhoun's installation he found the new Secretary "very happy and as much at ease, as quiet, and free from restlessness" as he had ever seen him.[12]

Calhoun had reason to feel at ease. The situation he found with respect to the Texas treaty was just such as the Texan Commissioner,

Isaac Van Zandt, had described to his own government immediately after Upshur's death. All important points had been agreed on. It remained only to whip the terms into formal shape, with such modifications as were necessitated under the final instructions from Texas. These were brought by J. Pinckney Henderson, who had arrived in Washington to associate himself with Van Zandt only a day or two ahead of Calhoun. The only significant stipulation was that already alluded to: that Texas must be fully protected from Mexico while the negotiations went forward and until the treaty had been ratified.

The American chargé in Texas, General W. S. Murphy, had found no difficulty in giving in the name of his government all the assurances desired. His report reached Washington after Upshur's death but before Calhoun had learned of his own appointment to the office. Attorney General John Nelson, acting as Secretary for the interim, repudiated Murphy's promise, informing the too co-operative diplomat that "you have suffered your zeal to carry you beyond the line of your instructions." He added, however, that the President was nevertheless "not indisposed, as a measure of prudent precaution . . . to concentrate in the Gulf of Mexico, and on the Southern borders of the United States, a naval and military force to be directed to the defence of the inhabitants and territory of Texas at a proper time," even though such forces could not be used against a friendly power. Calhoun repeated and clarified the American position in a note to Van Zandt and Henderson on April 11. "I am directed by the President to say that the Secretary of the Navy had been instructed to order a strong naval force to concentrate in the Gulf of Mexico, to meet any emergency; and that similiar orders have been issued by the Secretary of War to move the disposable military forces on our Southwestern frontier for the same purpose. Should the exigency arise . . . I am further directed by the President to say that, during the pendency of the treaty of annexation, he would deem it his duty to use all the means placed within his power by the Constitution to protect Texas from all foreign invasion." [13]

Houston was ready to call off the whole negotiation in event that Murphy's assurances were disavowed by the United States Government, but Van Zandt and Henderson were satisfied with the truncated assurances given by Calhoun. The treaty was formally signed on April 12, and the knowledge that American defense of Texas would be strictly limited to the constitutional powers of the President reached the Texan Capital only with the *fait accompli*.[14]

The possible fate of the treaty had meanwhile become a subject of considerable speculation in political circles. Upshur's conviction of January that two thirds of the Senate would ratify with votes to spare, which had been repeated to Calhoun as recently as March 5, was no longer sure. Under sectional and partisan pressures the opposition had been slowly rising until by April many doubted if the treaty could be ratified at all.[15] Calhoun refused to believe that public sentiment would permit such a result. He knew, however, that the threat of Mexico to regard annexation as an act of war was one of the factors that might operate against ratification. On Archer's advice, therefore, conciliatory dispatches were sent to Mexico City, and the treaty was temporarily held up. The original intention seems to have been to submit it to the Senate only after an answer had been received from Mexico, but after the New York *Herald* had published the terms of the document on April 16 delay seemed hazardous. The rumor quickly spread that it was deliberately being shelved until after the Democratic convention, and the whole Texas question threatened to be engulfed in party politics. It seemed better to face the issue boldly and at once, and so the treaty and its accompanying documents were sent to the Senate on April 22, 1844.[16]

4

While the Texas treaty was temporarily on ice, Calhoun turned to other unfinished business of his department, and one of the first things to meet his eye was a dispatch from Lord Aberdeen, transmitted through the British Minister, Richard Pakenham, just two days before Upshur's death. Pakenham himself was a newcomer, having reached the United States only in mid-February. He had formally taken over his duties on the twenty-first of that month, and three days later he read to Upshur the letter from Aberdeen which he transmitted in writing on the twenty-sixth. It was this letter that Calhoun found, unanswered, among the papers of his predecessor. Pakenham, it should be noted, had come with special instructions to negotiate on the Oregon question, but he came from a long previous assignment in Mexico City, and his first official business with the government to which he was accredited concerned not Oregon but Texas.[17]

The dispatch in question, dated December 26, 1843, took due note of American suspicions as to British intentions in Texas, and was no doubt intended to put those suspicions to rest. To a mind as acute as Calhoun's, however, and as obsessed with the problem of slavery, the effect was bound to be precisely the reverse. For though Aberdeen disclaimed any self-interested motives in Britain's attitude toward Texas other than the general one of commercial expansion, he avowed frankly the intervention of his government to gain Mexican recognition of Texan independence, and clearly implied that abolition of slavery in Texas would be an acceptable *quid pro quo.* As to slavery as such, "it must be and is well known, both to the United States and to the whole world, that Great Britain desires, and is constantly exerting herself to procure, the general abolition of slavery throughout the world." This did not mean, the Foreign Minister insisted, that his government had any intention of interfering in Texas, "provided other States act with equal forbearance," nor that Britain "sought in any way to stir up disaffection or excitement of any kind in the slaveholding States of the American Union." Not at all. She simply wanted to see slavery abolished, in the United States as well as everywhere else. And she would not think of interfering in the affairs of Texas, unless the United States interfered by, let us say, seeking to annex that country.

We must remember at this point that neither Calhoun nor any other Southerner, nor very many Northerners except perhaps the abolitionists themselves, really believed in the altruism of British policy. If Aberdeen wrote an official denial that Britain had any designs on Texas, or intended any interference with Southern institutions, the semiofficial patronage given to the abolitionists, the record of British commercial and diplomatic dealings, and especially the active interference with slavery in the Western Hemisphere, all spoke a different language. Evidence was not wanting that the British Government, weakening under pressure from organized abolitionists both in England and America, might well at any time block the whole annexation move, and there was nothing in Aberdeen's letter to say she would not. There was, moreover, in Calhoun's hands at that moment a voluminous report from Alexander H. Everett, whose brother Edward, at London, seemed so blind to the economic motivations of political behavior. It was a report based on many months of study by agents at first hand, and it proved to Everett, whose sympathies were wholly Northern, as clearly as it did to Calhoun, that British abolitionists, probably with the connivance of their government, were stirring up revolt in Cuba preparatory to British seizure of that island. Cuba, so far as slavery was concerned, stood in the same relation to Florida that Texas stood to Louisiana and Arkansas. Surely if Calhoun, knowing what he knew of economic and diplomatic history and of the actual situation in Mexico, Texas, Cuba, and Britain herself, had accepted Aberdeen's letter at its face value, he would have been unfit to be Secretary of State.[18]

He did not accept it, but on April 18 addressed a reply to Pakenham in language as suave as Aberdeen's own. His government was pleased to know that Great Britain had no intention of meddling in the affairs of the Southern states, but was deeply concerned over the Foreign Minister's avowal of British interest in world-wide abolition. "It is with still deeper concern the President regards the avowal of Lord Aberdeen of the desire of Great Britain to see slavery abolished in Texas," a desire that British diplomacy appeared to be furthering. From this point of departure he went on to argue that the danger to the South and therefore to the Union from abolition in Texas was so great that the United States was bound to interfere, leading up to an acknowledgment that a treaty of annexation had already been concluded.

Aberdeen had promised not to interfere in Texas provided nobody else did. Calhoun replied in effect: You have been interfering in Texas for a long time. That interference has become a threat to our security, and we are therefore going to put a stop to it by annexing Texas to ourselves. We are doing it in self-defense, and if there is any trouble over it between your country and mine, you started it.

No doubt he should have left it there, but he proceeded first with a brief justification of annexation on historical grounds and in terms of national defense; then with a lengthy defense of slavery itself. In view of the outspoken convictions of a large number of his own countrymen it was an error, and undoubtedly one that he would never have committed had he realized the letter would be published. He was impelled to say what he did, however, by his own innate honesty. He had long since reasoned himself into the position of justifying slavery not on grounds of expediency but on the far more infuriating ground that, given all the circumstances, it was right in itself as it existed in the Southern states. Calvinist that he was, and deeply religious in his own approach of life, he could not have defended it in any other terms; yet those were the very terms that aroused the antislavery forces to their highest pitch of moral indignation.

There was a further exchange between Calhoun and Pakenham, but without adding to or altering the basic points. Then both men hastened to transmit the correspondence, together with the Texas treaty and their own appropriate comments, to their respective London colleagues: Pakenham to Aberdeen direct, Calhoun to Everett to be called to Aberdeen's attention in the normal diplomatic way.[19]

5

The treaty of annexation, as we have seen, was sent to the Senate on April 22, 1844, with a special message from President Tyler and a sheaf of supporting documents. These began with Van Zandt's appeal to Webster of December 4, 1842, for American intervention to prevent further violations of the rules of war in the still pending struggle between Texas and her mother country. They proceeded with the evidence for British designs and the bearing of these on Southern security, as revealed in the official correspondence; detailed the origin and progress of the annexation movement under Upshur; and ended with Calhoun's letter to Pakenham and his dispatch explaining the situation to the authorities in Mexico. The President's message stressed the commercial and strategic value of Texas to the various sections of the Union, and the threat to peace, prosperity, and possibly to national existence that lay in permitting her to fall under British dominance.[20]

Message, treaty, and documents all were strictly confidential, and under the seal of confidence were ordered printed for the use of the Senate before being referred to Archer's Committee on Foreign Relations. Five days later, on April 27, 1844, the treaty and documents appeared in the New York *Evening Post*. The leak was quickly traced to Senator Benjamin Tappan of Ohio, a Van Buren partisan. The newspaper concerned was Van Buren's New York City mouthpiece, and the political implications of the episode were further underlined by the immediate concentration of editorial fire against the letter to Pakenham.[21]

The Pakenham letter was never intended for publication. It was not in any sense a complete statement of the case for annexation but only of so much of the case as was necessary to justify it in terms of the position taken by the British Foreign Minister. There seems no reason to doubt Calhoun's explanation that his purpose was merely to force the British Government to stop dealing with the abolitionists. He did not mean to imply that annexation could be sustained only by defending slavery; and he most certainly did not mean to advance the defense of slavery in that connection for the deliberate purpose of securing the defeat of his own treaty, with the ultimate object of taking the South out of the Union. Yet it was inevitable, as the Senator who revealed it and the editor who published it must both have known, that abolitionists like Giddings and Adams would not be able to see it in any other light. It was equally certain that shrewd and experienced opponents like Benton and Blair, adroit in the use of slander and misrepresentation as weapons of political warfare, would seize upon and enlarge the abolitionist view.

If Calhoun had realized the reaction his letter would provoke he would probably never have written it, and he would certainly not have allowed it to go to the Senate with the treaty. But his own genius here as in many other instances was his undoing. He was so sure, so confident in the correctness of his own views, that he failed to appreciate the fact that others who believed differently might be just as obsessed with their own rightness as he was. He could not doubt that American policy required the preservation of slavery, even as British policy required its destruction. Slavery, therefore, was the real stake in Texas, and he was fundamentally too honest to pretend it was anything else. With that proposition the abolitionists wholly agreed, and so, thanks to the Pakenham letter and the calculated indiscretion of an Ohio Senator, slavery was the issue that was fought out in the Senate in the guise of a treaty to annex Texas. On that basis it would have been doomed, even had the administration commanded a party and even had there been no Presidential election in the offing.

CHAPTER XIII

THE CAMPAIGN OF 1844

1

To UNDERSTAND more fully the nature of the rising sectional storm and its bearing on the Presidential contest, we must go back to the meeting of Congress in December 1843, and the sweeping victory of Van Buren's partisans in the organization of the House. Calhoun's intimates, for the most part, accepted a situation for which their own ineptitude was at least in part responsible, but they prepared to force the Northern Democrats to redeem long-standing pledges on the tariff and slavery questions. The pledges, of course, were strictly inferential: the votes of party leaders on sundry policy resolutions going back to 1838, and various unguarded promises made in the heat of past campaigns. The Southern Democrats were nevertheless justified in their insistence that pledges had been given. They had repeated over and over again that in return for their support of the party program in Congress, and of the party nominee in 1840, they expected a strictly revenue tariff and the retention of the gag rule; the Northern wing of the Democracy had accepted the support and had voted in the indicated manner.

The South first took alarm when Silas Wright voted for the tariff of 1842, but alarm approached panic when the New York and Massachusetts Democratic conventions adopted protariff platforms the following year. What the Southern contingent now prepared to do was to say in effect to their brethren in the free states: You cannot elect a President without our support. We shall give you that support if, but only if, the forthcoming party convention chooses a candidate and pledges a platform that we can approve. We will take any candidate, even Van Buren if there is no escape for it, providing you demonstrate to us by deeds *before the convention meets* that you do in fact mean to repeal the tariff of 1842 and keep the slavery question off the floor of Congress.

A few days after the session opened the Democratic majority consented to set up a committee under Henry A. Wise to revise the rules of the House. This work was still going forward when on December 21, 1843, Adams offered more firebrand resolutions from Massachusetts. This time they came from the legislature, and proposed to amend the Constitution so that Southern slaves would no longer be counted, not even three fifths of them, in determining representation in Congress. The Southern members, sensitive as raw flesh to anything that concerned their peculiar institution, saw the Massachusetts resolutions referred to committee and entered on the Journal by votes of Van Buren Democrats. As the new year began they learned that the legislature whence the resolutions came was also controlled by partisans of the ex-President.[1]

Immediately thereafter, on January 2, 1844, not Wise but Adams reported the amended rules, and one of the changes was the elimination of all barriers to the discussion of slavery. Two Van Buren Democrats on the nine-man committee voted with the majority in what Calhoun branded a piece of "political treachery almost without example." During the next two months the party leadership kept the question in abeyance, bringing it to a vote only on February 28. There were many absentees, some of them guests aboard the ill-fated *Princeton,* but the Democrats were in fact a large majority when they retained the gag rule by a single vote.[2]

The tariff question had also been reopened by Calhoun's partisans, and was pending while the rules were under discussion. Before the session was two weeks old Rhett moved instructions to the Committee on Ways and Means, looking to the repeal of the tariff of 1842 and the substitution of a uniform duty of 20 percent ad valorem. McDuffie in the Senate moved simultaneously to achieve the same purpose by restoring the compromise of 1833. Both propositions were received coldly by Northern Democrats, who felt more keenly year by year the pressure of the rising industrialism that was becoming the dominant economic force in the free states.[3]

The Ways and Means Committee, headed by James I. McKay of North Carolina, probably did the best that could have been expected in the circumstances. It strove to balance the various pressures against one another, it compromised and temporized and sometimes obfuscated issues, but it succeeded before the end of February in drafting a bill that did generally reduce the level of duties imposed by the act of 1842, though not uniformly, nor as low as 20 percent. But its provisions first became known when the rancorous battle over the twenty-first rule was at its bitterest, and it was inevitable that those predisposed to take offense would see in it no concession but only the conscious rubbing of salt into old wounds.

McKay himself showed a draft of the bill to the leaders of the Calhoun faction, apparently in entire good faith, and McDuffie and Woodbury in the Senate so accepted it. McDuffie, indeed, saw enough of concession in it to justify the Southern Democrats in supporting Van Buren. But Rhett reacted instantly in the opposite direction, and in terms of the logic Calhoun had trained his followers for almost a generation to pursue, Rhett was undoubtedly correct. Such a bill, he wrote Calhoun, "would be the grave of the free-trade cause forever . . . after a protective Tariff is made by the Whigs, and only modified by the Democrats, the principle will be supposed to be surrendered by both Parties." Calhoun saw the point and cautioned McDuffie, who promptly denounced Rhett as vain, self-seeking, and unsafe; but Rhett in the interval had burned his bridges with a letter to Van Buren that amounted to a threat.[4]

The McKay bill was brought to the floor March 8, 1844, two days after Calhoun's confirmation as Secretary of State, and was debated sporadically for two months while the Senate gave similar attention to McDuffie's bill to restore the compromise of 1833. When Calhoun arrived late in March he managed to quiet his followers enough to permit consideration of the Texas question, but the sectional split was already too deep to be healed. Before the end of April slavery itself was a party issue, and the McKay bill was tabled by Van Buren's men on May 10. The next day the *Spectator* attacked the Van Buren Democrats, and no one doubted Rhett's agency in preparing the article.[5]

2

The whole Texas question had already become a matter of party politics. Van Buren had undoubtedly been pondering the problem for some time, but he had been very careful not to tip his hand, even to his closest friends. It was taken for granted by many Democrats, especially by Van Buren's Southern followers, that he would of course favor annexation, largely no doubt because of Jackson's outspoken stand and the public support the old General had consistently given to his New York protégé. But the truth was that public opinion in New York, whipped up as it was continuously by the abolitionist press, was growing restive at the continued existence of slavery in the United States. A growing segment of New York voters leaned toward the antislavery side, even though it meant breaking the old party ties with the South, and Van Buren was not indifferent to the changing sentiment.

By early April the ex-President's mind was made up, but so far as the records go, he discussed his stand only with Silas Wright. The two men agreed that the slavery issue was more important for the future of the Union and for the ultimate fame of all concerned than was the outcome of any given election. Van Buren knew that if he came out against annexation he would probably destroy his chances of getting the Democratic nomination when the convention met in May, but he had shrewdly judged the temper of the times. He had had his measure of political success, and he preferred to take his case to history as the champion, though belatedly, of the better cause. That it would also be the winning side, so far as the political control of New York was concerned, was no longer open to question; and to those who, like Van Buren, had spent their lives in manufacturing and commercial states, it probably seemed equally clear that an ultimate triumph for abolition in the country as a whole was only a matter of time. He decided, in a word, that the slavery issue was overriding in American politics, and that he must therefore take a firm stand. His decision was essentially the same decision that Calhoun had reached a decade or more before. Van Buren simply took the opposite side, as befitted his place of residence and his economic ties.[6]

Van Buren's views as to Texas were announced in a very long letter that beat around the bush in masterly fashion, but in spite of its length, its circumlocutions, and its verbiage, its central point was clear. Annexation in the manner proposed was unconstitutional, and immediate annexation in any form ought not to be considered. Addressed to Mississippi Congressman W. H. Hammett and dated April 20, 1844, the letter appeared in the *Globe* for April 27. It was that same day that the New York *Evening Post* gave Calhoun's Pakenham letter to the world in what had every appearance of a carefully planned coincidence; that same day too that the *Intelligencer* carried a short letter from Clay, who also opposed annexation "at this time." Clay undoubtedly reflected the sentiment of the party that nominated him by acclamation a few days later. Van Buren's sentiment was strictly sectional and carried with it a conscious responsibility for splitting the Democracy.[7]

It has been argued many times that Calhoun forced Van Buren's hand on the Texas question, in a deliberate effort to break the ties between the Northern and the Southern Democracy. Indeed Blair even insisted in an almost incoherent letter to Jackson that Calhoun had written to Pakenham after he had read Van Buren's Texas statement in the *Globe;* written for the deliberate purpose of driving off the North, solidifying the South, and paving the way for secession of the slave states and for a new empire with himself at its head. Certainly such charges were of a piece with those Blair had tossed around so lavishly in the nullification days, but the logic was absurd. The Pakenham letter was written in Washington on April 18, and delivered the same day. Van Buren's Texas letter was dated from Kinderhook April 20, and published April 27. Calhoun could not possibly have seen it before he answered Aberdeen's dispatch; nor could Van Buren have known of Calhoun's letter, which did not go to the Senate until April 22, in time to change anything in his own, even though it was one of his Senatorial friends who gave it to the *Post*. Above all things Calhoun wanted the annexation of Texas, for therein he was now sure lay the only hope for Southern security and therefore for the permanence of the Union. It is hardly credible, even had it been chronologically possible, that he would do anything deliberately to alienate those on whose votes annexation depended.[8]

Clay's letter was only what had been expected, but the effect of Van Buren's pronouncement on his followers was catastrophic. Wright, of course, agreed fully, as did the bulk of the Northern Democracy; and Bancroft paid his usual lip service to the wisdom of his chief, even though he himself would very shortly move into the other camp. But the Southern Democrats were shocked and indignant. One of Polk's friends spoke for them all when he declared angrily that "Vans Letter has played Hell with us." [9]

3

A more decisive reaction to Van Buren's Texas letter came from Virginia. The document reached Richmond April 30, on the heels of sweeping Whig victories in local elections throughout the state. Long-standing friend of Van Buren though he was, Ritchie took the lead and called a meeting of the Shockoe Hill Democratic Association —the Richmond version of Tammany Hall—for May 1. Resolutions drawn by the old editor himself demanding immediate annexation of Texas were quickly pushed through, along with others urging the propriety of releasing the Virginia delegates to the Baltimore convention from their pledges. For the next three or four days letters poured in, commending the Richmond action and condemning Van Buren's stand. With these expressions of public opinion in hand, Ritchie wrote to the ex-President on May 5 telling him bluntly that he could not now carry Virginia and would be regarded by the Virginia delegates in Baltimore as unavailable.[10]

In South Carolina the State Central Committee had held a two-day meeting in the middle of March to reconsider its position consequent on the withdrawal of Calhoun from the Presidential contest. It was agreed that in protest against the mode of organizing the convention, no delegates should be sent to Baltimore. Not a few of Calhoun's friends deplored this action at the time, and after the appearance of Van Buren's letter many among them insisted that the Secretary of State be held up as a candidate once more. He himself, however, refused to depart from the position he had taken in his December letter to his supporters. He realized, unquestionably, that the effect of the Pakenham letter and of the savage onslaughts Blair began against him in the *Globe* would be to destroy his availability, if indeed he had ever been available, as surely as Van Buren had destroyed his own.[11]

In the North Van Buren's letter was well received, and there were a few personal supporters in the South and West who clung to him, most notable of them Benton and Blair. The line taken by these two was to denounce Calhoun with consuming bitterness, and to charge that the whole annexation project was a dastardly plot of the South Carolinian's to defeat Van Buren's nomination at Baltimore. But for the most part even Northern Democrats conceded that the little Dutchman was out of the running, and a new candidate must be found. The names of Cass, Buchanan, Johnson, and Woodbury were tossed into the pot and the brew was vigorously stirred.[12]

The Calhoun wing of the Democracy drew closer to Tyler, while the President courted Southern support and especially that of his powerful Secretary of State. The post of chargé d'affaires in Belgium, though it would not be vacant until August, was given to Thomas G. Clemson early in May; and Calhoun was allowed to dispose of the patronage of his department with a virtually free hand. The *Madisonian* defended the Texas treaty and the Secretary, and it was made known immediately after the publication of the Van Buren and Clay letters that John Tyler would seek the Democratic nomination. It was also indicated that there would be a Tyler convention in Baltimore at the same time as the regular Democratic gathering, and that if he were not the party nominee, the President would run as an independent Democrat.[13]

Calhoun's hand was strengthened in the Senate shortly before the Texas treaty was reported from committee on May 10. The veteran William R. King of Alabama had accepted appointment as Minister to France and his place in the Senate was taken by heavy-fleshed but nimble-witted Dixon H. Lewis. The sectional lines were already too sharply drawn, however, for one man's weight to alter the result—even a man who weighed four hundred pounds. The McKay bill was tabled in the House the same day the treaty reached the floor of the Senate, emphasizing once more the North-South rift in the Democracy, while the reaction to Van Buren's antiannexation letter and to Calhoun's Pakenham correspondence boded no good for the cause. Calhoun had in fact already primed Ingersoll to offer a joint resolution admitting Texas to the Union as a state if the treaty failed.[14]

For some two weeks the Senate debated annexation in various guises, with Benton attacking Tyler and Calhoun rather more than the treaty, while McDuffie and Walker carried the burden for the administration. The Senate majority, now made up of Northern Whigs and Van Buren Democrats, took time to reject W. S. Murphy as chargé in Texas by way of a harassing action, but the Baltimore convention was too close for any other serious business.[15]

4

Convention delegates began to arrive in Washington as early as May 21, and before they moved on to Baltimore each knew exactly what he was expected to do. The annexationists built their hopes on the two-thirds rule, which had the backing of the Calhoun group and was moved on the convention floor by Romulus M. Saunders, Calhoun's leader in North Carolina. It was the Virginia delegation, however, led and controlled by Ritchie's son, that forced the issue, aided and abetted by the Mississippians drilled by Senator Walker. The strategy was simple and effective, for even though a clear majority of the delegates were pledged to Van Buren many of those so committed could be induced to vote for the two-thirds rule, which would admittedly make the New Yorker's nomination impossible. Undoubtedly promises to favorite sons like Woodbury and Buchanan aided in bringing about this result. Perhaps also there were promises to Northern men that Oregon too would be "annexed." Jackson's insistence that only a pro-Texas man should be chosen influenced some, and others, even among Van Buren's partisans, no longer believed the ex-President could be elected if nominated.[16]

Feeling was bitter by May 27 when the convention met, and became more so with the actual adoption of the two-thirds rule on the second day, after hours of heated wrangling. As anticipated, Van Buren had a majority on the first ballot, but was far short of two thirds. Seven ballots were taken on the afternoon of May 28, with Cass quickly edging out Van Buren but also falling well below two thirds. Calhoun drew a scattering handful of votes but they were by courtesy only, his followers having reaffirmed throughout the preliminary discussions the Secretary's determination not to be a candidate. The also-rans included Buchanan, Woodbury, and Richard M. Johnson, but none of them had any real strength. As the long sitting drew to a close the whole convention threatened to break up in pandemonium. Tempers flared and individual fist fights looked for a time as though they would merge into a general free-for-all when the chairman lost all semblance of control. It was then that Bancroft and other Northern leaders approached the Tennessee delegation with the suggestion that Polk be brought forward as a compromise candidate.[17]

Polk's friends in the Tennessee delegation, especially Gideon J. Pillow, Cave Johnson, and S. H. Laughlin, and probably also Jackson's nephew, A. J. Donelson, had undoubtedly been working toward this result for several days, and it may well be that they had privately committed Ritchie and Walker before the convention met.[18] Polk had been from the start the leading candidate for Vice President, but before the Tennessee delegates left home Jackson himself had fixed on the former Speaker as the most available man for the first office. Polk was so informed by Jackson, and wrote to Cave Johnson on May

13 authorizing the use of his name for the Presidency if it seemed advisable. A second letter to Johnson, dated May 14, suggested confidential meetings with a member of each state delegation to plan strategy, and a third letter of the same date proposed that Johnson should show the second to Silas Wright.[19] It was not altogether a surprise, therefore, when Bancroft's suggestion was received. The next morning, no doubt after a night of feverish discussion, Polk's name was offered as a candidate for President, and drew 44 votes on the eighth ballot, the first taken that day.

As the ninth ballot was announced, various delegations retired for consultation. Then, halfway through the roll call, Benjamin F. Butler of New York, "Van Buren's drill sergeant," rose and read a letter from the ex-President, authorizing the withdrawal of his name. When the shouting and cheering had died down the roll call was completed, but before the result was announced, a call went up from the floor for South Carolina, the only state unrepresented. Pickens was recognized as he stood in the crowd at the rear of the room, and came forward in response to the cries of the delegates. To the accompaniment of thunderous cheers he pledged his state to the convention nominee, and Elmore emerged from among the spectators to second the pledge. Polk was then declared to be the unanimous choice of the convention for President of the United States.[20]

A few minutes later word of the nomination was received in a room in the Capitol over the magnetic telegraph. Samuel F. B. Morse himself handled the instrument in Washington while his partner, Alfred Vail, transmitted from the Convention Hall in Baltimore. The historic test message had passed over those same wires only five days earlier. A crowd of nearly a thousand persons read the news from placards held up to the window of the receiving room, and it was hard to tell from their reaction whether they marveled more at Polk's nomination or at the miraculous way they had learned of it. Senators and Congressmen crowded around the instrument, where Silas Wright was presently summoned to learn of his own unanimous nomination for Vice President. His prompt refusal was sent back over the wires at once, but had to be repeated several times before the committee in Baltimore would believe it. Even then they remained doubtful until a personal deputation had made the round trip to gain confirmation.[21]

On Thursday, May 30, the name of George M. Dallas of Pennsylvania was substituted for that of Silas Wright, and the convention adjourned on a note of general harmony. That same day President Tyler accepted with thanks his nomination at the hands of "a Democratic Convention" which had met in Baltimore on May 27, wound up its predetermined business in a few hours, and disbanded.[22]

5

Polk's nomination was accompanied by the adoption of a platform intended to unite the party. The platform of 1840, with which no faction could quarrel because all factions had then accepted it, was reasserted in its entirety. It called for strict construction of the Constitution, for economy in government, for separation from banks, and for liberality in the extension of the rights of citizenship; and it denied to the Federal Government any power to carry out internal improvements, to assume state debts, to "foster one branch of industry to the detriment of another," to charter a Bank, or to "interfere with or control the domestic institutions of the several States." To this earlier declaration of principles were now added resolutions opposing the distribution of the proceeds from the sale of public lands and upholding the veto power of the President. The platform concluded with a resolution asserting title to the whole of Oregon, and proclaiming "that the re-occupation of Oregon and the re-annexation of Texas at the earliest practicable period are great American measures, which this convention recommends to the cordial support of the Democracy of the Union."[23]

Van Buren's Locofocos could hardly refuse to support a candidate who adhered to the same platform on which their own favorite had stood four years earlier; Benton was the outstanding champion of Oregon; and Calhoun stood committed to Texas annexation. On the negative side, of course, there were points with which each faction would have to disagree; but the wording, especially on slavery, on the tariff, on Texas, and on Oregon was sufficiently equivocal so that no one need feel himself compromised by an endorsement of the entire declaration.

Common principles on paper do not, unfortunately, make a united party in fact. Although the convention had given unanimous support to its candidate, it had so intensified the internal cleavage between Northern and Southern wings that the Democracy threatened to be blown to fragments. Calhoun's *Spectator* was the first newspaper in the country to carry the Democratic ticket at the head of its editorial column, which only made the Van Buren partisans the more certain that Calhoun had engineered their defeat. Benton, Wright, Butler, and their friends were furious, and for a time considered rejecting the ticket altogether. "The Democracy of the North," wrote one disgruntled Locofoco, "owe a debt to T. Ritchie J C Calhoun—Lewis Cass & a few others—which they will some day repay with interest." The *Globe* was so cool that Polk asked Jackson to bring pressure on Blair. He received assurances, but there was little change in the attitude of the paper, official organ of the party though it was. The Calhoun partisans remained equally bitter over the way they had been deserted on the gag rule and the tariff; while the obliteration of the Texas treaty on June 8 by a vote of 16 to 35 added gunpowder to the fires of their resentment. Both Calhoun and Van Buren factions seemed bent on forcing Polk to take sides between them, which would have been in effect to read the loser out of the party. It would also have been to lose the election.[24]

Polk was equally determined to keep the fragments united at least long enough to beat Clay. In June he threaded his way gingerly between North and South in a guarded statement of his position on the tariff. His "Kane letter" was elicited by Pennsylvania Democrats, who could take comfort from the candidate's failure to pledge repeal of the existing law, and his avowal that he had "heretofore sanctioned such moderate discriminating duties, as would produce the amount of revenue needed, and at the same time afford reasonable incidental protection to our home industry." For the South he came out unequivocally against any tariff not designed first and foremost for revenue purposes, and fell back on his record: he had voted against the tariff of 1828 and for the compromise.[25]

The factional squabble reached its disruptive peak in late July and early August. In New York William Cullen Bryant of the *Evening Post* and other leading Democrats denounced the Baltimore platform and called for the election of antiannexationists to Congress. In South Carolina Barnwell Rhett and Isaac Holmes set in motion a new "resistance" drive to force tariff reform, which will be the theme of the next chapter. Both movements were equally threatening to Polk's chances, and again he sought Jackson's intervention. This time, however, Van Buren put his own house in order for the sake of his power in New York, and Calhoun whipped South Carolina into line after Pickens visited Nashville and received from Polk himself satisfactory assurances on the tariff.[26]

There remained only the threat of Tyler's independent candidacy, which the Polk managers undertook to deal with by direct approach. Tyler's partisans had forced the issue with a Fourth of July meeting in Philadelphia at which it was agreed to run state and local tickets under the "Tyler and Texas" banner. Democratic reaction was one of immediate alarm, and Senator Robert J. Walker of Mississippi called forthwith on the President. In "a conversation . . . of several hours" the two agreed, in effect, on the terms of Tyler's capitulation. The President's followers, whom he estimated optimistically to number 150,000, most of them former Whigs, were to be received into the Democratic party as full communicants; and the *Globe* and other Democratic papers were to cease their attacks upon the administration. Walker forwarded the terms to Polk, who placed in Jackson's lap the problem of how they might be carried out.[27]

With military bluntness, Jackson dispatched the business. To Blair he sent what amounted to an order: "support the cause of Polk and Dallas and let Tiler alone." The President he approached through John Y. Mason of the Cabinet, and through Major Lewis. To each of these he wrote his conviction that Tyler must withdraw without delay. He could not carry a single state, and his persistence would forever alienate him and his friends from the Democracy. Withdrawal, on the other hand, would be accepted as evidence of good will and would serve to unite him once more with his old party. Tyler was reluctantly convinced. "Your letter to Major Lewis was, as you requested, shown to me," he wrote to Jackson on August 18, "and your views as to the proper course for me to pursue in the present emergency of public affairs has decided me to withdraw from the canvass. . . . But every thing depends on the course of Mr. Polks friends and press. I have been so prominently the object of attack on the part of the Globe and so furiously assailed by Col. Benton, that without an immediate change in this respect I fear that no good will ensue to the Democratic party." Two days later his long, defensive, slightly petulant letter of withdrawal took up four columns in the *Madisonian*.[28]

6

As the Presidential campaign moved toward its climax, Texas became more and more certainly the issue on which it was to turn. The *Madisonian,* as the leading administration paper, kept up a steady barrage on the annexation question, emphasizing British designs and the perfidy of Northern abolitionists, and other pro-Texas papers followed the pattern. The *Globe* made a halfhearted attempt late in June to turn the spotlight from Texas to Oregon, but without success. All this was a planned propaganda campaign on which Calhoun, Ingersoll, and Tyler had agreed at the time the treaty was defeated. It was designed as an appeal to the country which was to be followed, if the response was satisfactory, by a special session of Congress to annex Texas by joint resolution.[29]

The drive to arouse popular support for annexation reached its critical phase at about the same date as the matter of Tyler's withdrawal, an event not altogether unrelated. The next move was discussed by the Cabinet about the middle of August, where the consensus was that a special session in September or October might damage Polk's prospects. Calhoun suggested calling the regular session to meet November 1, on the ground that as long as annexation was still open, Mexico might at any time attack Texas and Congress should be on hand to deal with any eventuality that might thereupon arise. This too was abandoned, however, for the same reason. The fact that a special session had been discussed somehow leaked out to the press, and wind of it reached Polk in Tennessee before the end of the month. His reaction was identical with that of the President's advisers, and he wrote urgently to Donelson to have Jackson once more interpose. Before any further steps were taken in Tennessee, Donelson received word from Calhoun that the project had been abandoned.[30]

Thereafter the tenuously united Democracy gained steadily. To offset the proslavery stigma that attached to the ticket in the Northern states, and incidentally to win the state elections in New York, Silas Wright was put on the ticket for Governor. Though it was not altogether in line with his personal preferences, Wright yielded for the good of the party, and by October Van Buren and Calhoun partisans were working closely together in New York City.[31] Whig confidence began to wane after Wright's nomination, and Clay's attempts to salvage Southern votes with further equivocations on Texas only drove the Northern antislavery men into the ranks of the Liberty party.

Calhoun's own part in the campaign was probably notable. As we shall see in the next chapter, he was primarily responsible for quieting a radical outburst in South Carolina, and he threw the full support of his own not inconsiderable organizations in the key states of Virginia and New York behind the ticket. He also had some hand in effecting the final union of Tyler's following with the Democracy. His Washington paper, the *Spectator,* gave consistent support to Polk, and continued to do so after it became the *Constitution,* under the editorship of former Virginia Congressman William A. Harris, in October.[32] Calhoun's efforts in behalf of the Democratic candidates were sufficiently conspicuous to lead to charges that he had already bargained with Polk for retention of his place and control of the administration. The Secretary of State immediately issued a public denial that he knew anything of Polk's intentions, or Polk of his, and declared flatly that there had been no correspondence whatever between them on the subject of that office.[33]

There was, however, direct contact between Calhoun and the Polk organization on matters of policy and campaign strategy, and it was certainly clear to the candidate after Pickens' visit in August, if it had not been clear before, that Calhoun's powerful aid was being given because the South Carolinian expected from a victorious Democracy not only annexation of Texas, but tariff reduction and an end to agitation of the slave question. To him these measures were parts of a single system designed to oppose the power of organized and united sectional minorities to the centralization of power in the general government, where it would inevitably become in the hands of a sectional majority an instrument of economic exploitation. From their own point of view the antislavery leaders entirely agreed, and so they could not support Clay any more than they could accept Polk.[34]

It was in the end these same antislavery men who elected Polk, by refusing to support the Whig candidates. The crucial contest was that in New York, where only the presence of Silas Wright on the state ticket carried Polk through, with a margin of barely 5,000 votes over Clay. But James G. Birney drew more than 15,000 votes, the bulk of which were nominally Whig, and it was these 15,000 Liberty party voters who gave New York and the Presidency to Polk. Birney's total popular vote of 62,300 was almost twice the difference between the two major candidates. Everywhere but South Carolina, where the legislature still chose the electors, the contest was close. Polk lost his own state of Tennessee, but won the largest blocks of electoral votes, from New York, Pennsylvania, and Virginia, to win out by 170 to 105. The popular vote stood 1,337,000 to 1,299,000.[35]

The Whigs blamed their defeat on foreigners and abolitionists, and there is little doubt that they were correct. The urban machines in New York and Philadelphia especially had made free use of unnaturalized or too quickly naturalized aliens, mostly Irish, in building up the Democratic totals. There had been riots and bloodshed in both cities earlier in the year as "Native Americans" and Irish immigrants clashed. But the real story was the story of rising hostility to slavery in the industrial states.

CHAPTER XIV

THE BLUFFTON MOVEMENT

1

THE DELIBERATE refusal of the Northern Democrats to reform the tariff, the high-handed resistance of the younger Southern members to any compromise on the issue, the sudden and bitter opposition to Texas annexation—all these were straws in a wind that had become a gale. Even as in the later 1820's Southerners were calculating the value of a union in which they constituted a permanent and hopeless minority. Again South Carolina was in the lead, with fiery orators and newspaper letter writers posing the issue, and there was more talk of disunion than there was of nullification.

The first overt act of separation between North and South actually came in May 1844. With sectional tension at its peak in Congress and on the whole political front, the question of slavery was humbly and prayerfully debated by a Methodist Conference gathered in New York. There was no meeting of minds, but the more numerous delegates from the Northern states carried every test by ballot. The Southern group seceded and thereby opened, though only to a crack as yet, the door Calhoun had so long and so resolutely kept barred and guarded.[1] With deep foreboding the Secretary of State observed the travail of disunion in the Methodist Church, which was still a source of anxiety to him when he learned of a new sectional outbreak along political and economic lines in his own state.

Under pressure from Calhoun, Rhett so far retraced his steps as to speak in favor of the McKay bill a few days before its irrevocable demise. When the bill was tabled he demanded action, and proposed that the South Carolina members address their constituents as they had so often done in the past. It was agreed that McDuffie, the veteran among them, should prepare a statement, but McDuffie was too ill and delegated the task to Rhett. When the document was passed around for signature Huger asked abruptly if Calhoun had been consulted. Rhett explained that he had felt such a course to be improper, since the Secretary of State was a part of the general government, "with which it was proposed to bring South Carolina into conflict." On Huger's insistence Calhoun met with the delegation, assured them that no man prized the Union more than he did, and convinced most of them that annexation of Texas was too important to be jeopardized by radical action that might cost Polk the election. McDuffie, Rhett, and Holmes agreed reluctantly, but Calhoun's will was not to be resisted at close quarters and the matter was dropped.[2]

The Congress had scarcely adjourned before the papers were featuring accounts of an eloquent denunciation of the tariff by McDuffie, who had stopped off in Richmond on his way home long enough to address the Democratic Association there. The South Carolina Senator had been careful to repudiate all charges that his state sought or desired disunion, but the whole effect was that of a resounding trumpet call to resist. A few days later came papers from Charleston, with an address to his constituents from Robert Barnwell Rhett: the same address that Calhoun had suppressed so short a time before. Rhett, it should be noted, was still in Washington directing the editorial affairs of the *Spectator,* but he was moving rapidly away from his old moorings. In his address he called for a convention of the Southern states to consider the Texas question, and for a separate South Carolina convention to meet in April 1845 and nullify the tariff if the incoming President had not by that date indicated an intention to repeal it.[3]

2

Calhoun's position in all this was difficult and unpleasant. The excitement was seized on by his enemies and charged to his account. Blair insisted that it was all part of the ancient Calhoun plot to destroy the Union, and repeated his recent charges that the Texas annexation had been deliberately so managed as to insure defeat and thereby give South Carolina an excuse to secede. At the same time the harassed Secretary received letters from friends and partisans urging him to intervene to quell the revolt before irreparable damage had been done.[4]

Calhoun understood well enough what lay behind the bombast. The price of cotton, which had started slowly climbing after the disastrous collapse of 1837, had gone down again with the passage of the tariff of 1842. The average of 6.2 cents the following year was the lowest ever recorded up to that date, and the trend was still down. His people were suffering the cumulative effects of a depression already seven years old, of continuous and pointed attacks upon their morality by those same persons whom they held responsible for their economic plight, and of aggravated frustrations in their attempts through the national legislature to solve their problems. When men reach that stage they are apt to reason that they have less to lose than to gain by the appeal to battle.[5]

Before Calhoun's conservative followers could interpose, Rhett's address was the subject of heated controversy throughout South Carolina and much of the South. It was not until July 16 that a brake could be applied, at a great mass meeting in Charleston. There Holmes followed Rhett and talked passionately of the crisis of the South, but Huger succeeded him on the platform to suggest peaceful remedies and to make it publicly known that Calhoun had already acted in Washington to curb the precipitousness of the radicals.[6]

In spite of Calhoun's quiet opposition the belligerent talk was snowballing, and it carried with it men who should have known better. Rhett abandoned the *Spectator* to its legitimate proprietor and hurried home, prepared to take personal command of the resistance element in South Carolina. An open invitation appeared in the *Mercury* shortly after his return, calling on citizens of St. Luke's parish to join in honoring their returning Representative with a public dinner, to be held on July 31 at Bluffton. Holmes, in the interim, followed up his Charleston speech with a too-specific answer to a question put to him by an anonymous letter writer in the press. "What," asked the writer, "is the proper remedy for the evils which afflict the South?" and Holmes replied: "I answer unequivocally, *Resistance—combined Southern Resistance,* if you can procure it. *If not, then State Resistance.*"[7]

Holmes, Rhett, Hammond, and those who acted with them were in fact bent on taking into their own hands the leadership of the South, and to "repudiate Mr. Calhoun's pacific policy" once and for all.[8] The Bluffton dinner was held as planned and the fiery Rhett aroused his auditors to a rebellious fury with his impassioned eloquence. He called again for a Southern convention, and for a state convention after Congress met, to nullify the tariff or if need be secede from the Union. Regretfully but pointedly he parted company with Calhoun, challenged the grip of the old leader, and appeared in the role of Moses about to lead his people from the old bondage to some new promised land. For a week the news spread by word of mouth and private letter. Then on August 7 the *Mercury,* for more than a dozen years accepted the country over as Calhoun's own house organ, came out with a ringing editorial in favor of separate state action. It was signed "J. A. S." and marked the return of Rhett's brother-in-law, John A. Stuart, to the helm after an interval of fourteen months. The text of Rhett's speech followed presently, and the battle was joined.[9]

3

Even before Rhett's July 31 speech gave the movement its name Calhoun was quietly working through Elmore, H. W. Conner, Henry Bailey, Ker Boyce, and other conservatives to bring pressure on the insurgents. Holmes and Rhett were asked bluntly whether they did or did not mean to support Polk and Dallas, and neither man was prepared to answer "no." Elmore then staged a great mass meeting in Charleston on August 19, which pledged the South Carolina Democracy to the party ticket, and reaffirmed the faith of the state in Calhoun and his leadership. Rhett conceded his discomfiture and went back to Washington and the *Spectator.*[10]

Pickens, meanwhile, had been dispatched to Nashville. The appeals for a Southern convention which had arisen in South Carolina and elsewhere immediately after rejection of the Texas treaty had been adroitly capitalized by Polk and his managers. The movement was skillfully shorn of its sectional implications, and it was presently announced that there would be held at Nashville on August 15 a great rally of the Democracy, North, South, and West. To this meeting Pickens went at Calhoun's direction, but he was to do more than merely appear as representative of South Carolina. He was to get from Polk positive assurances on the tariff, which could be used to quiet the Bluffton extremists. He was back early in September with a pledge that the principles of the compromise of 1833 would be restored, that the government would be reformed as that term was understood in South Carolina, and that nothing would be permitted to stand in the way of Texas annexation. The word was spread where it would do the most good, and the middle of the month found the state calm once more. For all this Calhoun took primary credit as he assured a Northern correspondent that the trouble was over.[11]

At this point Langdon Cheves, now nearing seventy and long considered one of the bulwarks of Southern conservatism, emerged from a twenty-year retirement with a letter to the editor of the *Mercury*. He was cautious and appallingly verbose, but in the course of seven newspaper columns Cheves managed to propound and document a basic thesis, about which there could be no misunderstanding. The struggle then going on between North and South, in his view, must come in the end of a choice for the South between abolition and secession. Both were evils, but of the two he preferred secession. Nothing but disaster, however, could come from the unsupported action of a single state, and there were signs that the Democratic party might yet take steps to redeem the interest of the South. There should therefore be united support for Polk, but as a long-range program the ground should be prepared in concert with the other slave states for an ultimate confederacy of their own.[12]

From Judge Cheves' letter both conservatives and radicals might take comfort, but the general effect was once more to alarm the Democratic leaders outside the state, and to encourage the less stable element at home to take up the cudgels again. Before the end of September McDuffie had kicked over the traces with a flaming speech at Edgefield, in which he called eloquently for resistance and proclaimed the "final crisis" to be at hand. Rhett left the *Spectator* for good, and proposed publicly that Cheves should be sent to the Senate in Huger's place. The *Mercury* took up the cry, and it was stopped only when Cheves categorically refused.[13]

Again the election seemed endangered, but Calhoun himself arrived on September 30, on his way home for a belated vacation. He spent only a day in Charleston, but a month at Fort Hill, and well before his visit was over the magic of his personality had prevailed once more. Holmes came back to the fold, and even Stuart was temporarily won over. Before October was out the *Mercury* was again a Calhoun paper, desirous of nothing so much as the election of James K. Polk to the Presidency. Stuart himself was sent to the state legislature in the October balloting, which saw Rhett's following cut from a majority in the lower House to a minor fraction. Rhett and McDuffie made no more speeches before the national election, and even

Hammond, though he refused to meet Calhoun and poured bitterness into his diary, held his peace.[14]

4

On his way back to Washington early in November Calhoun stopped over in Charleston long enough to discuss the political affairs of the state and of the South with some of those to whom the leadership would fall. Pickens accompanied him from the upcountry, and though he missed Elmore he saw most of the other conservative leaders. His views were passed on to Governor Hammond by James Hamilton, who was careful not to say they were Calhoun's. "The result of the presidential election," wrote Hamilton, who had himself sympathized pretty strongly with the 'Bluffton Boys,' "must be to put our State on a new line of policy. If we bluster, threaten resistance or disunion, we throw ourselves out of gear and cut ourselves off from all sympathy with the other Southern States. . . . I came to this conclusion from sheer policy—without the sacrifice of a single principle involved in the question." Calhoun understood the Governor's character only too well, and in Hammond's failure to call on him, or to meet him in response to a direct request, he undoubtedly saw reason for concern. He knew, of course, where Hammond had stood with respect to the resistance movement, and he wanted no ill-timed and perhaps politically fatal attempt on the part of the Governor to revive the Bluffton doctrines in his message to the legislature. His fears were fully justified, for just such a message had already been written and was in the hands of the printers when Hamilton transmitted Calhoun's warning as his own.[15]

Two days before his message was delivered Hammond wrote bitterly in his diary that Calhoun's friends "are extremely decided against State action & most of the rest are paralysed. Some have called on me. None—not even Stuart of the *Mercury* . . . are for action. *Wet-blanketed* by Calhoun & Co. . . . Doing nothing will in fact be going backwards & I fear the moral influence of So Ca will be sacraficed forever & with it all will be lost—A separation of the States at no remote period is inevitable. It might now be effected peacefully & properly—A few years hence it must take place in blood or the South remain in it as a subjugated region." [16] Brilliant, aristocratic, class-conscious, Hammond had leaped ahead to the ultimate end toward which Calhoun's own logic pointed. In Calhoun's personal reluctance to go so far, Hammond could see only motives of self-interest because he did not share and could not understand the older man's deep love for the Union.

Hammond's message, delivered on November 26, 1844, was a masterful performance, clear, concise, logical, and above all restrained.[17] He went as far as Rhett had gone at Bluffton, but he did it with a cold detachment that made it far more effective—and more dangerous—than Rhett's impassioned outburst. He began with reference to the severe agricultural depression that engulfed South Carolina and the South, tracing it to the tariff policy of the general government. This led him to the routine passages on the financial condition of the state, but he presently returned to the subject of federal relations. He spoke of the compromise of 1833 as a treaty "made between belligerent parties." He explained how this treaty had been violated by the reimposition of protective duties under the tariff of 1842, and how South Carolina had forborne to act in her own interest then but had awaited the election of a new Congress. The new Congress had considered the question but had refused to arrest the violation. It was now up to South Carolina to uphold in her own way the principles she professed.

He moved on to the Texas question, brushed aside the reasons offered for the rejection of the annexation treaty, and laid the loss entirely at the door of the abolitionists. To his mind it was only the ultimate proof of "the deep seated hostility of every portion, and almost every individual, of the North, to our system of Slavery, and their fixed determination to eradicate it." He concluded by facing squarely the disunion charges so often leveled at South Carolina, insisting on the loyalty of his people and their devotion to their ancient laws and customs. Their devotion, however, was not blind. The Union "was a compact for justice, liberty, and security. When these fail, its living principles are gone. . . . It is vain to sound it in our ears, and claim for it our allegiance. Our ancestors of the old world, waged a successful war against the divine right of kings; and our fathers of the revolution broke the yoke of Lords and Commons. Little has been gained for us, by these two noblest struggles which history records, if we are now to be overawed by the divine right of Union, and steeped in wretchedness under its violated charter."

5

Hammond's rebellious message was received by the assembled houses of the South Carolina legislature in stony silence. In the Senate the routine motion to print brought Pickens to his feet. Everyone knew that the former Congressman was an unofficial spokesman for Calhoun, and he was heard with attention and respect. He deprecated the tone the Governor had seen fit to take, expressed his confidence that Polk would meet South Carolina's wishes, and hoped that there would be no more threats or sword rattling from his countrymen. Then he offered resolutions directly contravening Hammond's position, declaring South Carolina's faith that Texas would be annexed and the tariff brought back to the revenue standard by the incoming administration.[18]

The resolutions expressed so fully the views that Calhoun had handed down to his partisans since the Bluffton movement first began that they were accepted without question as desired by him. They came up in the Senate after a lapse of one day, and almost without debate they were unanimously passed. Hammond was deeply mortified, for though he knew the majority was against him he had not expected unanimity.[19] The Governor was stronger in the House, but there too he was outgeneraled. The Committee on Federal Relations had been carefully packed by the Speaker to uphold the Bluffton views, but C. G. Memminger, who emerged in this session as one of Calhoun's ablest lieutenants, circumvented the whole strategy by getting the message referred to the Committee of the Whole. There the question could be debated by the full membership, and was so debated at intervals for three weeks.[20]

The Bluffton leaders rallied to Hammond's support, to become the nucleus of a radical disunion party in South Carolina; but Calhoun's friends showed their purposes and their power by electing William Aiken, conservative Unionist of the nullification days, to succeed Hammond as Governor. The Bluffton candidate was Whitemarsh B. Seabrook, who drew only 50 votes on the final ballot to 88 for Aiken and 24 more for another old Unionist, R. F. W. Allston.[21]

It was shortly after Aiken's election that news from Washington set the radicals aflame again, and found conservatives ready on one issue, at least, to join them. The Twenty-eighth Congress met for its final session on December 2, and old John Quincy Adams gave his perennial notice that he would on the following day move to rescind the gag rule. The motion was duly offered on December 3, but this time, without debate and while the clerk waited to read the President's message, it was passed. By a vote of 108 to 80 the House of Representatives repealed its eight-year ban on the reception of abolition petitions, and the cleavage was sectional rather than political.[22]

Immediately Pickens introduced new resolutions in the state Senate and again they were unanimously passed. They declared that the action of the lower house of Congress was "a flagrant outrage" upon the rights of the South; they denied that Congress possessed any power to legislate on that subject and insisted that "such legislation will be in fact a dissolution of the Federal Compact"; and they called upon the Governor, should Congress act in any manner on the slave question, to summon the legislature into special session "to decide upon the mode and manner in which we shall preserve and defend our ancient liberties."[23]

Hammond found sardonic pleasure in these sentiments, which he took to mean that his own message had been vindicated and that Calhoun at last had seen the light. But unfortunately for the ex-Governor's ego, Pickens was acting strictly on his own. The House, guided by Memminger's strong hand, did not act until the word came from Washington. Then, just before the final adjournment, Pickens' original resolutions opposing Hammond's message and expressing full confidence in the incoming Democratic administration, were passed by a vote of 57 to 39. By a similar margin the resolutions condemning the repeal of the gag rule were postponed to a date when the legislature would not be in session.[24]

6

The proceedings on Hammond's message were interrupted by another incident that revealed briefly the width of the chasm separating North and South. On November 28, 1844, Judge Samuel Hoar arrived in Charleston. Hoar was a distinguished Massachusetts lawyer, ranking professionally with Webster and Choate. He had served one term in Congress, the turbulent 1835-1837 term when the gag rule was first enacted. He was an outspoken abolitionist, and his present mission was to test in the courts the validity of South Carolina laws restricting free Negroes, even though they might be citizens of other states. Hoar came with a formal commission from the Governor of Massachusetts, in compliance with a resolution of the state legislature, and on the day of his arrival he notified Governor Hammond in writing of the nature of his mission. He was to determine what citizens of Massachusetts were being held in South Carolina without being charged with crime; and he was authorized to prosecute one or more suits on behalf of such citizens, at the expense of his state, "for the purpose of having the legality of such imprisonment tried and determined in the Supreme Court of the United States." [25]

Hammond saw Hoar's mission for what it undoubtedly was, a new and potentially most effective means of attacking the whole institution of slavery. The laws in question were common to most of the Southern states, and a Supreme Court decision invalidating them would at once bring the whole South into collision with the Federal Government; that, or it would expose the slave states to an inundation of free Negroes, carefully trained by the abolitionists and protected by the armed forces of the United States if and when a President with antislavery leanings chose to intervene. Hammond sent Hoar's letter with a special message to the legislature on November 30, and five days later, with only one dissenting vote, resolutions in line with the Governor's request were passed. These resolutions were in effect the declaration of a sovereign power as to its rights under international law, but they followed inevitably from the compact theory of the Constitution and its South Carolina glosses. The only deviation was the declaration, essential to support the case, that free Negroes were not citizens of the United States within the meaning of the Constitution. The Governor was directed to expel the Massachusetts emissary forthwith from South Carolina soil.

With only a few days of his term remaining, Hammond moved with the utmost speed to carry out the instructions of the legislature. His aide-de-camp, Colonel P. S. Brooks, was sent posthaste to Charleston with orders to confer with Attorney General Henry Bailey as to procedure. Every precaution was to be used to avoid violence, and Hoar was to be treated with consideration and respect; that is to say, he was to be considerately and respectfully, but firmly,

escorted aboard a vessel bound for Boston. Hoar did not wait for
his escort to arrive from Columbia. He noted the tendency of crowds
to gather around his hotel, and accepted the advice of the Charleston
authorities that he withdraw. His expulsion accomplished almost
as much for the cause he served as a more orthodox termination of
his mission would have done, and he was satisfied.[26]

7

The aftermath of the Bluffton movement was a new internal split
in South Carolina. The Rhett-Elmore machine of 1840 was destroyed, with Rhett now the leader of the radical wing and Elmore
aligned with the conservatives behind Calhoun. Hammond, who had
fought the machine until it elected him Governor in 1842, was now
teamed with Rhett, while most of the old Unionists of the nullification days welcomed Calhoun into their own camp. Yet there was in
reality little or no change of position. There had been fire-eaters in
1832 who would gladly have joined a Southern confederacy then, or
even have taken the state out of the Union by herself. Rhett was
one of these, and Hammond and Holmes and McDuffie had leaned
in the same direction. Calhoun had then invoked nullification as a
remedy short of secession which might be applied within the framework of the Constitution. He had been, in short, the conservative
throughout, not powerful enough to curb the radicals but strong
enough to compromise with them and thereby restrain them from
going too far. The parties stood at the end of 1844 more or less
where they had stood a dozen years before, but this time Calhoun
did not have to compromise. He was strong enough to stop the resistance movement outright, and stop it he did; or rather, he drove
it underground.

The radicals of 1832, however, had never agreed with Calhoun that
nullification was a peaceful and conservative remedy. To them it had
been a form of resistance to oppression, and so they could not see in
1844 why Calhoun held back. His opposition to the Bluffton approach was in their eyes desertion in the face of the enemy, and evidence either that he had been purchased by promises or that he was
suffering senile decay. In either case he seemed to them no longer
fit to be their leader, and they resolved to depose him when they

could. While he lived that time never came, and it is perhaps significant that while he lived neither Hammond nor Rhett achieved the Senate seat to which both aspired.

Chastened by Calhoun's prompt interference with their attempt to address their constituents in June, the South Carolina Representatives were silent when the gag rule was repealed, but McDuffie drafted a letter of protest for them all to sign. It was finally decided not to go through with it; and there again the hand of the Secretary of State was in evidence. McDuffie chafed under the restraints imposed upon him, but he knew and loved Calhoun too well to be disloyal now. The younger men condemned him out of hand and looked forward to a day when they would themselves hold the reins of power. They would know then how to defend their institutions. Among themselves they talked openly of a new confederacy of the Southern states, and their logic was only what they had learned from Calhoun, carried out against his wishes and his will to its predestined end.[27]

CHAPTER XV

TEXAS ANNEXED

1

THE CRUSHING DEFEAT of the Texas treaty found the State Department already prepared with a substitute. On June 11, 1844, McDuffie offered a joint resolution providing that the rejected instrument, whenever it should be ratified in Texas, should become the "fundamental law of union" between the two countries. On the same day the Senate confirmed Tilghman A. Howard of Indiana, friend of Jackson and former aide to Sam Houston, to be chargé in Texas in place of the rejected Murphy. The business of the session ended with a barbed exchange between Benton and McDuffie, and on June 17 Congress adjourned.[1]

The following day Calhoun sent instructions to the new chargé, and he did not mince words. Howard's task was to convince the Texan Government that the loss of the treaty did not mean the failure of the enterprise; that McDuffie's joint resolution, tabled for want of time, might yet be passed; that dire consequences would follow any yielding to British pressure. At the same time the Secretary prepared instructions for Wilson Shannon, the former Ohio Governor who was about to go out as Minister to Mexico. The special messenger who had gone to Mexico City in April with dispatches meant to be conciliatory reported back to the Department the evening of June 17. He brought with him what came perilously close to a blunt threat of war should Texas be annexed, and it was anybody's guess what the situation might be when Shannon reached his post. It was necessary, therefore, to give him large discretion. He was to emphasize the desire of the United States for friendly relations with her neighbor and to offer a liberal boundary adjustment, but he was to be firm that the mutual concerns of Texas and the United States, both independent nations, had nothing to do with Mexico.[2]

The Mexican Government saw things in a very different light. So far as it was concerned, Texas was still a province in revolt, being

199

aided and abetted by a foreign power. The existing armistice between Texas and Mexico had recently expired, and the unpredictable Santa Anna, through his army commander in the north, decreed renewal of hostilities forthwith. For the prosecution of the war the Mexican President revived his own decree of a year earlier which denied quarter to any foreigner invading the territory of Mexico, whether alone or as part of an army, and all Americans in Texas were understood to be of this category. The Texans in due season called on Howard, who arrived at his post on the first of August, to supply the protection promised by his predecessor. Howard pointed out that the guarantees confirmed by Calhoun were strictly circumscribed by the constitutional powers of the President, and extended only to the period during which the treaty was pending. He undertook, however, to get instructions to cover this new emergency as quickly as possible.[3]

While dispatches moved over the plains of Texas with intolerable slowness, British diplomacy moved quickly to block annexation by any available means. Aberdeen followed up his note of December 26, to which Calhoun's Pakenham letter was in reply, with special instructions to the British Ambassador in Paris. Guizot agreed to co-operate, and the French Minister in Washington, Alphonse Pageot, received his orders at about the time Calhoun took office. He was to make common cause with Pakenham, and the two were to warn the United States that their respective governments could not with indifference see Texas added to the Union. The contemplated joint protest was not delivered, but only because the two diplomats agreed that the treaty would be more certainly beaten if it were not officially announced that Britain and France desired that result.[4]

Without the knowledge of the American Minister in London, Lord Aberdeen gave positive assurances to the Mexican envoy late in May. He proposed that Mexico should recognize Texan independence, in return for which Britain and France would see to it that Texas neither joined the United States nor extended her boundaries beyond the Rio Grande. The same proposal was at once carried to Guizot, and shortly thereafter was made the basis of a formal offer to Ashbel Smith whereby the independence of Texas was to be jointly guaranteed by Britain, France, and Mexico. It was clear, however, that the co-operation of Mexico would be coerced if necessary, and that the probability of war with the United States was taken into account. Louis Philippe and his Foreign Minister agreed readily, and when in due season the proposition reached Texas it found that "Prince of Brigands," Sam Houston, also ready to agree.[5]

Through Smith and Van Zandt Calhoun knew enough of British and French designs by May to give William R. King a thorough oral briefing before the former Alabama Senator left for his post as Minister to France. By mid-July he knew virtually the whole story and conjectured shrewdly what he did not know. It seemed to him of the utmost importance that Houston be kept in line, and for that purpose he turned to Andrew Jackson, despite a mutual enmity of more than a dozen years. His intermediary, wisely chosen, was Major William B. Lewis, once of the Jackson "kitchen cabinet" and through four administrations a Treasury auditor. "Mr. Calhoun authorized me to say to you, *confidentially,*" wrote Lewis on July 19, "that he has received communications, in which he has the most implicit confidence, informing him that it is the intention of England, aided, it is said, by France, to *coerce* Mexico into an acknowledgment of the independence of Texas, provided the latter will . . . pledge herself to maintain a separate and independent Government. . . . That this information is correct I have not the shadow of a doubt, as I have it from *other sources* which I believe to be unquestionable." [6]

What his "other sources" were Lewis did not say, but Jackson could hardly have failed to understand the allusion. It was during his own tumultuous days of rule that Lewis' daughter had married Alphonse Pageot, then only a minor diplomat but now French Minister to the United States.

In Paris King fell back on the Monroe Doctrine and contrived to convey the impression that only interference by Britain or France would be needed to unite his own country solidly behind annexation, however divided Americans might appear from across the Atlantic. He adroitly suggested also that British and French interests in the matter of Texas were opposed, just as they had been in the earlier matter of the right of search, and expressed surprise that the two countries should now concur in policy. Calhoun received King's report early in August, and immediately followed it up with a lengthy dispatch of his own. It was destined to arouse as much controversy as had the Pakenham letter, but, right or wrong, it served its purpose. It drove so deep a wedge between England and France that Aberdeen himself abandoned all thought of aid from across the channel in case of war.[7]

Calhoun's letter to King was a pointed summary of the various arguments that had been developed over the past decade to buttress the defense of slavery. The analysis was in terms of world economy, penetrating, ingenious, and to modern ears cynical and amoral, but it struck close enough to the roots of British policy to create something of a sensation in Parliament when the full text appeared early in 1845. Reduced to its skeleton, the argument ran something like this: Great Britain does not want Texas annexed to the United States, because she hopes that her influence, if Texas remains independent, will ultimately secure the abolition of slavery in that country, and permit her to exert great pressure for abolition in the Southern states. This idea originated with the abolitionists in the United States, and was first called to the attention of the British Government through the World Antislavery Convention held in London in 1840. It is decidedly to the interest of France and of the other powers of continental Europe to oppose this British policy, because the motives behind it are not philanthropic as alleged but are concerned with the competitive position of British products in the world market.

Without minimizing the humanitarian factor in the abolition of slavery in the British West Indies, Calhoun insisted that an even stronger motive was the belief that Negro labor would be more profitable as the hired labor of free men who would then have money with which to buy British goods. In the actual event, however, the social and economic position of the Negro had not been improved, and the cost of raising the tropical products of the islands was greatly increased—so much so that the British possessions could no longer compete with the United States in their production, and huge investments of British capital were therefore jeopardized. As the only way of rescuing this capital, the Secretary continued, Britain now seeks to raise the cost of production in the United States, Cuba, Brazil, and other competing regions by abolishing slavery throughout the Western Hemisphere. France and other consuming nations will make up the difference in higher prices. From all of which it followed that the true interest of France lay in the annexation of Texas to the United States.

2

Late in August Howard's first dispatch arrived from Texas, with official word that Mexico had renewed the war against her quondam province and that Houston now demanded the military aid he insisted had been promised him. The situation was charged with danger, for an assumption of too much power on Tyler's part might cost him the support of Congress when the joint resolution finally came to a vote, but failure to defend Texas now might throw her into the arms of Great Britain. The two weeks that elapsed before instructions were sent to the United States chargé bespeak the anxiety with which the President approached the problem.[8]

In Calhoun's dispatch, dated September 10, 1844, Howard was commended for correctly interpreting the American commitment to Texas, but the commitment itself was now subtly enlarged. The President, explained the Secretary, "feels the full force of the obligation of this Government to protect Texas pending the question of annexation [not, as originally stated, "during the pendency of the treaty of annexation"] against the attacks which Mexico may make. . . . As far as it relates to the Executive Department, he is prepared to use all its powers for that purpose." Proper measures would be recommended when Congress met, but in the meantime a strong protest backed by a very thinly veiled threat of intervention was hastened by special messenger to Mexico City.[9]

At the same time the Texan chargé in Washington was privately informed that the orders to General Taylor and Commodore Stockton to stand by still held good. Indeed Charles H. Raymond, who had just succeeded Van Zandt, got a distinct impression that the administration would "do rather more for our protection and support, if necessary, than they desire should appear." "They don't like to leave themselves open to an attack by Congress," he explained to the Texan Secretary of State, "especially Wilkins, Mason and Nelson. Mr. Calhoun is case-hardened. When he thinks he is right he will go ahead, no matter how great the responsibility; and had he the power, the army would doubtless be ordered right into Texas, to repel any attack upon her." [10]

The responsibility was mounting. Tilghman A. Howard, on whom Calhoun relied so heavily to keep Texas pacified until Congress could be induced to act, had died of yellow fever almost a month before the Secretary addressed him. The news did not reach Washington until the Southern mail arrived on the evening of September 16. There was a hurried conference between President and Secretary of State, but in the mind of each there was only one man to be rushed to the vacant post. The next morning Calhoun tendered the place to Andrew Jackson Donelson, in terms of urgency not to be refused. The letter was accompanied by the official commission, a draft on New York for a quarter's salary in advance, and copies of the instructions and enclosures addressed only a week before to Howard. At the same time Tyler wrote to Jackson with similar urgency, explaining frankly that Donelson's old intimacy with Houston, his acceptability to all factions in the Democracy, and his position in Jackson's household would give him an influence no other American save the ex-President himself could command.[11]

There was every need for tact, diplomacy, and personal persuasion, and every demand for speed. Though the circumstances were not known in Washington, it was exactly one week after Donelson's appointment, and long before he could possibly reach Texas, that President Houston instructed his Secretary of State, Anson Jones, to conclude the agreement with England and France which would pledge Texas to independence and bind her to Europe rather than to the United States. Jones, who was already President-elect of Texas and was due to succeed Houston in December, disregarded the order. He favored annexation no more than did Houston, but he saw risks in signing at that time so great that he suspected Houston of a secret wish to break down his administration before it started. He also desired for himself whatever credit might flow from the British-French alliance. It was this subterranean feud between Jones and Houston that gave Donelson time to act.[12]

3

Simultaneously with the sudden crisis in Texan affairs, Calhoun was called on to begin the difficult and long-delayed negotiations over Oregon. The influx of American settlers in the territory and the bellicose attitude of Western Senators and Representatives gave the question a new urgency in British official circles. In Calhoun's policy of "masterly inactivity" Aberdeen saw the possible loss of the whole region, and early in March he advised Pakenham privately that a compromise on the forty-ninth parallel would now be acceptable, provided only that as a face-saving gesture Britain retained all of Vancouver Island. This would give an appearance of compromise and would justify Aberdeen in accepting a line his government had previously refused. It seemed necessary, however, in order to convey the notion of concession, that the offer come from the United States, and Pakenham was to maneuver the American negotiator into making it. When Everett called on the Foreign Minister later that month to inform him of Upshur's death, Aberdeen brought up the Oregon question, and managed to give the American Minister the same impression he had conveyed more directly to his own subordinate.[13]

Calhoun thus knew what Britain would be willing to concede well before Pakenham moved on July 22 to open the discussions. For a month the Secretary let the matter ride. He was personally preoccupied with the sudden resurgence of separatist agitation in his own state, and the British Minister's timing made it look very much like an attempt to divert attention from Texas. It was only after he had done what he could to drive a wedge between Britain and France that Calhoun accepted Pakenham's offer to negotiate on Oregon, and named August 23 for a preliminary conference.[14]

Six separate meetings were held over the next thirty days. At the second conference, on August 26, Pakenham repeated the standing British offer of the Columbia River as a boundary, with free access to ports south of forty-nine degrees and free navigation of the river itself. This was, of course, only a talking point, as Calhoun fully understood when he countered on September 2 with a detailed written statement of the American position. Briefly summarized, his argument was that under the law of nations the United States was entitled to the entire watershed of the Columbia on the basis of Captain Gray's discovery of that river in 1792, the exploration of it by Lewis and Clark, and the prior settlement at the river's mouth by agents of the American Fur Company. He also claimed for the United States under the Louisiana Treaty of 1803 with France and the Treaty of 1819 with Spain any and all interests of either or both of those powers by right of discoveries under their respective flags; and added a further argument based on territorial contiguity and the continental sweep of the original colonial grants. For the time being the Secretary did not press the American claim to the region north of the Columbia basin, which rested primarily on the validity of the earlier French and Spanish titles, but specifically reserved the right to advance these claims at a later date.[15]

The British case, according to Pakenham's rejoinder of September 12, was based on Vancouver's exploration of the Columbia immediately following Captain Gray's discovery of the river; and on a contention that the Spanish claims had in fact been passed on to Britain under the Nootka Sound Convention of 1790. Calhoun rejected this interpretation of the 1790 agreement in its entirety. Neither the Secretary of State nor the British Minister reached the point of compromise, and the discussions ended late in September with Pakenham seeking new instructions from his government while Calhoun visited Fort Hill. Pakenham's obvious reluctance to act on his earlier privately expressed instructions probably stemmed from the jingoistic reference to Oregon in the Democratic platform. Calhoun appears throughout to have been deliberately playing for time, which was so clearly on the American side; and this is borne out by Tyler's refusal in January 1845 to consider the offer of arbitration made by Aberdeen as a consequence of the apparent breakdown of negotiations.

4

Diplomatic relations between the United States and Mexico, meanwhile, were degenerating at an accelerating pace. Shannon reached his post late in August, and allowed Santa Anna to persuade him that the military preparations he saw on every hand had nothing to do with an attempt to reconquer Texas. He was brought rudely back to earth early in October by the arrival of Calhoun's blunt warning that "the President would be compelled to regard the invasion of Texas by Mexico while the question of annexation is pending, as highly offensive to the United States." Shannon was directed to inform the Mexican authorities "in strong language" of the American position, after which he was to repeat previous assurances of friendship and of willingness to adjust all outstanding differences including the boundary. By way of inducement he was to apply economic pressure in the form of a vigorous insistence on the payment of outstanding American claims.[16]

Shannon obeyed instructions to the letter, but all he got for his pains was a note from the Mexican Foreign Minister, Manuel Crescencio Rejón, which reviewed in a tone of bitter indignation and studied insult the history of past American attempts to seduce Texas from her allegiance. After another exchange Shannon, obviously beyond his depths, contemplated demanding his passports, but contented himself with rushing a messenger to Washington for instructions, while a duplicate set of the correspondence was forwarded to the United States chargé in Texas. Rejón continued the offensive through November by way of amplifying the record. If there should be a war he wanted to prove in advance that the United States had started it. A revolution had already broken out, however, and to Shannon's great relief Santa Anna was in exile by the end of the year.[17]

The Mexican correspondence through October went to Congress along with Tyler's fourth annual message, which called on the legislators to do forthwith by joint resolution what the Senate had refused to do by treaty. By this time, however, the Democratic factions were openly at war and the line of cleavage was dangerously close to the line that separated slave from free soil. The gag rule had already been repealed by Northern Democratic votes, and both the *Globe* and the New York *Evening Post* were savagely attacking the administration and the annexation treaty. As soon as the organization of Congress was completed McDuffie reintroduced his joint resolution of the previous session, while Ingersoll offered one to the same effect in the House. Benton countered with a bill authorizing negotiations with Mexico and Texas, and the eventual division of Texas into slave and free states. The issue was quickly reduced to a battle between Calhoun and Benton for control of the next administration and of the Democratic party. Behind Benton stood the growing but divided power of the free states; behind Calhoun the static but increasingly concentrated power of the South.[18]

There were rumors in the Capital a day or so after the opening moves had been made in Congress that the President would shortly send in a war message, and there were sharp-tongued critics who were not sure he had not done so when he laid before the legislators on December 19 the Mexican correspondence received since the start of the session. Tyler called attention to the "extraordinary and highly offensive language which the Mexican government has thought proper to employ" in reply to his own remonstrance against renewal of hostilities against Texas. He pointedly abstained, however, from "recommending to Congress a resort to measures of redress," contenting himself with "re-urging upon that body prompt and immediate action on the subject of annexation." Then followed what Adams called the "brawling correspondence between Calhoun, Shannon, and . . . Rejon." In it all the aged ex-President, with his own particular form of sectional bias, saw only "the subjugation of the Union to the double slave-representation." [19]

5

Back in Texas matters were rapidly coming to a head. Donelson reached Galveston November 10, but he knew Houston was away so he proceeded to the Texan Capital at a leisurely pace, sounding out the people as he went. He arrived at his post on the twenty-first and was received by Houston three days later, within fifteen minutes of the Texan President's own return. Donelson skillfully brought the interview around to the talk he had heard of opposition to annexation in Texas. He knew that General G. W. Terrell who had recently been named Texan Minister to France, was an antiannexationist, and he had heard of similar feelings on the part of the commercial groups that were gaining and hoped to gain more by trade with Europe. He did not say, but let Houston infer, that there were even some in high quarters who believed the Texan President himself was against joining the United States. This Houston denied utterly, indicating that he was merely following a very devious route to arrive at the end both men desired.[20]

So much of the story reached the State Department on December 28. In each of Donelson's dispatches there was assurance that the plain people of Texas were still overwhelmingly in favor of annexation, and that if there were no further incident at home there would be no question of ratification there.

Ten days or so after the first interview between Houston and Donelson—an interval put to excellent account by the American in the cultivation of members of the Texan Congress—the Shannon-Rejón correspondence arrived from Mexico City. This was shown at once to the Texan Government as evidence of the extent to which the United States was willing to sustain Texas against Mexico. The effect was excellent; but Donelson was by that time sure that British mediation with Mexico on terms very favorable to Texas was available whenever the Texans chose to avail themselves of it. All was still well, but the question of annexation must not be allowed to go over to another Congress. To fail now would be to fail for good.[21]

Donelson had done all he could for the moment. Anson Jones succeeded Houston on December 9, and Ashbel Smith was recalled from Europe to become Secretary of State. Donelson was assured that nothing would be done until Smith arrived, and as his own personal affairs were pressing he solicited a brief leave of absence. Then without waiting for a reply he set off on a flying trip to Tennessee. At New Orleans he passed Captain Charles Elliot, the British chargé in Texas, ostensibly on his way back to his post, and heard rumors that Elliot was indeed now empowered to offer liberal terms from his government for the maintenance of Texan independence. Still Donelson was not unduly alarmed, realizing that Elliot too must await the return of Ashbel Smith; but he knew, and warned Calhoun, that there must be no further procrastination in Washington.[22]

The documents constituting this second chapter of Donelson's mission reached the State Department on January 2, 1845. That evening the Democratic members of the House held a caucus on strategy, and we may be sure that the leaders were informed of the urgent tone of Donelson's dispatches. The caucus agreed that the rules should be suspended the following day so that the House could go into Committee of the Whole on the Texas question.[23]

Ingersoll set the tone for the debate when he led off on January 3 with a dispassionate plea for annexation as a great national measure, of importance to every portion of the country. It was a Southern Whig speaking three days later in opposition who brought it down once more to the level of sectional antagonism and personal intrigue. Thomas L. Clingman of North Carolina attacked not only annexation and all those who favored it, but devoted his forensic skill especially to the Secretary of State, whom he charged with having consciously pursued over the past dozen years a course looking to the destruction of the Union and the substitution of a Southern confederacy. Clingman was answered in a maiden speech by William Lowndes Yancey who now held the Alabama seat made vacant by the elevation of Dixon H. Lewis to the Senate. It was fitting that Yancey, whose father had read law in Calhoun's Abbeville office, should speak in the Secretary's defense; ironical because it would be the work of William Lowndes Yancey more than that of any other man that would create the Southern confederacy he was now properly to deny that Calhoun ever contemplated or desired. The verbal clash culminated in a bloodless exchange of shots near Beltsville, Maryland—another milestone in the steady progress of the South toward unity and a nationalism of her own.[24]

The House, relentlessly driven by the party leadership, proceeded with the Texas debate day after day as though nothing had happened. The familiar arguments for and against the measure were expounded with varying degrees of heat. Alternatives to Ingersoll's joint resolution continued to be offered as the terms of the debate broadened. By the middle of January it seemed to be agreed that Texas was to be admitted to the Union as a state rather than annexed as a territory. Isaac Holmes, whose sword rattling of the previous summer had so alarmed Calhoun, took the floor on January 14 to make what the hostile Adams called "the most powerful and most eloquent speech in favor of annexation" that had yet been heard, and it was notable that Holmes like Ingersoll stated the national rather than the sectional case. The even more bellicose Rhett confined himself to legal questions when he spoke a week later. Joshua Giddings, zealot that he was, used Texas as the text for another of his perennial attacks on slavery and all who maintained it; and was answered by a first-term member from Tennessee, Andrew Johnson.[25]

After three weeks of almost continuous debate, annexation came to a vote in the House on January 25, 1845. Ingersoll's original joint resolution incorporating the text of Calhoun's treaty had been dropped along the way and the vote was actually taken on a modified version of a resolution offered by Milton Brown of Tennessee. By a count of 120 to 98 the consent of Congress was given to the people of Texas to form a state government, providing they did so before January 1, 1846. The boundaries were to be adjusted by the Federal Government, but Texas was to retain her public lands and to pay her own public debt. Provision was also made for splitting off up to four additional states, with the consent of Texas, but slavery was to be prohibited in such of them as lay north of the Missouri Compromise line.[26]

That evening Blair shouted hosannas in the *Globe*, pronouncing the action of the House to be "an extinguisher of agitation," which established "peace and good will between the different sections of our Union too firmly to be shaken by religious fanaticism or political phrenzy." But those who represented Northern and Southern interests on the floor of Congress knew better. A Whig from western New York condemned bitterly the nine Southern members of his own party who had voted for annexation, complaining that in "all matters touching slavery the south moves in solid phalanx, and the north, by its own divisions, will always fall an easy prey." Southerners of both parties seemed to him to be exulting "as if they had vanquished a foreign enemy." Yet those same Southern Representatives felt only that they had postponed for a little longer their own inevitable doom. "I confess frankly," wrote one of them three days after the Texas vote, "that I regard the Union as it is, a degrading and ruinous alliance to the South, and if she have spirit, or self respect, she will not endure the dishonor and shame of submission. I would await the fate of annexation and some of its consequences before I would determine *what* it becomes the South to do. That she must do something, he is blind not to see." [27]

6

At the very climax of the Texas debate in the House Calhoun was taken ill. Overwork no doubt contributed to his condition, but he had always been subject to bronchial ailments. He was no longer young, and a cold, disregarded, quickly became pneumonia. It was a very fortunate thing indeed that Mrs. Calhoun, Patrick, and Cornelia were with him, because he needed all the care and attention they were able to give. It was indeed commonly stated in the Northern papers that he could not survive. Floride wrote to James on February 1 that his father was better, but admitted that he had been "very sick for several days." He continued sick for many days more. When the weather was fine he rode out in a carriage, but not for long at a time. By February 4 he was able to attend to the more important business of his department from his bedchamber; and on the sixteenth he called briefly on both President and President-elect, but it was February 20 before he returned to his office, and then only for a few hours at a stretch. [28]

During the critical phase of Calhoun's illness the joint resolution passed by the House moved over to the other end of the Capital.

There had been two significant changes in the Senate since the previous session, both of them from New York. John A. Dix—he who
as a young lieutenant in the army twenty years before had been one
of Calhoun's most loyal followers—was chosen to finish out the four
years of Silas Wright's term. N. P. Tallmadge had been appointed
Governor of Wisconsin Territory, and to fill out the remaining weeks
of his term the New York legislature chose Daniel S. Dickinson,
Bouck's Lieutenant Governor. After a sharp factional fight, Dickinson was also named to the succeeding six-year term. Dix represented
the radical faction of Wright and Van Buren; Dickinson was a
Hunker. But the votes of both would be needed to carry the annexation of Texas through the Senate.[29]

For a time the prospect looked utterly hopeless. Archer on February 4 reported unfavorably from the Committee on Foreign Relations,
not only as to the House action but with respect to all similar bills and
resolutions previously moved in the Senate, McDuffie's and Benton's
among them. The next day Benton reopened the question by withdrawing his bill and substituting another almost as impractical. He
no longer insisted on the assent of Mexico, but he still clung to his
demand that the territorial limits of Texas and the terms of the
cession be subject to negotiation between Texas and the United States
before annexation could take place. Blair praised Benton's bill as
extravagantly as he had praised the House resolution a few days
earlier; but the delay it involved, if Donelson had correctly judged the
situation, would be fatal to the project.[30]

Hardly more than two weeks of the session remained when the
Senate took up in earnest the most bitterly contested sectional issue
since the Missouri Compromise itself. Archer was unwell, so the
burden of upholding the Committee on Foreign Relations fell to
James T. Morehead of Kentucky, while Buchanan, the minority
member, led the fight for annexation. Morehead was supported by
the Whigs generally, with Woodbury, Colquitt, Walker, McDuffie,
and others of the Calhoun bloc serving as reserves for Buchanan.
Benton was strangely silent. It was evident from the newspaper
accounts, if not from the speeches themselves, that the real contest was
a personal one. The issue had become, not annexation itself, but
what plan of annexation would be followed. The House plan
promised speed and speed was essential, but Benton and the *Globe*

were striving mightily to salvage prestige and the Whigs hoped to defeat the measure by keeping the Democrats divided.[31]

The President-elect reached Washington the evening of February 13, and shortly thereafter a change began to show itself. Polk kept his own counsel on appointments, but there is no doubt that he used his position as a lever to bring pressure to bear on dissident Senators. As Calhoun slowly regained his strength, he too brought all the weight of his position and his personality, all his political experience and shrewdness to the battle. He realized more keenly than any of the others concerned how urgent the question really was, but even he did not know the whole story. Houston had in fact already indicated to Smith that if Congress did not pass an acceptable annexation act by March 4 he would himself take the stump against any further move to join the United States. King wrote from Paris, on receiving word that annexation had passed the House, to report France using all her influence behind the scenes to keep Texas an independent power. In Britain Calhoun's August letter to King, published with the President's annual message, furnished the text for a lively debate in Commons, with Sir Robert Peel himself going far toward authenticating the American Secretary's analysis of British policy.[32]

As the session moved into its final week the Senate began to sit in the evening, still devoting most of its time to Texas, but it was February 27 before the proannexation forces were fully concentrated. On that day Walker offered a compromise solution of the difficulty, proposing to amend the House resolution by adding Benton's bill to it as an alternative choice. The President, in other words, was to be given two options: he might offer statehood to Texas at once upon the approval of the properly constituted authorities there; or he might send commissioners to negotiate terms on which Texas was to enter the Union. It was then mid-afternoon. There were immediate objections, but the Senate agreed to recess until six o'clock.[33]

There is no record of what went on in the interval, but somehow the necessary votes were whipped into line. It was known that the division would be very close, but with an even number in the Senate and no Vice President, a margin of two was necessary. A tie would be defeat. The Washington correspondent of the Charleston *Courier* believed on February 25 that the vote of Senator Dix of New York would be the crucial one, and the *Mercury's* correspondent wrote the

next day that Dix's vote had been secured by a promise from Polk
that Calhoun would not be retained in the Cabinet.[84] Whatever the
persuasion may have been, the New York Barnburner voted with his
Hunker colleague and the Southern Democrats on the crucial issue.
So did Benton, and the amended resolution was carried 27 to 25.
After a sharp but unsuccessful fight to avoid a vote, the Senate
amendment was accepted in the House the next day, 132 to 76.[85]

7

Tyler signed the joint resolution for the annexation of Texas on
March 1. Immediately thereafter Calhoun called at the White House,
and the President and his Secretary of State reviewed the possible
courses open to them. Calhoun, with his detailed knowledge of the
probable course of the Texan Government and of the avowed policy
of Britain and France, had no doubt whatever that to reopen negotiations would be to lose Texas altogether. His immediate reaction,
therefore, was that despite the impending change of administration,
Tyler should exercise the option given the President, and act under
the House resolution. Tyler was equally sure that the first option
should be followed, but wondered if propriety did not require him to
leave the actual execution of the matter to his successor.[36]

Tyler did not doubt that Polk favored the same mode of completing
the annexation proceedings, and of course realized, as did Calhoun,
that Polk's behind-the-scenes influence had been in all probability the
deciding factor in passing the resolution through the Senate. The
Secretary argued, however, that the need for speed was too great
to admit of delay. He already knew that he himself was not to be
retained in the new Cabinet, and it is quite likely that he feared Polk
might be induced by commitments to the Benton-Blair interest to
choose the second alternative and lose the cause. In any event, he
convinced Tyler, and a special meeting of the Cabinet on Sunday,
March 2, confirmed the decision unanimously. To put Tyler's qualms
at rest Calhoun called on the President-elect after the meeting to
explain the action being taken and the reasons for it, but Polk
declined to comment. The next day the necessary instructions were
rushed off to Donelson, with the unnecessary warning that he would
have to act before Britain and France could interfere.[37]

Calhoun remained in the State Department for a few days until his successor, James Buchanan, could take over the work, but for all practical purposes his connection with the annexation of Texas ended with his March 3 dispatch to Donelson. Three days after that date, Juan Almonte, the Mexican Minister in Washington, asked for his passports. At the same time Polk requested copies of both the joint resolution and the dispatch to Donelson; and unknown to Calhoun directed the envoy not to act on his instructions until further notice. A few days later, however, the new Cabinet gave unanimous approval to the action taken by the Tyler administration and Buchanan then confirmed the instructions of his predecessor. Donelson, waiting at New Orleans, received both the original instructions and the confirmation of them on March 24, and reached Galveston in three days' time.[38]

The rest of the Texas story is Donelson's. He learned at New Orleans that Elliot, the British chargé, had just returned from a secret mission to Mexico City. At Galveston he found that Elliot had been joined by Saligny, the French envoy, and that the pair had already departed for the Texan Capital. Donelson chartered a steamer and set off in pursuit. He found his worst fears largely confirmed. In an interview with Ashbel Smith he learned that the Secretary of State was officially on leave of absence, and that he was to negotiate with Ebenezer Allen, the Attorney General. He found President Anson Jones cool and ex-President Sam Houston hostile. He learned also the terms of the British offer, confirmed by Jones himself. They were the same as those discussed by Aberdeen with the Mexican Minister in London the preceding May: Mexico was to recognize Texan independence, with a boundary to be adjusted, and Texas was to pledge herself not to accept annexation to the United States. It was understood that rejection of these terms would probably mean an attack by Mexico. To lend more urgency to the matter, Smith presently set out for London, and a sizable British fleet appeared off Cuba.[39]

Polk, meanwhile, had sent Tyler's Postmaster General, Charles A. Wickliffe, to Texas as confidential agent to concentrate on the counteraction of British and French blandishments. Archibald Yell, former Governor of Arkansas and Congressman-elect from that state, who had carried Buchanan's instructions to Donelson, also proceeded on to Texas for the same purpose, though without official credentials. Donelson, Wickliffe, and Yell were joined in their endeavors by

Commodore R. F. Stockton, whose American fleet lay not too far off Galveston. Ashbel Smith insisted later that these four had gone up and down the length of Texas, promising internal improvements, river and harbor works, fortifications, and public offices.[40]

Whatever the technique they used, it was effective, but it is not likely that much in the way of political bribery was needed. The rank and file of the Texans were overwhelmingly in favor of annexation, and Donelson used this popular feeling as a lever to force the reluctant government to act. The last hitch was overcome when Polk recalled Shannon from Mexico, and ordered General Zachary Taylor to take up a position on the Sabine. Commodore Stockton was directed at the same time to hold his fleet in readiness near the mouth of that river. As soon as Texas ratified the joint resolution both troops and ships were to be disposed as Donelson and the Texan authorities thought best for the defense of Texan soil, and Texan soil was emphatically declared to extend to the Rio Grande. In event of a Mexican invasion threatening to disrupt the ratification procedure, the military forces were to move in anyway.[41]

As the pressure of public opinion and the cross fire of international complications built up to the danger point, Jones yielded gracefully. Early in May a convention was called to meet in Austin on July 4. Houston then threw in the sponge, and departed on a pilgrimage to the Hermitage, where he arrived on June 8, a few hours after Jackson's death. The Texas Congress, called into special session, passed its own joint resolutions consenting to annexation on June 23, subject to the approval of the convention, and that body ratified on July 4 with only one dissenting vote.

Donelson stayed another month to see to the disposition of Taylor's forces, then sailed for home, having completed the work begun by Upshur and so single-mindedly carried forward by Calhoun.

CHAPTER XVI

POLK AND THE DEMOCRATIC SCHISM

1

POLK AND DALLAS reached Washington together on the evening of February 13, 1845, having met by prearrangement in Baltimore. The word was sent ahead by telegraph from the relay house thirty miles away, and made known by booming cannon on Capitol Hill. There was an official deputation, and the streets were lined with cheering spectators. When the ceremonies were over the President-elect walked from the railroad station to the National Hotel on the arms of Tennessee Congressman Aaron V. Brown and John Heart of the *Constitution*. To visitors he was affable and friendly but he gave no hint as to his Cabinet or the policy he meant to pursue.[1]

The task Polk faced was formidable: to escape a partisan dilemma whose horns were Benton and Calhoun. Both factions had contributed to the slender margin of his victory, and each sought now to control his administration. For a month following the election he had kept his own counsel in the seclusion of his Tennessee home. Then on December 7, 1844, he offered the Treasury Department to Silas Wright. He placed the choice on the ground that the problems of the administration would make the Treasury the key position, but he belied his own argument with a postscript offering the New Yorker his choice of Cabinet seats, should he prefer "the State or some other." Then he changed his mind and recopied the letter without the addition. Yet he must have known that Silas Wright, whose vote in the Senate had carried the tariff of 1842, would be to the South the most objectionable man to whom the Treasury could be given. Wright declined, explaining with apparent sincerity that he had accepted the governorship in order to unite the party in New York, and that if he did not now serve out his term the sacrifice would be in vain. Both letters were cordial. If Polk knew all along that Wright would take nothing less than the first place in the Cabinet he

217

gave no evidence of it, nor did Wright give any indication that he thought he was being smoothly pushed aside.[2]

At the same time A. V. Brown was busy sounding out Calhoun through third parties as to whether he would accept the British Mission. Polk seems never to have considered retaining the strong-willed Carolinian in his official family, but gave much thought to the problem of how he might be dropped without offending the South. Through trusted lieutenants like James Hamilton and A. B. Long-street Calhoun had already managed to let Polk know what he wanted and where he stood. He would remain in the State Department if Polk desired it, and if they agreed on policy; but if the incoming President wished to put someone else in that position, he would leave the Cabinet without regret. He wanted only a concrete assurance that the tariff would be reduced to the level prescribed by the compromise of 1833, an assurance that might be given either in the inaugural address or in the composition of the Cabinet. He even let it be known by indirection that he was quite willing to re-nounce any future Presidential aspiration for himself if Polk would satisfy him as to policy, conveying thereby an implied threat to run for the succession and thus become the focal point for an opposition if the policy were not satisfactory. He was undoubtedly aware, how-ever, that the only guarantee acceptable to the South as a whole would be his own retention in the Cabinet. "If you mean to take a decided stand against the tariff," wrote Longstreet to the President-elect, "retain Mr. Calhoun; if you do not, by all means dismiss him." In either case the South would know what to expect, and would be guided accordingly.[3]

After he received Wright's refusal, Polk wrote Van Buren for advice as to available New Yorkers. He wanted a New York man for Treasury or State, and he wanted advice on the Cabinet generally. It was perhaps significant that he sought no advice from Calhoun; but Cave Johnson, at least, was exploring the soothing possibilities inherent in offering the War or Navy Department to Elmore or Pickens. The Charleston *Courier's* usually well-informed correspond-ent in Washington even promoted Elmore to the Treasury, but that would have brought reprisals from the North as surely as Wright's appointment would have brought them from the South. The tariff policy of the administration would inevitably be deduced from the known views of the Secretary of the Treasury. Van Buren wrote cordially to suggest B. F. Butler for the State Department, or A. C. Flagg or C. C. Cambreleng for the Treasury. Convinced by Polk's request that Calhoun was being dropped and that policy would incline toward the Northern interest, the ex-President was off guard. He remained unsuspicious when Polk replied that he was on his way to Washington and would make no decision until he had looked over the situation for himself.[4]

Calhoun was still confined by illness to his room when Polk arrived, but he wrote to Hunter the next day that he thought no members of Tyler's Cabinet would be retained. On the sixteenth he was well enough to call briefly on the President-elect, but the Cabinet was not discussed. Even had his original plans been otherwise, Polk might well have hesitated when he saw the emaciated frame and feeble step, the glazed eye and hectic cheek of his visitor. Calhoun's health was visibly failing, and more than any personal reward he needed rest.[5]

The next day Polk formally tendered the State Department to Buchanan, and the Pennsylvania Senator accepted promptly. On the nineteenth a letter was drafted offering the post of Attorney General to Senator Robert J. Walker of Mississippi; and as late as February 22, when he wrote once more to Van Buren, Polk intended the Treasury for George Bancroft, whom he regarded as a Northern man acceptable to the South. That left only the War and Navy Departments for New York to choose from, and Polk asked Van Buren if Butler or Marcy would take one or the other. Without waiting for an answer he selected Butler, and wrote the ex-President again to solicit his good offices in gaining an acceptance. Van Buren answered tartly that nothing less than State or Treasury would be good enough for New York, and Butler, echoing his chief's words, declined the offer.[6]

On March 1 Polk wrote Van Buren that he had tendered the War Department to William L. Marcy, who after Wright and Butler was the best known of the New Yorkers. He went out of his way to praise Marcy's talents and to insist that he knew of no difference of views between the former Governor and the former President, but that, of course, Van Buren did not for one moment believe. The factional squabbles of the New York Democracy were too well known for Polk to have been in ignorance. Van Buren was furious and coldly turned his back on the party he had himself once led.[7]

Somewhere along the line the pressure from the South prevailed, and Walker moved up to the Treasury. The Navy Department went to Bancroft, who would have preferred a foreign mission. Tyler's Navy Secretary, John Y. Mason of Virginia, was retained as Attorney General, perhaps primarily because he and Polk had been classmates at the University of North Carolina and he could fill the role of personal confidant. The Post Office, traditional seat of the party patronage dispenser, went to Cave Johnson of Tennessee. Each Cabinet post was offered on specified conditions. There was to be no electioneering, and no long absences from Washington; and there was to be concurrence on policy as laid down in Polk's inaugural address, a copy of which went in confidence to each of the appointees for approval.[8]

Calhoun did not officially know his own fate until February 26, when he called on Polk by request. He was received with every mark of consideration, was informed that an entirely new Cabinet would be appointed, and was urged to accept the mission to London. This he again declined, but insisted that he felt no dissatisfaction, and was happy to return to the retirement he had left reluctantly a year ago. The next day he formally resigned the office, effective whenever a successor should have qualified. At the same time he directed his friends and editors not to make his removal a ground for criticism.[9]

Shortly thereafter A. V. Brown called on Calhoun as emissary from Polk to urge the British Mission once more on him, and Buchanan sent Isaac Holmes to tell him the Oregon negotiations would be placed entirely in his hands. He would yield to no importunities, and undoubtedly he was correct in so doing, for reasons unvoiced by him as well as for those expressed. His stated reasons were those he had already given to Polk: that his health was poor, that he could not afford the scale of living that would be required, that the Oregon negotiations could be better carried on in the United States, and that any treaty which bore his signature would be defeated by the Benton bloc in the Senate. More potent than any of these, however, was the knowledge that the South looked to him for leadership, either for or against the administration as its policies might require, and he could not desert his people in their hour of need.[10]

2

The rain poured down on the morning of March 4, 1845, and the afternoon was damp and overcast. The quadrennial thousands jammed the streets of Washington, nonetheless, till the Avenue was a moving sea of umbrellas. At the designated hour Polk and Tyler rode to the Capitol together in an open carriage, followed by Tyler's Cabinet with the lean, graying Calhoun at their head, though he should not have ventured out at all on such a day, so recently recovered from serious illness.[11]

The inaugural address was the lure that had brought him to brave the elements; for the Cabinet offered in itself no promise of tariff reform, and only a forthright pledge could now win Southern confidence. The address, delivered from the east portico of the Capitol to a canopy of umbrellas, was only a cautious restatement of the party platform. On the tariff Polk repeated and reaffirmed the doctrine of the Kane letter. He favored a tariff for revenue, and strongly opposed a tariff for protection; but as strongly he upheld discrimination for protection within the revenue framework. The Kane letter had been accepted by Pennsylvania and South Carolina alike, each recognizing its equivocations as being designed to win votes from the other. In its expanded form the doctrine satisfied neither, implying too much protection for the South and not enough for the North, but the presence of Buchanan and Marcy in the Cabinet tended to outweigh the uncommitted Walker, who had himself been born in Pennsylvania. On the Oregon question Polk also echoed the party platform, declaring the title of the United States to the whole territory to be "clear and unquestionable." The country was filling up with American settlers and it was therefore the duty of the government to protect them and to give them the benefit of the laws and institutions to which they were by citizenship entitled.[12]

Within a week Polk knew where he stood with respect to the contending factions in his own party, and it is not unlikely that it was where he meant to stand. North and South were nicely balanced in the official family and the official policy was as nicely weighed, with a revenue tariff for the one, Oregon and incidental protection for the other. The extremes were deliberately cut off in hopes of attracting the more moderate friends of each to the new alignment.

Although the Cabinet was not altogether satisfactory to him, Calhoun took issue with the President primarily on his tariff and Oregon statements. On the tariff the South Carolinian's position was so well known that no one could possibly have mistaken it. On the Oregon question he had been explicit as to his predilection, both to Polk and to Buchanan, well in advance of the inauguration. To declare a clear title to the whole country after previous offers to compromise at forty-nine degrees left nothing to negotiate, and to set up a territorial government would be to abrogate the existing treaty of joint occupancy and leave the issue to be resolved by force. It would be to sacrifice the advantages time was steadily piling up for the United States. Lest there be any doubt, however, he let Polk know that he regretted the attitude the President had seen fit to take.[13]

Van Buren's objections were to people rather than to policies, and he too was at pains to inform the President of his dissatisfaction. He did it so bluntly as to preclude any possibility of a change of heart. The appointment of Marcy, the ex-President wrote to Bancroft for Polk's eye, "is an evil which neither civil words nor the disposition of patronage can repair and which, under the circumstances, nothing can justify." [14]

Deeply disappointed though he was at Polk's failure to come up to expectations on the tariff and Oregon questions, Calhoun gave no public sign of opposition or offense, and permitted none of his partisans to do so. He remained in the State Department until March 10 at Buchanan's request. When at last he stepped down, his parting with the President was cordial and frank, and before he left the city on March 11, each of the new Cabinet officers called on him at his lodgings to pay his respects and to bid him adieu. Once more he was going into retirement, and taking with him the homage due to his talents, his services, and his position in the small galaxy of elder statesmen. But even in retirement he would be a more powerful force in the political life of his country than most of those he left behind in harness.[15]

3

A major complication on the road to Democratic harmony was the policy and practices of the Washington *Globe*. Blair had managed in the course of the campaign to identify himself with Benton. He had, moreover, been outspokenly for Van Buren up to the very hour of Polk's nomination, and had never been more than lukewarm and occasionally openly hostile toward the party candidate. Except for the interval of truce between 1837 and 1842 Blair had been bitter and completely without scruple in his attacks on Calhoun, and his methods of chastising dissenters of whatever faith were ruthless. The heritage, after almost fifteen years of a journalistic career unrivaled for its vituperative fervor or its calculated use of falsehood as a weapon of party warfare, was one of animosity and distrust.

It was clear to Polk and his advisers from the date of the election that the *Globe* could no longer be retained as the official paper. The Benton-Van Buren group wanted Blair kept on, and Jackson himself warned that the editor's removal would wreck the party; but too many Southern leaders had been branded as traitors, blackguards, and bullies in the editorial columns of the *Globe,* and these threatened to wreck the party on their own account if Blair continued in his place as editor.

Before the end of December 1844 the post of party editor was offered to Thomas Ritchie, who had refused a similar offer at Van Buren's hands some seventeen years earlier. The Richmond publicist refused once more, and for a time the matter remained in abeyance. The Calhoun following, however, with Duff Green acting as Washington spokesman, was insistent, and Polk himself was determined that Blair must go. During March the basis of a deal was perfected. Ritchie came to Washington to talk to Polk, and finally promised to undertake the job if a satisfactory associate could be found to share the labor. Blair agreed very coldly and very reluctantly to sell out if Jackson so advised. On March 28 Polk confirmed an invitation to Andrew Jackson Donelson to join the venture as associate editor.[16]

When Donelson declined, Ritchie again grew reluctant, and Polk almost decided to let Blair remain, inviting W. A. Harris of the *Constitution* to move in with the veteran. John P. Heiss of the Nashville *Union* had meanwhile been selected as business manager of the Ritchie-Donelson paper. Heiss refused to give up when Donelson proved unavailable. Lewis S. Coryell, Pennsylvania businessman who was an old personal and political friend of Calhoun's, then guaranteed funds to buy and merge the *Constitution* and the *Madi-*

sonian, or to set up a new press altogether, should the *Globe* deal fall through, and Heiss went to Richmond to talk Ritchie around. Jackson at last advised Blair to sell, and early in April Ritchie capitulated, having been convinced that the future unity of the party, on which depended the ultimate safety of the South, was at stake. Calhoun's followers, and Calhoun himself, were not wholly satisfied with Ritchie, but accepted him as the lesser evil, while Polk kept open a place for Donelson should he change his mind.[17]

The financing of the deal was handled by Simon Cameron, Buchanan's successor as Senator from Pennsylvania, but the method was open to question. We know, at least, that $13,000 was actually advanced to Ritchie by William Selden, the Treasurer of the United States, presumably on Cameron's account, and it is more than likely that all the funds immediately needed came by way of advances from the Treasury, to be written off later against the public printing contracts that would accrue to the paper in its official capacity. The whole transaction was confused, and perhaps deliberately so. According to Harris the ownership of the *Union,* as the *Globe* was rechristened, was divided originally among Ritchie, Heiss, Cameron, and J. Knox Walker, nephew and private secretary of President Polk. Cameron, however, was forced by the others to sell out, and the share originally in his name was transferred to that of Coryell, who was also a financial guarantor of Heiss. Coryell, nevertheless, assured Harris that he really did not have any pecuniary interest in the paper. By this he presumably meant that he had invested no money in it; but apparently nobody did except the taxpayers.[18]

Blair announced the impending change in the issue of the *Globe* for April 14, 1845, and that paper ceased to publish on April 30. The first issue of the *Union* appeared on May 1. The Washington *Constitution,* which with its predecessor, the *Spectator,* had carried Calhoun's colors for the past two years, lapsed into a semiweekly when it became obvious that there was no prospect of becoming the administration organ, and went out of existence altogether after Congress met and did in fact vote the public printing to Ritchie. The *Madisonian* also changed hands and character, avoiding party controversy for a space as the *United States Journal,* and then disappearing. For the next few critical years Washington journalism centered in the *Union* and the *National Intelligencer,* official spokesmen respectively for Democrats and Whigs.

JAMES K. POLK

LEWIS CASS   SILAS WRIGHT

LEVI WOODBURY   JAMES BUCHANAN
by G. P. A. Healy

4

Calhoun's homeward route took him by way of Richmond, where Ritchie himself presided at a dinner of intimates and the Carolinian was flattered by toasts that looked ahead to 1848. But he advised his Virginia followers to assume in their public utterances that Polk meant to restore the tariff compromise, and Barbour warned the President a few days later that Democratic victory in the forthcoming state elections would mean that Virginia expected him to do just that. In Charleston the retiring Secretary was the guest of the city, but declined the inevitable public dinner. He was back at Fort Hill on March 21, prepared to wait until the President showed his hand before deciding on his own future course.[19]

It was on appointments and on declarations of policy alone that the new administration could be judged, in advance of the meeting of Congress eight months distant, and neither faction meant to give Polk that much time to consolidate his position if he chose the wrong road. The indications began to filter back to Fort Hill shortly after Calhoun's own arrival there. His friend and supporter, Lemuel Williams, for whom the ex-Secretary was believed to have interceded personally, was displaced as collector of customs at Boston, and lesser officers also began to go. Yet other Calhoun adherents, such as Henry A. Wise in Brazil, Clemson in Belgium, William R. King in France, retained their places. The Pendleton *Messenger*, while it regretted the number of removals being made, continued to credit Polk with independence and good intentions.[20]

Early in April the British Mission was offered to Elmore, and refused because of the pressure of personal affairs. The more potent reason, however, was that Buchanan's tariff views would not permit the negotiation of such a commercial treaty as Calhoun's policy required. The mission was then tendered to Pickens who also refused it, with the pointed comment that he could not accept any Federal office so long as the tariff of 1842 remained in force. By that time news had come from England, with accounts of the sharp reaction in both houses of Parliament to Polk's blithe assertion of the "clear and unquestionable" nature of American claims to all of Oregon.[21]

Polk became alarmed at last and proposed as a good will offering toward both Britain and New York to give the mission to Martin

Van Buren. Buchanan tried to interpose, on the ground that Calhoun's powerful following would be alienated. On the heels of the British dispatches had come news from Richmond of smashing victories for the State Rights Democrats in the April elections. Hunter and Seddon led the parade, winning Congressional seats in districts gerrymandered against them by the Van Burenites only two years before. Calhoun's partisans would control the legislature and the delegation in Congress, and would have the selection of a Senator in their hands. Polk persisted in his offer to Van Buren, using Bancroft and Butler as intermediaries, but the ex-President declined as firmly as had Calhoun. At this point Polk seems to have considered Calhoun once more, and Duff Green undertook to learn the terms on which the Carolinian would take the place. They were not acceptable to Polk, nor could they have been. Levi Woodbury received the next refusal of the job; and finally, near mid-June, the London mission was reluctantly accepted by Louis McLane, perhaps the best choice that could have been made.[22]

By his Delaware birth and Maryland residence, McLane was Southern, but not so identified with the South as to invite Northern hostility. He had served under Jackson both as Secretary of the Treasury and as Secretary of State, as well as in the diplomatic post to which he was now to return, but had not held office under Van Buren. As President of the Baltimore and Ohio Railroad he had been associated for a decade with an economic interest that cut across sectional lines. The B & O expected to tap the rich Western market and help move the grain that would go to England from eastern seaports. Railroad extension called for cheaper iron than the protected domestic industry could supply, but the rails that would carry transportation to the West might well come from England, in exchange for Western breadstuffs and for Southern cotton.

Before the British Mission was settled, criticism of Presidential appointments was general and the *Union* was on the defensive. Ritchie could not explain to the satisfaction of either Benton or Calhoun men the principles behind the distribution of offices; and he could not, or would not, rise above generalities on Oregon or the tariff. John S. Barbour of Calhoun's Virginia following visited Washington, and concluded after long personal interviews that President, Cabinet, and editor all were well disposed; but the New York *Herald* insisted that Calhoun men were proscribed in that state, and similar word came from Pennsylvania and New England. The Benton partisans were equally dissatisfied, and began a strenuous agitation for the return of Blair and the *Globe*.[23]

The loss of patronage as the President wavered between factions, the deliberately noncommittal program, and the still smoldering embers of revolt at home combined to force the Calhoun managers to a decision. They had promised Polk in the waning days of Tyler's regime that they would once and for all withdraw the Carolinian from Presidential competition in return for a strictly revenue tariff, but the guarantee of tariff reform was to be his retention in the Cabinet. So they concluded, when their leader was replaced by the pro-tariff Buchanan and Calhoun supporters lost Federal offices in the Northern states to the Albany Regency, that they had fought the long battle for free trade in vain.

On the evening of May 8, 1845, representatives of the group that had managed Calhoun's 1844 campaign met at Elmore's home in Charleston: Elmore himself, who combined political sagacity with the talents of a business promoter; the obscenely fat but clearheaded Dixon H. Lewis; James Hamilton, handsome and volatile, who had conveyed their terms to Polk six months before; Ker Boyce of the Charleston Bank; Henry Gourdin, banker and businessman, who provided a link to the low-country aristocracy; and as a gesture of appeasement toward the Blufftonites the brothers Rhett, Robert Barnwell, brilliant but unstable, and the younger but more evenly gaited James. Their purpose, as Lewis put it, was to decide on a course that would put Calhoun in the best position for 1848. They proposed, in short, to renew the implied threat of the November correspondence with Polk by using Calhoun's presumptive candidacy as a club to force action on the tariff from the administration, and to make that candidacy actual if they failed. To all of this Calhoun agreed.[24]

The New York Barnburners, skilled and seasoned politicians that they were, expressed their own displeasure with Polk's appointments in more forthright fashion. They were not willing to share the patronage in the state with the Hunkers, and despite Marcy's presence in the Cabinet they forced the President to accept their terms. The method was characteristic. They let Polk know that unless they had their way the New York Representatives in Congress would prevent the choice of Ritchie as public printer, and to underline the threat they began raising money to put Blair back in business with a rival sheet. The dubious means by which the *Union* had been financed made it imperative that Ritchie receive the public printing, and Polk was compelled to give in. The New York radicals appeared to be strengthening their own machine at Polk's expense preparatory to going into opposition.[25]

The Bluffton rebels were also preparing to go into opposition. Rhett went off to Europe, and the others kept quietly in the background while the *Mercury,* now edited by Stuart's former partner, J. Milton Clapp, built up through letters to the editor the case they would in due season make their own. "The Bluffton Boys have been silenced, not subdued," wrote "Bluffton" on the anniversary of the famous dinner; "the fire is not extinguished; it smoulders beneath, and will burst forth in another glorious flame that shall overrun the State and place her light again as of old, upon the watch tower of freedom." And Hammond, in private letters, poured out his discontent. A Southern confederacy could have been formed the previous winter, had a convention for that purpose been called (or so the ex-Governor now insisted), and his fondest hopes would have been realized. "The Union dissolved—the South out—the world at our feet entreating for our staple & our trade—abolition treason against God & man. But we failed then & if it was not too late would fail now. So. Ca. belongs to Calhoun. *He will not agitate.*"[26]

5

As the younger leaders in South Carolina moved further toward radical action, events were shaping themselves to give a new direction to the administration's policies. The persistent pressure from the Van Buren faction became in time unbearable. The wholesale proscription within the party, ruthlessly carried out by the Barnburner leaders who now controlled the Federal patronage in New York, alarmed Marcy and brought a rising tide of protest from the Calhoun following. In the Cabinet Walker gradually gained an intellectual ascendancy, and the President turned to South and West to sustain him against the spoilsmen of New York and Pennsylvania. The South wanted tariff reform, and the West was ready to go along if its territorial desires could also be gratified.[27]

The shift meant that the emphasis of the administration would be placed on tariff reform, and by the beginning of August the *Union* was attacking the whole protective system. The *Mercury* and its votaries rejected all overtures. On his way home from England Rhett stopped over in Washington long enough to talk with Polk, Walker, and Buchanan. Sure as he already was that the administration would not go far enough to suit him, these conferences did not change his mind, and he asked Calhoun bluntly what course South Carolina was to take. Then, without waiting for a reply, he declared at a Virginia watering-place that his state would nullify if the tariff was not at once reduced to the revenue level. If Calhoun would not go along he would be shelved.[28]

Calhoun's position, both in relation to the administration and with respect to the resistance movement in South Carolina, precluded his making any public statement that might be construed as having a political bearing. McDuffie, however, was under no such restraint and his early sympathy with the Bluffton movement put him in an even better position to combat it now. So an unnamed correspondent, professing alarm at the attitude of the *Mercury*, asked McDuffie what he thought the administration would do about the tariff. The Senator's answer, dated September 27, was promptly turned over to the *Mercury*, whose editor had no alternative but to publish it. The letter was something of a masterpiece, which fully expressed Calhoun's own views. In essence it was a concise, documented statement of the free-trade position; but at beginning and end, and woven through the whole, were assurances that the President could not, and of course would not, be false to his own record, to his promises, to the policy and expectations of his party, and to the true interests of the country.[29]

6

Through all the pulling and hauling of conflicting interests and rival factions during Polk's first six months of office, Calhoun's future course was a matter of deep concern, to his partisans, to his enemies, and to himself. A growing number in and out of South Carolina took it for granted at the time of his retirement from the Cabinet that he would resume his Senate seat. Webster and John M. Clayton had already rejoined the Whig ranks in that body while the Democrats had been materially weakened by the loss of Buchanan and

Walker to the Cabinet and Wright to serve New York as Governor. In part this loss was offset by the election of Lewis Cass from Michigan, but the Whigs would clearly have the preponderance of ability, and the Democratic leadership; for better or for worse, would almost certainly go to Benton.[30]

When Calhoun's return to the Senate was first bruited early in 1844, Huger had offered to resign to create a vacancy, and on March 24, 1845, he renewed the offer. Calhoun deliberately left the matter open pending developments, but the volume and pertinacity of his correspondence on that subject in the succeeding months left little doubt what his partisans desired. Their arguments were various but always boiled down to this: the place of leadership in the Senate was open, and if Calhoun did not seize it, it would fall to Benton who would bully and browbeat a weak administration for his own purposes —purposes that did not include tariff reform and might eventually extend to abolition.[31]

John S. Barbour of Virginia was perhaps the most eloquent among them, and showed the keenest insight into the character of the man he would persuade. "To stand with folded arms and yield the battlement to the enemy, in the frail hope of a redeeming energy in the virtue of the people," he wrote late in June, "is neither the duty nor the policy of patriotism. In the Senate the administration has to stand the brunt of a powerful combination of talent and celebrity. It is *there* that the fate of the country is to be settled. . . . Your retirement is ruin and annihilation to us. In the whole South we have not a man who has the elements of a commander, neither in Congress nor out. . . . You can save the Country & no other man can do it." And in mid-August, when the resurgent Blufftonism was at its peak, Barbour wrote again: "It is *your* power (inherent & not transmissable), that stands out in the South—like the Fort above the valley—for its protection, & not for your elevation. It is your character & strength alone, that can give hope, & overawe treachery." [32]

Calhoun was genuinely reluctant to return to the political hustings, but the state and the Union still required his services. McDuffie's always precarious health took a turn for the worse, threatening further to weaken Democratic strength in the Senate. Many of those who would be Calhoun's colleagues, should he return, added their voices to the general plea; while editors and political confidants earlier opposed to the step swung over to the affirmative side. More important still, the Oregon question began to look increasingly threatening. Calhoun probably did not know that the President himself was consistently overruling all efforts of the Secretary of State to compromise the issue, but the *Union* began in August to intersperse its antitariff articles with reiterated demands for all of Oregon. It was then that "fifty-four-forty or fight" became a battle cry and Buchanan indicated to his predecessor that he feared the business would not be settled by the parties to it.[33]

Sometime in the first half of September Calhoun made up his mind, and in a letter to Armistead Burt dated September 17 he placed himself at the disposal of his friends. "Since you left me," he began, "I have received several letters from different parts, some expressing their regret, that I left the Senate, others praying my return. One in particular, from one of the most intelligent and devoted friends from Ohio, who last winter advised me by no means to return to the Senate, but whose impression now is entirely changed." The allusion is significant, for it could refer only to Ellwood Fisher of Cincinnati, whose recent letter summed up the views of Calhoun's supporters with admirable succinctness. It was the universal belief, wrote the Quaker editor, that "if thee were absent Benton would be too prominent and pernicious." [34]

A new argument was added when Judge Joseph Story died, and Polk named Levi Woodbury, next to McDuffie the ablest free-trade man left in the Senate, to the Supreme Court seat thus vacated. The growing tension between the *Mercury* and the *Union,* and the presence of Benton in Washington where he seemed to be in familiar contact with the administration, gave the final push, and on October 9 Calhoun accepted Huger's long-standing offer to resign in his favor. Even then, although the impending event was widely rumored, it was not certainly known until the legislature validated it late in November. There were only four dissenting votes, all blanks.[35]

It was fitting, perhaps, that among those who expressed a desire for Calhoun's return to the Senate were Daniel Webster and William B. Lewis. Webster, his perennial opponent but lifelong friend, indicated his wishes to Isaac Holmes, who passed them on. Lewis addressed Calhoun direct. "We need, at the present crisis," wrote the former third auditor, "men in the Senate not only of distinguished ability but of purity and undisputed patriotism." One wonders if Calhoun, as he read those lines, allowed his mind to dwell on the charges of treason manufactured for his destruction in the early 1830's by this same Major Lewis.[36]

CHAPTER XVII

THE NEW SOUTH-WEST ALLIANCE

1

POLK'S STATEMENT of policy in his first annual message was precisely such as his inaugural address foreshadowed, unmodified by any of the intervening circumstances.[1] The annexation of Texas was hailed as "the deliberate homage of each people to the great principle of our federal union," and the President pointed with characteristic American pride to the great extent of territory thus peaceably acquired. The adverb would soon prove to be in error, but at the moment a new minister was on the way to Mexico City and a resumption of friendly relations was expected shortly. The Oregon controversy seemed more threatening. Polk reported that he had resumed negotiations in deference to the convictions of his predecessors; that he had offered to compromise the boundary at the forty-ninth parallel; and that his offer had been rejected by the British Minister in Washington without even the courtesy of a reference to his government. The President's answer was to call on Congress to give the twelve months' notice required to abrogate the treaty of joint occupancy, and in the interim to take all permissible steps to protect United States citizens in Oregon and on the road thither. This portion of the message ended with a classic reaffirmation of the Monroe Doctrine.

On the domestic side Polk asked that the tariff be reduced to the revenue level and that ad valorem be substituted for specific duties; but he insisted still on the right of Congress to discriminate between articles so long as the revenue standard was not exceeded.

The Oregon and tariff issues were so intimately related that they will be treated together in another chapter. The question of Mexican relations, the events that grew out of them, and the bearing of those events on the past and subsequent career of John C. Calhoun, will also be reserved for separate treatment. The present chapter will be concerned primarily with the economic and political forces, both sec-

233

tional in their nature, that formed the background of these far-reaching controversies, and bore decisively on their solution.

2

Since 1830 Southern leaders, with Calhoun foremost among them, had been consciously bidding for Western support in their long battle against the tariff, offering in return markets and cheap transportation. The natural waterway of the Great Lakes, supplemented by the Erie Canal, had diverted much of the Western produce to New York. Southern hostility to public improvements at government expense delayed the development of internal communications, and the advantages in winds and ocean currents enjoyed by Southern ports were more than overcome by the general use of steam over the shorter great-circle routes to Europe from Boston and New York. But the Mississippi remained the greatest single artery of trade, and as the surpluses of Western grain piled up, the pressure increased from both directions: for relief from trade restrictions so that these surpluses could be sold abroad, and for better transportation, which meant dredging river channels and importing railroad iron.

Calhoun had never relinquished his own far-flung scheme of internal transportation, based on Albert Gallatin's report of 1808. Early in his term as Secretary of War he had put forth, and strenuously defended, his plans for communication with the West, and he had seen some of them carried out. The Northern route, of which the Erie Canal was the key, had been built by the state of New York. The most important of the central routes was building by private capital in the form of rails from Baltimore to the Ohio River. But the Southern routes still lagged. Too much of Southern capital was tied up in land and labor. There were mutual jealousies and disagreements over surveys. Calhoun had sought to overcome the capital deficit by depositing the federal surplus of 1836 with the states, but the panic of the following spring put an end to the surplus. With his eyes on the remoter West he had powerfully supported a railroad route from Charleston skirting the lower end of the Appalachian chain in Georgia, and swinging up through Alabama, Tennessee, and Kentucky to strike the Mississippi opposite St. Louis. The reorganization of the South Carolina Railroad under James Gadsden in 1840 was a forward step, but the vital rails that would link the destinies of

South and West remained unlaid for want of money, and plans were modified to terminate the road at Memphis.[2]

As the country slowly emerged from the long depression, there was renewed activity in railroad building and revived interest in water transportation. The westward movement of the population was enormously accelerated by the hard times, and the census of 1840 re-emphasized the political power of the Western states. The sectional struggle between North and South was to be decided in the West, and the victory would follow the lines of economic advantage. So the South renewed its bid for a political alliance with the West, with free trade the goal and rail and river transport as the tools. Such was the atmosphere when Captain H. D. Bingham of Arkansas visited Memphis in March 1845 in quest of support for a military road to the Indian frontier. A convention to consider the problem was held in July, but by that time the horizon had broadened and the possibilities for useful action extended far beyond the mere opening up of the Indian country. The convention adjourned to reconvene in November, with larger representation and more comprehensive agenda.[3]

During the intervening four months the sponsors of the Memphis Convention prepared to seal once and for all the political and economic alliance of South and West. The newspapers played up the coming meeting and railroad promoters like Gadsden were indefatigable in their efforts. The advance publicity indicated agreement that the convention should discuss not merely railroad connections between the Mississippi Valley and the South Atlantic states, but the military and naval resources of the valley, the improvement of the river and its tributaries, a ship canal connecting with the Great Lakes, and in general the whole question of agriculture, manufacturing, and transportation in the South and West.[4]

Late in September Senator Edward A. Hannegan of Indiana visited Washington and confided to Duff Green the terms on which the West would join the South for tariff reform. "He says," Green reported to Calhoun, "that the West will be united and will demand funds for the improvement of their harbours, rivers and the Cumberland road, and the graduation of the price of the public lands, and that if the South will give these to the West the West will go with the South on the tariff." Hannegan also called at the White House, and we may be sure that the President also listened to his version of the Western terms.[5]

The effectiveness of the Memphis Convention as a means of developing a program mutually advantageous to West and South would depend largely on the distinction and potency of the delegates who attended, and the convention managers prepared the list with care. Calhoun must have received an invitation before he made his decision to return to the Senate, but he doubted the propriety of attending, and even after Governor Aiken named him as an official delegate from South Carolina he questioned the wisdom of his going. For more than a month he hesitated, while Gadsden, Elmore, Hamilton, and others used every argument at their command to persuade him. Early in October he left with Floride and John for a leisurely visit to Andrew's Alabama plantation, but the insistent letters followed him.

"I look to this meeting," Gadsden urged on October 6, "as calculated to begin to bind the bonds of union between the South & West and your presence must have a powerful influence." The next day he wrote again with news of the Governor's appointment, which was to remove all question of propriety; and a third letter followed on the ninth. "Your presence would be very important to your Native State, and to all those projects in which she has so deep a stake. We are on the eve of realizing all the fond hopes and expectations of 1836: and this is not the time for our strong and leading men to falter. . . . Now is the time to meet our Western friends at Memphis —to set the ball in motion which must bring the Valley to the South: and make them feel as allies of the Great Commercial and Agricultural interests—instead of the Tax gathering and Monopolizing interests of the North." Elmore talked of personal prestige as well as of public duty, and Gadsden amplified his case in further letters as the time drew near.[6]

Calhoun realized as well as those who urged him forward how potent was the Western influence in Congress, and how essential it was to have that influence wielded on the side of the South; but he saw dangers, too, which were for the present unexpressed. If he conceded to the West the internal improvements demanded as the price of tariff reform, could he consistently oppose similar expenditures of public money in the North? And would not those expenditures quickly mount to a figure that would require more revenue and so render tariff reform meaningless? If the Western Congressmen voted for the low duties so dear to the South as a result of any activities of his, would they not also expect him to insist with their own people

on all of Oregon? And in that case could war with Britain be avoided
—war that would destroy Southern commerce and devastate Southern coasts? Would his appearance at Memphis be regarded as electioneering for 1848, which would weaken his hand in the Senate
later? It was near the end of October before he made up his mind,
but he yielded at last, and about November 1 he set out for the
Tennessee metropolis.

3

Calhoun's journey to Memphis was one long personal triumph,
sufficient, he wrote later to Clemson, "to gratify the feelings of any,
the most illustrious for talents and public services." There were
demonstrations in his honor at every stopping place. In every village
and hamlet along the way he was treated as a guest and "passed without expense or charge." A committee of citizens from New Orleans
met him in Mobile, to carry him in triumph to their own bustling city.
Governors and mayors turned out to do him honor, and from places
as far from his route as Galveston, Nashville, and St. Louis came
pressing invitations to extend his journeyings.[7]

Accompanying Calhoun were his sons, Andrew and Patrick. Andrew went as an official delegate from Alabama, and Patrick for his
own pleasure, although he was promptly seated as one of the South
Carolina delegates. They left New Orleans on November 10, aboard
the river steamer *Maria*—"a perfect moving palace" one member of
the party called it. General Edmund P. Gaines was with them, as a
delegate from Louisiana, and there were others from the Gulf coast
region. On the afternoon of the twelfth, an hour or so from her des-
tination, the *Maria* was met by a sister ship from Memphis with hundreds of cheering spectators aboard, and the two steamers finished
the trip together. Calhoun's coming was proclaimed by the firing of
cannon when the *Maria* was still ten miles down the river, and thousands lined the shore and crowded the wharf to see the great Carolinian. Only with difficulty was a way cleared for the carriage that
was to take him to his rooms at the Gayoso House, and he was not
spirited away until night had fallen, nor before hundreds of well-
wishers had grasped his hand.[8]

The convention held its first session before Calhoun reached Memphis, but the delegates were only marking time until he came. The

first order of business on November 13 was his unanimous election as permanent president. Among the fifteen vice presidents were former Senator C. C. Clay of Alabama; General A. C. Dodge of Iowa Territory, who would be first Senator from that state; General Gaines from Louisiana, the Army's second-ranking officer, whose perennial squabble over precedence with General Winfield Scott had cost Calhoun many an uneasy hour in his War Department days; and B. B. Minor, Virginia journalist and editor of the *Southern Literary Messenger*. One of the secretaries was J. D. B. De Bow of Charleston, lately one of the editors of the *Southern Quarterly Review,* whose famous *Commercial Review of the South and West* was about to make its appearance in New Orleans. Altogether fifteen states and two presumptive states, Iowa and Texas, sent delegates that included Senators, Representatives, Governors, editors, army officers, and local politicians and businessmen of various degrees of importance, without regard to party. Colonel Gadsden was there from South Carolina, and there were two Calhoun editors, Shadrach Penn from St. Louis and Ellwood Fisher from Cincinnati. The large Tennessee delegation included James C. Jones, who had twice beaten Polk for Governor; and John Bell, who had been Speaker of the House and Secretary of War. There were almost six hundred in all, constituting as imposing an array of talents as anyone could wish.[9]

Calhoun set the tone for the convention when he took the chair, with a speech that advanced a wide-ranging program for West and South. Prosperity for the agricultural states he held to be dependent on an extensive market, and that in turn depended on safe and inexpensive transportation, internal, continental, and world-wide. He proposed, therefore, to protect the sea-bound commerce of the Mississippi and the Gulf with a naval base at Pensacola and fortifications to guard the narrow passage through the Straits of Florida.[10] He would connect the valley with the South Atlantic coast by rail, thus cutting off nearly two thousand miles of hazardous voyaging; and with the Lakes and the St. Lawrence by ship canal. Supplemented by railroads moving beyond the Mississippi toward the Rockies and eventually to the Pacific itself, and with the main tributaries of the great river kept clear of obstructions and improved for navigation, the whole Union would be served by cheap and rapid transportation in peace and war.

The politically explosive question of Federal aid he evaded for the time being, save only to suggest that the steamboat had in effect converted the Mississippi into an inland sea, which might well be placed on the same footing as the Great Lakes and the navigable waters of the Atlantic and Gulf coasts. The building of railroads he held to be beyond the power of Congress, but even there substantial aid might legitimately be given. As landowner the government might grant alternate sections of the public domain to railroads and canals, since such grants would enhance the value of the lands retained; and it could reduce the duty on railroad iron, which under the existing tariff added $2,000 a mile to the cost of construction. On the land question Calhoun's views were well known, and he merely repeated his desire to see the price of the public lands scaled downward, and to see the Federal Government surrender its holdings to the states "as early as it can be practically effected," save only such sites as were necessary for military works and public buildings. As long as its proprietorship remained, however, he did not doubt that the Federal Government should contribute, in proportion to the percentage of its overflowed lands, to the cost of building levees for reclamation purposes.

The program outlined was too sweeping to be reduced to proposals for tangible action in the brief four days the convention was to last, nor was an assembly of such size, in which the states were so disproportionately represented, a suitable forum to discuss at large such controversial topics. The major themes were therefore divided among various committees whose reports were made part of the official record. One committee, of which Governor Jones of Tennessee was chairman and Gadsden, C. C. Clay, and Ellwood Fisher members, reduced the mass to a series of resolutions; and in compliance with one of these Calhoun appointed a five-man committee under Colonel Gadsden to prepare a memorial to Congress.

After the Memphis Convention closed its sessions on Saturday, November 15, Calhoun played host in his rooms at the Gayoso House until far into the night. With graciousness and tact and the disarming simplicity so characteristic of him, he received all visitors. Hundreds of them were ladies, who had been excluded from the convention sittings and so had enjoyed little opportunity during the earlier days of his visit to see one of the most talked-of men in America. There was music and dancing in the hotel, and over the whole an air of gaiety and accomplishment, and perhaps a little of the sense of destiny. The next morning the Carolinian boarded the trim and stately *Maria* once more, and the vessel steamed out into the channel pointing down-river. "His visit," said the Memphis *Eagle,* "has been a most agreeable one to our citizens, and the impressions left behind him . . . are such as have much increased the profound regard entertained towards him by our entire community." [11]

4

The Memphis Convention served to touch off once more the smoldering rebellion against Calhoun's leadership in South Carolina. The day after his election to the Senate, resolutions were offered in the legislature condemning federally financed public works in general and the Memphis proposals in particular. In the subsequent debate Calhoun was a direct target, and the resolutions were tabled only after assurances had been received that the first newspaper reports of his speech were incorrect. The *Mercury* pronounced the Memphis demands a Western raid on the Treasury, and held the doctrine behind them to be the same Federalist-Whig consolidationism that South Carolina had so long and so valiantly opposed under the leadership of her great Senator. It was the same doctrine, according to the editor, as that on which the tariff rested, and the South was weakened in the antitariff battle to precisely the extent that she had now been associated with the philosophy of power.[12]

This highly critical response from his own side of the fence was undoubtedly anticipated by Calhoun, and was probably one of the factors responsible for his relatively long delay in deciding to go to Memphis in the first place. He had no desire to perpetuate the internal dissension in South Carolina, or to turn any substantial portion of the South against his leadership. For almost a score of years he had been striving for sectional unity, and his was hardly likely to be the hand that sowed new seeds of discord if any alternative were possible. What, then, did he expect from the Memphis Convention, that would outweigh the sense of betrayal on the part of those who had learned at his own feet to fear above all things the centralization of power in Washington?

We must remember that Calhoun by 1845 had been obsessed for a decade with one fixed idea. He had convinced himself that the South with all that term implied of culture, homeland, way of life, and livelihood, could survive only with the institution of Negro slavery as its foundation. He believed also that the South could maintain itself economically only under a system of free trade. The renewed impulse given to the abolitionist movement as a consequence of the annexation of Texas, with the able and plausible restating of the issues by Hammond in his Clarkson letters; the Bluffton movement, which threatened disruption of the Union; the equivocal tariff statements of the President and of the administration press—all these things combined to convince Calhoun that the South was in great and imminent danger. He had long been aware that the only hope of destroying the protective policy lay in the concurrence of the West, but free trade was fast coming to be as much in the Western as in the Southern interest, so that no virtue would long remain in such an alliance. For the West to take full advantage of a new and extensive foreign market, however, cheap and convenient transportation was needed—especially transportation that could still be be used in winter when the Great Lakes route was ice-locked.[13]

The Western states would have their internal improvements at government expense sooner or later in any event, because sooner or later they would be strong enough to vote themselves the necessary funds. To give them what they wanted a few years ahead of time would be only to anticipate a little, yet it could create a good will of incalculable value. It could establish free trade, create so brisk an exchange of goods that the revenue even at lower rates of duty would be ample to take care of the expense involved, and above all, it could tie the dominant trans-Mississippi states to the South in interest and in culture, and so preserve domestic slavery. For the Northwestern states, peopled largely by New England stock, already leaned toward the abolitionist side in sentiment, and it was only too clear to so acute a mind as Calhoun's that if the South did not make this gesture to the West, and make it quickly, the Northern states would. In cultural and commercial alliance with the North, the antislavery sentiment would sweep the prairies and the South would be left to choose between slavery and the Union.

All Calhoun's hopes for the perpetuation of that Union now lay in mutual concession within the federal framework, and such he conceived the Memphis program, with its tacit acceptance of tariff reform, to be. The younger men who now challenged his leadership wanted no concessions of any kind and already looked on a separate national existence as preferable for the South. A failure of South and West

to get together now, especially if that failure were precipitated by
Southern men, could result only in giving new impetus to the Bluffton doctrines. Calhoun's alarm was therefore understandable when
the *Southern Quarterly Review,* published in his own state and controlled by men prominent in her affairs, came out in January 1846
with a trenchant criticism of the whole internal improvement scheme
and a thinly veiled attack upon himself for advocating it.[14]

The theme of the article, which set Whigs and Benton Democrats
to chuckling, was the division of power between federal and state
governments as Calhoun himself had expounded it. The argument
was meant to show that the Memphis plans were sectional, not national, in character; that the money to carry them out would come
from the very customs duties that tended to impoverish the South
even while they gave to the North monopoly profits for manufactured
goods; and that they would therefore operate not to improve but
further to impair the fortunes of the South. There were pointed references to "unholy ambition" and to "Memphis politicians," after
which—by way of contrast, we must suppose—there was a long quotation from a five-year-old speech of Francis Pickens, which the
writer professed to believe conclusive on the constitutional question.

Calhoun believed Pickens himself to be the author and was in no
way shaken in his belief when Pickens denied it before he was charged
with the offense. Whether he had had any hand in the matter directly
or not, Pickens admitted having seen the article shortly before its
appearance, and professed to agree with the abstract position taken.
That alone, to Calhoun's mind, was enough to align Pickens with
the Bluffton rebels and to destroy forever after his usefulness as a
lieutenant.[15]

It was only after Congress had actually passed a revenue tariff with
Western votes in July that the South Carolina radicals came to a
tardy realization of Calhoun's purposes and returned, albeit reluctantly, to the shelter of the oak. The *Mercury* led the way, Pickens
followed with indecent haste, and even Rhett retracted in the fall.[16]

5

Calhoun took his seat in the Senate on Monday, December 22,
1845. He had read the President's message on the way to the Capital, and had followed the proceedings of Congress up to that point

so far as the newspaper reports permitted. He knew, therefore, that the Oregon and tariff questions loomed as the major business of the session; and he knew also that he had himself been named in anticipation of his coming as chairman of the important Committee on Finance that would have tariff revision in charge. The state of his health did not permit him to serve, and he was excused on January 7, 1846, on his own motion.[17]

By the time Calhoun himself arrived in Washington, the Senate had been enlarged by two members: David Levy and James D. Westcott, Jr., from Florida. Levy, who by act of the Florida legislature would thenceforth be called David Levy Yulee, had been Territorial Delegate in the past two Congresses. The Texas Senators, Thomas Jefferson Rusk who was a native of Pendleton, South Carolina, where he had been a protégé of Calhoun's, and Sam Houston, did not take their seats until the end of March 1846, when the final details of annexation were completed. Iowa had not yet adopted a constitution, and would send no Senators to Washington until the Thirtieth Congress. The Senate thus boasted for the first and only time in its history an actual preponderance of members from slaveholding states.

Calhoun presented Gadsden's Memphis Memorial on February 3, 1846. He praised the ability with which the document was drawn up and noted the importance of the matters with which it dealt, but qualified his approval with becoming caution. There were recommendations in it which he held to be outside the constitutional power of Congress, and there were others with which he simply did not agree. He then asked that it be referred to a select committee of five members. Vice President Dallas appointed the committee with Calhoun himself as chairman, the others being David R. Atchison of Missouri, James Semple of Illinois, Alexander Barrow of Louisiana, and Joseph W. Chalmers of Mississippi. It was a committee "well inclined to carry out all the leading views of the Convention." [18]

It was also a committee well inclined to follow the lead of its chairman. Its report, presented late in June, was unanimous but it was entirely Calhoun's work.

The long delay between the referral of the Memphis Memorial and the report on it was owing to the great pressure of other matters, which will be the theme of succeeding chapters. Through February, March, and April Congress debated the Oregon question with its persistent threat of war with England; and in May the government faced an actual war with Mexico. On each of these questions Calhoun had positive views, and in all the discussions he took a leading part. It was therefore about the first of June before he found time to work on the Memphis report. He was interrupted again by the final settlement of the Oregon controversy in the middle of that month, but had his long, detailed report ready for presentation on June 26. One would never guess to read it that it was written as the country narrowly escaped one war crisis and plunged headlong into another.[19]

The Memphis Memorial itself was only an elaboration of the resolutions of the convention, with suitable arguments bearing on the need for the various improvements asked. Calhoun largely ignored it in his report, developing instead a detailed statistical and constitutional basis for the recommendations he had himself made in his Memphis address. There was a brief summary of the memorial, since it offered the only excuse for the committee's existence, but the rest was pure Calhoun.

The bulk of it was devoted to establishing the power of the Federal Government to improve the navigation of the Mississippi and its principal tributaries. To this great river network, offering cheap and easy transportation, Calhoun attributed the spectacular growth of the valley in the past half century. He forecast continued growth and progress to equal or exceed that of any other spot on the globe if only the waterways were kept clear of obstructions and open for navigation to an ever growing flotilla of steamboats. On the point of what should be done, he found no disagreement. The only problem was who should do it.

Clearly the improvement of the river system was beyond the power of individuals; and it was equally beyond the power of the states, if they acted separately. Yet they could not act together without violating the constitutional prohibition against entering into any "treaty, alliance or confederation." If the power existed at all, and it must exist since it was necessary and had been exercised in the past, it must belong to the Federal Government. Calhoun then went on to examine the possible basis for Federal authority to improve river navigation, and found what he sought in the power to "regulate commerce with foreign nations and among the several States." He explored the meaning of the terms by determining what functions had been performed under this heading in the days of the Confederation, and concluded that supplying aids to navigation was foremost among them. That brought him to his Memphis rationalization, that the Mississippi with its major tributaries was a sort of inland sea, and that whatever powers the general government possessed with respect to navigation extended to the great river system even as they had long since been conceded to extend to the Great Lakes. It followed that snags and rocks could be removed from the Mississippi under the same power by which lighthouses were established and harbors protected by jetties and breakwaters along the Atlantic coast.

Accompanying Calhoun's report was a bill providing for the creation of a three-man board of engineers, one to be of the army and two from civil life, who were to survey the Mississippi and its major tributaries to determine in what way navigation was obstructed and how it might be improved. There was also in the bill a provision for the gradual reduction of the price of inundated or overflowed public lands in the states bordering the river.[20]

6

River and harbor improvements already formed the subject of two bills then pending in the Senate. Both of them arose more or less directly, as had Calhoun's report, out of the proceedings of the Memphis Convention, but neither realized the objectives the South Carolina Senator sought. The first was a bill to provide for improving navigation of the Ohio, Mississippi, Missouri, and Arkansas rivers, introduced by John J. Crittenden, the veteran Kentucky Whig. The other was a masterpiece of old-fashioned pork-barrel politics from the House, embracing individual projects from Maine to the headwaters of the Missouri and from the Great Lakes to the Gulf, to a total cost of nearly a million and a half dollars.[21]

Also awaiting action in the Senate was a bill to graduate the price of the public lands, another measure for which Western members had been pressing insistently for two decades. The land bill had been discussed in Committee of the Whole only twice before Calhoun's report on the Memphis Memorial. When it came up again Calhoun moved to strike out everything after the enacting clause and substitute a new bill, remarkably like the scheme he had fathered back in Van Buren's time. It provided for an immediate reduction in the price of lands that had been on the market for ten years, a further reduction of price for those that still remained unsold after another three years had passed, and so on by increments. Those still unsold on March 1, 1859, were to be ceded to the states. John M. Clayton, with the backing of the whole Whig contingent, secured deletion of the provision for final cession to the states, but with that alteration Calhoun's amendment was adopted on July 8, and the next day the bill was passed by 25 to 19.[22]

On July 13, a little more than two weeks after Calhoun's report on the Memphis Memorial and four days after passage of the graduation bill, Crittenden's proposal for improvement of the Mississippi and its main tributaries came up for debate. Calhoun moved that it be tabled, as his own bill covered the subject in better form, but Crittenden objected that there was probably not time left to pass the South Carolinian's version, whereas the bill before the Senate was too familiar to require debate. Calhoun then withdrew his motion, and proposed to amend the Kentuckian's bill by adding to it the first two sections of his own, namely, the provision for a survey and that for defraying the expenses thereof. The amendment was accepted by the Senate without a roll call, and the bill then passed by 32 to 12.[23]

The following day the Senate bill was forced to a quick vote in the House on motion of Hannibal Hamlin of Maine that it be rejected. "A bill," the caustic Adams called it, "for the improvement of the Ohio, Missouri, Mississippi, and Arkansas inland seas—a notable device of the political mountebank John C. Calhoun." It was not on that ground, however, that the House rejected it promptly and overwhelmingly, but because their own rivers and harbors bill already passed covered the same ground and much, much more.[24]

Ten days later the House pork-barrel version was adopted in the Senate by a thumping majority of better than two to one, with Calhoun voting "no." Within a week the tariff reduction also passed, but the South-West alliance was not thereby concluded. The rivers and harbors bill was not the *quid pro quo* the West had been promised for antitariff votes, but a wholesale grab for Federal funds. Polk held it the full ten days allowed him while the tariff revision was forced through the Senate. Then he returned it without his signature. The House retaliated by tabling the graduation bill. The Western men felt they had been cheated by the South and inevitably turned to the free states for an offer. The Northern price was the exclusion of slavery from the territories.[25]

CHAPTER XVIII

OREGON AND FREE TRADE

1

IT WAS the threat of war over Oregon rather than concern about the tariff that brought Calhoun back to the Senate, but both problems were in his mind, and in the minds of those who urged the step upon him. It could hardly have been otherwise, for the two were so closely interrelated as to be almost mutually interdependent. Both were closely connected, also, with the repeal of the Corn Laws, with internal transportation, and with the more general question of the future relations between Great Britain and the United States. At the time that Polk took over the reins of government from Tyler these various elements in the pattern of Anglo-American relations were beginning to merge and the final crisis was drawing near.

The text of Polk's inaugural address reached England on April 1, 1845, and precipitated the sharp reaction we have already noted. The moderation of the new President's tariff references, however, struck a more responsive chord. In May and June Corn Law repeal was again discussed, but without any action being taken. In July Louis McLane presented his credentials as United States Minister to the Court of St. James's; and on the twelfth of that month, in Washington, Buchanan offered to settle the Oregon boundary at the forty-ninth parallel. The face-saving device for Polk, in this case, was the fact that the United States on three previous occasions going back to 1818 had offered this same boundary, and the President could therefore consider himself committed by the acts of his predecessors in spite of his own assertion of title up to 54° 40'. This offer Richard Pakenham, the British Minister in Washington, took it upon himself to reject without referring it to his government, although he had been privately directed by Aberdeen more than a year earlier to seek just such a settlement. On Polk's orders Buchanan reluctantly withdrew the offer on August 30, and again the Oregon question threatened war. This was the situation that brought Calhoun back to the Senate.[1]

Pakenham had not yet informed his government of the abrupt termination of the Oregon negotiations, when the Secretary of the Treasury told him plainly that the duties were to be reduced. Walker explained for the Britisher's benefit that recent elections had insured a clear majority for the administation in the House, and there was a small majority in the Senate. He left Pakenham with the definite impression that it would be easier and more certain if Great Britain would agree to admit maize or Indian corn without duty. Pakenham passed all this along to his government in the same mail that carried Buchanan's note of August 30 withdrawing the offer to settle the Oregon boundary at 49°. Aberdeen and Peel were both distressed by this turn of events, and blamed Pakenham for his failure to refer the matter to them, but Walker's hint offered a possible way out of the impasse.[2]

By the time these dispatches reached the Foreign Office at the end of September, it was known in London that the Irish potato crop had failed and that a serious food shortage threatened. Possible courses of action were already under discussion when Aberdeen broached the question of waiving the duties on maize by an Order in Council. Peel felt that Parliament would have to be called if such a step were to be taken, but he did not see how the duties on wheat could in such a case be maintained. When the Cabinet met on October 31 Peel had resolved to go all the way, and suggested suspension of the Corn Laws, with legislation to be introduced into the next Parliament to make the repeal permanent over a period of time. The Cabinet demurred, then met again on November 6, still without agreement. On November 22 came the famous letter to the Electors of London in which Lord John Russell, leader of the opposition, denounced the Corn Laws and called on the Government to take steps to avert famine. A few days later the Cabinet reconvened, and after a week of discussion Peel offered an outline of the specific repeal measures he had in mind. The next day Aberdeen wrote once more to Pakenham, assuring him that an Oregon settlement could yet be worked out. "Many things," he wrote, "may shortly occur to improve the prospect of affairs very considerably. The access of Indian corn to our markets would go far to pacify the warriors of the Western States."[3]

Aberdeen's optimism was premature, for Peel had not fully reckoned with his party. Protection had been identified with the Tories too long to be lightly cast aside by a Tory Prime Minister. Lord Stanley, the Colonial Secretary, threatened to resign, and Peel realized that he could not carry out the contemplated reform. He therefore tendered his own resignation on December 5, 1845.

2

In the United States, meanwhile, the policy of the Polk administration had taken definite shape, thoroughgoing in favor of free trade but uncompromising on the Oregon issue. In both instances the course of events in England was tacitly if not overtly a factor. News of the British food crisis, in exaggerated and therefore all the more impressive form, reached New York on October 28. Three days later the Washington *Union,* with the full force of the party in power behind it, launched a propaganda drive for all of Oregon. Polk certainly knew by that date, both through Pakenham and through McLane in London, that the British Government would welcome an opening for renewal of the Oregon negotiations. The President simply realized as clearly as did Aberdeen and Peel that Pakenham's unfortunate failure to refer Buchanan's July offer to his government had left the Americans in the better position; and the news from England probably convinced him that country was in no position to fight for Oregon. He was, as he later expressed it, looking John Bull "straight in the eye," having first made sure that the bull was hobbled.[4]

The party press generally followed the lead of the *Union,* and "fifty-four-forty or fight" was soon firing the enthusiasm of young men from Maine to Iowa. Except as a pure piece of propaganda for bargaining purposes, however, the whole business was quite inconsistent with the pacific nature of the report that the Secretary of the Treasury read to the Cabinet November 11, with its heavy emphasis on free trade and particularly on the prospects for an increasingly important commerce with Great Britain.[5]

Walker's report went to Congress on December 3, and the bulk of its twenty pages of text constituted as forthright a free-trade document as could have been asked by either Cobden or Calhoun. The basic principle laid down was that no duty should be imposed on any article "above the lowest rate which will yield the largest amount of revenue." Below this point there might be discrimination downward, but the objectionable word "protection" was not used, and all duties were to be levied as a percentage of actual market value. The whole revenue system, moreover, was to be so designed "as to operate as equally as possible throughout the Union, discriminating neither for nor against any class or section." [6]

Walker demonstrated, lucidly and unanswerably, that there could be no flat horizontal scale because the maximum revenue duty would necessarily vary from article to article. Then followed a discourse on the economics of international trade, ending with a denial that tariffs were necessary to countervail those of foreign countries. On the contrary, in the Secretary's view an example of free trade in one country would almost necessarily be followed by others. "If we reduce our tariff, the party opposed to the corn laws of England would soon prevail, and admit all our agricultural products at all times freely into her ports, in exchange for her exports. And if England would now repeal her duties upon our wheat, flour, Indian corn, and other agricultural products, our own restrictive system would certainly be doomed to overthrow." He noted with satisfaction that England was already moving toward free trade, and insisted that "her present bad harvest, if accompanied by a reduction of our tariff, would lead to the repeal of her corn laws, and the unrestricted admission, at all times, of our agricultural products."

For the time being the tariff question rested there, with a declaration of good intentions on the part of the President and friendly committees in House and Senate. The Oregon question was more pressing.

3

Calhoun, not yet in Washington, agreed that the "present scarcity of provision in Europe" would greatly improve the chances of substantial tariff reduction, but Oregon was another matter. "I cannot doubt," he wrote to his brother-in-law, "if the recommendation of the Message be carried out into acts, the termination will be war with England." [7]

When he reached the Capital on December 20 Calhoun found ample matter for confirming both his judgments. As earnest of tariff reform he had himself been elected chairman of the Senate Committee on Finance, with Dixon H. Lewis as the ranking member who would succeed to the chairmanship on Calhoun's withdrawal. But two days before the Carolinian's arrival William Allen of Ohio, chairman of the Committee on Foreign Relations and high priest of the "54-40's," had introduced a joint resolution authorizing the Executive to give formal notice abrogating the treaty of joint occupancy. On the same day David R. Atchison of Missouri moved a series of resolutions looking toward effective occupation and government of Oregon; and these were followed by a more bellicose version in the House, from the hand of Stephen A. Douglas of Illinois.[8]

There were other resolutions and motions on the subject in both houses but the effect of them all would be the same. Unless the British quietly withdrew from Oregon, war could hardly be avoided. Calhoun certainly looked on these various moves to carry out the recommendations of the President in that light, and every mail that came in from North, or West, or South brought additional evidence that conservative men the country over expected him to interpose. It was high tribute to his character, his abilities, and his prestige, and he set out without delay to justify it, so far as lay in his power.[9]

On the night of December 20, only a few hours after his arrival, Isaac Holmes and Robert M. T. Hunter called on Calhoun, to brief him on the course events were taking. They believed that the Democratic members of both houses would uphold unanimously the President's claim to all of Oregon, and they were convinced Calhoun would be isolated and his usefulness to the South destroyed unless he too went along with the administration program. Calhoun did not see it that way. He had come back to the Senate to prevent war over Oregon. Pacifically minded men throughout the land expected him to prevent it, and so far as one individual could influence the fate of nations he meant to keep faith with himself and with those who relied on him. He must, therefore, however reluctantly, in this particular oppose the avowed purposes of the administration. By midnight when the two visitors left both had been converted. The former Speaker carried the word to his Virginia colleagues, and won from them a pledge of support. Holmes went to the Whig leaders on the Senate side, and before Congress reconvened at noon on Monday he had received assurances that if Calhoun would take the lead they would support him.[10]

As early on Monday morning December 22 as the proprieties permitted, Calhoun called on the President. "He appeared to be in a fine humour," Polk noted. But the South Carolina Senator intended more than a courtesy call, and he soon had the conversation turned to Oregon. He stated his own objections to denouncing the existing treaty, and asked the President to restrain the warlike enthusiasm of his followers. Polk, tight-lipped and secretive as he always was, agreed to nothing and promised nothing, but he confided to his diary that night his belief that Calhoun would soon be in opposition to the administration.[11]

For the next few days Calhoun was very busy outside the Senate chamber, seeking to delay aggressive action and to bring about a resumption of the interrupted Oregon negotiations. Veteran press correspondents in Washington, and the President himself, believed that leading men from both West and South had fallen in with the South Carolinian's views. It was probably also at his instigation, directly or through others, that Senator William S. Archer, former chairman of the Foreign Relations Committee and now its ranking Whig member, and William W. Corcoran, powerful Washington banker, called on Pakenham. Both assured the British Minister that an offer from his government to fix the boundary at 49°, with all of Vancouver Island to be British and free navigation of the Columbia for a term of years, would be referred by the President to the Senate, and would there be approved. Pakenham was the more ready to believe it because he was sure Corcoran spoke for a member of the Cabinet, and because Benton assured him that he would support such a treaty. There was already a noticeable change of atmosphere when Congress resumed its sittings on December 27, after the Christmas recess, and Calhoun's move to gain time by referring Atchison's resolutions to the Committee on Foreign Relations was unopposed.[12]

On the next legislative day, Monday, December 29, Hannegan offered resolutions similar to those that Douglas had tossed into the hopper in the House. The Senate version declared that all the country west of the Rockies and lying between 42° and 54°40′ was a part of the territory of the United States; that the government possessed no power to alienate the soil or transfer the allegiance of United States citizens; and that to give up any portion of Oregon would be to abandon the "honor, character, and the best interests of the American people." Hannegan called them up the next day, and asked that they be made the special order for a week later. Archer asked further delay, and Hannegan obligingly changed his motion to make it the third Monday in January. Then, at Calhoun's request, the motion was withdrawn, and the South Carolina Senator took the floor.[13]

Calhoun pointed out the dangerous implications of Hannegan's position, and its complete inconsistency with the many previous efforts that had been made to divide the territory in equitable fashion. He proposed a substitute set of resolutions which affirmed the power of the President and Senate to make treaties, and declared that the treaty-making power extended to boundary questions. As for Oregon itself, Calhoun's version stated calmly that there were conflicting claims to the territory, which had been a frequent subject of negotiation; that these claims might be adjusted by treaty; and that the President, in renewing lately an offer to fix the boundary at 49°, was within his constitutional powers. In the ensuing debate there was "some snarling" from the Western members, but the reporters who knew the Senate best counted a clear majority for pacific measures. When the views of the contestants had been sufficiently aired both sets of resolutions were tabled on Hannegan's motion. Pakenham was particularly gratified with Calhoun's remarks on this occasion, and not less so with the "long and friendly conversation" between the two men shortly thereafter.[14]

Calhoun was now sure of his own power to manage things so as to avoid a clash, but for the sake of the tariff reform he held to be essential to Southern prosperity, he sought to conciliate both the West and the administration. On the evening of January 4, 1846, Representative James A. Black of South Carolina made an unscheduled but urgent call at the White House, and Polk departed from his customary practice to see him. Black pointed out the danger of a split in the Democratic ranks over the termination of joint occupancy in Oregon. He gave the President to understand that if the notice was not pressed the South would support the other recommendations of the message, including land grants to Oregon settlers with provision for adjustment after a boundary should have been fixed. He did not say he came from Calhoun, but Polk had no doubt of it. The President replied only that he had fully expressed his views in his annual message, and had not altered them. It was in this interview that he made the classic remark about looking John Bull in the eye.[15]

For the next week the Senate was occupied with other matters, and on January 10 Calhoun himself called on the President. He argued powerfully that giving notice would be interpreted as closing the door to compromise, while the President maintained his own belief that Britain would yield only to a show of strength. They were still debating the point when members of the Cabinet began to assemble for their regular meeting. On Polk's invitation the South Carolina Senator remained, and the discussion continued on a more detailed basis. Calhoun's position, reduced to its essentials, was that the British claim under the Nootka Sound convention was not valid; but that the American claim under the Spanish Treaty of 1819 was not valid either, north of the Columbia Valley. The clearest title was that gained by discovery and settlement, and on this basis the British title to the Fraser River watershed was as good as that of the United States to the Columbia basin. The obvious compromise was to draw a line between the two rivers, which coincided neatly with 49°.[16]

Again Calhoun met with no response other than a polite willingness to listen to his views, and so he prepared to move in his own way. By argument on the floor and quiet persuasion outside the halls of Congress he had already won enough Senators to his position to risk a test vote, and it was taken on Monday, January 12. The question at issue was fixing a time for debating Allen's resolution to terminate joint occupancy. Allen suggested January 27. The newly formed bipartisan bloc that stood for delay substituted February 10, and by a smashing vote of 32 to 18 they carried it. "The future," wrote Webster that evening, "may & will, probably, much depend on what we hear by the next steamer." [17]

4

In England events had been moving rapidly toward a climax. Sir Robert Peel's resignation on December 5, 1845, was followed by an invitation to Lord John Russell to form a Ministry. The Whig leader realized, however, that he would have to work without a majority, and he waited a full week, during which there were many

conferences with members of the outgoing government, before he
consented. Then, on December 20, Russell informed the Queen that
he could not form a Cabinet. The stumbling block, though he did
not say so, was Lord Palmerston's refusal to accept any post but
the Foreign Office, where his aggressiveness and truculence had been
a constant embarrassment to his colleagues of the old Melbourne
government. Peel was perforce asked to try again, and a new Tory
Cabinet was formed with Gladstone replacing the uncompromising
Stanley as Colonial Secretary.[18]

None of this was yet known in the United States when Edward
Everett wrote to Lord John Russell just before the end of the year.
Everett's term as United States Minister in London had given him
an understanding of both party politics and personalities in Britain,
and from the detachment of private life he wrote to the leader of
the opposition as to a friend. His theme was the supreme importance
to both countries of an amicable adjustment of the Oregon dispute,
and the reasonableness of a settlement on the forty-ninth parallel to
the sea. He wanted Russell to assure Peel in advance that the Whigs
would approve such an arrangement, and thus keep the issue above
politics. At the same time but without collusion Duff Green wrote
to John McGregor, Canadian-born Secretary to the Board of Trade
and an economist of note. Green urged on the Tory officeholder as
Everett did on the Whig chief the importance of compromising the
Oregon dispute at 49°, but added as Everett did not that repeal of the
Corn Laws would make it easier for the United States to accept that
line.[19]

By the time these letters were delivered the Peel Ministry had fallen
and had been reinstated; Parliament had met; and a bill to repeal the
Corn Laws had been introduced by the Government. Russell was
already bound by his own acts and the traditional tenets of his party
to support Corn Law repeal; and he had already taken a stand on
Oregon by rebuking Pakenham in the House of Commons for his
summary rejection of the American compromise offer. He passed
Everett's letter along to Palmerston, but he did not wait for the negative reply he knew would come before he gave his own assurances
to Aberdeen that Oregon would not be regarded as a party issue. To
the leaders of both parties in England the substantial modification
of the American tariff was worth more than a few hundred square
miles of wilderness. The crop failures of the past fall revealed an

alarming dependence on imported foodstuffs; they were already dependent on imported cotton; and the United States badly needed the iron rails that British manufacturers had learned to make in overabundance. It was time to compromise.[20]

Thereafter the British problem was how to find an opening for resuming the Oregon negotiations, while the American problem, from the point of view of Calhoun and his conservative following, was how to delay aggressive action until the opening had been found.

On January 19, 1846, by telegraph from Baltimore where the news had come in part by rail and in part by wire, Washington learned of the fall of the Peel Ministry. The telegraph message, received at one in the afternoon, was rushed immediately to the White House. That evening the *Union* carried full details as set forth in the British press up to December 13, 1845. The next news came on the *Hibernia* which docked in Boston January 22. The enterprising James Gordon Bennett had arranged a special express relay system, and had the whole story in the New York *Herald* on Saturday morning, January 24. Official Washington knew that night that Peel had returned to power in circumstances that seemed to mean the certain repeal of the Corn Laws. The same steamer also brought official diplomatic correspondence and private letters, including dispatches from McLane to Buchanan and a long unofficial letter to Calhoun.[21]

McLane expressed his pleasure that Calhoun was back in the Senate at so critical a time, and for the South Carolinian's future use he gave a full résumé of attitudes and reactions in Great Britain. He thought the "tough" tone of Polk's message had made an impression that would on the whole tend in the direction of peace. Aberdeen was prepared for the giving of notice, and looked on such a step by Congress as favorable. It would, at least, allow a year for settlement. McLane made much of the growing interest in reciprocal trade between the two countries, and gave it as his conviction that a settlement on the basis of the forty-ninth parallel, with some modifications, would be accepted.[22]

Calhoun had already determined on his own strategy. He realized that the notice was certain to pass, but it could be so amended as to invite reopening of negotiations. McLane's letter confirmed him in this approach, but there were still dangers of which he was only too well aware. There was a rising bitterness between the "54-40's" and the "49's." The support for Calhoun's position, while it was substan-

JOHN C. CALHOUN IN 1845
by Clark Mills

YOUNG YANKEE-NOODLE TEACHING GRAND-
MOTHER BRITANNIA TO SUCK EGGS.

A British jibe at the Oregon settlement, from *Punch*, 1846

tial, came from a combination of Southern Democrats who were decidedly antitariff and Whigs like Webster and Clayton and Crittenden who were last-ditch protectionists. Yet the Oregon settlement was so intimately bound up with free trade that the press in both countries discussed them as though they were mutually interdependent. Most dangerous of all, thoroughgoing abolitionists like Adams and Giddings, though classed as Whigs, led the fight for all of Oregon in the House, and avowed frankly that they hoped thereby to counterbalance Texas and add to the preponderance of free soil.[23]

Despite this confusion of purposes, and a steady pressure from the administration, a qualifying clause was added in the House to the resolution giving notice to terminate joint occupancy. On February 7 a dispatch from McLane was sent in, carefully expurgated to give a threatening rather than a pacific view of British sentiment, and the House was kept in session for fourteen hours in an effort to drive through the notice in unmodified form. But Hunter, Holmes, and others of the Calhoun bloc held their ground and prevented action. When the members resumed their seats on Monday, February 9, the warlike mood had passed. The resolution was amended to declare that "nothing herein contained is intended to interfere with the right and discretion of the proper authorities of the two contracting parties to renew or pursue negotiations for an amicable settlement of the controversy respecting the Oregon territory." It was then passed by a margin of three to one.[24]

5

In the Senate where debate began on February 10 the extremes were represented by Hannegan's resolutions declaring all of Oregon to be United States soil, not disposable by the President or Congress; and by Calhoun's countering declaration that it was within the constitutional power of the Executive, with the advice and consent of the Senate, to determine a boundary by treaty. Inevitably the whole question was lumped for purposes of debate, the real issues being, first, whether the notice should be given at all; and second, if it was given, whether it should be in the naked form proposed by Allen, in modified form as adopted by the House, or in some such form as that offered by Crittenden, which amounted to an instruction to the President to resume negotiations.[25]

Each point of view had its advocates, in a Senate of unusual ability. Lewis Cass, whose surprisingly strong bid for the Democratic Presidential nomination in 1844 had given him high rank among the party leaders, joined Allen and Hannegan in the camp of the "54-40's." Calhoun led a combination of Whigs and Southern Democrats against notice in any shape, lest war result and the consequence be the collapse of the elaborate free-trade structure that now seemed so close to completion. Benton, who saw the Western leadership slipping from his own hands to those of Cass, became a peace-loving moderate— a position the easier to take because he privately agreed with Calhoun's analysis that the British title to the Fraser River was as good as the American title to the Columbia. There were Whigs like Crittenden who realized the great importance of national unity in international affairs, and Democrats who understood the value of party regularity even at the expense of personal conviction. The stage was set for a slashing factional battle, with the mitigating circumstance the very general belief among the people at large that a fair compromise ought to be made.[26]

The next news from England reached Washington on February 20, a group of New York papers having intercepted the mail packet at Halifax. The Queen's speech from the Throne at the opening of Parliament was pacific in tone, and Peel's program, with its unequivocal demand for repeal of the Corn Laws, was pronounced by the *Union* to be "one of the most victorious vindications of the freedom of commerce" ever seen. Polk and his Cabinet agreed on the peaceful character of the news, while the Whig press wailed that peace was to be purchased at the cost of the American manufacturer. John Quincy Adams, now nearing the end of his long and stormy career, expressed it better than any of the editors. "It is evident," he wrote in his diary, "that the Oregon question will be settled by the repeal of the corn laws and the sacrifice of the American tariff; a bargain, both sides of which will be for the benefit of England, and to our disadvantage." [27]

By the same steamer came the usual diplomatic dispatches and private letters. McLane reported at length an interview of January 29 with Aberdeen at the latter's request. The American Minister was sure that the boundary adjustment so often privately discussed on both sides of the water would be accepted. He thought Aberdeen might even propose it, if there were any assurance that it would be well received in the United States, and if a suitable opening for renewal of negotiations could be made. At the same time McLane wrote privately to Calhoun, enclosing English papers with accounts of the proceedings in Parliament, and repeating his own conviction that the policy recommended by Polk in his annual message would not be regarded in Britain as warlike. "On the contrary it might do great good; whereas a refusal by Congress to sustain the President would have a mischievous tendency. There will be a year after the notice to settle the question, and unless one side be *bent* on war that *cannot* be difficult." [28]

Undoubtedly influenced by McLane's views and by the whole tenor of the advices from England, Calhoun and those who followed his lead considered the strategy of seeking to push a resolution through the Senate in Executive session, advising the President to reopen negotiations on the basis of compromise, or specifically on the basis of 49°. Calhoun and Webster both discussed the matter with Pakenham, and both were sure that such a resolution would pass by a very large majority. Calhoun, however, was unwilling to make the move without taking the President into his confidence. Polk objected on the ground that it would tie his hands, but he had already been warned by Senator Haywood of North Carolina, an old personal friend of his college days, that Benton would oppose any such move to keep Calhoun from getting credit for it.[29]

The President condemned Calhoun's course roundly, seeing nothing in it but political ambition; but Buchanan's next dispatch to McLane showed the impact of the South Carolinian's power in the Senate. The Secretary of State notified the American Minister, for Aberdeen's benefit, that the door to compromise was still open, and that any reasonable proposition, such as the forty-ninth parallel, would be submitted to the Senate regardless of the President's personal views. A private letter accompanied the official one, and intimated that whatever offer the British might make, providing only that it did not include perpetual navigation of the Columbia, would be shown to the Senate in advance of the signing of a treaty.[30]

The same vessel carried Pakenham's reports, including his estimate that "a very gratifying sensation" had followed the publication in the United States of the "intended alterations in the Commercial Policy of England." By way of reciprocity Pakenham enclosed a manuscript copy of Walker's as yet unpublished tariff bill, and the letter by which the Secretary of the Treasury had transmitted it to him. "The Cotemporaneous and reciprocal reduction of the British & American Tariff," Walker explained, "would be an event more important in securing the blessings of peace, and advancing the best interests of mankind, than any which has occurred during the present Century." [31]

The debate moved slowly along for another two weeks, revealing a dangerous tendency toward party disintegration along sectional and economic lines and an unwholesome lack of confidence between President and Senate. An apparent stalemate had been reached by March 12 when Calhoun indicated that he would speak on the Oregon question at the next sitting, which would be Monday, March 16, 1846. The galleries were already overflowing, the rotunda and anterooms were full, and disappointed hundreds had been turned away by nine o'clock of the appointed day, though the Senate did not meet until noon and would have still an hour or so of business before reaching the special order.[32]

Calhoun's purpose when he took the floor was to find a common ground on which the contending factions could unite. The President's message, he argued, was clearly premised on the belief that after Pakenham's rejection of the American offer of 49°, no compromise was possible; but the course of events since December, both in Britain and in the United States, revealed a new willingness to adjust the question. If as now appeared an equitable boundary settlement could be drawn by mutual agreement, the year's notice to terminate the existing arrangement, if given in conciliatory language, would constitute an invitation to negotiate, and as such would command his support.

To save face for the President rather than for himself, he urged eloquently that true consistency was to act in accordance with circumstances, rather than to cling obstinately to the same position when circumstances changed. His own policy of "wise and masterly inactivity" would in time have won the whole country through settlement, but that policy had not been followed and the issue had been joined so that now there remained only compromise or war. He devoted a few minutes to painting a vivid picture of the horror and cost of a conflict that might well last for years only to end in so altering the form of the government that victory itself would be defeat. The alternative picture was a vast panorama of material progress, through perfection and extension of the new forces already revolutionizing the world—the forces let loose by steam transportation on land and sea, and the magic of communication by electricity. He saw his country in no long space of years dominating the commerce of both oceans and perhaps controlling the destinies of the world.[33]

The immediate response was electrifying, but the President was resentful and a little sullen. First to congratulate Calhoun on the Senate floor was Hannegan, who shared with Cass and Allen the leadership of the "54-40's," and others were close behind. Duff Green, with the partiality of long intimacy, pronounced it "the crowning effort of your eventful life." Parke Godwin, already widely known for his contributions to the New York *Evening Post* and to the *Democratic Review,* wrote with equal fervor: "Had you done nothing else to deserve well of your country, . . . your efforts to prevent the awful calamities of war would have raised you an eternal monument in all noble minds." The *Mercury* was unstinting in its praise, and the able Washington correspondent of the *Courier,* a few days after the event, wrote that Calhoun's appeal had settled the question and that notice in conciliatory form would now be passed. The directors of the New York and Boston Magnetic Telegraph Association voted him their thanks for his appreciative reference to telegraphic communication in his "eloquent & patriotic speech upon the Oregon question." For weeks the messages of praise continued, and a majority of them came from the North.[34]

The pacific effect was heightened by the news from England, published in Washington on March 20, that Corn Law repeal had passed the House of Commons late in February with a margin for the Government of nearly a hundred votes. Indeed, the impetus to compromise was almost more than Polk could withstand. The *Union,* nevertheless, renewed its attacks upon the Senate dissidents and demanded once more that notice be given without any qualification. For another month the administration and its Senate supporters kept the argument alive, but it was a losing battle. On April 16 the House version of the notice was amended and passed. In its final form a preamble recited the circumstances of joint occupancy, and proclaimed it desirable "that the respective claims of the United States and Great Britain should be definitely settled." The President was then authorized "at his discretion" to give the notice, but the reason for giving it was clearly stated to be "that the attention of the Governments of both countries may be the more earnestly and immediately directed to renewed efforts for the amicable settlement of all their differences and disputes in respect to said territory." The vote on the amended resolution was 40 to 14.[35]

6

While the Senate debated the Oregon question between early February and mid-April 1846, the House Committee on Ways and Means was occupied with the related question of tariff reform. The Secretary of the Treasury himself directed the strategy, with a nice sense of timing and a very shrewd insight into the factors involved. Walker had called to his aid experienced officers, without regard to party or economic predilection, from the larger customhouses, and for months they had been quietly at work seeking to determine on the basis of experience, past customs receipts, and the responses to questionnaires, the maximum revenue duty for each separate item of import—the point, that is, beyond which importation of the article would fall off and the revenue decline.[36]

As the schedules neared completion the press took up the subject. The *Democratic Review* set the tone in its February issue with a sweeping indictment of the whole protectionist system. The *Union* followed with a column and a half on February 14 in praise of Walker's December report, and the announcement that a bill, prepared with "great care, and precision, and clearness" by the joint efforts of the Treasury Department and the Committee on Ways and Means, would be reported in a few days.[37]

The expectation was overoptimistic, reflecting rather the administration's hopes as to the passage of the Oregon notice than any time schedule for the tariff bill itself. Walker did not want the question debated on the floor until the fate of Corn Law repeal was known, and Polk did not want attention diverted from the Oregon issue. The bill was therefore kept closely guarded in committee, and all attempts to print it for the use of the members were voted down lest there be a leak to the press. The terms of Peel's free-trade proposals reached Washington, as we have noted, on February 20, and the same mail brought word that Walker's report had been reprinted in England as a Parliamentary document. On February 21 the *Union* called on the Democratic party to respond in kind, and even to set an example for the mother country. It was on February 25 that Walker furnished

Pakenham with a manuscript copy of the tariff bill, as given to the Committee on Ways and Means, to be forwarded by the March 1 mail steamer to London, but still the bill was not published nor brought onto the floor of the House.[38]

The same silence prevailed when the next mails from England brought word late in March that the Corn Law repeal had passed the Commons. There were rumors of changes and modifications, even of disagreements between McKay and Walker. New England textile manufacturers and Pennsylvania ironmasters were descending in numbers upon Washington to lobby for protection, and on the other side an exhibition of British goods was displayed in a Capitol committee room. The *National Intelligencer* led the Whig press in what began to assume the proportions of a crusade to retain protective duties, and friends of free trade wondered if the long delay was not a deliberate sellout. But the truth was that the fate of the tariff was too closely joined to the Oregon question to be debated before some settlement of the Northwestern boundary was in sight.[39]

By early April the administration was apparently satisfied as to Oregon. Polk had determined to consult the Senate on any British proposition approximating those discussed by the advocates of compromise, and the advices from London indicated that a proposition would be made whenever the notice was received there. The Senate debate was drawing to a close, and the country was impatient to see the tariff schedules.[40]

McKay introduced the long-awaited bill on April 14. Spirits and cordials were to pay ad valorem duties of 75 percent. Other articles were divided into categories paying ad valorem duties of 30, 25, 20, 15, 10, and 5 percent. There was a free list, and a provision that articles not specifically mentioned should pay 20 percent. There could be, and were, objections from free-trade men, but they were minor matters of detail. On the whole the bill was theirs, and they recognized it as such. So did the protectionists, and before the second reading could be called for, a motion to reject was made, only to be voted down. McKay declined to set a day for commencing the debate, and the matter rested once more.[41]

The *Union* launched a full-scale propaganda drive to put the bill over, and predicted that debate would begin about May 1. The prediction again proved erroneous. The Charleston *Mercury* presently got out of hand, and Ritchie read it out of the party on May 6. It was about that date that news from Mexico became critical, and the sudden outbreak of hostilities served both to drive tariff arguments from the papers and to produce still further delay. It was late in May before the campaign for tariff reform was resumed, culminating in a caucus agreement on the evening of May 29 that the Walker-McKay bill would be brought to the floor June 8. The date was almost immediately changed to June 15, and so it transpired.[42]

At noon that same June 15 the *Great Western* docked in New York with word that Corn Law repeal had passed its crucial test in the House of Lords, and thanks to the telegraph the word reached Washington before Congress adjourned for the day.[43]

7

The opening of the tariff debate in the House also coincided exactly with the final settlement of the Oregon dispute. It was none too soon.

After a conference committee had agreed on the Senate version of the notice, and both houses had accepted the conference report, Calhoun still doubted whether the notice would actually be used to reopen negotiations. He saw the result as a victory for the Senate over the President, but he was not at all sure that Polk would accept that outcome. A caustic editorial in the *Union* on April 23 gave ground for his suspicions, but created so much alarm among conservatives that the President himself drafted a follow-up for the next day's paper in more conciliatory tones.[44]

Calhoun need not have been concerned, for neither McLane nor Aberdeen had stood on ceremony. The American Minister, without authority and without waiting for instructions, had already reopened negotiations on a purely informal basis, and Aberdeen had written out a proposal for settlement in his own hand on May 18. McLane had by that date received the notice but had not delivered it, though of course its terms were carried in full in the British papers. It was still undelivered the next day when Aberdeen's instructions went off to the British Minister in Washington.[45]

McLane's summary of the British terms was discussed at length in a special Cabinet meeting the afternoon of June 4; and two days later the formal proposal, as delivered by Pakenham, was debated in detail. The terms were substantially those so often mentioned in the past as fair and reasonable: 49° to the sea, and a line dividing the Straits of Fuca, leaving all of Vancouver Island to Britain; free navigation of the Straits to both parties; and free navigation of the Columbia River to the Hudson's Bay Company, whose charter would expire in 1859. There was also provision for guaranteeing individual property rights lawfully acquired, and that was all. Polk hesitated and Buchanan procrastinated, but the Cabinet, with Walker the moving spirit, voted to submit the terms to the Senate in Executive session for advice in advance of any formal signing of a treaty.[46]

The proposition was duly submitted on June 10. Allen moved reference to the Committee on Foreign Relations, but could muster only nine votes for what would have amounted to a death sentence. A proposition to print the documents for confidential use of the Senate, which would probably have resulted only in delay, was tabled, and a motion by Hannegan to postpone consideration until June 15 was roundly beaten. No more was done that day, but the way was cleared June 11 when Senator Haywood moved a resolution advising the President to accept the British terms. Attempts to amend were defeated and on June 12 the Haywood resolution was passed by 38 to 12. Calhoun was inclined to take the major credit for this outcome to himself, and there were many who were willing to let him have it.[47]

When the Senate resumed sitting on Monday, June 15, Senator Allen, who had so long carried the burden of the battle for fifty-four-forty, resigned his place as chairman of the Committee on Foreign Relations. The Whigs offered to support Calhoun for the post and many urged him to take it. He declined, and two days later George McDuffie was elected to the vacant chairmanship. In the interim the Oregon treaty was signed exactly as it came from Aberdeen's hand, and was submitted to the Senate. A last-ditch effort by Hannegan to alter the terms commanded only five votes, and on June 18, 1846, the treaty was ratified by 41 to 14.[48]

The news of the outbreak of war between the United States and Mexico reached London almost immediately after the instructions to Pakenham had been dispatched, and many Americans, Calhoun among them, believed that this time lag was crucial. "It is now known," wrote the South Carolinian early in July, "that had the English proposition been delayed 5 days, until the news of our declaration of War against Mexico had arrived, the Settlement could not have been made." It would at least have been more difficult, and delay of another six weeks might well have been fatal. On June 25 the House of Lords finally passed the repeal of the Corn Laws. In the Commons, on the same day, the Government was badly beaten on the Irish Coercion Bill. Four days later the Peel Ministry resigned, this time for good, and it fell to the reluctant Palmerston to pass on to McLane the actual ratification of the Oregon treaty.[49]

His work completed, McLane's earlier expressed desire to return home was heeded and he was given permission to leave his post in mid-August. Polk offered the London Mission to Senator John A. Dix of New York, who delayed an answer until he had consulted Governor Wright; but the President was not in the good graces of the Albany Regency and Dix was told to decline. The post then went to George Bancroft, who welcomed the opportunity to escape the arduous duties of the Navy Department in wartime. The Massachusetts historian had coveted the British assignment from the start, and he was more than happy to give the Navy back to Mason.[50]

8

While the Senate was busy with the Oregon treaty the tariff debate got under way in the House. The lines were clearly formed by the middle of June. Free trade had been made a party measure by the President's message and the report of the Secretary of the Treasury, and the party character of the bill that was finally brought to the floor was emphasized by Walker's hand in it and by the efforts made in its behalf by the administration press. Generally speaking, therefore, the Democrats favored and the Whigs opposed, with Democrats from the manufacturing states seeking modifying amendments to rescue what they could of the protective system and a handful of Southern Whigs willing to see the bill pass though for partisan reasons not willing to argue for it.

The dissident note came, as usual, from South Carolina, where the *Mercury,* already cut off from the party counsels, attacked the bill introduced by McKay as less than Walker had asked for and as not strictly a revenue measure. To some extent the *Mercury* was right, for changes had been made in committee. They were made, however, with the consent of the Secretary and possibly even at his instigation. The bill was admittedly not perfect, but its basic principles should have been satisfactory to those who had opposed so strenuously the blatent protectionism of 1828 and 1842. The whole object was to get the best bill that could be passed—not a perfect bill that was bound to fail.[51]

For two weeks the protectionist forces whittled away at the bill in Committee of the Whole, with the administration leaders conceding modifications where they must, but holding firm on the major points. The manufacturers' lobby gathered in the city, and augmenting daily, made no great effort, preferring to concentrate on the Senate where the division would be nearly even. As the debate neared its close, excitement ran high, with the bitterest opposition coming from Northern Democrats, especially those from New York, Pennsylvania, and Ohio. Every parliamentary device was used to shift favored articles of local production from lower to higher categories, and to drop noncompetitive items like tea and coffee to the free list. Some succeeded, others failed. A break was near on July 3, the final day of argument, but the administration rallied its forces, and forced a vote. It was carried, 114 to 95.[52]

The bill as passed was not the bill Walker had drafted, nor quite the bill the free-trade advocates desired. But it was undoubtedly the nearest approach to free trade that could possibly have been passed at that date, and it was actually better than many of the antitariff men had believed possible. According to the *Union's* analysis the bill on the final vote was supported by six Democrats in Maine, three in New Hampshire, and 16 out of 21 in New York, together with the entire Southern and Western party contingents. The heavy opposition, as was of course inevitable, came from the dominantly manufacturing states of Pennsylvania, New Jersey, Delaware, Ohio, Massachusetts, Connecticut, and Rhode Island, with the border states of Maryland and Kentucky also in opposition. It was truly, as Ritchie noted, a combination of South and West—the long-planned alliance that had flowered at Memphis. It will be remembered that the rivers and harbors bill had already passed the House and was looked on as sure in the Senate.[53]

9

There were still dissident voices in South Carolina after the tariff had passed the House, but Calhoun was jubilant. He anticipated a stiff fight in the Senate, but thought the bill would ultimately pass, and as usual gave himself due measure of credit for creating a situation that would make such an outcome possible. If the protectionists are wise, he wrote to Clemson shortly before the bill came up in the Senate, "they will agree to the best terms they can now get. The longer the adjustment is postponed the worse for them. . . . The South and the West have never been so strongly united before. . . . To this desirable result, my report on the Memorial of the Memphis Convention has greatly contributed. The improvement of the navigation of the Mississippi was the great barrier, which kept them assunder and threw the West into the arms of the east. I hope I have forever removed it, by showing that the power is clearly embraced by that of regulating commerce among the states." [54]

Calhoun did not overestimate the intensity of the coming contest, which was to be the last great tariff controversy before the Civil War. The House bill reached the Senate floor on July 13, presented by Dixon H. Lewis of Alabama, chairman of the Committee on Finance. For the next two weeks Lewis led the forces of free trade, with powerful aid from such rugged campaigners as Calhoun and McDuffie, while the assault was led by the peerless Webster. The protectionists followed the well-worn path, with memorials and meetings and personal visits from manufacturers all purporting to show that American business could never survive the blow to be inflicted by this bill. The administration concentrated on theory, on the advantages of reciprocal trade with Britain, on appeals to the sectional interests of South and West, with such assistance in individual cases as the party in power may always command. [55]

The protectionists also applied direct pressure to individual Senators. The division was so nearly even that a shift of one or two votes would make the difference, and the weak spot was quickly found. William Haywood, Polk's college classmate, had been chosen Senator from North Carolina early in 1843 when a Democratic caucus deadlocked over candidates sponsored by Van Buren and Calhoun. He was a vain man, proud of his friendship with the President but capable of believing that he too had a mission. Perhaps it came about without any suggestion from the outside at all, but two days after the tariff bill reached the Senate, Haywood indicated to Polk that he could not support it without amendment. He wanted the effective date made March 4, 1847, significantly, after another session of Congress would have met and adjourned. Polk, in common with Congressional strategists of both parties, believed that the bill would be lost if the Senate returned it to the House with any major alteration in it, and he so informed Haywood, but without noticeable effect. Members of the Senate also failed to talk the North Carolinian around, as did Judge Mason of the Cabinet, another college classmate.[56]

After a week of increasingly heated debate in the Senate, Polk was sure that the fate of the bill rested on Haywood's vote, and he was ready to entertain a compromise offer made to him by a group of Pennsylvania manufacturers. The "compromise" suggested was a reduction of 20 percent, or if necessary 33 1/3 percent, in the 1842 schedules instead of the drastic reductions included in the Walker-McKay bill. The proposal was discussed again at the White House on July 22; and two days later Vice President Dallas gave it more specific form and commended it to his chief. All duties above 30 percent under the tariff of 1842 were to be reduced by 25 percent of the excess at once, and by another 25 percent at the end of five years. At the end of ten years the duties were to be fixed as in the Walker-McKay bill. Haywood, meanwhile, had called on Polk on July 23, and expressed his intention not to vote for the bill as it stood. After his departure, the President talked to McDuffie, Lewis, and McKay, who agreed that the fate of the bill would depend on Haywood's vote, unless Whig Senator Jarnagin of Tennessee voted for it, as instructed to do by his legislature. In that case there would be a tie, and the Vice President would have to choose between his home state and his party.[57]

The city was still speculating on the prospects for compromising on a bill that was already a compromise, when Haywood threw a bomb into the proceedings. The North Carolina Senator appeared in his seat as usual on the morning of Saturday, July 25, and listened for an hour or so to a speech by Webster. Then abruptly he wrote a brief note which he sent to the Vice President's desk, and walked from the room. The note was his resignation.[58]

The administration press, the party leaders, the low-tariff men, all were at first hotly indignant, then alarmed. Haywood's seat could not possibly be filled in time for the vote. The number in the Senate was now uneven. Jarnagin would decide the question one way or the other, and that last political ace, the casting vote of the Vice President, could not be used. What happened next might be called a comedy of errors, or a complex bit of double dealing.

At one o'clock Saturday afternoon, July 25, Jarnagin appeared at the White House along with a member from the lower chamber to present various enrolled bills for signature, among them the pork-barrel rivers and harbors bill. Buchanan asked Jarnagin about the prospects for passing the tariff and remarked that the city was speculating on the Tennessee vote. Jarnagin immediately replied that he had been instructed to vote for precisely such a bill as this, and would do so. He had assured Polk as early as July 13, the day before the debate opened, that he intended to obey his instructions, but the tone and emphasis were now different, and the President for the first time believed him. Jarnagin presumably did not know of Haywood's action until he returned to his seat in the Senate, since word did not reach the White House until three-thirty. The resignation put the Tennessee Senator in a difficult position. It is one thing to cast a vote that merely creates a tie, giving the final responsibility to someone else, and quite another thing to be oneself the ultimately responsible party.[59]

Webster, meanwhile, was already at work, bringing to bear upon the hapless Jarnagin the full weight of his prestige, his political power, and his matchless eloquence; and on Sunday, July 26, the Tennessee Senator promised the Whig members from his own state that the bill would not be allowed to pass. His stipulation was that the Vice President was to be forced to go on record, and that same afternoon Webster outlined a method, to which Jarnagin agreed. It was this: When the Massachusetts Senator, who was entitled to the floor, finished his speech on Monday, he would move to strike out a portion of one section of the bill. Jarnagin was to vote for this motion, which would thereby carry, to be followed by a motion to engross. This time Jarnagin was not to vote. If the engrossment carried by Dallas' casting vote, Jarnagin would then move to lay the bill on the table, the Whigs would carry it by one vote, and that would end the matter.[60]

When the Senate convened on Monday, July 27, Webster curtailed his speech and made the agreed motion. Before it could be voted on, however, John M. Clayton of Delaware moved to recommit the bill, with instructions to restore the duties laid down in the act of 1842. This motion took precedence over Webster's under the rules, and the Whigs felt in duty bound to vote for it, which automatically ended proceedings until the Finance Committee had acted. That evening, when Whig leaders sought to prepare a new strategy, Jarnagin could not be found. According to Webster's account, written down two days later, the Tennessee Senator was at the White House, and when he returned to his lodging about ten in the evening he would not talk. Polk, though he has bitter comments to make, does not mention any such visit in his diary, but if the result was as Webster implied, he probably would not have mentioned it. Webster, meanwhile, had written as strongly as he could, which was very strongly indeed, "beseeching" Jarnagin to carry through his agreement of Sunday. At nine o'clock on Tuesday morning Webster received an almost agonized note in reply. The harried Tennessean would not vote on engrossment, even as they had agreed, but on the final passage, it was his unfortunate duty to vote "aye." [61]

It happened in exactly that way. Lewis opened the debate on Tuesday, July 28, by asking in behalf of the majority of the Committee on Finance that they be discharged from the instructions. There was no time to write a new bill. It was this one or none at all. There was a lengthy and excited debate, but at last the Committee's request was granted, 28 to 27, with Jarnagin on the majority side. Webster then renewed his motion to strike out a portion of one section—actually of little moment—and that motion too was carried by Jarnagin's vote. The test vote then came on Reverdy Johnson's motion to refer to a select committee. This time Jarnagin rose in his place when the roll was called and denounced the bill in unmeasured language. He would, he said, obey his instructions and vote for it on final passage, but it was strictly a party measure, and it should be saved from destruction by party votes. There was a bitter and angry exchange between the two Tennessee Senators before Jarnagin stalked from the floor without voting. Dallas unhesitatingly broke the resulting tie against commitment. The engrossment was then carried, also by the Vice President's vote, after which Dallas made a dignified and moving statement in justification of his course. It was a difficult and courageous thing for a Pennsylvanian to do and richly deserved the tribute he received from his fellow Democrats. There was a little more jockeying, some further talk, and the bill was passed by Jarnagin's vote, 28 to 27.[62]

Under the Walker tariff most duties were fixed at 30 percent ad valorem, with a few as high as 40 percent, and a few down to 25 and 20. It was by no means the uniform 20 percent level that Calhoun and his fellow Nullifiers had written into the tariff compromise of 1833 as the ultimate goal, nor even the bill Walker had sent over from the Treasury, but it was a large concession—indeed a very large concession—to the point of view of the Southern Democrats, and they accepted it with good grace. The iron shapes and products that had ranged from 73 to 168 percent under the 1842 schedules were now fixed at 30 percent; the duty on shirtings was dropped from 95 to 30 percent; and that on cordage from 120 to 25 percent. The South and the West could not fail to prosper, under the joint operation of these relaxed trade barriers in England and the United States.

The President signed the tariff bill on July 30, and his sweeping legislative program was completed a few days later with the re-establishment of the Independent Treasury, destroyed during the Whig extra session of 1841. It was only then, after the administration measures had been enacted, that Polk on August 3 vetoed the rivers and harbors bill. It is hardly likely that the tariff could have passed the Senate, had the internal improvements anticipated by the West been struck down before the final disposal of the Walker-McKay bill, and ill feeling was thereby engendered that was to crop up a few days later in a new and dangerous form. For the most part, however, the country was satisfied with what had been done. The South especially was in high spirits and was inclined to give the credit not to Polk but to Calhoun. So were large segments of the party elsewhere throughout the nation, and the South Carolinian became once more, for a brief interval, a favored choice for President of the United States.

CHAPTER XIX

MANIFEST DESTINY

1

IN HIS FIRST annual message to Congress Polk had forecast an early resumption of friendly relations with Mexico. As in the case of Oregon, however, he relied on power diplomacy, and this time Calhoun could not muster enough strength in the Senate to rescue the President from the consequences of his own precipitance. The issue of Texas annexation was still in doubt when Polk sent a confidential agent to Mexico late in March 1845. Dr. William S. Parrott was a familiar figure in the Mexican Capital, where he had extensive business connections to conceal his diplomatic character. His instructions were to urge the mutual desirability of harmony between the two countries, and to find out whether a new United States Minister would be received. Shannon's recall went off on the same boat that carried both Parrott and the departing Mexican envoy, Juan Almonte.[1]

Parrott found the government of acting President José Joaquín Herrera well disposed but weak, with General Mariano Paredes in the background, ready to interfere at the first conciliatory gesture. He found also that his mission was not so secret as it was supposed to be, with the more outspoken element openly calling him a Yankee spy. For three months he entertained members of the Mexican Congress, talked to civil and military officials, kept an eye on the British Minister, and read the newspapers, sending back reports that went erratically up and down with the changing fortunes of the Herrera government. The crisis came late in July when news of the Texan acceptance of annexation reached Mexico City. For a few anxious days a declaration of war against the United States seemed probable, but the martial fever quickly subsided. By the end of August Parrott was sure that Herrera desired a peaceful clarification of the situation, and he noted hopefully a rising popular sentiment in favor of receiving an American commissioner.[2]

273

As soon as annexation had been officially ratified by the people of Texas, General Zachary Taylor took up a position at Corpus Christi near the mouth of the Nueces. He was there encamped with the small force he deemed adequate for his needs when Parrott's dispatches of late July, with their accounts of warlike demonstrations, reached Washington. There was a special meeting of the Cabinet on August 29, and another the following day, after which new orders were rushed by special messenger to General Taylor and to Commodore David Conner in command of the Gulf squadron. Taylor was to regard as an act of war any Mexican crossing of the Rio Grande in force, and Conner, on receiving word of any outbreak of hostilities, was to blockade or seize Mexican Gulf coast ports.[3]

The next advices from Dr. Parrott were of a very different character, indicating that the excitement had subsided, and that the Mexicans were again preoccupied with their own internal difficulties. Dispatches from the United States consuls at Mexico City and Vera Cruz confirmed Parrott's impression that an opening for the resumption of diplomatic relations would be welcomed. The new situation was discussed in Cabinet meeting on September 16, and it was agreed that the mission to Mexico should be tendered to John Slidell, Spanish-speaking member of Congress from Louisiana. Slidell was directed to hold himself in readiness to leave on twenty-four hours' notice, pending word from John Black, the consul in Mexico City, that he would be received. Black's inquiry brought a courteous and affirmative reply from the Mexican Foreign Minister and the prearranged machinery of diplomacy swung into action early in November.[4]

In the interim Polk had sent Lieutenant A. H. Gillespie of the Marine Corps on a secret mission to California with instructions for Thomas O. Larkin, the United States consul at Monterey. Larkin's own sporadic dispatches indicated a disposition on the part of the Californians to cut loose from Mexico, and a suspicion that British agents on the ground intended in such circumstances to "protect" them. For the consul's guidance Buchanan spelled out the Monroe Doctrine in detail. Larkin was warned that he must not do anything that might incite the local inhabitants to rebellion, but he was at liberty to let them know that should they "desire to unite their destiny with ours, they would be received as brethren, whenever this can be done without affording Mexico just cause of complaint." John Charles Frémont was already in California at the head of a small detachment of "explorers," and more inclined to follow instructions from his powerful father-in-law, Senator Benton, than those received from the War Department.[5]

Slidell was given explicit and detailed information as to the nature and extent of the acknowledged but long unsatisfied claims of American citizens against the Government of Mexico, was reminded that Mexico was in no position to pay, and was directed to use these claims for bargaining purposes. For a treaty fixing the boundary between the United States and Mexico at the Rio Grande as defined by act of the Texan Congress in 1836, the American negotiator was authorized to assume the claims for payment by the United States. For an extension of the line to include Santa Fé and the valley of New Mexico, he might add an inducement of $5 million. If a strip to the Pacific coast that would include the Bay of San Francisco were added, the sum might be raised to $20 million; and for Polk's preferred boundary, following the Rio Grande to El Paso and thence west on the thirty-second parallel to the ocean, Slidell was authorized to offer $25 million, in addition to assuming the outstanding claims.[6]

2

Slidell left Pensacola on a naval vessel November 20, 1845, and sailed into Vera Cruz ten days later. In another week he was in Mexico City, but his reception there was very different from any he had been led to expect. John Black, the United States consul, met the arriving Minister-designate at the outskirts to warn him of the changed complexion of Mexican affairs. Privately the government still wished to receive the American envoy, but in the two months since that decision had first been taken the weakness of Herrera's administration had become more obvious and the strength of the opposition, urged on by popular clamor, had grown. It was now impossible to carry out the earlier promise, and it would soon be impossible to carry on the government at all.[7]

Greeting Slidell's arrival were posters scattered throughout the city announcing that he came to buy Texas and California, and that to receive him would be treason. The government was cowed and fearful, and the Foreign Minister temporized. He had agreed, he said, to receive not a plenipotentiary but only a commissioner to negotiate a boundary between Texas and Mexico; the American's powers were insufficient; the question of reception would have to be considered by the Council of Government. The Council met, weighed the power of General Paredes, assessed the force of public opinion, and gave its recommendation in the negative. Mindful of his instructions to bear much for the sake of his mission, Slidell kept his temper and urged on the Mexican Government the outstanding American claims, just as though he had been received; but Herrera and his ministers were too busy saving their own skins to be distracted. The long-threatened revolution erupted bloodlessly. Herrera resigned during the night of December 29-30, and by January 2, 1846, General Paredes was in full control.[8]

Slidell would have left the city then, but that it was unsafe to travel and undignified to flee. As soon as conditions permitted, however, he established himself at Jalapa near the Gulf coast to await further instructions. His first dispatches, meanwhile, had reached Washington on January 12, and formed the primary topic at an animated Cabinet meeting the following day. Polk reacted by sending new orders posthaste to the military and naval forces nearest the scene of action. General Taylor was ordered under date of January 13 to move his camp from Corpus Christi to the Rio Grande; and the warships in the Gulf were augmented to the proportions of a "strong fleet." Slidell was necessarily given large discretion, but if circumstances permitted he was to wait things out, and in the event of revolution, to try his fortunes with the new regime.[9]

Another Cabinet session on the subject was held January 17, unofficial news from the South indicating more strongly still the possibility of revolution, and additional orders were sent to the Gulf fleet to concentrate at Vera Cruz. Within a few days Washington reports had ferreted out enough to startle their readers, and the news that Slidell would not be received was public property. To Calhoun it heralded all too surely the approach of war with Mexico, and that at a time when the issue with Britain over Oregon was still in doubt. He would have been more certain even than he was, had he seen the dispatch that went out to Slidell on January 28. The envoy was to seek recognition once more, this time from the Paredes government, and he was to "wait patiently for a final decision." Should he, however, be finally refused, nothing would remain "but to take the redress of the injuries to our citizens and the insults to our Government into our own hands." He was in that event to demand his passports, and the President would call on Congress for suitable measures to avenge the nation's wounded honor.[10]

It was about two weeks later that Colonel A. J. Atocha called on the President. The Colonel was a naturalized citizen of the United States, but he had been with Santa Anna at the time of his expulsion from Mexico, and only a month back had visited the former dictator in his Cuban exile. The conversation continued for some hours on each of two days, and it covered many points, but the upshot was that Santa Anna, should he be restored to power, would for a trifling consideration of perhaps $30 million make such a treaty as Polk desired, relinquishing both Texas and California. Paredes was misrepresented as a sort of stalking horse for Santa Anna, who would ease the path for the returning exile. To be sure it was Paredes who had driven Santa Anna out in the first place, but things like that happened in Mexico, and Polk seems to have accepted the explanation. The President had no doubt that Atocha actually came as an emissary from Santa Anna, and was strongly influenced by the picture thus painted for him of Mexican affairs.[11]

While all this was going on Slidell was cooling his heels at Jalapa. It was there, on February 27, that he received Buchanan's latest instructions. Delighted with the prospect of doing something to end the impasse in which he found himself, Slidell at once addressed a note to the new Foreign Minister. Dated March 1, 1846, it was more of an ultimatum than a request, with its clear implication that he must be received or there would be an open rupture, for which Mexico would be responsible. The note was delivered by Black, who had remained in the capital, and the answer, dated March 12, came back through the same channel. It was the blunt refusal that Slidell might have learned from the files of his own legation was the only answer Mexican diplomats ever returned to threats and blustering; and it was accompanied by the familiar recital of American aggressions against her neighbor, adding now to the older list the movement of American troops to the frontier and the presence of American naval squadrons off both coasts.[12]

Slidell had now no alternative but to demand his passports, which he did on March 17, and a few days later he was on his way home aboard the warship *Mississippi*. It was only when the *Mississippi* put into Vera Cruz on March 29 that he received Buchanan's further instructions of March 12. These new instructions found in the instability of the Paredes government a justification for delaying still further any final action, and suggested the probable efficacy of a discreet offer of immediate cash. They undoubtedly reflected Polk's talks with Santa Anna's emissary, but they reached Slidell too late for him to retract what he had done. The Mexican Government had already published the correspondence, and public sentiment made further delay out of the question.[13]

Back in Washington the knowledge that Taylor had advanced to the Rio Grande had become general, and Calhoun, who knew no reason for it, thought it but further evidence of a drift toward war. Polk's own assurance as to the rightness of his show of force remained unshaken, for Colonel Atocha had quoted Santa Anna as advising that very thing. The fallen dictator's advice was perhaps also in Polk's mind when he followed the precepts of good politics and consulted leading Senators as to the possibility of getting an appropriation to be used in negotiating a Mexican treaty. Allen, Cass, and Benton were all asked for an opinion, and then, at Cass's insistence, Calhoun too was taken into the President's confidence.[14]

Calhoun called at the White House by request on the evening of March 30, and Polk explained what he had in mind, tracing on a map the boundary he hoped to secure from Mexico. He asked Calhoun if it was worth $25 million, and the Carolinian indicated that for such a boundary money would be no object. Polk then broached the question of having a specific sum appropriated by Congress to be paid over on the signing of a treaty. Calhoun feared that no matter what care was taken, the object of the appropriation would become known, and it might create new difficulties in the Oregon settlement. He agreed, however, to consider it and promised to give the President an answer later, after he had discussed it confidentially with McDuffie. It was April 3 before Calhoun rendered his opinion. He approved the purpose but thought it inexpedient to ask money for it at this time. Allen then advised the President to drop it, which for the time being he did.[15]

3

With a Mexican war now highly probable, Polk needed more than ever a friendly Congress and a united nation. Secretive and taciturn by nature, he seems to have done nothing about Mexican affairs for some forty-eight hours after receiving word that Slidell had asked for his passports. Then on the evening of April 9 he explained the situation to Senator Benton. The next day the President sent for the colorful and potent Sam Houston, who had taken his seat as Senator from Texas only ten days before; and Houston was followed by William Allen, still chairman of the Senate Committee on Foreign Relations. With each he discussed the gravity of the impending rupture with Mexico. He had already made up his mind to send no message on the subject to Congress until he received confirmation that Slidell had actually sailed from Vera Cruz. The Cabinet, on April 11, unanimously approved his course.[16]

The news preceded the dispatches by a day, and Washington knew on April 15 that Slidell had left Mexico. The same mails carried word that Taylor was now encamped near the mouth of the Rio Grande, opposite the Mexican town of Matamoros, where he might at any moment be attacked. Although he was still under fire in the administration press for his part in modifying the Oregon notice, Calhoun called on the President the evening of April 18. He was not happy about the prospect of war, nor was he in agreement with what seemed to be the President's policy. He wanted no warlike move until the Oregon question was settled once and for all, and was sure that if war could be delayed so long, it need not occur. The basis for this judgment was a belief that Great Britain did not desire war between the United States and Mexico, which might seriously interfere with her own new commercial policy, and that once her own differences with America were settled, she would use her good offices to prevent the impending conflict. In an atmosphere of mutual distrust the President and the Senator reached no common ground. Polk did agree to hold back a message on Mexican affairs as long as possible, but he would not promise to wait for an Oregon treaty.[17]

As the days passed the President grew impatient with delay, and toward the end of April he told the Cabinet that "we must take redress for the injuries done us into our own hands." There were no new "injuries" nor further aggravation of old ones since Slidell's departure. Indeed the latest word from Consul Black indicated a turn for the better. He noted a friendly disposition on the part of the British Minister in Mexico City, and thought that Paredes himself, uneasy in his seat of power, would now like to get things adjusted with the United States if a way could be found. With the Oregon affair well on the way to settlement, however, Polk could afford to be more warlike. His own position as head of a divided party seemed to require some positive step that would unite at least the bulk of the Democracy, and territorial acquisitions had always been popular. So the situation that might have justified a declaration of war on April 16, when the President was first officially notified of it, was held on April 28, after its force had been somewhat mitigated, to be insoluble except by the sword.[18]

There were dispatches on April 29 from what Polk called "the army of occupation" on the Rio Grande, indicating that Taylor faced an obviously hostile Mexican force across the river, but the President was still uncertain as to the outcome of this power diplomacy of his. On May 3 he once more consulted Benton, who advised, as had Calhoun two weeks earlier, that matters should be delayed until an Oregon settlement was reached. "He expressed a decided aversion to a war with Mexico if it could be avoided consistently with the honour of the country," and Polk insisted that he too was anxious to avoid a conflict. He proposed to lay the whole case before Congress as soon as he had seen Slidell, who was daily expected. Slidell, it should be remarked, had been taking his time, not having been summoned. He had reached New Orleans on the eighth or ninth of April, but took a month to come on to Washington.[19]

The next news from the Rio Grande came on May 6. General Ampudia, one of the best of the Mexican officers, had arrived in Matamoros and had given the Americans twenty-four hours to withdraw. Taylor had replied by directing his naval support to blockade the mouth of the river. The probabilities, as Polk noted in his diary, were "that hostilities might take place soon." The President was still studying the documents when Slidell arrived on May 8. The Cabinet met the next day and agreed that Polk should ask Congress for an immediate declaration of war, "if the Mexican forces . . . committed any act of hostility." Polk saw no reason for waiting, and before the Cabinet rose all except Bancroft had accepted his proposal to ask for a declaration of war on the following Tuesday, May 12.[20]

Any doubts or reservations that may still have existed in the minds of any of the Presidential advisers were quickly dispelled. At six o'clock Polk received further dispatches from General Taylor, with word that on April 25 Mexican troops had crossed the Rio Grande and had fallen upon a scouting party of 63 dragoons, all of whom were killed or captured. So far as Taylor was concerned, it was now war, and he had called upon the Governors of Texas and Louisiana for additional men. The President agreed that it was war. The Cabinet was back in session at seven-thirty that evening, and the *Union* was presently on the streets with news that American blood had been shed on American soil. Polk, Buchanan, and Bancroft set to work on a war message as soon as the Cabinet meeting broke up around ten o'clock, and completed it the next day. It went to Congress at noon on Monday, May 11, 1846.[21]

4

The President's message was adroit or ambiguous, according to the point of view. He reviewed the course of relations between the United States and Mexico since the beginning of the session, emphasizing the friendly feelings that had prompted him to seek resumption of diplomatic intercourse. Mexico had agreed to receive a minister, and had then rejected him. After this and other grievances had been detailed at some length, Polk told of the attack on a detachment of Taylor's army. "The cup of forebearance had been exhausted even before the recent information from the frontier of the Del Norte. But now, after reiterated menaces, Mexico has passed the boundary of the United States, has invaded our territory and shed American blood upon the American soil. She has proclaimed that hostilities have commenced, and that the two nations are now at war." He did not, it will be noted, ask for a declaration of war, but merely proclaimed that war existed and asked for the means of prosecuting it. "As war exists, and, notwithstanding all our efforts to avoid it, exists by the act of Mexico herself, we are called upon by every consideration of duty and patriotism to vindicate with decision the honor, the rights, and the interests of our country." [22]

Leading members of both houses had been informed in advance what the President expected, and were prepared to do their part. In the lower chamber everything went as smoothly as Polk could have asked. The message was read, and a reading of the accompanying documents—the diplomatic and military correspondence in the case—was dispensed with. The House then resolved itself into a Committee of the Whole, where a bill authorizing the President to accept volunteers was already pending. There were objections and expostulations based on the constitutional provision that Congress alone could declare war, the leaders being Jefferson Davis of Mississippi, who was soon to cover himself with glory at Buena Vista, and Holmes and Rhett, the perennial dissenters from South Carolina. All opposition was brushed aside under the operation of the previous question, the bill before the committee was amended into an act "providing for the prosecution of the existing war between the United States and the Republic of Mexico," and was passed 174 to 14. The negative votes came from Adams, Giddings, and the tight little band of abolitionists who saw in war with Mexico only the extension of slavery.[23]

The Senate moved with more deliberation. There too a reading of the documents was dispensed with, but they were ordered printed for use of the members, and it was understood that no decision would be taken until there had been time for consideration. Calhoun was one of the first to claim the floor, and his remarks were typical. There was no war, he argued, until Congress declared one, but only hostilities arising out of an invasion of American soil. Such an invasion the President was fully empowered to repel; he was not empowered to make war. The question was too grave to be decided without informed debate. He called on the Senate to "weigh everything calmly and deliberately, and do all that the Constitution, interests, and honor of the country may require."[24] Allen and Cass failed completely to whip up a war spirit. The message was divided between the committees on Foreign Relations and Military Affairs, and with all the "forebearance, dignity, and calmness" Calhoun asked of it, the Senate turned to routine business.

The nature of the referral made Allen and Benton, the chairmen of the two committees concerned, the key Senators. Benton had called on the President during the morning of May 11, before the Senate met. He had been allowed to read the message in advance, and had then indicated to Polk that while he would vote men and money to defend the soil of the United States, he was not prepared to vote for aggressive war against Mexico. He did not believe that American territory really extended west of the Nueces, and did not approve of the movement of Taylor's army to the Rio Grande. After the day's proceedings in Congress, Benton called again, ostensibly for information as to the number of men and the amount of money needed for the defense of the country. Neither the President nor the Secretary of War had any idea, but the Missouri Senator was assured that it would be a quick war. A reference to the bill passed that day in the House brought from Benton only the remark that so serious a subject required more consideration than the House had given it. Polk concluded that Benton would oppose the bill in the Senate. He was already sure that Calhoun would oppose, and began to believe that these two, with the Whigs, could prevent a declaration of war altogether.[25]

That is as far as Polk's diary enlightens us, so we do not know what agency if any the President may have had in the sequel. At any rate Benton gathered together his Committee on Military Affairs early the following morning, and from a newspaper text the members approved the House bill. Sometime before the Senate met at noon a Democratic caucus also concurred in what the House had done. The bill came before the Senate at once, and Calhoun sought in vain to split it. He was ready and eager to vote supplies and men to repel invasion, but he would not vote a declaration of war without an opportunity to see the documents on which the necessity for it was alleged to rest. Benton announced that the Committee on Military Affairs would have reported the bill as it was, embodying both the declaration of war and the means of prosecuting it. Allen said the Committee on Foreign Relations would have done the same. All efforts to refer were voted down. All protests that war ought not to be declared without knowledge of the facts were shouted down. Calhoun pleaded for time to weigh the situation, to examine the alternatives, to determine for themselves as the Constitution bade them do whether war was indeed the only way out of the situation. He was heeded only by the reporters. One after another, limiting amendments were rejected by an unchanging margin of 26 to 20, Calhoun and McDuffie voting with the Whig minority. Then the vote was taken and the war bill was passed by a majority of 40 to 2. Thomas

Clayton of Delaware and John Davis of Massachusetts were the dissenters; but Berrien of Georgia, Evans of Maine, and Calhoun sat silently in their seats when their names were called.[26]

There were many who did not believe that the Rio Grande was really the Texas boundary. The best treatises of the time held otherwise, and the Texan Republic, though it had asserted jurisdiction beyond the Nueces, had never been able to govern there. Others, who believed with all honesty and sincerity in the uttermost extent of the Texan claims, still felt that ordering General Taylor to occupy the disputed ground was a deliberate provocation, at a time when forbearance might have secured all that was wanted through diplomatic channels. Calhoun believed that the vote of Congress had set a precedent whereby any President could in future make war, and insisted that not 10 percent of the Senate would have voted for it if the issue had been fairly presented. The Senate had, as Dix of New York put it, "voted not merely on *confidence*, which is bad enough in great matters of public concern, but on *faith*, which the Scripture tells us 'is the evidence of things unseen.' " No one in either house had read the actual documents, on which Polk's recitation of wrongs was based, before they voted war.[27]

5

Calhoun was very well aware that his course on the war bill would be unpopular in many quarters, and would be represented as an act of hostility to the administration and to the party. He had acted as he always did, according to his convictions and his judgment, and he was prepared to take whatever consequences might follow. The *Mercury,* itself read out of the party, commended his stand, and there were appreciative letters from other sections of the country, but by and large his opposition to the immediate blind declaration of war asked by the President was condemned. Some old friends, like J. S. Barbour, pleaded with him not to place himself again on the unpopular side; others, of the newer crop, quietly slipped away to attach themselves to men with better prospects. Through it all he remained unmoved, supporting the war measures but continuing to believe that the end sought could have been achieved without resort to arms.[28]

Polk signed the declaration of war on May 13, 1846, then sent for

General Winfield Scott to offer him personal direction of the Mexican campaign. On the same day, however, the President tried his hand at the back-door approach by dispatching to Commodore Conner an order to permit the exiled Santa Anna to pass the blockade, should he seek to return to Mexico. He was acting, of course, on the hints given him by Colonel Atocha, and on reports from the United States consuls in Mexico City and Vera Cruz that Santa Anna was a likely candidate to succeed Paredes. In a few days the Secretary of War was impatient and disgusted with General Scott's careful planning, with his insistence on co-ordination of supply services, transportation, and all the other details of war, on training for the recruits, on attention to climate and terrain. All this meant delay to the Secretary's mind, and the President wanted a quick war. Then came a sharp comment of the General's in a private letter about a fire in his rear, which was most annoying to Polk. The news of Taylor's initial successes arrived about this time, and Scott found himself relegated to a desk with the field command bestowed on his junior General. In early July Commander A. S. Mackenzie called on Santa Anna, having first talked to Polk, and everything was in order for the next act.[29]

Polk continued to play at politics and to dabble in international intrigue, but the whole affair was really out of his hands almost from the start. What the President intended, what leading Senators desired, what editors hoped, was quickly submerged in what the rank and file of the people intended to get. The news of Taylor's early victories at Palo Alto and Resaca de la Palma fired the popular enthusiasm, and the man in the street, particularly in the West and Southwest, talked of California as though already American soil. In fact, it was, for all practical purposes, thanks to such as Frémont, Gillespie, Commodore Stockton of the Navy, and a handful of adventurers who were engaged in taking formal possession of it. Everywhere except perhaps New England the war was popular, as victorious battles accompanied by the acquisition of rich and all but unoccupied lands are always popular. The land is a form of loot in which the people share, and realize after a fashion the age-old dream of something for nothing—nothing, that is, but a little blood, which no one ever believes will be his own.

"Our people," wrote Calhoun, after learning of Taylor's first victories, "are like a young man of 18, full of health and vigour and disposed for adventure of any description, but without wisdom or experience to guide him." [30] If the South Carolina Senator under-rated his compatriots, perhaps it was because the changing times had passed him by. The tide of settlement, however thin it might be in spots, had swept across the continent with unbelievable speed. The railroad and the telegraph and countless other devices like Howe's sewing machine and McCormick's reaper opened limitless possibili-ties. American ships were on every sea, and Americans themselves were pushing their way into the commercial and cultural stream the world over. They were conscious of a new and larger world even before the vast Western prairies and mighty mountains, designed by nature for the habitation of the American people, brought home to those with imagination the certainty of destiny. The Mexican war was adventure, and its cost in lives and money a trivial thing to pay for the Bay of San Francisco, for all California, for half a continent, for the dominance of both oceans and eventually of the destinies of the globe. The prospect charged young men with fire and purpose that the petty gains and losses of politics could not sway.

Calhoun would have been foremost among them thirty years ago, but now the recklessness of youth was gone. He would not welcome change for the sake of change, but with the grim tenacity of his Scotch forebears he would hold fast to that which he found to be good. He still foresaw a great destiny for his country, but only in unity and union. That meant, to him, the protection of slavery in the South, just as it meant to Adams, Giddings, and their compeers the final end of slavery. But the young men who left the city offices, the farms, the colleges, to storm the enchanted gateways to the West cared nothing for slavery, one way or the other. They were wooed and won by adventure, empire, the boundless freedom of an unsettled land, the sheer magnetism of the setting sun.

CHAPTER XX

RESTRICTION OF SLAVERY

1

CONGRESS had been sitting for an almost unprecedented eight months and was within three days of adjournment when the incident occurred that would set the stage for the sectional struggle of the next decade and a half, and lead at last to fratricidal war.

The Oregon treaty had been signed and ratified; the first genuine revenue tariff since Jefferson's time had been enacted into law; the lavish appropriation for public works that was the price of Western support for tariff reform had been vetoed; war with Mexico had begun in a questionable border incident and had been made official by the force of public opinion. The basic acts of a major program had been carried through, and Polk wanted to complete the work by acquiring California. He still believed it could be done with a sum of cash in hand for bargaining purposes, and with the concurrence of party leaders he asked Congress on August 8, 1846, for two million dollars "for the purpose of defraying any extraordinary expenses which may be incurred in the intercourse between the United States and foreign nations." Such a bill was offered in the House in the early afternoon, and it was agreed before the three o'clock recess that it would be taken up at the evening session.[1]

When the bill reached the floor Whig spokesmen complained that they had not been told the purpose of the appropriation. They charged the President with intending to buy or bribe additional territory from Mexico—almost the literal truth, though the language was somewhat disrespectful. If such was the case, they argued, it would be territory in Southern latitudes. Hugh White of New York and Robert C. Winthrop of Massachusetts, the latter Whig leader in the House, made it plain that the money would not be appropriated except with a guarantee that none of it would ever be used to extend slavery.

After vigorous debate the bill was withdrawn and McKay supplied

287

a substitute, but David Wilmot, thirty-two-year-old Representative from Western Pennsylvania, moved to amend the new version in the same language he had already offered as an amendment to the original bill. He was supported by Western members who thought they had been cheated by Polk's veto of the rivers and harbors bill a few days earlier; by Democrats who believed they had been promised all of Oregon in return for Texas; by Northerners who recognized the potentialities of the South-West alliance and would divert the political power of the West to the service of their own sectional aims; and by antislavery men of all political complexions. The amendment was adopted without a roll call and the amended bill was passed. The President, so far as the House was concerned, could have his two million dollars, *"Provided,* That, as an express and fundamental condition to the acquisition of any territory from the Republic of Mexico by the United States, by virtue of any treaty which may be negotiated between them, and to the use by the Executive of the moneys herein appropriated, neither slavery nor involuntary servitude shall ever exist in any part of said territory, except for crime, whereof the party shall first be duly convicted." [2]

That was Saturday night, and the two houses had agreed to adjourn at midnight of Monday, August 10. There was the usual last-minute log jam on the final day. The accumulated irritations and overwork of the long session revealed themselves in short tempers and wandering attention. There was confusion in the Senate and business moved with intolerable slowness. The hands of the Senate clock (ten minutes behind the House clock) were nearing eleven-thirty before Dixon H. Lewis, chairman of the Finance Committee, heaved his ponderous bulk erect and secured the floor to present the bill passed by the House on Saturday night. When the Senate agreed to consider it, Lewis moved to strike out the proviso. John Davis of Massachusetts wanted to know why, and Lewis replied that the time was too short for explanations. The Senate had less than half an hour to amend the bill, pass it, and return it to the House for concurrence. Davis knew it very well; he had cast one of the two votes against the war, and he objected to giving two million dollars of unallocated funds to James K. Polk or anyone else to prosecute it. He had the floor and there was no cloture rule to force him off it, so he continued to talk, despite frequent interruptions, until word came that the House had adjourned. The bill was thus filibustered to death, and the President was furious; but neither President nor Congress had heard the last of the Wilmot Proviso.[3]

2

When Calhoun reached Fort Hill after a brief vacation with members of his family at White Sulphur Springs, he found the President-makers active and his own partisans determined to push his claims for 1848. He knew that his popularity had risen high; but he knew also that the issues on which it rested—the report on the Memphis Memorial, the tariff settlement, the Oregon treaty—all would now be overshadowed by slavery. In the Wilmot Proviso he saw "an apple of discord" that would "do much to divide the party," and as the fall elections came on, he warned a Northern correspondent that the Union could not survive the continued assault on Southern institutions.[4]

More important in his eyes than any Presidential election was the preservation of the Southern way of life, and to that end unity was the first essential. So in the fall of 1846 the grim-visaged, ironhanded Senator put personal ambition aside and tightened his grip on South Carolina, yielding neither to the rising trend toward popular democracy with its faith in numbers, nor to the growing separatism of the feudally organized planter-aristocracy whose spokesmen had issued their challenge at Bluffton two years earlier.

An act of Congress fixing a uniform day for holding Presidential elections gave him an opening for expressing his views. The law required some change in South Carolina, where the legislature which still chose Presidential electors did not meet until three weeks after the day fixed by Congress. The alternatives were retention of the existing system through a quadrennial special session of the legislature; direct choice of electors by general ticket; and direct choice by election districts. A full-scale controversy was soon in progress with candidates for office taking sides. Though earnestly solicited for an opinion, Calhoun refused to comment until after the state elections had been held, lest he be accused of seeking to influence the outcome. Then in a long and carefully phrased letter published in the Pendleton *Messenger* in November, he came out strongly for the system as it was.[5]

Calhoun rested his case on the moral obligation to preserve the compromise between upcountry and low country as it had been written into the South Carolina Constitution of 1808, but he was thinking also of the infinitely more important compromises between North and South that had ushered the Constitution of the United States into being. On the basis of his own arguments advanced during the preconvention campaign of 1843 he should have favored the district system for choosing electors, but this method he now rejected because it would tend to destroy the sectional balance within the state. Both Presidential electors and Governor were supposed to reflect the will of South Carolina, but that will, Calhoun insisted, could not be determined by a numerical majority of the voters, nor even by majorities in elections districts. Under her constitution the will of South Carolina could only be made manifest by the concurrent voice of her two major interests—the low-country planters and the upcountry farmers; and this concurrent voice could be expressed only through the legislature, where each interest controlled one house.

If the argument was abstract the application was nothing of the sort. Taking the fall line as the traditional division between sections, the upcountry could outvote the coastal plain in the ratio of five to four, but two thirds of the slaves were concentrated in the lower districts. On the basis of popular election by distric; the state would be divided and that unity of action so important to her role in national affairs would be gone; popular election by general ticket would mean that the upcountry, with its lesser interest in preserving slavery, would control the state. While the sectional balance was preserved the slave interest would predominate and as long as he lived Calhoun would speak for a single interest. Let the balance be broken and the way would be open for driving a wedge between slavery and freedom. The influence of South Carolina and eventually her leadership of the South would be weakened by internal dissension and the cause to which Calhoun stood dedicated would be lost.

The question was debated for ten days in the legislature, but no action was taken and the old conservative system that now formed the bulwark of Calhoun's power remained intact.[6]

The same session of the legislature showed the influence of Calhoun's conservatism in another particular. About the time Congress adjourned McDuffie's precarious health took a turn for the worse, and his long-rumored resignation was presented in November. The leading candidates for the Senate seat thus vacated were Robert Barnwell Rhett and James H. Hammond, but on both the Bluffton taint was strong. It took only four ballots to elect Judge Andrew Pickens Butler, Unionist of other days; and the governorship went to Judge David Johnson, who had once ruled the test oath of the Nullifiers unconstitutional.[7]

The state was in process of consolidation, the better to serve her destined purpose as the sword and buckler of slavery. Throughout the South the Wilmot Proviso had shocked men of all shades of opinion, and local differences were being set aside in the face of a common danger.

3

Back in Washington the President was being forced to reconsider his own position. His heart was set on a short war, and he received without enthusiasm the news of Taylor's victory at Monterrey. In Polk's view, a thousand rugged miles from the battlefield, the General had been wrong to permit the beaten Mexicans to retire with their arms, and doubly wrong to grant an armistice. The news from Monterrey was followed by word that Santa Anna, having taken advantage of his safe-conduct, was back in power, but far from offering peace and territory, he was personally leading the armies in the field and vowing destruction to the invaders. Polk tartly ordered Taylor to get on with the war, while he looked around for another general. Benton by this time was a familiar at the White House, and was freely discussing military strategy with the President and the Secretary of War. They agreed that the conflict would be most quickly ended by striking directly at Mexico City by way of Vera Cruz.[8]

General Scott, still under the ban of Polk's displeasure, was busily urging the same operation, and from sheer necessity he was restored to the command. Privately, however, the President promised Benton the honor of leading the attack if Congress could be persuaded to revive the rank of lieutenant general to give him precedence.[9] Even more than the blunt and taciturn Taylor, Scott was a potential President: a Whig whose claims were not to be advanced by a Democratic administration. Tall, well-built, flamboyant, and astonishingly well informed on everything, he was precisely the kind of man to repel the small, secretive, intellectually narrow Polk. But he was a thoroughly competent soldier, a brilliant commander, and whether the President liked it or not, Winfield Scott was still the ranking officer of the United States Army. He would have to do until Benton could be elevated over him.

When Congress reconvened December 7, 1846, Polk did his best to justify the situation in a long, argumentative message. There was little he could say, however, except to expound once more the causes of the war and to ask for money and men to bring it to a close. American armies, inadequately supplied and reinforced and deep in difficult and hostile territory, faced the best of the Mexican military leaders in a dubious cause. Worse than that, the fall elections showed strong Whig gains, with the crowning blow the defeat of the popular Silas Wright in New York. Polk thought it best to consult party leaders before he asked Congress to give him a lieutenant general.[10]

Within two weeks the President knew that his chances of altering the top military command were very slim indeed. He knew also that he would never get his bargaining fund from Congress unless he could divorce it from the Wilmot Proviso. Among those consulted was Calhoun, who still believed the war could have been avoided had administration leaders allowed so much as twenty-four hours for consideration. The South Carolina Senator held his Missouri colleague for no military genius but a political mountebank, without fidelity to principles or party. He knew, too, from his War Department days how professional soldiers jealous of their prestige, like Scott and Taylor, would react to the appointment of a civilian, or at best a superannuated lieutenant colonel, to be their superior officer. The President was convinced of nothing save the power of the opposition, and he presently summoned Benton to call off the deal. Polk's record of the interview is brief, but it is clear that he found Benton's heart set on the coveted honor, and he dared not face the formidable reprisals that would come if he dropped the project now. He made one more unsuccessful effort to persuade Calhoun, following a Christmas Eve dinner party at the White House; then made the formal request in a special message to Congress January 4, 1847.[11]

Ten days later, with a minimum of debate and an appearance of casual routine, the bill to revive the rank of lieutenant general was tabled in the Senate by a vote of 28 to 21. Calhoun and those who constituted his special following voted with the majority. Polk held the South Carolinian personally responsible for this rebuff to his administration, and Benton never forgave Calhoun for depriving him of his chance to reach the White House on the wings of military glory.[12]

4

Calhoun was far more disturbed over the slavery issue than he was over the matter of who should command the army. In his eyes it was no longer a struggle for power between North and South, because the North was already preponderant. It was now a struggle, and probably the final one, for the preservation of a way of life, an economic and social system, a culture. The Wilmot Proviso was a symbol, asserting in a sentence all that the minority most dreaded. Its adoption would mean that the majority would thereafter wield its power without regard to the interests and desires of the weaker section. Calhoun realized that slavery could not survive much if any beyond the area it then occupied, and he stoutly denied that he sought its actual extension. But he understood, as many of his contemporaries did not, that the moral obloquy of the quarantine the Proviso would impose would soon make the position of the South in the Union intolerable. He understood also that the admission of new free states would in time mean amendment of the Constitution to abolish forever the peculiar institution of the South, if indeed the dominant majority saw fit to bother with the forms of law at all.[13]

Prepared as he was for the issue, Calhoun could not have been surprised when Preston King, forty-year-old Representative from Silas Wright's home district in upstate New York, hurled the incendiary torch into the House on January 4. King forestalled the appointed business of the day by asking unanimous consent to introduce a bill on a different subject: a bill to give the President two million dollars to negotiate with Mexico, and to provide at the same time that there should be "neither slavery nor involuntary servitude in any territory which shall hereafter be acquired by or annexed to the United States." Consent was not granted, but the following day King again obtained the floor, this time to make a personal explanation. In the guise of answering a paragraph in the *Union* of the previous evening, the New Yorker read a prepared statement in which he insisted that slavery must never be allowed to extend beyond its existing limits. He conceded that Congress had no power to abolish slavery and affirmed the exclusive jurisdiction of the states, but he would not risk the possibility of any new state adopting a proslavery constitution by permitting Negroes to be carried into any territory from which a state might someday be made.[14]

Preston King professed to speak only for himself, but those who followed the political scene with attention, from the President down to the Washington reporters, recognized the move for what it was: a manifesto by the Northern wing of the Democracy, which originated somewhere in the neighborhood of Kinderhook. It meant that Polk had failed in his efforts to unite his party and must now choose between the contending factions or face the opposition of both. It meant that the differences in principle between Northern Whig and Northern Democrat were less than the differences between North and South and that the line of division between parties would in time be the Mason and Dixon line.[15]

The subject was resumed a few days later in more specific form, when the House debated a bill to set up a territorial government in Oregon. The bill included a provision to extend to that territory the terms of the Ordinance of 1787, which had barred slavery forever from all lands lying north and west of the Ohio. To this provision Armistead Burt of South Carolina proposed to add the words: "inasmuch as the whole of the said territory lies north of 36°30′ north latitude, known as the line of the Missouri compromise." Burt's relationship to Calhoun made him one of the accepted spokesmen for the South, and in this case, although it was not yet publicly avowed, he was acting on Calhoun's instructions.[16]

Burt's argument was an ingenious demonstration, buttressed by legislative precedent and Supreme Court decisions, that the Ordinance of 1787 was not binding, even on the states carved from the territory to which it referred, after they had been admitted to the Union, because the sovereignty of a state could not be impaired by an act of Congress. It followed that Congress could not, under the Constitution, prohibit slavery anywhere. Burt then recited the various steps in the antislavery agitation, noted the increasing pressure upon the South, and called for an end to sectional hostility. The Missouri Compromise was without constitutional foundation, but it stood as a workable agreement between North and South which the states had accepted. Let it, then, be extended to the Pacific and let the subject once and for all be abandoned.

John Pettit of Indiana answered Burt, and the next day the amendment was voted down by the substantial majority of 113 to 82. It was after all reference to the Missouri Compromise had been thus eliminated and the bill was up for final passage that Robert Barnwell Rhett elaborated his colleague's argument. Rhett concentrated on a single point: that Congress had no power to restrict slavery in the territories. The case rested on the familiar State Rights interpretation of the Constitution. The sovereignty, defined as supreme ultimate authority, rests not in Congress nor even in the general government of which the Congress is a part. It rests with the states. The taking and holding of territory is a sovereign act, and the territories accordingly do not belong to the general government but are the joint property of all the states. The delegated power to make "needful rules and regulations," therefore, cannot extend to the exclusion of some of the states from participation in the joint property of them all.[17]

The argument may seem finespun and legalistic, but it was in fact the only valid ground the South could oppose to the Wilmot Proviso. If it also excluded the Missouri Compromise, so much the worse for the North. Burt, with Calhoun's blessing, had offered to abide by the ancient line, extralegal though it was, for the sake of peace, but the offer had been rejected. Now there was to be no line and no restriction. The issue was joined for all the territories, in whatever latitude they might lie. All were to be open to slavery, or slavery was to be excluded from them all; and in the latter eventuality, the South would be forced to look to her own protection.

On January 16 the House passed the Oregon bill with slavery excluded and Rhett had his answer.

The President fretted and fumed and complained bitterly to anyone who would listen that vital war measures were being neglected or set aside while Congress spent "day after day and week after week in a worse than useless discussion about slavery." A "mischievous & wicked agitation," Polk called it; but for all his impatience he was beginning at last to see what a whirlwind was to follow in the wake of his own expansionism. The Northern Democracy had issued its manifesto; the Southern offer to compromise had been rejected; and the party schism was too wide for Polk or any other man to bridge.[18]

As the President vacillated on the crucial slavery issue, abdicating to squabbling factions the leadership that was rightfully his, the tension rose and the Southern members, because they had been placed on the defensive, drew closer together. The Charleston *Mercury* found no essential difference between the positions of Robert Toombs, Georgia Whig, and James A. Seddon, Calhoun Democrat from Virginia. It was an issue on which they would draw closer still until both would serve in the Cabinet of Jefferson Davis. It was the evidence of sectional unity against them, regardless of party, that so alarmed the South.[19]

But perhaps we should pause once more to explain why these chivalrous gentlemen were so outraged. It was because they knew that if the antislavery sentiment in the North was strong enough to break down the barriers between Democrat and Whig, if it was potent enough in Congress to bar slavery from the territories, it was or one day would be powerful enough to abolish slavery. It was this day that these Southern intellectuals could not face; that they would leave the Union rather than endure. For abolition did not mean to them the relatively peaceable shift from payment for labor in quarters and subsistence to payment in cash; it did not mean the mere surrender of physical control, which would in part be balanced by the surrender of economic and moral responsibility. To them it meant a holocaust of blood. It meant a ruthless and pitiless war of extermination waged between blacks and whites in which, whoever won, the land would be laid waste and the stench would rise to high heaven to torment the nostrils of generations yet unborn. It was only this conviction that could lead men as intelligent as Burt to appeal on the floor of the House to his fellow Southerners not to wait "till their hearthstones were drenched with the blood of their wives and children." Say they suffered from the deepest of guilt complexes; say they failed abysmally to understand the character of the Negro; say that their fears were the groundless nightmares of bad boys. They nevertheless believed that the slave, once freed, would rise and slay his master, and because they believed it, they reacted as they did to what appeared a settled purpose on the part of the majority to expose them to this danger.[20]

5

While the House ignored the war to debate the slavery question Polk received another visit from the ubiquitous Colonel Atocha, who succeeded in convincing the President, the Secretary of State, and Senator Benton that he was actually and unquestionably a personal agent of Santa Anna. The Mexican dictator was represented as desiring peace and as willing to deal with commissioners for the cession of California to the United States. There were various terms, of course, and there would be fifteen or twenty million dollars involved in the transaction, but Polk was too eager to end the war to quibble. Atocha was hustled to Vera Cruz in a United States revenue cutter, with a dispatch for the Mexican Foreign Minister; and identical bills to give the President three million dollars "to bring the existing war with Mexico to a close" were quickly introduced in both houses of Congress by the chairmen of the respective committees on foreign relations.[21]

It was this "three-million bill" as it came to be called—the same bill, with the addition of an extra million, that had been lost at the previous session because the Wilmot Proviso was attached to it—that gave Calhoun the springboard he wanted for making his own views known. Before he spoke on it, however, he had been officially read out of the party, and was again the lonely but powerful maverick he had been in Jackson's time.

The break with the President came when Calhoun and the small band of Southern Democrats who followed his lead forced an unwelcome amendment to one of Polk's cherished measures. The bill in question, as it came from the House, provided for recruiting and equipping ten additional regiments for the duration of the war, and gave the President the power to appoint commissioned officers during the recess of Congress. Calhoun held such a delegation of authority to be unconstitutional, and for a time it appeared that the whole bill would be lost between the houses before an acceptable compromise was worked out. The day before an agreement was reached the President pronounced Calhoun "the most mischievous man in the Senate" and that evening the *Union* featured the apparent loss of the ten-regiment bill through the obduracy of a handful of Senate recalcitrants. "If it is to be lost," Ritchie's editorial concluded in ominous echo of the President's words, "let the country understand by whose hands the sacrifice is made." [22]

That was February 8, 1847, and Calhoun was already scheduled to speak on the three-million bill the next day. With the small group that followed his lead he held the balance of power in the Senate,

and he knew before he took the floor that he had been excommuni-
cated by the President.

The galleries were jammed and the Senate floor itself was crowded
with visitors, members of the other house, officials, and guests of
Senators, when Calhoun rose to speak. His step had lost some of its
spring, his coarse hair was now iron-gray and worn long rather
than close-cropped as in the past, his lanky frame was more ema-
ciated-looking than ever, but his dark, deep-set eyes still flashed the
inner fire that was remarked by all who saw him, his voice was
strong and clear, and his sentences tripped over one another with
all their old-time fluency. In his opening words he waived discussion of the sectional issue until a later time, proposing to confine
himself to the more immediate question of how to achieve the objects
of the war.

The topic gave him room for gentle irony. No one, he observed,
had ever explained just what were the objects of the war, but from
a study of the President's messages and of the act of Congress declaring that war existed because Mexican forces had invaded American soil, he concluded that the executive and legislative branches
agreed on three purposes to be accomplished. The first, clearly, was
to repel the invasion; the second was to establish the Rio Grande as the
boundary; the third and least important was to secure indemnity for
the claims of American citizens against the Mexican Government.
The first two were already achieved, for the invading armies had been
hurled back at every point and the United States was in firm control of
the Rio Grande from its mouth to its source. Nothing remained,
then, but the idemnity, and even there the means of satisfying the
wildest claims were already in American possession. Did we not
hold Mexican territory far greater in value than any claims? What,
then, remained to be done but to set up a defensive line and go
on about our business until Mexico decided to sue for peace?

His arguments were practical ones, designed to appeal to practical
men. Such a line as he proposed could be held, he thought, with a
minimum of men at a relatively trifling cost, and could be easily
and quickly supplied. It would end the uncertainty and hazard and
permit the country to enter that prosperous state that only the war
now prevented. It would be the most generous and forbearing course
toward Mexico, a neighbor whose good will we must have. The

much-talked-of campaign for Vera Cruz and Mexico City would be hazardous and costly, and there was little reason to hope it would be decisive even if it succeeded. The war might then last for years, bleeding the resources of the country, destroying its youth, its industry, its growth, building up a mountain of debt and in the process giving England the advantage in the race for commercial supremacy.

And the line he would hold? He had selected it with care, though he professed much diffidence and an inadequate knowledge of the geography involved. He would hold the Rio Grande to the line of 32° of north latitude, thence along that parallel to the Gulf of California, and down the gulf to the sea. It was precisely the line that Polk had told the South Carolinian repeatedly (and probably every other Democrat in the room) he meant to secure as a boundary. It was already conquered, every mile of it, and being held. The whole scheme, moreover, was identical with that suggested by Calhoun to the President in December, and unanimously endorsed by the Cabinet at that time. It could hardly fail to appeal to all who wanted an end to fighting, an end to borrowing and heavy taxes, an end to uncertainty and tension. It was bound to appeal also to those who feared the power placed in the President's hands by the military patronage and financial perquisites that were now his.[23]

Polk was unmoved because his mind was already made up. The Union had forecast what was to come in its comments of February 8 on the ten-regiment bill. On February 9 the full text of Calhoun's speech appeared, only a few hours after its delivery. There was no specific comment, save a very generally worded denunciation of "the opposition" for what Ritchie was pleased to call its desire to surrender California to Great Britain. But a contributed article signed "Vindicator," to which the editor called the attention of his readers, was caustic. No names were named and the reference was specifically to the ten-regiment bill, but the purpose was unmistakable. In the field, declared the writer, the American forces are everywhere triumphant, but on the floor of Congress "the cause of Mexico is maintained with zeal and ability." "In the Senate of the United States, on yesterday," Vindicator continued, "the Mexicans achieved another victory. . . . If Santa Ana, Ampudia, or any other Mexican general could snatch from our soldiers a corresponding victory, we should place them upon the same elevation where their compatriots,

friends and fellow-soldiers in the Senate of the United States stand."
It was a calculated challenge that Ritchie knew full well would not
be overlooked.

6

The Senate met as usual at noon on February 10, and as soon as
the routine business was out of the way David Yulee of Florida, one
of the most faithful of Calhoun's followers, rose to a question of
privilege. He moved that the editors of the *Union,* having "issued
and uttered a public libel upon the character of this body," be
excluded from the floor of the Senate, a privilege they enjoyed by
virtue of their position as public printers. By agreement the question was carried over for a day, and was then once more postponed
in what was probably a deliberate attempt to provoke the administration into making a personal attack.[24]

In a Senate closely balanced as to party Calhoun's position was
very strong, and to the administration dangerous in the extreme.
For no concession Polk could have made, short of yielding up to
the dominant Carolinian the actual partisan leadership, would have
won him over, and any such concession, even had Polk been willing
to make it, would have alienated an equally potent group under
Benton's leadership. Polk had hoped, temporized, and experimented,
but Calhoun's stand on the declaration of war had shown the President that he could delay no longer. He had then made his peace
with Benton and set out to eliminate Calhoun. From the start
of the session the *Union* had pressed harder and harder upon the
Senate, and always the attacks were pointed toward the group of
conservative Southern Democrats who held the deciding voice.

As the weeks went by the tone of the *Union* had grown sharper
until the climax of February 8, when Ritchie threatened to expose
publicly those Senators who were in the administration's view ob-
structing the war. It was the start of a full-scale campaign against
Calhoun and his followers, but the South Carolinian realized that
his own strength would be the greater if he could force Polk into
the open. When names were named he could show that he had in
fact voted for every war measure except two. On the declaration
itself he had not voted at all; and on the creation of the lieutenant
generalship he had opposed. He could show, in short, that it was

not what he had actually done but what his position made it possible for him to do if he chose, that made him so obnoxious to the administration.

Yulee opened the debate on his resolution of expulsion on February 12, and he made out a very good case, anticipating the organized cries of "censorship" and "infringement of freedom of the press" that would come from Ritchie and his defenders. It was not proposed to evict the *Union's* reporters, who would occupy their places as usual; and the venerable editor himself might still sit at the reporter's table, or in the gallery as a citizen-visitor. What the resolution was designed to do was to withdraw from him the privilege of a seat on the Senate floor. It was a privilege that had been extended by courtesy, had been abused, and should therefore be revoked. Allen and Sevier talked generally about freedom of the press, with sundry not very apropos references to the Alien and Sedition Laws of infamous memory. Then the fireworks began.[25]

Hopkins L. Turney, the Democratic Senator from the President's own state of Tennessee, secured the floor and trained his batteries directly on Calhoun. Ritchie had, to be sure, permitted his correspondent to use some rather unguarded language, but had he in any particular gone beyond the truth? Was it not true that there was in the Senate a "balance of power party, which . . . gives shape and form to every measure?" Yulee egged him on and Turney elaborated, getting closer and closer to the point until at last he allowed his own eloquence to carry him away. Calhoun suddenly rejoined as though he had in fact been personally attacked, and Turney was trapped into the avowal before he could recover his guard. In the course of the five-hour wrangle that followed Calhoun himself was charged with responsibility for the war, through his handling of the Texas annexation; and Turney took a verbal beating from Butler that had even the administration Senators shaking with laughter.[26]

The next day Westcott of Florida, another of the "balance of power party," brought the debate back to Ritchie and the libel. He pointed out that while no one had defended Vindicator, three days had gone by without retraction or apology. On the contrary, the *Union* had lashed out at all concerned in what seemed all too surely an attempt to whip into line those who would not blindly follow the administration. He even insinuated that the President himself was "Vindicator," and perhaps he was.

The debate consumed the remainder of the day, but it ranged far beyond the immediate point at issue. When it was over it was clear that Calhoun and his followers had been read out of the party because they would not support the war with suitable enthusiasm; but it was also clear that in the minds of Southern men the war was now inextricably bound up with the Wilmot Proviso. They were unwilling to aid in the acquisition of territory from which they were themselves to be excluded, and which would be used only to make further war upon their domestic institutions. Before they voted men and money for the conquest of Mexico they wanted the administration to give evidence of its own good faith by taking a stand against restriction. Ritchie was expelled by a vote of 27 to 21, with Butler, Calhoun, Westcott, and Yulee voting with the Whigs to make the majority. But the whole tenor of the debate, and particularly Westcott's summation, left no doubt that the vote of censure was meant not for Ritchie but for Polk.[27]

CHAPTER XXI

SENTINEL OF THE SOUTH

1

THE WILMOT PROVISO was adopted in the House of Representatives for the second time on February 15, 1847, this time by a margin of 115 to 106, in the form of an amendment to the bill that would give the President three million dollars to negotiate a peace with Mexico. The majority was made up of Northern Democrats as well as Northern Whigs. The voting was accompanied by a flood of resolutions from the legislatures of the free states calling on Congress to exclude slavery from any territory acquired as a result of the war.[1]

Calhoun undertook to answer with countering resolutions of his own on February 19, and his brief speech of explanation was a definitive statement of the Southern case. In his incisive fashion he brushed aside the question of restriction to go directly to the real issue that lay behind it. The slaveholding states, he pointed out, were already a minority in the House of Representatives and in the electoral college, and would be a minority in the Senate also when the members from Iowa and Wisconsin took their seats in the next Congress. The fixed purpose of this growing majority was openly declared to be the complete exclusion of slavery from all the remaining territory of the United States, including all that might be acquired in future, which meant that, even without new acquisitions from Mexico, the ratio in favor of the free states would before long be two to one.[2]

"Sir," he continued, "if this state of things is to go on—if this determination, so solemnly made, is to be persisted in, where shall we stand, as far as this Federal Government of ours is concerned? We shall be at the entire mercy of the non-slaveholding States. Can we look to their justice and regard for our interests? I ask, can we rely on that? Ought we to trust our safety and prosperity to their mercy and sense of justice? These are the solemn questions which

303

I put to all—this and the other side of the Chamber." For answer, if indeed they need look beyond the Proviso itself, he referred his auditors, quiet and attentive all of them, and a little apprehensive, to the history of the tariff.

He stood there, straight and slender, his seamed face tense, his shaggy hair shaking with the vehemence of his speech, his brilliant eyes fixed on handsome George M. Dallas in the chair, and the hand of prophecy was on him. "Sir, the day that the balance between the two sections of the country—the slaveholding States and the non-slaveholding States—is destroyed, is a day that will not be far removed from political revolution, anarchy, civil war, and widespread disaster. The balance of this system is in the slaveholding States. They are the conservative portion—always have been the conservative portion—always will be the conservative portion; and with a due balance on their part may, for generations to come, uphold this glorious Union of ours. But if this scheme is to be carried out—if we are to be reduced to a handful—if we are to become a mere ball to play the presidential game with—to count something in the Baltimore caucus—if this is to be the result—wo! wo! I say, to this Union."

He sought then, as the weaker side has always sought, for safety in the Constitution, in which he solemnly affirmed the states were equal partners, and the territories the joint possession of them all, from which none could be legitimately excluded. And when the territorial stage was passed, each new state had an inviolable right to determine for itself what institutions it would countenance, provided only that its form of government be republican. The Missouri Compromise he considered an error, "highly injurious to the South, because it surrendered, for mere temporary purposes, those high principles of the constitution upon which I think we ought to stand." He would nevertheless have been willing to extend the compromise line to the Pacific, "in order to preserve, under the present trying circumstances, the peace of the country." It had been at his suggestion, he now explained, that such a proposal had been made in the other house, but it had been decisively defeated. Perhaps it was as well.

"I see my way in the constitution; I cannot in a compromise. A compromise is but an act of Congress. It may be overruled at any time. It gives us no security. But the constitution is stable. It is a rock. On it we can stand, and on it we can meet our friends from the non-slaveholding States. It is a firm and stable ground, on which we can better stand in opposition to fanaticism, than on the shifting sands of compromise."

He would ask the Senate then to endorse resolutions expounding the meaning of the Constitution in terms that would protect the South and assure her equality within the Union. And if the Senate rejected his interpretation, what then? He would not undertake to decide. "It is a question for our constituents, the slaveholding States—a solemn and a great question. If the decision should be adverse, I trust and do believe that they will take under solemn consideration what they ought to do. I give no advice. It would be hazardous and dangerous for me to do so. But I may speak as an individual member of that section of the Union. There is my family and connections; there I drew my first breath; there are all my hopes. I am a planter—a cotton planter. I am a Southern man and a slaveholder —a kind and merciful one, I trust—and none the worse for being a slaveholder. I say, for one, I would rather meet any extremity upon earth than give up one inch of our equality—one inch of what belongs to us as members of this great republic."

Embodied in the categorical form of resolutions, his views were then laid before the Senate.

2

The President could not permit the slavery question to overshadow the war. However much he might personally resent the intrusion of the Wilmot Proviso, he could neither endorse it nor take a stand against it. Polk's responsibility was to the whole, and he could not permit a vote on Calhoun's resolutions without putting his administration, through its adherents in the Senate, into a sectional position. The attack on the Senate dissidents had already been renewed on February 16 when "Vindicator" returned to the columns of the *Union*. The editor denied that the earlier blast had been aimed at Calhoun, but there was no doubt about these new strictures.

As soon as Calhoun's resolutions had been read, Benton waved them angrily aside as "a string of abstractions" and demanded that the important business of the session proceed without interruption. There was a brief, but barbed, interchange between the two Senators; then the resolutions were ordered printed and debate on the three-million bill resumed. The speaker for the day was rugged and weather-beaten Sam Houston, who left his eternal whittling to play the partisan role assigned to him. He started by chiding the opposition for losing sight of the purpose of the bill in its zeal to crucify Ritchie, but that was only persiflage. He switched quickly and adroitly to the history of Texas, and the bulk of his speech was an elaboration and documentation of Turney's charges that Calhoun, by his actions in the State Department, was the real author of the war.[3]

Ritchie took up the cudgels again on Monday, February 22, with the most savage attack yet hurled at the South Carolina Senator, the purpose being once more to blackguard Calhoun on the basis of his State Department record. As the end of the Congress drew near and partisan fervor rose to a shrill crescendo, it seemed almost as though not Mexico but John C. Calhoun was the country's foremost enemy. It was only fitting that the privilege of delivering the *coup de grâce* against the South Carolinian should be assigned to Benton. When the frustrated lieutenant general presumptive was absent from his seat for three days it was quickly rumored that he was preparing most carefully for the grateful role of executioner, and the announcement that he would speak on the twenty-fourth brought the usual crowd of eager onlookers. "Long Tom" Ritchie was in the gallery and the entire Cabinet found seats on the Senate floor.[4]

Benton's speech contributed nothing new, not even its obvious rancor, and was no more than a restatement of the charges already made by Houston, Turney, and Ritchie. They were stated, perhaps, in more arresting form, and certainly delivered with greater forensic skill, but they failed to annihilate as advertised, or even seriously to wound. The administration, declared the fluent Missourian, was in no way responsible for the war. The blame fell solely on the Senator from South Carolina, who had procured the annexation of Texas not in Benton's way but in his own. The treaty of 1819, by which Texas was alleged to have been given up to Spain, was now laid not at Adams' door but at Calhoun's, and the South Carolinian was charged with an inveterate hostility to the West. There was in all this planned and careful method. Benton, as we have already seen, had taken his own stand with the Northern Democracy, and he was seeking, as the Wilmot Proviso men were generally seeking, to break down the alliance that had flowered at Memphis between South and West and to turn the West once more into the Northern sphere of influence. That was the real point Benton desired to make. The letters and documents he read had most of them been heard already in the course of the debate, and so had the hostile résumé of Calhoun's career.[5]

Calhoun answered immediately, his calm, confident manner the more striking in contrast to the bombastic style of his opponent. He began by thanking the Senator for at last yielding him the credit for annexing Texas; and professed to see in this eagerness to fix on him the responsibility for the war an indication that the war was no longer popular. Then he took up the charges one by one as Benton had elaborated them, answering each in turn and adding now and then a thrust at his adversary's record. He was not crushed, nor even shaken, by all the power at the President's command, and he emerged from the contest stronger than he had been before. The attack on him served only to pose the sectional issue in a new form, and to show Southern conservatives that there was no alternative within the Union but to follow the road Calhoun would have them take.[6]

In sober mood the Senate rejected the Wilmot Proviso the evening of March 2 by a vote of 32 to 21, and the three-million bill was then passed by a five-vote margin, Calhoun and all his following voting "aye." There was no further incident until the closing day, when Allen moved to take up the Oregon bill. The slavery restriction imposed in the House had been stricken out by the Judiciary Committee, and so the bill was tabled by Northern votes. It was then that Allen "broke into a most indignant invective" against those whom he charged with seeking now to force Oregon out of the Union after failing in their first design to give that fair region to Great Britain. So pointed were some of the Ohio Senator's remarks that Calhoun felt obliged to notice them. Though suffering from a cold and so hoarse he could hardly speak above a whisper, he was heard to say that "so far as this imputation of motive fell on him, he would suffer it to pass by him as the idle wind." [7]

3

Calhoun left Washington the evening of March 4, in good spirits and hopeful that the Democracy would yet make concessions to the South for the sake of harmony.[8] He knew, however, that nothing would be yielded until he could say positively to the North that without concessions there would no Southern votes for party measures in Congress and none in any Presidential nominating convention. He had been preaching Southern unity already for twenty years without any real accomplishment, but now it was not only livelihood but the Union itself that seemed to be at stake. The issue was not the war, nor organization of the territories, nor even the existence of slavery, but whether the South could maintain her social and economic structure within the united framework or would be forced to seek security in a political organization of her own. Divided she would be crushed; united the slave states might yet act as a brake upon the radicalism of the North and save both the Union and themselves. It was therefore on Southern unity that Calhoun's thoughts were fixed as he journeyed homeward.

He arrived in Charleston on the Wilmington boat at six o'clock in the morning of Saturday, March 6. Despite the hour he was met by the Mayor, and by sundry deputations and committees of citizens who escorted him to the Carolina Hotel. There he was installed as the guest of the city, and there he rested over the week end with Floride, who had been awaiting his arrival. Arrangements had been made for a formal reception at the City Hall, where the distinguished guest would receive his admirers, but he was compelled to cancel the ordeal because of the severe cold he had brought with him from Washington. For the same reason a meeting scheduled for the evening of the eighth at the New Theatre was postponed until the following evening. Though Calhoun was still hoarse and a little shaky, the meeting was held on the ninth, and the Senator laid down a program for the South.[9]

The meeting was said to be one of the largest ever held in Charleston. Long before the appointed hour of seven every seat was occupied and every vantage point from which one might conceivably be able to hear was taken up. The steps were jammed and the street itself was full by the time the gavel fell. The crowd roared its welcome when Calhoun stepped out on the stage, men and women vying with one another, and it was some time before John E. Carew, the new publisher of the *Mercury,* could establish order and turn the meeting over to its permanent chairman, Henry Bailey. He was flanked by sixteen vice presidents, including Huger and Aiken, Elmore and Boyce and Gadsden. There was a "forcible and eloquent" committee report, presented by Colonel Isaac W. Hayne. When the protocol was satisfied a deep hush fell over the great hall as Calhoun rose to speak.[10]

His words were solemn and straight to the point. There was no longer any doubt in his mind that large majorities of both parties in the free states were determined to exclude the South from all terri-tory belonging to the Union. Neither was there any doubt that they had the numerical strength to do it. Only the Constitution, inter-preted as he and his followers had expounded it in the past session of Congress, stood in the way, and even there mere words were not enough. There was a way, however, in which the danger might be met.

The apparent unity of the North in opposition to slavery had come about, in Calhoun's view, because parties were so evenly matched in strength that the small minority of organized abolitionists—per-haps 5 percent of the whole—could sway elections in the free states. Their votes had therefore been sought by the politicians until they had come to dictate policy to Whigs and Democrats alike. The only remedy was an equally united front. The South must demonstrate to Northern partisans that "the immediate and necessary effect of courting abolition votes" would be to lose those of the slave states.

The South, he argued, had thus far been impotent because she was herself divided into parties, bent like their Northern allies on winning elections. Each party, at the critical moment, would fail to take a decisive stand on the disputed issue lest the abolitionists be offended and the vote of New York or some other populous Northern state be lost. It was time, Calhoun thought, to be done with all this. First of all the nominating convention should be dropped and the choice of President left "where the constitution placed it—to the Electoral College." By its numerical superiority the North would dominate any convention that could be held, and by its unity on the slave question it would exclude the South. Since both parties in the North were united "to divest us of our just and equal rights in the public domain, it is time that both parties with us should unite in resistance to so great an outrage. Let us show at least as much spirit in defending our rights and honor, as they have evinced in assailing them. . . . Henceforward, let all party distinction among us cease, so long as this aggression on our rights and honor shall continue, on the part of the non-slaveholding States. . . . It is thus, and thus only, that we can defend our rights, maintain our honor, ensure our safety, and command respect."

He repeated again as he had often reiterated in the past that his object was to preserve the Union if it could be done without yielding the equality of the slave states, but he saw in the current agitation a danger too great to be disregarded. If this danger were not met "promptly and decidedly, the two portions of the Union will gradually become thoroughly alienated, when no alternative will be left to us as the weaker of the two, but to sever all political ties, or sink down into abject submission. It is only by taking an early and decided stand, while the political ties are still strong, that a rally of the sound and patriotic of all portions of the Union can be successfully made to arrest so dire an alternative."

Calhoun's speech was not published in full until March 23, after he had himself written it out, but the Charleston papers carried summaries which gave Polk and his supporters a new text for denouncing the South Carolina Senator. They saw in his appeal for Southern unity no more than the desire to create a sectional party whose purpose would be to raise Calhoun to the Presidency, and they condemned it in unmeasured terms. In justice to Polk be it said that he equally condemned the sectionalism of Silas Wright and his New Yorkers; but like Jackson whom he was trying to emulate, he failed to come to grips with the real problem. The question of slavery, as he correctly noted, had been settled by the Constitution, but who was to enforce the settlement if the Executive and majorities in both houses of Congress chose to violate it? [11]

Even in the South there were many who saw in the Charleston speech only a new bid for the Presidency. As the controversy raged around him Calhoun protested in vain that he sought nothing but peace and safety for his country and retirement for himself. In vain he pleaded for a settlement of the moot slavery question before sectional antagonism and hostility became so great that peaceful settlement would be impossible. He succeeded only in fanning the flames he would have quenched and in filling his own few remaining years with anxiety and toil.

4

Colonel Atocha, whose glib tongue had already produced untold damage, returned from his mission to Santa Anna on March 20. The answer he carried was that Mexico would not even consider negotiation until all United States warships were withdrawn from her coasts and all American soldiers from her soil. Polk was thus left with no alternative but to order a crushing blow at the heart of Mexico. He must have been greatly relieved when he received word on April 1 of Taylor's smashing victory at Buena Vista, and ten days later the official news that Vera Cruz and its defending fortress had surrendered to Scott, even though both feats had been accomplished by Whig generals. As quickly as possible the President dispatched Nicholas P. Trist, Chief Clerk of the State Department, to Scott's headquarters, with instructions as to peace terms and power to negotiate a treaty when the Mexicans had been sufficiently beaten.[12]

On the home front everything seemed to bear a sectional cast. Business and commercial activity in Charleston showed a steady rise from the fall of 1846, apparently coincidental with the operation of the Walker tariff. Railroad building along the pattern urged at Memphis moved rapidly forward, and only the war seemed to stand in the way of long-continued prosperity. But the war was now inevitably associated with the rising opposition to slavery, and Northern men would not be content to see the commerce of the West diverted to Southern ports.

July 5 saw another internal-improvement convention called to order, this time at Chicago under the auspices of men from the North and Northwest whose interest lay in improving transportation between the grain states and the great seaport cities of the East. President of the convention was Edward Bates of Missouri, who would be Lincoln's Attorney General. Lincoln himself was there, a comparative unknown, as one of the delegates from Illinois; and from New York came the potent Whig editors, Thurlow Weed and Horace Greeley. There were also letters from leading politicians who thought it expedient not to attend in person. Van Buren was noncommittal; Silas Wright approved harbor development on the Lakes at Federal expense, and many river improvements, but recognized that the dividing line was difficult; Benton denounced local raids on the Treasury, but came out strongly as the champion of great national works such as connecting the Mississippi with the Lakes. Webster, with a sly thrust at Calhoun's Memphis subtleties, favored internal improvements by the general government without distinctions, and so did Clay. Cass found a reason for absence but in writing his excuses cautiously neglected to say where he stood.[13]

The Chicago Convention was aimed in part at Calhoun and his Memphis doctrines; it was aimed in part at President Polk, who had vetoed two river and harbor bills; but most of all it was directed toward a political alliance of North and West to the exclusion of the South, and opposition to slavery would inevitably be one of its tenets. The Washington *Union* loyally supported the administration's position, as laid down in the internal-improvement vetoes; but the radical wing of the New York Democracy—the Barnburners of Van Buren and Wright, Flagg and Hoffman and Dix—looked on the movement not unfavorably. They had already made up their minds that the future belonged to freedom, and that the Wilmot Proviso would be the breaking point.[14]

The war, meanwhile, moved rapidly ahead, and Polk became more and more deeply engrossed in its political aspects. News from California, while satisfactory enough from the military point of view, made it clear that Lieutenant Colonel John Charles Frémont, presuming perhaps on the political potency of his father-in-law, had been insubordinate and possibly mutinous, and sooner or later an issue on that score would have to be made with Benton. Trist had not been tactful on arriving in Scott's camp, and the President's emissary and the commanding general were presently insulting each other by letter. Polk ordered the general reprimanded, and would have recalled him, had he dared.[15]

Calhoun too feared the political consequences of the war, but he saw it from a different point of view from that of the President. To the Southern champion Scott's easy conquest of Vera Cruz meant that there would be no stopping the conflict short of the complete conquest of Mexico, and he dreaded what must happen then. In any solution that could be adopted he saw grave danger to the American system of government as he understood it, and he visualized a generation of military dominance.

5

As Calhoun intensified his efforts to unite the South for her own political defense, he renewed earlier attempts to establish a proslavery newspaper in Washington. There had been many discussions of the theme during the winter of 1846-1847, and a committee had been set up under Elmore's leadership to raise a fund of $50,000. But there was indifference and delay, and opposition from those who held the whole venture to be a tactical blunder or perhaps just a maladroit bit of electioneering. It was the end of March before a prospectus was issued and the campaign for funds got under way.[16]

Robert Barnwell Rhett and Isaac W. Hayne were suggested as possible editors, and Duff Green advanced his own claims to that position with vigor if not with modesty. For the time being, however, no decision was made. Hayne was inexperienced while Rhett and Green were unacceptable to many of those from whom financial support would have to come. Calhoun himself refused to express any preference, insisting only that the venture must be supported by the whole South rather than by a small group in the vicinity of Charleston.[17]

Additional impetus was given to the project by sharply rising sectional hostility. A Pennsylvania law of March, protecting fugitive slaves with great legal ingenuity, had rendered slave property insecure in Maryland and northern Virginia. A request from the Maryland Governor for the return of fugitives was refused, and tension between neighboring states neared the breaking point before midsummer. The directors of the Baltimore and Ohio Railroad decided to avoid Pennsylvania soil entirely by striking the river below Wheeling instead of at Pittsburgh, and the *Mercury* pronounced on the significance of this change of plans. "Leading Northern men are yielding step by step to Abolition, and thereby cutting one by one the ties that unite us. . . . They have invaded our political rights—they trample on our social relations—they excommunicate and drive off our Churches, and now most naturally follows our trade and commerce. Is it not time for men of thought and influence to reconsider and retrace their steps?" Calhoun noted "that the conflict between North and South is every day becoming more pointed and determined"; and on the other side, Joshua Giddings, as narrowly obsessed in one direction as Calhoun was in the other, pronounced in favor of a strictly Northern party.[18]

The ominously growing sectional hostility was reviewed in detail in a printed circular of August 2, 1847, sent out from Charleston and signed by former Senator Daniel E. Huger and more than thirty other prominent South Carolinians. With it went a subscription pledge for the proposed Southern paper, and it was mailed to influential men throughout the South. Partisan politics was set aside and the appeal was put on a frankly sectional basis.[19]

Dispassionately, and the more effectively because of it, the various steps in the "progress of the Anti-Slavery spirit" were reviewed. There was the "inundation of Congress with petitions for the abolition of slavery in the District of Columbia"; the disregard of the fugitive slave law, and finally its statutory nullification in Pennsylvania; and Hoar's mission to South Carolina "to obstruct the execution of the local laws." Then came the Wilmot Proviso, twice adopted by the House of Representatives and urged on Congress by the legislatures of eleven states; and the repudiation of the Missouri Compromise in the rejection of Burt's amendment to the Oregon bill. In language reminiscent of Calhoun's Charleston speech, the circular went on to show how all this was possible because of the unity of purpose of a relatively small band of abolitionists, supported by an able and zealous press. Yet there was no paper of general circulation in the South, none in the free states, none in Washington, to counteract these views.

The purpose to be achieved by a paper in the Capital to represent Southern interests was then explained. "We want a paper whose polar star shall be the sentiment, 'that danger to our Institutions can only be averted by jealously watching our rights under the Constitution; by insisting upon the proportionate influence intended to be secured to us by the compromises of that compact; and, above all, by maintaining, at all times, and at all hazards, our equality full and complete with whatever communities we hold connection.' We wish a paper which we can *trust*, firm and fearless, which cannot be bribed, cajoled, flattered, or frightened, into furling, for an instant, the banner of SOUTHERN EQUALITY." The proposed paper was to be free from all party influences, and it was hoped that it would be generally supported by men who had no political ends to seek. The appeal for funds followed.[20]

As General Scott moved rapidly along the road to Mexico City, and the Northern press insisted with growing unanimity that, whatever the territorial acquisitions of the war, slavery should advance no farther, the time seemed to Calhoun to be getting dangerously short. He wanted the paper to be set up and ready when the new Congress met, and his partisans in South Carolina, Georgia, Alabama, Mississippi, and Louisiana intensified their efforts. Calhoun himself distributed circulars, and brought all of his matchless powers of persuasion to bear on the doubters. New names were considered for the editorial post, among them William L. Yancey of Alabama, Richard K. Crallé of Virginia, Muscoe R. H. Garnett, brilliant young nephew of Robert M. T. Hunter, and Ellwood Fisher of Cincinnati. By September two thousand circulars had been distributed in the slave states, and pledges from South Carolina alone had reached $20,000. But the response elsewhere was less encouraging and though Conner ranged as far afield as New York City he could not stretch the total beyond $30,000.[21]

It was not enough; nor did other projects for combating the anti-slavery activities of the North fare better. One suggestion was that the law prohibit the collection of debts due to citizens of states unwilling to render up fugitive slaves. Calhoun himself proposed that the ships of the offending states be barred from Southern ports, in an application of economic pressure. But without unity no form of retaliation would succeed, and Calhoun insisted on laying that firm foundation before the superstructure was put up.[22]

By mid-September South Carolina had news of the battles of Contreras and Churubusco in the outskirts of Mexico City, where Colonel Pierce M. Butler of the Palmetto Regiment had lost his life; and the end of the month brought word that the Capital itself had fallen to General Scott. Yet peace seemed as far away as ever. In Washington Polk showed his own dissatisfaction by determining to recall Trist, who had failed to make the treaty that was his mission, and prepared to push hostilities to the limit once more. Calhoun looked only to the fearful aftermath. "If we should succeed in conquering the whole what shall we do with it," he wrote Clemson late in October, "or what can [we] do with it without ruin to our institutions? If we fail where shall we be?"[23]

The territorial question was certain to be again the major issue before Congress, and Calhoun foresaw another session of "great distraction and confusion." He was confirmed in his own course, however, by trustworthy reports coming in from the free states. Conner returned from his Northern trip convinced that the people and politicians alike were alarmed at the stiffening attitude of the South, and were ready to drop the Proviso. Ellwood Fisher wrote in similar vein from Cincinnati where he found the people uniformly hostile to slavery and in favor of restriction, but unwilling to risk disunion for such a cause. "Much will depend," he wrote, "on the manner in which the issue is presented—but more far more will depend on the union and firmness of the South. If they are clearly displayed the South will have friends enough here of both parties to assert her equality. . . . But if she waivers or divides she is lost." The *Mercury* stated it more ominously: "It is from [the Northern] organization and success that we are made to see that our safety in the Slaveholding States consists alone in *confidence in each other, and* UNION AMONG OURSELVES. *The Potomac may yet be as celebrated as the Rubicon.*[24]

CHAPTER XXII

WAR, POLITICS AND PEACE

1

THE MEXICAN WAR and the bitter sectional struggle that grew out of it tended for a long time to overshadow the Presidential contest, even while providing the issues in terms of which the political battle would be fought out. It was only after Congress had adjourned in March of 1847 that political speculation became general. By the end of that month the election, still a year and a half away, seemed to many as good as over, for it was on March 30 that news of the battle of Buena Vista reached the Capital.

From the very first victories of the war Zachary Taylor had been mentioned in various quarters as a Presidential possibility. Blunt and uncompromising, a lifelong professional soldier with so little political experience that he had never even cast a ballot, "Old Rough and Ready" was certainly more at home in the camp than on the hustings, and he had been himself the first to ridicule the idea of his being Presidential timber. Yet circumstances and a handful of men wise in the ways of politics contrived by the spring of 1847 to make him decisively the choice of the masses and to overcome in large measure his own reluctance.

There had been nothing brilliant in Taylor's career, but his record was one of solid achievement in his chosen vocation. After years on the western frontier he was shifted to Florida in the late 1830's where he brought the long Seminole war to a successful close after better-known officers had failed. It was there that he won his first star and his first national renown. He had two stars when Polk's orders sent him from Corpus Christi to the Rio Grande early in 1846, but he was still a soldier's soldier—a squat, homely figure in battle fatigues, easily riding Old Whitey at the head of his dragoons. He did not fire the imagination as Jackson had done, but he inspired the implicit confidence of his men, and he won battles. Tales of his prowess, of his rugged independence, of his great simplicity of char-

317

acter, began to drift back from Resaca de la Palma and Palo Alto, and after Monterrey he was a popular hero. It was the sharp criticism of the President following the victory at Monterrey that first fixed in the General's mind the notion that he was being unjustly treated by the administration, and the idea grew apace when he was stripped of much of his fighting force in the interest of Scott's projected attack on Vera Cruz. In the eyes of the average American, whose sympathies have always been with the underdog, Taylor was being sacrificed for political reasons, and in his own eyes he was being sacrificed to the ambitions of his superior officer, the vain and gaudy Winfield Scott.

Then came Buena Vista, where Taylor faced a picked Mexican army outnumbering his own forces four to one and commanded by the Napoleon of the West himself: the redoubtable Santa Anna, who but for Polk's interference might have remained in harmless exile. After two days of the most dogged and bitter fighting of the war Santa Anna fled the field and Zachary Taylor became the favorite of the masses for President of the United States.[1]

He became the favorite also with certain politicians, who saw in him precisely the qualities demanded by the times. He had as yet avowed no party affiliation, though the Whigs took it for granted he was one of them if only because he had suffered humiliation at the hands of a Democratic administration. He was personally popular in the North, where the war itself was often strenuously opposed. Better still, he was a Southerner and a slaveholder, the Virginia-born master of Cypress Grove plantation on the lower Mississippi near Baton Rouge. In a day of unprecedented sectional tension and partisan animosity, Zachary Taylor was a man to win votes from all parties and in every section. He would need, to be sure, the advice and careful handling of men who knew their way in politics, but this he was destined to have—had already, in fact, in the person of able and honest Senator John J. Crittenden of Kentucky.

2

In South Carolina where, thanks to incessant publicizing of the issue, the danger to the Southern way of life was most keenly felt, Taylor's candidacy posed a special problem. A bare three weeks before the news of Buena Vista launched the Taylor boom in earnest,

Calhoun had shown how the South might force both parties to protect her interests by herself remaining aloof from party. Here was a Southern man without partisan ties and with great personal popularity in all sections of the country. Could the South hope for more or even for as much from any other quarter? Rumors were quickly afloat in Washington that the South Carolina Senator would decline any form of Presidential nomination for himself in favor of General Taylor. It was precisely the course Polk expected Calhoun to take after his Charleston speech of March 9, and the President added his own private denunciations to those appearing almost daily in the *Union*.[2]

Calhoun did not come out for Taylor, however, either in public or in private. He accepted his own ejection from the Democratic party by Ritchie and the administration without complaint. He realized that his opposition to the war made that result inevitable, and even saw sardonic humor in the fact that the hero of the war seemed likely to unseat the President who made it. "Had Polk & his administration dreamed that sending Taylor to the del Norte would make him President, we would have had no war," he wrote in mid-May to one of his political lieutenants. But he insisted still that safety for the minority he represented lay only in maintaining a balance between the two great parties, and he would not sacrifice that position to endorse a man whose views he did not know. He would not go beyond conceding that circumstances might at some future time make it expedient to support the General. "The fact, that he is a slave holder, a Southern man, & cotton planter, is one of no little importance at the present moment. . . . Let us, then, treat him kindly and wait for developments of events. It is the course, that would be most dignified, most consistent with our character & principles, & best calculated to give us the control of events." [3]

Calhoun's partisans were presently divided into two groups, one ready to back Taylor unreservedly as the best man for the South, and the other waiting for some more explicit indication of views than any of the General's noncommittal pronouncements had yet given. Conner and Hammond were in the Taylor camp. Rhett and Dixon H. Lewis were in cautious correspondence with Taylor's friends, such as Balie Peyton of New Orleans and Jefferson Davis, and were prepared to offer a conditional support so long as Taylor did not accept a formal Whig nomination. Others, such as Elmore and James L.

Orr, were impressed but skeptical, and awaited Calhoun's lead before they took a stand.[4]

These differences of opinion were but reactions, not always consciously taken, to a sweeping realignment of parties along sectional lines. Calhoun was absorbed in forging a united South to oppose the growing unity of the North in relation to the all-important slavery issue. To the average mind unity meant political unity, and the *Union* trumpeted far and wide the warning that Calhoun was seeking to build a purely Southern party. For propaganda purposes if for no others it was easy for opponents to argue that Zachary Taylor was to be the beneficiary of this political sectionalism, and so Taylor's candidacy unwittingly accelerated moves already under way for a strictly Northern party, of anti-extension if not outright antislavery complexion. It is not fair to say, however, that this Northern sectionalism was only a reaction to the similar sectionalism Calhoun was preaching to the South. Each aggravated the other, but each arose more or less independently out of a common situation: the unwillingness or inability of two widely divergent societies to face and seek to solve in a spirit of mutual forbearance a problem that was rapidly driving them to conflict.

When Benton urged on the Democracy the necessity of nominating a Northern man he was only making public clamor of what every Democratic politician knew. It served, however, to draw the sectional line more sharply still, and to pose the Presidential election itself as an issue between slave and free states. It increased the bargaining power of the abolitionist leaders, who prepared to offer their support to Silas Wright if he would take a stand in favor of the Wilmot Proviso. And Wright had in fact done just that, though the time was not yet ripe to make it known.[5]

3

Silas Wright died suddenly toward the end of August 1847. Although he himself had often denied any political ambitions, it had been almost universally assumed that the former Senator and New York Governor would be the Presidential choice of the Northern Democracy. His views on public questions had been eagerly sought, even after his retirement at the beginning of 1847, and while he

DANIEL WEBSTER

HENRY CLAY

JOHN M. CLAYTON

ZACHARY TAYLOR
by John Vanderlyn

ANNA CALHOUN CLEMSON
by De Bloch

always demurred, protested, and otherwise displayed more or less genuine reluctance, he usually wrote the desired letter. His views on the Wilmot Proviso were carefully guarded, but they were fully explained in a letter to his friend James H. Titus, dated April 15, 1847.[6]

In the Titus letter Wright came out unequivocally against permitting slavery in any territory acquired in future, from Mexico or any other country, his position being essentially that taken by Preston King, the Representative from his home district, in the recently concluded session of Congress. The canny New Yorker, however, did not see fit to permit the publication of his views at that date. He informed Titus that he might pass the letter on to William Cullen Bryant, editor of the New York *Evening Post,* but Bryant was not to publish. That meant, of course, that he was not to publish just then, for there would have been no point in giving him the letter at all, or even in Wright's having written it, if it was not intended for ultimate publication. Wright's death left the matter in Byrant's hands, and he chose the time best suited to the interests of the radical wing of the New York Democracy: the Barnburners, whose official mouthpiece he was.

By the date of Wright's death the sectional controversy had reached alarming proportions. The administration was frankly concerned, and began through the columns of the *Union* a vigorous drive to settle the territorial issue by extending the Missouri Compromise line. In keeping with the President's views, but in the interest of his own candidacy for the succession, Buchanan took the same position in a political letter to the Democracy of Berks County, Pennsylvania. Dated August 25, Buchanan's letter was featured in the *Union* for the thirty-first, the day following Ritchie's eulogy on Silas Wright.[7]

Armed with Wright's Titus letter, Byrant immediately challenged the policy laid down by Buchanan and so eloquently espoused by the administration press. Ritchie and the truculent New York editor were soon engaged in a battle royal, in the course of which Wright's views were made public and became the platform of the Northern radicals. After Preston King's activities in the House of Representatives, there had been little real doubt as to where Wright stood, but now it was official and it is probable that this posthumous pronouncement carried a potency the living voice could never have achieved.

As the fall elections drew near the Barnburners turned back to Van Buren to champion their cause, and the Southern reactionaries prepared to force the Proviso men out of the Democratic party.[8]

Matters came to a head for the Northern Democracy late in September when New York Democrats met at Syracuse to nominate a party ticket for the November election. The Hunker forces had been immeasurably strengthened over the past nine or ten months by Marcy's influence in the distribution of patronage. It was the resurgence of the Hunkers perhaps more than any other single factor that had compassed Wright's defeat in the fall of 1846, and the Barnburners were mustering all their forces for a new trial of strength when Wright's death deprived them of their ablest and most popular leader. The choice of delegates to the Syracuse convention was bitterly contested all over the state, and when the day came, five counties sent rival delegations. The real struggle for power was over the seating of these disputed delegates, and after three days of heated wrangling the Hunkers gained a ten-vote margin.[9]

Before the hectic five-day session was over James S. Wadsworth of Geneseo had bluntly accused the Hunkers of the murder of Silas Wright; and David Dudley Field, brilliant young New York lawyer who had been one of the dominating figures at the Chicago internal-improvements convention three months earlier, had moved a resolution approving the Wilmot Proviso. The majority held firm, and the convention wound up its work on October 3 with the nomination of a complete Hunker ticket for state offices. Perhaps the action most bitterly resented of all was the dropping of Azariah C. Flagg, who had served the party as comptroller since the heyday of the Albany Regency. "The radicals," wrote the convention correspondent of the New York *Herald* in his final dispatch, "are exasperated beyond all bounds." [10]

Their exasperation was quickly converted into action with a call for a new convention to meet at Herkimer on October 26. Although Van Buren and Flagg both professed to disapprove, it was notable that Churchill C. Cambreleng, intimate of them both, was chosen to preside, and the "address" of the convention was the work of John Van Buren—"Prince John" who had danced with the young Queen Victoria, and had served as New York's Attorney General during Wright's regime. The long list of eighteen resolutions, including a ringing endorsement of the Wilmot Proviso, was the work of Field, and the principal invited speaker was Wilmot himself.[11]

The Herkimer Convention and those who sponsored it were savagely denounced in the *Union,* while the Washington correspondent of the Charleston *Courier* predicted an independent nomination of Van Buren for the Presidency. Some held the whole affair a mere matter of New York State politics, others saw in it Van Buren's revenge for his failure to win the Democratic nomination in 1844, but all agreed on the probable result, which was not long in coming. The New York elections were held on November 2, and the Whigs swept all before them. The Barnburners had put up no ticket of their own, but they would not vote for Hunkers, and either cast Whig ballots or wrote in taunts at their Democratic rivals. The powerful comptrollership went to Millard Fillmore of Buffalo, and was a factor in carrying the state for Taylor in 1848.[12]

4

Whig victories the country over were impressive enough to challenge the control of Congress. The Senate, to be sure, would remain nominally Democratic, but Calhoun and his growing band of Southerners still held the balance of power. Benton's position, too, was doubtful. He had forced the President's hand in the Frémont case, but it was all too clear that he would be satisfied with nothing less than a complete vindication for his son-in-law, and he let it be known before Congress met that he was not satisfied with Marcy's handling of the court-martial then in progress. It was notable that if Benton chose to align himself with the two Van Buren Barnburners in the Senate, Dix of New York and Niles of Connecticut, he too might hold a balance of power on critical questions.[13]

In the House of Representatives the division was so close that a handful of absentees might swing the Speakership to either party, and with it the control of the committees. So might one or another of the insurgent blocs whose members could not be counted on to vote for party measures. One such group, as in the Senate, was made up of Calhoun's adherents; another was a splinter from the Whigs, its steel core consisting of three militant abolitionists, Joshua Giddings of Ohio, Amos Tuck of New Hampshire and John G. Palfrey of Massachusetts. The two last were newcomers whose election reflected the rising power of the antislavery forces. Palfrey in particular, former pastor of Brattle Square Unitarian Church in Boston, and for eight years editor of the *North American Review,* was famous for his crusading zeal and skill.

In summary, then, there were four distinguishable parties in each House: Whigs, Democrats, a proslavery party, and an antislavery party, each with shifting adherents and uncertain relationship to the administration.

A scant three weeks before Congress met, the most reliable tabulation available showed the membership of the House to consist of 115 Whigs, 112 Democrats, and one Native American, Lewis C. Levin of Philadelphia.[14] There were actually 220 members present when the gavel fell at noon on December 6, 1847. The Whigs had already held a caucus and had agreed on personable Robert C. Winthrop of Massachusetts. The leading Democrat was Linn Boyd of Kentucky, but initial Democratic strength was scattered among several candidates. The first ballot gave Winthrop 108, three short of a majority, with the abolitionist trio throwing away their votes. In advance of the balloting Palfrey had asked the caucus nominee if he would so arrange the committees "as to secure respectful answers to petitions from the people of the free States touching slavery." That, at least, is how Giddings explained it afterward. The contemporary account was that the abolitionists wanted control of either the Committee on Territories or the Committee on the District of Columbia. Whichever it was, the answer was not satisfactory, and so the three withheld the votes that would have made up the necessary margin of victory. On the second ballot Winthrop's total climbed to 109, the addition coming from John W. Jones, a Georgia Whig who had thrown away his first vote. At the same time Patrick W. Tompkins, Mississippi Whig who could not decide between party loyalty and sectional interest, left the floor, thereby cutting the majority needed to 110. On the third ballot Levin moved into the Whig column, and Winthrop was elected.[15]

In both houses there were new faces and most of the changes served to emphasize the rising sectional tension. Among the more important new members in the Senate were John Bell, one of the founders of the Whig party and for a term Speaker of the House, who replaced the vacillating Jarnagin from Tennessee; leather-lunged and iron-nerved John P. Hale of New Hampshire, the first avowed abolitionist to reach the Senate, though others like Corwin and Dix had long leaned in that direction; and Robert M. T. Hunter of Calhoun's Virginia following, who replaced the veteran William S. Archer. From Illinois came that short, powerfully built, human dynamo, Stephen A. Douglas, promoted to the Senate at thirty-four after serving two terms with distinction in the House. And from Mississippi, by appointment of the Governor to fill out an unexpired term but soon to be unanimously elected in his own right, came handsome, swarthy Jefferson Davis, still limping from a wound received at Buena Vista and one of the individual heroes of the war. There were also new faces in the House, but most of those who were destined for important roles during the next ten or fifteen years had already served at least one term. Among these we may mention Howell Cobb, Alexander H. Stephens, and Robert Toombs of Georgia. Most notable of the first-termers, although obscure enough at that time, was lanky Abraham Lincoln of Illinois.

5

With the prospect of a stormy session ahead Polk took great pains in the preparation of his message, submitting it in advance to leading members of both houses. He reviewed the current status of the war, including the breakdown of negotiations and Trist's recall, and asked for means of crushing Mexico to end the conflict. He asked also that territorial governments be established in the already conquered provinces of New Mexico and California. He did not mention the slavery issue that would inevitably arise in that connection, but his views were embodied in resolutions offered in the Senate on December 14 by Daniel S. Dickinson of New York.[16]

Dickinson represented the conservative element of the New York Democracy, and his resolutions constituted both an answer to the Herkimer rebels and a new attempt to reach an adjustment acceptable to both North and South. The desirability of annexing territory was affirmed, and the right of new states to enter the Union without conditions was upheld. Dickinson then proposed that in the organization of territorial governments all questions of "domestic policy" be left to the legislatures chosen by the people of the territories. It was this view that came to be known as "squatter sovereignty" because it meant that those first on the scene—the "squatters" in the argot of the West—would determine what institutions each territory would have.[17]

Many moderate Southerners were satisfied with this solution, but Calhoun saw that the Dickinson formula would destroy slavery as certainly as would the Wilmot Proviso. In practice the territorial legislatures that would decide the issue would be made up of pioneer settlers, adventurers, and those of Spanish and Mexican origin already on the ground, and there were few if any slaveholders among them. Slavery would inevitably be excluded, Southerners would not migrate to the territories without their human chattels, and so the states ultimately carved from the conquered lands would be free. The three-quarters majority needed to amend the Constitution would be just as sure in the end as though Congress itself had excluded slavery from the territories.[18]

Calhoun had already prepared a set of resolutions designed to avert the dangers he saw in the complete subjugation of Mexico demanded by the President, and he introduced them the day after Dickinson's had been offered, both as a counterweight and as a means of forcing debate on the policy of the war itself before the territorial question was discussed. His point was that a conquered Mexico could neither be held as a province nor incorporated into the Union without eventually destroying the American system of government, and he asked the Senate to resolve that "no line of policy in the further prosecution of the war should be adopted which may lead to consequences so disastrous." [19]

A direct attack on the administration by the South Carolina Senator seemed to be in prospect when Dickinson waived consideration of his own resolutions and the Senate agreed to debate Calhoun's on January 4, 1848. The lines were sharply drawn before that date arrived when Cass publicly declared in favor of self-determination by the people of the territories and the administration press pronounced the Michigan Senator's position to be the true Democratic doctrine.[20]

By the time Calhoun rose to speak on the appointed day the President was thus committed to the principle of Dickinson's resolutions, and was committed also by his own annual message to Congress to the complete conquest of Mexico. These circumstances alone made the South Carolinian's speech one of the most important he had ever delivered. The galleries, hallways, and approaches had already been jammed to suffocation for three hours, and the privileged seats on the floor were full. Only one Senator was absent—Benton, who was attending the Frémont court-martial as counsel for the defendant. Tall, erect, impressive, with thick, shaggy gray hair falling almost to his shoulders and dark, piercing eyes sweeping the semicircular chamber, Calhoun had never been a more dominant figure or a more potent force than he was this day. Standing aloof from party, he could yet by the power of his argument, his great prestige, his unquestioned integrity and pre-eminent abilities, sway parties to his will. He spoke quickly and without notes, as he always did, but with an unwonted depth of feeling, to an audience unusually quiet and attentive.[21]

His purpose, he explained, was neither to aid the administration nor to strengthen the opposition, but to discharge an imperative duty to the country. He had, as his audience well knew, seen from the start grave dangers to American institutions in the prosecution of the war. He had sought to prevent it, but had failed. He had then offered at the last session a plan to minimize the danger by converting the conflict into a defensive, holding action, but in that also he had failed. His present resolutions were designed to accomplish the same purpose in a different way.

It was not of the past, however, but of the future that he wished to speak. Bills already authorized and others before the Congress would increase the total strength of the Army in Mexico to not less than 70,000 men, and would raise the cost of the current campaign to some $60 million. He reviewed the economic status of the country, the shift of the balance of exchange with Europe from favorable to unfavorable within the past year, the rising interest rate, and the danger if the money could be raised at all of precipitating a new financial crisis in the process, with a return to the paper system and the overthrow of free trade—the destruction in fact of all the principles for which the party in power professed to stand. And even if the economic hazard could be overcome, would the object the President professed to seek be attained?

Calhoun then reverted to his own often expressed fear that it would be impossible to call a halt short of absorbing all of Mexico. For the vigorous prosecution of the war to force the signing of a satisfactory peace could lead only to the overthrow of all legitimate Mexican authority. Peace would be made, not with an independent republic but with a puppet government set up for that purpose by the conquerers and by them kept in power. In the end it would have to come to one of the two alternatives the resolutions under discussion were intended to prevent—holding Mexico by force of arms as a conquered province, or incorporating it into the American Union— and either course would be equally fatal.

He enlarged on both dangers—that of converting a union of self-governing states into an empire by holding in enforced dominion a large, heterogeneous, and alien population, existing meagerly in a rugged and largely sterile land; and that of giving equality to millions of illiterate and ignorant Indians and half-breeds more inclined to live by plunder than by honest toil. Either way, in his view, meant loss of liberty at home.

He concluded with a recapitulation of his earlier arguments, to which new emphasis was now given, for holding a defensive line along the thirty-second parallel and cutting loose from Mexico. Such a policy he saw still as the only alternative to that of the President, with all the grave dangers that entailed. The Whig preference for taking no territory at all he dismissed out of hand, because he thought public opinion so overwhelmingly against it that to press it would be merely to reinforce the policy of the administration. To Democrats and Whigs alike he appealed to sustain him, before events moved beyond control and no action they might take could effect the outcome.[22]

The impression made by Calhoun's speech was profound, and the response, from all over the country and without reference to party lines, was gratifying. He had forced the alternatives into the open, had compelled the administration to disavow any intention of annexing all of Mexico, and had probably turned the current of popular opinion in favor of a defensive line. But he did not alter in the least the President's policy of conquest. The hapless Polk, with the Frémont court-martial entering its third month of bitter recrimination, was so harassed and bedeviled by the problems that multiplied around him that he scarcely noticed the Carolinian's remarks. His former law partner, Gideon J. Pillow of Nashville, now a Major General in Mexico, had brought charges against Scott, and Scott had cast aspersions on General Worth. Again the President had no alternative but a court of inquiry involving all three generals, with the command devolving meanwhile on Major General William O. Butler, who was at least a Democrat. If the war was really to go on as Polk had proclaimed in his message, all this was military madness; and in any event, in a campaign year, it came near to political suicide for the party in power. Even this, however, was not the end of the President's woes, for Trist, although recalled, had coolly declined to come home and persisted in negotiating a treaty. With the burdens of his office and his war closing in on him, Polk was beyond caring what Calhoun might say, and left in Ritchie's hands the defense of the administration's policy.[23]

When Dickinson's resolutions finally came up for decision, Yulee moved an amendment asserting the territories to be the common possession of all the states, and denying the right of the "territorial community" to exclude the citizens of any section. Hale countered with a motion to substitute the Wilmot Proviso, and the whole explosive subject was tabled as the administration forces retreated from the issue they had themselves first raised. With Benton going into opposition and Southern Democrats being wooed by the Taylor managers, Polk saw his party disintegrating before his eyes, and through intermediaries made overtures to Calhoun.[24]

6

The administration was saved almost in spite of itself by what can only be called an extraordinary bit of good fortune. On February 18 news reached the State Department in fragmentary form, by telegraph from the South, that the much reprobated Trist had in fact concluded a treaty of peace, which had been duly ratified in Mexico and was on its way to Washington. The news was quickly confirmed, and the next evening the treaty itself arrived. Polk held it over for careful study before submitting it to the Senate. Considering the circumstances of its origin, he was not sure that he ought to submit it at all. He was still debating the problem with his Cabinet on February 21, when old John Quincy Adams suffered a stroke at his desk in the Hall of Representatives, and was carried unconscious into the Speaker's room. For two days Congress met only to adjourn, while the distinguished ex-President lingered on in a coma. On the evening of February 23 Adams died.[25]

In the interval, Polk made up his mind. He prepared a special message on February 22, and the next day the Senate sat in Executive session just long enough to receive it, and to arrange for the confidential printing of the treaty and accompanying documents.

The Treaty of Guadelupe Hidalgo was precisely the treaty that Trist had been directed to make, but he made it in defiance of his own later instructions, after he had been recalled and had so notified the Mexican authorities. The Mexican Government, moreover, could claim little more in the way of authority than could the repudiated American negotiator. Santa Anna had long since fled once more, and as Calhoun had forecast in his speech of January 4, the Mexican commissioners derived such power as they possessed only from the willingness of the conquering army to recognize them. It was the right treaty but it had been drawn up and ratified by the wrong people in circumstances that gave it questionable validity.

In the end Polk's anxiety to end the war overcame his pride and the objections of the two dominant members of his Cabinet. Both Buchanan and Walker opposed the treaty on the ground that it was no longer adequate as to indemnity. There had been too much blood spilled in the interval since Trist's instructions were issued. Walker notoriously now wanted all of Mexico, and Polk himself would have been glad to extend the boundary southwest to the Sierra Madres, giving most of the Gulf coast to the United States. The President was politically astute enough to realize, however, that to reject a treaty made in accordance with his own instructions without even submitting it to the Senate would be an act of folly that neither he nor his party could survive. A majority of the Cabinet agreed, and the treaty was sent in with a message explaining Trist's dubious position and recommending that with certain modifications the document be ratified.[26]

The terms differed from those most often discussed in and out of Congress only in leaving Lower California in Mexican possession and in making the Rio Gila the boundary west of El Paso, allowing Mexico to retain a land connection at the head of the Gulf of California. For the territorial concessions the United States was to assume the claims of her own citizens against Mexico, and was to pay the sum of $15 million.[27]

In the Senate the treaty met with immediate opposition, based ostensibly on the unauthorized manner of its negotiation but actually on a variety of political considerations. Of the five members of the Foreign Relations Committee, only the chairman, Ambrose H. Sevier of Arkansas, wanted to ratify it as it was, modified only in accordance with the President's recommendations. The other members—Benton,

Webster, Hannegan, and Mangum—wanted the President to appoint forthwith a proper commission to proceed to Mexico and negotiate it all over again. It was a process that, as Polk was quick to see, would probably put off the whole question until after the election. And as if this opposition from the majority of the committee were not enough, it was generally believed in Washington that Buchanan and Walker were also diligently working behind the scenes to defeat the treaty.[28]

For a time the President despaired of getting the document ratified, but gradually doubtful and even hostile Senators swung over. Calhoun backed it vigorously from the outset, and popular opinion soon made itself felt in favor of acceptance. As the days dragged on in debate behind closed doors, the general anxiety was manifest and business virtually ceased while the outcome was in doubt. The end came a little after nine o'clock on the evening of Friday, March 10, when the Senate ratified by a vote of 38 to 14, with four not voting. Senator Sevier and Attorney General Clifford set out at once for Mexico City, where the modifications were accepted on May 25, 1848.[29]

After two years the war was over, but its most bitter battles were yet to be fought out, not on the field but in the halls of Congress. "The slave question will now come up & be the subject of deep agitation," Calhoun wrote to his son Andrew. "The South will be in the crisis of its fate. If it yields now, all will be lost." [30]

CHAPTER XXIII

SLAVERY AND WORLD REVOLUTION

1

By 1848 the preservation of the social and economic structure of the South had become, under Calhoun's guidance, the one vital, all-absorbing objective of Southern leaders in all walks of life. To understand why this was so we must pause briefly in our narrative to examine the forces that were molding Western civilization.

We have already seen how the growth of industrial capitalism in England influenced British policy in the direction of general emancipation, simply because mass production requires a mass market, which can be supplied only by free workers with money to spend. The advance of the nineteenth century brought these same forces into play in Europe generally, and in the United States. As Marx was to argue in the *Communist Manifesto* in this very year of 1848, and as Calhoun had shown in his own *South Carolina Exposition* twenty years earlier, the tendency of the capitalistic system in the absence of modifying factors was to concentrate wealth in relatively few hands, to drive down wages, and eventually to pauperize the workingman. In Europe and in the industrial areas of the United States the class distinction between owner and operative was already drawn when the widespread depression of the late 1830's and early 1840's set in.

The inevitable result was to give to the 1840's a revolutionary character. Men everywhere inquired anew into the meaning and purposes and rightful ends of government. In Europe and particularly in France the doctrines of socialism were developed in various forms, giving an ethical content to the political unrest that always arises out of economic catastrophe. In the United States the hardier and more independent among the dispossessed moved west to new lands, pioneering on to the Pacific coast in Oregon, settling the open spaces of Wisconsin and Iowa, and swarming onto the plains of Texas. Those who stayed home, and the intellectuals who always seem to gravitate to mass movements, experimented with imported socialisms and developed new ones of their own, drawing freely on the egalitarian philosophy of the Jeffersonian era, on the religious impulse set in motion by the great revival of the early 1830's, on their own inventiveness and ingenuity.

Along with utopian communities and religious migrations went the development of a workingman's anticapitalist literature, usually with French inspiration but often with indigenous materials and slanted to measure the American scene. Most effective of the radical writers were journalists like William Leggett and Parke Godwin, both associated with the New York *Evening Post*. The central theme was always a plea for equal rights, opposition to economic monopoly, revolt against exploitation by a ruling class, whether politicians or industrial magnates. The terminology of the Jackson era fitted the pattern very well, and elements of imported economic radicalism were presently absorbed as part of the body of doctrine espoused by the Northern Democracy.

The revolt against monopoly took a variety of forms, not always welcomed by the party leaders. Most spectacular, perhaps, was the Dorr rebellion in Rhode Island in 1842, in which the Northern Democratic leaders frankly took sides with the rebels and roundly condemned President Tyler's intervention in behalf of the established government. The antirent agitation among tenant farmers in the Hudson Valley proved more embarrassing, and it fell eventually to the lot of Governor Silas Wright, the darling of the radicals, to suppress the rioters and to imprison their leader for murder. It was one of the causes that contributed to his defeat in 1846. Another expression of the times was a Nativist movement, accompanied by anti-Catholic, anti-Irish demonstrations with rioting and bloodshed, and powerful enough in Philadelphia to elect a Congressman by 1844.

The decade and a half between the British emancipation act of 1833 and the fall of Louis Philippe in 1848 was characterized both in literature and in action by the upsurge of the common man. In Europe he would make his bid for power in 1848. In the United States, in theory, he held power already, but in practice the checks and compromises of the Constitution still balked his efforts. Now it was the South that insisted on and forever put in play these checks and compromises, with her eternal appeal to State Rights to frustrate the popular will. It was the South, with her working class made up of human chattels, her wealth concentrated in the hands of a very small

fraction of her population, her conservative and virtually self-perpet-
uating system of local government, that formed the core of resistance
to the whole egalitarian doctrine of the time. When Calhoun stood
forth as the leading critic of the right of the numerical majority to
govern, he struck at the very basis on which the political power of the
Northern Democracy had come to rest.[1]

The Southern planter was no greater beneficiary of the capitalist
system than was the Northern millowner, but because he was the
master of slaves and slavery was the extreme form of the exploitation of labor, he was especially vulnerable. Thus it was that much of
the idealism and reforming zeal that were turned in Europe to the
overthrow of monarchy and to the destruction of serfdom was directed in the United States to an attack on slavery and on the political
structure that maintained it. It was no accident that an observer as
acute as Orestes Brownson could couple the terms "socialist" and
"abolitionist" as though they belonged in the same context. They
were indeed both expressions of the same mass movement whose
philosophy was equality and whose political base was the preponderance of numbers.[2]

2

The philosophy of the abolitionists was that of the *Declaration of
Independence,* supposedly fundamental and indisputable in the American creed. But the South, with its rigid class structure and its feudal
social institutions, could never accept either the dogma of natural
rights or the equality of men. Placed at first on grounds of expediency and economic and social necessity, the defense of slavery shifted
in the middle 1830's to moral grounds and there the issue was sharply
and clearly drawn. There is undoubtedly truth in the often repeated
contention that Calhoun's insistence on slavery as a positive good
encouraged the North to go to extremes; but Calhoun realized that
the Southern position must in the end be defended on that ground or
not at all. Once you admitted that slavery was an evil to be eventually
abandoned, you would be challenged to take steps to get rid of it,
and when you did that you had surrendered at discretion. Or, if you
delayed laying the ground for eventual abolition, your own admission
of the evil nature of the institution would justify action by the majority in Congress. No, if slavery was to be retained at all, it must be

on grounds of moral worth; and if it was good, then naturally it should be made permanent.

As the egalitarianism of the Revolution became in the industrial states an instrument for attacking the propertied classes, the deeply class-conscious planters of the South abandoned such lingering doubts as they may once have entertained and made common cause against the leveling tendencies of the age. Every misgiving, each sign of hesitation, was but evidence of weakness, which would only encourage the abolitionists to greater exertion. So Hammond could write in the fall of 1845 that a "Southern man who falters—who apologises— much less who denounces Slavery & regards abolition as inevitable is in my opinion our *very worst enemy*"; and Calhoun could "look back with pleasure to the progress, which sound principles have made within the last 10 years in respect to the relation between the two races." [3]

As recently as 1840, if we are to accept the statement of a Quaker abolitionist who visited him in May of that year, Calhoun freely conceded "the superiority of freedom to slavery, even in a pecuniary point of view." He insisted then, however, as he had argued in the Senate earlier, that the gulf between Negro and Caucasian races was too great to be bridged; that they could in no circumstances live together in relatively equal numbers except in the relationship then obtaining in the South.[4] It was the argument John Randolph had used many years before: the argument that led straight to the position already noted in these pages, that emancipation would inevitably be accompanied by bloody and barbaric interracial war. It led also to the more abstract contention that slavery was, in the circumstances as they existed in the Southern states, a positive good. It was this point at which conflict became inevitable.

By 1848, when the smoldering unrest in Europe burst at last into the flame of revolution, the Southern position had become fixed, and was accepted with virtual unanimity by the ruling caste in the plantation states. The Southern aristocrat held with the French socialists that capitalism tended to divide society into classes. In this, however, he saw no evil but a natural and proper development, to be encouraged for the good of all. Human slavery was in fact a violation of all the tenets of an age that called itself civilized. It simply could not be extended, nor in the long run allowed to remain in existence anywhere. But generations of living with the system had brought sincere, intelligent, and honorable men to a contrary view. In time they convinced themselves that their Negro slaves constituted the best and most efficient labor force in the world; that slavery was sanctioned by God and man, in the Bible and in the long record of human history; and that the Negro in bondage in the South was better off physically and morally than the free Negro anywhere else, or for that matter than the free white laborers in the mill towns of Europe and the Northern states. They did not expect to convince their critics with such arguments, but they did not doubt that Northern dependence on Southern staples would decide the issue in their favor.[5]

In many respects the Southern slave undoubtedly was better off, in a physical sense, than the "wage slave" of the North. But the Northern worker could vote, could agitate for the improvement of his lot, could use such leisure as he had for study and self-improvement. He could team with his fellows to strike for better conditions, and if worst came to worst, as it often did in the 1840's, he could always make a new start in the West. The new doctrine of equal rights so eloquently explained in the columns of the New York *Evening Post,* and in Horace Greeley's *Tribune,* made him restive, and he tended to look to the radical Democrats for aid and comfort. So his employer came to feel sympathy for the Southern planter, and eventually to ally himself with his fellow conservatives of the cotton kingdom against all forms of radicalism.[6]

3

If we accept the thesis that the antislavery crusade was but a phase of the social upheaval that spread throughout the Western world toward the middle of the nineteenth century, it becomes easier to understand the gradual shift of political forces that accompanied it. Slavery was a sectional phenomenon, peculiarly the labor system associated with the cultivation of cotton, sugar, and rice, just as the protective tariff was specifically the doctrine of an industrial economy. The defense of slavery and opposition to protection went together in the South, and so did the two contrary positions in the North. By the spring of 1847 when Calhoun appealed for Southern unity in defense of a way of life, he was simply giving expression and leadership to a movement already on the way to being an accomplished fact. In the North by that date both parties stood for protection and free soil; in the South majorities in both upheld free trade and domestic slavery.

It is probably not possible to identify the precise point at which slavery became a political issue. Certainly it played a part in local elections early in the 1830's, and it was a major factor in the election of Seward as Governor of New York in 1838. The annexation of Texas, however, put the question on new ground. For the first time the possibility of actually extending the area of slavery was raised, and the subsequent storm of protest from the already powerful and well-organized antislavery forces made it a national issue. Politicians were forced to take sides, and the antiannexation letters of Van Buren and Clay precipitated sectional splits within both major parties which subsequent events did nothing to heal. Many in the North considered themselves aggrieved by settlement of the Oregon dispute short of 54°40'; and the Walker tariff, with its frank abandonment of the protective policy, had even sharper sectional repercussions. When the Mexican War was represented as being for conquest in the interest of the South the stage was set for the Wilmot Proviso, for Calhoun's call for a united South, and for the organization of a new Northern party to combat the extension of slavery.

The social philosophy long since developed in the South was the very antithesis of the egalitarianism so soon to plunge most of Europe into revolution, and Southern theorists had identified their own doctrines with those of the founding fathers. The defense of their system was always in terms of the Constitution, in which they found first no warrant for the protection of domestic industry, then a prohibition against any interference with or agitation of the slavery question, and finally an injunction against any legislation on that subject in the territories or in the District of Columbia.

The institution of slavery had already spread beyond profitable limits although it is unlikely that many Southerners realized it. They admitted readily, however, that even in New Mexico and southern California slavery would not supplant but only supplement free labor. The real issue raised by the Wilmot Proviso was not the extension but the extinction of slavery; and behind that issue lay another still more basic: Did the Constitution of the United States contemplate a government in which the will of the majority was to rule? Or did it provide a government by a balance of interests which the popular will could not overstep? If it was legitimate for the Dorrites, because they were numerically a majority, to seize the reins of power in Rhode Island in defiance of law and constitution, would it not also be legitimate for the workers, who surely outnumbered those who hired them, to vote into their own hands the control of New England's textile mills, or Pennsylvania's iron foundries? If all men were equal, and the majority was to rule, then the Negroes of the plantation states would be the political masters of the South.[7]

When the news reached America late in March of 1848 that Louis Philippe had fallen and a "popular" government was in control of France, there were many things at hand to remind conservatives of the direction toward which the leveling doctrines pointed. The morality of the Dorr rebellion had just been argued before the Supreme Court, with Nathan Clifford, the Attorney General of the United States, upholding the rebels while Daniel Webster presented the case for the established government.[8] The Democratic party had split in two in the most populous state in the Union, with an ex-President of the United States leading the portion that stood for government by the will of the numerical majority. And a treaty had just been ratified that must soon force Congress to decide whether the Constitution was a mere instrument of the popular will or a conservative check upon the exuberance of the masses.

4

The abdication of the French King and the establishment of the Second Republic under the auspices of radical theorists like Louis Blanc filled the Washington papers on March 21, 1848. To those who believed in popular democracy it was the great triumph of their cause, and they acclaimed it with unrestrained enthusiasm. Calhoun also recognized its far-reaching importance, for France, for Europe, and for the world, but he would not call it good. "No one can say where it will stop," he wrote. "France is not prepared to become a Republick." [9]

Although he read no foreign language, Calhoun followed events in Europe more closely than most of his contemporaries. His year in the State Department had given him background, and in addition to the obvious sources of information—the British papers and journals, and the members of the diplomatic corps in Washington—he drew freely on the knowledge and experience of his son-in-law,

Thomas G. Clemson, who continued as United States Chargé in Brussels. He had long been aware of the political unrest in Europe, as of its counterpart in his own country. "What I dread is," he wrote to Anna Clemson late in 1846, "that progress in political science, falls far short of progress in that, which relates to matter, and which may lead to convulsions and revolutions." [10]

He had reflected deeply on the nature and problems of government, and he applied his conclusions freely to the passing scene. "We make a great mistake in supposing all people are capable of self-government," he declared in his Mexican War speech of January 1848. "It is a sad delusion. None but a people advanced to a high state of moral and intellectual excellence are capable in a civilized condition, of forming and maintaining free governments; and among those who are so far advanced, very few indeed have the good fortune to form constitutions capable of endurance." And only two weeks before he learned of the Paris revolution, he summed up his observations in a letter to his daughter in Belgium. "I am not surprised," he wrote, "that the powers of Europe so much dread changes. They are right; because what are called reform[s], will lead to anarchy, revolution and finally to a worse state of things than now exists, through the most erroneous opinions now entertained both in Europe and this country by the . . . popular party, as to in wh[at] liberty consists, and by what means, it can be obtained and secured. Their opinion of liberty is, neither more nor less, than Dorrism." [11]

It was one of those who believed in Dorrism that first brought the French Revolution to the official attention of the Senate, after the establishment of a provisional republic had been confirmed. William Allen of Ohio offered a joint resolution congratulating the people of France; Hale moved an amendment especially commending the emancipation of slaves in the French colonies; and Calhoun intervened with a trenchant plea for delay. The revolution, he argued, was not yet over. The old government had been overthrown but congratulations would not be in order until a better one was firmly established in its place. "Whether the result shall prove to be a blessing or a curse to France and the world, depends upon what is coming, rather than upon what has been already done." [12]

Calhoun then moved to lay the resolutions on the table, but was voted down by a margin of more than two to one, without relation either to party or to sectional lines. The question next turned on fixing a day for debate, and Douglas of Illinois summed up the popular view. "All republicans throughout the world have their eyes fixed upon us. Here is their model. Our success is the foundation of all their hopes. . . . Shall we cast a damper on their hopes by expressing a doubt of their success?" The subject was dropped for the time being to attend to more pressing matters but the imagination of the masses had been fired, and the direction of public sympathy was clear.[13]

When the Senate again took up the question of congratulating the French people, it was merely to ratify a step already taken. Richard Rush, the American Minister in Paris, had faced an emergency that allowed him no time to seek instructions. He had therefore drawn on his own knowledge of his people, his own not inconsiderable experience, and his own judgment of the men who composed the provisional government of France, and had recognized the new regime in the name of the United States. Polk sustained the Minister in a special message to Congress on April 3, and three days later Allen's resolutions were unanimously passed, after the virtually unanimous rejection of Hale's amendment. It was notable, however, that Calhoun and all but two of those who had earlier voted with him to table the resolutions left the chamber before the vote was taken.[14]

The Allen resolutions passed the House by 174 to 2 on April 10, and jubilant Democrats celebrated with a torchlight procession through the streets of Washington. Secretaries Marcy and Mason took part, and President Polk greeted the marchers from an upper window of the White House. The French Revolution was on the way to becoming a triumph of the Democracy.[15]

While Americans concentrated their attention on France, the revolution spread to Austria, to Germany, to Italy. Calhoun watched with penetrating, if skeptical, eyes, appraising what he saw in terms of his own conservative social theory. For France he had little hope, and predicted by May that the Second Republic would end as had the first, in imperial government. For Germany he saw better prospects because the new regime took the form of a confederacy not unlike the political structure of the United States. In his eyes the essential distinction was that the government of France was based on the will of the numerical majority, while that of Germany provided local checks to centralized power.[16]

Intelligent, widely read in history and government, inclined to

fatalism, and all too well aware of the intellectual and moral shortcomings of the human species, Calhoun simply did not believe that
the mass of mankind could ever govern themselves in any genuine
sense. It was right and proper for the common man to advance and
improve his condition, but he did not thereby narrow the gap between
himself and the uncommon man in whose hands all real progress lay.
To narrow that gap would be to level the peaks rather than to uplift
the plain.

5

The revolutionary surge in Europe, with its broad humanitarian
base and its egalitarian philosophy, could hardly fail to stimulate anew
the abolitionist movement in the United States. When resolutions
congratulating the French people were first read in the House, Giddings seized the occasion to chide the mover of them for not including
such a clause as Hale had offered in the Senate: a special commenda-
tion for emancipating the slaves of the French colonies. The fiery
Ohio abolitionist was quickly embroiled with Southern members, and
before the debate closed he had managed to provide another text for
the antislavery crusade.[17]

Perhaps some hardy soul in the gallery was inspired then and there
to take action in the cause of freedom; perhaps there existed no connection whatever. Action there was, however, within two weeks, on
a grand scale and with a boldness that must have given those who had
eyes to see a glimpse behind the curtain of the future. On Saturday
April 15 the schooner *Pearl* slipped from her Georgetown wharf, and
after nightfall took aboard nearly eighty Negro slaves belonging to
residents of the District of Columbia. The vessel then hoisted sail
and made for the river's mouth, for Hampton Roads and the open
sea, and ultimately for some friendly Northern port. On Sunday
afternoon thirty irate citizens commandeered a steamboat and set off
in pursuit. As luck would have it the winds were unfavorable, and
the schooner was overhauled near the mouth of the Potomac. Pursued and pursuers returned together, and Tuesday April 18 saw three
white men and 77 Negroes from the *Pearl* lodged in the District jail.[18]

Angry mobs gathered in the streets of Washington, and for three
or four days federal employees teamed with local police to stop the
rioting. Giddings' rooms were twice searched and he was warned that

he would be lynched if he was caught. The presses of the *National Era,* the antislavery weekly that Gamaliel Bailey had been publishing in the Capital since the beginning of 1847, were threatened with destruction, and Bailey himself for a time shared Giddings' danger. The episode touched off a three-day debate in the House which Giddings called "the most profitable to the nation that had ever occurred in Congress," and in the Senate brought Calhoun into direct conflict with Hale as the high spot of a daylong wrangle.[19]

John P. Hale was already the nominee of the Liberty party for President when he asked leave on April 20 to introduce a bill for the protection of property in the District of Columbia. Benton tried to ward him off, but Calhoun demanded that the bill be read. The language of it, as Hale pointed out, was the same as that used in similar laws in Maryland and other states. It provided that full damages for property injured or destroyed "by any riotous or tumultuous assemblage of people" might be recovered by suit against the local authorities. The property Hale meant thus to guard from damage was not the human chattels of Washington slaveholders but Gamaliel Bailey's antislavery press.[20]

Calhoun replied, going straight to the underlying issue. "I suppose," he began, "no Senator can mistake the object of this bill, and the occurrence which has led to its introduction." He recalled his own past warnings against agitating the slavery question, and insisted now that the very nature of Hale's bill indicated that a crisis was at hand. As he warmed to his subject he must, indeed, have seemed a man possessed. He could hardly have been more eloquently indignant if Northern Senators had been caught in the very act of inciting one of his own slaves to cut his throat. The Southern position becomes credible only when we realize that they regarded the work of the abolitionists in just that light. To them it was incitement to murder and they and their families were the potential victims.

In a moment of weariness Calhoun chided his younger colleagues from the South for leaving him still to bear the burden in defense of their common way of life. Then he switched back to his theme. "I trust that we will grant no leave to introduce this bill; that we will reject it; and that if anything be referred to the Committee on the Judiciary, it will be to make penal enactments to prevent these atrocities, these piratical attempts, these wholesale captures, these robberies of seventy-odd of our slaves at a single gasp." He would meet the whole issue directly, and went on to propose that Northern ships might be excluded from Southern ports if the fugitive-slave law continued to be annulled in the free states. "If you do not regard the stipulations of the Constitution in our favor, why should we regard those in your favor?"

Calhoun's reproach brought Westcott of Florida and Davis of Mississippi to their feet, and they were quickly joined by Davis' colleague, Henry S. Foote, while Hale played a lone hand and seemed to enjoy it. Soon there were personalities and bitterness and venom. Foote invited Hale to Mississippi and promised the outspoken New Englander that he would there "grace one of the tallest trees of the forest, with a rope around his neck, with the approbation of every virtuous and patriotic citizen." If necessary Foote undertook to help pull the rope, and thereby earned for himself the title of "Hangman Foote." As things went from bad to worse Calhoun re-entered the debate long enough to say that he would "just as soon argue with a maniac from bedlam, as with the Senator from New Hampshire" on the slave question. There were cries of "Order! Order!" but they did not prevent Hale from returning the compliment in kind.

First Crittenden, then Mangum, interposed to recall the combatants to the dignity that belonged to the Senate. Calhoun took the responsibility on himself for the direction the debate had taken, but that did not deter him from entering the lists again, to insist on the efficacy of the frontal attack against the abolitionists. This time it was Douglas who interposed. Did not the Senator from South Carolina realize that by his insistence on agitating the question he was creating antislavery votes for the Senator from New Hampshire? He knew such would be the consequence in Illinois. Calhoun denied it almost scornfully, as though Douglas were a young upstart presuming more than his position allowed—just such a young upstart as Calhoun himself had been in 1812!

It was Hannegan of Indiana, a man not noted for his tact or suavity, who at last poured soothing oil on the troubled waters. Butler then explained the position of the South in language less irritating than Calhoun's had been. He saw no possibility of resisting this tide of antislavery sentiment so rapidly rising in the free states. Only the Constitution and its compromises stood between the South and inevitable doom, and the laws now in force in almost every state north of Maryland for the protection of fugitive slaves gave ample evidence that solemn convenants would avail nothing when the North was ready. He left it there, and on Crittenden's motion the Senate adjourned.

The net effect was to draw all slaveholders closer together, and to add further strength to the growing unity of the North; to drive deeper still the chasm opening between the sections. Southern leaders did not fail to link the "disturbances in Europe" with the "late abolitionist movements in Washington." Friendly observers in the free states warned that hostility to slavery was becoming more inveterate and wider spread. It was against this background that President Polk, the slaveholder from Tennessee, and Senator Calhoun, the planter from South Carolina, encountered each other while taking an early morning walk. For the first time since the session had opened they exchanged greetings and shook hands.[21]

CHAPTER XXIV

CONCILIATION FAILS

1

THE SUMMER OF 1848 was unbearably hot in Washington, and there was a concerted effort to force an adjournment of Congress. It was not the heat alone but the slavery question that inspired the legislators with a sudden desire to go home, at least until after the election was over. Nothing came of it, and at last the dreaded issue could be evaded no longer. A bill to set up a territorial government in Oregon was called up in the Senate on June 23, together with an amendment offered by Hale that would forever bar the introduction of slavery.[1]

The next day Senator Hannegan called at the White House for advice and instructions. Warned by the fate of Dickinson's resolutions six months earlier, the President abandoned the notion of territorial self-determination and reverted to his original preference, which was to settle the sectional conflict by extending the Missouri Compromise line to the Pacific. The party nominating conventions, to which we shall recur in the next chapter, had revealed that the Democratic split was fast becoming irreconcilable, and time was dangerously short. Over the week end Polk talked to other Senators, including Turney of Tennessee, Breese of Illinois, and Bradbury of Maine, seeking to commit as many as possible to his views. The debate was resumed on June 26 with Senator John A. Dix, recognized spokesman for the Barnburners, arguing the case for restriction. Calhoun then asked that further consideration be postponed until the next day to give him time to prepare, and of course the request was granted.[2]

The next morning Senators Jesse D. Bright of Indiana and Henry S. Foote of Mississippi called at the White House, and Foote took down from the President's own dictation an amendment to the pending bill. Bright, who was acting as chairman of the Committee on Territories in the absence of Stephen A. Douglas, then copied it so

345

that it would be in his hand when submitted. The two Senators were back at the Capitol in time for the opening gavel, and as soon as the order of the day was reached, Bright offered the amendment that came to bear his name. Slavery was to be prohibited in all territory lying north of 36°30′, including Oregon, New Mexico, and California; but "any person escaping into the same whose labor or service is lawfully claimed in any State or Territory of the United States" was to be returned.[3]

Bright's amendment thus formed the backdrop, although it was not the occasion, for Calhoun's remarks, which were made immediately thereafter. As was always the case when it was known in advance that Calhoun would speak, the Senate chamber was jammed, and had been so for hours—rare tribute indeed in that small, stifling room on one of the hottest days in the memory of Washington old-timers. It was so still when the great Carolinian rose that one reporter insisted a feather could have been heard dropping to the newly laid matting covering the floor. He spoke with all his accustomed energy and fire, the words tumbling from his wide, mobile lips in a perfect torrent, but with more feeling and gravity than was usual, even for him.[4]

It was characteristic of Calhoun that he should scorn all evasion, indirection, logic chopping, and face squarely both the real issue before the Senate and the consequences of his own reasoning in relation to it. He added little in the way of argument to a position already fully developed by many speakers over a period of two years, but he summed up the whole case in cogent and compelling form, and stated explicitly the unvoiced premises on which in the end it rested. The South, he said, wanted no law nor governmental action of any kind. They were willing to leave the question as the Constitution left it, with the joint territory of all the states held open to citizens of all to settle as long as the territorial status remained. The North, on the other hand, demanded a law giving exclusive rights of settlement to their own citizens, by forbidding those who came from slave states to bring with them the property on which their way of life rested. This demand had been incorporated into the twelfth section of the bill under discussion—the section for which Bright's amendment had just been offered as a substitute.

From this starting point Calhoun went on to deny that any authority existed in the Congress to enact any such law. The power to make "needful rules and regulations respecting the territory and other property of the United States," on which Dix had relied in his speech of the day before, had reference in Calhoun's view solely to public lands; to territory as property rather than as an extension of sovereignty. The Ordinance of 1787 did not cover the case, even if it were conceded for the sake of argument that it remained binding under the Constitution, because, as he demonstrated at some length, that ordinance was actually a compact between North and South, the North undertaking for her part to return fugitive slaves. This she had not done, and so the agreement with respect to the other party was void.

On the Missouri Compromise he had Jefferson's famous letter of April 22, 1820, to John Holmes read from the clerk's table, embodying the prophetic forebodings of the aged philosopher-statesman when the Compromise was passed: "This is a reprieve only, not a final sentence." He disposed of "squatter sovereignty" almost with a wave of the hand. It meant, if it meant anything at all, that sovereignty over the territories belonged, not to the states of the Union but to the inhabitants of the territories. In that case the "first half-dozen squatters" would have full dominion, and the "conquered people of New Mexico and California" would take over as sovereigns as soon as those territories passed to the United States, in which capacity they might if they chose exclude their conquerors. The only escape was divided sovereignty, which by very definition was absurd.

With great solemnity he addressed directly the Senators from the Northern states: "What are you prepared to do? Are you prepared to prostrate the barriers of the constitution, and in open defiance of the dictates of equity and justice, to exclude the South from the territories and monopolize them for the North? If so . . . vote against striking out the 12th section. We shall then know what to expect. If not, place us on some ground where we can stand as equals in rights and dignity, and where we shall not be excluded from what has been acquired at the common expense, and won by common skill and gallantry. All we demand is to stand on the same level with yourselves, and to participate equally in what belongs to all. Less we cannot take."

With equal solemnity he turned to his colleagues from the slave states, and bade them prepare to meet the issue. "The time is at hand, if the question should not be speedily settled, when the South must rise up, and bravely defend herself, or sink down into base and acknowledged inferiority; and it is because I clearly perceive that this period is favorable for settling it, if it is ever to be settled, that I am in favor of pressing the question now to a decision—not because I have any desire whatever to embarrass either party in reference to the Presidential election. At no other period could the two great parties into which the country is divided be made to see and feel so clearly and intensely the embarrassment and danger caused by the question. Indeed, they must be blind not to perceive that there is a power in action that must burst asunder the ties that bind them together, strong as they are, unless it should be speedily, settled."

He repeated his plea that there should be no restriction of any kind, assuring Northern Senators that the division between free and slave soil would actually be very close to 36°30', and that it would be a far more satisfactory line for being dictated by nature and not by Congress. From every point of view, even that of party, he saw in simple justice and the Constitution the best and safest road. To what better principles could appeal be made, more likely to rally the people on election day? He challenged both parties to try that road at least, repeating his deep conviction that the Union was threatened by the only question potent enough to work its destruction. The critical point was rapidly approaching, and if that point were passed, the Union would be gone. "In uttering these opinions, I look to the whole. If I speak earnestly, it is to save and protect all. As deep as is the stake of the South in the Union and our political institutions, it is not deeper than that of the North. We shall be as well prepared and as capable of meeting whatever may come, as you."

2

Like Bright's amendment, Calhoun's speech dealt not with Oregon alone but with California and New Mexico as well, and the arrival of the ratified treaty from Mexico City quickly broadened the scope of the whole debate. In a special message to Congress on July 6, Polk called for the "immediate establishment of Territorial governments" in the provinces embraced by the Mexican cession, and invoked "that spirit of concession, conciliation, and compromise in your deliberations in which the Constitution was framed, in which it should be administered, and which is so indispensable to preserve and perpetuate the harmony and union of the States." [5]

The next three days were devoted once more to the bill to organize a territorial government for Oregon. Despite Polk's plea for compromise and his repeated conferences with Bright and other members, the often amended bill grew more objectionable as the debate proceeded. The spirit of conciliation seemed infinitely remote from the Senate chamber on July 12, when John Middleton Clayton gained the floor. Though only in his early fifties, Clayton was one of the older Senators in point of service. Like Calhoun and Benton, he remembered vividly the bitterness that preceded the tariff compromise of 1833. With Webster and Calhoun and Vice President Dallas he had served on the Select Committee that had brought about a peaceful settlement, and he now reminded his fellow Senators of those troubled times. He proposed that the territorial question then before them be referred in similar fashion to a select committee, to be composed of eight members chosen by ballot. He would have two Whigs and two Democrats from the South, and a like bipartisan representation from the North. The suggestion was immediately adopted by a vote of 31 to 14, all of the nays coming from Northern states, and nine of them from New England.[6]

Needless perhaps to explain, Clayton's proposal and the large vote sustaining it did not come about spontaneously. There had been a "private consultation" among leading Senators and Representatives of both parties the previous day. Clayton was chosen to take the lead in part on the basis of experience, in part because he did not belong to the administration party, but above all because he came from the most nearly neutral of all the states on the slave question. Delaware, where slavery was legal but little practiced, was variously counted the northernmost of the Southern states and the most southerly of the Northern. We are not told the names of those who discussed the matter, but it is a safe guess that there was a pretty general coincidence between the Senate members of the original group and the committee selected by ballot on July 13.[7]

Before naming the compromise committee, a few major changes in the composition of the Senate must be noted. In February 1848 Herschell V. Johnson had taken the seat voluntarily relinquished by Walter T. Colquitt of Georgia; late in April Solon Borland replaced Sevier from Arkansas, the latter having gone as Commissioner to Mexico; and the other Arkansas seat, vacated by the death of Chester Ashley, was filled on the last day of May by William K. Sebastian. Of greater significance than any of these was the appearance on June 12 of Hannibal Hamlin, outspoken and tenacious antislavery Democrat, elected by the Maine Legislature to the seat formerly held by John Fairfield. The twentieth of the same month saw the relatively unimportant Thomas Fitzgerald succeed Lewis Cass, who had given up his seat when he received the Democratic Presidential nomination late in May; and the following week witnessed the arrival of two newcomers, Henry Dodge and Isaac P. Walker from Wisconsin. Both the Wisconsin Senators were Democrats, but Dodge at least belonged to the Barnburner faction. On July 3 Thomas Metcalfe replaced Crittenden, who had resigned to devote himself to his own campaign for Governor of Kentucky. The last change came on the very day the Territorial Committee was set up, the able and experienced William R. King returning from Alabama to succeed Arthur P. Bagby, recently appointed Minister to Russia. In none of these changes were there any alterations in politics, the Wisconsin Senators giving the Democrats an actual gain of two; but in fact the antislavery forces were strengthened, both in ability and in numbers.

The Select Committee on Territorial Governments was probably as strong a group as could have been chosen for the purpose. Clayton of course was chairman; and the others, neatly divided to balance section and party, were Jesse D. Bright of Indiana, Calhoun, John H. Clarke of Rhode Island, David R. Atchison of Missouri, Samuel S. Phelps of Vermont, Daniel S. Dickinson of New York, and Joseph R. Underwood of Kentucky. The day after their appointment the members selected a committee room and held a meeting behind closed doors. The "Compromise Committee," as it quickly came to be called, was immediately the center of interest in Washington, and a sort of lodestar to the peacefully inclined the country over.[8]

It is notable that although later generations have come to look on Calhoun as the obstinate and immovable barrier to any compromise settlement of the slavery question, his colleagues and contemporaries in the summer of 1848 regarded him as conciliatory, and he amply justified the confidence they showed in him in placing him on the Compromise Committee. It was undoubtedly at Calhoun's instigation that Franklin H. Elmore, who happened to be in Washington, paid a call on the President during the morning of July 14, while the committee held its first meeting. Elmore's task was to pave the way for a visit by Calhoun, and on Sunday July 16 the two South Carolinians called together. They were back again the following evening, and on both occasions the work of the Clayton committee was fully discussed together with Polk's views on the problems faced.[9]

The committee's relatively few sittings were protracted, and every possible solution of the territorial problem was explored. There were strongly held differences of opinion and on more than one occasion it seemed as though no common ground could ever be reached. Yet each time a fresh start was made, some concession offered, some moot point yielded, and at last an agreement was achieved. Late in the afternoon of July 18 Clayton and his seven collaborators returned to the Senate chamber, and the Delaware Whig reported a bill "to establish the Territorial Governments of Oregon, California, and New Mexico." He paid moving tribute to the patience, industry, and conciliatory spirit of his colleagues, reviewed the history of their deliberations, and tendered the compromise on which six of the eight had agreed as the best in the circumstances that could be had. The bill was very long, but its main features were clear. Oregon was to have a territorial government immediately, without restriction as to slavery. In California and New Mexico temporary governments were to be set up, also without restriction, but with an appeal to the Federal Courts if a slave brought into the territory should claim his freedom. The issue between North and South was thus resolved into a constitutional question, to be determined in the manner usual in such cases.[10]

For the next ten days the compromise bill, and many thought the fate of the nation, hung in the balance. The *Union,* speaking for the administration, hailed it as a "rainbow of peace," and the Charleston *Mercury,* usually regarded as the organ of the Southern extremists, pronounced it satisfactory. Calhoun believed, and said in the Senate, that it would prove a permanent solution for the most dangerous question ever to divide the country, and in this view moderate Northerners like Phelps and Dickinson concurred. The attack came from those already bent on the organization of a sectional, anti-slavery party: Corwin of Ohio, Hale of New Hampshire, Niles of

Connecticut, Dix of New York, Hamlin of Maine. But those who had prepared the bill with so much patience and labor were sure of their ground, and confident that a large majority of their fellow Senators sincerely desired an amicable settlement of the question. The members of the Compromise Committee confined themselves for the most part to brief explanations whenever they seemed to be required, letting the bill speak for itself.[11]

There was some preliminary discussion on July 19, but the debate did not begin in earnest until Saturday, July 22, after which it was pushed relentlessly to a conclusion. The test finally came on Thursday, July 27, at eight o'clock in the morning, the Senate having sat in continuous session for twenty-one hours. Just before the vote was taken, Bright of Indiana, who made the closing speech for the bill, paid spontaneous homage to the senior Senator from South Carolina. "He said that he, in common with many others, had entertained strong doubts as to Mr. Calhoun's attachment to the Union, but he now felt it due to justice and truth to declare, that in his late course in the Select Committee, and on the floor, he had exhibited a spirit so fair, so just, so noble and patriotic, as to win the heartfelt admiration and esteem of all who acted with him." [12]

The bill passed substantially as it came from the hands of the Clayton committee by a count of 33 to 22, with Webster, Pearce of Maryland, and Cameron of Pennsylvania the only absentees. It was sustained by 26 Democrats and seven Whigs, opposed by eight Democrats and 14 Whigs, giving it too largely the character of a party measure. In sectional terms the affirmative votes included 23 from slave states and only ten from free soil, while 19 of the 22 negative votes were cast by Northern men. Polk heard the news at breakfast from his nephew and private secretary, J. Knox Walker, who had sat out the night in the Senate gallery.[13]

One incident of this nightlong debate must be recorded for the use that has been made of it. In the course of a prepared speech against the compromise Dix endeavored to show that Calhoun, who now denied the power of Congress to prohibit slavery in the territories, had been of a contrary opinion at the time the Missouri Compromise was enacted. Dix read a letter of Monroe's tending to show that the President had asked written opinions from the members of his Cabinet, and that these opinions had been unanimous as to the right of Congress to control slavery as long as the territorial status con-

JOHN C. CALHOUN
Attributed to Thomas Buchanan Reid

WILLIAM H. SEWARD

STEPHEN A. DOUGLAS

JEFFERSON DAVIS

ROBERT TOOMBS

tinued. Calhoun interposed to explain that he remembered no occasion during Monroe's administration when written opinions had been given. He had a vague impression that they had once been asked, but for some reason he could not recall the request had been withdrawn. According to an eyewitness account, the South Carolina Senator made a positive and peremptory denial; and was much embarrassed when Dix then read a corroborating passage from the diary of John Quincy Adams, supplied him by the late ex-President's son. The opinions, according to Adams, were to be filed in the State Department, but Dix conceded that they had not been found there. Calhoun then gave his own recollection of the circumstances, and the incident passed off. In the opinion of the Northern antislavery men it was a distinct triumph for Dix, though even the most hostile of them, Francis Preston Blair alone excepted, did not question the Carolinian's sincerity or his fundamental honesty. The truth was, as Calhoun himself admitted, that he had come to see in the Constitution by 1848 a great deal that had escaped his less pertinacious eye in 1820.[14]

The Clayton Compromise met short shrift in the House, where Alexander H. Stephens of Georgia, slight and sickly of body but keen of mind, moved to lay it on the table. There were various delays, including a call of the House and some remarks on procedure, but the vote on Stephens' motion was presently taken. The result was that the bill was tabled hardly thirty hours after it passed the Senate—tabled without debate, by a vote of 112 to 97. In this majority of 15 the votes of Stephens and seven other Southern Whigs were quickly singled out as making up the margin of defeat; but it might just as well have been the eight Van Buren Barnburners from New York. As had been the case in the Senate the vote was both sectional and partisan, with only 21 Northern votes, all Democrats, to save the bill and only 8 Southern votes, all Whigs, to kill it. So another opportunity was lost and another marker blazed on the road to Appomattox.[15]

4

During the final days of the Senate debate on the Clayton Compromise, as though in anticipation of what they were about to do, the House resumed consideration of its own bill for establishing a territorial government in Oregon. Untouched since May, the bill was taken up on July 25, and a week later it was passed by a strictly sectional majority, substantially in the same form as the bill that had been tabled in the Senate on the last day of the previous Congress. It was silent on the great, agitating question, but it extended to Oregon the provisions of the Ordinance of 1787, and validated all laws passed by the existing legislative body, which included one barring slavery.[16]

The House Oregon bill was read in the Senate on August 3, and on Clayton's motion was referred to the Committee on Territories. It was not referred, however, before there had been some angry references to the summary disposal of the compromise in the lower chamber, and some sharp personal exchanges among the Senators. Clayton, with the permission of the Senate, made what might be called the final speech in favor of the compromise, detailing the difficulties encountered by his committee and surmounted only by a spirit of tolerance and a will to preserve the Union. He answered at once the whole series of speeches that had been made on the other side during the closing days of the Senate debate, and did not hesitate to express his belief that Presidential politics had been placed above patriotism in the defeat of the measure.[17]

Two days later, on Saturday, August 5, Stephen A. Douglas, chairman of the Committee on Territories, reported the Oregon bill with amendments, most important of them being the Missouri Compromise. The phrasing was virtually identical with that used by Armistead Burt in the House when he had sought to amend the same bill in the same way eighteen months before: the provisions of the Ordinance of 1787 were made applicable to Oregon *because* that territory lay north of 36°30′ north latitude. The bill was called up and the amendments debated on August 7, but the time was rapidly running out. August 14 had already been fixed as the date of adjournment, and the debate was necessarily abbreviated in the extreme, reaching a significant level only on the afternoon of August 10, shortly before the bill was passed.[18]

On this occasion Calhoun delivered one of his greatest speeches, as profound, as solemn and foreboding in its tone as any words he had ever uttered.[19] The question arose on the amendment validating free soil in Oregon because the territory lay north of 36°30′. He would not, Calhoun told his fellow Senators, vote for the amendment in that form because it was ambiguous. "Where the stronger party refuses to be explicit . . . the weaker . . . will in the end be deceived and defrauded." To accept it in this naked form, without any guarantees as to California and New Mexico, would be to yield the disputed point and concede to Congress a right to exclude slavery from the territories. He offered, nevertheless, to acquiesce in the re-enactment of the Missouri Compromise, with its more precise language, providing the first move came from the North, and came in a spirit of harmony. For such an amendment he would vote, though he would not vote for the bill, even when so amended.

Calhoun went on then to trace more incisively than he had ever yet publicly done the causes as he conceived them of the impending sectional conflict: the growing conviction in the North that slavery was sinful; the gradual subversion of the whole concept of liberty until a free man had come to mean everyone, everywhere, who was not a chattel slave; the identification of universal liberty at last with emancipation in the Southern states. He showed how the growth of abolition sentiment had paralleled and gained impetus from the increasing centralization of government; how slavery had been accepted as merely a local institution as long as the Union was regarded as a confederacy of sovereign states, but was now felt by the people of the North to be their responsibility because they had come to look on the confederation as a consolidated whole. He thought not accidental the coincidence in time between the sweeping assertion of central power embodied in the Force Bill of 1833 and the militant attack on slavery that began when the South was flooded with incendiary publications two years later. Then he exposed the fanaticism that lay behind the antislavery impulse, and traced the persistence of the movement to its political importance.

The analysis of the political process followed the same general lines as those already made familiar in his Charleston address of the previous year, but it was more polished, more condensed, more aptly turned to the situation at hand. The strictly Northern, antislavery party he had then feared would arise was now a reality, and at the very moment he spoke was holding its first national convention at Buffalo. The potency of the abolitionist vote had already proved great enough to influence the actions of a majority in the House, where the last hope of compromise had been rejected without even the courtesy of a hearing. It was manifest that a sizable majority of both parties in the Northern states was bent on carrying out the principles of the Wilmot Proviso, and even should another session of Congress see the Missouri line extended, it would be done not as a matter of right or by way of equitable compromise but as an act of temporary concession on the part of the stronger interest.

Calhoun reminded the Senate that nearly forty years of his own life had been spent in the service of the Union. "If I shall have any place in the memory of posterity it will be in consequence of my deep attachment to it." But he saw no hope of saving what he held to be the best of governmental structures unless the stronger portion ceased to encroach upon the weaker. "It is not for us who are assailed, but for those who assail us, to count the value of the Union. To us, without the observance of the guaranties of the constitution, the Union would be a curse instead of a blessing,—a sword to assault, and not a shield to defend. It is for our assailants to count whether the Union, with the observance of its guaranties on their part, is of sufficient value to them to be preserved or not. If, in their estimate, it would be so small as to put its safety at stake, rather than be restricted to the observance of its guaranties, how could they expect us to cease resistance to their aggressions, when the Union, if they should succeed, would be to us the greatest of curses, instead of being one of the greatest blessings, as it would be with strict adherence to the constitution?"

Shortly after Calhoun's speech the Senate recessed, but the debate was resumed in the evening, and late that night the disputed amendment was rejected with only two votes in its favor. The Missouri Compromise as such was then moved as Calhoun had asked, by an authentic spokesman for the North: Douglas of Illinois. It was adopted by a substantial majority, with Calhoun, Butler, and their friends voting for it. The distinction was that the form in which the Committee on Territories had reported the amendment, and as Burt had first offered it in the House at Calhoun's own instigation, left open the whole question of New Mexico and California. The form adopted, while forbidding slavery north of 36°30', left the decision with respect to territory south of that line up to the states to be made from it.[20]

At the last moment, just before the final vote on the bill was taken, Jefferson Davis moved to strike out everything after the enacting clause and substitute the Clayton Compromise, but Berrien, Metcalfe, and others persuaded him to withdraw the motion. The amended Oregon bill was then passed by 33 to 22, with Calhoun voting in the negative.[21]

The next day the House rejected the Senate amendments, again by a strictly sectional vote, and it was all to do over again. The bill came up on Saturday, August 12, with adjournment already set for Monday noon. Douglas called for a committee of conference, but Benton forestalled him with a motion to recede, which took precedence. Berrien pleaded for one last effort at conciliation, and Calhoun declared once more that failure to compromise the slavery issue now would place it beyond compromise. "Gentlemen may do with this bill as they please. If they will not give now what the South asks as a compromise, she will, at the next session, demand all, and will not be satisfied with anything less." [22]

Debate raged hotly until the recess, and resumed at the evening session with fury unabated. Benton and Houston, in prepared speeches, denounced Calhoun and all he stood for, Benton in particular growing more arrogant and violent as the night wore on. The inevitable collision occurred shortly after midnight when Benton pronounced Butler a liar, and received for his pains a challenge to settle it with pistols. After that the swaggering Missourian calmed down enough so that business could proceed, and the wrangle went on through the night. It was nearly 10 o'clock Sunday morning, after a session of twenty-four hours, when a vote on receding from the Missouri Compromise amendment was taken, and was carried by 29 to 25. Benton, Houston, and Presley Spruance of Delaware were the only Senators from slave states who sided with the majority, and their votes were decisive. The Senate amendment was set aside, and the bill stood passed as the House had first enacted it.[23]

5

At every step the South had lost. The egalitarian philosophy that had overturned the old monarchies of Europe, only to replace them with governments that would rule more powerfully and more ruthlessly in the name of the numerical majority, was in firm possession of the populous Northern states. The antislavery movement was no longer confined to a handful of impractical zealots but had become a potent political engine, before which the Southern way of life faced ultimate extinction. On their way home Calhoun, Butler, and Burt addressed a mass meeting in Charleston the evening of August 19, 1848, and their analysis of the congressional session just ended was pessimistic in the extreme. Calhoun professed to see a faint ray of hope in what he called the "spirit of anarchy and misrule" pervading the industrial states: the Fourierists and other socialistically minded groups opposing the supremacy of the ruling class. But the South could not wait for revolution to come and be put down in the North. She must look out for herself, and internal unity was now the only possible road.[24]

He was following still the political maxim he had tardily learned from his ancient foe, John Randolph of Roanoke, that power can only be overcome by power. He saw with the utmost clarity where events were leading, he saw the alternatives, and he began to marshal his troops for the next battle. "There can be no rational doubt," he wrote to Conner after he returned to Fort Hill, "that the time has arrived, when we must make up our mind, to give up our slaves, or give up all political connection & association with either of the existing parties at the North, and rely on ourselves for protection. . . . The only real practical question is; What should be done to bring the South to the same conclusion, & to rally on support of her domestick institution?" To that end he would wean the South from party allegiance and wield her strength as a gigantic pressure group within the federal structure. It was in furtherance of this purpose that he sought to revive the project for a pro-slavery press in Washington, that he called upon Southern legislatures to act in concert, that he began to work actively for a Southern convention. But even now he was not seeking a dissolution of the Union. "In whatever we do," he concluded, "we must act in good faith, to save the Union if we can, consistently with our liberty & safety; but, if not, to save ourselves at all events." [25]

Conservative that he was, he simply could not face the social, economic, and political upheaval that would inevitably follow abolition of slavery in the South. He could not make peace with the revolution, and so the revolution would pass him by and execrate his name.

CHAPTER XXV

THE FREE-SOIL CAMPAIGN

1

THE ANTISLAVERY MOVEMENT came of age politically with the campaign of 1848. The Liberty party, to be sure, had placed a candidate in the field in 1840, and in 1844 had won enough votes in New York to influence the outcome of the election; but it was never much more than a tool of the American and Foreign Anti-Slavery Society, and its backers were zealots rather than practical politicians. The New York Barnburners who endorsed the Wilmot Proviso in the fall of 1847 included among their number some of the country's most successful manipulators of men and issues. The Herkimer convention was followed by a new Liberty nomination—no longer the publicist and propagandist James G. Birney, but tough and able Senator John P. Hale of New Hampshire. When the Barnburners again repudiated the Democratic organization in February 1848 and chose a rival set of delegates to the Baltimore convention, the way was opened for a new Free-Soil party.[1]

The growing political strength of the antislavery forces was not lost on either Whig or Democratic leaders. Before the end of March it was known that delegates to both party conventions would include more than a sprinkling of abolitionists, and Calhoun reasoned that Southern men could not unite with them without giving tacit assent to their doctrines. The numerical strength of both parties lay in the free states, where both courted the antislavery vote. The process would operate to reduce with each quadrennium the relative weight of the slave states in party conventions. It followed that the South could not adhere to party without accepting candidates opposed to her vital interests, and so Calhoun bade his followers stay away from Baltimore.[2]

Whig leaders in the South chose a less forthright road, but with the Allison letter of April 22 they gave Zachary Taylor a commanding lead. Addressing his brother-in-law, Taylor professed no object but to serve his country and modestly conceded his own unfamiliarity with the details of politics. He would make no promises that he might later regret as he became better acquainted with the points at issue, preferring to be guided by broad principles. He saw no need for more. "One who cannot be trusted without pledges cannot be confided in merely on account of them." He then stated a position calculated to win over the maximum number of Democrats while losing the minimum number of Whigs. He was, he declared, a Whig, but he would "feel bound to administer the government untrammelled by party schemes." He would defer to the wisdom of the elected representatives of the people on all such leading questions as tariff, currency, and internal improvements, interposing a veto only in cases of clear violation of the Constitution.[3]

His profession of Whig allegiance and his no-veto pledge were enough for the North; the South would be satisfied with his Southern birth and residence. So he could avoid all reference to the Wilmot Proviso or to slavery. From that date until the Whig convention met early in June, Taylor's strength increased.

The Democrats had no such standout. Torn by internal dissension, the party had as many candidates as it had factions. Cass and Buchanan were the leaders, but the South favored Judge Woodbury or Dallas. Secretary Walker commanded a following, but it was generally conceded to be the North's turn to have the candidate. The Barnburners of New York tended to favor Benton or their own Senator John A. Dix, who was on the way to inheriting the mantle as he had already inherited the seat of Silas Wright. Generals William O. Butler of Kentucky and John A. Quitman of Mississippi also were spoken of by way of offset to Taylor's military fame, but both were Southerners which made their chances slim. In the confusion of candidates there were those who anticipated a deadlock, and Polk was besought not to commit himself irrevocably against a second term. He might prove to be the only man on whom they could agree.[4]

Calhoun personally thought most highly of Woodbury among Northern men, but he was unwilling to take any action that might later be construed as a commitment. He would not support a man who might be forced by geographical position to give pledges to the abolitionists; and he would not have South Carolina attend a party convention lest she be bound thereby to support the convention nominee. His advice was to wait until the late stages of the campaign, when the candidates would have been chosen, their views made known, and the issue to be tried by ballot had been clarified. Then he would act as circumstances dictated.[5]

Back in South Carolina his views were privately circulated, and the question was discussed in the *Mercury*. It was not for the moment pushed, however, because public sentiment seemed to lie in another direction. The other Southern states were sending delegates to Baltimore, and there was a strong current of feeling that South Carolina should do the same, if only to be acting with her sister states. Calhoun revealed once again the iron hand inside the velvet glove. He imposed his will on his state, but not without temporary mutiny in the ranks. Rhett, Simpson, and at least one other South Carolina Representative talked with Edmund Burke of New Hampshire, the Commissioner of Patents, who acted in Woodbury's interest. Rhett gave assurances that his state would be on hand at Baltimore, and that after a complimentary first ballot vote for President Polk, they would unite on the Supreme Court Justice. The incident revealed that many of the younger men who had followed Calhoun's banner in 1844 could no longer be counted among his political friends. The politician's reward is place and power, but neither comes from backing a consistent loser.[6]

By May, with the convention only three weeks away, Ritchie sought heroically to unite the Democracy, making it clear that strenuous and wholehearted support of the nominee was to be the test of party fidelity. But the schism was too deep. The *Mercury* was explicit as to why South Carolina would take no part in the nomination and why she would reserve judgment on the nominee. The Barnburners were equally blunt in announcing that they would not go into the convention at all save as the rightful and only delegation from New York. Francis P. Blair, still a power in the Democracy despite the supplanting of the *Globe,* and himself a convention delegate from Maryland, let it be known that he favored the Barnburners. On the eve of the Baltimore meeting Ritchie made a last valiant effort to minimize factional differences by playing up achievements of the party in its days of unity; but there was no longer any common ground on which Northern radicals and Southern conservatives could stand.[7]

2

The Democratic National Convention met in Baltimore on May 22, 1848. The claims of the two New York delegations were immediately submitted to a Committee on Credentials, but the rival leaders, Churchill C. Cambreleng for the Barnburners and Senator Daniel S. Dickinson for the Hunkers, vowed they would accept no compromise. The case of South Carolina was less difficult. One lone delegate was there: J. M. Commander of Georgetown, who had been selected at a local meeting attended by only a handful of voters and had been authorized to cast the single vote of his Congressional district. Passing through Washington, Commander had pointedly avoided Calhoun and had announced his intention of casting the whole nine votes to which South Carolina was entitled. A majority of the delegates agreed that he should do so, and he was also named one of the convention vice presidents. With the aid of Morse's magnetic telegraph the news came quickly back to Washington, where it did nothing to sooth the already embittered South Carolinians.[8]

The second day of the convention saw the two-thirds rule adopted after lengthy debate. The Committee on Credentials then reported that no decision could be made between the New York delegations until both pledged themselves to support the party nominee. The Barnburners refused in a vigorously worded written statement signed by Cambreleng and Jared Wilson, the two delegates-at-large. The Hunkers, however, announced that they had been pledged from the start to support the convention choice, whereupon the committee recommended that they be seated. An adjournment was quickly taken, but the wrangle resumed on May 24. It lasted all day and on into the evening, when a resolution to seat both delegations and split the vote was carried by a majority of two. This time the Hunkers protested but the question was soon resolved when Cambreleng, Preston King, young Sam Tilden, and the others rounded up their forces and withdrew from the convention.

The formal balloting got under way on May 25. With 168 necessary for a choice, Cass led on the first try by a wide margin over Buchanan and Woodbury. Out of belated respect or pure impishness, Commander gave South Carolina's nine votes to Calhoun. On the second and third ballots the Georgetown delegate shifted his nine-fold strength to Woodbury, but Cass was gaining fast and on the fourth and last ballot South Carolinia appeared in the winning column. Cass was chosen by 179 votes out of a possible 253. At the evening session that same day General William O. Butler of Kentucky was nominated for Vice President on the second ballot.

The final day was given over to platform making, with the finished product almost as equivocal as the Allison letter. The resolutions of 1840 and 1844 were reaffirmed and new ones added. The late war was pronounced to have been just and necessary, commenced by the act of Mexico; officers and men of the victorious armies were extravagantly praised; and in fulsome terms the French people were congratulated on their successful assertion of popular sovereignty. The convention pledged the Democracy, "as the party of the people, to sustain and advance among us constitutional liberty, equality, and fraternity, by continuing to resist all monopolies and exclusive legislation for the benefit of the few at the expense of the many, and by vigilant and constant adherence to those principles and compromises of the Constitution which are broad enough and strong enough to embrace and uphold the Union as it was, the Union as it is, and the Union as it shall be, in the full expansion of the energies and capacity of this great and progressive people." The achievements of Polk's administration were then listed, the outgoing President and Vice President were duly congratulated, and Cass and Butler were recommended to the American people as suitable successors.[9]

It was a platform not calculated to satisfy the Calhoun wing of the party, and William L. Yancey of the Alabama delegation promptly offered an amendment declaring that the "doctrine of non-interference with the rights of property of any portion of the people of this confederacy . . . by any other than the parties interested in them" was the true republican faith. Yancey spoke eloquently in favor of this strictly Southern gloss, but his amendment was overwhelmed by 216 to 36. Only a fraction of those from the South and none at all from the North or West sustained him.[10]

The Democratic convention brought no harmony to a distracted party, but succeeded only in driving the extremes farther apart. The nomination of Cass made the defection of the New York radicals irreconcilable; for Cass had allowed himself to be run against Van Buren in 1844, he had been supported in New York at that time by Marcy and the Hunkers, and when his own position had become hopeless he had thrown his strength to Polk though Van Buren could have won easily with only a portion of the Cass delegates. The South Carolinians were offended by the platform and found the candidate almost as unpalatable as did the Barnburners. The Congressional delegation decided in caucus to take no stand, either as a group or as individuals, until after the Whig convention had met, but the sentiment of the state was fairly expressed in the ovation given Yancey, who spoke in Charleston on his way home from Baltimore.[11]

The Whig convention met in Philadelphia on June 7 and proved to be almost as hectic as that of the Democrats. On the first ballot Taylor polled 111 votes to 97 for Clay and 43 for Winfield Scott, with Webster, McLean, and Clayton the also-rans. Thereafter Taylor climbed steadily to 171 on the fourth, while Clay dropped out of the picture to leave Scott second high with 62. Taylor had more than enough, and the old Kentucky champion never forgave those who had deserted him when he might have won the long-coveted honor.[12]

But the truth was that here, as with the Democrats at Baltimore, slavery was an issue. Clay was unacceptable to the South because he had gone too far in the direction of free soil, but the Northern men, albeit some of them reluctantly, were willing to swallow Taylor, slaves and all, because they believed he could be molded in their image. Such qualms as they might have were put at rest by the nomination of Millard Fillmore for Vice President—Fillmore who, as Whig chairman of the House Committee on Ways and Means had authored the tariff of 1842, and had given more ground than most to the abolitionists. The New Yorker defeated Abbot Lawrence of Boston on the second ballot.

The initial Southern reaction to Taylor's nomination was varied. In South Carolina Henry W. Conner cast in his lot with the Whigs, and so did Hammond, though he wanted to make an independent ticket of it with Woodbury in the place of Fillmore. In Virginia the Calhoun leaders accepted Cass, in spite of his drawbacks, as decidedly preferable either to Taylor or to a third ticket. But in Alabama, where Southern extremism was beginning to dominate, the third-party idea found backers, the preferred ticket being Littleton W. Tazewell of Virginia and Jefferson Davis of Mississippi. Calhoun was asked by Yancey to sound out the Virginia veteran, who had been in retirement since Jackson's time, but before the request could be acted on the Northern radicals put their own independent ticket in the field. Again the political climate was changed, and again the South marked time.[13]

3

The Barnburners gathered in political conclave in Utica on June 22 and 23, just a month after the Baltimore nomination of Lewis Cass. After they had surrendered the thirty-six seats reserved for New York to the triumphant Hunkers, the radical delegates paused in their homeward journey long enough to hold a mass meeting in New York City. The attendance was large and enthusiastic—so much so as to convince the leaders they headed a popular cause. It was there that resolutions calling for a convention of their own were offered, and passed by a significantly large majority. The Utica gathering was the result.[14]

The work of the Utica convention was pretty much predetermined. The party leaders had been satisfied in advance as to Van Buren's receptiveness, and the whole affair was in the hands of his friends. John Van Buren was one of the moving spirits, as were Cambreleng, King, Tilden, and others who had walked out at Baltimore. B. F. Butler headed the platform committee, which produced a standard Democratic document with the Wilmot Proviso added. There was a smoothness about it all that bespoke careful preparation, including the attendance on such short notice of delegates from Connecticut, Massachusetts, Ohio, Indiana, and as far away as Illinois and Wisconsin. When the ground was properly laid, Van Buren was nominated for President and Dix for Governor. The Vice Presidential nominee was Senator Henry Dodge of Wisconsin, who declined the honor.[15]

On the same day that the Barnburners gathered at Utica a statewide antislavery convention met at Columbus, Ohio, and issued a call for a national convention of all those in favor of free soil.[16]

News of the Barnburner nominations reached Washington in the midst of the Senate debate over slavery precipitated by the Oregon bill. In that context, its significance could hardly be overlooked. Polk called it "more threatening to the Union" than anything since the Hartford Convention, and Ritchie elaborated that view in the columns of the administration paper. There was no mistaking the genuineness of the crusty old editor's feelings as he recalled his own unwavering devotion to Van Buren's cause. Together they had fought against all sectional tendencies, but now the little New Yorker was the godfather and candidate of "a sectional northern party, the most dangerous of all parties in a confederacy of States." It was a party, moreover, whose very reason for existence was the agitation of the most disrupting question ever to confront the country. There could not be, and there was not any further doubt that a growing splinter in the North was bent on the abolition of slavery in the South, and no one—not even the prime movers of the agitation—believed that could be done without rocking the Union to its core, if not destroying it entirely.[17]

Calhoun had been so long aware of the concentrating antislavery forces that he made no special comment when his own direct prophecies came true. The immediate effect of the third-party movement in the North would be, he thought, to elect Taylor. The long-range effect, if the movement persisted, would be the abolition of slavery or the destruction of the Union, or both. To many in the South, however, who had not heeded the warnings of their own Cassandra, the news came as a sudden shock. Calhoun was besieged with questions, urged to come out for Cass or Taylor, asked to tell South Carolina and the South what to think and what to do. As his friends divided into Cass and Taylor groups, Calhoun continued to advise a hands-off policy. He saw one hope, and only one. If the disputed slavery question could be settled before the election, the Van Buren Barnburners would die away for want of an issue, and the choice between Taylor and Cass could be made in terms of the traditional party differences.[18]

In the North, and particularly in New York, there was a reaction of a different sort. Van Buren, who had twice been honored by his party's Presidential nomination and had held the most distinguished offices in the power of the Democracy to bestow, had bolted. Van Buren, who had made a fetish of regularity and had brought the party purge to a state of perfection, had calmly walked out of the party and become the standard-bearer of a rebel organization. Northern Democrats demanded that all Barnburners be dismissed forthwith from federal offices, and particularly that Benjamin F. Butler be removed as United States Attorney in New York.[19]

The President, under pressure from Senator Dickinson, Secretary Marcy, and the few loyal House members from New York, agreed with them wholly, but insisted on being himself a regular organization man. He consulted the Cass managers as to the effect of such removals on the chances of the party nominee, and was advised that they would be hurtful. He determined, therefore, to wait. The long-contemplated call for a general convention of all the antislavery forces had meanwhile gone out, and the Barnburners had agreed to attend at Buffalo on August 9. The date was less than two weeks away when the Clayton Compromise, Calhoun's last hope for sectional peace, was defeated in the House—defeated, as we have seen, by eight votes that might have been those of Taylor Whigs, but might just as well have been the eight Barnburners from New York who voted to table the bill. The dismissal of all officeholders yielding allegiance to the Van Buren faction was immediately urged once more, backed this time by the administration leaders in the Senate. Polk promised that Butler, at least, should go as soon as the Buffalo convention was over.[20]

4

The Free-Soil convention met beneath a great tent in the outskirts of Buffalo on August 9, 1848. It was humid and sweltering as western New York can sometimes be in August, and the delegates and visitors milled around uncomfortably. There were more than a thousand of them, altogether—in itself enough in cramped quarters and unusual heat to stir a restless spirit; but there were other reasons for acute discomfort. There were men there who had spent half a lifetime hating and distrusting one another, yet here they were, uniting in a common cause, or rather in a joint crusade. There were Liberty men whose single aim was the abolition of slavery and who would not count the cost; there were radical Democrats from New York, New England, and the Western states; there were "conscience" Whigs who could not support Taylor because he owned slaves and who would not support Cass because he was a Democrat and in their eyes a trimmer. Reformers and politicians, editors and farmers and men of affairs, breezy Westerners and New Englanders as cold and hard as their own granite hills, all rubbed elbows and jostled one another as the convention got under way. Every free state was represented, and delegates had even come from the border states of Delaware, Maryland, and Virginia.

Van Buren and John P. Hale, the nominees of the two largest

groups represented, were not themselves present. Neither was Senator Bradbury of Maine, though he was chosen to a convention office, nor Senator Dix of New York, though he was officially listed. These men could not leave their seats in Washington while the debate on restriction in the territories was going on, lest their own cause be lost in their absence. But John Van Buren was there, and Preston King; Samuel J. Tilden and David Dudley Field, and the slashing, unforgiving editor of the Barnburners, William Cullen Byrant of the *Post*. Charles Francis Adams came from Massachusetts to mingle fraternally with his father's lifelong foes. From Ohio came bull-necked and bullheaded Joshua Giddings, his white mane of hair and ruddy face standing out in any crowd; and Salmon P. Chase who had already won at forty a reputation as one of the best legal minds in the anti-slavery movement. He it was who argued for runaway slaves before the Supreme Court of the United States, over which he would himself one day preside as Chief Justice.[21]

After some preliminary discussion of principles Adams was chosen permanent president, and a committee on nominations was named. The next morning the committee reported Van Buren its unanimous choice and in open balloting that afternoon the ex-President was nominated with 159 votes to 129 for Hale, the only other candidate. The Vice Presidential nomination went to Adams by acclamation.

The platform repudiated any desire to interfere with slavery in the states where it existed, but there were to be no more slave states. The Clayton Compromise was roundly condemned and a blunt warning was hurled in the general direction of those Senators who had voted for it "in open violation of the known will of their constituents." There were to be no more compromises with slavery. After demanding "freedom and established institutions" for Oregon, New Mexico, and California, the platform moved on to points of public policy unconnected with the slave question, and a curious mixture of Whig and Locofoco principles came forth. Retrenchment, economy, and free land for actual settlers went hand in hand with river and harbor improvements and upward revision of the tariff. In short, the interests of the Free-Soil party were those of the North to the exclusion of the South, and the West was to be won over with free land and cheap transportation. The practiced hand of Benjamin F. Butler was visible in all this, and the South resented it the more on that account. Not even the presence of Frederick Douglass, the distinguished ex-slave turned abolitionist orator, infuriated Southerners so much as the spectacle of Butler and Giddings publicly clasping hands when the platform was ratified.[22]

Hale withdrew as the Liberty party candidate, and the Liberty party itself passed out of existence. There were various degrees of acceptance on the part of the disparate elements that made up the Free-Soil party, but all agreed on the direction in which it pointed. It was not, in Garrison's view, the party that would abolish slavery; but it was the precursor of that party. "The day of prophesy is passed; that of fulfilment is come." Perhaps Ritchie meant the same thing when he damned it as "the vilest and most mischievous party which has ever arisen in the republic." Polk pronounced Van Buren "the most fallen man I have ever known"; and Calhoun foresaw the gravitation of forces into "two great sectional parties" with results "which may lead to great changes." Hammond, brilliant and intractable, wondered if it would not be best for all concerned to elect Van Buren and bring on the crisis at once.[23]

5

When Calhoun appeared in Charleston on his way home from Congress in August, leaders of both political factions tried to win his support, but he would take no stand either for Cass or for Taylor. He was concerned only with the preservation of slavery, and with the threat to the South implied by Van Buren's candidacy. "Such a man," he explained in his speech on the evening of the nineteenth, "would never have consented to be placed in that position unless he was convinced there was a firm foundation for the movement, and saw that the North had determined to rally on this great question of sectional supremacy." On that question neither Cass nor Taylor could be trusted, and so Calhoun called on his fellow Carolinians to take no part in the election but to work instead for a nonpartisan unity in the South—a sectional party to oppose the partisan sectionalism of the free states.[24]

But South Carolina was already divided into Cass Democrats, Taylor Democrats, and Taylor Whigs. No politician who expected to retain his grip, much less to advance in the hierarchy of office, could be neutral in such a contest. Calhoun was a law unto himself, but the younger men still had too much to gain from party to eschew partisanship now. On Monday, August 21, immediately after Calhoun's departure and against his advice, there was a great Cass meeting in Charleston, with Isaac Hayne and Henry Bailey and Ben Rhett playing prominent roles. The Taylor men tried to break it up. Speakers were hooted off the platform and missiles flew freely, but order was at last restored, with the Cass men in control. The same day the *Mercury,* widely recognized outside South Carolina as a Calhoun organ, came out for the regular Democratic ticket, and closed its columns to Taylor contributors.[25]

The letter writers, of course, immediately set about demonstrating each to his own satisfaction that while Calhoun had called for neutrality as a matter of principle, he really favored one or the other candidate, who would surely get South Carolina's vote. The pressure from Northern Democrats to join openly in their cause was renewed with all suitable assurances, and in sheer self-defense Calhoun found it necessary to state his position more specifically than he had yet done. "If my friends, on both sides," he wrote to the editor of the *Mercury* on September 1, "would regard me as taking no part between the two candidates, and as standing on independent ground, ready to support or oppose the successful, as his measures may or may not accord with the principles and views of policy which have long governed me, they would avoid all misapprehension. I see much to condemn and little to approve in either candidate." In his eyes the very existence of the Free-Soil party demonstrated that the coming struggle for power would be along sectional rather than party lines.[26]

Calhoun's aloofness baffled some and infuriated others, but it was generally taken to mean that South Carolina would go for Cass. The dominant group in the state had acted too long with the Democratic party to be weaned away by anything less than a positive expression from Calhoun. As the election drew near, A. P. Butler, Rhett, Simpson, and even Armistead Burt declared for the Baltimore nominee. Late in September James Hamilton published a long letter in Cass's favor, and the Whigs, with varying degrees of bitterness, counted South Carolina as lost.[27]

Elsewhere over the country the *Union* had set the tone for the Democratic campaign, and a surprisingly negative tone it was. Ritchie seemed to find little or nothing to say in favor of Cass but much against Taylor and Van Buren, Fillmore and Adams. Polk finally got around to removing B. F. Butler from his federal job in New York, but that merely made him a martyr to the vindictiveness of faction and if anything strengthened the Free-Soil cause.[28] The Whigs had their last fears put at rest early in September when Taylor explained away the public support he was being given by Southern Democrats. In a second letter to Captain Allison the Whig candidate reiterated that he was truly and completely a Whig, in doctrine as well as name. He had accepted nominations from local Democratic meetings in the same spirit that he would accept Democratic votes, without sacrificing any of his personal beliefs. When he had allowed it to be said that he was not a party candidate, he had meant only that if elected he would be the President of the whole people and not merely of a party.[29]

As the Whig campaign gained momentum, the Democrats lost ground, and by mid-October Calhoun, at least, was ready to concede a Taylor victory. It was an outcome to which he professed to be indifferent, save in so far as defeat for the Democracy might make internal reform possible. In his eyes the Democratic creed was still the old State Rights doctrine of half a century back, and the party was doomed unless it could be brought once more to its original base.[30]

6

Behind Calhoun's attitude toward the election, so inexplicable to his friends, lay the shadow of the Free-Soil party. There were those who held Van Buren's bolt to be motivated solely by political hostility to Cass, but whatever the purposes of their candidate, the purpose of the rank and file of the party was the extinction of slavery in the United States. Moved by the same forces that were releasing the energies of the European masses into political channels, the free-soil movement, to the bulk of those who participated in it, was a great crusade. Even as Calhoun would restore the Jeffersonian doctrines of 1798, the Free-Soilers would return to the simpler and nobler Jeffersonianism of 1776. As an official campaign document phrased it, "The old party issues are for the most part settled. A new one has arisen, appealing to new and higher motives than the old. It takes direct hold on the purity, if not the very existence, of our civil and religious freedom as a nation." If the meaning was obscure, it was amply clarified by reference to "the late events in Europe, which have so deeply stirred our national sympathy," and to the "solemn and heart-stirring facts connected with the legislation of the fathers and founders of this republic." [31]

In his refusal to take a stand for either Presidential candidate, Calhoun was seeking primarily to lessen partisan hostility in his own state and section, because he believed that in the unity of common purpose alone could the South protect herself. He stood again as he had stood in 1832 and 1844, between the radicals of left and right. The solid and unwavering South he sought was to achieve her safety within the constitutional framework by the political potency of her unanimity, and was thereby to avoid the extremes of giving in to the abolitionists or seceding from the Union. During the final months of the campaign Calhoun's mail brought him ample evidence that the younger men, and some of the older ones as well, were ready to take the final step; and however dissatisfied, however fearful of the future, he might become, it was an extremity he did not wish to see. The union of Northern Whigs and Northern Democrats to exclude the South from the territories he would counter with a union of Southern Democrats and Southern Whigs to compel observance of the compromises of the Constitution. The Northern convention of antislavery forces at Buffalo he would answer when the time was ripe with a Southern convention of proslavery men.

The state elections in South Carolina were held early in October. In the Charleston parishes of St. Philips' and St. Michaels' the Whigs put up no ticket but merged their strength with that of the Taylor Democrats, who won handily. Isaac E. Holmes was re-elected to Congress as a Taylor man, and thirteen of the seventeen seats allotted to the district in the lower house of the state legislature went to Whigs. Elsewhere in the state, however, the regular Democratic ticket carried the day, insuring a substantial majority for Cass when the legislature met in special session to choose Presidential electors. The actual count was 129 for the Cass ticket, 27 for the Taylor ticket, and eight blanks. The Democracy had carried South Carolina without aid or comfort from Calhoun.[32]

Over the country as a whole the results were very different. Cass divided both New England and the South with Taylor, and carried most of the Western states, including Ohio with her 23 electoral votes. But Taylor carried New York and Pennsylvania, and that was enough. The electoral vote stood 163 for Taylor and 127 for Cass. New York's 36 electoral votes made all the margin of victory, and in

New York Van Buren and the Free-Soil ticket ran ahead of the regular Democrats. In that key state the popular vote stood at 218,-000 for Taylor, 120,000 for Van Buren, and 114,000 for Cass.[33] Van Buren did not carry a single state, but he rolled up more than 10 percent of the aggregate popular vote, and by defeating Cass in New York he gave the election to the Whigs. As in 1844, the abolitionists elected a Southern slaveholder to the Presidency. This time, however, he was a Whig, and the Whig doctrine of central power would mean in time the triumph of their cause. None knew it better than John C. Calhoun.

CHAPTER XXVI

THE WIDENING RIFT

1

THE FAILURE of Congress to provide a government for California before the adjournment in August 1848 was more dangerous than any member knew. The fateful nugget had been taken from Sutter's millrace in January, and the word had spread. More gold was found, and more. By summer all other activity in California was at a standstill as men dropped whatever they were doing and hurried to the diggings. Soldiers deserted their posts, sailors abandoned their ships, and even the editors left their presses in a mad scramble for the mines. The first scattered rumors began to appear in the Eastern papers before the first of October, and by the date of Taylor's election, everybody knew that there was gold in California. An official report from the military governor reached Washington in December about the time Congress met, together with samples which the Philadelphia Mint pronounced to be of high purity.[1]

As the great gold rush got under way, even the perennial slavery question was driven from the papers momentarily, but the net effect was to intensify the sectional conflict. California could not be left much longer without a government, and both free-soil and proslavery forces concentrated for what each recognized as the crucial test. Everywhere through the fall and winter of 1848 there were local meetings, resolutions, protests, and demands, always emphatic in their expressions of opinion on the great question dividing the country. In South Carolina early in November meetings at Fairfield and Orangeburg denounced the Oregon bill for its inclusion of the Wilmot principle, and proposed measures of redress should it become a precedent. The favorite suggestions were concerted action by Southern legislatures, and a convention of the Southern states; but both meetings resolved to accept the Missouri Compromise as a gesture of peace.[2]

Governor David Johnson's message to the South Carolina Legis-

374

lature, cleared in advance with Calhoun, was firm but moderate. Johnson endorsed a Southern convention as the best means for promoting unity among the slave states; he approved full and free discussion; but there would be time enough for action when the issue between the sections was actually decided against the South. Calhoun himself stopped over in Columbia for two or three days early in December, and his influence was thrown against the passage of resolutions looking to state action. A day or two after his departure a caucus of legislative leaders agreed on the terms of a single resolution designed admittedly to meet his wishes. The *Mercury* came out for radical action by South Carolina, pronouncing it impossible to get the Southern states into a convention together and condemning as futile anything less than that. There was a brief revolt in the legislature by those who wanted to recall the Congressional delegation if the Proviso should be adopted; but the conservatives quickly regained control, and the caucus resolution was unanimously adopted. It called for resistance "at any and every hazard" to exclusion from the territories, but went no further than to declare that South Carolina was "prepared to cooperate with her sister states" to that end.[3]

2

The first session of the Thirtieth Congress had shown a surprisingly strong trend in the antislavery direction. The second session, meeting as it did after a Free-Soil party had been organized, carried the trend still further, yet with little change in the actual membership. In the House the only important new member was Horace Greeley, editor of the New York *Tribune,* who was filling out an unexpired term. In the Senate the principal change was the loss of Dixon H. Lewis, who had died suddenly late in October. His interim successor was another State Rights Democrat, former Governor Benjamin Fitzpatrick. The roster was completed shortly before the end of December when the Senators from Iowa finally took their seats two years after the admission of the state into the Union. Both were Democrats and neither was any stranger in Washington. Augustus Caesar Dodge, son of Senator Henry Dodge of Wisconsin, had served more than three terms as Territorial Delegate; George W. Jones had served as Delegate from both Michigan and Wisconsin.

Within a week Congress got down to business on the major question. The point of departure for the Senate was a bill offered by Douglas to bring all the territory acquired from Mexico into the Union as a single state of California, reserving to Congress the right to carve additional states at some future time from that portion lying east of the Sierras. Though he was not yet thirty-six and had served only one session in the Senate, Douglas had already made himself spokesman for the conservative wing of the Northern Democracy. His dynamic personality, his skill and tact in off-the-floor maneuvering, his grasp of issues and his judgment of men, combined to give him a leading place in a body of unusual distinction. He had discussed his purpose privately with influential members of both houses before the session opened, and he explained it frankly to the Senate when the bill was read on December 11. The presence of gold in California had materially altered her status and vastly increased her population. Some kind of government was necessary, and only immediate statehood would avoid the difficulties that had defeated three different territorial bills at the previous session. That evening Douglas called at the White House and in the course of the next few days received assurances of administration backing, providing he would draw the eastern boundary of his proposed state at the Sierras.[4]

Calhoun arrived in the city the day Douglas' bill was presented, but did not take his seat until the twelfth. He looked healthier than he had for many a day, a striking and ominous figure with his tall, gaunt frame, his shaggy mane of iron-gray hair, his strong features marked by a prominent, aggressive jaw jutting out over a short fringe of white beard, mouth straight and grimly set, eyes large, luminous, and piercing. He called on the President the next morning and listened attentively to Polk's views, though he confessed that he had as yet read neither the annual message nor the bill giving statehood to California. He was careful, therefore, to express "no decided opinion" save an anxiety to settle the territorial question at that session.[5]

He took no part in the debate when the Douglas bill was referred to the Judiciary Committee, but he voted with the majority. Douglas had asked reference to his own Committee on Territories, but Berrien of Georgia blocked the move on the technical ground that the admission of a state required evaluation of her constitution, which was a judicial function. The real point was, however, that the Committee on Territories boasted a majority from the free states. The Judiciary Committee was dominated four to one by the deep South.[6]

In the House, where the strength and talents of the Free-Soil movement were largely concentrated, the underlying issue was being simultaneously debated in a much more direct, and to the South more dangerous, form. A surprise move by Palfrey to abolish slavery in the District of Columbia and another by Giddings with the same purpose had been made and lost by threateningly narrow margins when the Committee on Territories reported according to instructions on December 20. The committee's chairman was Caleb Smith, Indiana Whig who was reputedly close to the President-elect. He would one day sit in the Cabinet of his fellow Representative in this Congress, Abraham Lincoln of Illinois. The bill Smith reported was patterned on the Oregon bill of the past session, including the disputed twelfth section which now extended to the people of California the provisions of the Ordinance of 1787.[7]

It was the following day, December 21, that brought the explosion. The Southern members were irritable and uneasy over the course of events so far when Daniel Gott, New York Whig, moved one of the familiar antislavery resolutions in a new form. "Whereas," began his preamble, "the traffic now prosecuted in this metropolis of the Republic in human beings, as chattels, is contrary to natural justice and the fundamental principles of our political system, and is notoriously a reproach to our country throughout Christendom, and a serious hindrance to the progress of republican liberty among the nations of the earth: Therefore,

"*Resolved*, That the Committee for the District of Columbia be instructed to report a bill, as soon as practicable, prohibiting the slave trade in the said District."

Hugh Haralson of Georgia moved to lay the resolution on the table. Wentworth of Illinois and Gott demanded the yeas and nays, which were ordered and Haralson's motion was lost by 81 to 85. The previous question was invoked and sustained, and the resolution passed, 98 to 88. It was quickly pointed out that prominent Northern Whigs, notable among them Truman Smith of Connecticut and Caleb Smith of Indiana, were present but had not voted. Their failure to do so was a violation of the House rules, but one for which the rules provided no remedy. They could not now be recorded unless the vote should be reconsidered. The motion to reconsider was duly made, but the Speaker, after some discussion of the point, ruled that it could not be debated until it had lain over for a day. In the course of this discussion Isaac Holmes invited Southern members to leave the hall, but nothing came of it until the next day.[8]

3

It was probably before Gott's resolution was offered and purely with reference to the House version of the California bill that a group of Senators representing ten of the fifteen slave states held a private caucus of their own. They drew up and signed a resolution naming a committee of five "to ascertain who amongst the Southern members are willing to unite in an address to the Southern people advising firm, prompt, and manly opposition to the Wilmot proviso in the event of its being applied by law to the territory acquired from Mexico south of 36°30′," and authorizing the committee to call a meeting of the Southern members "when in their opinion it is proper to do so." The members of the committee were Hunter of Virginia, Rusk of Texas, and Foote of Mississippi from the Democratic side, Johnson of Louisiana and Berrien of Georgia from among the Whigs. Calhoun was one of the signers and may have been the prime mover, but the first signature was that of Jefferson Davis.[9]

After the passage of Gott's resolution the committee decided that the time had come to call a Southern meeting. There was an air of tension and excitement when the House met at noon on December 22. Senator Foote was in the House chamber, passing a paper among the members from slave states asking them to meet together that evening. Whigs were as excited as Democrats, as indignant over the proceedings of the previous day, and almost if not quite so willing to sign the circulating paper. Members drifted restlessly from the hall until for a time there was no quorum present to do business. It was easy and logical to attribute the movement to Calhoun, but the evidence seems to show that he was not informed in advance that the meeting was to be called.[10]

The meeting was held with all formality in the Senate chamber at seven in the evening. There were eighteen Senators present and fifty-one members of the House, every slave state except Delaware being represented without distinction as to party. Calhoun and Butler were there, and so were five of the South Carolina Representatives: Wallace, Simpson, Woodward, Burt, and Holmes; but conscious of the reputation of their state, they remained in the background. General

Thomas Metcalfe of Kentucky, Whig successor to John J. Crittenden, was called to the chair; vice presidents were David Atchison of Missouri, the President pro tempore of the Senate, and Whig Representative John Gayle of Alabama; the secretary was Democratic Representative Abraham W. Venable of North Carolina.[11]

Representative Thomas H. Bayly of Accomac, Virginia, successor in the House to the volatile Henry A. Wise, started the business of the evening by moving a set of resolutions, hastily prepared that afternoon. They were a compound of all their predecessors, back as far as the Virginia and Kentucky Resolutions of 1798, and belonged in the same tradition. There was the preliminary expression of "a firm determination to maintain and defend the Constitution of the United States against every aggression," followed by a solemn declaration of "warm attachment to the union of the States, agreeably to its obvious and real intention," expounded in the familiar contractual terms. After stating the limits of delegated and reserved powers, Bayly's version went on to resolve that Congress had no authority "to impair or destroy the right of property in slaves either in the States, the District of Columbia, the Territories of the United States, or any other place whatever." Then came the immediate issue: recent efforts to interfere with slavery, both in the District and in the Territories, and the support "of a dangerous character" given to such moves in the free states. When the list of grievances was complete, Bayly concluded with a declaration that the Congressional delegations from the aggrieved states had "exhausted their power of resistance in vain," and that it remained only for them to explain the danger to their constituents who must now decide what course to take. He proposed that a committee of one from each slave state be named to draw up a suitable address.

Alexander H. Stephens then moved that the whole problem confronting the South be referred along with Bayly's resolutions to the suggested committee, with instructions to report on or before January 15, 1849. A general discussion followed, in which many individuals took part. The most important remarks of the evening, however, were those of Calhoun. The South Carolina Senator commended Bayly's effort as very creditable considering the brief time allowed for preparation, but he thought the whole ground was not covered. He expressed himself, therefore, as favoring Stephens' motion. An address to their constituents he considered indispensable, and the sooner the better—if possible while some of the Southern legislatures were still in session; for it was the states themselves and not their Congressional delegations that would have to do whatever was done. He noted the rapidity with which sentiment in the North was crystallizing: "Who believes that propositions which have, within a few days past, commanded the support of a majority of the lower House of Congress, would even three years ago have been tolerated by any respectable portion of either House?" [12]

To Calhoun's clear and logical mind, with his conviction that the American Union was indeed a confederacy of sovereign states, the question at issue was the survival of the confederacy; for the actions against which he and his fellows were protesting would reduce the states they represented from a position of equality to one of colonial dependence. There could, he thought, be no idea of submission, but he would still be conciliatory and moderate. "The action of the South should be united, temperate, but decided—our positions must be taken deliberately, but held at every hazard. We wage no war of aggression. We ask only for the constitution and union and government of our fathers. We ask our Northern brethren to leave us those rights and privileges which our fathers held, and, without securing which to their children, all know they would not have entered into this union."

The only real point at issue among those attending the meeting was whether or not the time for action had come. Foote led the fire-eaters, who were for passing Bayly's resolutions then and there. Others held that no separate Southern action should be taken unless and until the objectionable measures had been enacted into law. Calhoun's position, as always, was dead center. They should explain to their constituents what was taking place, and what dangers were involved, but the people of the states should determine what course to take. He would suggest nothing, save that "it should be temperate, mild, and decided."

Stephens' motion was then adopted and a committee of fifteen, one from each slaveholding state, was named by the chair. The members were Alexander H. Stephens of Georgia, chairman; John C. Calhoun of South Carolina; Edward C. Cabell of Florida; William R. King of Alabama; Henry S. Foote of Mississippi; Solomon W. Downs of Louisiana; Thomas J. Rusk of Texas; William K. Sebastian of Arkansas; David R. Atchison of Missouri; Charles S. Morehead of Kentucky; John M. Clayton of Delaware; John G. Chapman of

Maryland; Thomas H. Bayly of Virginia; Meredith P. Gentry of Tennessee; and Abraham W. Venable of North Carolina. It was as judicious a selection as could have been made. Eight were Senators, seven were members of the House; nine were Democrats, at least nominally, and six were Whigs. Three of the Senators had served on the Compromise Committee of the previous session: Clayton, Calhoun and Atchison; and these three, together with King of Alabama, were men of long experience in public life, national and international reputations, and consummate ability.

4

The Committee of Fifteen met promptly the day after its appointment, confirmed Stephens in his chairmanship, and after a general exchange of views and discussion of procedure, a subcommittee of five was named to draft an Address to the People of the Southern States. Again the choice of members was conservative and judicious: Calhoun, Clayton, King, Morehead, and Bayly. It was no secret that Calhoun would prepare the address. For the next few weeks the content was one of the favorite topics of speculation in the Capital, but the mere fact that it was being prepared seems to have had a salutary effect. The veteran correspondent of the Charleston *Courier* noted that he had "never witnessed more good feeling among the members of Congress of all sections than was manifested . . . in the cordial greetings upon the opening of the new year." [13]

Washington was still speculating as to the nature of the forthcoming address when Gott's resolution came up for reconsideration in the House on January 10. It was then that the Illinois first-termer, tall, gangling, good-humored Abraham Lincoln secured the floor to read an amendment he proposed to offer to the resolution, should the House agree to reconsider. Gott's resolution instructed the Committee on the District of Columbia to bring in a bill abolishing the slave trade. Lincoln proposed to abolish slavery in the District altogether, over a period of years, provided a majority of the white, male inhabitants agreed to it. The mere suggestion of such a thing had Southern members breathing fire, even though the Lincoln version did have a stiff section on the return of fugitives. [14]

After further debate the vote on Gott's resolution was reconsidered by a substantial majority of 119 to 81, and was again before the

House. A move by Botts of Virginia to table it was beaten, but the House adjourned without further action and the resolution was not again called up. In the South, at least, this sudden change of front on the slavery question was attributed solely to the decisive stand of the Southern members. It appeared to justify Calhoun's often repeated belief that the North would not press the issue if the South showed a united determination to resist it.[15]

That same evening the Committee of Fifteen met to consider the report of the subcommittee. The Address as prepared by Calhoun was read and discussed at length. No decision on it was reached, and the committee agreed to reconvene on the morning of Saturday, January 13. At the second meeting two members were absent—King, for whom Downs was authorized to act as proxy; and Sebastian, who was represented by Foote. There was more discussion, but a quick test when Chapman, the Maryland member, offered a resolution to the effect that it was inexpedient at this time to publish any address at all. It was defeated, seven to eight, those favoring it being Chapman, Clayton, Cabell, Gentry, Morehead, Rusk, and Stephens—all six of the Whig members of the committee, Rusk being the only Democrat. Bayly then moved that Calhoun's Address be reported to the general meeting scheduled for the fifteenth, and the motion was carried by exactly the same division. It was carried, in other words, by the exclusively Democratic votes of Atchison, Calhoun, Downs for himself and King, Bayly, Foote for himself and Sebastian, and Venable.[16]

The fine frenzy that had brought these able Southerners together subsided quickly after the vote on Gott's resolution was reconsidered, and they resumed their normal pursuit of political advantage. Consider the course of Alexander H. Stephens, for example. The Georgia Whig was one of the dominant figures in the whole affair, had chaired the Committee of Fifteen, and had appointed a subcommittee sure to favor some kind of address. Yet he voted against the expediency of any address at all when proceedings reached that stage. Like his fellow Whigs he was far more interested, once the immediate threat to the South seemed to have been stayed, in protecting the interests of President-elect Zachary Taylor. As the Whigs lined up against an address, the Democrats were almost automatically thrown onto the other side. In the interval between the adoption of the document by the Committee of Fifteen and the reassembling of the general meeting, Polk was pressed by Southern Democrats who wanted to know what course to follow. The President wanted no sectional caucus, no report or address or action of any kind outside the constituted channels, and he particularly did not want any document signed only by Democrats. His advice was to go to the meeting and try to prevent any action at all; but in no circumstances to sign anything.[17]

5

The Southern Address, as it came from Calhoun's hands, is not an inflammatory document, or one designed to stir unduly the antagonism of the sections. It is a very sober, very dignified, and very frank recital of the points at issue between North and South. The growing danger facing the South as a result of repeated failure to settle these outstanding difficulties is clearly pointed out, and that is all. There is no appeal to arms, nor to passions; indeed, there is no appeal at all save for unity in whatever it might be determined to do—unity that might of itself be enough.[18]

The Address pointed out that the difference of opinion between North and South on the question of slavery was already present when the Constitution was framed, and was one of the major problems faced by the framers. It was a problem compromised by counting three fifths of the Southern slaves for purposes of representation and of direct taxation; by protecting the slave trade until 1808; and by guaranteeing the return of fugitives who might cross state lines. Without these provisions explicitly recognizing and protecting slavery, the Southern states would never have ratified the Constitution. When the Northern states ratified, they accepted these provisions and were bound by them.

The Address then took up the provision regarding the rendition of fugitive slaves and demonstrated as clearly as language allowed that it was now a dead letter, in palpable and open violation of the Constitution.[19] Adroitly Calhoun quoted Northern Justices Story and Baldwin, whose language was as strong and as unequivocal as any he himself had ever used. The injury was only compounded by the existence of organized groups whose purpose was to entice slaves from their owners and hurry them secretly from the country. Scarcely less a breach of faith was the systematic agitation of the whole question of slavery, designed as it was admittedly to force emancipation upon the South. The methods employed were briefly detailed, in-

cluding every device for molding Northern opinion and the direct
instigation of discontent among the slaves. One of the purposes for
which the Constitution was established was to "insure domestic tranquillity"; but the Northern states looked on or even aided, while their
citizens deliberately sought to destroy the domestic tranquillity of the
South. Between independent nations, no one would question the right
of remonstrance with an ultimate resort to arms in such a case.

The Address turned next to the history of the Missouri Compromise, which was the means adopted to put at rest the first agitation
of the question of slavery in the territories. With the annexation
of Texas and the Mexican War the agitation was renewed in a
more decided form. The North now repudiated the Missouri Compromise, originally adopted by her own nearly unanimous vote, and
proposed to exclude slavery from all the territories, wherever they
might lie, at the same time charging the South with a desire to extend
the peculiar institution. This Calhoun and his co-signers bluntly denied. They held rather "that the Federal Government has no right
to extend or restrict slavery, no more than to establish or abolish it;
nor has it any right whatever to distinguish between the domestic
institutions of one state, or section, and another, in order to favor one
and discourage the other. . . . What then we do insist on, is, not to
extend slavery, but that we shall not be prohibited from migrating
with our property, into the Territories of the United States, because
we are slaveholders."

Passing to still more recent events, the Address argued that the
passage of the Oregon bill of the past session, with the President's
exposition of his reasons for signing it, constituted an agreement by
the South to accept the Missouri Compromise once more as a solution,
but the events of the present session revealed that the North had no
such intention. This paragraph was stricken out before the signing,
as tending to criticize the President and the Northern Democracy.

The recent series of events in the House was then reviewed, and
the sectional division between yeas and nays was duly noted. The
conclusion was that all of the constitutional stipulations and guarantees intended to protect the South were already set at naught; and
that if the measures pending in the House should be carried out,
emancipation could not long be prevented. There would be too many
easily accessible asylums for runaways, and too rebellious a temper
among the slaves, to permit the institution to endure for long, even

should the agitators not force Congress itself into taking the ultimate step. Indeed, the exclusion of the South from the territories alone would be enough, for it would mean the ultimate admission of enough states imbued with the antislavery philosophy to amend the Constitution as they pleased. The abolitionists already counted a majority in the House of Representatives, and the end toward which they aimed was bound to be achieved before long unless some action were taken. A few paragraphs enlarging on the fate of the British West Indies and forecasting even greater calamities for the South if ever slavery was abolished brought the narrative to an end, with a final exhortation to unity.

"If you become united, and prove yourselves in earnest, the North will be brought to a pause, and to a calculation of consequences; and that may lead to a change of measures, and the adoption of a course of policy that may quietly and peaceably terminate this long conflict between the two sections. If it should not, nothing would remain for you but to stand up immovably in defense of rights, involving your all—your property, prosperity, equality, liberty, and safety. . . . We hope, if you should unite with anything like unanimity, it may of itself apply a remedy to this deep-seated and dangerous disease; but, if such should not be the case, the time will then have come for you to decide what course to adopt."

6

The Southern Senators and Representatives, eighty-eight of them this time, met again in the Senate chamber on the evening of January 15. A motion to admit reporters and the public was decisively beaten. Then Calhoun's Address was read by Venable, the secretary, and a prolonged debate followed. Clayton, Stephens, and Toombs led the opposition; Calhoun himself, Westcott, Bayly, and Jefferson Davis were the more important speakers favoring the Address. Clayton, who had disapproved of the document at every step, finally moved to table it, but the motion was beaten, 28 to 60. A motion by Senator Berrien of Georgia, one of the top-ranking Southern Whigs, to recommit with instructions fared somewhat better. There was considerable jockeying, but the Address was recommitted by a vote of 41 to 40, after Calhoun had expressed his willingness to accept any modifications that would not impair its truthfulness nor materially alter its character. There were no instructions, but it was informally agreed that the narrative portion of Calhoun's draft should stand.[20]

Stephens made one last attempt to drop the whole matter by moving adjournment sine die, but he was overwhelmingly voted down. Stephens, Chapman, Rusk, Morehead, and Clayton then asked to be excused from further service on the Committee of Fifteen, and the first four were excused accordingly. Senator Metcalfe, the chairman, refused to release Clayton, insisting that his skill and integrity were needed. He was, in brief, the best man the Whigs had as a counterweight to Calhoun, and they could not afford to let him go. The others were replaced, Stephens by Berrien, Rusk by Representative David S. Kaufman, Morehead by Representative Samuel O. Peyton, and Chapman by Senator James A. Pearce. No change in the Whig-Democratic line-up was involved. An adjournment was then taken until January 22.[21]

The reconstituted Committee of Fifteen held its first meeting the morning of January 18, when William R. King was chosen to succeed Stephens as chairman. Pearce, Clayton, Peyton, and Foote— three Whigs and a Democrat—were absent, but this time there were no proxies. When they got down to business, a motion by Berrien to change the orientation, making it an Address to the People of the United States rather than to the South alone, was carried seven to four, with Atchison, Bayly, Calhoun and Venable constituting the minority. Also on Berrien's motion, and by the same vote, the Address was referred to a new subcommittee of five, composed of the Georgia Senator as chairman, Atchison, Cabell, Bayly, and Calhoun. Only Bayly and Calhoun remained from the first subcommittee, but the majority was still Democratic. They were to report to the Committee of Fifteen at 6 P.M. on Saturday, January 20.[22]

By this time Calhoun was feeling the strain of his intense application, and his advancing years. His health had appeared excellent when he reached Washington in mid-December, but events had conspired against him. He could not relax, he could not let others carry the load when his own most profound convictions were involved. He had begun to regard himself as indispensable—to feel that in his exertions alone lay the salvation of the South. He acknowledged no indisposition, nor even undue weariness, but his intimates noticed that he was not quite himself. They were not therefore wholly unprepared when on January 19, the day following the first meeting on the recommitment of his Address, he collapsed in the Senate, falling suddenly to the floor. He insisted—to his absent family, at least—that it was only a temporary faintness, which quickly passed and left him as well as ever; but to Rhett, who found him feverish and exhausted in the Vice President's room, he admitted frankly that his career was nearly done. Dr. Hall was summoned, and the Senator was assisted to his rooms where for several days he was closely confined. The immediate diagnosis was a stomach upset, but it was complicated by bronchitis, and the beginnings of heart disease were observable.[23]

Calhoun's illness prevented his attendance at the January 20 meeting of the Committee of Fifteen. In his absence the committee took no action on a substitute Address prepared by Berrien, but voted to submit both versions to the general meeting. Calhoun's draft had already been modified, with his consent, to meet some of the objections made to it.[24]

At the general meeting of January 22 King reported both documents. Berrien's was read by its author, but the reading of Calhoun's was dispensed with, since it was already familiar to the participants. Stephens then moved that it was inexpedient to issue any address, but the motion was tabled, 59 to 18. After some further parliamentary maneuvering and some "red hot debating" King moved that Berrien's draft be approved. By this time many of the Whigs had withdrawn from the meeting, and the motion was rejected, 27 to 33. Calhoun's Address was then adopted, and at one in the morning the meeting adjourned. It was agreed that signatures would not be affixed until everyone interested had been given ample time for meditation.[25]

Calhoun was well enough by January 23 to get around, though he did not resume his seat in the Senate until the twenty-fourth, and did not fully recover during the remainder of the session. Indeed, we may say that it was the beginning of his final illness, and that he never fully regained his health. For the moment, however, he was carried along by nervous excitement and the overwhelming inner drive that had marked his whole life. His present task was to get as many signatures as possible on the Southern Address before it was released to the press. The widespread interest and curiosity aroused over the past month meant that publication could not be long delayed, but his cause was aided by the passage of vigorous resolutions in the legislatures of Virginia and North Carolina.[26]

Altogether he secured only 48 signatures out of a total representation from the slaveholding states of 121. It was less than he had hoped but he was reasonably well satisfied. Out of a possible total of 73 Democrats, 46 had subscribed their names, despite the full weight of the administration against it. The name whose absence he regretted most was that of Thomas J. Rusk, his own protégé and now regarded as one of the strong men of the South. Neither Benton nor Houston signed, but it had not been anticipated that they would. Benton, indeed, had attended none of the meetings, nor had he been invited. Among Senators the list of signers included Hunter and Mason of Virginia, Butler and Calhoun of South Carolina, Herschell V. Johnson of Georgia, David L. Yulee of Florida, Downs of Louisiana, Borland and Sebastian of Arkansas, Turney of Tennessee, Atchison of Missouri, King and Fitzpatrick of Alabama, Davis and Foote of Mississippi. The Representatives also comprised an able group, including two lone Whigs, Gayle of Alabama and Tompkins of Mississippi. Calhoun had gone so far as to offer his support to the Taylor administration if the Southern Whigs would assure him that the General would take a State Rights position, but this they could not do. By the same token, they could not sign.[27]

The proceedings of the various meetings and the full text of both addresses, Calhoun's and Berrien's, were published in the Washington *Union,* January 28, 1849, and Ritchie in a long editorial took the Whigs sharply to task for their failure to support the movement. The editor had roundly condemned Calhoun some two years back for calling on the South to unite in defense of her domestic institutions. Now, however, he saw nothing sinister in the identical proposal, but rather a necessary step for the protection of a system in which he too believed. He had opposed in 1847 lest the movement create a deeper schism in the party and jeopardize Democratic chances in the coming election. For a similar reason the Whigs opposed it now. They had just elected a Southern President, and they could not risk a split between their own Northern and Southern wings before he had even been inaugurated. They must give Taylor a chance, without embarrassing the very commencement of his administration.[28]

7

While the Southern Address was in process of preparation and promulgation, the major business of Congress was more or less at a standstill. The Douglas bill giving statehood to California was reported without amendment on January 9, but with a recommendation from the Judiciary Committee against its passage. The Southern majority of the committee held that, while they might admit a properly organized state into the Union, they could not constitutionally create a state where none existed. A minority report was submitted a few days later, and both reports were printed, but no further action was taken until after the final meeting of the Southern delegates.[29]

The decisive form taken by the reaction of Southern members to the new aggressiveness of the abolitionists seems to have taken the President by surprise. There had been caucuses of Southern members on various phases of this question over a period of a dozen years, but this was the first time proceedings had continued for more than two or three days. By January 15, when Calhoun's Address was recommitted, Polk had identified in his mind a resolute opposition to sectional action and an earnest wish to get a government in California in some manner that would avoid raising the slavery issue. Thereafter he threw all his personal influence and the whole weight of his administration against any Southern Address and in favor of the Douglas bill.[30]

Administration forces in the Senate succeeded in getting the bill called up on January 24, and in substituting for it a revised version from the same hand designed to overcome the objections of the Judiciary Committee to the earlier draft. Butler insisted, however, that it must now be treated as a new bill and recommitted. Senate parliamentarians agreed, and Clayton then moved reference to a select committee to be appointed by the chair. After some discussion the motion carried, and Vice President Dallas named a carefully balanced group with Douglas as chairman. Clayton, Reverdy Johnson of Maryland, and Badger of North Carolina represented the Whigs. Flanking Douglas on the Democratic side were Jones of Iowa, Jefferson Davis of Mississippi, and John M. Niles, the Connecticut Barnburner.[31]

The select committee did its work quickly, laying before the Senate on January 29 an amendment that was still another substitute. This new approach divided the territory acquired from Mexico by a roughly diagonal line. The northern boundary of California was to be the forty-second parallel to a point east of Great Salt Lake, whence it followed Frémont's route southwest to the 117th meridian of west longitude, and cut west to the Pacific. The arrangement gave the towns of San Diego and Los Angeles to New Mexico, which thus gained a substantial outlet on the ocean. California was to be brought into the Union by Presidential proclamation as soon as she had provided herself with the necessary constitution and government; New Mexico whenever her population was large enough. In the meantime the laws of the United States, so far as they were not locally inapplicable, were extended to the entire region.[32]

The touch of a master hand was there, for the laws of the United States, extended to both California and New Mexico, protected property in slaves. The territorial enactments of California, forbidding slavery, were specifically not validated, and the Mexican laws prohibiting the institution were superseded by the American. Theoretically both territories were thus opened for settlement by slaveholders. Practically California would be in the Union and free to regulate her own concerns long before any slaveholders could take advantage of the permission thus granted them. The South would doubtless occupy New Mexico in force, so that in effect the Mexican cession would be divided into two states, one free and one slaveholding; and the line of division, though irregular, would approximate that of the Missouri Compromise. The choice, moreover, would be that of the inhabitants in both cases. Neat as the arrangement was, it was such as neither extreme could now accept, and the bill was never called up.

The Southern Whigs preferred to make their own bid for a settlement of the territorial issue in the House. They served notice of their intention on January 22, before final action was taken on the Southern Address, when William Ballard Preston indicated that the question would be taken up at an early date. The forty-three-year-old Preston, serving his first term as Representative from Virginia, was a cousin of William C. Preston, the former South Carolina Senator, and also of Governor John B. Floyd of Virginia. He was a strong Taylor Whig, but his connections and his personal ties gave him strength with Southern Democrats. Other matters crowded the calendar, and when Preston finally found an opportunity to offer the proposition on which the Southern Whigs had agreed, it was in irregular fashion. A fortifications bill was before the Committee of the Whole when on February 7 Preston abruptly changed the subject. He proposed that all of the territory acquired from Mexico be erected into a single state, provided the necessary convention had been held and a constitution adopted before the first of October 1849. It was a compound of the various versions of the Douglas bill, and it was no more acceptable to the Calhoun faction, despite the able and conciliatory speech in which the young Virginian pleaded for it. Toombs professed optimism as to its chances, but actually it had no chance at all.[33]

The difference of opinion within the ranks of the Southerners themselves was fundamental and not to be bridged by expedients. Neither Preston's bill nor the Douglas bill could possibly satisfy those who believed, with Calhoun, that it was the whole institution of slavery that was under attack. Either of these bills would have resulted ultimately in the creation of enough free states, by partition as the population grew, to amend the Constitution. Both Douglas and Preston avoided the Wilmot Proviso, but both ignored the larger issues between North and South that were so clearly set forth in the Southern Address. Calhoun, in the obduracy of his defense of what was rapidly becoming a hopeless position, could no longer accept any solution that compassed only the territorial question. To himself and to those who clustered around him, more like devotees of a cult than followers of a party, he was the great bulwark between the South and chaos. To those not under his spell, even men of his own party and section, he seemed an immovable barrier in the way of any adjustment whatever.[34]

For the next two weeks both houses of Congress were occupied with other matters, but the time was getting short. The session was nearing its end, and with it would end Polk's administration and the control of the Democratic party in national affairs. The *Union* renewed its pleas for a government in California, printing startling stories of the prevalence of murder, violence, and lawlessness of all kinds in the territory. The Senate had been debating a routine appropriation bill for some days when Isaac P. Walker, Wisconsin Democrat, offered an amendment authorizing the President to set up a temporary government in California and extending over that territory the Constitution and laws of the United States. A move by John Bell of Tennessee to substitute the Whig version of the Douglas bill was voted down, and after a week of debate the Walker amendment in somewhat modified form was adopted. Calhoun was not in the chamber when the vote was taken, but Butler, Hunter, and other Calhoun men supported it. The amended bill was passed on February 28, and sent back to the House.[35]

The Senate debate was still in progress when the House finally got around to its own California bill on February 24. Preston offered his substitute, but it was quickly set aside, and three days later, by the substantial margin of 126 to 87, the bill was passed essentially as Caleb Smith had first offered it. It set up a territorial government for California, with an area limited on the east by the Sierras, and extended to that territory the provisions of the Ordinance of 1787.[36]

The session was now in its final days. The House bill was referred in the Senate to the Committee on Territories, where it remained until March 3. The Senate then refused by a vote of 25 to 28 to take it up, and there it ended. The Senate's own solution for the California problem could not be so lightly put aside, since it was attached to a bill appropriating funds to operate the government for the next fiscal year. There was, indeed, more than a little suspicion that a combination of Whigs and Free-Soilers meant to embarrass the President by adding the Proviso to the Walker amendment, thereby forcing him to violate his principles or leave the government without funds.[37]

The tension was if anything heightened by the presence in Washington of the President-elect, who was frequently consulted by members of his party but remained noncommittal. As much could not be said, however, for William H. Seward, who was to succeed Dix as Senator from New York on March 4. Seward had been in Washington since January, and was often seen in the Capitol lobbies, where he was thought by some to have more influence than any of the members. What hand he played, if any, in the history of the Walker amendment is obscure. It was later charged, however, that a word from Taylor would have secured its passage, but that Seward saw to it the word was not spoken.[38]

The House rejected the Walker amendment on March 2. The Senate insisted and asked a conference, but there was no agreement, and the next day the Senate amendment was again before the House. It was at this point that the worst suspicions of Southern Democrats were borne out. In a wild and unruly sitting the amendment was amended to validate until July 4, 1850, both the existing military government and the existing laws of California, which excluded slavery. It was already evening when the House took this way of showing its power, and it was past midnight when the Civil and Diplomatic Appropriation Bill, with its amended amendment for the government

of California, came back to the Senate. The time had already run
out, but the Senate continued to sit until seven in the morning of
March 4. Sometime before dawn, during a sitting of almost unprecedented excitement, confusion, and disorder, the Senate receded from
its own amendment, by a vote of 38 to 7. Calhoun, still unwell, had
long since left the chamber, but his followers voted with the majority.
The government would have operating funds for another year, but
California would have no government.[39]

Another action of that last hectic night of James K. Polk's administration was the passage of a bill creating a new Cabinet post: a
Department of the Interior, split off mainly from the Treasury, with
public lands its chief concern, though it would also take over patents
and the census from State and Indian Affairs from War. The bill
was largely the work of the retiring Secretary of the Treasury, Robert
J. Walker, who insisted that the operations of his department had
simply grown too big for any one man to handle. The principal sponsor of the bill in the Senate was Jefferson Davis, but Calhoun opposed
it to the last. To him it was another evidence that the central government was getting out of hand—another step in the consolidation
of power where it would inevitably be wielded by a majority hostile
to the interest he particularly represented.[40]

CHAPTER XXVII

UNIFICATION OF THE SOUTH

1

ZACHARY TAYLOR was inaugurated at noon on March 5, 1849. The fourth fell on Sunday and the General had the ceremony postponed. The address, inaudible to most of those who milled about in front of the Capitol bundled up against the rain and snow, had the supreme merit of being short, but aside from breathing a spirit of lofty patriotism it said nothing. The new President, like all those who had preceded him, pledged adherence to "those great republican doctrines which constitute the strength of our national existence." He asked for conciliation and harmony among conflicting interests, and promised to co-operate with the co-ordinate branches of the government in whatever their wisdom might dictate. That was all. Northern Whigs who wanted a positive commitment on tariff and national bank were as disappointed as those from the slave states who wanted assurances on the territorial question.[1]

Taylor and his predecessor rode to the Capitol together for the inauguration, and Polk understood the General to say that it would be better for both California and Oregon to be independent of the United States.[2] Such views were not uncommon among men of Taylor's generation, but the composition of the Cabinet belied the statement, even as it gave a clue to policy in other matters. The State Department went to John M. Clayton of Delaware, after Crittenden refused the place. The Delaware Senator was identified with both bank and tariff, but had established himself as a leading peacemaker in the sectional struggle. He had ability, experience, and industry, marred to be sure by a taste for strong drink, but he was, nevertheless, regarded by many Whigs, including himself, as future Presidential timber. The Treasury also went to a bank and tariff man, William M. Meredith of Philadelphia. He was an able lawyer, long associated with such luminaries of the bar as Horace Binney and John Sergeant, but his chief qualification for the Cabinet was a relatively neutral position in a factional battle among Pennsylvania Whigs. The War Department went to former Governor George W. Crawford of Georgia, who belonged to the same group as Toombs and Stephens but was less well known and less able than either. Ballard Preston of Virginia, first slated for the Attorney Generalship, wound up with the Navy Department after Taylor had been convinced that he was too inexperienced for a job that would pit him against the great lawyers of the day. The new Interior Department went to Thomas Ewing, the former Ohio Senator who had served a few months in the unhappy Harrison-Tyler Cabinet as Secretary of the Treasury. Ewing, too, was a bank and tariff man, who had been scheduled for the Post Office until the passage of the Interior Department bill during the night of March 3-4 made a better spot for him. The Post Office then went to former Congressman Jacob Collamer, a simon-pure Vermont Whig. Ablest of them all was probably the Attorney General, Senator Reverdy Johnson of Maryland, a last-minute choice after Taylor decided the job was too big for Preston.

Whatever doubts there may have been on the personal side, and there were many, the Cabinet reflected faithfully the traditional Whig policies. It stood also for California statehood, to which Clayton, Preston, and Johnson had all committed themselves in the past session of Congress.

Another portent was evident when the new Senate met in extra session to act on Presidential appointments. The two Barnburner Democrats, Dix of New York and Niles of Connecticut, were gone, but their successors were antislavery Whigs of courage and ability: William H. Seward and Truman Smith, the latter promoted from the House. Cameron of Pennsylvania was succeeded by a Whig, James Cooper; and Clayton's place went to another Whig, John Wales. The one Democratic Senator from Georgia, Herschell V. Johnson, had been defeated by William C. Dawson, a Whig; and Westcott of Florida had also surrendered his seat to a Whig, Jackson Morton. Hannegan of Indiana had lost to a fellow Democrat, James Whitcomb, but slavery had been the issue and Whitcomb had won on a free-soil platform. Sidney Breese of Illinois was replaced by General James Shields without change of party, but the Irish-born Shields had not been long enough a citizen of the United States, and for a time was not seated. Cass reclaimed his old seat from Michigan, and there was a Democratic gain in Louisiana, where Pierre Soulé replaced Henry Johnson. There would also be a Democratic gain in Maryland, where David Stewart was presently appointed to the seat vacated by Reverdy Johnson. A vacancy from Alabama would be filled by Jeremiah Clemens of the Calhoun faction. Unoccupied seats from Kentucky and Ohio would shortly be taken by men of preeminent abilities, aging but still commanding Henry Clay, and the most brilliant of all the Free-Soilers, Salmon P. Chase. The Democrats would still control the Senate in December, but the Whigs would be stronger, and the Free-Soil contingent, now heavily on the Whig side, would be larger and abler than ever before.

Calhoun paid a friendly visit to the new President a day or two after the inauguration, and left Washington toward the end of March convinced that Taylor was "well disposed to settle" the slavery question. He was prepared to co-operate with the administration "in any feasible plan" for accomplishing that end, but he saw no evidence that the Whigs had any common policy on the disturbing issue.[3]

They had a policy as to California, however, which they set about putting into effect as soon as the extra session of the Senate had adjourned. The invariable rule up to that time had been that the first Senators and Representatives from a new state were of the party in power in Washington at the time the state was organized. The Whigs had every reason to suppose that California would follow the normal pattern, and the administration badly needed strength in both Houses of Congress. Former Illinois Representative Edward D. Baker, who had resigned his seat in the Twenty-ninth Congress to lead a regiment of volunteers to Mexico, stated the case most frankly. "Every thing I see & hear," he wrote Clayton two weeks after the inauguration, "convinces me that California should be a State *at once*. The permanency of Whig ascendency may depend on it." To bring about that desirable result he proposed that he be sent forthwith to California to organize it for statehood. His letter was endorsed by his successor from the seventh Illinois district, Abraham Lincoln, who assured the Secretary of State that Colonel Baker would be just the man for such a mission, should it be regarded by the administration as practical.[4]

Administration strategists were thinking along very similar lines, but a choice of agent had already been made before Baker's letter arrived. The man selected was Georgia Congressman Thomas Butler King, who set out for San Francisco with instructions dated April

3, 1849. So far as the records go, he was merely a bearer of dispatches to the naval and military commanders in California, but charged with the additional duty of collecting as much information as he could about the country and its people. He was also, however, to convey to the Californians the assurances of the President that he would do all in his power, within the limitations of the Constitution, the Mexican treaty, and the relevant acts of Congress, to extend to them the benefits of civil government. "You are fully possessed of the President's views," the instructions went on, "and can with propriety, suggest to the people of California the adoption of measures best calculated to give them effect." [5]

General Bennet Riley, acting under orders that antedated the Taylor administration, had meanwhile succeeded to the dual office of military commander and governor in California. He was quickly convinced that an organized civil government was imperative, and waited only long enough to learn that Congress had not acted before he called a convention for that purpose. His proclamation, fixing September 1 as the convention date and prescribing the manner of electing delegates, was issued from Monterey on June 3, the day before King docked in San Francisco.[6]

The intent of Secretary Clayton's instructions to King was undoubtedly to encourage—if necessary, to stimulate—a constitutional convention in California at an early date. The legal objections of the previous session to the Douglas bill would thus be overcome. The move was so clearly indicated as the next step that external stimulus was hardly necessary, nor was there any concealment as to the President's expectations. That in itself was enough to arouse the South, but it was by no means all. The President outdid any of his predecessors in "rotating" public officials. Men who had supported the Taylor campaign went out with those who had not, and there were more offices to fill than any President up to that time had commanded. In the distribution the Taylor Democrats of the South went unheeded. There was little pattern in the appointments, and political obligations were often ignored. For a time even Crittenden was disgruntled. By summer the Southern Democrats were largely disillusioned and ready to go as far as Calhoun would take them toward sectional unity. Southern Whigs, and many Northern ones as well, saw the President they had labored to put in office on the way to wrecking the party. The Cabinet commanded less and less confidence as the weeks went by. Ritchie used every device of an opposition press to fan the discontent, and Southern Whigs in growing numbers began to regret their failure to support Calhoun's Address.[7]

2

The Southern Address was, and was intended to be, an appeal to conservatives, and to Calhoun's great gratification it was quite generally so understood. Toombs had asserted when the Address was first read to the assembled Southern delegates that a united South ought not to be sought until they were ready to dissolve the Union, but older and more experienced men, not all of them in the slave states, agreed that only the direct threat of secession backed by a unanimous South would stop the attacks on slavery and thereby render the Union secure.[8]

So those who sincerely desired, like Calhoun himself, to settle the issue within the constitutional framework, and those who looked forward to an eventual Southern confederacy joined to express their approval. All over South Carolina meetings were held to endorse the document and to consider ways and means of backing it up. There was a meeting at Pendleton on February 22; one in Charleston February 27; one at Kershaw March 3; and others in quick succession thereafter. About them all there was a standard pattern. Resolutions were passed approving the Address, condemning the Wilmot Proviso, denouncing the nonenforcement of the fugitive slave law, denying the power of Congress to legislate in any fashion on the subject of slavery and pledging co-operation with the other slave states in any joint endeavor looking to their collective security. In each community a Committee of Vigilance and Safety was appointed from among the leading men, and was instructed to correspond with like committees elsewhere. The Kershaw meeting of March 3 called for a general convention to organize on a state-wide basis, and the movement was well under way by the time Calhoun reached home.[9]

More than a hundred delegates chosen by committees of safety in twenty-nine state election districts met at Columbia on May 14, 1849. The roster of those present included many of the most distinguished of South Carolina names, representing both sides of bygone political battles. Former Governor J. P. Richardson opened the meeting and former Senator Daniel E. Huger was chosen permanent president. A Committee of Twenty-one to report a plan of action was headed by Elmore and included among its members such outspoken antinullifiers of the past as Richardson, R. F. W. Allston, Robert Cunningham, and Benjamin F. Perry. A standing Executive Committee of five members, chosen by ballot, was made up of Elmore as chairman, Wade Hampton, D. J. McCord, James Gadsden, and Francis W. Pickens.[10]

The State Executive Committee was Calhoun's suggestion, and his thinking also lay behind the resolutions adopted. He was not personally present, but his personality pervaded the two-day meeting, and his views, carefully committed to paper, charted the course of the delegates.

"You ask my opinion as to the course the Meeting should take," he wrote to John H. Means who headed the Fairfield delegation. "Before I give it, I deem it due to candour and the occasion to State, that I am of the impression that the time is near at hand when the South will have to chose between disunion, and submission. I think so, because I see little prospect of arresting the aggression of the North. If anything can do it, it would be for the South to present with an unbroken front to the North the alternative of dissolving the partnership or of ceasing on their part to violate our rights and to disregard the stipulations of the Constitution in our favour; and that too without delay. I say without delay; for it may be well doubted whether the alienation between the two sections has not already gone too far to save the Union; but, if it has not, there can be none that it soon will, if not prevented by some prompt and decisive measure."[11]

The measure he thought most likely to succeed was a convention of the Southern states. "That, and that only could speak for the whole, and present authoritatively to the North the alternative, which to choose." If even that failed to halt the attack upon her institutions, the South would then, he felt, be justified in dissolving a partnership no longer consistent with her safety. A Southern convention would be at once the "indispensible means" of warning the North against further aggressions, and of organizing for separate national existence should the warning not be heeded. The object of the Columbia meeting should therefore be "to adopt measures to prepare the way" for such a convention, and to groom South Carolina to take her part in it.

The delegates did substantially as Calhoun advised, ending the meeting with the unanimous adoption of resolutions that followed the familiar pattern. By this date almost any proslavery politician could draft a set without leaving his seat at whatever meeting he happened to be attending. The rising tide of abolitionism was noted, the Southern Address was approved, and the governor was requested to call the legislature into special session should Congress enact the Proviso or interfere with slavery or the slave trade in the District of Columbia. Governor Whitemarsh B. Seabrook, who did not wait for any meeting to instruct him, was already in correspondence with other Southern governors as to their common problem. The Executive Committee was also quickly engaged in interstate business, including the purchase of additional arms for South Carolina.[12]

3

It was only natural that the most unyielding opposition to the Southern movement should come from the opposite extreme, the Northern Free-Soilers; and it was equally natural that Thomas Hart Benton, because of his position in a slave state, should be the spearhead. Benton may or may not have been fighting for an ideal, but there was no doubt that he was fighting for his political life. As the slavery issue came more and more to transcend all others in national politics, Missouri tended to side more definitely with the South. She was a border state, her losses in runaway slaves were disproportionately high and the reasoning of the Southern Address met with wide acceptance. Benton was up for re-election in 1850, and his avowed sympathies with the radical wing of the Northern Democracy put him out of step with his constituents. It was widely believed in the North that Benton was to be the next Free-Soil candidate for President, but to win that place he had first to win his own state.[13]

During the winter session of 1848-1849 the Missouri legislature followed the Southern trend, passing strong resolutions on the slavery question and instructing her Senators to vote in conformity with them. Benton bluntly refused to obey, and came home to face down an irate constituency. He spoke at Jefferson City on May 26, 1849, not in defense of himself but in opposition to Calhoun. In the bombastic and aggressive manner so well known to his fellow Senators, he began by declaring the Missouri resolutions to be no more than a copy of those introduced into the Senate by the South Carolinian in February 1847. Their purpose, he said, was disunion, and so he could not obey them. The rest of the speech was a review of Calhoun's public career from the days of Madison's administration forward, emphasizing and often distorting out of all recognition every shift of view and every change of ground. By a species of rhetorical legerdemain he made Calhoun responsible for the protective system and for the national bank, for the alleged cession of Texas to Spain by the treaty of 1819, and for the Missouri Compromise of the following year, for the Free-Soil movement, and even for the Wilmot Proviso.[14]

In everything the Carolinian had ever said or done Benton professed to see a deep-laid plot to destroy the Union—a plot brought to a head in the meeting of Southern Senators and Representatives in Washington the past winter. The speech was compounded of many earlier philippics in the Senate, and particularly that of January 24, 1847, with seasoning by Sam Houston and garnish by F. P. Blair. The only distinction was that on this occasion, since Calhoun was not present to reply and the audience was presumably less versed in political history than members of the Senate, the charges were a little more fantastic than usual.

A newspaper text of the first half of Benton's "Calhouniac," as he himself called it, reached Washington early in June, where Senator Foote of Mississippi read it in the *Intelligencer* office. Foote saw danger in it, and as soon as the full text was available he sent it on to Fort Hill, urging the necessity for a reply. Behind the bombast, the obvious personal malice, the vicious slanders, lay a potentially effective attack by indirection upon the whole Southern resistance movement. For Benton had artfully contrived to make Calhoun appear as the prime and only important mover of Southern unity in opposition to free soil, and he had used every trick in the prosecutor's bag to discredit the South Carolinian, both in the North and in the South. For the North he was held up as an archtraitor who had for thirty years been plotting and conniving his country's overthrow; for the South he was painted as a selfish and ruthless politician, sacrificing his fellow slaveholders to his own inordinate ambition.[15]

Calhoun quickly saw the point, and the Pendleton *Messenger* announced on June 29 that "a communication from Mr. Calhoun" would appear in its next issue. Foote meanwhile had decided to answer Benton on his own, and did so in the guise of a letter to Henry A. Wise, whose Accomac district had come in for special notice from the Missouri Senator. Dated June 23, the letter appeared in the *Union* the following day. Foote confined himself to a defense of the Southern meetings and of those who signed the Southern Address, suggesting that Calhoun might prefer to repel the personal attack himself. The defense, however, was merely nominal. The heart of the letter turned Benton's tactics against Benton by a series of quotations from his leading speech in the great debate of 1830. The method afforded an opportunity to show that while Benton now pooh-poohed the idea that slavery was in any way endangered, he had been quite sure twenty years ago (when he was trying to bring the West into the Southern rather than the Northern orbit) that only united Southern action could save the peculiar institution from the hostility of the North. Foote's letter was featured in the Pendleton *Messenger* on July 6, Calhoun's "Address to the People of the Southern States" being held over for another week on that account.[16]

By the time Calhoun's statement appeared, in the *Messenger* for July 13, the whole country had been apprised that it was coming, and it was eagerly awaited. The New York *Herald* arranged by telegraph for a special express to get the document as quickly as possible, but the Post Office slipped up somewhere along the way, and it was July 21 before the *Herald* printed it in full. At that Bennett was a day ahead of the *Union,* and only four days behind the Charleston papers, which featured it on July 17. The Address filled close to two full pages of newsprint, but it was amply rewarding for those who read it.[17]

The tone was set at the very beginning. He had, Calhoun said, made a practice of taking no notice of Colonel Benton, if it could be avoided consistently with his public duty. "I regard him in a very different light from what he seems to regard me, if we may judge from the frequency and violence of his attacks upon me. He seems to think I stand in his way, and that I am ever engaged in some scheme to put him down. I, on the contrary, have never for a moment thought of raising him to the level of a competitor, or rival, nor considered it of any importance to me whether he should be put down or not. He must think he has something to gain by assailing me; I, on the contrary, feel that I have nothing to gain by noticing him, and, when compelled to do so, am satisfied if I escape without some loss of self-respect." The blow in this case, however, was aimed not at Calhoun personally but at the people of the South. "He strikes at me for the double purpose of weakening me in your confidence, and of striking at you and your cause through me, which he thinks can be done more effectually indirectly than directly."

Benton's charges were then taken up seriatim, and ridiculed as only a master of debate could do it. Calhoun was alternately grave and sarcastic, quoting resolutions and documents to show how their meaning had been distorted, and time and again carrying the offensive to his antagonist by holding up to the bright light of his own logic inconsistencies and damaging admissions within Benton's speech itself. Calhoun did far more than was necessary in his own defense, for the basic charge that he had raised the territorial issue for disunion purposes was amply refuted, as he did not fail to mention, by his exertions in behalf of the Clayton Compromise. But he was quite obviously enjoying himself, and determined to make the most of this opportunity to discredit Benton as Benton had sought to discredit him. It is a document that cannot be abstracted but must be read to appreciate the art of its composition.

He ended with a careful and clear restatement of his interpretation and application of the Constitution—the compact theory, with sovereignty remaining in the states, and the territories the joint property of these several sovereigns. He insisted, as he had insisted many times in the past, that his own efforts were and had been from the start directed not to the destruction but to the preservation of the Union—the Union as he understood it : a confederation of sovereign states. He deplored as much as Benton that parties should come to be geographical. "But to avoid geographical designation of parties it is indispensible that each section of the Union should respect the rights of the others, and carefully abstain from violating them. Unless that is done, it will be impossible to avoid it; aggression will and ought to lead to resistance on the part of those whose rights are trampled upon and safety endangered. Sectional assault on one side, and sectional resistance on the other, cannot fail to lead to sectional designation of parties. The blame and responsibility rightfully falls on the section that assails, and not on that which repels. Which that is in the present case admits of no doubt."

The response on the whole was exactly what Foote and others who had urged him on had expected. The *Mercury* spoke for the Southern Democracy generally, declaring that "a more powerful defense of the course pursued by the South has never fallen from any pen." Those who had joined Calhoun in signing the Southern Address of January were satisfied that their own course had now been fully vindicated, and that the net effect would be to advance the Southern convention movement. In the North, Byrdsall wrote that there was "not a weak point in it"; and the powerful James Gordon Bennett, in the New York *Herald,* publicly commended Calhoun and his followers for their efforts in behalf of the Union.[18]

4

The controversy between Benton and Calhoun was but one skirmish in the more general battle between Northern free-soilers and the proslavery forces of the South. Everywhere through the slave states the lines were being drawn between the signers and nonsigners of Calhoun's Address, and the movement for Southern unity gained momentum with every new evidence that Zachary Taylor could not be trusted on the crucial issue.

From California and New Mexico the news came very slowly, but it was generally known by June that men and money were at work in both territories in the interest of quick organization without slavery. In another month the South heard that the administration had sent an emissary to California, and understood his purpose to be to get up a constitution and avoid the Proviso by immediate statehood. The end of July brought confirmation in the form of General Riley's proclamation calling a constitutional convention, and the text of speeches by Thomas Butler King and others at a great rally in San Francisco. To Calhoun and to many other Southern leaders all this meant that California could not be kept out of the Union, for the administration was committed and enough Southern Whigs would back their President to carry the day in alliance with Northern men of both parties. After California would come New Mexico and Utah, Minnesota and Nebraska and Oregon. The South would be overwhelmed by sheer numbers, and would be forced to accept whatever fate was meted out to her.[19]

A further irritation grew out of the administration's handling of foreign affairs. The California gold rush reopened the whole question of a canal between Atlantic and Pacific oceans. The United States had transit rights across the Isthmus of Panama by treaty with New Grenada, as Colombia was then called, but Nicaragua was thought to offer the more favorable terrain. A British protectorate over the Mosquito Indians, occupying the Carribean coast of that country, blanketed the eastern terminus of the latter route, and set the stage for a new conflict between the two powers. At the same time the importance of Cuba was enhanced by her position astride the water passage to California. For decades Americans had been haunted by the fear that Great Britain would secure sovereignty over Cuba, and with it control of the commerce of the Gulf of Mexico. The South feared also that Cuba in British hands would become another experiment in emancipation, and she did not relish the prospect of a second Santo Domingo off her shores. With Spain unable to pay huge debts to British nationals, and the bellicose Palmerston in the Foreign Office, there was new threat of seizure, and new Southern agitation for annexation. Before he retired from the Presidency Polk offered the tottering Spanish government $100 million for the island, but the offer was peremptorily rejected.[20]

It was in this setting that Narciso López undertook to lead a band of Americans to the conquest of Cuba. López had already made an abortive attempt to revolutionize the island, but was convinced that the people would rise and assert their independence as soon as armed assistance reached them. During the summer of 1848 he had talked to Southern leaders in Washington, among them Calhoun, Davis, and Foote, each of whom expressed sympathy for the Cuban cause if nothing more. López, incurably sanguine, did not doubt that the South would back him, and in sentiment it most certainly did. He was busily engaged in raising a small army of "liberation" when his activities were rudely halted by a proclamation from President Taylor in August 1849. The embattled South took it as further proof that Taylor was under Northern influence, and another contingent of Southern Whigs fell away.[21]

Polk's sudden death three months after his retirement paved the way for the final blow, which came with the reunion of Barnburners and Hunkers in September. Taylor had already strengthened the free-soil faction among the Whigs by giving the New York patronage to Seward, and the reconciliation between radical and conservative Democrats in the same state seemed to imply that the Democracy too would be dominated by free-soil sentiment. The slaveholders of the South, smarting under Northern attacks and driven on by their own compulsion to maintain their system, turned in increasing numbers to the idea of unity as their strongest and by now their only defense. Calhoun's Southern Address pointed the way, and became an issue in state elections over the South. The Whigs, who had relied on Taylor and refused to take part in the Southern movement, lost eight seats and with them control of the House of Representatives in the next Congress. A hint that Calhoun might again retire to private life brought such passionate protest from friends of the Southern cause that the idea was dropped.[22]

So great was the excitement through the South that James Gordon Bennett sent a special correspondent to investigate and report on conditions for the New York *Herald*. Bennett had begun his own newspaper career on the staff of the Charleston *Courier,* and his personal sympathies at this time lay strongly with the South. His decision was made in May after a long conference with Thomas G. Clemson, who was returning to his Belgian post after a visit home. The reporter selected was Joseph A. Scoville, who had been closely associated with Calhoun's 1844 Presidential campaign, and was later a clerk in the State Department during the South Carolinian's regime as Secretary. Scoville was about to sail for Europe, but changed his plans at the urging of Bennett, the Clemsons, Ellwood Fisher, and other friends of Calhoun's then in New York. His orders were to write what he pleased, and to spend as much time as possible at Fort Hill, where he was to be at Calhoun's disposal. Scoville began his tour in Charleston, and his letters, signed "Commissioner" and "Northerner," began to appear in the *Herald* on June 19, where they were given featured position on the front page. He was at Fort Hill before the end of June, and probably served Calhoun as amanuensis in the composition of the reply to Benton. He was in and out for the next two months, moving on to Alabama around the middle of September. He stayed in the South until about the time Congress convened, sending back some forty letters to the *Herald*.[23]

5

In Mississippi a state convention was called to meet at Jackson early in October, and Calhoun was asked for advice as to the course to be pursued. He answered in detail on July 9, repeating substantially the position he had taken in April when his views had been sought in connection with the South Carolina Convention of May 14. "In my opinion," he wrote to a Mississippi correspondent, "there is but one thing that holds out the promise of saving both ourselves and the Union; and that is a Southern Convention. . . . All our movements ought to look to that result. For that purpose, every Southern State ought to be organized with a Central Committee, and one in each county. Ours is already. It is indispensible to produce concert and prompt action. In the mean time, firm and resolute resolutions ought to be adopted by yours, and such meetings as may take place before the assembling of the Legislatures in the fall. They, when they meet, ought to take up the subject in the most solemn and impressive manner." The objects of such a Southern convention as he had in mind were to set forth the grievances of the South, to admonish the free states most solemnly as to the consequences if they were not redressed, and to prepare to back up the admonition with action. "The call should be addressed to all those who are desirous to save the Union and our institutions, and who, in the alternative, should it be forced on, of submission or dissolving the partnership, would prefer the latter." In his eyes it was a "great conservative movement." [24]

With the endorsement of both Democratic and Whig organizations, plans for the Mississippi Convention were perfected during the summer. Calhoun, watching closely from Fort Hill, amplified his views in letters to various state leaders, and these letters, privately shown where they would be most effective, fixed the lines within which Mississippi acted. The convention met on October 1, with Chief Justice William L. Sharkey, a leading Whig, in the chair. Congressman Daniel Wallace of South Carolina, sent by Governor Seabrook as an observer, was invited to a privileged seat, and took an active part behind the scenes. [25]

Judge Sharkey's opening address was only a restatement of Calhoun's position, with the emphasis of a jurist on the constitutional argument, and the same views were incorporated into a formal "Protest" and a list of resolutions. The Protest included a trenchant exposition of the theory of state sovereignty, and made the further point that in rejecting the Clayton Compromise the majority in Congress had refused the arbitration of the courts on the points in dispute, leaving no recourse but power. The resolutions included the familiar declaration of "devoted and cherished attachment to the Union"; the usual assertions as to the powers and limitations of Congress on the slave question; and a warning that enactment of the Wilmot Proviso, or the abolition of slavery in the District of Columbia, would of themselves so far violate the "federal compact" as to throw the slave states on their own resources, and to make enemies of the free states. A Convention of the Southern States was called to meet at Nashville, the first Monday in June 1850; organization on state and county levels was recommended; and the legislature was asked to instruct the Governor to call a state convention immediately upon the passage by the Congress of the Wilmot Proviso or any other of the reprobated acts. The Address of the Convention was prepared after the adjournment by Judge Sharkey. It was an elaboration of the Protest, with the addition of a defense of slavery on Biblical grounds, and a documented amplification of the constitutional argument.[26]

The Mississippi resolutions undoubtedly helped to clarify the whole situation, North and South. In the slave states many who had relied on Taylor were now disillusioned, and the convention call was well received. Calhoun gave his blessing and promised that the Nashville Convention could yet save the Union if only the South would forget party and back the movement to the full. The Charleston *Mercury* and the Pendleton *Messenger* were quick to deny that any new party or Presidential nomination was contemplated, and Calhoun himself rebuked one editor for suggesting it. In response to a direct question posed by Foote, North Carolina Whigs were committed by Clingman and Mangum to the resistance doctrine, should the Proviso or other antislavery measure pass Congress. It was the more significant when we remember that less than five years back Thomas L. Clingman had charged in the House that Calhoun's course led straight to disunion, and for his pains had exchanged shots with Yancey. Only ten months earlier he and Mangum and dozens of their fellows had refused to sign the Southern Address, yet here they were where they had so recently impeached Calhoun for standing. In Georgia, too, the nonsigners were "alarmed & sick of their position," ready now to "cooperate in energetic action." [27]

Governor George W. Towns of Georgia took the lead when the legislature of that state met on the first Monday in November. In his annual message he reviewed the sectional crisis, and in forceful language declared that "further aggression was not to be endured." Following the Mississippi recommendations, he asked authorization to call a state convention should any measure inimical to Southern security be enacted by Congress. A week later Governor Reuben Chapman of Alabama also came out boldly and clearly for resistance to any act of the Federal Government calculated to impair the equality of the states within the Union, or to infringe in any way the rights of the people of Alabama.[28]

In South Carolina Governor Seabrook went further still in his annual message of November 27, 1849. The language was such as Calhoun himself might have used, so thoroughly had his thinking permeated the state. Seabrook commended the Nashville Convention in the highest terms, declaring its purpose to be the preservation of the Union. Only if that should prove impossible should the next step be taken; but he left no doubt as to what he considered the next step to be. He asked that the Governor be empowered to summon the legislature should the Wilmot Proviso or any other anti-slavery measure be enacted by Congress; he called for the creation of a new militia division; he proposed spending $50,000 for arms and ammunition for the state; and he requested a $30,000 appropriation for the contingent fund.[29]

The legislature did not give him all he asked, but the power to call a special session in the indicated circumstances was granted, and $7,500 was voted for the purchase of arms. More important was the ending of a long fight over the State Bank. Calhoun himself, under prodding from Elmore, suggested the importance of the institution in event of conflict with the general government, and Memminger's bill to wind up the Bank's affairs was defeated by a single vote. Elmore was then re-elected President of the Bank by a substantial majority over Benjamin F. Perry.[30]

The Nashville Convention was taken up first at a legislative caucus on December 7. Four delegates-at-large were selected, and the choice was unanimously ratified at a joint session of the two houses three days later. Those named were Langdon Cheves, Franklin H. Elmore, Robert W. Barnwell, and James H. Hammond. All were men who had served in Congress and enjoyed national reputations. It was a selection designed to show the South and the country as a whole that South Carolina would take the Nashville Convention very seriously.[31]

Even before the South Carolina delegates were chosen, the Vir-

ginia legislature met, and Governor Floyd's message echoed Seabrook's. The Northern press still professed to regard the Southern
movement as a gigantic bluff, manipulated by ambitious men for their
own advancement; but before the Thirty-first Congress was organized the shadow of the Nashville Convention lay ominously over
Washington.[32]

CHAPTER XXVIII

THE THEORY OF GOVERNMENT

1

CALHOUN'S INSISTENCE on Southern unity and his personal efforts in the late 1840's to bring it about were based on a complete and logically constructed theory of government, which he was committing to paper at precisely this time in the spare moments available to him. His activities toward the close of his life will become clearer if we digress for a chapter to examine this theory and the background out of which it arose.

From the date of his intensive study of the Constitution of the United States and of the philosophy of government generally in the summer and fall of 1828, Calhoun's speeches, reports, and letters form a consistent body of doctrine. His approach to the widely varied problems of the subsequent years was always in terms of this broad theory of government, and it was his emphasis on first principles that led so many of his contemporaries to dismiss him as a mere "abstractionist." The campaign *Life* of 1843 and the volume of speeches that accompanied it should have cleared him of any suspicion of impracticality. From the writings emerged a broad and stable concept of the nature of man in society, while the career at every point displayed the same principles in action.[1]

He had already decided to reduce his views on what he called "political science" to systematic form by the time he selected the speeches for the campaign volume late in 1842. In the fall of that year Rhett told Senator William H. Roane of Virginia that Calhoun meant to write a book on government. Calhoun himself passed through Richmond on his way to Washington that winter, and when Roane asked him about it he discussed the project freely, giving Roane the impression that the result was to be "John Taylor of Caroline with metaphysical variations." [2]

He probably got started on the composition of the treatise during the summer or fall of 1843, after his retirement from the Senate;

411

but the demands on his time precluded much in the way of progress until after his withdrawal from the Presidential campaign that winter. His return to public life as Secretary of State followed too quickly to have offered much leisure for composition, but he undoubtedly brought something in the way of a manuscript or notes with him when he came to Washington late in March 1844. At least he had enough done by February 1845 so that he could discuss it with Francis Wharton as a work upon which he was engaged.[3]

Thereafter the references become more frequent. He picked up the threads almost immediately after his retirement from the State Department. To Charles Jared Ingersoll, who was then at work on his distinguished history of the War of 1812, Calhoun wrote not only as a fellow actor in those stirring scenes, but also as a fellow author. "I, on my part," he explained on April 12, 1845, "have commenced an enquiry into the elements of political science, preliminary to a treatise on the Constitution of the U. States; but I know not whether I shall ever have time to finish it." Though the project had thus grown in scope, his pessimism was gone when he wrote to Anna Clemson six weeks later, and he was able to report "good progress toward finishing the rough draft" of the preliminary disquisition. He expected shortly to move on to the "treatise on the Federal Constitution" which he hoped to finish "in the course of the year, if I can remain at home." He vouchsafed no details as to the ground he was covering, but his friends were not backward in letting him know what they expected. "The friends of constitutional law and of true political science, expect much from you," wrote Wharton in April. "We want a full, thorough, and just, disquisition on the theory of our constitution, and we want, in addition to it, what Hallam has given to Great Britain, a sketch of our constitutional history." [4]

Before he got much further other matters crowded his schedule, and the winter of 1845-1846 found him back in the Senate giving all of his time and energy to the serious domestic and foreign questions then facing the country. It was fairly generally known, however, that Calhoun was writing a book on government in his spare time, and an occasional reference to the fact found its way into the newspapers over the next two or three years.[5]

He was at work on it again in the summer of 1847, and he seems to have hoped that the leisure afforded by the short session of Congress would permit him to go to press that fall. He was undoubtedly stimulated to renewed exertions by the terms in which the slavery question was then being agitated in the North, by the Wilmot Proviso, and by the Mexican War. But again other demands on his time were too great, and once more he carried an unfinished manuscript to Washington in the winter of 1847-1848. In the revolutions that swept the continent of Europe in the spring he saw an opportunity to test his theories, and although the rough draft of the preliminary treatise—the one we know as the *Disquisition on Government*—was finished, he proposed to withhold it for the time being. He was the more willing to do so because he felt, no doubt correctly, that "the publick mind" was not so well prepared for his conservative doctrine as it would be after the reaction he anticipated had set in abroad.[6]

As the great struggle over slavery gathered momentum with the rise of the territorial issue, Calhoun developed at length in his speeches the dogma of a federation of sovereign communities, united by a treaty called a constitution. Under the Marshall-Story-Webster doctrine of a national state, with sovereignty inhering in the people as a whole to be exercised by their majority through the general government, the Southern economy, and the whole Southern way of life, was doomed, and it became a matter of practical necessity to arrest the trend. It was this purpose that the South began to visualize as being served by the treatise Calhoun was known to be writing. "You must not die if God spares you two years longer," wrote A. B. Longstreet on Independence Day 1848, "without writing a commentary on the Constitution. That Story's is lamentably faulty, I know; but if I could prove it the weight of his character would bear me down—at least for many long years. Not so with you." [7]

When he got back to work in the spring of 1849 Calhoun knew exactly what he had to do. The basis of his argument was clearly laid down in his speeches and writings of the past decade. Ill health gave a sense of urgency, and on June 14, 1849, he completed the final revision of the *Disquisition on Government*. "It takes 125 pages of large foolscap closely written for me," he explained next day to Anna. "I am pretty well satisfied with its execution. It will be nearly throughout new territory; and, I hope, to lay a solid foundation for political Science. I have written, just as I thought, and told the truth without fear, favour, or affection." He proposed to rest only briefly before going on with the longer but less difficult *Discourse on the Constitution and Government of the United States*. It was already blocked out and he thought could be completed in four or five months. Some of it, no doubt, was dictated to Scoville who turned up at Fort Hill late in June, and spent much of the next two months making himself useful. Before the end of July Calhoun was confident he could finish the job before he left for Washington in November.[8]

Harper and Brothers meanwhile had asked for copies of his recent speeches in order to reissue the 1843 volume in enlarged form, and Calhoun undoubtedly had some correspondence or other contact with them in the course of the summer of 1849. At any rate we find him proposing in late July to take the manuscript with him to Washington, to be "put to press in New York, early next year"; and the Harper name was coupled with the venture in newspaper references. The two treatises on government and a new selection of speeches and other writings were to constitute a single work, to be published in "two moderate size Octavo volumes" not later than the summer of 1850.[9]

In Washington he devoted all of his spare time to the project during the early weeks of the session, and the work was in fact substantially done before he was forced by illness to put it aside. Richard K. Crallé, who had planned to visit the Capital in the spring in search of materials for a biography of Calhoun, came hastily in March to take final instructions as to the manuscripts from his dying friend. It was Calhoun's own desire, reiterated by the family after his death, that Crallé should edit the work, and Crallé it was who brought it to South Carolina. If he was aware of any commitment to Harper he was not at liberty to carry it out. The state of South Carolina assumed the responsibility, and with true bureaucratic slowness published in handsome form the posthumous works of her great Senator. Instead of the summer of 1850 the volume was distributed only when the South Carolina legislature met in November 1851.[10]

2

The *Disquisition on Government,* which constitutes Calhoun's introduction to political science, is the mature statement in universal terms of the premises on which his own public career since the middle

1820's had been based. It is at the same time an original and significant contribution to the literature of political thought.[11]

Government, for Calhoun, was inseparable from human nature, and
he took a realistic view of both which was completely devoid of
romantic illusions. His point of departure, derived from what he
called "universal experience," was that man cannot exist without
some kind of government. The law of self-preservation requires us
to pursue our own interests more assiduously than we pursue the
interests of others. The natural consequence is a tendency to conflict
among individuals that would destroy society and make life itself
insupportable, were it not in some manner controlled. The controlling force, whatever form it takes, is government. The powers of
government, however, must be exercised by those same self-interested, quarrelsome creatures whose tendency to conflict brought about
the restraints they are to administer, and so it follows that the very
qualities in human nature which make government necessary also
make inevitable a tendency to the abuse of its powers. Unless safe-
guarded in some fashion, the power given to the rulers to prevent
injustice and oppression will be used by them to oppress the ruled.

With that clear, marching logic which characterizes everything he
wrote, Calhoun goes on to show that the abuse of power can be
prevented only by the internal structure of the government itself.
Those so constructed that the ruled may resist the abuses of the
rulers he calls limited or constitutional governments. All others are
absolute. In neither category does it make any difference whether the
ruler is a single individual, an oligarchy, or a majority.

A constitutional government, as Calhoun visualizes it, must be
based on suffrage; but the right of suffrage alone is not enough to
prevent absolutism. By means of popular elections the actual seat of
power may be shifted from the rulers to the body of the community,
but the abuse of power will not thereby be prevented unless the individual interests of the whole citizen body are the same. Where
interests are many and varied, the right of suffrage merely intensifies
the tendency to conflict, for each interest strives to gain control of
the powers of government as a means of protecting itself. This leads
to combinations and arrangements, until the whole community is
divided into hostile parties.

Indeed, the community would be so divided, even if interests were
otherwise the same, by the action of the government alone. To fulfill

its purpose, government must be strong. It must, therefore, employ officers, collect taxes, and spend money in numerous ways. It is difficult if not impossible to collect taxes in equal proportions from the whole citizen body, and they are never spent equally. The community will thus be divided into opposing interests by the fiscal action of the government alone. The majority, moved by the same self-interest as the individuals who compose it, will inevitably seek to aggrandize itself at the expense of the minority. The fact that the two may change places by the process of elections only intensifies the tendency to conflict and disorder.

Suffrage, then, is not enough to prevent the abuse of power. There must be some other provision that will prevent any single interest or combination of interests from gaining exclusive control of the machinery of government. The identification of this provision is the heart of Calhoun's political theory, and his greatest contribution. He would take "the sense of each interest or portion of the community, which may be unequally and injuriously affected by the action of the government, separately, through its own majority" and would "require the consent of each interest, either to put or to keep the government in action." The government, in short, would be so constituted as to "give to each division or interest, through its appropriate organ, either a concurrent voice in making and executing the laws, or a veto on their execution." The will of the numerical majority would be supplemented by concurring majorities in each of those "interests, orders, classes, or portions, into which the community may be divided," the two types of majority together comprising the elements of constitutional government.

Each of these two ways of measuring the popular will, Calhoun explains, collects the sense of the majority. "But one regards numbers only, and considers the whole community as a unit, having but one common interest throughout; and collects the sense of the greater number of the whole, as that of the community. The other, on the contrary, regards interests as well as numbers; considering the community as made up of different and conflicting interests, as far as the action of the government is concerned; and takes the sense of each, through its majority or appropriate organ, and the united sense of all as the sense of the entire community." The one he calls the numerical or absolute majority, the other the concurrent or constitutional majority.

To govern by the numerical majority alone is to confuse a part of the people with the whole people, and is in fact no more than the rule of the smaller by the larger part. A written constitution offers no restraint to the majority will, unless the power to enforce its provisions is given to those it is designed to protect, for the stronger party will always construe broadly the powers it is to exercise. Neither will the separation of powers preserve the constitution, so long as each branch is controlled by the numerical majority. The concurrent majority, on the other hand, gives to each portion of the community a negative on the others. "It is this negative power,—the power of preventing or arresting the action of the government,—be it called by what term it may,—veto, interposition, nullification, check, or balance of power,—which in fact forms the constitution. They are all but different names for the negative power. In all its forms, and under all names, it results from the concurrent majority. Without this there can be no negative; and, without a negative, no constitution." If a concurrent majority were required, to act at all the government would need the consent of the various interest groups of which it is composed. Its conservative principle would therefore be compromise, whereas the only principle by which absolute governments may be preserved is force.

Such, in broad outline, is Calhoun's system of political philosophy. He found a classical basis for it in the separate representation of patricians and plebeians in ancient Rome, where each had a veto over the acts of the government; and a more recent illustration in the balance of classes or estates in British parliamentary practice. In his own country he found that the basic distinction between interests, though still along economic lines, followed an essentially geographical pattern. They were not stratified as classes or estates, but were localized as sections or regions in terms of the prevalent source of livelihood, this in turn being a product of climate and natural resources. The states were most nearly representative of this division, so it was to the states, in their character as members of a federation, that Calhoun accorded a concurrent veto.

The dogma of State Rights, with its correlatives of nullification and secession, was but a restatement of the general doctrine in terms of the familiar American institutions—a restatement given its definitive form in the *Discourse on the Constitution and Government of the United States.*

3

The *Discourse* is considerably more than an exposition of the compact theory of the Constitution, though it starts with a well-nigh irrefutable demonstration that the fundamental law, at least in the understanding of those who made and ratified it, was indeed a contract or joint agreement among sovereigns for the creation of a federal system. It is more than a belated answer to Marshall's constitutional jurisprudence, to Story's *Commentaries,* to the nationalistic doctrines of Webster and Jackson. In the context of its time and place it is basically an interpretation of the American government in terms that made the Southern Address and the forthcoming Nashville Convention logical and proper steps that followed inevitably from the premises laid down in the preliminary *Disquisition.*

With wisdom greater than their own, the founding fathers, so Calhoun reasoned, had actually devised a government of the concurrent majority. The numerical element was of course expressed through the House of Representatives, but the great interests of the country—the slave-based agriculture of the South and the commercial-industrial complex of the North—had each a concurrent veto on legislation through their equal representation in the Senate. There were other factors, of course, that entered into the full delineation of the system, such as the amending process, the mode of electing President and Vice President, the two-thirds vote required to override a Presidential veto, and the participation of the Senate in the treaty-making and appointing powers. Step by step and point by point, Calhoun demonstrated, to his own satisfaction at least, that these provisions were devised with the deliberate intention of giving to each major interest, localized in sectional terms, a negative voice.

It was clear, however, that the working of the system so defined rested on the maintenance of a permanent sectional balance, which the operation of the government itself soon began to upset. The industrial and commercial enterprises of the Northern states, artifically stimulated by legislation, invited greater concentration of population, which soon overflowed into more westerly regions. The balance threatened to be lost, and so the Missouri Compromise was made, to preserve the equal power of the sections in the Senate. The more rapidly growing population and wealth of the nonslaveholding states nevertheless continued to increase the relative influence of the North in the lower house of Congress and in the electoral college. Many of the intentions of those who made the Constitution were evaded by the party system, and the more drastic negative of state interposition was required to compel a new compromise.

We cannot here summarize the argument of the *Discourse* in any detail, but enough has been said to indicate the direction in which it pointed. The operation of the concurrent majority principle as incorporated into the Constitution of the United States or deducible from it depended on a balance between sections. The balance was gone, and the government was being transformed into one resting on numbers alone, with no restraint of any kind to prevent its degenerating into absolutism—an absolutism that would disregard the interest of the South and emancipate the slaves. The conservative principle of constitutional governments, as the *Disquisition* had shown, was compromise; and the government of the United States might yet be saved in that fashion. It could be accomplished, however, only by a clear and united demand from the weaker interest, backed up in the only way that now remained—a threat of withdrawal from the federation. By such means only, since men were moved by self-interest, and governments by the interests of the men who dominated them, could the power to protect themselves be restored to the slaveholding states, through some new compromise or constitutional provision.

In the *Discourse,* though it is throughout as detached in tone as a legal commentary ought to be, Calhoun was writing from the point of view of a conscious minority. He was here, as in the speeches of the later years, a deliberate sectionalist; but he was so in no narrow or invidious sense. He had drawn a concise outline of what he believed to be the most perfect form of government that imperfect human intelligence could devise, and he had shown that this ideal scheme could exist only when each of its parts could guard itself against encroachment by the others. He had ingeniously if not always with historical accuracy fitted to the pattern the government of his own country, in which the parts were geographical divisions. It followed necessarily that since the preservation of the whole depended on the concurrent veto of the parts, the sectional approach was the highest patriotism.

4

If Calhoun's library had been preserved it might be possible to trace the germ of his political ideas in his reading, but we know enough of his preference in books to give a general idea of his intellectual antecedents. We know that he knew Plato and Aristotle, Machiavelli and Hobbes and Locke; we know that he studied institutional history, particularly that of the Greeks and Romans and Hebrews, the history of the Italian republics and of Great Britain; we know that he had high admiration for Burke. He was thoroughly steeped in the literature of political controversy produced in his own country, from the Revolutionary pamphlets through the *Federalist,* the State Rights controversy that preceded Jefferson's rise to power, John Taylor of Caroline, and the constitutional commentaries and glosses of his own time; and he was on familiar terms with the economic doctrines that had burgeoned since the days of Adam Smith. According to his brother-in-law, who knew him as intimately as anyone ever did, he was far more widely read than was generally believed, but seldom gave that impression because he did not quote or cite authorities in his speeches and public papers.[12]

His reading undoubtedly entered into his thinking, but the quality of his intellect led Calhoun almost inevitably to generalize from his experience, and to set up his generalizations in the form of universal laws. His unshakable self-confidence, his unquestioning certainty that he was right, led him to evaluate the actions of others and in large measure to determine his own on the basis of these general principles. His own political philosophy, in short, was a framework on which he hung his reading of history and in terms of which he interpreted the economic and political forces of his time. By the same token it is also a pattern which gives consistency and direction to a career that appeared to his enemies and often to his friends to be erratic and without principle. His course was not determined by simple reactions to people and events but was rather derived from a system of philosophy into which people and events had first been neatly fitted and arranged.

Calhoun belonged to an age of revolution, of intellectual ferment, of political and economic experimentation. He was born before the close of the American struggle for independence. When he was a precocious lad of six his father opposed ratification of the new Constitution of the United States because it gave too much power to a central government. The French Revolution was the overshadowing fact of his youth. He was nearing maturity when Virginia rebelled against the autarchy of the Alien and Sedition Acts, and he had already entered preparatory school when the explosive force of that rebellion carried Thomas Jefferson to the Presidency. He was in college when Bonaparte completed the transition from successful military commander to First Consul to Emperor, and we know from his letters that the young Carolinian watched the process and its aftermath with interest and concern.

Equally suggestive of conflict and upheaval is Calhoun's early political career. He entered public life at a time when his country was being forced to choose sides in a world-wide struggle for power. He sat in a war Congress and grappled there with the problems of foreign invasion and internal revolt. He saw, and encouraged, the rise of industry in the Northern and Middle states, but in the process he had ample opportunity to observe the interaction of economic forces and political events. From the vantage point of a Cabinet seat he witnessed the rising sectional tension between North and South, and he recognized the Missouri Compromise for what it was—an internal balance of power. It was an age of wonderful technological advances, which seemed to go hand in hand with crumbling social institutions: an age when active minds went back to fundamentals, and thinking men sought new interpretations of the world order.

Calhoun's own search for first principles undoubtedly began at an early stage of his career, but it was not until the summer and fall of 1828, when he made his first intensive study of the Constitution in search of an answer to the tariffs that were eating away the prosperity of his native state, that the broad outline of the political theory ultimately refined and perfected in the *Disquisition* and *Discourse* was worked out. The first statement of it came in the *South Carolina Exposition and Protest* of that year, with refinements and amplifications being added as the nullification controversy unfolded, to conclude with the great debate with Webster on the Force Bill and on the nature of the Constitution.

There was further enlargement of the doctrine in the course of the three-year controversy with Jackson over the removal of the deposits from the Bank of the United States, in the course of which the focus shifted from legislative to executive power. The reports on incendiary publications and on executive patronage of 1835 and 1836 built up the background. The return of the Whigs to power with the election of 1840 led Calhoun to consider the whole question of centralization in the general context of a Hamiltonian program, while the Dorr rebellion in Rhode Island showed him how an unchecked numerical majority might operate. By 1842, when the tariff compromise was swept aside at the bidding of local interests, an understanding of the forces that were changing the whole scope and structure of government as they changed the face of nature had begun to loom more important in his eyes than even the Presidency itself. It was then that he conceived the idea of writing a book on government and prepared to rest his place in history on his analysis of the political process.

He anticipated many of the arguments of the *Discourse* in his speech on the veto power in 1842. By the summer of 1843, when he probably began the tentative blocking out of the systematic treatises, the precise ideas of the *Disquisition* and some of its phrasing began to appear in his speeches and in his familiar writings. The analysis of man in relation to society first appeared in his letter to William Smith on the Rhode Island controversy, dated July 1843. In the State Department the following year he became fully aware for the first time "of the immense influence, which may be exerted through it on foreign and domestic relations"; and before he left the Cabinet he was talking of "concurrent majorities" as being the "essence of the constitution." [13]

In retirement and at work on his treatises once more, he reflected sharply in his private letters on the influence of patronage as he had seen it grow in the Tyler administration. "The truth is," he explained to J. R. Matthews in August of 1845, "that the office holders & the office seekers govern the country, & the struggles between the parties have degenerated into a mere contest for the spoils, without a particle of regard on either side for principles or country." He enlarged on the theme the following spring, in the midst of the battle for the Walker tariff, in terms such as might have gone into the *Disquisition*. "I have seen enough of publick men," he wrote to his brother-in-law in May 1846, "to come to the conclusion, that there are few, indeed, whose attachment to self is not stronger, than their patriotism, and their friendship." He was prepared, however, to make allowances, comparing this personal self-love to the friction in a machine. "We

must take men as they are, and do the best we can with them. . . .
If all were disinterested patriots, there would be very little difficulty in
constructing or managing the political machine; and very little merit
in doing either." It was later that same year that he prepared his
elaborate exposition of the constitution of South Carolina as a perpetual balance of interests.[14]

His speeches and writings on the Mexican War, and on the territorial and slavery questions growing out of it from 1847 on, display
the theory pretty much in its final form, with the language used being
the same or very similar to that in which the posthumous treatises are
expressed. His starting point in 1828 had been the defense of a
conscious minority against exploitation by a legislature in the hands
of a stronger interest. Twenty years later he was still defending that
same minority, now relatively weaker than before, against not mere
exploitation but destruction at the hands of a numerical majority
fired with crusading zeal. In the interval he had broadened and en-
riched and universalized his principles as he watched them work themselves out with almost mathematical precision to ends he had foreseen.

5

What Calhoun was actually doing was rationalizing the governmental process as he had seen it at work in his own time. From his
own experience he generalized that certain basic premises would
always be true—that governments tend to become absolute, that
rulers tend to abuse their powers, that the honors and emoluments of
government are in themselves enough to fix party lines and to precipitate a struggle for power. All these propositions were deductions
from the nature of man, but they were far more than that to the grim-
visaged realist from South Carolina. They were also obvious facts
that anyone could see for himself in the day-to-day operations of the
government of the United States. The history of his own country
was both the source and the practical proof of his theory.

In making the generalizations on which his political theory rested,
Calhoun was not concerned with the motives or morals of individuals, nor with those by-products of the process that have seemed
good to later historians, steeped in an altogether different social
philosophy. He did not look on the extension of the franchise as a
forward step in raising the condition of the common man; he saw it

as one of the means by which irresponsible power passed to a numerical majority, to be wielded by a small group of politicians for partisan
ends. He did not see in the destruction of the Bank of the United
States any popular victory over entrenched privilege and private
monopoly; to him it represented a dangerous extension of executive
power, more potent for evil than for good. He did not regard the
protective tariff as a means of building up industry, increasing the
national wealth, and raising the standard of living for the masses;
he saw it rather as a tremendous engine of political bribery whereby
the stronger was permitted to exploit the weaker interest in return for
votes. In his eyes the antislavery agitation and the Wilmot Proviso
were not elements in a great moral crusade; they were simply the
final proof that constitutional guarantees and property rights were
alike worthless in the face of a hostile majority.

Contemporary history as he wrote his treatises only made Calhoun's case seem the stronger. The popular revolutionary governments in Europe gave way to new and more powerful absolutisms
almost before the tumult died, because the weaker interests had not
been clothed with power to protect themselves. And the election of
Zachary Taylor to the Presidency of the United States offered only
another illustration of the political process in action. Democrats dissatisfied with Polk's administration, some of them friends and erstwhile followers of his own, went over to the Whigs to swell the margin of victory. Taylor Democrats they called themselves, and made
their case on principles; but what were they in reality but partisans
who had failed to get what they wanted in the way of office, or special
legislation, or protection for some special interest? They thought of
themselves as standing for truth and justice against political corruption, but was not their concept of truth and justice, in reality, only
their own self-interest?

From the hot August day in 1846 on which the Wilmot Proviso
made its first appearance it became increasingly evident with each
session of Congress and with each election that a sectional majority
in the Northern states would not permit slaves to be carried into any
territory of the United States. To the South, already a minority in
numbers and in wealth, sensitive because world opinion condemned
her labor system and on the defensive because of the long crusade her
co-partners in the Union had been waging against it, the Proviso

could mean only one thing. Slaveholders were to be held rigidly within their existing bounds, while the millions of acres acquired by the common military effort were to be applied to making the stronger interest stronger still.

True, Northern spokesmen denied over and over again that there was any intention, then or ever, of interfering with slavery in the states where it existed; but how could a man who read history as Calhoun read it have any illusions on that score? Politicians of both parties in the North had been forced step by step to follow the abolitionists, and the abolitionists had decreed that slavery must go. It was inherent in the political process itself, which in turn was an inescapable concomitant of human nature, that the stronger interest would abuse its power at the expense of the weaker. There could be only one possible answer: power to resist; a concurrent veto to be applied by a united South through the Nashville Convention, or by state interposition, or by the threat to secede from the Union. A numerical majority in control of the general government had defined the powers of that government as sovereign. From that claim, if it were allowed to stand, would flow not only the abolition of slavery and the economic ruin of the South, but also the practical destruction of political liberty in the United States.

6

The problem with which Calhoun came to grips was the perennial problem of government—how to achieve a working adjustment between liberty and power. Liberty was the goal, because it was the liberty of the individual to seek his own betterment, to develop his own talents and skills, to realize his own fullest potentialities, that led to every advance in civilization and thereby improved the condition of the whole society. But power was necessary to curb the conflicts arising out of the inherent selfishness of men. Because of that inherent selfishness, however, power was inevitably subject to abuse, which could be curbed only by power itself. The answer, in the abstract terminology of political theory, was a kind of pluralism, whereby the sovereignty lay not in the whole but in the parts or classes or elements of which the whole was composed. In the language of governmental structure it was a form of federalism, geographical in the terms of Calhoun's time and place but functional in concept, since he thought of the states and sections as economic interests rather than as mere areas of land.

The concurrent veto in operation is a negative variation of the pressure-group approach, which persists in one form or another in all diverse societies. Is it not in this fashion that we have come in our time to the public purchase and destruction of foodstuffs in order to raise prices to fantastic levels in the interest of a special group? Is it not thus that we have come to pay wages for work unperformed, and rent for land unused? Is it not in these terms that we have raised the cost of government beyond the wildest nightmares of our ancestors and bought partisans to keep in power the generous patrons of our own selfishness? The effectiveness of the approach clearly depends on the relative power of the opposing interests, with the weaker being compelled to make up in organization and unity what it lacks in strength. The Southern movement of 1849-1850 was just such an attempt of a weaker to bargain with a stronger interest. The power of the individual states, as nullification had shown, was purely negative, and could be easily crushed by a majority. But if the Southern states could be brought to unite they could perhaps save their institutions, their way of life, their source of livelihood. Remember Calhoun and his fellow planters were quite sure that the South was economically more necessary to the North than the North was to them.

The real issue of constitutional interpretation—of liberty against power—has been obscured by the fact that the test was made in defense of an unworthy cause. Let us, therefore, assume a hypothetical case. Let us assume that manufacturing has been concentrated in a dozen states, with no more than a third of the population; and that the physical conditions are such as to preclude its extension to other localities. If for any reason the rest of the Union gradually became imbued with the idea that the private ownership of manufacturing was immoral, and launched a vigorous agitation aimed at nationalization with a distribution of the profits pro rata among the whole population, would not the manufacturing states react exactly as the South reacted to the abolitionist crusade? Would not the manufacturers fall back on constitutional limitations, on group pressure, and ultimately on secession from the Union?

In retrospect, Calhoun's policy for the South, leading as it did to civil war, seems suicidal, and his defense of slavery, to use the mildest term, amoral. Yet what were the alternatives? It seems indisputable that Southern acquiescence in the kind of legislation being introduced at every session of Congress by the Northern majority would, as Calhoun argued, have ended in the abolition of slavery. Suppose, then, that Calhoun had accepted abolition as inevitable, and had persuaded the South to free her slaves without waiting to have the inevitable forced upon her. Would that have changed the Northern majority in Congress, or prevented the passage of laws in the interest of the dominant section? Surely the history of Reconstruction, of the postemancipation tariffs, of railroad rate discrimination and other forms of economic exploitation, proves the contrary. The picture of the stronger interest abusing the powers of government to exploit the weaker has been materially altered only as major economic interests have come to transcend state and regional boundaries. Even this alteration does not change the substance, but only poses the original problem in a different form.

If we accept Calhoun's estimate of human nature, it is difficult to escape his conclusion that the majority will always exploit the minority unless the weaker portion has power to protect itself. The concurrent veto was to give them that power. The theory remains today what Calhoun himself conceived it: a defense of the minority—any minority—against the arbitrary exercise of power. It was, and is, effective to precisely the degree that the moral and physical cost of coercion seems to the majority to outweigh the gain. The great South Carolinian was defending an eighteenth-century form of society that had already been rendered obsolete by the technological developments of his own time. But his basic fear of power was justified, and the scientific advances that he failed to take into full account have only accelerated the tendency he recognized for governments to become absolute. As he clearly saw, an issue may be compromised only so long as both sides are strong. When one is weak, no matter how noble its cause, it will be crushed: for men are still moved by love of gain, and power still corrupts. Let us not forget that the accretions of power we yield to government to promote our safety and our welfare may also be used for our destruction.

CHAPTER XXIX

TWILIGHT AT FORT HILL

1

A NORTHERN TRAVELER who visited Fort Hill in the summer of 1849 did not guess that Calhoun's personal affairs were in chaotic state. He was impressed by the great beauty of the surroundings, the rapidly changing moods of forest and cultivated field and distant mountain; he admired the highly developed agriculture and was struck by the large community of people—family, overseer, and some eighty slaves—whose living came from these eleven hundred acres; and most of all he marveled at the incredibly rich conversation and dynamic energy of his host.[1] He yielded as people invariably did to the spell of Calhoun's personality, the inexhaustible fertility of his mind, the sheer power that seemed to emanate from him. To anyone who had known him only in Washington the master of Fort Hill seemed but distantly related to Senator Calhoun. On his farm, among his own people, he seemed less austere, no longer the living embodiment of an idea but a rounded human being of flesh and blood. He was still intense, still dominant. His quick and restless mind still roamed at large over all creation, not, as one neighbor put it, like a well-stocked reservoir but "like a never-failing spring gushing fresh and free from the mountain side."[2] But surrounded by his family he seemed to shed some of the burden of public responsibility, and to relax.

Yet he was under pressure in that critical summer of 1849 such as he had never endured before. The rapidly approaching crisis over slavery, and his concern for the definitive expression of his reflections on the nature of government, were but two of the many cares that weighed on him. Over the past four or five years his duties as a father had not always been easy. There had been endless financial troubles and a mounting burden of debt which he vainly hoped with the eternal optimism of his nature to liquidate with each succeeding crop. He had battled failing health, surmounted domestic storms and filial indiscretions, faced floods and droughts and falling prices for his crops with unruffled calm. Now he was nearing the end of his road, his lungs diseased, his property encumbered, his sons unsettled, his best-loved Anna weeks away in Europe, his country facing the gravest crisis of her existence. Yet he held his head high, rose as usual at four in the morning, rode or walked over his rolling acres in the gray of dawn, worked long close hours in his study, entertained his guests and delighted his friends with his brilliance, his graciousness, his warmth of hospitality.

2

Calhoun's financial troubles could be traced directly to the purchase of Andrew's Alabama plantation early in 1839. The money borrowed from Clemson at that time had never been more than partially repaid. Notes jointly signed by Calhoun and Andrew had been conveniently ignored by the younger man when they fell due. Before his departure for Belgium in 1844 Clemson had purchased the Canebrake plantation from the estate of Eldred Simkins. He had turned, naturally enough, to his father-in-law for funds, but the needed money could not be raised. In the end Arthur Simkins took a note, jointly signed by Clemson, Calhoun, and Andrew, and secured by a mortgage on the property. It was understood among them, however, that the responsibility was Andrew's and that he would make partial payment in the spring of 1845, to be charged against his debt to Clemson.[3]

Andrew neglected the obligation, and he failed also to take up or even to pay interest on the $8,500 note given by him and his father to Clemson, payable in March of that same year. A long overdue note held by Ker Boyce was similarly ignored. Boyce and Simkins threatened lawsuits, and Clemson said some harsh things about Andrew, but Calhoun mediated between son and son-in-law, and borrowed money to pacify the more belligerent creditors. John Ewing Bonneau, Calhoun's cousin and Charleston factor, took care of Simkins for the time being, and Elmore arranged for a loan of $4,000 from the State Bank, at least a part of which presumably went to placate Boyce.[4]

Behind this typical bit of financial juggling—borrowing from Peter to repay Paul—lay a sort of cumulative gamble involving all the imponderables of cotton planting. Each season, if the weather was not too dry and not too damp, if the worms did not come, if the hands remained healthy, and if the price of cotton did not fall too low, the planter could break even. If the price went up a little, he could make money; and if only he had more land in cotton when that price rise came, he could pay off all his debts and live in luxury. This was Andrew's way, and Calhoun endorsed it, or at least he registered no protest. So instead of paying off his debts as they fell due, Andrew invested such profits as there were in land and Negroes, and year after year increased his cotton acreage.

The 1844 crop, held over until the spring of 1845, brought less than five cents a pound, netting something under $5,000 for the four hundred bales that represented the combined output of the Alabama Canebrake and Fort Hill. There would be no debts repaid this year; but surely the price of cotton would have to go up. "The very low price must discourage its production, while it must greatly increase its consumption." So Calhoun reasoned in the familiar terms of classical economics, and promptly forgot his disappointment in his pleasure over a new Devon bull, and the excellence of the wheat and rye, planted this year on the Seneca bottoms.[5]

The summer of 1845 was a sort of second retirement for him. He had left the State Department in March and it was well along in the fall before he decided to return to the Senate. In the intervening months he was simply a skillful and ingenious planter whose main concern and primary interest in life was agriculture. He explained to Hammond his method of hillside ditching to prevent erosion and invited inspection at any time. He boasted of one decidedly rolling field now bearing its thirteenth crop yet still unscarred by wash or gully. He sent to Columbia, and as far away as Baltimore, for the latest in improved farm machinery: a straw cutter; a circular saw to operate either by steam, water, or horsepower; a threshing machine; a "corn and cob crusher" to be attached to the gristmill. Early in 1846 a new "cow house" and a smokehouse were completed.[6]

Calhoun was in Alabama in late October of 1845, and when the cotton harvest was half complete he wrote cheerfully to Clemson of a new debt adjustment. The crop would run to 300,000 pounds at the least, he thought. "Should the present price continue," he went on, "we shall be able to apply $15,000 to our debts." He proposed to take up Clemson's share of the debt to Simkins when it fell due, to pay off Bonneau, and to pay the interest on the outstanding debt to Clemson.[7]

It was all premature. The upswing in the price of cotton quickly subsided as Polk's aggressive policy threatened to produce a rupture with England, and Andrew looked about for more Negroes to increase his output. He needed a thousand bales to show a profit at six cents, instead of the 700 bales he could make with available labor. The 1845 crop was held over the winter and into the spring of 1846, with Calhoun again forecasting a price rise as the Oregon difficulty neared a settlement and war with Mexico broke out. In May he advised Andrew to meet the next steamer at Mobile and to sell if he could get seven cents. At the same time he found it necessary to chide his son for another financial lapse—his failure to take up a note, probably Boyce's, in Charleston, or to square accounts with Bonneau, both of which Andrew had promised to attend to at the proper times.[8]

Andrew simply didn't have the money, and when the crop was sold the profit went back according to practice into the land. So we find Calhoun in the summer of 1846 again approaching the bankers, hat in hand. The applause of two nations was still ringing in his ears for his part in averting war over Oregon, and those not swept away by the lure of easy conquest and rich spoils were at that very moment urging him to interpose to end the war with Mexico. Mere money cannot be weighed against the services of such a man, yet money he required. He first spoke to Elmore before the end of May, and by July he was $14,000 deeper in debt to the State Bank. The new note, like most of Calhoun's borrowings, was for six months, but renewable for another six months to allow time for selling an extra cotton crop. Elmore, perhaps with a view to protecting the aging statesman from the looser financial morality of his son, placed very little of the money in Calhoun's hands. Instead the Bank paid for him $3,000 against Boyce's claim and something like $8,000 to Bonneau. The remaining $3,000 was earmarked as part payment of a personal debt to a Pendleton neighbor, Mrs. Jasper Adams, a widow whose daughter Angie would a few years later become Mrs. John C. Calhoun, Jr.[9]

For a month or two everything seemed clear sailing. Then caterpillars, army worms, bollworms moved in simultaneously. Fort Hill suffered little damage but the Canebrake cotton crop for 1846 was cut to a third of the expectation. Before Calhoun left for Washington in November of that year he was forced to ask Bonneau to honor his drafts though he had neither funds nor cotton to back them; and before the end of the year he was compelled to renew his $14,000 note at Elmore's bank.[10]

The long-hoped-for rise in the price of cotton actually came in 1847, partly as a result of the Mexican War and partly because the widespread destruction of the crop the previous fall had reduced the supply. In the summer of 1847 Bonneau sold the Fort Hill crop at twelve cents, and Calhoun advised Andrew to wait for a still better price. He moved at the same time to offer a new basis for settling the old debt to Clemson, who was now pressing hard for payment. Clemson disputed the figures, and before a new agreement could be reached the price of cotton had tumbled again, on the heels of a bumper crop.[11]

The year 1848 saw increasing financial pressure, arising out of large government borrowing to meet the expenses of the war and aggravated by unsettled conditions in Europe. To avoid the growing unpleasantness of strained relations between Clemson and Andrew, Calhoun would gladly have borrowed whatever was needed to pay his son-in-law in full; but money was too scarce and interest rates too high. Andrew again ignored both interest and principal of the debt to Boyce (who now had a court judgment in his favor), and Calhoun's language was almost uniquely tart as he called his son's attention once more to the oversight. Yet to Clemson he praised Andrew's skill and industry, and attributed the persistent failure of Canebrake to pay its way to the prolonged depression in the price of cotton.[12]

He was borrowing again before the end of June, this time by way of extending a note at the Bank of Charleston over which Henry W. Conner presided. A "free and full conversation" with W. W. Corcoran, the Washington banker, convinced him that a long-term loan at legal interest could not be had anywhere in the North. As the cotton harvest approached that fall, with prospects of a good crop in Alabama, Calhoun advised Andrew to sell as fast as the bales could be packed and shipped, and to take 6½ cents if he could not get more. The proceeds were to be applied as quickly as received to the servicing of their joint debts, including at least $1,000 against Boyce's judgment and a similar sum to Mrs. Adams. As for Clemson, he and Anna would soon be there in person on their first visit home since they went to Belgium, and an adjustment could no doubt be reached.[13]

The situation was almost desperate by the time Calhoun was ready to leave for Washington and the final session of the Thirtieth Congress. The various obligations, even the most pressing of them, had not been met, because Andrew had not sold the Alabama cotton. He could not get the 6½ cents his father had set as a minimum. The best Mobile price was 4¾ cents and the Charleston prices ranged from 5 to a little less than 6. Only in New York was the price above 6 cents in the late fall of 1848, and so great was his need that Calhoun even toyed with the notion of shipping his output to that city. He was willing now that Andrew should sell at 5 cents—almost anything to get a little cash. Yet he took pains to deny any loss of confidence in his eldest son, or any jealousy on the part of others in the family. As earnest of his good faith he explained that he meant to set aside his own portion of the Alabama property under Andrew's control, to be divided as part of his estate only after the joint debts incurred on it were liquidated. When the word of criticism finally came, it was in characteristic manner. "Let me entreat you," he concluded, "to write me fully and often, and keep me early informed of all remittances you may make, or arrangements you may make, in reference to our debt, and the sales you may make of our cotton & the funds that are or will probably be at your disposal. In reference to all these, you have been negligent, which has embarrassed me much, & crippled my efforts to support our credit." He assured Andrew that he need not fear to frighten his father with the truth as to "the utmost extent of your difficulties." "I would always rather know the worst. I am not easily disheartened." [14]

3

Clemson's visit to the United States late in 1848 was primarily to attend to personal business, of which the future disposition of his Edgefield plantation and a financial adjustment with Calhoun and Andrew constituted prominent items. The status of the plantation no less than the status of the debts had changed from year to year and almost from month to month, as that inevitable barometer of the Southern economy, the price of cotton, rose or fell. Brilliant in his chosen field of science and hardheaded in business matters, Clemson was in other respects unstable and erratic. He blew hot and cold by turns, and could never quite make up his mind whether he wanted to be a Southern planter, a scientist, or a career diplomat. It was Cal-

houn's own buoyant temperament that prevented serious difficulties
—Calhoun's temperament and Anna's complete devotion to her
father as well as to her husband.

As early as the spring of 1845 Clemson talked of selling his plantation, in order to reinvest his capital in more profitable industrial
enterprises. Calhoun was understandably reluctant to see his son-in-
law sever his economic ties with South Carolina, meaning as it probably did that in his declining years Anna and her children would not
be near him. He nevertheless accepted Clemson's decision, and in
October offered to buy the Canebrake slaves himself for $12,000, or a
little over $300 each, on three years' credit. Clemson countered with
a proposition of his own, which Calhoun found "fair and equitable,"
but passed along to Andrew for final decision. Andrew rejected the
terms, but offered $14,000 for the Negroes—an offer turned down
by Clemson with equal curtness, and there the matter rested.[15]

By the middle of 1846 Clemson had decided he would prefer settling
down in a government job to the hazards of agriculture, and so
informed Calhoun. The Senator replied that under the spoils system
permeating the whole governmental structure jobs were hard to get
and harder still to hold. Clemson then suggested that since he was
already in the diplomatic service, his politically potent father-in-law
might use his influence to get him promoted to a better post than
Brussels. But Calhoun had long since lost any influence he might
once have had with the Polk administration, and he answered that
Clemson would have to stay where he was, or come home. In the
latter eventuality he would need both plantation and slaves, so he
had better hold on to them. Calhoun felt bound to transmit an offer
he had received for Canebrake; but to Anna he wrote of his great
desire to see her and her family, and of his hopes that "circumstances
will justify your early return." [16]

When the price of cotton rose in the summer of 1847 Calhoun once
more urged the Clemsons to come home, holding out the prospect of
enlarging Canebrake by draining adjacent swamplands as Hammond
had done so successfully at Silver Bluff. By 1848 his impatience to
see Anna and her children led him to urge on Clemson a visit home
in the summer or fall, "notwithstanding the state of things in Europe." He recurred again and again to that theme. When Clemson
explained somewhat testily that he wanted to sell the plantation, settle
his personal affairs, and see his ailing mother, but couldn't afford to

bring his family, Calhoun himself, hard-pressed financially as he was, borrowed forthwith and remitted through Corcoran and Riggs $600 to insure passage for Anna and her children. Clemson's return, he wrote to his daughter, "without you & the children would have been a cause of great greif to us all. Had the sum required been ten times greater it would be remitted to prevent it." He did not tell her that he had been forced to ask Elmore, as a personal favor, to discount another note for him at the State Bank.[17]

4

Calhoun had his problems, too, with other members of his family. Johnny, who had entered the University of Virginia in the spring of 1843, did not return the following year, but his place at Charlottesville was taken by his younger brother, Jimmy, in the fall of 1844. Again the patronage of Judge Henry St. George Tucker was forthcoming, and for a time Jimmy applied himself to study. He had a fair degree of native ability, and some thought he resembled his father more than did any of the other Calhoun boys, but he was restless and not really interested. He was, moreover, utterly unprepared for the curriculum of a ranking university. In Pendleton Academy he had been allowed to study as he pleased, which was not very often nor very much. He was quickly beyond his depth and departed abruptly toward the end of April 1845, leaving behind him sundry items of furniture, a box of personal effects, and acknowledged debts to the sum of $164.95.[18]

Patrick was a handsome and dashing figure in the gaudy uniform of the dragoons. He was twenty-four years old early in 1845, on detached duty in Washington where the social life was always gay during a session of Congress. The opportunities for enjoyment were almost limitless in his position, even his perennial lack of funds being in large measure compensated for by his prestige as the son of the Secretary of State and the fact that his mother, in the Capital that season, was one of the town's most popular hostesses. As one might expect, Pat was "constantly employed among the ladies," but presently singled out for his special attentions Kate Wilkins, daughter of the Secretary of War. There was even an engagement before Polk's administration supplanted Tyler's, and Calhoun was delighted. Miss Wilkins, he wrote to Anna, was "a very fine sweet tempered girl" and the army was "a dangerous place for the habits of a Batchelor." But Pat was not ready to settle down, and nothing came of it. In March he went with his mother and sister to Philadelphia, where Cornelia was being treated by a specialist, and escorted them home in April. By summer he was back in harness again, as aide-de-camp to General Gaines in New Orleans, and the fascinations of Miss Wilkins were forgotten.[19]

In the fall of 1845 Calhoun decided to send James and Willie, the latter just turned sixteen, to Erskine College, at Due West near Abbeville. The principal virtue of the place was its location, remote from any distracting influence. At Erskine, so their worried father thought, there would be nothing to keep the boys from studying, and their morals would be safe. He hoped that, in a year or two, they would acquire habits of study and be prepared to enter some other school with higher academic standing. The pair had already left Fort Hill for their favorite haunts at Millwood with Uncle James, and to Uncle James their father relievedly transferred the responsibility for getting them to Erskine at the proper time.[20]

They got there in good order, and Willie, who had had no previous experience with college, liked the place better than he had expected to. He even made serious gestures toward his books and for the moment put aside thoughts of the ladies, a department in which he seems to have sought to emulate his brother Pat. Jimmy was not so easily pleased. He took one brief, disapproving look at Erskine and bolted. When Calhoun learned of it on his return from the Memphis Convention, Jimmy was back at Millwood, not particularly contrite and definitely not unhappy, though he seems to have felt it desirable to avoid his father for the time being. Calhoun visited Due West on his way to Washington in December and got the whole story, or as much of it as was available for paternal consumption, from Willie. James's excuse was that the course of studies did not suit him, and his father accepted it without comment. Calhoun knew that Jimmy was almost as extravagant with money as Patrick was, and about as eager to fall into bad company. He had just paid bills that came drifting in from Charlottesville, and he seems to have known a great deal more about his boys than they assumed he knew. Uncle James had more influence with Jimmy than anyone else had, and so the harassed father proposed that he stay at Millwood for the time being, where James Edward, senior, undertook to look after his namesake's education himself. By the spring of 1846 Jimmy was doing so well under this avuncular tutelage that Calhoun sent Willie to Millwood for a course of the same treatment.[21]

General Gaines, who commanded the Southern Division of the Army, was ordered to Washington for consultation when Zachary Taylor was sent to the Rio Grande early in 1846, and Pat Calhoun came along. After the declaration of war in May his official duties took more time than heretofore, and his father, absorbed as he was in the pressing problems of the day—Oregon, the tariff, Mexican hostilities, river and harbor improvements—had little time to keep an eye on his soldier-son. Pat was in and out of the city on the business of his chief, chafing like many another young officer who finds himself on headquarters staff duty while his fellows are winning glory and promotion on the field of battle. Later in the year, apparently without his solicitation, Pat was chosen Colonel of a New York City regiment of volunteers, and he spent fruitless weeks in Washington trying to persuade the War Department to let him accept without losing his regular commission in the line. Calhoun, though he opposed the war, was reconciled to his son's fighting in it and was suitably proud of this honor which would make Patrick the youngest Colonel in the service. But alas for Calhoun's pride and Pat's ambition, the Fifth New York Volunteers were never called up, and their elected Colonel remained a Lieutenant in the line, staff Captain by brevet, until the war was over.[22]

Willie returned to Fort Hill in August 1846 to await the arrival of his parents and sister Cornelia. The Calhouns had gone for a short rest to White Sulphur Springs after the long first session of the Twenty-ninth Congress finally ended. They returned home by way of Wythe County, Virginia, where they stopped for a few days at the ancestral seat of the Calhouns, and altogether did not reach Pendleton until September. They found Willie down with fever; but James was deep in his books, and so much improved in manners and habits that Calhoun agreed that he should enter South Carolina College for the fall term. Willie, after a relapse and slow recovery, was sent back to Millwood in hope that a miracle would happen to him too.[23]

The first report on Jimmy's progress was a noncommittal note from Francis Lieber early in November. The boy was in his class but it was still too early to judge of his prospects. Then James expressed his own satisfaction with the school; William C. Preston, still president of the college, took an interest in him; and Calhoun allowed himself to hope. "Be studious," he advised, "stand aloof from the idle & vicious, & cultivate the acquaintance of the deserving, and you will acquire the esteem of the wise and good, and, what is more important, the approbation of your own conscience." James had asked for twenty or thirty dollars. His father sent him $40 and a caution: "I hope you will spend as little as you can. Indeed, it has become necessary you should, in consequence of the great failure of our Alabama crop. As great as Andrew expected it would be, it has turned out to be much greater." Calhoun sent James another $100 in December, and $60 more in January 1847, repeating his cautions about being economical. He was clearly pleased, however, with the substantial progress this once wayward son was making. "Willie writes, that the members of the Legislature from Pendleton report you to be at the head of your class. Go on my son. Acquire knowledge & good habits & cultivate honorable sentiments." [24]

5

With James seemingly squared away at last, Willie shuttling among Alabama, Fort Hill, and Millwood, and John, though spending much time with Andrew, beginning to take a serious interest in a scientific career, the family wild oats must have seemed to Calhoun to be just about sown. Then, in the spring of 1847, Patrick fell back into his old ways. He wrote from New York in April that he was going to Kentucky in all probability the following month, and might there be married to a daughter of former Congressman (now Colonel) John W. Tibbatts. The young Captain seemed as reluctant and as undecided as to the matrimonial side of the venture as he had ever been in such matters; and it is perhaps needless to say that he did not marry Miss Tibbatts, nor anybody else. About the financial requirements of his projected Kentucky trip, on the other hand, he had no doubts. "My funds," he explained to his father with becoming candor, "have run very low and some additional means will be necessary to me— If you will therefore advance me such an amount as you may deem proper, it will be a great relief to me." Pat had another idea that struck him as perhaps likely to produce a greater sum, so he proceeded: "It would be just as convenient if you will authorize me to draw on brother Andrew through his Factors—and notify him of it—

If you conclude to do so, let me know who they are—I can manage it through Cousin Edward Boisseau." [25]

Patrick had more than once drawn on Edward Boisseau, Floride's indulgent cousin whose thriving commission house in New York gave him access to ready funds, and the process was so easy that it gave him ideas. On this particular occasion Calhoun either gave him money or authorized the draft on Andrew. At any rate we hear of no further difficulties until late in the year. On his way to Washington Calhoun saw Patrick briefly in Charleston, and realized at once from his son's demeanor that something was wrong. It was only later that he learned to his great mortification that Pat had actually drawn unauthorized on Andrew's factors for $600. He knew, of course, that the necessity must have been great; and he knew that it arose from gambling or some other unwise pursuit of pleasure. Indeed, he feared, from his memory of Pat's low spirits, that the $600 he had drawn was probably less than he needed. Yet often as Pat had promised to mend his ways, and often as he had broken his promise in the past, Calhoun's reaction was the same as it had always been—reasonable, gentle, understanding.

"I am uneasy about him," he wrote to Andrew of this latest escapade. "I have heard nothing from him since he left Charleston. I hope the draft was taken up. But you must write him, that he must not again draw without my consent. Write him kindly, but firmly & state the reason, why you cannot hereafter honor his drafts, except through me. Carefully avoid any thing like censure, and all unkind expressions. He is at a critical point; and it will require great judgment & discretion to give him a right direction. . . . As he has drawn for an amount greater than what you were to remit me, I must endeavour to get along without that." [26]

There were many items on the credit side that winter of 1847-1848, and Calhoun and the others were quick to forgive and forget. Lieber wrote with real enthusiasm of James's work before the year was out, and the lad was class orator in March. Willie, like James before him, was doing so well under the personal direction of his devoted uncle at Millwood that he too was scheduled to enter South Carolina College in the fall of 1848. John Caldwell, Jr., had at last channeled his scientific leanings in the direction of medicine, and after various courses in Charleston, went to Philadelphia in March 1848 to complete his work for the medical degree. Between December 1847 and

April of the following year Patrick wrote seldom, but cheerfully. He was again contemplating matrimony, and from other sources his father learned that he looked very well and moved much in high society.[27]

It was just at this time—the spring of 1848—when the fortunes of the Calhouns were approaching their lowest ebb, that Patrick slipped again. "Patrick, I am sorry to say, has made another & quite a heavy call on me," Calhoun wrote to Andrew on April 26, "but in terms expressive of great distress & deep mortification. I had to borrow money to meet it. I wrote him in kind, but strong terms, stating the great inconvenience to which it subjected me, & the injustice it was doing the rest of the family, accompanied by a strong expression of the absolute necessity of his living hereafter within the limits of his pay. I trust, and think, it will have the desired effect. I wish he was married to some good girl with property to live on, and was out of the army." Calhoun did not mention the amount of Patrick's requirements, knowing how short-tempered his older son was inclined to be, but it developed later that he had borrowed for Pat's use upward of a thousand dollars.[28]

It was shortly thereafter that Calhoun managed to raise another $600 for Anna's passage money home, and the anticipated pleasure of seeing her made Pat's dereliction easier to bear. Then in July Johnny arrived from Philadelphia with a new diploma proclaiming him a Doctor of Medicine, and the family rejoiced once more.[29]

There was an interval of quiet, but October found Pat in deep trouble again. This time he wrote to Andrew, who promptly passed the letter on to his father with caustic comments of his own. Calhoun replied at once. "I have just received your letter covering one from Patrick, which I have read with pain; & I now write, without a moments delay to say, that if he draws for the amount stated, it must be met. He is at a critical point, and I cannot but hope, if he gets through his present difficulties, he will see the necessity of a reform in his habits [and] expenses. He has good sense & many excellent qualities. His misfortune is, his fondness for pleasure." Calhoun proposed to write to urge "in the most solemn manner" the necessity for reform— as if he had never urged it before—and hoped that with Pat in Washington he could establish some control over him that winter. The amount of the new demand is not specified in the available letters, but Calhoun estimated that it brought "the larger advances I have made to him" to a total of more than $4,000. Though he himself continued to treat Patrick as a wayward child, he approved Andrew's more blunt approach. "It is proper he should be made to feel sore, but not to be alienated." [30]

6

Calhoun looked forward to a real family reunion when the Clemsons arrived in the fall of 1848, and confidently hoped that he, Clemson, and Andrew could straighten out their financial tangle in some manner satisfactory to all. But the Clemsons were delayed by storms at sea, and it was early November before their crippled vessel docked in New York. There was further delay while the young diplomat reported to the State Department in Washington, and his plans called for a visit to the ironworks at Clarksville, Georgia, before he finally established himself at his Edgefield plantation. Anna and the children did not make the Clarksville trip, but even so it was the end of November before they reached home.[31]

Floride, John, and Cornelia left for the Clemson plantation on the twenty-third, and Calhoun joined them there before Anna arrived. The waiting was irksome, but she showed up at last and her father stayed on another two days. He thought her "much improved in appearance . . . full & plump without being fat." The children, at least in the partial eyes of their grandfather, were "well grown, very good looking, & smart." He left the family "quite comfortably fixed in a new House" and prepared to remain there until February, when they would have to return to Europe. Floride, Cornelia, and John stayed with Anna after Calhoun's departure, but John was to leave shortly for New Orleans, where he seems to have hoped he might set up a medical practice.[32]

On his way to Washington Calhoun stopped briefly in Columbia to visit South Carolina College where James was a senior and doing very well, and where Willie had just enrolled as a sophomore after passing "an excellent examination." James Rion was there, too, and he also came in for Calhoun's attention. There was a special convocation in honor of the distinguished Senator, who entered on Preston's arm and responded gracefully to a speech of welcome by one of the students.[33]

In Washington Calhoun seems to have explored further the possibility of borrowing money in New York. Specie was coming in from Europe, and he thought this favorable balance of trade combined with the "extraordinary deposites of gold found in Calafornia" would ease the money market, at least enough to permit funding his debts at 6 percent instead of the 7 or more he was then paying. If he and Andrew could commit their cotton to some large New York factor or commission merchant in return for a loan they could at least settle with Clemson, and New York could hardly be a worse market than Mobile had proved to be. He was full of this project a few days after he reached the Capital, and urged Andrew to come on for a settlement. He suggested late February, when Anna and the children as well as Clemson expected to be in Washington; but Andrew did not see fit to come.[34]

The grueling meetings of Southern Senators and Representatives soon absorbed all of Calhoun's time and strength, but he managed to interpose a parental veto against James's latest scheme. From December 1848 on the papers were filled with notices of parties organizing for the gold fields of California, and the South Carolina papers were as forward in this department as any. Reading them, and the stories of rich and ever richer treasures in the new El Dorado of the West, James found his old restlessness come back upon him, and he proposed to go forthwith to California. Calhoun's reply, dated January 17, 1849, reveals as well as anything he ever wrote the deep conservatism of his nature.

"You must give up all idea of going to Calafornia. The mines may be rich, but more will be ruined by them than will make fortunes. Nothing is more uncertain than gold mining; but if you should be ever so successful, the enormous prices of every thing there will take away the greater part of your profit. Besides, the danger of violence, sickness & loss of life is great; to say nothing of the great expense and the fatigue & difficulty of going there. It would suit persons of hardy constitution, and of desperate circumstances to go there, but not any one, who has a reasonable prospect of doing well here. I trust you will give up all idea of going, & stick to your studies, which will be of vastly more advantage to you in the end, than you could get ever by going to Calafornia." [35]

It was two days later that Calhoun was stricken in the Senate chamber, but he concealed details and made light of the whole episode, as he always did when writing to those dear to him. He called the seizure a "momentary faintness . . . owing principally to the bad air & heat of the room" which had passed in a minute and left him "as well as usual." But after three days, when he wrote those deprecating words, he was still not well enough to attend the final and most important of the Southern meetings, and his attendance in the Senate where he had once been the most punctual of members was never regular again.[36]

Floride, who was still with Anna at the South Carolina Canebrake, and Anna herself read of Calhoun's illness in the papers before they heard from him, and were greatly alarmed, as were friends and relatives and the conservative planters of the South generally. It was Anna who best understood his psychology, and so she wrote for her mother and herself, urging him in terms of shameless flattery to relax and take care of himself. "Setting aside your family, you are too important to the whole country, & the South in particular, not to feel your health a sacred deposit. What will become of the country if you . . . are not there to give them timely warning of the breakers towards which they are rushing?" [37]

7

Shortly after he returned home in the spring of 1849 Calhoun secured a loan from private sources—$5,000 on demand, and $12,000 or $13,000 more to come. He paid Mrs. Adams in full, made part payments on other obligations, and looked forward to getting reasonably clear of his more pressing obligations. If Clemson would be satisfied with interest, the State Bank could be paid off; or if Clemson insisted, the balance could be used to pay him.[38]

Perhaps it was this temporary respite from financial pressure, perhaps the calming effect of the rolling hills and distant mountains he loved so well, that brought about an improvement in his health. He began taking the "water cure" under the direction of his doctor-son, and professed to feel the better for it. John had just returned from Milledgeville, Georgia, where he had been taking the cure himself and learning the technique. Like his father, whom he did not long survive, John suffered from "consumption." As Calhoun described the process, it consisted of wrapping the patient in a damp sheet and covering him heavily with blankets, thereby producing a sort of vapor bath. He hoped it might prove an effective substitute for brandy toddy and hot punch, which he disliked.[39]

Anna put more faith in toddy. "I was very anxious about you," she wrote from Philadelphia on April 15, "knowing what a fatiguing journey you had before you, till I received a letter from Pat at Charleston, giving such excellent accounts, that I was entirely relieved. The complete establishment of your *strength,* (for I am happy to think your health is as good as ever,) now depends upon yourself, & you must be careful for all our sakes. To aid in this good work, Mr. Clemson begs me to tell you, that he has sent you some of the best Port Wine, & Brandy, Philadelphia contains. The Brandy, in particular, he says is as old as—(I forget what,) but 'old as the hills' will do. In short he speaks of it as something extraordinary, which I hope it will prove. Don't forget the miracles I performed with the warm toddy on going to bed & stick to it. Take exercise, but don't fatigue yourself— Study, but don't worry yourself, & don't write too much, (*except to me*). Live generously, & go to bed early. There are some 'golden rules' for you! I am sure no doctor could better them, & if you follow them I shall know you love me." [40]

Anna was on her way back to Europe with her husband and children, and her father was serving out the remainder of his earthly time, which he knew would not be long. Both understood that their chances of seeing each other again were very slender, and beneath the cheerful surface of their letters lay a deep unhappiness. Anna wrote from New York just before they sailed, gossiping of the lavish hospitality of cousin Edward Boisseau, giving more advice as to health and welfare, expressing her disapproval of the water cure. Europe was no longer novel, and she did not want to leave her father. "I know all I [am] to see & expect, & how little there is in that all, to recompense me for my separation from my family." [41]

Calhoun replied in kind. "We all felt, my dear daughter, as you described your feelings to be, at your departure. It is, indeed, distressing to be so far off and for so long a time from those so dear to us; but let us rather look forward to when we shall again meet, than to indulge in unavailing sorrows. I trust two years, at the utmost, will terminate your residence in Europe, and return you all again safe to our country. It is due to the children, that your stay should not be longer. Their habits and mode of thinking will, by that time, begin to be formed; and it is important, that they should be such, as to conform to the conditions of the country, which is to be their home. I often think of them, and how delighted they would be, to be enjoying themselves in our green and shady yard." He went on to describe the beauties of Fort Hill in an almost rhapsodic strain that only Anna could evoke from him: a lush meadow, a green field of oats, corn already tall and sturdy on the bottoms, shocked wheat on the hill, cotton in serpentine rows on the upland. "I ride or walk, according to the weather twice a day, morning and evening over it, for the double purpose of exercise and superintendence. . . . I would be delighted to have you and the children with me occasionally, in my walks." He wanted her to write to Andrew, who was again quarreling with his mother; partly to let her brother know that the rest of the family understood and did not share Floride's hostility; partly to comfort him because Andrew, Jr., was hopelessly ill.[42]

It was shortly after this that Joseph A. Scoville arrived at Fort Hill, largely in response to Anna's urging; and the time until Congress met again was taken up with the reply to Benton, with work on the *Discourse on the Constitution,* with correspondence relating to the Mississippi Convention and to the projected meeting of Southern leaders at Nashville that came out of it. For months Calhoun was immersed in politics, directing, suggesting, explaining, from the quiet remoteness of his study, but still his children occupied a share of his time and thoughts.

James had finished his work at South Carolina College, and Willie had completed the sophomore year at the head of his class, despite poor health. Both the younger boys were at home during the summer, and so was John, at intervals. John was married in July to Angie Adams, an impending event which may have had something to do with Calhoun's eagerness to pay off his debt to Angie's mother. General Gaines had died, and Calhoun was worried about Patrick, who had not been heard from since. So the summer passed and the fall of 1849 came on, with another poor cotton crop in Alabama, and more financial pressure in consequence. James got started in the winter of 1849-1850 on a course of reading for the bar, and promptly relapsed into his old-time habits, running up debts after Patrick's fashion to his father's deep distress.[43]

Anna wrote long and frequent letters from Brussels, full of advice and misgivings, and breathing an affection bordering on idolatry.

Her news of Calhoun as the session of Congress advanced came mostly from the papers, and it was uneasy news. By mid-February of 1850 she knew he was ill, and urged him as only she could to resign and go back to Fort Hill. "You have spent a long life in the service of your country, & it is now time to take care of yourself for our sakes." In the last letter of the series—one that perhaps he never saw—she spoke of her son, who had begun to show some physical resemblance to his grandfather. "If my son only resembles you in every thing, dearest father, I shall have nothing to wish for him." [44]

8

Up to the very end of his life the mounting financial obligations of the preceding decade plagued Calhoun and gave him no rest. He was still hoping as late as the winter of 1849-1850 to settle in full with Clemson from the proceeds of the next crop, if only the yield were large and the price were high; and within two weeks of his death, when he was too ill to write in his own hand, he was dickering once more with the Bank of Charleston.[45]

His concern over financial matters undoubtedly aggravated his recurrent illness, and was a source of alarm to his South Carolina friends, who felt that his life could be prolonged and his usefulness to state and country extended if only he could be freed from worry and could be persuaded to leave the Senate and travel for a time in some climate less afflicting to diseased lungs. Early in 1850 a small group in Charleston, headed by Daniel E. Huger, Henry W. Conner, and Henry Gourdin, quietly set about raising money on their great Senator's account. The original intention seems to have been simply to send him to a better climate, but shortly before his death it was decided to pay his debts as well. His consent was to be obtained by not asking for it; the debts were simply to be paid.[46]

He died before the required sum had been raised, but the self-constituted committee went on with its task, and on July 8, 1850, a total of $26,798.10, less printing costs of $15.00, was tendered to Mrs. Calhoun, who accepted it gratefully. Calhoun's notes held by the State Bank and by the Bank of Charleston amounting to a little over $20,000 were paid, and the balance of $6,739.68 was turned over to the widow. It was enough to enable Floride to retain possession of the heavily mortgaged Fort Hill property.[47]

There was no mention of debts to private individuals. Perhaps the Charleston committee had no knowledge of them. On some if not all of these personal notes Andrew was cosigner, and he may have assumed them all. The best evidence available seems to indicate that these personal debts were about equal in extent to the bank loans paid off by the dead Senator's friends, bringing his total obligations at the time of his death to something in the neighborhood of $40,000. All of it had been contracted since 1839.[48]

Although he had spoken from time to time of settling his estate, Calhoun actually died intestate, and the property was divided by agreement. Calhoun's interest in the Alabama property went jointly to Andrew, Patrick, James, and William, the two latter selling out to Andrew and Patrick for their bonds. Fort Hill went to Mrs. Calhoun and Cornelia. Available records do not show what share the others received. We know only that there continued to be ill feeling between Andrew and Clemson as well as between Andrew and his mother, and the family affairs soon became as tangled as they had ever been.[49]

For our purposes we need pursue the property no further, save only to note that Fort Hill fell eventually to the Clemsons, and is today a part of the beautiful campus of Clemson College.

CHAPTER XXX

NO COMPROMISE

1

CALHOUN MADE early preparations for the first session of the Thirty-first Congress, which was to meet on December 3, 1849. It was to be, he thought, the most important ever held, for this Congress would decide, by positive enactment or by default, whether the Federal Union was to endure. It was the solemn conviction of thoughtful men that if a satisfactory adjustment of the slavery question could not be reached now, it could not be done at all. The Southern states sooner or later would denounce the constitutional compact, and the Union would be destroyed—destroyed as effectively by the coercion as by the secession of the South. The Nashville Convention was to meet in June, and what it might do would depend in large measure on what Congress did before that date.

Calhoun felt as he had never felt before the overwhelming responsibility of his position. As profoundly as any man of his time he had studied and reflected on the process of government, and its well-springs in the nature of man. He carried with him the finished manuscript of his *Disquisition on Government,* and the draft of the *Discourse on the Constitution* which he hoped to find time to revise before the session ended. It was this matured concept of the nature of political society that was to form the basis of his final appeal for Southern equality within the Union. He knew it was to be his final argument; that the books were to be his legacy and his justification to posterity. Perhaps in one of those luminous prophetic moments of his he even saw how quickly his own path would be lost in the valley of the shadow, but he would not have needed any premonition to tell him that there would be no further chance. His own incisive reasoning, covering four hundred foolscap pages; the course of history in the large as it stretched backward into the seventeenth century; the experience of forty crowded and fateful years in public life—all these

448

added up to only one answer. It was time to draw the line and face the consequences.

He reached Washington the last day of November, looking better than he had for years. It was still three days in advance of the actual opening of the session, but the city was already thronged with excited partisans, Democrats determined, Whigs apprehensive, Free-Soilers belligerent. House members held their respective party caucuses on December 1 to decide on candidates for Speaker. With eighty Representatives present, the Democrats put up Howell Cobb of Georgia, despite the opposition of the Calhoun faction. The Whigs showed even less unanimity in renominating the incumbent, Robert C. Winthrop of Massachusetts. Robert Toombs had called on Taylor a few days earlier, and had left the interview convinced that the President would not veto the Wilmot Proviso. The disillusionment of the big Georgian was complete, and most of the Southern members followed him out of the Whig caucus when the majority refused to pledge the party to oppose any restriction upon slavery in the territories. A small but potent little knot of thirteen Free-Soilers named Wilmot as their candidate for the Speakership.[1]

The Senate met on December 3, as prescribed by the Constitution, but until the House was organized there was little that could be done. As the members straggled in, the immediate center of attention was genial and smiling Henry Clay, a personality to be reckoned with still, by the administration, by the Democracy, by the North, and by the South. Webster greeted the new Kentucky Senator warmly, though relations between them had not been altogether cordial for several years. So, too, did Calhoun walk across the aisle that separated Whig from Democratic seats to salute his old antagonist despite the coolness that had long existed between them. They were under no illusions, these three giants of an earlier and simpler age. Their day was past. Calhoun was already living on borrowed time, and the others would not linger long behind him. Tired and feeble, all of them, they were here only because each, from his own special point of view, saw danger to the Union, and had come to offer his last strength to save it if he could.[2]

At the other end of the Capitol the House was almost full, with an unprecedented 223 of its 230 members in their seats when the clerk called them to order on opening day. They proceeded at once to ballot for Speaker. It was the start of a three weeks' battle that did more to unify the South than all of Calhoun's logic and entreaties over as many years. After the roll call the two leading candidates, Cobb and Winthrop, stepped off the floor, leaving 221 members with 111 needed to elect a Speaker. Cobb had 103 on the first trial, Winthrop 96, Wilmot 8. Meredith P. Gentry of Tennessee was supported by a handful of Southern Whigs, including the now militant Toombs and Stephens; and there were scattering votes for a half-dozen other candidates.[3]

By the end of the week twenty-eight ballots had been taken, but no Speaker had been chosen. On the third day of the balloting Winthrop took over the lead from Cobb, and on the sixth day the bulk of the Democratic strength was thrown to Emery D. Potter of Ohio, but the deadlock remained unbroken. With the thirty-second ballot, taken on Monday, December 10, William J. Brown of Indiana supplanted Potter as the Democratic choice. One day and six ballots later he had climbed to 109, the highest total any candidate had yet received. Winthrop then withdrew his name, and when the House adjourned on December 11, it was with a very fair prospect of achieving an organization when they reconvened. The first ballot taken the next day was the fortieth, and with 114 now needed for a choice Brown commanded 112 votes. He would have had the necessary majority but for a last-minute switch by Seddon of Virginia and Wallace of South Carolina, who had both supported him the previous day.

There were numerous conferences and caucuses throughout the whole Speakership fight, with proslavery men and Free-Soilers alike determined not to support anyone acceptable to the other side. Unsavory rumors were already afloat before the fortieth ballot was taken, gaining credence when Wilmot followed Winthrop's example and withdrew his name. As the roll was called, first Allen of Massachusetts, then Giddings, then Preston King, all unwavering Wilmot men, voted for Brown. There were hurried conferences in whispers, and as the end of the alphabet neared, Seddon and Wallace switched to prevent a choice. In the succeeding discussion it developed that Brown had given a written pledge to Wilmot as to the crucial Committees on Territories, the Judiciary, and the District of Columbia.[4]

No more voting was done that day, and little on the next. The good humor of the first week was gone, and so were mutual trust and common courtesy. December 13 opened with a motion by Albert

Gallatin Brown of Mississippi to declare Howell Cobb of Georgia the Speaker. He appealed to the Whigs for the necessary margin of votes and expressed his willingness to see a fair division of offices between the two major parties. He succeeded only in starting an argument as to which party should give way to the other. Tempers were rising when Richard K. Meade of Virginia said plainly what everybody knew—that it was no partisan question but a battle to control certain committees of the House, and to prevent them from introducing bills threatening to the peace of the country. Growing more excited as he talked, the Virginian called on all conservatives to unite and stop the agitation. But it was no longer possible. The struggle had already been too long dragged out, and members had heard from their constituents. There was to be no compromise. The debate went on until William Duer, a New York Whig, called Meade a disunionist, and then, for denying it, a liar. Meade sprang at Duer, and for a few minutes there was only "indescribable confusion."

When order had been restored, and Duer had finished what he had to say, Toombs gained the floor. It was Toombs more than any other single man who had kept the Southern Whigs from signing Calhoun's Address less than a year before, Toombs who for party's sake had blocked the way to Southern unity, Toombs who had insisted that Taylor would make everything right. He declared himself now unwilling to turn over the "great power of the Speaker's chair without obtaining security for the future." He saw no reason to hurry the organization of the House, if it was only to result in harm to his constituents. He would not give to the North control of the purse through the Committee on Ways and Means until grievances were redressed and pledges given. It was time for men to speak out, and he declared himself as plainly as any man could. "Sir, I have as much attachment to the Union of these States, under the Constitution of our fathers, as any freeman ought to have. I am ready to concede and sacrifice for it whatever a just and honorable man ought to sacrifice— I will do no more. . . . I do not, then, hesitate to avow before this House and the country, and in the presence of the living God, that if by your legislation you seek to drive us from the territories of California and New Mexico, purchased by the common blood and treasure of the whole people, and to abolish slavery in this District, thereby attempting to fix a national degradation upon half the States of this Confederacy, *I am for disunion.*" [5]

After another week of fruitless balloting amid turbulence and disorder the two major parties, each in separate caucus, agreed to set up a joint committee to explore the situation. A report was offered on December 22, and by a margin of 113 to 106 was adopted by the House. It proposed that three more ballots should be taken, and if a choice had still not been made then a plurality should elect. Immediately the original order of things was restored, with Cobb and Winthrop back in the lead. Both sixtieth and sixty-first ballots were indecisive, and the sixty-second found the caucus candidates tied with 97 votes each. The agreed rule was then invoked, and on the sixty-third ballot Howell Cobb of Georgia was elected Speaker of the House by a plurality of 102 out of 221. He was chosen, Calhoun wrote caustically, by Northern Democrats, because of all Southern men he was least true to the South.[6]

In the Senate adjournments had been taken from day to day, because no business could be done until the House was organized. The Senators could do no more than organize themselves, and the process revealed cleavages as deep as those in the lower chamber. As had been the custom for several years, a caucus of the majority party selected the chairman and majority members of all committees, while the minority members were similarly chosen by themselves. In the past the full slate of names had been unanimously ratified by agreement, but this time agreement was not forthcoming. Calhoun did not attend the Democratic caucus on December 16, but enough of his friends were there to register strong protest against making Benton chairman of Foreign Relations. The next morning Calhoun and Foote entered personal objections potent enough to bring about a new caucus at which William R. King was designated as the party choice for the disputed post. On the eighteenth Mangum moved appointment of committees in the usual way, but Hale objected, and so there had to be a separate vote on every name. It was no more than a delaying action, for the caucus lines held firm; but the dissidents ranged from four to seven, meaning there were that many who would not follow either party line.[7]

2

President Taylor's first and only annual message was delivered on Monday, December 24, 1849, three weeks to the day after Congress met. It was listened to most attentively by Southern members, and they found little enough in it to their liking. The Cuban question and the improvement of communications across the Isthmus of Panama were dealt with in a routine review of foreign relations. Then the President plunged boldly, as became an old soldier, into the whirlpool of domestic issues. He gave his approval to the protective policy, and recommended revision of the tariff to produce more revenue, including restoration of specific duties in place of the ad valorem system. The fate of the subtreasury he left to "the wisdom of Congress," but pronounced "important modifications" to be necessary if it was to be retained. He proposed a further extension of governmental activity by way of a bureau in the new Interior Department to foster and encourage agriculture. He endorsed a wide-ranging program of river and harbor improvements. California took only a few lines. Her people, "impelled by the necessities of their political condition," had met in convention to form a state government, and would soon present a constitution and apply for admission to the Union. The application, when it should come, was recommended to the favorable consideration of Congress; and so was that of New Mexico whenever her people should follow the example of the Californians. In the meantime Taylor hoped there would be no further discussion "of those exciting topics of a sectional character which have hitherto produced painful apprehensions in the public mind." He closed with a strong declaration of faith in the permanence and value of the Union, and avowed himself ready to "maintain it in its integrity to the full extent of the obligations imposed and the powers conferred" upon him by the Constitution.[8]

There was little disagreement as to the purport of the message. Webster saw it as "a good Whig Document." Ritchie, meaning the same thing, called it a negation of all the Democracy had accomplished over the past decade—a frank return to the principles of Hamiltonian Federalism. The radical Southern press agreed, but laid stress on the California question. Recalling the mission of Thomas Butler King, the *Mercury* charged that the prospective state had been organized on orders from Washington, to give the North "the triumph of the Wilmot Proviso without the trouble of enacting it."[9]

By the time Congress got down to business after New Year's, opinions were reasonably clear. The consensus in the North was that the issue could be settled by admitting California as a state and by giving territorial governments without restriction to New Mexico and Deseret, but there was a strong disposition to insist on restriction everywhere. Among Southern men of both parties, the admission of California to statehood with an antislavery constitution seemed the ultimate indignity, and they pledged themselves to block it. California and Oregon between them could be divided into enough free states to rewrite the Constitution; and even if that danger did not exist, there would still be the open nullification of the fugitive slave laws and the attacks on slavery in the District, both all the stronger for a Northern victory in California. The Nashville Convention assumed greater importance as the days went by, for it seemed to Southern conservatives their only chance to arrest a course of events they were powerless to control through Congress.[10]

In an atmosphere of rising tension the next few weeks were devoted almost exclusively to the slavery question. There were memorials and resolutions from state legislatures, and petitions from the territories. Foote offered a "compromise" that would establish territorial governments for California, Utah, and New Mexico and create a new slave state in Texas, but it was not satisfactory to either side. Mason offered a bill for the return of fugitive slaves, and Butler argued for it though he knew it could never be enforced save by the free states themselves. Before the end of January Senators were debating as though they were emissaries of hostile powers, bent not on avoiding but on precipitating war.

It was time, and high time, either to make peace or to part company. The session was nearly two months old, and there had been long and earnest discussions outside the halls of Congress. All but a few extremists on each side were willing to compromise if a common ground could be found. So it was that Henry Clay took the floor on January 29, 1850. He was now almost seventy-three years old, his long straight hair little more than a silver fringe around a balding skull, his mellow voice not quite so full and resonant as of old and his step no longer quick, but his personal magnetism and his mastery of tactics were unimpaired by age, and his timing, as always, was flawless. That morning the Democratic *Union* had charged the President with shirking his responsibility and had pleaded earnestly and powerfully for a settlement of the whole slavery question. Clay could not speak for the administration, but he could command a substantial following. He had his scheme worked out and ready, and when the right moment came, he offered the outlines of a compromise, embodied in a series of eight resolutions. There was little or nothing new, but many propositions coming at various times from both sides of the chamber and either side of the Potomac, brought together in such a fashion as to show their mutual interdependence.

One at a time Clay read his resolutions, and offered some explanation with each one. First, California, despite the irregularity of her case, was to be admitted to the Union without restriction or compulsion as to slavery. The second declared it inexpedient to adopt any restriction or conditions as to slavery in the remainder of the territory acquired from Mexico, on the express ground that slavery did not then exist there and was not likely to. The third defined the western boundary of Texas well short of her claims, while the fourth proposed to assume the Texan public debt in return for acceptance of this boundary. The fifth resolution pronounced it inexpedient to abolish slavery in the District of Columbia without consent of the people, both of the District and of Maryland, or without just compensation to the slaveowners. The sixth declared it expedient to abolish the slave trade in the District; the seventh called for better provisions for the restitution of fugitive slaves; and the eighth denied the power of Congress to interfere with trade in slaves between the states.[11]

Clay asked for a week's delay before the resolutions should be debated, and it was granted; but not before objections had been filed by Rusk and Foote, Mason and Davis, King and Downs and Butler, all Southern Senators and all Democrats. They agreed with various individual provisions, including the abolition of the slave trade in the District. The burden of their complaint was that there was no compromise, but only further concessions by the South. Indoors and out, the reaction of Southern leaders was the same. They were hopeful of a settlement, but they expected it to come about not by sectional reciprocity in the Senate but because the South was at last showing a determined and united front.[12]

3

Calhoun did not hear Clay's remarks on the introduction of the compromise resolutions. For two weeks he had been confined to his rooms at Hill's boardinghouse across the street, dangerously ill. Only within the last day or two had he begun to mend. The truth was that his apparent good health when he arrived in Washington was illusory, an appearance of health brought about by eight months of rest and outdoor life on his farm. The tan of his skin masked a growing weakness, of which he himself was very much aware. It was this consciousness of failing strength that had led him to take quarters as near as possible to the Capitol.[13] For the first month, while the bitter Speakership fight went on in the House of Representatives, Calhoun's Senatorial duties were light, and he experienced no physical difficulties. Even so, however, he did not attend the New Year's levee at the White House, but received at his lodgings the host of friends and acquaintances and well-wishers who called to pay their respects.[14]

He attended the Senate faithfully during the first two weeks of 1850, when the slavery controversy was beginning to unfold in all its fury, though he took little part in the discussions. His letters showed the same bold, confident penmanship of earlier years, but he could no longer work the long, steady hours he had been accustomed to. He was in his seat when the Senate convened on January 16, and remained at least long enough to vote with the majority in favor of tabling a motion to receive an antislavery petition offered by Seward. It is probable, however, that he withdrew shortly after, and was not present when Foote's territorial bill was presented. Three days later he was down with a severe attack of pneumonia, and for a week or more Calhoun's health was the most important topic discussed in Washington. Dr. Hall attended him, and Representative Abraham W. Venable of North Carolina, who occupied an adjoining room at Hill's boardinghouse and held a medical degree, acted as nurse and assistant physician. It was the end of January before his recovery was assured, and not until February 18 did he resume his seat in the Senate.[15]

Calhoun was still too ill to be present, even as an auditor, when the debate on Clay's compromise resolutions began. He heard none of Clay's great speech of February 5 and 6—one of the greatest in the Kentuckian's brilliant career; but it spurred him on to resume his place and take his share in the crucial debate he saw ahead. On the day Clay finished Calhoun wrote to his son-in-law, making light of his illness and promising to be back at his post in a few days. No doubt he followed the proceedings closely in the papers, and of course he received firsthand accounts from other Senators: Jeremiah Clemens of his own mess, Butler, Hunter, and the many others who called at frequent intervals.[16]

It was a crisis to bring patriotic men together, whatever their past differences may have been. Clay set the tone in his opening remarks, which fell with the greater solemnity for the age and experience and obvious feebleness of him who uttered them. "Mr. President, never, on any former occasion, have I risen under feelings of such deep solicitude. I have witnessed many periods of great anxiety, of peril, and of danger even to the country; but I have never before arisen to address any assembly so oppressed, so appalled, so anxious." Within a few days Thomas Ritchie called on Clay by invitation, though an open hostility had existed between them for many years. Among the older men, at least, the animus of party feeling tended to be forgotten in a common purpose—to avert the catastrophe that seemed so surely to impend.[17]

There were various interruptions before the compromise debate went forward, but on Monday and Tuesday, February 11 and 12, Berrien replied to Clay. As had been the case from the beginning, the utmost courtesy prevailed. The Georgia Senator spoke with suavity and grace, and with the learning that had earned him renown at the bar. He was very careful to inflict no personal wound, but the core of his speech expressed the new, inflexible temper of the deeper South. There was a point beyond which the slave states could yield nothing without in fact surrendering everything, and that point was rapidly being approached.[18]

Webster took notes as Berrien spoke, but did not attempt to secure the floor when the Georgian finished. Neither did any other Senator, for it was understood that Calhoun wished to speak, and if physically able, would do so the next day. He was not strong enough, despite his hopes and all his reassurances to family and friends. So Jefferson Davis took the floor instead, and was perhaps not too disappointing to those who had packed the galleries in anticipation of hearing the great Carolinian. A new element of urgency had been added a few minutes before Davis rose by a brief message from the President, transmitting an authenticated copy of the constitution of California. Davis finished on February 14, and the question of referring the California matter to committee took up the rest of the week.[19]

When the gavel fell at noon on Monday, February 18, Calhoun was in his seat, and his appearance there was specially noted in the *Con-*

gressional Globe, unusual as such a procedure was. That day and the next, Downs held the floor on the compromise, but Calhoun heard only the first part of the speech. The nineteenth was cold and damp, and the South Carolina Senator wisely kept to his rooms, but despite his precautions he was coughing and feverish again on the twentieth. Once more he minimized his symptoms when he wrote to Anna on February 24, brushing off his relapse as no more than a cold, with "nothing serious about it." But he doubted his ability to speak in the Senate, and he was most anxious to be heard. It was then that he decided to write out a speech that could be read for him by someone else.[20]

4

During these weeks of Calhoun's illness the tension between North and South had been rising until in the last few days of February 1850 the breaking point appeared to be very close. The apparent obliteration of party lines in the slave states and the overt threat of secession posed by the Nashville Convention acted for a time as a damper upon Northern agitation. Through January volatile Southern members of the House denounced Northern aggression, making the most of their constitutional position which they backed up with threats to leave the Union, or to withhold appropriations until a satisfactory settlement was reached. Northern members appeared to wither under the blast, and enough of them sided with the South on crucial issues to make a majority. A resolution in the House instructing the appropriate committee to prohibit slavery in the territories was tabled by 30 votes on February 4; yet it was precisely such a resolution as had passed at the previous session by a margin almost as large.[21]

Within two weeks the whole temper of the Northern members changed. They had heard, and heard peremptorily, from their constituents. Memorials and petitions gave them excuse to speak, and speak they did in bitter denunciation of the politics of slavery and all who indulged in it—not Free-Soilers alone, but staid and hitherto conservative party stalwarts. By the date of Calhoun's relapse the House was as factious and as uncontrollable as it had ever been; and the Senate kept order only because of the preponderance among its members of men of distinctly superior quality. Ritchie was crying out once more that the Union was in danger, and calling on all reasonable and patriotic men of whatever party or sectional ties to unite for its preservation. In the Senate Foote proposed that all questions touching slavery be referred to a select committee, to keep provocative debate to a minimum; but the motion itself only provoked new arguments on basic questions.[22]

At this point Calhoun determined to write out a speech; his last, few doubted, for ill as he had long been it was hardly possible he could retain his Senate seat even if he recovered. Washington was soon speculating at large on the course the South Carolina Senator would pursue and on what Webster would say when finally he took the floor. The *Union,* giving a correspondent of the Baltimore *Patriot* as its authority, stated on February 26 that Calhoun had completed the writing of a speech, which would be printed and read in the Senate by Judge Butler. The Washington correspondent of the *Courier* was more specific still, announcing in his dispatch of that day that Butler would read his colleague's speech on the twenty-eighth.[23]

Both announcements were premature. No doubt the speech was already well formulated in Calhoun's mind by that date, but February 26 was actually the day on which he began to commit it to paper. James Gordon Bennett was in Washington at that time, and to the New York publisher Calhoun addressed a brief note. He knew that Scoville had gone to Richmond on assignment for the *Herald.* Would Bennett tell him when he returned that the South Carolina Senator would be glad to see him? Scoville returned that same day and was already on his way to Calhoun's rooms when Bennett encountered him. That evening Calhoun began dictating the speech, with Scoville transcribing as the Senator talked. It was probably completed the following day, and the final corrections were added by its author.[24]

Before the Senate resumed its debate on Clay's compromise resolutions February 28, Butler rose to ask on behalf of his absent colleague that he be allowed at one o'clock the following Monday, March 4, to present his views. He explained that Calhoun's friends thought it not advisable for him to attempt to speak in person, and he therefore desired the privilege of having his remarks read by some friend. Butler was interrupted by Dickinson of New York, who assured him that the mere request was enough. Clay rose to express his "hearty concurrence"; and King declared that no motion was necessary.[25]

Two days later, on Saturday, March 2, Daniel Webster called at

Calhoun's rooms, and for two hours the veteran Senators who had broken so many lances in the past were closeted together. Webster had probably also been there a day or two earlier; at least he had a very clear idea on March 1 what Calhoun's speech was to cover. Both men were sincerely desirous of saving the Union and stopping the agitation. They did not see things in quite the same way, but they were near enough in their objectives to confide in each other. It was presumably at this time that Webster outlined the main points of his own forthcoming speech, with which Calhoun expressed himself to friends as being perfectly satisfied. Though full agreement was not possible, it seems probable that a general understanding had been reached.[26]

It appears to have been Calhoun's intention that Butler should read the speech, and such certainly would have been the normal procedure, as the Senate apparently took for granted. Butler's eyes were too weak for the task, however, and so he suggested one of his own messmates, the younger and more vigorous James M. Mason of Virginia. Mason asked that the speech be put in type, to avoid any possible slip in the reading; and Scoville scurried about on Sunday to find an available printer.[27]

5

Few speeches have ever been delivered in circumstances more solemn or in a setting better calculated to impress those who listened with the awful gravity of the situation. The Senate chamber was crowded, with galleries and privileged seats and places on the floor all filled with ladies, with officers of the government, with members of the lower house and distinguished visitors to the city. The Representatives from South Carolina were there, and so were many from free soil. It was a bright springlike day outside, but there was no gaiety, no excited chattering, no hint of the festive air that had in the past so often attended a great speech in the Senate. This was an occasion the like of which had never before occurred in the Congress of the United States, and might never occur again. Unless the deep sectional chasm that had called forth this day's business could somehow be bridged, the United States would cease to be.

Calhoun came in a few minutes after twelve, on the arm of General James Hamilton of South Carolina. He was emaciated and feeble, his sallow cheeks sunken, his long hair now almost white, his step short. Only the brilliant, flashing eyes and the grim, straight lips remained of the old Calhoun. It was a shock indeed to those who had not seen him since his illness. Senators crowded around to greet him and welcome him back—Clay and Webster, King and Mangum and Berrien, Atchison and Dickinson, Davis and Douglas and Rusk —friends and antagonists of twenty and thirty years' standing; and younger men whose thankless task it would be to carry on when these were gone. Calhoun quickly sank into his seat and pulled his long cloak about him, to await the appointed hour of one. Not a Senator was absent save only Sam Houston, who was then in Texas.[28]

When the moment came, Calhoun rose in his place as straight for all his feebleness as he had been forty years before, and in a voice calm, distinct, and clearly audible he thanked the Senators for their indulgence. He had reduced to writing what he intended to say, and without further remark would ask the favor of his friend, the Senator behind him, to read it.

The ghostlike figure sank into his seat. He had no ambition now to gratify, no hope to fulfill, no further duty to perform this side of the grave. He would never speak again, and so his words as they rang out in Mason's bold and challenging tones were taken by almost all who heard them for what they were—the final effort of a dying man to serve his country. There were no rolling periods, nor emotional exhortations. There was only cold, blunt realism; logical analysis of the situation as he saw it in terms of his concept of the nature of the Union. The philosophy was that of the *Disquisition on Government* that lay with his papers in his room; the premises were those of the *Discourse on the Constitution,* the final revision of which he had temporarily dropped to prepare this very speech. Age had not softened him, disease had not dimmed his inner vision, experience had not left him any illusions as to the nature of man.

"I have, Senators, believed from the first that the agitation of the subject of slavery would, if not prevented by some timely and effective measure, end in disunion. . . . The agitation has been permitted to proceed, with almost no attempt to resist it, until it has reached a point when it can no longer be disguised or denied that the Union is in danger. You have thus had forced upon you the greatest and the gravest question that can ever come under your consideration—How can the Union be preserved?"

Before giving his answer—before stating, in effect, the terms on which the South could remain in the Union—he undertook to trace the steps by which the present crisis had come about. The danger to the Union arose, he thought, from the "almost universal discontent" pervading the Southern states; and that discontent had originated in and had grown with the agitation of the slavery question. The people of the South now believed that as things then stood they could not remain "consistently with honor and safety" in political alliance with the North.

The "great and primary cause" of this feeling he found in the fact that the original equilibrium between the two sections had been destroyed. At the beginning of the government the slaveholding and nonslaveholding states were equal in number, and very nearly so in population. Through her more rapid growth the North had long dominated in the House of Representatives and in the electoral college. She now dominated also in the Senate and would soon control overwhelmingly every branch of the government.

The South would have no reason to complain, he thought, had time alone worked this great disproportion, but it had in fact been brought about by the action of the Federal Government, charged though it was with the welfare of all. There were three classes of measures by which this result had been achieved. First was the exclusion of the South—by which he meant slaveholders—from large portions of the public domain; by the Ordinance of 1787, by the Missouri Compromise, and prospectively by the Wilmot Proviso. Second was the financial system, based on a protective tariff, which had operated to build up the power and wealth of the manufacturing states at the expense of those engaged in agriculture. Third was the gradual alteration of the whole character of the government, paralleling the destruction of the equilibrium between the sections. Instead of a confederacy of sovereign states, a majority now firmly believed that the general government had the right to determine the extent of its powers, and might rightfully resort to force to make good its claims.

It followed as a matter of course, in Calhoun's realistic view of the nature of man, that wherever there was a diversity of interest between sections, the interest of the weaker would be sacrificed to that of the stronger. Slavery was such a case. "Every portion of the North entertains views and feelings more or less hostile to it." Some regarded it as a sin, which they were under a sacred obligation, to the extent of their power, to extirpate. To others it was a crime against humanity, which they were bound to eliminate if they could. Even those least hostile felt it to be "a stain on the character of what they call the Nation." The South, on the other hand, regarded the existing relation between white and Negro races "as one which cannot be destroyed without subjecting the two races to the greatest calamity, and the section to poverty, desolation, and wretchedness; and accordingly they feel bound, by every consideration of interest and safety, to defend it."

He then traced the rise of abolition sentiment and its conversion into political power in terms similar to those he had used on former occasions. The antislavery movement had now gone so far that if it were not promptly arrested it would of itself destroy the Union. "It is a great mistake to suppose that disunion can be effected at a single blow. The cords which bound these States together in one common Union, are far too numerous and powerful for that. Disunion must be the work of time. It is only through a long process, and successively, that the cords can be snapped, until the whole fabric falls asunder." But the process had already begun. The churches were divided, and the ties of party were beginning to give way. When spiritual, political, social ties were gone only force would remain to hold the Union together. "But, surely, that can, with no propriety of language, be called a Union, when the only means by which the weaker is held connected with the stronger portion is *force*. It may, indeed, keep them connected; but the connection will partake much more of the character of subjugation, on the part of the weaker to the stronger, than the union of free, independent, and sovereign States, in one confederation, as they stood in the early stages of the Government, and which only is worthy of the sacred name of Union."

With this analysis Calhoun arrived at the main question: How could the Union be saved? Not by Clay's plan, as others had sufficiently shown, for the Kentucky Senator had not gone to the roots of the difficulty. Neither could it be saved by the scheme of the administration, which would bring California into the Union in defiance of the express provisions of the Constitution. Only Congress could authorize the people of a territory to form a state government, and Congress alone could fix the manner and mode of calling a convention. The Union could yet be saved, by adopting "such measures as will satisfy the States belonging to the Southern section, that they can remain in the Union consistently with their honor and safety," but it could be done in no other way. He had no compromise to offer and no concession to make. The South would be satisfied only by "a full and final settlement, on the principle of justice, of all questions at issue between the two sections." Such a settlement could easily be made, but only by the North. The South could not even protect herself.

"The North has only to will it to accomplish it—to do justice by conceding to the South an equal right in the acquired territory, and to do her duty by causing the stipulations relative to fugitive slaves to be faithfully fulfilled—to cease agitating the slave question, and to provide for the insertion of a provision in the constitution, by an amendment, which will restore to the South, in substance, the power she possessed of protecting herself, before the equilibrium between the sections was destroyed by the action of this Government. There will be no difficulty in devising such a provision—one that will protect the South, and which, at the same time, will improve and strengthen the Government, instead of impairing and weakening it." It was, then, squarely up to the North to decide her course. She would have no difficulty in agreeing to all this, if her people had half the love for the Union they professed to have. So he called directly on the Northern Senators to show their hands.

"It is time, Senators, that there should be an open and manly avowal on all sides, as to what is intended to be done. If the question is not now settled, it is uncertain whether it ever can hereafter be; and we, as the representatives of the States of this Union, regarded as governments, should come to a distinct understanding as to our respective views, in order to ascertain whether the great questions at issue can be settled or not. If you, who represent the stronger portion, cannot agree to settle them on the broad principle of justice and duty, say so; and let the States we both represent agree to separate and part in peace. If you are unwilling we should part in peace, tell us so, and we shall know what to do, when you reduce the question to submission or resistance. If you remain silent, you will compel us to infer by your acts what you intend. In that case, California will become the test question. If you admit her, under all the difficulties that oppose her admission, you compel us to infer that you intend to exclude us from the whole of the acquired territories, with the intention of destroying, irretrievably, the equilibrium between the two sections. We would be blind not to perceive in that case, that your real objects are power and aggrandizement, and infatuated not to act accordingly."

6

As this powerful and prophetic final utterance of the great South Carolinian was read, Calhoun himself sat motionless in his chair, sweeping the chamber now and again with deeply sunken luminous eyes. Throughout the reading Webster leaned forward in his chair, intently absorbing every word of it. Clay, his hand resting on his temple, was equally attentive; and Benton, rigid as granite, did not miss a syllable. Cass lolled in his seat, the very picture of gloom; and Truman Smith, the administration leader, followed the printed text as Mason read it.[29]

The speech concluded, Walker of Wisconsin rose, but yielded to Webster. There was something almost awesome in the way younger men of whatever political faith deferred to these giants of a dying age—Calhoun, Webster, Clay. Benton, Cass, Berrien, were as old; King and Mangum almost as long in public life. Yet none but the great triumvirate commanded this spontaneous veneration, the unconscious tribute men pay to genius. Webster disclaimed at once any desire to reply. He had risen to express his pleasure at seeing, "the honorable member from Carolina able to be in his place today," and to voice his own prayer that Calhoun would "yet have an opportunity to perform much public service for the benefit of all portions of the country." There was some conversation between Walker, Webster, Seward, and Hale as to the allocation of time for the remainder of the week. It was agreed that Webster should speak on Thursday March 7, and the Senate adjourned.

The next day Henry S. Foote of Mississippi secured the floor to give notice that he would press his motion for a select committee to consider the whole slavery question as soon as Webster had made his forthcoming speech. Being up, however, he seized the opportunity to move to another, not unrelated, topic. He spoke of Calhoun's performance of the day before, and of his great respect and friendship for the author of it, but he wanted to make clear that he had not been consulted and that he did not agree with all that the South Carolinian had said. He did not agree that the entire North was hostile to the South; and more important still, he did not agree that any amendment of the Constitution was necessary. To make the alteration of the charter a *sine qua non* was, he feared, to make disunion inevitable. It was at this point that Calhoun entered the room and took his seat. Foote's tone changed immediately, but not his substance. When he had finished, Butler, who had not seen his colleague come in, rose to reply but turned the task over to Calhoun as soon as he discovered his presence. Calhoun expressed his regret that Foote had seen fit to raise this question in his absence, and inquired if he was being accused of disunion. Foote, of course, disclaimed vehemently any such intention.[30]

Calhoun thought the Mississippi Senator a little anxious to misconstrue, but gravely corrected the accusation of unfairness toward the North. He had not said that all Northerners were hostile to the South, but to the institution of slavery. Foote denied it, and Calhoun declined to argue the point. As to the amendment, he simply asked if Foote thought, in the existing circumstances, the South might safely remain in the Union without further guarantees than she then possessed. Foote thought she might; and again Calhoun dropped it without argument. The nature of the guarantees he would require by way of amendment to the fundamental law, he was careful not to specify; but clearly the strategy of such a proposal required that the terms be left open until the reaction of the country was known.

In a long, defensive speech in the Senate on December 18, 1851, Foote contended that he had received a hint from Willie P. Mangum —who was present, and assented—that the amendment Calhoun had in mind was a dual executive: a President elected by each section, each with a veto. In support of his contention Foote read a passage from Calhoun's *Discourse on the Constitution,* which had been published earlier that year.[31] It has since been taken for granted by most historians that this was, indeed, what Calhoun had in mind. It was, certainly, one of the devices he was considering; but his very refusal to be explicit seems to imply that he had not settled on the terms of any particular amendment. Rather, he was prepared to wait until the temper of the various parties concerned might develop in the course of the discussion. Remember he was not acting completely alone. Others, including Webster, knew his intentions before he spoke, and he in turn knew what Webster was going to say on the Northern side. He was, moreover, satisfied with it. Does it not appear, then, that he had simply made in the clearest and strongest possible language the opening speech for his side in what was to be a full-scaled debate?[32] Surely his hope was that after Webster had rejoined, the common ground might be worked out in general discussion, and possibly an agreement could be reached. He could not, therefore, commit himself in advance to specific terms. Those were to be the end product of the debate. He meant by his remarks only that he wanted the agreement, if one acceptable to both parties could be reached, to be embodied in the Constitution.

The passage in the *Discourse* on which Foote based his conclusion was illustrative only. "The nature of the disease is such, that nothing can reach it, short of some organic change,—a change which shall so modify the constitution, as to give to the weaker section, in some one form or another, a negative on the action of the government. . . . How the constitution could best be modified, so as to effect the object, can only be authoritatively determined by the amending power. It may be done in various ways. Among others, it might be effected through a reorganization of the executive department; so that its powers, instead of being vested, as they now are, in a single officer, should be vested in two. . . ." As we have seen, Calhoun was working on the *Discourse* at this precise time, and there were undoubtedly many among his friends who had seen part or all of the manuscript, or with whom he had discussed specific points. Mangum was no doubt one of these; and it was presumably on the basis of a conversation with someone who had seen the manuscript that the Washington correspondent of the Charleston *Courier* guessed in his dispatch of March 15 that Calhoun meant a dual executive.[33]

Calhoun had been very careful in his speech, however, to leave the road open for any proposal that might be made. "There will be no difficulty in devising such a provision—one that will protect the South, and which, at the same time, will improve and strengthen the Government, instead of impairing and weakening it." The idea of amending the Constitution in the interest of the South had been suggested more than once before. Yulee had pondered the problem only the previous summer, holding that the "elementary antagonism in the social structure of the two sections" made political connection impossible on any other basis. Rhett had made a special point of it as long ago as 1838, when he proposed to make more explicit those provisions on which there was difference of opinion. The Charleston

Mercury thought Calhoun intended something of this nature. Stephen A. Douglas thought he meant only to insist on the admission of a slave state with every free state, to maintain the balance in the Senate; and the Charleston *Courier* quoted a "very grave and enlightened and quite conservative Northern Senator" to the effect that the proposition was to be full representation for slaves instead of the three fifths then counted.[34]

Calhoun was not a man to accept misinterpretation or misunderstanding of his views, if it was in his power to clarify them. As Webster noted in his Seventh of March speech, "What he means he is very apt to say." And Calhoun responded, "Always, always." Certainly he was aware of all this speculation, ill though he was, and had deliberately parried Foote's effort to smoke him out—something he would never have done had his purposes been fixed. He would, in fact, have stated explicitly what he meant in the first instance if he had intended to offer a specific amendment. The conclusion is inescapable that he did not. Practically, he wanted some form of guarantee to the South that her economic and social structure would not be destroyed by the superior power and hostile morality of the North; theoretically, he wanted, in terms of his own political philosophy, a concurrent veto for the weaker interest. He was an old, a dying man, content to leave the details to others. In South Carolina, certainly, where the question of amending the Constitution had often been discussed, Calhoun's meaning was not a subject of speculation. It was taken for granted that he intended only to make effective the guarantees already provided in the basic law.[35]

In laying down what the North could hardly fail to regard as an ultimatum, Calhoun was following his own ripe wisdom and mature judgment. He had no desire to see the Union fall. His life had been coextensive with the independent existence of his country, and bound inextricably with it. The failure of constitutional government in the United States would mean the end of popular government everywhere, perhaps for centuries to come, and with it all the high hopes of the past century for the future of mankind. He did not seek it, he did not want it; but he saw more clearly and more distantly than his fellows, and he knew that the line must now be drawn or never. He rejected the compromise schemes of Clay and Bell and Foote because he was realist enough to see that no compromise is or ever has been possible between a strong and a weak party. Compromise is possible only between equals, and the South was no longer the equal of the North in any aspect of material or political power. She must be given the power to protect herself, or she must hazard the uncertain road of separation. The alternative was not merely the abolition of slavery, but reduction to colonial vassalage for the economic benefit of the stronger interest.

7

The day after Foote's attack had revealed a new schism in the South, Webster called again at Hill's boardinghouse. This time the two Senators were in private conference together for six or seven hours, neither appearing in the Senate at all.[36] Calhoun had laid down an ultimatum, stating in effect the terms on which the South could remain in the Union, and appealing to the North to use its admitted power to meet those terms. Webster was to answer for the North, not yielding all the South Carolinian asked, but not refusing, either. He was rather to state the minimum terms of his section, but was to do it in conciliatory fashion, leaving room for mutual adjustment.

There are many touching stories of how Calhoun, more haggard and ill than ever, rose from what everyone knew to be his deathbed, and made his way to the Senate chamber to hear his great antagonist and friend; of how Webster did not see him enter, and alluded to his absence with regret; of how Calhoun painfully raised himself and made his presence known, to the evident pleasure of the speaker. The stories have lost nothing of pathos nor gained anything of truth in the telling. The best evidence we have is that Calhoun was actually present from the beginning or very near the beginning of Webster's speech, but in the overcrowded room it was some time before the great Massachusetts orator became aware of it.[37]

With that superb theatricalism of which he was past master, Webster fixed the attention and captured the imagination of his hearers from the start—and the attention of the country, too: the larger audience he had to reach to be effective. "Mr. President, I wish to speak to-day, not as a Massachusetts man, nor as a northern man, but as an American, and a member of the Senate of the United States. . . . I speak to-day for the preservation of the Union. 'Hear me for my cause.'" In this lofty vein of patriotism he continued, until

Senators and guests and visitors alike were deeply under his spell. Then he came to the point. He held the South clearly right about the fugitive slaves, about the propaganda of the abolitionists, even in large measure about the territories. He did not defend slavery. He knew it to be abhorrent to his people and he himself rejected it on principle. But the South on this question was correct. Slavery existed. It antedated the Constitution and was guaranteed by it. The North must live up to her obligations.[38]

The Wilmot Proviso he held a needless insult, and so was every other legislative device to prevent the spread of slavery. Nature had already taken care of that, and her determination would in the end be decisive. California and New Mexico were destined to be free soil. He thought it, moreover, the duty of Congress to subdivide that part of Texas lying south of 36°30′ into additional slave states when the population warranted, as the act of admission provided. There was an offhand colloquy between Webster and Calhoun over points of history in the annexation of Texas. Then the speaker resumed. The North, too, had grievances. When the constitutional compact had been entered into, the South no less than the North regarded slavery as an evil, and there was therefore no expectation of any future effort to add new slave states. The South had been highhanded in her treatment of respectable citizens like Judge Hoar, and tactless in the needless insults she hurled at the working classes of the North by contrasting them unfavorable with her slaves. He closed on the theme with which he had begun—the permanence and value of the Union. He ridiculed the notion that the states might separate, and denied utterly that there was any right of peaceable secession.

It was indeed, as almost all the editors joined to call it, a remarkable performance. For what Webster had done was to accept most of Calhoun's ground with respect to the immediate—though not the ultimate—causes of Southern discontent. He insisted, however, that the disruption of the Union would not be a remedy. It would be, on the contrary, the inevitable road to bloody and destructive civil conflict in which everyone would lose. And in the course of his speech, without ever explicitly saying so, he had endorsed as feasible and worthy of consideration virtually all of Clay's compromise proposals. At the end there was some further discussion between Webster and Calhoun, involving Florida, Louisiana, Texas, and eventually the right of peaceable secession. Old and wise in the ways of

debate, each as familiar with the other's views as with his own, the
two weary gladiators gracefully dropped it there. There were many
in the crowded chamber who must have been sorely disappointed,
when these two greatest advocates of conflicting theories of government agreed that they had debated those issues often enough in the
past, and had no desire to do it now.

In the South the reaction to the Seventh of March speech was about
what Calhoun and Webster must have looked for. It was taken as a
peace offering. The *Mercury,* long slanted toward the radical side, saw
hope at last that the sectional controversy could be ended. The *Union*
and the New York *Herald* were equally emphatic; but Northern
sentiment was against any form of concession to slavery, however
hollow. For days no other topic was talked of in Washington, but
Northern members freely admitted their inability to follow their
own convictions. The *Liberator* opened its heaviest batteries of
scorn; Whittier wrote his shameful "Ichabod"; and the olive branch
withered and was trampled under foot.[39]

After Webster's speech Calhoun returned to the Senate only once,
on March 13. Foote's motion for a compromise committee was the
order of the day. Cass gained the floor, and spoke ramblingly of
nonintervention in the territories. He said he had listened with great
regret to Calhoun's speech, because of its unnecessarily gloomy tone,
and attributed the South Carolinian's pessimism to his illness.[40]

Calhoun took up the challenge at once, apologizing that his poor
health required him to be brief. He denied categorically that he had
ever advocated disunion. He had done no more than state the terms
on which, in his judgment, harmony and good feeling could be restored between the sections. He was going to the root of the matter,
whereas the Senator from Michigan was dealing in palliatives. Cass
tried to postpone further discussion until the next day, but Calhoun
insisted on finishing it then and there. With that peculiar prescience
of his, he knew he would not be there the next day, nor the next. He
had asked for an amendment to the Constitution. Was that disunion?
Was that treason? The slow-witted Cass fumblingly tried to explain,
and presently Foote came to his rescue.[41]

The point of the argument shifted to the ground of March 5, and
Foote accused Calhoun of trying to make a compromise out of doors,
without consulting other Southern Senators. Calhoun revealed then
that he had consulted many others before his speech was made, then

charged that Foote had informed no one before he moved his own plan for a select committee. The South Carolinian was manifestly feverish and exhausted, and there were fears that he would collapse and perhaps die on the spot if the excitement was not curbed. Jefferson Davis and A. P. Butler interposed, Foote was silenced, and Calhoun retired. It was his last appearance on the Senate floor.

CHAPTER XXXI

WHAT MANNER OF MAN?

1

BACK IN HIS ROOMS Calhoun talked to the many who called on him, freely and gravely, and as fully as his strength allowed. No other way was left him to impress his fears and his convictions on those who would inherit the sorely divided country he was so soon to leave. Until very close to the end of his life he believed the Union could be saved. He clung doggedly to his belief in the efficacy of Southern unity, and explained the purpose of the Nashville Convention as being consultative, to secure a meeting of minds on the problems facing the South, and an agreement on remedies.[1] Though he never said so, it is probable that he expected this assembly to propound the terms of the constitutional amendment for which he had asked. Such had been the course of the Hartford Convention half a lifetime earlier, and the proceedings there were the model for those at Nashville.

For a time he seems to have had high hopes that Webster's conciliatory attitude would make possible a settlement in Congress; but the sharp antagonism of Foote and others from the South to his own forthright position, and the bitter reaction of the North to Webster's speech, led him to give up hope. "Can anything more clearly evince the utter hopelessness of looking to the North for support," he wrote Conner on March 18, "when their strongest man finds himself incapable of maintaining himself on the smallest amount possible of concession to the South;—and on points too clear to admit of Constitutional doubts?" It was probably then that he told Mason the Union was doomed, predicting that the end would come "within twelve years or three Presidential terms," and that the crisis would probably be brought on over an election.[2]

His conversations, in fragmentary and garbled form, were spread about Washington, and men drew conclusions according to their prejudices. Benton professed to believe the South Carolina Senator was malingering, avoiding a return to the Senate lest he be forced

to encounter Houston or the rugged Missourian himself in debate.
Blair spread the rumor that Calhoun was dictating another speech,
or was preparing a constitution for a Southern confederacy, to be
promulgated at Nashville. Others believed he was writing, or had
written, a paper showing the advantages of secession to the South.
He was preparing nothing, however, but a series of resolutions embodying the points made in his March 4 speech: that, and the manuscript of his *Discourse on the Constitution,* which was to be his
legacy to his country and to mankind.[3]

2

From the time he first became ill, Calhoun was attended constantly
by devoted friends, and for the last month of his life they vied with
one another for the privilege of waiting on him. General Hamilton,
who came to Washington about the middle of February, was a daily
visitor until the last week in March, when business called him home.
Scoville was there from late February on; and Calhoun's messmates,
Venable of North Carolina, James L. Orr who represented Pendleton
district, Senator Clemens of Alabama, and half a dozen others took
turns in looking to his wants. The other South Carolinians in Congress, particularly Butler and Armistead Burt, were daily visitors,
and so was Robert M. T. Hunter of Virginia. When the illness persisted, and Calhoun overtaxed his strength in going to the Senate,
Burt provided a competent nurse, and the sick man's doctor-son,
John Caldwell, Jr., came on to share the duties of physician with Dr.
Hall and with the medically trained Venable. Ellwood Fisher was
another daily caller; and in March Richard K. Crallé came up from
Lynchburg to spend most of his time by the bedside of his old friend
and patron.[4]

After that last grueling session in the Senate, Calhoun slipped
back, and Burt sent hastily for Floride. She was expected about the
first of April, but an unduly optimistic report from the sick chamber
led her to defer the trip in the expectation that her husband would
soon be able to come home to convalesce. Duff Green, who then had
a home in Washington, tried to persuade his old friend to move there,
but he would not, and so Mrs. Green attended him every day where
he was. For three weeks or more Orr's room, which connected with

Calhoun's was used by Scoville, John Calhoun, and Crallé to rest in the intervals between bedside watches.[5]

The various firsthand reports agree that Calhoun did not realize how serious his condition was. According to Burt's account, Dr. Hall believed he would recover, and Calhoun never gave any indication that he himself thought otherwise. It is hardly likely, however, that so thorough a realist would have had any illusions as to his actual condition. Hamilton knew that there was no hope whatever before he left; and Calhoun must have known it too. He knew, at least, that his heart was diseased and that "consumption," or tuberculosis, was eating out his lungs at an accelerated rate. There were marked changes from day to day. On March 22 he was "extremely low," but two days later he appeared much better. He sat up for an hour and a half, and with assistance managed to walk across the room.[6]

On the morning of March 30 he took a turn for the worse, and sank slowly through the day. Toward evening he experienced that singular clarity of mind which sometimes comes to dying men, and made to those around him the often quoted remark: "If I could have but one hour to speak in the Senate, I could do more good than on any previous occasion of my life." About four in the morning, Sunday, March 31, he felt himself sinking rapidly. He gave John directions as to his papers; refused medicine on the ground that he was now beyond medical aid; and spoke the last words that were audible: "I am resting now, very easily." He died three hours later, completely conscious to the very last; died with the quiet composure and perfect serenity that comes only to those who have no fear of death.[7]

3

The death of John Caldwell Calhoun was announced in the Senate on April 1, 1850, by his surviving colleague, Andrew Pickens Butler. The news had already spread over the United States as far as the telegraph lines extended. In Charleston the bells of St. Michael's tolled all day long; and everywhere, even in those places where his doctrines were most abhorred, he himself was mourned as a man truly great in his own time. There were those, even in his native South Carolina, who felt that it would now be easier to achieve a settlement of the slavery problem; there were those in the North who piously noted the passing of what they were pleased to call a misspent life; but these were the exceptions. More common was the feeling of irreparable loss. Not since the death of Washington had the passing of any public figure so profoundly affected the country.[8]

Butler, in a singularly restrained and appropriate eulogy, recounted the high points of Calhoun's career and paid tribute to his character and his great abilities. He then moved the resolutions customary on such occasions: that a committee be appointed to superintend the funeral at noon the next day; that members of the Senate wear crape on the left arm for one month; and that the Senate adjourn as a further mark of respect.[9]

Henry Clay rose to second the resolutions, and to add his tribute to the dead. The tall Kentuckian, silvered and bent with age and well knowing that his own remaining time was short, recalled those gallant days of 1812 when he and Calhoun and other free and youthful spirits had shared a mess and had known one another as comrades. He recalled the many times they had labored together, and without asperity now, the many times they had been opposed. He spoke of the transcendent talents, the great personal charm, the spotless integrity, and high patriotism of the departed Senator. "I was his senior, Mr. President, in years—in nothing else. According to the course of nature, I ought to have preceded him. It has been decreed otherwise; but I know that I shall linger here only a short time, and shall soon follow him." And in his own incomparable fashion, Clay called on his fellow Senators to profit by the melancholy occasion, and substitute harmony for discord among themselves.

Clay was followed by Webster, who delivered a touching, all but perfect tribute to his departed antagonist and friend. He spoke with deeper emotion than he had been known to show in the Senate, and no one who heard him—no one, indeed, who reads his words today —could doubt the genuineness of his respect, his admiration, his affection for the South Carolinian.[10] Like Clay, Webster spoke of his long acquaintance with Calhoun, going back to his own first appearance in the House of Representatives in 1813. "From that day to the day of his death, amidst all the strife of party and politics, there has subsisted between us, always, and without interruption, a great degree of personal kindness." They had differed widely on many points, but their differences had not marred their personal relations. Webster went on to speak of Calhoun's talents in debate, of his gifts of leadership, of his undoubted genius. He paid an orator's tribute to the style and manner of his friend when speaking, and his demeanor on the Senate floor. "No man was more respectful of others; no man carried himself with greater decorum, no man with superior dignity." He spoke of Calhoun's austerity of life, his great application, his constant employment in matters bearing on his public duty, his only recreation being the exercise of his extraordinary colloquial powers.

Webster dwelt longer than had Clay on the personal character of the dead Senator. "Mr. President, he had the basis, the indispensable basis, of all high character; and that was, unspotted integrity—unimpeached honor and character. If he had aspirations, they were high, honorable, and noble. There was nothing groveling, or low, or meanly selfish, that came near the head or the heart of Mr. Calhoun. Firm in his purpose, perfectly patriotic and honest, as I am sure he was, in the principles that he espoused, and the measures that he defended, aside from that large regard for that species of distinction that conducted him to eminent stations for the benefit of the republic, I do not believe he had a selfish motive or a selfish feeling."

While Webster was speaking, Thomas Hart Benton ostentatiously turned his back. He too, as the oldest continuous member of the Senate, should have said at least a word, and Webster himself had urged it on him, but Benton remained unyielding, even in the presence of death. He insisted still that Calhoun's doctrines were treason, and that he could make no distinction between the treason and the traitor.[11] Thomas J. Rusk spoke briefly, as one who had fallen under Calhoun's magnetic spell while yet a lad. Jeremiah Clemens placed Alabama high in the mourning column. The resolutions were unanimously passed, and the Senate adjourned.

There were similar observances in the House of Representatives, which had recessed while the Senate proceedings were in progress. Isaac E. Holmes, senior member of the South Carolina delegation, announced the death and pronounced a eulogy a little long and florid, after which he moved the usual resolutions. Winthrop spoke for the North, Venable for the South, and the House too adjourned.[12]

Funeral ceremonies were conducted from the Senate chamber on April 2. The desks had been removed to make room for a larger audience, hushed and seemingly overawed with a sense of public loss. It was this common feeling that dominated the room, and subordinated all the impressive and solemn pomp of a state funeral. Vice President Millard Fillmore was in the chair; on his left was the

Speaker of the House, on his right the President of the United States. In the rows of seats that filled the room were the members of the Senate and of the House, the Cabinet, the diplomatic corps, the Supreme Court Justices. The simple metal casket was brought in accompanied by the pallbearers: Willie P. Mangum, Henry Clay, Daniel Webster, Lewis Cass, William R. King, and John M. Berrien. There was an impressive sermon by the Reverend C. M. Butler, the Senate Chaplain, and the whole cortege accompanied the casket to the Congressional Cemetery, where it was laid in a vault to await instructions from the family.[13]

4

Three weeks later, with public buildings of the Capital still draped in black, the body of South Carolina's greatest son began its journey home. With Calhoun on this final passage were twenty-five distinguished South Carolinians named by Governor Seabrook; Senators Mason of Virginia, Dickinson of New York, Clarke of Rhode Island, Davis of Mississippi, and Dodge of Iowa; Representatives Venable and Holmes; and two of the dead Senator's sons, Andrew and Patrick. Webster, whose own health had compelled him to decline a position on the Senate committee, followed the procession to the Virginia landing, and so did William Winston Seaton, joint editor of the *National Intelligencer* and perennial Mayor of Washington.[14]

There were solemn ceremonies at every city along the route where the black-shrouded steamer touched, but on April 25 the journey ended in Charleston harbor. The tall spires of St. Philip's and St. Michael's pierced the fog as revenue cutters and harbor craft moved out to escort the funeral vessel to her mooring. The lifting mist revealed a city draped in black, and the body was brought to rest on its native shore to the accompaniment of tolling bells and minute guns. In Charleston John M. Berrien, the sixth member of the Senate committee, joined the funeral party.

The body of the dead Senator was carried first to Citadel Square, where silent thousands bared their heads as the somber procession drew near. There the Senate committee passed its trust to the state authorities, and after elaborate ceremonies the mortal object of all this veneration was moved to the City Hall. The black-draped hearse was followed through otherwise deserted streets by the men and women of Charleston. In the City Hall the body lay in state for a day, and an unbroken line of mourners filed past, from dawn to nightfall. The burial service was read in St. Philip's Church the following day by Bishop Christopher Gadsden, and John C. Calhoun was laid to rest in the quiet churchyard across the street. It was not his wish to lie there, but the spontaneous demand of South Carolina's greatest city. A committee of twenty-five friends and neighbors had come from Pendleton to bring him home, but they were disappointed, and the legislature eventually decreed that he should remain where he was.[15]

So he lies beneath a graying monument, all but obscured by the more pretentious memorials to the dead of later days—lies among others, great in the history of South Carolina and of the nation, rather than beneath the rich soil of his own Fort Hill. To him it would make very little difference, for he never meant his monument to be of stone, nor his final resting place to be of bricks and sod.

5

"Mr. Calhoun's death has deified his opinions," wrote a Northern jurist in June of 1850, "and he is therefore more dangerous dead than living." [16] The choice of adjective is significant. For the last twenty years or more of his life Calhoun's views as to the nature and limits of the government of the United States were regarded by a growing body of his countrymen as "dangerous." Dangerous to the Union, they would have explained, but that was not really what they meant. Calhoun's ideas were dangerous because they threatened the growth and prosperity of the Northern states, the spread of industrialism with its quickly mounting profits, the rapid conquest and exploitation of the continent. They were dangerous not because they challenged the existing order of things but because they would tend to make that order permanent and inhibit change.

Calhoun was as sincerely anxious to preserve the Union as any of his critics, but he wanted to preserve it as he had known it in the days of the Virginia Dynasty. His model was Jefferson, but he built on only one facet of the Jeffersonian tradition, enlarging the doctrine of the Kentucky Resolutions of 1798 into a complete philosophy of government. Intelligent, sincere, incorruptible, in many ways a man of prophetic vision, Calhoun was both a magnificent and a tragic figure, battling to maintain the economic prosperity of an agrarian world in the face of the industrial revolution.

It was inevitable that men who held his ideas to be dangerous would come in time to question his motives. The single-minded zeal and ingenuity with which he fought could not fail to make enemies; and his defense of slavery, by-product though it was, lent a moral stigma to his cause that made hostile evaluation certain. His influence, both as statesman and as thinker, was deep and lasting, and was freely acknowledged in his own time, but his contemporaries disagreed almost violently as to whether its tendency was good or evil. He symbolized a basic conflict between two widely different forms of society, and so he was and still remains a controversial figure.

Immediately following Calhoun's death and throughout the next decade interpretations of his career and influence, both publicly and privately expressed, were as far apart as the poles. There were Northern intellectuals who lamented his passing but thought the course of his later years disastrous to the country, while leaders of thought in the South regarded his death as breaking the last link with the political ideals of the Revolution. It was possible for Southerners like Henry S. Foote to charge him with a conscious wish to disrupt the Union, and for Northerners like William Plumer to bracket him with Adams, Webster, and Clay as one of the great men of his time. Reactions to him were emotional, conditioned by personal relationships, by place of residence and economic ties, by ambitions thwarted or advanced through his intervention or the impact of his thought.

As the South rushed headlong toward the ultimate test of Calhoun's logic, opinions as to his motives and the direction of his influence became still more sharply divided. The South, as plans for a Confederacy of her own took firmer shape, came to look on the great Nullifier not as the unwilling prophet but as the active partisan of secession, while the North, with the twisted history of Blair and Benton for confirmation, laid at his door all the evils of the rising sectional conflict. Jefferson Davis, when he took leave of the Senate in January 1861, was at pains to clarify the distinction between Calhoun's position and his own, but it was far too late to convince men inflamed by decades of sectional hostility that the South Carolina Senator had sought only to preserve the Union. Though ten years dead he still personified the slave states, and the slave states were in rebellion. The Northern press, with the license of war, built up the case for his long-standing treason, and survivors of the Jacksonian days like Blair and Kendall and James A. Hamilton, reinterpreted the partisan struggles of the past in the light of the ultimate result.[18]

When hostile armies faced each other in the field at last Calhoun's doctrines, consciously distorted on the one side and imperfectly understood on the other, were accepted by North and South alike as the intellectual genesis of the Confederacy, and they did not survive the final test of battle. The sovereignty passed once and for all from the states to the national government, and Calhoun became to an embittered people the symbol of defeat and destruction. The war had been fought in defense of his ideas, and in the eyes of those who had lost their homes and their loved ones, the responsibility was his.[19]

The ground was thus prepared for the publication of Adams' diary in the 1870's, and for the bitter condemnation of Von Holst in the next decade. It was not until 1900, when the first volume of Calhoun's correspondence was issued under the aegis of the American Historical Association, that it became possible to penetrate the emotionalism of fratricidal war and consider what manner of man this was who aroused such abiding passions in so many breasts.

6

The years of Calhoun's active political life—roughly from 1810 to 1850—were years of expansion and change more rapid and more sweeping than any the world had previously known. It was during this period that the shift from an agrarian to an industrial economy was assured, with all that shift implied in the evolution of social and political institutions. It was a period of intellectual ferment in which the old mercantilist and planter world was cracking beneath the mighty blows of industrial capitalism and technological change. The Constitution of the United States represented the best in seventeenth and eighteenth century political thought, but without reinterpretation it could never have survived the first half century of its existence. The strong national government against which Calhoun fought so long and so ingeniously was the only kind of government that could exercise jurisdiction over an economy wealthy and powerful beyond the wildest imaginings of the founding fathers, but it was nothing inherent in the American idea, or in the Anglo-Saxon race, or in the continental sweep of the environment that brought about the ultimate centralization of power. It was not the decisions of John Marshall nor the arguments of Webster, but the industrial revolution itself that won the day. The enduring bonds of union were not a common heritage nor even a common speech, but the steamboat, the railroad, the telegraph, and all the scientific progeny that followed.

The economic and cultural differences between North and South, had it not been for the development of rapid communication, would undoubtedly have become greater rather than less. The period between the American Revolution and the Civil War was one of sociological differentiation, such as had come about in Europe following the breakup of the Roman Empire. But for the technological advances of the early nineteenth century the process would probably have run its course and the continent would have seen not two or three but a dozen nations, each with its own national characteristics and economy.

It was a process familiar enough to Calhoun's generation. The American Revolution, the French Revolution, the Napoleonic wars, the revolt of the Spanish colonies in the Western Hemisphere, the Texan revolution, and the European uprisings of 1848 all occurred within the span of a long lifetime. To those who lived through any substantial portion of this period, governments must certainly have appeared to be unstable things and regional self-determination the natural order of events. The *Declaration of Independence* had stated the case as clearly as it would ever be stated, and it was inevitable that Southerners who felt themselves oppressed should compare their grievances with those against which their fathers had rebelled. They were undoubtedly correct in their contention that the economic impact of the tariffs of 1828 and 1842 was more damaging to the cotton states than ever the taxes of George III had been to the colonies, and the antislavery agitation, in economic terms, was more disastrous still.

Calhoun was the most articulate and clearest-headed of Southern spokesmen but his influence was consistently thrown to the side of union. He used the real grievances of the planters not to inspire a separatist revolt but to consolidate a pressure bloc whose aim was to secure concessions from the stronger interest. In 1833 and again in

1846 he did secure modification of the tariff, but the antislavery agitation, because of the moral base on which it rested, was not to be stopped that way. It is true that Calhoun's logic justified the ultimate secession of the South; true also that the very stubbornness of his defense of slavery intensified the zeal of the abolitionists and increased their political power. It is not likely, however, that the result would have been materially changed had he never lived. He did not create but only formulated and expressed the attitude of the planter class to which he belonged, seeking always to direct Southern discontent into nonviolent channels.

In the process he developed and refined a constitutional doctrine that would in itself be an adequate defense of the old agrarian order, but it was a doctrine incompatible with the powerful national state required by the industrial economy of the North. This is not to say that Calhoun's reasoning was in any way responsible for the Civil War, even though the end product was the supremacy of the Federal Government. The basic cause of the sectional conflict was a fundamental antagonism between two divergent economies, and as long as the cause remained the conflict was bound to come, sooner or later, no matter how the two contestants rationalized their positions.

Calhoun's genius lay in his awareness of the problem his country faced, and his greatest contribution was his long and patient effort to explain it in terms that would make a peaceable solution possible. The United States was the first great modern nation in which agriculture and industry were both major interests. Calhoun more than any other man drove home the point that policies designed to foster and encourage the one would be ruinous to the other, and we have come at last, though by a different route, to his position. We have recognized the necessity, in a nation embracing many economic interests, for equalizing what he called the burdens and bounties of government. We have done it by direct action through taxation and subsidies, and in the process we have made the central government powerful beyond Calhoun's most gloomy fears; but we have at least recognized the problem with which he struggled, and we have arrived at a solution, however tentative, within the framework of the Constitution—not the Constitution he so painstakingly limited lest the society he cherished be destroyed, but one better suited to the needs of a more complex age and perhaps not less responsive to the welfare of those who are governed by it.

The federation of sovereign states that seemed to Calhoun the only practical way to reconcile the conflicting demands of agriculture and industry was essentially static, without adequate room for the development of a dynamic society. The concurrent veto was negative, defensive, designed to preserve the order of things as they were. In action it could only obstruct, until obstruction became intolerable and had to be swept aside. Thoroughgoing conservative that he was, Calhoun came at last to place security for his class above all other considerations, and when security becomes an end in itself the society is doomed.

In his rejection of the democratic dogma, and in his failure to appreciate the moral values in the antislavery crusade, Calhoun was following out the premises of his own mechanistic theory of society. His estimate of human nature was low, but his analysis of the political process is still largely valid, and is nowhere better illustrated than in his own career. His defense of the minority against the weight of numbers is timeless in its application, and his insistence that the power of government must somehow be controlled is a universal condition of human freedom.

For himself and in his own time his path was marked by repeated failures, but his place in history cannot be determined in terms of his own political fortunes. As statesman he came to grips with the basic problems of government, and clarified the issues for a half century of partisan conflict. As political theorist he showed more clearly than any other American has ever done how the political process works.

NOTES, BIBLIOGRAPHY, ACKNOWLEDGMENTS
AND INDEX

NOTES

CHAPTER I

[1] *Niles' Weekly Register,* LVIII, 152-159.

[2] Henry A. Wise, *Seven Decades of the Union,* 174-179.

[3] *Niles,* LVIII, 147-152.

[4] *Historical Statistics,* 245, 297; G. R. Taylor, "Wholesale Commodity Prices at Charleston, S. C., 1796-1861," *Journal of Economic and Business History,* IV, part 2, 848-868, appendix, table I; Samuel Rezneck, "The Social History of an American Depression, 1837-1843," *American Historical Review,* XL (July 1935), 662-687.

[5] R. C. McGrane, *Foreign Bondholders and American State Debts,* 6.

[6] J. P. Bretz, "Economic Background of the Liberty Party," *Am. Hist. Rev.,* XXXIV (January 1929), 250-264; Dwight L. Dumond, *Antislavery Origins of the Civil War,* 83ff.

[7] The extravagances of the campaign may be conveniently followed in the files of the *National Intelligencer* (Whig), the *Madisonian* (Democratic Whig), the Washington *Globe* (Democratic), and the Charleston *Mercury* (State Rights). See also James A. Hamilton, *Reminiscences,* 314-315; Duff Green to Calhoun, Aug. 21, 1840, J. Franklin Jameson, ed., *Correspondence of John C. Calhoun,* 828-829 (hereafter cited as *Correspondence*); Joseph Story to Mrs. Story, Feb. 9, 1840, W. W. Story, *Life and Letters of Joseph Story,* II, 328.

[8] *Congressional Globe,* 26th Cong., 1st sess., 433; Calhoun to James Edward Calhoun, Feb. 1, 1840, *Correspondence,* 445; to J. H. Hammond, Apr. 2, 1840, *ibid.,* 452; to Andrew P. Calhoun, June 8, 1840, *ibid.,* 460; to J. M. McCalla, *et al.,* June 27, 1840, Charleston *Mercury,* Aug. 7, 1840; to James Blake, *et al.,* July 3, 1840, Washington *Globe,* Sept. 5, 1840; to J. E. Scott, *et al.,* Aug. 11, 1840, Charleston *Mercury,* Sept. 15, 1840.

[9] *E.g.,* Oran Follett to Thurlow Weed, Sept. 18, 1840, Historical and Philosophical Society of Ohio, *Quarterly Publications,* XI, No. 1, 23; Levi Woodbury to Cyrus Barton, Oct. 13, 1840, Woodbury Papers.

[10] See, *e.g.,* D. Torrence to George P. Torrence, Aug. 4, 1840, Historical and Philosophical Society of Ohio, *Quarterly Publications,* III, No. 3, 89-90; and Harrison's Carthage, Ohio, speech of Aug. 20, 1840, *Niles,* LIX, 42-43.

[11] Hunter to his constituents, June 29, 1840, Charleston *Courier,* July 13, 1840; McDuffie to A. Burt, Aug. 27, 1840, McDuffie Papers, Duke.

[12] Calhoun to Virgil Maxcy, Mar. 28, July 20, 1840, Maxcy Papers; to A. P. Calhoun, Sept. 25, 1840, *Correspondence,* 465; to Burt, Aug. 20, 1840, *ibid.,* 463.

[13] See, *e.g.,* James M. Walker to J. H. Hammond, Aug. 22, 1840, Hammond Papers.

[14] Washington *Globe,* Nov. 9, 1840; Charleston *Courier,* Nov. 11, 1840.

[15] Calhoun to Burt, Nov. 2, 1840, *Correspondence*, 465-466; Hammond to Judge Harper, Oct. 6, 1840, Hammond Papers; Charleston *Mercury*, Nov. 16, 1840; Charleston *Courier*, Dec. 7, 1840.

[16] Calhoun to F. H. Elmore, Nov. 24, 1840, Elmore Papers.

[17] Calhoun to A. P. Calhoun, Nov. 22, 1840, *Correspondence*, 467.

CHAPTER II

[1] Benton to Moses Dawson, Dec. 6, 1840, *Niles*, LIX, 310; Washington *Globe*, Nov. 11, 14, 24, Dec. 3, 1840; Jackson to Van Buren, Nov. 12, 24, 1840, J. S. Bassett, ed., *Correspondence of Andrew Jackson*, VI, 82, 83; to Blair, Dec. 18, 1840, *ibid.*, 85. Also J. L. Petigru to Hammond, Dec. 14, 1840, Hammond Papers; W. B. Slaughter to W. C. Rives, Jan. 5, 1841 [misdated 1840], Rives Papers; Calhoun to Virgil Maxcy, Feb. 19, 1841, Maxcy Papers.

[2] Harrison to Clay, Nov. 15, 1840, Calvin Colton, ed., *Works of Henry Clay*, V, 446.

[3] Clay to Francis Brooke, Dec. 8, 1840, *ibid.*, 446-447; Glyndon G. Van Deusen, *Life of Henry Clay*, 337-338.

[4] Harrison to Webster, Dec. 1, 1840, *Writings and Speeches of Daniel Webster*, XVIII, 90-91; George Ticknor Curtis, *Life of Daniel Webster*, II, 48. Cabinet speculations may be followed in the newspapers of the day and in the correspondence of leading partisans.

[5] Washington *Globe*, Feb. 9, 1841; New York *Herald*, Feb. 11, 12, 1841; A. O. P. Nicholson to James K. Polk, Feb. 12, 1841, Polk Papers.

[6] Calhoun to Mrs. Thomas G. Clemson, Feb. 17, 1841, *Correspondence*, 474-475; to Virgil Maxcy, Feb. 19, 1841, Maxcy Papers; E. F. Ellet, *Court Circles of the Republic*, 284.

[7] *Cong. Globe*, 26th, 2nd, 14. Clay's platform was set forth during the campaign in a widely publicized speech in his native Hanover County, Virginia. See *Niles*, LVIII, 322-326; and Van Deusen, *Clay*, 335-336.

[8] *Cong. Globe*, 26th, 2nd, 19-23; Calhoun to James Edward Calhoun, Dec. 26, 1840, *Correspondence*, 469.

[9] *Cong. Globe*, 26th, 2nd, 65, 90-91, 105, 130.

[10] *Cong. Globe*, 26th, 2nd, 120, and Appendix, 123-126; R. K. Crallé, ed., *Works of John C. Calhoun*, III, 560-583.

[11] Webster's speech was not reported but Calhoun summarized the points made for the benefit of his son-in-law. See Calhoun to Clemson, Jan. 26, 1841, *Correspondence*, 473-474.

[12] *Cong. Globe*, 26th, 2nd, 134, and Appendix, 135-139; Calhoun's *Works*, III, 583-609.

[13] Calhoun to Burt, Jan. 24, 1841, *Correspondence*, 472.

[14] Gilbert H. Barnes, *The Anti-Slavery Impulse*, 178.

[15] New York *Herald*, Feb. 3, 1841; Nicholson to Polk, Feb. 2, 1841, Polk Papers; J. M. Niles to Gideon Welles, Feb. 7, 1841, Welles Papers.

[16] Peter B. Porter to Clay, Jan. 28, Feb. 20, 1841, Clay's *Works*, V, 448-450; New York *Herald*, Feb. 25, 26, 1841.

[17] There are numerous accounts. The text follows the Whig versions of the New York *Herald*, Mar. 5, 1841; *National Intelligencer*, Mar. 5, 1841, conveniently reprinted in *Niles*, LX, 18-19; Allan Nevins, ed., *Diary of Philip Hone*, 530; C. F. Adams, ed., *Memoirs of John Quincy Adams*, X, 439 (hereafter cited as Adams, *Diary*); and Nathan Sargent, *Public Men and Events*,

II, 114. The characterization of the horse is from Adams. The *Intelligencer* called it a "white charger."

[18] *Senate Journal*, 26th, 2nd, 250-251.

[19] J. D. Richardson, comp., *Messages and Papers of the Presidents*, 1860-1876; Charleston *Mercury*, Mar. 9, 1841. See also Washington *Globe*, Mar. 4, 1841; *Madisonian*, Mar. 6, 1841; *National Intelligencer*, Mar. 9, 1841; Charleston *Courier*, Mar. 9, 1841; J. H. Hammond, *Diary*, Mar. 17, 1841, Hammond Papers.

[20] J. M. Niles to Gideon Welles, Mar. 6, 1841, Welles Papers.

[21] Nicholson to Polk, Mar. 8, 1841, Polk Papers; Van Buren to Jackson, Mar. 12, 1841, Jackson's *Correspondence*, VI, 93; Clay to Harrison, Mar. 13, 1841, Clay Papers; Harrison to Clay, Mar. 13, 1841, *ibid.*; Clay to Harrison, Mar. 15, 1841, Clay's *Works*, V, 452-453; New York *Herald*, Mar. 11, 19, 1841; *Madisonian*, Mar. 19, 1841; *National Intelligencer*, Mar. 20, 1841; Sargent, *Men and Events*, II, 116; Van Deusen, *Clay*, 339-342.

[22] Adams, *Diary*, X, 444; Poinsett to Van Buren, Mar. 24, 1841, Van Buren Papers.

[23] Washington *Globe*, Mar. 29, Apr. 1, 2, 3, 5, 1841; *National Intelligencer*, Mar. 31, Apr. 1, 2, 3, 1841; *Madisonian*, Mar. 30, Apr. 1, 3, 6, 1841; W. B. Lewis to W. C. Rives, Mar. 31, Apr. 1, 2, 3, 4, 1841, Rives Papers; H. D. Gilpin to Van Buren, Apr. 3, 1841, Van Buren Papers; Poinsett to Van Buren, Apr. 4, 1841, *ibid.*; Adams, *Diary*, X, 454-456.

[24] Lewis to Rives, Apr. 4, 1841, Rives Papers; T. Allen to Rives, Apr. 4, 1841, *ibid.*; L. Rogers to Rives, Apr. 4, 1841, *ibid.*; W. B. Hodgson to Rives, Apr. 4, 1841; *ibid.*; Forsyth to Van Buren, Apr. 3, 4, 1841, Van Buren Papers; Gilpin to Van Buren, Apr. 3, 1841, *ibid.*; Poinsett to Van Buren, Apr. 4, 1841, *ibid.*; Pendleton *Messenger*, Apr. 16, 1841.

CHAPTER III

[1] Washington *Globe*, Apr. 6, 1841; Charleston *Courier*, Apr. 12, 1841. The *Courier's* Washington correspondent, Elias Kingman, was one of the very best of the Capital's early newsmen, and his stories are often more detailed and almost invariably more objective than those in the Washington papers. See also L. G. Tyler, *Letters and Times of the Tylers*, II, 11-12.

[2] See, *e.g.*, Adams, *Diary*, X, 456-457; *Cong. Globe*, 27th, 1st, 4-5.

[3] Adams, *Diary*, X, 456-457; N. Niles to W. C. Rives, Apr. 4, 1841, Rives Papers; Hone, *Diary*, 534-535; N. Carroll to W. P. Mangum, Apr. 7, 1841, Mangum Papers; Gov. John Davis to Webster, Apr. 23, 1841, Webster Papers; W. C. Preston to Mangum, May 3, 1841 [misdated 1840], Mangum Papers; Charleston *Courier*, Apr. 8, 1841; New York *Herald*, Apr. 6, 7, 1841; Washington *Globe*, Apr. 5, 1841. Also F. P. Blair to Jackson, Apr. 4, 1841, Jackson's *Correspondence*, VI, 98.

[4] Hammond, *Diary*, Apr. 9, 1841, Hammond Papers; F. W. Pickens to Hammond, Apr. 13, 1841, *ibid.*; Charleston *Mercury*, Apr. 15, 1841; Pendleton *Messenger*, Apr. 23, 1841.

[5] Wise, *Seven Decades*, 181-182; Duff Green, *Facts and Suggestions*, 139; Green to A. P. Upshur, Dec. 29, 1842, Tyler, *Times of the Tylers*, II, 25-26; Charleston *Courier*, Apr. 12, 1841. The Address is in Richardson, *Messages and Papers of the Presidents*, 1889-1892.

[6] *Madisonian,* Apr. 13, 23, 1841; Washington *Globe,* Apr. 29, 1841; Hone, *Diary,* 542; Blair to Jackson, May 16, 1841, Jackson's *Correspondence,* VI, 113; David Hoffman to Green, May 17, 21, 23, June 6, 1841, Green Papers; W. B. Lewis to Rives, Apr. 13, 1841, Rives Papers.

[7] Adams, *Diary,* X, 465; Ewing to Clay, May 8, 1841, Clay Papers.

[8] Richardson, *Messages and Papers of the Presidents,* 1893-1904; *Cong. Globe,* 27th, 1st, 8, and Appendix, 6; Washington *Globe,* June 1, 1841.

[9] *Cong. Globe,* 27th, 1st, 11, 12, 52.

[10] *Ibid.,* 2-63, *passim;* Clay to E. M. Letcher, June 11, 1841, Mrs. Chapman Coleman, *Life of John J. Crittenden,* I, 156-157; A. V. Brown to Polk, June 12, 1841, Polk Papers; Charleston *Mercury,* June 14, 1841; S. H. Butler to Hammond, June 16, 1841, Hammond Papers.

[11] *Cong. Globe,* 27th, 1st, 22; Washington *Globe,* June 24, 1842.

[12] *Cong. Globe,* 27th, 1st, 13-14, 21, 36; Calhoun's *Works,* III, 615-618; Woodbury to Mrs. Woodbury, June 9, 1841, Woodbury Papers.

[13] *Cong. Globe,* 27th, 1st, 39, 48-49, 79-81; *Senate Documents* 17 and 32.

[14] *Cong. Globe,* 27th, 1st, Appendix, 61-64; Calhoun's *Works,* III, 629-648.

[15] *House Journal,* 27th, 1st, 175, 188, 222, 234, 241; *Senate Document* 46.

[16] *Senate Journal,* 27th, 1st, 100; *Cong. Globe,* 27th, 1st, Appendix, 123-125; Charleston *Mercury,* July 23, 1841; Calhoun's *Works,* IV, 1-13.

[17] *Senate Journal,* 27th, 1st, 125; *House Journal,* 324, 302, 344-345; Mangum to Mrs. Mangum, Aug. 3, 1841, Mangum Papers. See also Charleston *Mercury,* July 12, 1841; and Calhoun to Micah Sterling, July 24, 1841, Calhoun Papers, SCL.

[18] Wise to N. B. Tucker, June 5, 1841, Tyler, *Times of the Tylers,* II, 37-38; Green, *Facts and Suggestions,* 139-140; Clay to E. M. Letcher, June 11, 1841, Coleman, *Crittenden,* I, 156-157; *Madisonian,* June 8, 1841; *Cong. Globe,* 27th, 1st, 48-49; *Senate Document* 17.

[19] A. V. Brown to Polk, June 12, 1841, Polk Papers; Nicholson to Polk, June 14, 1841, *ibid.; National Intelligencer,* June 14, 1841, *et seq.*

[20] *Cong. Globe,* 27th, 1st, 79-81; *Senate Document* 32; *National Intelligencer,* June 22, 1841.

[21] Silas Wright to J. M. Niles, June 27, 1841, Welles Papers; to Van Buren, June 21, July 10, 1841, Van Buren Papers; Clay to F. Brooke, July 4, 1841, Clay's *Works,* V, 454; Wise to Tucker, July 11, 1841, Tyler, *Times of the Tylers,* II, 52; *Cong. Globe,* 27th, 1st, 133, 140, 152; Charleston *Courier,* June 28, July 5, 1841; New York *Herald,* July 13, 1841.

[22] *Senate Journal,* 27th, 1st, 123; W. L. Marcy to Van Buren, July 20, 28, 1841, Van Buren Papers; Charleston *Courier,* Aug. 2, 1841.

[23] Thomas Ewing, "Diary," *Am. Hist. Rev.,* XVIII (October 1912), 99; Charleston *Courier,* Aug. 18, 1841; D. Seldon to Mangum, Aug. 12, 1841, Mangum Papers; R. McClellan to Van Buren, Aug. 15, 1841, Van Buren Papers; Calhoun to A. P. Calhoun, Aug. 14, 1841, Calhoun Papers, Duke; J. R. Ingersoll to V. Maxcy, Aug. 11, 1841, Maxcy Papers.

[24] Woodbury to Mary E. Woodbury, Aug. 16, 1841, Woodbury Papers; Nicholson to Polk, Aug. 16, 1841, Polk Papers; "Memorandum regarding the Bank Bills & the Vetos," in Webster's hand, Webster Papers; Richardson, *Messages and Papers of the Presidents,* 1916-1921; *Senate Journal,* 27th, 1st, 165-169; *National Intelligencer,* Aug. 17, 1841; Charleston *Courier,* Aug. 20, 1841; Wade Hampton to Clay, Aug. 20, 1841, Clay's *Works,* V, 455; Hone, *Diary,* 552-553;

Charleston *Mercury*, Aug. 20, 1841; Pendleton *Messenger*, Aug. 20, 27, 1841; Hammond, *Diary*, Aug. 22, 1841, Hammond Papers; Washington *Globe*, Aug. 16, 1841. Also Wise, *Seven Decades*, 184.

25 *Cong. Globe*, 27th, 1st, 339-342, 346, and Appendix, 344-345; Marcy to Van Buren, Aug. 17, 1841, Van Buren Papers; Webster, "Bank Memorandum," Webster Papers; Ewing, "Diary," *op. cit.*, 99-103; *Madisonian*, Aug. 19, 1841; Charleston *Courier*, Aug. 19, 23, 1841; Tyler, *Times of the Tylers*, II, 71-103; O. P. Chitwood, *John Tyler*, 228-229.

26 *Cong. Globe*, 27th, 1st, 352, and Appendix, 222-224. The speeches of Clay and Rives are more fully reported in *Niles*, LX, 403-406, and LXI, 6-10. See also the *Madisonian*, Aug. 21, 1841; and Claude M. Fuess, *Caleb Cushing*, I, 303-304.

27 Webster, "Bank Memorandum," Webster Papers; Webster to Tyler, Aug. 20, 1841, Webster's *Writings*, XVI, 354; *Cong. Globe*, 27th, 1st, 363-364.

28 Webster, "Bank Memorandum," Webster Papers; Ewing, "Diary," *op. cit.*, 104; Webster to H. Ketchum, Aug. 22, 1841, Webster's *Writings*, XVIII, 109; *House Journal*, 27th, 1st, 409; Wise, *Seven Decades*, 189. The choice of Wise for intermediary was no doubt because he was Sergeant's son-in-law as well as Tyler's confidant.

29 *Cong. Globe*, 27th, 1st, 369-370, and Appendix, 332-337; Calhoun's *Works*, IV, 13-43. See also Washington *Globe*, June 24, 1842; and Calhoun's remarks in the Senate, Mar. 16, 1842, *Works*, IV, 105-106.

30 *Cong. Globe*, 27th, 1st, 385; Ewing, "Diary," *op. cit.*, 104-106; New York *Herald*, Aug. 26, 27, 1841; Charleston *Courier*, Aug. 30, 1841; Adams, *Diary*, XI, 3-4; *Senate Journal*, 27th, 1st, 234, 237; *House Journal*, 461-462.

31 Richardson, *Messages and Papers of the Presidents*, 1921-1925; *Cong. Globe*, 27th, 1st, 444.

32 Webster to Ketchum, Sept. 10, 11, 1841, Webster's *Writings*, XVIII, 110, and XVI, 356-358; Adams, *Diary*, XI, 14; Hone, *Diary*, 560. A typical query was addressed by Webster to Peter Harvey, then a Boston merchant, on September 10: "Do the Whigs of Mass. think I ought to quit or ought to stay? Yrs, D. W." *Writings*, XVI, 356.

33 Crittenden to R. P. Letcher, Sept. 11, 1841, Coleman, *Crittenden*, I, 165-166; Washington *Globe*, Sept. 11, 1841; Charleston *Courier*, Sept. 14, 15, 1841; New York *Herald*, Sept. 14, 1841; Tyler, *Times of the Tylers*, II, 96, 97.

34 *National Intelligencer*, Sept. 11, 13, 1841; *Madisonian*, Sept. 16, 1841; *Niles*, LXI, 35-36.

35 Duff Green to Judge John McLean, Aug. 26, 1841, McLean Papers.

36 *Madisonian*, Sept. 14, Oct. 9, 1841.

37 *National Intelligencer*, Oct. 16, 1841; Calhoun to Maxcy, Sept. 13, 1841, Maxcy Papers.

CHAPTER IV

1 Charleston *Courier*, Feb. 11, 13, 1840; Charleston *Mercury*, Feb. 12, 14, 1840.

2 Charleston *Courier*, Feb. 13, 1840; Charleston *Mercury*, Feb. 14, 1840.

3 For background see C. M. Wiltse, *John C. Calhoun, Nullifier, 1829-1839*, 405. The whole episode is documented in the Hammond Papers for the first eight or nine months of 1840, and in the files of the South Carolina papers,

particularly the *Courier* and the *Mercury,* for the same period. While individual letters and newspaper issues will be cited as occasion seems to require, no attempt will be made to list all that are relevant.

⁴ Pickens to Hammond, Jan. 22, Feb. 1, 1840, Hammond Papers; Butler to Hammond, Jan. 30, Feb. 5, 1840, *ibid.*

⁵ Charleston *Mercury,* Feb. 14, 1840; Pickens to Hammond, Feb. 18, 19, Mar. 8, 1840, Hammond Papers; S. H. Butler to Hammond, Feb. 19, Mar. 6, 1840, *ibid.;* Calhoun to Hammond, Feb. 23, 1840, *Correspondence,* 448-450; F. H. Elmore to J. Rogers, Feb. 14, 1840, Elmore Papers; Elmore to Pickens, Feb. 24, 1840, *ibid.;* Rogers to Elmore, Feb. 25, 1840, *ibid.;* Pendleton *Messenger,* Feb. 28, 1840.

⁶ The Calhoun-Hammond correspondence, with some omissions, is in *Correspondence,* 451-462, and 818-828, *passim.* The omissions may be checked in the Hammond Papers. See Hammond Papers generally for March-May 1840, especially Pickens to Hammond, May 28, 1840, and S. H. Butler to Hammond, May 29, 1840.

⁷ Charleston *Courier,* and Charleston *Mercury,* August-October 1840; Hammond to Pickens, Sept. 8, 1840, Hammond Papers; to T. T. Player, Sept. 9, 1840, *ibid.;* Player to Hammond, Sept. 16, 1840, *ibid.;* B. M. Pearson to Hammond, Oct. 7, 1840, *ibid.;* Pickens to Hammond, Oct. 16, 1840, *ibid.*

⁸ Hammond to Isaac Hayne, Jan. 21, 1841, Hammond Papers; to Pickens, Jan. 27, 1841, *ibid.*

⁹ M. E. Cam to Hammond, Feb. 15, 1841, Hammond Papers. In a letter dated Nov. 18, 1841, *ibid.,* Cam states explicitly, on Albert Rhett's authority, that the original proposition to Hammond "came from Mr. Calhoun through R. Barnwell Rhett."

¹⁰ See especially Hammond to Cam, Mar. 18, June 20, 1841, Hammond Papers; Cam to Hammond, Sept. 2, 1841, *ibid.;* J. M. Walker to Hammond, Oct. 6, 1841, *ibid.;* and entries in Hammond's diary for Mar. 25, June 20, July 17, 21, and Sept. 10, 1841, *ibid.*

¹¹ Calhoun to A. Burt, Nov. 28, 1841, *Correspondence,* 495-497.

¹² Charleston *Mercury,* Oct. 28, 1841, Feb. 10, 1842; D. D. Wallace, *History of South Carolina,* II, 476; Hammond, *Diary,* Dec. 16, 19, 1841, Hammond Papers; A. Rhett to Hammond, Feb. 6, 26, 1842, *ibid.;* Hammond to Rhett, Feb. 13, 1842, *ibid.*

CHAPTER V

¹ St. George L. Sioussat, "Duff Green's 'England and the United States,' " American Antiquarian Society, *Proceedings,* n.s., XL (October 1930), 175-276, is the most complete account.

² For much of the economic background in this chapter I have relied on Thomas P. Martin, "The Upper Mississippi Valley in Anglo-American Anti-Slavery and Free Trade Relations: 1837-1842," *Mississippi Valley Historical Review,* XV (September 1928), 204-220; and to a lesser extent upon the same writer's "Free Trade and the Oregon Question, 1842-1846," *Facts and Factors in Economic History,* 470-491. I am also indebted to Dr. Martin for many stimulating discussions of the points here treated.

³ See Calhoun's speech of Feb. 5, 1840, in *Works,* III, 407-439. Also New York *Herald,* Jan. 9, 1840.

4 McGrane, *Foreign Bondholders and American State Debts,* treats all aspects of the problem. See especially Chaps. 1 and 2. Also F. W. Pickens to J. H. Hammond, Apr. 4, 1840, Hammond Papers.

5 Thomas A. Bailey, *Diplomatic History of the American People,* 213-215. For Calhoun's activities in this episode see *Correspondence,* 644.

6 T. P. Martin, "Some International Aspects of the Anti-Slavery Movement, 1818-1823," *Journal of Economic and Business History,* I (November 1928), 137-148. Eric Williams, *Capitalism and Slavery,* is illuminating on this whole problem. See especially page 135ff.

7 Martin, "Upper Mississippi Valley in Anglo-American Anti-Slavery and Free Trade Relations," *Mississippi Valley Historical Review,* XV (September 1928), 208-211; "Free Trade and the Oregon Question," *Facts and Factors in Economic History,* 471-478; Gilbert H. Barnes, *The Anti-Slavery Impulse,* 171ff; Julian P. Bretz, "Economic Background of the Liberty Party," *Am. Hist. Rev.,* XXXIV (January 1929), 250-264.

8 See *Senate Document* 119, 26th, 1st, and Calhoun's speech on the *Enterprise* case, Mar. 13, 1840, *Works,* III, 462-487.

9 *Cong. Globe,* 26th, 1st, 233, and Appendix, 266-270; Calhoun's *Works,* III, 462-487; Calhoun to Mrs. Clemson, Mar. 24, 1840, *Correspondence,* 451.

10 Calhoun to Virgil Maxcy, Mar. 28, 1840, Maxcy Papers; Richard Rush to Andrew Stevenson, Apr. 8, 1840, Stevenson Papers; Washington *Globe,* Mar. 23, 1840; Charleston *Mercury,* Mar. 28, 1840.

11 Sioussat, *op. cit.,* 182ff; Duff Green, *Facts and Suggestions,* 119ff.

12 Richardson, *Messages and Papers of the Presidents,* 1930-1931.

13 Albert B. Corey, *The Crisis of 1830-1842 in Canadian-American Relations,* 27-37.

14 *Ibid.,* 130ff. Relevant documents are in William R. Manning, ed., *Diplomatic Correspondence of the United States, Canadian Relations,* III.

15 Corey, *op. cit.,* 139-140; *Cong. Globe,* 26th, 2nd, 170-171; *House Document* 33; Green, *Facts and Suggestions,* 143; Adams, *Diary,* X, 422.

16 Manning, *op. cit.,* 616-620, 624-626, 136-146. See also Jared Sparks to W. H. Prescott, Mar. 9, 1841, Roger Wolcott, ed., *Correspondence of William Hickling Prescott, 1833-1847,* 213; Hone, *Diary,* 537-538.

17 Corey, *op. cit.,* 141-145; Charleston *Mercury,* June 30, July 20.

18 Sioussat, *op. cit.,* 180-181; Green, *Facts and Suggestions,* 142ff; Everett to Webster, Dec. 31, 1841, Manning, *op. cit.,* 685-686.

19 Sioussat, *op. cit.,* 182-192; E. F. Baker, *Henry Wheaton,* 197ff.

20 Sioussat, *op. cit.,* 192-199; Baker, *Wheaton,* 200-201.

21 *Cong. Globe,* 27th, 2nd, 110, 203-204; *Senate Documents* 51, 137; Theodore Weld to Angelina G. Weld and Sarah Grimké, Jan. 9, 1842, Gilbert H. Barnes, ed., *Letters of Theodore Dwight Weld, Angelina Grimké Weld, and Sarah Grimké,* 891; Weld to A. G. Weld, Jan. 15 [?], 1842, *ibid.,* 893.

22 Weld to A. G. Weld, Jan. 9, 1842, *Weld-Grimké Letters,* 891.

23 See *Cong. Globe,* 27th, 2nd, 158-215, *passim,* for the whole episode. Also Adams, *Diary,* XI, 75-88; Weld to A. G. Weld, Jan. 23, 25, 30, Feb. 3, 6, 9, 1842, *Weld-Grimké Letters,* 897-917; Washington *Globe,* Feb. 3, 4, 5, 10, 11, 12, 1842. The characterization of Adams is in Calhoun to Mrs. Clemson, Apr. 22, 1842, *Correspondence,* 513.

24 *Cong. Globe,* 27th, 2nd, 342, 344-346, 349; *House Journal,* 784. See also George Ticknor to H. S. Legaré, Mar. 4, 1842, A. Ticknor and G. S. Hillard, *Life,*

Letters and Journals of George Ticknor, II, 199-200; *Southern Quarterly Review,* II (July 1842), 67.

[25] My account, unless otherwise noted, follows C. A. Duniway, "Daniel Webster," *American Secretaries of State and their Diplomacy,* V, 20-49. The documents are in *Cong. Globe,* 27th, 3rd, 2-30; and there is a convenient selection in Webster's *Writings,* XI, 270-328, and XII, 3-64. See also H. G. Soulsby, *Right of Search and the Slave Trade in Anglo-American Relations,* 78-117.

[26] Ashburton to Clay, Apr. 11, 1842, Clay's *Works,* V, 460; Calhoun to Mrs. Clemson, Apr. 22, 1842, *Correspondence,* 513; Ashburton to Webster, undated, in Curtis, *Webster,* II, 120; Adams, *Diary,* XI, 156.

[27] Isaac Holmes tells the story in his Eulogy in the House at the time of Calhoun's death. See J. P. Thomas, ed., *Carolina Tribute to Calhoun,* 30.

[28] The date is not given at all in the *Congressional Globe,* 27th, 3rd, Appendix, 49-53, where the executive proceedings of the previous session are first printed, and is given incorrectly as Aug. 28, 1842, in Calhoun's *Works,* IV, 212. The Washington correspondent of the Charleston *Courier* refers to it in the issue of that paper for Aug. 23, his dispatch being dated Aug. 16, but this is also incorrect. Aug. 16 was a Sunday, and the debate did not start until the following day. A four-day gap was about right for dispatches from Washington in the *Courier,* and in the days of hand-set type a nine might easily be inverted without attracting the notice of a proofreader. Conclusive, however, seems to be the fact that all the other incidents mentioned in the article in question as part of the day's news may be verified from the Senate and House proceedings of the 19th. Calhoun could not have spoken later than that day because the treaty was ratified on the 20th. It could conceivably have been on the 18th, following Benton, but the Missourian's speech, characteristically, was so long as to make such a supposition incompatible with the 9:00 P.M. adjournment. The inexactness of the record is owing to the exclusion of reporters from executive sessions.

[29] Holmes's Eulogy, *Carolina Tribute,* 30; Charleston *Courier,* Aug. 23, 1842; *Madisonian,* Aug. 24, 1842; Webster to Edward Everett, Jan. 29, 1843, Curtis, *Webster,* II, 175; *Senate Executive Journal,* VI, 131. See also Hone, *Diary,* 616-617.

[30] See, *e.g.,* Duff Green to Calhoun, Jan. 24, Aug. 2, 1842, *Correspondence,* 841-844, 846-849; Calhoun to James Edward Calhoun, Nov. 1, 1841, *ibid.,* 494; to Hammond, Dec. 31, 1841, *ibid.,* 502; to Green, Apr. 2, 1842, *ibid.,* 506-508; James Macqueen to Calhoun, Feb. 3, 1842, C. S. Boucher and R. P. Brooks, eds., *Correspondence Addressed to Calhoun,* 170-171 (hereafter cited as *Correspondence II*). Also Duff Green to Sir Robert Peel, July 27, 1843 (draft), Green Papers; and T. P. Martin, "Free Trade and the Oregon Question," *Facts and Factors in Economic History,* 470-491.

CHAPTER VI

[1] See Samuel Rezneck, "Social History of an American Depression, 1837-1843," *Am. Hist. Rev.,* XL (July 1935), 662-687.

[2] *Madisonian,* Nov. 6, 1841. First choice for administration editor was Horace Greeley of the New York *Tribune,* who dickered with Tyler's advisers for a month or more before he finally declined. See Greeley to Thurlow Weed, Dec. 7, 15, 1841, Thurlow Weed, *Autobiography,* 469-471. Also R. K. Crallé

to Calhoun, Oct. 8, 1841, *Correspondence II*, 161-162; David Lambert to Willie P. Mangum, Oct. 14, 1841, Mangum Papers; Clay to John M. Clayton, Nov. 1, 1841, Clayton Papers; B. L. Bogan to Rives, Nov. 3, 1841, Rives Papers; Tyler to A. J. Donelson, Nov. 16, 1841, Donelson Papers.

[3] Tyler to Webster, Oct. 11, 1841, Tyler, *Times of the Tylers*, II, 126; to Tazewell, Nov. 2, 1841, *ibid.*, 129-131; Upshur to Tucker, Nov. 5, Dec. 23, 1841, Jan. 12, 1842, *ibid.*, 153-155, and notes; *Senate Document* 18, 27th, 2nd.

[4] Richardson, *Messages and Papers of the Presidents*, 1927-1942.

[5] Weed to Webster, Dec. 18, 1841, Webster Papers; Jackson to W. B. Lewis, Dec. 28, 1841, Jackson's *Correspondence*, VI, 130-131.

[6] For the contemporary analysis see Calhoun to Nicholson, Dec. 18, 1841, *Correspondence*, 498-499; to Wilson Lumpkin, Dec. 26, 1841, *ibid.*, 499; to Clemson, Dec. 31, 1841, *ibid.*, 500; to Hammond, Dec. 31, 1841, *ibid.*, 501-502; and files of the *National Intelligencer, Madisonian,* Washington *Globe,* and Charleston *Mercury.*

[7] *Cong. Globe*, 27th, 2nd, 69-126, *passim; Senate Journal*, 86, 183-184; John Catron to Polk, Jan. 2, 1842, Polk Papers.

[8] *Senate Journal*, 27th, 2nd, 58, 164-165; *Cong. Globe*, 69, 235-236.

[9] *Cong. Globe*, 27th, 2nd, Appendix, 106-107; Calhoun's *Works*, IV, 44-73. In both sources the speech is misdated Jan. 25, though it was actually delivered on Saturday, Jan. 22, 1842. See *Cong. Globe*, 27th, 2nd, 160; *Senate Journal*, 115-116; and Calhoun to Clemson, Jan. 22 [misdated Jan. 23], 1842, *Correspondence*, 502-503.

[10] *Cong. Globe*, 27th, 2nd, 266, and Appendix, 164-168; Calhoun's *Works*, IV, 74-100.

[11] Calhoun to Mrs. Clemson, Mar. 20, 1842, *Correspondence*, 505; to Clemson, Apr. 3, 1842, *ibid.*, 508; to A. P. Calhoun, Apr. 3, 1842, *ibid.*, 510-511; Hammond, *Diary*, Mar. 16, 1842, Hammond Papers; Charleston *Mercury*, Mar. 14, 1842. The 46,000 copies of the speech circulated from Washington in three weeks are to be compared with 40,000 copies of Webster's second reply to Hayne in 1830, over a four-month span. See Wiltse, *Calhoun, Nullifier*, 66.

[12] *Cong. Globe*, 27th, 2nd, Appendix, 225-230; Calhoun's *Works*, IV, 100-139; Calhoun to Mrs. Clemson, Mar. 20, 1842, *Correspondence*, 505.

[13] Richardson, *Messages and Papers of the Presidents*, 1959-1964.

[14] *Cong. Globe*, 27th, 2nd, 376-377; Sarah Mytton Maury, *Statesmen of America*, 215; Sargent, *Public Men and Events*, II, 160-161; Oliver Dyer, *Great Senators*, 235; Ellet, *Court Circles*, 337-338.

[15] *Cong. Globe*, 27th, 2nd, Appendix, 296-298; Calhoun's *Works*, IV, 140-157.

[16] Benton to Van Buren, Apr. 14, 1842, Van Buren Papers; Wright to J. M. Niles, Apr. 18, 1842, Welles Papers; *Madisonian*, Apr. 30, 1842.

[17] *Cong. Globe*, 27th, 2nd, 574; *Madisonian*, June 2, 4, 1842; Benton to Van Buren, June 8, 1842, Van Buren Papers.

[18] *Cong. Globe*, 27th, 2nd, 591, 634-637, 675-679, 688.

[19] Richardson, *Messages and Papers of the Presidents*, 2033-2036. See also *Madisonian*, June 6, 1842; and Washington *Globe*, June 24, 1842.

[20] *House Journal*, 27th, 2nd, 1080-1110; *Cong. Globe*, 760-763. The House rules were well suited to such class and sectional and special-interest legislation. As it worked in this case, amendments were taken up in Committee of the Whole without a recorded vote, and any that had been rejected, if brought up after the Committee had reported to the House, were excluded by the previous

question. Thus the individual member was forced to take no personal responsibility for rejected amendments before his constituents. See Washington *Globe*, July 16, 1842; and Charleston *Courier*, July 21, 1842.

[21] Calhoun to Clemson, July 10, Aug. 3, 1842, *Correspondence*, 514; R. McClellan to Van Buren, July 24, 1842, Van Buren Papers; *Senate Journal*, 27th, 2nd, 514.

[22] *Cong. Globe*, 27th, 2nd, Appendix, 620-621, 771-775; Calhoun's *Works*, IV, 164-171, 171-201; Charleston *Courier*, Aug. 9, 1842.

[23] When the speech was available in pamphlet form Calhoun sent a copy to his Yale classmate of almost 40 years before, Micah Sterling, in Western New York. The speech, he wrote, "contains my deliberate views of the operation of the prohibitory system, after having watched it with vigilance for more than 20 years. I fear we may not agree, but I feel the deepest conviction, that on their adoption depends the peace & liberty and prosperity of the country." Calhoun to Sterling, Aug. 23, 1842, Calhoun Papers, SCL. See also Charleston *Mercury*, Aug. 23, 1842.

[24] Webster to Tyler, Aug. 8, 6 o'clock, 1842, Webster's *Writings*, XVI, 381; Richardson, *Messages and Papers of the Presidents*, 2036-2042.

[25] *Cong. Globe*, 27th, 2nd, 868, 871-873; *House Journal*, 1254-1255; Hone, *Diary*, 615.

[26] *House Journal*, 27th, 2nd, 1343-1352. Cf. Wiltse, *Calhoun, Nullifier*, 217-218.

[27] Richardson, *Messages and Papers of the Presidents*, 2043-2046; *House Journal*, 27th, 2nd, 1458-1463.

[28] *Cong. Globe*, 27th, 2nd, 925-926; *House Journal*, 1380-1386; Charleston *Courier*, Aug. 26, 1842; Pendleton *Messenger*, Sept. 23, 1842.

[29] *Cong. Globe*, 27th, 2nd, 950-955.

[30] *Ibid.*, 958-960; *Senate Journal*, 629; Calhoun's *Works*, IV, 201-212.

[31] See Calhoun to Duff Green, Aug. 31, 1842, *Correspondence*, 515; R. K. Crallé's introductory remarks on Calhoun's Texas and Oregon papers in Calhoun's *Works*, V, 319, 414; and Rhett to Crallé, Oct. 25, 1854, *Am. Hist. Rev.*, XIII (January 1908), 311. Also T. P. Andrews to Donelson, Sept. 2, 1842, Donelson Papers.

[32] Calhoun to A. P. Calhoun, Aug. 30, 1842, Calhoun Papers, Duke; to Duff Green, Aug. 31, 1842, *Correspondence*, 516; to Hammond, Sept. 24, 1842 [misdated 1841], *Correspondence*, 489-493; Hammond, *Diary*, Oct. 25, 1844, Hammond Papers.

CHAPTER VII

[1] See reference in John A. Stuart to Calhoun, Nov. 19, 1841, *Correspondence*, 834.

[2] Letters received from these political correspondents make up the bulk of the Calhoun Papers for the last months of 1841. See especially Wilson Lumpkin to Calhoun, Oct. 26, 1841, *Correspondence II*, 164-166; and J. H. Howard to Calhoun, Oct. 27, 1841, *Correspondence*, 829-832. The quotation in the text is from Calhoun to John Van Buren and others, Sept. 29, 1841, *ibid.*, 493-494.

[3] Pickens to Woodbury, Oct. 17, 1841, Woodbury Papers. See also Pickens to Calhoun, Oct. 7, 18, 1841, Calhoun Papers, CC; and Oct. 12, 1841, *Correspondence II*, 163-164.

[4] R. K. Crallé to Calhoun, Oct. 8, 1841, *Correspondence II,* 161-162; Calhoun to James Edward Calhoun, Nov. 1, 1841, *Correspondence,* 495. Also Calhoun to A. Burt, Nov. 28, 1841, *ibid.,* 497; to J. R. Matthews, Nov. 1841, Calhoun Papers, LC.

[5] Pickens to Calhoun, Oct. 23, Nov. 6, 1841, Calhoun Papers, CC; J. A. Stuart to Calhoun, Oct. 11, 1841, *Correspondence II,* 162-163; Stuart to Calhoun, Nov. 19, 1841, *Correspondence,* 834-838; J. H. Howard to Calhoun, Nov. 13, 1841, *Correspondence II,* 166-167. See also Thomas Ritchie to Calhoun, Nov. 24, 1841, *Correspondence,* 838-841.

[6] Poinsett to Van Buren, Nov. 28, Dec. 26, 1841, Van Buren Papers.

[7] Calhoun to Virgil Maxcy, Dec. 26, 1841, Maxcy Papers. Cf. to Wilson Lumpkin, Dec. 26, 1841, *Correspondence,* 499-500; to Clemson, Dec. 31, 1841, *ibid.,* 500-501; to Hammond, Dec. 31, 1841, *ibid.,* 501-502.

[8] Charleston *Mercury,* Jan. 31, Feb. 5 *et seq.,* Mar. 29, 1842; J. M. Howry to Polk, Feb. 15, May 10, 1842, Polk Papers; A. V. Brown to Polk, Mar. 22, 1842, *ibid.;* Pickens to McDuffie, Mar. 12, 1842, Calhoun Papers, SCL; Benton to Van Buren, Apr. 17, 1842, Van Buren Papers; Wright to J. M. Niles, Apr. 18, 1842, Welles Papers; D. H. Lewis to C. F. Fisher, Apr. 20, 1842, Fisher Papers; Lewis to Crallé, May 10, 1842, Crallé Papers, CC; F. H. Elmore to Polk, May 12, 1842, Polk Papers.

[9] For the whole Rhode Island story see A. M. Mowry, *The Dorr War,* Chaps. 9-11.

[10] Tyler to Gov. S. W. King, Apr. 11, 1842, *Niles,* LXII, 116-117; Hone, *Diary,* 596-603, *passim;* Jackson to Blair, May 23, 1842, Jackson's *Correspondence,* VI, 153; D. H. Lewis to Crallé, May 30, 31, 1842, Crallé Papers, LC; and files of the Washington *Globe, National Intelligencer,* and *Madisonian* for Apr. and May 1842.

[11] The *Democratic Review,* XI, 201-205, for Aug. 1842 honored Dorr to the extent of a steel engraving and nine columns of text. He is called "the representative of a great and true democratic principle" whose only sin was failure.

[12] *Cong. Globe,* 27th, 2nd, 445-472, *passim;* Adams, *Diary,* XI, 142.

[13] *Cong. Globe,* 27th, 2nd, 496-630, *passim;* Richardson, *Messages and Papers of the Presidents,* 2012-2013. In practice the law was nullified with impunity, as Silas Wright had predicted in debate that it would be.

[14] Washington *Globe,* July 18, 1842; *Cong. Globe,* 27th, 2nd, 849-850; Benton to Van Buren, Aug. 16, 1842, Van Buren Papers.

[15] See, *e.g.,* J. A. Scoville to R. M. T. Hunter, Sept. 11, 1842, C. H. Ambler, ed., *Correspondence of Robert M. T. Hunter,* 41-48 (hereafter cited as *Hunter Correspondence*). The operations of the various committees are detailed in the correspondence of those concerned, especially Hunter, Maxcy, Lewis, Crallé, Woodbury, and Calhoun himself.

[16] Hammond, *Diary,* Sept. 11, 1842, Hammond Papers; Poinsett to Van Buren, Sept. 13, 1842, Van Buren Papers; J. H. Wheeler to Woodbury, Sept. 13, 1842, Woodbury Papers; Poinsett to Donelson, Oct. 24, 1842, Donelson Papers.

[17] Wheeler to Woodbury, Nov. 8, 1842, Woodbury Papers; John Bragg to [Van Buren], Oct. 10, 1842, Donelson Papers.

[18] Hunter to Calhoun, Nov. 7, 1842, Calhoun Papers, CC; Pickens to Calhoun, Nov. 15, 1842, *ibid.;* Richmond *Enquirer,* Dec. 15, 1842; W. H. Roane

to Van Buren, Sept. 11, 1843, Van Buren Papers; C. H. Ambler, "Virginia and the Presidential Succession, 1840-1844," *Turner Essays*, 176-182.

[19] Bancroft to Van Buren, Sept. 28, Nov. 23, 1842, *Mass. Hist. Soc. Proc.*, XLII, 392, 394-395; Isaac O. Barnes to Woodbury, Nov. 22, 25, 1842, Woodbury Papers; Barnes to Calhoun, Jan. 27, 1843, *Correspondence II*, 181-182; Arthur B. Darling, *Political Changes in Massachusetts, 1824-1848*, 284ff.

[20] H. D. A. Donovan, *The Barnburners*, 32-34.

[21] New York *Herald*, Sept. 8, 1842.

[22] Scoville to Hunter, Aug. 29, Sept. 11, Nov. 21, Dec. 11, 1842, *Hunter Correspondence*, 39-57, *passim;* Calhoun to Hunter, Sept. 30, 1842, *ibid.*, 48-49; Rhett to Calhoun, Oct. 13, 1842, *Correspondence*, 851-855; Scoville to Calhoun, Oct. 25, 1842, *ibid.*, 855-857; Elmore to Calhoun, Nov. 2, 1842, *ibid.*, 857-861.

[23] Rhett to Calhoun, Oct. 13, 1842, *Correspondence*, 851-855; D. H. Lewis to Calhoun, Nov. 2, 1842, *Correspondence II*, 181; W. H. Roane to Van Buren, Sept. 11, 1843, Van Buren Papers. John P. Branch, Jackson's first Secretary of the Navy and one of the early victims of the "Eaton Malaria," was one of those who realized the vote-getting potential of Jackson's name. In the fall of 1842 Branch's son, who lived in Nashville, quoted Jackson to the effect that he had done Calhoun an injustice, and that the South Carolina Senator was an honest and patriotic man whom the old General would be glad to see in the White House. The story may have been pure fabrication, or may have had some foundation in an unguarded remark or partially misunderstood question, but whatever its origin Branch made such use of it as he thought best calculated to help Calhoun. Soon papers friendly to the South Carolinian were quoting other papers on this new reconciliation between the chief Nullifier and the author of the Force Act. It was late November before Jackson heard of it, and repudiated it with his customary vigor, but the story continued to circulate. John Bragg to [Van Buren], Oct. 10, 1842, Donelson Papers; Charleston *Mercury*, Nov. 8, 1842, Jan. 25, 1843; Jackson to Van Buren, Nov. 22, 1842, Van Buren Papers; Pendleton *Messenger*, Jan 29, 1843.

[24] Charleston *Courier*, Dec. 5, 1842.

[25] *Ibid.;* Pickens to Hammond, Dec. 1, 1842, Hammond Papers; R. F. W. Allston to his wife, Dec. 10, 1842, J. H. Easterby, *South Carolina Rice Plantation*, 90.

[26] Hammond, *Diary*, Dec. 8, 1842, Hammond Papers; A. Rhett to Hammond, Dec. 9, 1842, *ibid.;* A. Patterson to Hammond, Dec. 9, 1842, *ibid.;* Charleston *Courier*, Dec. 10, 1842; Charleston *Mercury*, Dec. 10, 1842; J. L. Petrigru to Susan Petigru, Dec. 17, 1842; James P. Carson, *Life, Letters and Speeches of James Louis Petigru*, 222-223; Wallace, *History of South Carolina*, II, 487.

[27] Charleston *Courier*, Dec. 12-15, 1842; Charleston *Mercury*, Dec. 13, 1842.

[28] Charleston *Mercury*, Dec. 17, 19, 24, 1842; R. F. W. Allston to his wife, Dec. 15, 1842, Allston Papers; [Albert Rhett] to Armistead Burt, Dec. 23, 1842, McDuffie Papers, Duke. This letter is mistakenly classified as from McDuffie but it is unmistakably from Albert Rhett. See also Hammond, *Diary*, Dec. 19, 1842, Hammond Papers.

CHAPTER VIII

[1] New York *Herald*, Jan. 4, 1843; Ellet, *Court Circles*, 342-343, 349.

[2] Washington *Globe*, Dec. 19, 1842; Savannah *Republican*, Dec. 23, 1842; *Niles*, LXIII, 282; H. L. Turney to Polk, Dec. 8, 1842, Polk Papers.

8 Rives to Cass, Dec. 1, 1842, Rives Papers; Bancroft to Van Buren, Dec. 9, 1842, *Mass. Hist. Soc. Proc.*, XLII, 395-396; Marcy to Van Buren, Dec. 10, 1842, Van Buren Papers; Cass to Rives, Jan 7, 1843, Rives Papers; Levi R. Jones to W. B. Lewis, Jan. 11, 1843 [misdated 1842], *ibid.;* Lewis to Jackson, Jan. 26, 1843, Jackson's *Correspondence*, VI, 183-184; Charleston *Courier*, Jan. 28, 1843. Also *Sketch of the Life and Services of Gen. Lewis Cass of Ohio*, Harrisburg, Pa., Jan. 9, 1843.

4 *National Intelligencer*, Jan. 5, 1843; Washington *Globe*, Jan. 5, 12, 1843; Blair to Jackson, Jan. 29, 1843, Jackson's *Correspondence*, VI, 185-186.

5 Scoville to Hunter, Nov. 21, 1842, *Hunter Correspondence*, 51-55; J. F. Hutton to Hunter, Feb. 18, 1843, *ibid.*, 59-60.

6 T [?] R to Hunter, Jan. 2, 1843, Hunter Papers, CC. Cf. Wm. Deming to Hunter, Jan. 6, 1843, *ibid.*

7 *Democratic Review*, XII, 93-95. The writer was presumably Orestes Brownson whose *Boston Quarterly* had only recently merged with the *Democratic Review*. Brownson's outspoken preference for Calhoun cost him his place on the *Review's* staff later in the year.

8 *E.g.*, B. Brown to Van Buren, Dec. 31, 1842, *North Carolina Historical Review*, XV (April 1938), 141-142; Kendall to Van Buren, Jan. 3, 1843, Van Buren Papers; S. Penn, Jr., to Van Buren, Jan. 4, 1843 [misdated 1842], *ibid.;* Poinsett to Van Buren, Jan. 6, 1843, *ibid.;* H. Turney to Polk, Jan. 10, 1843, Polk Papers; Bancroft to Van Buren, Jan. 12, Feb. 16, 1843, *Mass. Hist. Soc. Proc.*, XLII, 396-398; C. Johnson to Polk, Jan. 29, 1843, Polk Papers. Cf. A. P. Stinson to Woodbury, Mar. 4, 1843, Woodbury Papers; and A. Ten Eyck to Van Buren, Mar. 30, 1843, Van Buren Papers.

9 Richardson, *Messages and Papers of the Presidents*, 2047-2062.

10 *Cong. Globe*, 27th, 3rd, 198-201; Adams, *Diary*, XI, 301. Calhoun's speech is in the Appendix to the *Cong. Globe*, 138-141, and in his *Works*, IV, 238-258, in both sources misdated as Jan. 24. For correct dating see the *Cong. Globe*, 27th, 3rd, 227, and the account in the New York *Herald*, Feb. 2, 1843.

11 Washington *Globe*, Feb. 14, 1843; Webster to Everett, Jan. 29, 1843, Webster's *Writings*, XVI, 393-396; Sidney Breese to Van Buren, Mar. 21, 1843, Van Buren Papers.

12 The shift in Northern sentiment is nowhere better revealed than in the diary of that prince of merchants, Philip Hone. Though he had once seen commerce as the key to all American prosperity, and had admired Calhoun for promoting it, Hone could yet write in December 1842 of the Democratic aspirants to the Presidency: "Anybody but Calhoun, even Van Buren. I am a Northern man, and a New Yorker. As such I can never consent to be ruled by one whose paramount object is one of opposition to the interests and prosperity of this part of the Union." Hone, *Diary*, 638-639. Yet Hone and those who thought with him could never see in this attitude of their own any trace of sectionalism!

13 See files of the Charleston *Mercury* from December 1842 on. The Hammond Papers give the best picture of South Carolina sentiment. The best and most thorough secondary analysis is C. S. Boucher, "Annexation of Texas and the Bluffton Movement in South Carolina," *Mississippi Valley Historical Review*, VI (June 1919), 4ff. See also Wallace, *History of South Carolina*, II, 486-487.

14 Charleston *Mercury*, Jan. 25, 1843; New York *Herald*, Jan. 26, 1843; *Niles*, LXIII, 358-360. Also Laura A. White, *Robert Barnwell Rhett*, 60.

15 D. H. Lewis to Crallé, Dec. 28, 1842, Crallé Papers, LC; R. McClellan to

Van Buren, Feb. 3, 1843, Van Buren Papers; Calhoun to E. A. Brown *et al.*, Jan. 26, 1843, *Niles*, LXIV, 167; Charleston *Mercury*, Feb. 8, 1843.

[16] Calhoun to Hunter, Sept. 30, 1842, *Hunter Correspondence*, 49. H. C. Flagg to Calhoun, Sept. 30, 1842, Calhoun Papers, CC, also requests material for a biographical sketch, which apparently was to be issued by "the Messrs. Babcock" [of the *Palladium*] in New Haven, but Scoville had anticipated him.

[17] J. F. Hutton to Hunter, Jan. 25, 1843, *Hunter Correspondence*, 58; Scoville to Hunter, Feb. 16, 1843, *ibid.*, 59; Hunter to ———, Feb. 20, 1843, *ibid.*, 61; *Niles*, LXIII, 386. The contract is in the Maxcy Papers. It is entirely in Scoville's hand, including an assignment of all "right, title and interest in the above agreement" written across the bottom with a blank for the name of the assignee, presumably Maxcy, since the document is in his papers. Witness to the assignment was Horace P. Russ.

[18] Calhoun to Mrs. Clemson, Feb. 6, 1843, *Correspondence*, 524; to James Edward Calhoun, Feb. 28, 1843, *ibid.*, 525; to Hunter, Feb. 1, 1844, *ibid.*, 562.

[19] Rhett's assertion in his letter of Oct. 25, 1854, to Crallé, and Gaillard Hunt's conclusion from it that Calhoun wrote the *Life* himself, seem even less credible to me than they did when I challenged that thesis in the first volume of the present work. See *Calhoun, Nationalist*, Appendix A, 401-402. I had not at that time seen the Maxcy sketch in the *United States' Telegraph*, Apr. 25, 26, 1831, the manuscript of which is in the Maxcy Papers. See *Calhoun, Nullifier*, 107. The parallelism in organization, sequence, and language between this document and the first half of the campaign *Life* is too close to be accidental. Calhoun, of course, could have made the expansion even though we know he did not write the shorter version, but the internal evidence points to someone who was not personally familiar with the political scene before the 1830's. For example, Calhoun would never have spelled the name of Langdon Cheves as "Cheeves" (*Life*, 11, 17) because he was too accustomed to pronouncing the name as it was pronounced in South Carolina: "Chiv'-is." The name is correctly spelled in the Maxcy sketch, and in other references in the *Life*. Calhoun also knew that his late friend and colleague William Lowndes, for whom one of his own sons was named, was not "a few years" older than he (*Life*, 28), but only a bare five weeks older. The first draft of the last half of the *Life*, covering the period from Jackson's first election to 1843, could still have been written by Calhoun himself, and there is no way of proving, to those not convinced by the evidence thus far, that it was not. The critical reader, however, should have little difficulty in satisfying himself that the style is wrong. The whole idea, moreover, is out of character. His egotism would no doubt have been equal to the degree of self-laudation involved, but it simply would have seemed to him undignified and improper, just as he thought it undignified and improper to go around making stump speeches in his own behalf. He was quite willing to supply the material— in fact, he insisted on supplying it, so that he knew it was as he would have it —but the job itself he would assign to one of his followers. My personal guess, for what it may be worth, is that Scoville did the first expansion of Maxcy's sketch, that Anna Clemson wrote the first draft of the remainder, and that Hunter revised the whole, undoubtedly doing a great deal more along that line than Rhett gives him credit for.

[20] Harper and Brothers to Maxcy, May 22, June 13, 1843, Maxcy Papers; Maxcy to Calhoun, Aug. 29, 1843, Calhoun Papers, CC.

[21] James Broom to Hunter, March 4, 1843, *Hunter Correspondence*, 62; Scoville

to Maxcy, Mar. 12, 1843, Maxcy Papers, second series; Hunter to Maxcy, Mar. 18, 1843, Maxcy Papers; Washington *Spectator,* Mar. 18, 1843. For Heart's association with Blair see Washington *Globe,* May 13, 1841.

[22] Washington *Spectator,* Mar. 18, 1843, *et seq.;* W. B. Lewis to W. C. Rives, Mar. 19, 1843, Rives Papers; Charleston *Mercury,* Mar. 23, 1843; Washington *Globe,* Mar. 25, 1843.

[23] *Senate Executive Journal,* VI, 175-190, *passim.* On the first vote Wise was rejected 12 to 24 and Cushing 19 to 27. On the final vote each man received only two ayes, from Cuthbert of Georgia and Walker of Mississippi. Calhoun and McDuffie had both left the chamber before the third nominations were made. See also Adams, *Diary,* XI, 330.

[24] J. F. Hutton to Hunter, Feb. 18, 1843, *Hunter Correspondence,* 59; W. B. Lewis to Rives, Mar. 15, 1843, Rives Papers.

[25] New York *Herald,* Mar. 9, 15, 1843; *Madisonian,* Mar. 14, 1843; W. B. Lewis to Rives, Mar. 15, 1843, Rives Papers.

[26] New York *Herald,* Mar. 17, 18, 1843; *Madisonian,* Mar. 20, 22, 1843.

CHAPTER IX

[1] The nostalgic references in his letters are frequent. *E.g.,* Calhoun to Mrs. Clemson, Feb. 6, 1843, Calhoun Papers, CC (in part in *Correspondence,* 524). For his arrival in the South see Charleston *Courier,* Mar. 10, 1843. He presumably left Washington on Mar. 4. See Calhoun to David Hubbard, Feb. 28, 1843 [misdated Nov. 28], Calhoun Papers, SCL.

[2] Pickens County, S. C., Plat Book G-1, 454. For this reference I am indebted to Professor A. G. Holmes of Clemson College. See also Pendleton *Messenger,* Dec. 16, 1840; Clemson to Calhoun, Dec. 27, 1840, *Correspondence II,* 160; Wiltse, *Calhoun, Nationalist,* 341; and the map of Fort Hill that comprises the end papers of *Calhoun, Nullifier.*

[3] Patrick Calhoun, youngest of the brothers, died in October 1840; William, the oldest, followed in December of the same year; and James, who stood between William and John in age, died in January 1843. See "Inscriptions from a Calhoun Burying Ground," *South Carolina Historical and Genealogical Magazine,* XXVII (October 1925), 185.

[4] Mary Boykin Chesnut, *Diary from Dixie,* 17; Calhoun to M. Sterling, July 1, 1840, Calhoun Papers, SCL.

[5] Washington *Spectator,* Apr. 29, 1843. It was a visiting Frenchman who commented that Calhoun had "better manners than his colleagues in the Senate." Chevalier de Bacourt, *Souvenirs of a Diplomat,* 192.

[6] Mary Bates, *Private Life of Calhoun,* 11-12.

[7] Mrs. Calhoun's temperament and character have been discussed more at length in *Calhoun, Nullifier,* 160-161, 164, where sources are given.

[8] Calhoun to Mrs. Clemson, June 28, 1841, *Correspondence,* 480.

[9] Calhoun to Mrs. Clemson, Dec. 23, 25, 1841, Calhoun Papers, CC; Mrs. Clemson to Calhoun, July 1, 1842, *ibid.*

[10] Calhoun to Mrs. Clemson, July 16, 1842, *ibid.;* to James Edward Calhoun, Aug. 18, 1842, *ibid.;* to A. P. Calhoun, Aug. 30, 1842, Calhoun Papers, Duke.

[11] Mrs. Clemson to Calhoun, Dec. 21, 1840, Jan. 24, 1841, Calhoun Papers, CC.

[12] Calhoun to Mrs. Clemson, Dec. 25, 1841, *ibid.;* Mar. 20, 1842, *Correspondence,* 506.

[13] Calhoun to Mrs. Clemson, Jan. 16, 25, 1842, Calhoun Papers, CC; Mar. 20, 1842, *Correspondence,* 504-505.

[14] Calhoun to Mrs. Clemson, May 30, 1842, Calhoun Papers, CC.

[15] Calhoun to Mrs. Clemson, Feb. 6, 1843, *ibid.* (in part in *Correspondence,* 524).

[16] Calhoun to Mrs. Clemson, Feb. 17, 1841, Calhoun Papers, CC (in part in *Correspondence,* 475); June 28, 1841, *Correspondence,* 479-480; to Clemson, July 11, 1841, *ibid.,* 481.

[17] H. St. G. Tucker to Calhoun, no date [March 1843 may be postulated by a reference to the campaign *Life*], Calhoun Papers, CC; John C. Calhoun, Jr., to ————, Mar. 22, 1843, Calhoun Papers, Duke; Calhoun to Tucker, Mar. 31, 1843, *Correspondence,* 526-528.

[18] Calhoun to A. Burt, Aug. 8, 1840, Calhoun Papers, Duke; Kate Townes to McDuffie, Mar. 4, 1842, McDuffie Papers, Duke, seems to imply that Mc-Duffie's motherless daughter, Mary, also went to school to Miss Bates. And see Mary Bates, *The Private Life of John C. Calhoun.*

[19] Dave Sloan, *Fogy Days,* 78-80.

[20] See Wiltse, *Calhoun, Nullifier,* 322-323, for this transaction. This is perhaps as good a place as any to correct an error with regard to Andrew's education which appeared in the foregoing volume, p. 31. I there stated that while Calhoun's intention had been to enter his eldest son at Yale in the fall of 1829, Andrew had not been able to get to New Haven in time for the fall term, and had gone instead to South Carolina College. Andrew did indeed enter Yale in the fall of 1829, though too late to be listed in the classbook, but was dismissed in the summer of 1830 for his involvement in a "conic sections rebellion." It was in the fall of 1830 that he entered South Carolina College. For this information I am indebted to Professor Hollon A. Farr, curator of the Yale Memorabilia Room, Yale University Library.

[21] Calhoun to Mrs. Clemson, Apr. 29, 1840, Calhoun Papers, CC (in part in *Correspondence,* 454).

[22] Calhoun to James Edward Calhoun, May 22, 1841, Calhoun Papers, CC.

[23] Clemson to F. Markoe, Oct. 2, 1841, Maxcy Papers; Calhoun to Mrs. Clemson, Jan. 16, 25, 1842, Calhoun Papers, CC; Mar. 20, 1842, *Correspondence,* 504-505.

[24] See Wiltse, *Calhoun, Nullifier,* 320-321.

[25] Calhoun to Matthews, May 22, 1842, Calhoun Papers, LC.

[26] D. H. Lewis to R. K. Crallé, June 10, 1842, Crallé Papers, LC (in part in Southern History Association, *Publications,* VII, 358-360); Charleston *Mercury,* June 20, 1842; Pendleton *Messenger,* July 1, 1842; *Niles,* LXII, 256.

[27] Clemson to Calhoun, June 23, 1842, Clemson Papers; Pendleton *Messenger,* July 1, 1842; Charleston *Courier,* July 6, 1842.

[28] Clemson to Calhoun, June 28, 31 [sic], July 9, 25, 31, 1842, Clemson Papers; Mrs. Clemson to Calhoun, July 1, 1842, Calhoun Papers, CC. Clemson described the mine for the scientist in *The Orion,* IV (April 1844), 65.

[29] Clemson to Calhoun, Aug. 9, 1842, from the private collection of Mrs. A. G. Holmes.

[30] Clemson to Calhoun, Jan 23, 1843, Clemson Papers; Calhoun to A. P. Calhoun, July 6, 1843, Calhoun Papers, SCL; to Mrs. Clemson, Jan. 6, 1844 [misdated 1843], Calhoun Papers, CC; to James Edward Calhoun, Feb. 14, 1844, *ibid.* (in part in *Correspondence,* 569); B. M. Milner to Calhoun, Feb. 11, 1844, Calhoun Papers, CC.

³¹ Deed of conveyance, July 8, 1842, Clemson Papers; Calhoun to Mrs. Clemson, July 16, 1842, Calhoun Papers, CC; Clemson to Calhoun, Aug. 9, 1842, from the private collection of Mrs. A. G. Holmes. Clemson's partners in the Iron Works were James R. Wyly, the firm of Dobson and Frasier, and John R. Matthews.

³² Pickens to Hammond, Apr. 13, 1841, Hammond Papers; Calhoun to James Edward Calhoun, Aug. 18, 1842, Calhoun Papers, CC. In this letter Calhoun expresses himself as "much afflicted" by Eliza's death, and speaks of her "excellent parents, the best & most devoted friends." Maria also died within two years. See Pickens to Calhoun, Apr. 22, 1844, *ibid*.

³³ J. S. Barbour to Calhoun, Mar. 12, 1843, Calhoun Papers, CC; Calhoun to A. P. Calhoun, Apr. 20, 1843, Calhoun Papers, SCL.

³⁴ Barbour to Calhoun, Apr. 26, May 11, 1843, Calhoun Papers, CC.

³⁵ Undated statement in Clemson Papers. The probable date is determined by a reference in Clemson to Calhoun, Oct. 14, 1847, *ibid*. See also Calhoun to James Edward Calhoun, Nov. 11, 1843, Calhoun Papers, CC.

³⁶ Calhoun to James Edward Calhoun, Nov. 11, 1843, Calhoun Papers, CC.

CHAPTER X

¹ Richmond *Enquirer*, Mar. 4, 1843. See also C. H. Ambler, *Thomas Ritchie*, 229-230; and the same writer's "Virginia and the Presidential Succession," *Turner Essays*, 182-184.

² Richmond *Enquirer*, Mar. 7, 11, 1843.

³ Calhoun to Hunter, Apr. 2, 1843, *Correspondence*, 528-530. Cf. Calhoun to H. St. G. Tucker, Mar. 31, 1843, *ibid.*, 526-528; to Hunter, June 3, 1843, *ibid.*, 534-536; to Clemson, July 6, 1843, *ibid.*, 538-540; to T. W. Gilmer, July 28, 1843, *William and Mary Quarterly*, XX (July 1911), 8-10.

⁴ Ambler, *Ritchie*, 230; Ambler, "Virginia and the Presidential Succession," *Turner Essays*, 184; Seddon to Hunter, Apr. 1, 1843, *Hunter Correspondence*, 63-64; to Rives, Apr. 8, 1843, Rives Papers.

⁵ Richmond *Enquirer*, May 16, 1843; *Niles*, LXIV, 180; Hunter to Calhoun, May 23, 1843, *Correspondence II*, 184-185.

⁶ Charleston *Courier*, May 24, 25, 26, 1843; Charleston *Mercury*, May 26, 27, 1843; Washington *Globe*, May 30, 1843; *Niles*, LXIV, 236-237, 248-252. See also Hammond to M. C. M. Hammond, May 13, 21, 1843, Hammond Papers.

⁷ Scoville to Maxcy, Apr. 6, 1843, Maxcy Papers, second series; J. M. Brodhead to Woodbury, Apr. 9, 1843, Gist Blair Papers.

⁸ Elmore to Maxcy, May 2, 1843, Maxcy Papers; Hunter to Calhoun, May 23, 1843, *Correspondence II*, 184-186.

⁹ Scoville to Maxcy, May 12, 1843, Maxcy Papers. The Woodbury circular was undoubtedly only one of many indiscreet or ill-considered issuances from Scoville's hand. There is, for example, one dated Apr. 24, 1843, which amounts to a political catechism for local Calhoun workers, the questions having to do with the allegiance of local postmasters, editors, and other leading citizens. (Gist Blair Papers). And there is one in May, in the Maxcy Papers, which calls on all leading Democrats to organize local committees to help propagate the Calhoun doctrines. There was nothing wrong with either of these circulars, except political ineptitude, but in politics ineptitude is a graver sin than venality.

¹⁰ Hunter to Calhoun, May 23, 1843, *Correspondence II*, 184-186; Maxcy to Calhoun, May 27, 1843, Calhoun Papers, CC; to Woodbury, May 28, 1843, Gist

Blair Papers; Pickens to H. W. Conner, May 29, 1843, Conner Papers; Heart to Maxcy, June 3, 15, 1843, Maxcy Papers; James Simons to Maxcy, June 7, 1843, Maxcy Papers, second series; Hunter to Calhoun, June 16, 1843, *Correspondence,* 865-866.

[11] Webster to Tyler, May 8, 1843, Webster's *Writings,* XVI, 404; Tyler to Webster, May 8, 1843, *ibid.,* 404-405; Tyler, *Times of the Tylers,* II, 263-264.

[12] Webster to Nicholas Biddle, Mar. 2, 1843. R. C. McGrane, ed., *Correspondence of Nicholas Biddle,* 345, indicates that the decision to retire had been taken by that date. Calhoun's advice to Upshur is referred to in Calhoun to Duff Green, Mar. 19, 1843 [misdated Feb. 19], *Correspondence,* 525-526. The evidence that Calhoun declined the State Department is tenuous, but James Gordon Bennett, whose familiarity with the inner workings of the Tyler administration was notorious, stated in the New York *Herald,* Mar. 9, 1844, that he had "every reason to believe" Tyler had offered the department to Calhoun at the time of Webster's retirement. Duff Green to Calhoun, Sept. 29, 1843, *Facts and Suggestions,* 85 (in part in *Correspondence,* 884-885), indicates that the place was still open for Calhoun to take at any time he saw fit. See also Charleston *Courier,* Nov. 22, 1843. For the proposed British mission, see the Washington column of the *Courier,* Dec. 25, 1843: "It was contemplated last year to send a special minister to England. . . . It was then the wish of Mr. Webster, and, I believe, of the President also, that Mr. Calhoun should take this special mission." Also Bancroft to Van Buren, June 6, 1843, *Mass. Hist. Soc. Proc.,* XLII, 406.

[13] *Madisonian,* June 8, 22, 1843; Washington *Globe,* June 21, 22, 1843; Charleston *Courier,* June 24, 1843; *Niles,* LXIV, 261, 268-271, 281-284; Hone, *Diary,* 660; Bancroft to Van Buren, June 22, 1843, *Mass. Hist. Soc. Proc.,* XLII, 409.

[14] Bancroft to Van Buren, June 22, 1843, *Mass. Hist. Soc. Proc.,* XLII, 410; Jackson to Blair, July 14, 1843, Jackson's *Correspondence,* VI, 223; W. B. Lewis to Rives, July 30, 1843, Rives Papers; Gideon Welles to Van Buren, Aug. 1, 1843, Welles Papers; Darling, *Political Changes in Massachusetts,* 302-305.

[15] Charleston *Mercury,* July 26, 1843; *Madisonian,* Aug. 15, 1843; O. D. Lambert, *Presidential Politics in the United States, 1841-1844,* 125-126.

[16] Maxcy to Calhoun, May 27, 1843, Calhoun Papers, CC; Woodbury to Maxcy, June 29, 1843, Maxcy Papers, second series; Calhoun to W. M. Corry, *et al.,* July 9, 1843, *Niles,* LXV, 11.

[17] Charleston *Mercury,* June 29, 1843; *National Intelligencer,* July 8, 12, 15, 19, 1843. The Charleston *Courier,* July 8, 1843, also charges suppression.

[18] Washington *Spectator,* July 15, 1843; Washington *Globe,* July 15, 1843. The *Spectator* appeared in the morning, the *Globe* late in the evening.

[19] Calhoun to the editors of the *National Intelligencer,* July 28, 1843, in that paper for Aug. 5, 1843. Also in *Niles,* LXIV, 383. The letter from Harpers, dated July 17, 1843, is in the *Intelligencer* for July 21.

[20] *National Intelligencer,* Aug. 9, 1843.

[21] Washington *Globe,* July 20, 1843.

[22] Elmore to Maxcy, Aug. 18, 1843, Maxcy Papers; Henry Gourdin to Calhoun, Nov. 9, 1843, Calhoun Papers, CC. There is a copy of the subscription circular dated Aug. 18, 1843, accompanying Gourdin's letter.

[23] Elmore to Calhoun, Sept. 4, 1843, *Correspondence,* 872-874; A. Rhett to Calhoun, Sept. 5, 1843, Calhoun Papers, CC; Elmore to F. Byrdsall, Sept. 9,

1843, Hammond Papers; W. B. Lewis to Rives, Sept. 5, 1843, Rives Papers. See also Hunter to Maxcy, Aug. 25, 1843, Maxcy Papers.

[24] Elmore to Maxcy, Aug. 18, 1843, Maxcy Papers; to Calhoun, Sept. 4, 1843, *Correspondence*, 872-874; A. Rhett to Calhoun, Sept. 12, 1843, Calhoun Papers, CC; J. L. Martin to Van Buren, Sept. 19, 1843, Van Buren Papers; Hunter to Calhoun, Sept. 19, 1843, *Correspondence*, 881-884; R. B. Rhett to Calhoun, Oct. 7, 1843, *ibid.*, 885-887.

[25] J. F. Hutton to Maxcy, Sept. 11, 1843, Maxcy Papers; S. A. Lawrence to Calhoun, Sept. 13, 1843, *Correspondence*, 878-881; R. B. Rhett to Calhoun, Sept. 21, 1843, Calhoun Papers, CC.

[26] New York *Herald*, Aug. 18, 19, Sept. 5, 1843; J. F. Hutton to Maxcy, Aug. 31, Sept. 4, 6, 8, 1843, Maxcy Papers; S. A. Lawrence to Calhoun, Sept. 13, 1843, *Correspondence*, 878-881. Brownson's "Address" is in *Niles*, LXV, 54-55. Maxcy's pamphlet was entitled simply "Democratic National Convention," was unsigned, and bore no publisher's imprint or date, though it actually came from the presses of Harpers. Authorship is fixed by the Hutton correspondence cited above.

[27] New York *Herald*, Sept. 8, 1843; Washington *Globe*, Sept. 11, 12, 1843; *National Intelligencer*, Sept. 9, 11, 1843; *Madisonian*, Sept. 12, 1843; *Niles*, LXV, 41-42; W. B. Lewis to Rives, Sept. 10, 1843, Rives Papers. The Calhoun men continued to produce well-written pamphlets, the best of the post-Syracuse crop being Rhett's "Compromises of the Constitution considered in the Organization of a National Convention," which appeared in the *Spectator*, Sept. 16, 1843.

[28] Bancroft to Van Buren, Sept. 14, 1843, *Mass. Hist. Soc. Proc.*, XLII, 413-415; Washington *Globe*, Sept. 18, 1843; Darling, *Political Changes in Massachusetts*, 305-311.

[29] *E.g.*, J. F. Hutton to Hunter, Sept. 26, 1843, *Hunter Correspondence*, 64-65; C. M. Ingersoll to Calhoun, Sept. 29, 1843, Calhoun Papers, CC; H. P. Barbour to Calhoun, Nov. 23, 1843, *ibid.*

[30] W. B. Lewis to Rives, Oct. 11, 1843, Rives Papers; J. Garland to Rives, Nov. 6, 1843, *ibid.*; Calhoun to McDuffie, Dec. 4, 1843, *Correspondence*, 554. The Edgefield letter is discussed in *Calhoun, Nullifier*, 359-361; and the Webster-Clay deal is fully documented in the Clay Papers for September-November 1843.

[31] Cave Johnson to Polk, Nov. 28, 1843, Polk Papers; Maxcy to Calhoun, Dec. 3, 10, 1843, *Correspondence*, 896-897, 900-904; Silas Wright to Van Buren, Dec. 6, 1843, Van Buren Papers; Rhett to Calhoun, Dec. 8, 1843, *Correspondence*, 898-900; A. V. Brown to Polk, Dec. 9, 1843, Polk Papers; New York *Herald*, Dec. 5, 1843; *Niles*, LXV, 230; White, *Rhett*, 64-65.

[32] *House Journal*, 28th, 1st, 7-8; Wright to Van Buren, Dec. 6, 1843, Van Buren Papers; A. V. Brown to Polk, Dec. 9, 1843, Polk Papers; S. H. Laughlin to Polk, Dec. 18, 1843, *ibid.*

[33] Calhoun's *Works*, VI, 239-254.

[34] Calhoun to Hunter, Dec. 22, 1843, *Correspondence*, 555-557; to Burt, Dec. 23, 1843, *ibid.*, 557-559; to James Edward Calhoun, Dec. 24, 1843, Calhoun Papers, CC; Pickens to Calhoun, Dec. 27, 1843, *ibid.*; Maxcy to Calhoun, Dec. 31, 1843, *ibid.*; McDuffie to Calhoun, Jan 3, 1844, *Correspondence II*, 198; J. A. Campbell to Elmore, Jan. 4, 1844, Calhoun Papers, CC; Green to Calhoun, Jan. 6, 1844, *ibid.*; Green to Elmore, Jan. 6, 1844, *ibid.*; Maxcy to Calhoun, Jan. 7, Feb. 2, 1844, *Correspondence II*, 200-201, 207-208; Elmore to Cal-

houn, Jan. 9, 13, 1844, *Correspondence*, 908-913; Hunter to Calhoun, Jan. 19, 1844, *ibid.*, 914-916; J. B. I'On to Calhoun, Jan. 24, 1844, Calhoun Papers, CC; Pickens to Calhoun, Feb. 7, 1844, *ibid.*; A. Mazyck to R. K. Crallé, Sept. 13, 1854, Southern History Association, *Publications*, VII, 420-421; Charleston *Mercury*, Jan. 27, 29, 1844; Pendleton *Messenger*, Feb. 9, 1844.

[35] J. B. Nicolson [?] to Van Buren, Feb. 6, 1844, Van Buren Papers; John Slidell to Van Buren, Feb. 2, 1844, *ibid.*; Burt to N. L. Griffin, Jan. 10, 1844, *Am. Hist. Rev.*, XLII (October 1936), 80-82; Burt to Green, Jan. 27, 1844, Green Papers; Washington *Spectator*, Feb. 1, 2, 1844; *Madisonian*, Feb. 2, 1844; New York *Herald*, Feb. 3, 1844; Pendleton *Messenger*, Feb. 9, 1844; Charleston *Courier*, Feb. 13, 1844; Charleston *Mercury*, Feb. 15, 1844. See also J. H. Hammond to Van Buren, Dec. 24, 1843, Van Buren Papers.

[36] Seddon to Calhoun, Feb. 5, 1844, *Correspondence*, 923-927; Hunter to Calhoun, Feb. 6, 1844, *ibid.*, 927-931; Cave Johnson to Polk, Feb. 6, 1844, Polk Papers; Ritchie to Howell Cobb, Feb. 8, 1844, U. B. Phillips, ed., *Correspondence of Robert Toombs, Alexander H. Stephens, and Howell Cobb*, 55; Ambler, "Virginia and the Presidential Succession," *Turner Essays*, 190-192. J. S. Barbour to Rives, Jan. 4, 1844, Rives Papers, indicates a preliminary overture by Ritchie. The Calhoun delegates at Richmond issued a separate "Address" of their own that attracted wide attention. See *Spectator*, Feb. 10, 12, 1844.

CHAPTER XI

[1] Benton, *Thirty Years' View*, II, 581-619; Adams, *Diary*, XI, *passim*. Unless otherwise noted, the account here followed is that of Justin H. Smith, *The Annexation of Texas*.

[2] *Cong. Globe*, 27th, 2nd, 173-176.

[3] A. Smith to Anson Jones, June 8, 1842, Yanaguana Society, *Publications*, V, 155-157; Smith to Jones, July 3, 1842, G. P. Garrison, ed., *Diplomatic Correspondence of the Republic of Texas*, II, 971-976; Smith, *Annexation of Texas*, 84-86.

[4] *Ibid.*, 86-88; Sioussat, ed., "Duff Green's 'England and the United States,'" American Antiquarian Society, *Proceedings*, n.s., XL (October 1930), 175-276. See also Chapter 5 above.

[5] Jackson's letter to Brown, dated Feb. 12, 1843, was not published until more than a year later, in the Richmond *Enquirer*, Mar. 22, 1844. There is a draft in Jackson's *Correspondence*, VI, 201-202, dated Feb. 9, 1843. The Bentonian thesis that the procuring and withholding of the letter was a Calhoun plot is the figment of a highly colored imagination. Gilmer, though friendly to Calhoun, was a Tyler partisan, and was working in Tyler's interest. Aaron V. Brown, in so far as he was concerned with Presidential politics at all at this date, was working strictly for James K. Polk for the second place on the ticket. As will appear later, the real purpose of the Jackson letter was to make it easier for Northern Democrats to vote for annexation of slave soil, and to serve that purpose it had to be published just before the question came to the voting stage. Cf. Benton, *View*, II, 581ff.

[6] *Niles*, LXIV, 173-175; Adams, *Diary*, XI, 336-371, *passim*.

[7] A. Smith to A. Jones, July 2, 1843, *Texas Diplomatic Correspondence*, II, 1099-1103; Smith, *Annexation of Texas*, 116-117; T. P. Martin, "Free Trade and the Oregon Question," *Facts and Factors in Economic History*, 480.

[8] Smith, *Annexation of Texas*, 117-121. The only Ashbel Smith letter in the Calhoun Papers is an excerpt from a dispatch to Anson Jones of July 31, 1843. Upshur's letter to Calhoun, quoted in part below, clearly refers, however, to a communication from Smith, forwarded by Calhoun. The dispatch of July 2, 1843, fits exactly, both for timing and content, and I have therefore assumed this or one very similar to it to be the item referred to. In a letter to A. J. Donelson, May 23, 1845, *Correspondence*, 658-659, Calhoun says specifically that he received two letters from Ashbel Smith in 1843. Tyler later attributed the decision to annex Texas to the replies made by Peel to Everett's inquiries as to British financing of emancipation in Texas. See Tyler to Calhoun, June 5, 1848, *Correspondence*, 1172-1174.

[9] Upshur to Calhoun, Aug. 14, 1843, *William and Mary Quarterly*, n.s., XVI (October 1936), 554-557; Calhoun to Upshur, Aug. 27, 1843, St. G. L. Sioussat, "John C. Calhoun," *American Secretaries of State and their Diplomacy*, V, 141-144. Cf. Tyler to Waddy Thompson, Aug. 28, 1843, *William and Mary Quarterly*, XII (January 1904), 140-141.

[10] Green to Calhoun, Sept. 2, 29, 1843, *Correspondence*, 871-872, 884-885; Green to Calhoun, Oct. 18, 1843, *Correspondence II*, 188-190.

[11] Tyler was correct in his statement to Robert Tyler in 1856 that Calhoun had nothing to do with originating the measure for Texas annexation, but it was absurd or incredibly naïve to say that "knowledge of what was designed was confined to Upshur, Nelson (who served as Secretary of State *ad interim* during March 1844) and Van Zandt." Tyler, *Times of the Tylers*, II, 297. So many people knew what was going on that the administration press was almost open about it by December 1843. Virtually the entire Senate had been sounded; Jackson and Houston knew; so did officials in Mexico and London; and so did Tyler's leaders in the House, Wise and Gilmer. More important still, Francis Preston Blair knew, because Jackson told him, and through him the whole Locofoco wing of the Democracy knew. Calhoun knew as much about it as anyone, and he had learned it through the State Department itself, with Tyler's knowledge.

[12] Jackson to Lewis, Sept. 18, Oct. 31, 1843, Jackson's *Correspondence*, VI, 228-230; 238-239. For the position of the Liberty party see Dwight L. Dumond, ed., *Letters of James Gillespie Birney, 1831-1837*, II, 766-773.

[13] Hunter to Calhoun, Oct. 10, 1843, *Correspondence II*, 186-188; White, Rhett, 65; Ambler, "Virginia and the Presidential Succession," *Turner Essays*, 186-188.

[14] Upshur to Calhoun, Nov. 4, 30, 1843, Calhoun Papers, CC.

[15] Richardson, *Messages and Papers of the Presidents*, 2113-2115.

[16] *Senate Executive Journal*, VI, 211, 227, 229, 236. For more detailed analysis see C. S. Boucher, "The Annexation of Texas and the Bluffton Movement in South Carolina," *Mississippi Valley Historical Review*, VI (June 1919), 3ff; and *"In Re,* that Aggressive Slavocracy," *ibid.*, VIII (June 1921), 24ff.

[17] R. J. Walker to Jackson, Jan. 10, 1844, Jackson's *Correspondence*, VI, 255; Upshur to W. S. Murphy, Jan. 16, 1844, Tyler, *Times of the Tylers*, II, 284.

[18] Webster to certain citizens of Worchester, Mass., Jan. 23, 1844, *Niles*, LXVI, 53-55; Walker to George N. Sanders, *et al.*, Jan. 8, 1844, Washington *Globe*, Feb. 3, 1844. It is perhaps worth noting here that Calhoun, replying to the same query that brought forth Walker's letter, declined comment on the

ground that the Texas question was understood to be the subject of negotiations between the two governments which might be prejudiced by publicizing the opinions of others. To a second query on Oregon, however, he answered bluntly, though that part was ignored by Walker. "I can by no means agree with you on your Oregon plan," Calhoun wrote to Sanders. "I regard it as neither Constitutional, nor expedient. We of the Slaveholding States must never compromise with the fell spirit of abolition. The slave question is one exclusively for our own decision, and all attempts at interference by others ought to be promptly and indignantly repelled." Calhoun to George N. Saunders [sic], Feb. 3, 1844, Calhoun Papers, LC.

[19] Upshur to Murphy, Jan. 23, 1844, *Tyler's Quarterly,* VI (April 1925), 227-228; Houston to Jackson, Feb. 16, 1844, A. W. Williams and E. C. Barker, eds., *Writings of Sam Houston,* IV, 265; Smith, *Annexation of Texas,* 160-169.

[20] Van Zandt to Anson Jones, Mar. 5, 1844, *Texan Diplomatic Correspondence,* II, 261.

[21] Best and fullest eyewitness account is that of George Sikes, member of Congress from New Jersey and close friend of Gilmer whose guest he was. See St. G. L. Sioussat, ed., "The Accident on Board the U.S.S. 'Princeton', February 28, 1844: A Contemporary News-Letter," *Pennsylvania History,* IV (July 1937), 161-189. See also *Madisonian,* Feb. 28, 29, 1844; Washington *Globe,* Feb. 28, 29, Mar. 1, 1844; *National Intelligencer,* Feb. 29, 1844; Benton, *View,* II, 567-569.

[22] Isaac E. Holmes to James G. Holmes, Charleston *Courier,* Mar. 4, 1844; Calhoun to Mrs. Virgil Maxcy, Mar. 9, 1844, Maxcy Papers.

CHAPTER XII

[1] Wise, *Seven Decades,* 221-225. All the other accounts usually cited as sources are based directly or indirectly on Wise. See especially Tyler, *Times of the Tylers,* II, 293-295 (1885); Poore, *Perley's Reminiscences,* I, 314-315 (1886); and Frank G. Carpenter, "A Talk with a President's Son" [John Tyler, Jr.], *Lippincott's,* XLI (March 1888), 416-421. Chitwood, *Tyler,* 285ff, accepts the story uncritically although he is normally justifiably critical of Wise as a source. It is also accepted by Sioussat, "John C. Calhoun," *American Secretaries of State,* V, 127-128.

[2] McDuffie to Calhoun, Mar. 5, 1844, *Correspondence,* 934-935; D. H. Lewis to Calhoun, Mar. 6, 1844, *ibid.,* 935-938; Rhett to Calhoun, Mar. 5, 7, 1844, Calhoun Papers, CC; Holmes to Calhoun, Mar. 6, 1844, *ibid.;* Wise to Hunter, Mar. 6, 1844 [misdated Mar. 7], *ibid.* Some three years later, apropos of a newspaper slur, Tyler went out of his way to inform Calhoun that his appointment had been determined on without consulting anybody; and later still, at a time when he was inclined to be very critical of his old associates, Tyler took great credit to himself for having made it. See Tyler to Calhoun, Mar. 23, 1847, *Correspondence,* 1106-1107; and "Edmund Ruffin's visit to John Tyler," *William and Mary Quarterly,* XIV (January 1906), 205-206.

[3] Charleston *Courier,* Mar. 7, 8, 9, 1844; New York *Herald,* Mar. 5, 1844.

[4] McDuffie to Calhoun, Mar. 5, 1844, *Correspondence,* 934-935.

[5] See Rhett to Calhoun, Mar. 5, 1844, Calhoun Papers, CC. That Tyler did, indeed, expect some sort of political support from Calhoun seems to be indicated. The elusive James Watson Webb of the New York *Courier and Enquirer,*

for example, reported evidence of friction to Willie P. Mangum on Apr. 11, 1844, before Calhoun had been two weeks in office. He described a patronage discussion between Robert Tyler and James G. Clinton, Democratic Congressman from New York. Clinton, according to Webb's account, "told Master Bob that although a Calhoun man, the moment Mr. Calhoun was out of the question, he is thoroughly for Mr. Clay. This was quite astounding to Bob, & he had the folly to say that 'Mr. Calhoun had disappointed his father & would be turned out in thirty days!'" Mangum Papers. Webster had also heard and credited the story. See Webster to Haven, Apr. 22, 1844, Webster's *Writings*, XVI, 427. Of similar origin, in all probability, is the statement of John Tyler, Jr., in 1888 that Calhoun's appointment was his father's greatest regret. Carpenter, "A Talk with a President's Son," *Lippincott's*, XLI (March 1888), 418.

[6] Tyler to Calhoun, Mar. 6, 1844, Calhoun Papers, CC. An earlier letter of the same date, offering the post and stating that the nomination had been sent to the Senate, is in *Correspondence*, 938-939.

[7] His letter to Armistead Burt, Mar. 9, 1844, *Correspondence*, 572-573, does not mention either matter, so we may assume he knew nothing of either when the letter was written, probably early in the morning, as was his habit. Also dated Mar. 9, however, is the draft of a letter, probably to McDuffie, giving his reply to the question of his availability. This letter indicates that the one to which it is in reply has brought him the first news of the *Princeton;* and also that he has received at least one other letter in the same mail on the subject of the State Department. *Ibid.*, 573-576. The mail time between Washington and Fort Hill was 6 to 10 days, although a man could travel it under pressure in four.

[8] Calhoun to [McDuffie?], Mar. 9, 1844, *ibid.*, 573-576; to Mrs. Clemson, Mar. 15, 1844, *ibid.*, 576. The Senate seat was tendered by Governor Hammond on Huger's offer to resign in Calhoun's favor. See McDuffie to Calhoun, Feb. 22, 1844, *ibid.*, 932-933; Huger to Calhoun, Feb. 22, 1844, *Correspondence II*, 210; Hammond to Calhoun, Mar. 1, 14, 1844, Calhoun Papers, CC; Calhoun to Hammond, Mar. 5, 1844, *Correspondence*, 571-572.

[9] Calhoun to Mrs. Clemson, Mar. 15, 1844, *Correspondence*, 576; to Tyler, Mar. 16, 1844, *ibid.*, 577; to Clemson, Mar. 16, 1844, *ibid.*, 577-578; to James Edward Calhoun, Mar. 19, 1844, Calhoun Papers, CC. A cross section of the letters received by Calhoun at this time will be found in the two volumes of correspondence, under dates of Mar. 6, 1844 on. The main body of the letters is in the Clemson collection.

[10] W. E. Dodd, *Statesmen of the Old South*, 145-147; George M. Bibb to Calhoun, Apr. 26, 1844, Calhoun Papers, CC. For the extent of Northern fears as to Texas, see Webster to Charles Allen, Mar. 13, 1844, Webster's *Writings*, XVI, 417; and Judge Story to Ezekiel Bacon, Apr. 1, 1844, *Story*, II, 481. Cf. Boucher, "Annexation of Texas and the Bluffton Movement," *Mississippi Valley Historical Review*, VI (June 1919), 15.

[11] Cave Johnson to Polk, Mar. 6, 1844, Polk Papers; Wright to Van Buren, Mar. 22, 1844, Van Buren Papers; *Madisonian*, Mar. 6, 30, 1844; Washington *Globe*, Mar. 6, 1844; Washington *Spectator*, Mar. 16, 28, 1844; *National Intelligencer*, Mar. 7, 19, 1844; New York *Herald*, Mar. 9, 1844; Charleston *Courier*, Mar. 11, 13, 19, 29, 1844; Charleston *Mercury*, Mar. 12, 20, 27, 28, 1844; Pendleton *Messenger*, Mar. 22, 29, 1844. See also Hone, *Diary*, 690; Tyler, *Times of the Tylers*, II, 301; *Democratic Review*, XIV (April 1844), 423-430.

[12] Meigs, *Ingersoll*, 272-273. We know of Calhoun's relations with the House Committee Chairman because Ingersoll kept a diary. That relations with Archer were equally cordial must be inferred from the record, but it could hardly have been otherwise, in view of the importance of the Senate for foreign relations and of Calhoun's long service in that body. For Wright's comment, see Wright to Van Buren, Apr. 8, 1844, Van Buren Papers.

[13] *Senate Document* 349, 28th, 1st; Smith, *Annexation of Texas*, 175-176.

[14] *Ibid.*, 176; Calhoun to Murphy, Apr. 13, 1844, State Department, Texas, Instructions, I.

[15] Memucan Hunt to Mangum, Mar. 27, 1844, Mangum Papers; W. B. Lewis to Jackson, Mar. 28, 1844, Jackson's *Correspondence*, VI, 275-276; Webster to F. Webster, Apr. 1, 1844, Webster's *Writings*, XVIII, 188; Wright to Van Buren, Apr. 14, 1844, Van Buren Papers; Giddings to Oran Follett, Apr. 14, 1844, Historical and Philosophical Society of Ohio, *Quarterly Publication*, X, 15.

[16] Calhoun to B. E. Green, Apr. 19, 1844, William R. Manning, ed., *Diplomatic Correspondence to the United States, Inter-American Affairs*, VIII, 149-151; Tyler to Jackson, Apr. 18, 1844, Jackson's *Correspondence*, VI, 279; W. B. Lewis to Jackson, Apr. 19, 1844, *ibid.*, 279-280; Tyler to Brantz Mayer, Aug. 1, 1847, Boston Public Library, *Bulletin*, VII, 321-322; Tyler, *Times of the Tylers*, II, 298; New York *Herald*, Apr. 16, 1844. See also Benton, *View*, II, 608; and Smith, *Annexation of Texas*, 198-199.

[17] *Madisonian*, Feb. 14, 21, 1844. The Pakenham correspondence is most readily available in Manning, *Diplomatic Correspondence, Inter-American Affairs*, VII, 252ff, 18ff; and in Calhoun's *Works*, V, 330ff.

[18] A. H. Everett to Calhoun, Apr. 13, 1844, State Department, Miscellaneous Letters. Also Annie H. Abel and Frank J. Klingberg, eds., *A Side-Light on Anglo-American Relations, 1839-1858*, being the correspondence of Lewis Tappan and others with the British and Foreign Anti-Slavery Society.

[19] Pakenham to Calhoun, Apr. 19, 30, 1844, Manning, *Diplomatic Correspondence, Inter-American Affairs*, VII, 256-258; Calhoun to Pakenham, Apr. 27, 1844, *ibid.*, 22-25; Calhoun to Everett, Apr. 27, 1844, *ibid.*, 25-26; Everett to Calhoun, May 18, 1844, *ibid.*, 258-260.

[20] *Senate Journal*, 28th, 1st, 421-425; *Senate Document* 341.

[21] For the leak see report of the investigating committee, *Senate Journal*, 28th, 1st, 439-441.

CHAPTER XIII

[1] *House Journal*, 28th, 1st, 9-12, 52-53, 93; *Madisonian*, Jan. 2, 1844; E. J. Black to Calhoun, Jan. 8, 1844, *Correspondence II*, 202-204.

[2] *House Journal*, 28th, 1st, 142, 498-499; Black to Calhoun, Jan. 8, 1844, *Correspondence II*, 202-204; R. K. Crallé to Duff Green, Jan. 10, 1844, Green Papers; Calhoun to Hunter, Feb. 1, 1844, *Correspondence*, 562-564; to Burt, Mar. 9, 1844, *ibid.*, 572-573.

[3] *Cong. Globe*, 28th, 1st, 44, 47, 98; *Madisonian*, Dec. 19, 1843; Charleston *Courier*, Dec. 23, 1843, Jan. 8, 1844; A. Burt to N. L. Griffin, Jan. 10, 1844, *Am. Hist. Rev.* XLII (October 1936), 80-81; Boucher, "Annexation of Texas and the Bluffton Movement," *Mississippi Valley Historical Review*, VI (June 1919), 10-11.

[4] Rhett to Calhoun, Feb. 21, 1844, *Correspondence II*, 209-210; McDuffie to Hammond, Feb. 24, 1844, Hammond Papers; Rhett to Van Buren, Feb. 26, 1844, Van Buren Papers; McDuffie to Calhoun, Mar. 10, 1844, *Correspondence II*, 214-215; White, *Rhett*, 68-70.

[5] *House Journal*, 28th, 1st, 895-896; Washington *Spectator*, May 11, 1844.

[6] See Wright to Van Buren, Apr. 8, 1844, Van Buren Papers. Van Buren's correspondence with Bancroft, who was writing a campaign life of the ex-President (abandoned when Van Buren failed to get the Democratic nomination), indicates that although the Massachusetts historian tried hard to find out where his subject stood on Texas, he got no satisfaction. See Bancroft to Van Buren, Mar. 28, Apr. 16, 22, 1844, *Mass. Hist. Soc. Proc.*, XLII, 422-425.

[7] Both Van Buren and Clay letters are in *Niles*, LXVI, 152-157. Their simultaneous appearance, in the light of Van Buren's visit to Ashland in the spring of 1842, has led some to conclude that they were issued by tacit agreement. The only possible reason for such collusion, however, would have been to keep Texas out of the campaign, and it was already much too late for that. Had Van Buren won the Democratic nomination a third, pro-Texas candidate would have been inevitable. See Van Deusen, *Clay*, 366, 373-375; Fuess, *Cushing*, II, 10; Coleman, *Crittenden*, I, 219. To me, at least, the simultaneous publication by Van Buren's New York editor of the pirated Pakenham letter seems much more significant. For Clay's nomination, see *National Intelligencer*, May 2, 1844.

[8] See, *e.g.*, Benton, *View*, II, 588-590; and Blair to Jackson, May 2, 1844, Jackson's *Correspondence*, VI, 281-282. Blair himself, having come out in favor of annexation on April 15, was caught flat-footed, and for a few days was literally speechless. On April 29 he published a letter from Benton to the members of the Texas Senate which argued the new party line, but he himself did not comment until May 1, when he began attacking Calhoun as the author of the whole Texas "plot."

[9] Bancroft to Van Buren, May 2, 1844, *Mass. Hist. Soc. Proc.*, XLII, 426; Wright to Van Buren, May 13, 1844, Van Buren Papers; Kendall to Van Buren, May 13, 1844, *ibid.*; H. S. Turney to Polk, May 14, 1844, Polk Papers.

[10] Ambler, "Virginia and the Presidential Succession," *Turner Essays*, 195-200; Ambler, *Ritchie*, 237-240; Ambler, ed., "Virginia and Texas, 1844," *Branch Papers*, IV, No. 1, 116-137. Also Ritchie to Howell Cobb, May 23, 1844, *Toombs, Stephens, Cobb Correspondence*, 59.

[11] Charleston *Mercury*, Mar. 2, 19, 1844; [Orestes Brownson], "Mr. Calhoun and the Baltimore Convention," *Brownson's Quarterly Review*, I (April 1844), 257-269. Also Brownson's personal tribute at the Jackson Jubilee in Boston, Washington *Spectator*, Apr. 22, 1844. For the resurgence of Calhoun's partisans, see J. S. Barbour to Calhoun, Apr. 27, May 11, 21, 1844, Calhoun Papers, CC; D. H. Lewis to Calhoun, May 6, 1844, *ibid.*; J. Wishert to Crallé, May 6, 1844, Crallé Papers, CC; J. D. Morris to Crallé, May 7, 1844, *ibid.*; James Gadsden to Calhoun, May 3, 1844, *Correspondence*, 952-953; J. H. Howard to Calhoun, May 2, 1844, *Correspondence II*, 224-225; E. Prescott to Calhoun, May 11, 1844, *ibid.*, 225-226; L. A. Hoe to Calhoun, May 11, 1844, *ibid.*, 226-227; J. H. Campbell to Calhoun, May 14, 1844, *ibid.*, 227-228. For Calhoun's own unwillingness to re-enter the contest, see Calhoun to Mrs. Clemson, May 10, 1844, *Correspondence*, 585-586; and Ingersoll's diary, May 7, 18, 1844, Meigs, *Ingersoll*, 266-267.

[12] J. Hall to Woodbury, May 6, 1844, Gist Blair Papers; Jackson to F. P.

Blair, May 7, 18, 1844, Jackson's *Correspondence*, VI, 283-285, 293-294; Cave Johnson to Polk, May 12, 1844, Polk Papers; Donelson to [Van Buren], May 16, 1844, Donelson Papers; W. B. Lewis to Jackson, May 22, 1844, Jackson's *Correspondence*, VI, 294-295.

13 Calhoun to Mrs. Clemson, May 10, 1844, *Correspondence*, 585-586. Clemson's nomination was not sent to the Senate until June 17, the last day of the session, when it was promptly confirmed. *Senate Executive Journal*, VI, 351, 352. The Tyler boom may be followed in the columns of the *Madisonian*. See especially Apr. 29 and May 4, 1844, *et seq.*

14 *Senate Journal*, 28th, 1st, 427; Ingersoll's diary, May 6, 7, 1844, Meigs, *Ingersoll*, 265-266.

15 *Senate Executive Journal*, VI, 291, 293.

16 Bancroft to Van Buren, May 23, 24, 1844, *Mass. Hist. Soc. Proc.*, XLII, 428-430; [John C. Rives] to Van Buren, May 24, 1844, Van Buren Papers; Bancroft to Van Buren, May 25, 1844, *ibid.;* Wright to Van Buren, May 26, 1844, *ibid.;* Gideon Pillow to Polk, May 22, 24, 25, 1844, *Am. Hist. Rev.*, XI (July 1906), 835-840; Jackson to B. F. Butler, May 14, 1844, *ibid.*, 833-834; Clark E. Persinger, "The 'Bargain of 1844' as the Origin of the Wilmot Provisio," American Historical Association, *Annual Report*, 1911, I, 189-195; Ambler, *Ritchie*, 242; H. D. Jordan, "A Politician of Expansion: Robert J. Walker," *Mississippi Valley Historical Review*, XIX (December 1932), 370-371; J. G. de R. Hamilton, *Party Politics in North Carolina, 1835-1860*, 96.

17 See Pillow to Polk, May 28, 1844, *Am. Hist. Rev.*, XI (July 1906), 840-841; and Bancroft to I. G. Harris, Aug. 30, 1887, *ibid.*, 841 n. For proceedings as a whole up to this point, see J. M. Niles to Gideon Welles, May 28, 29, 1844, Welles Papers; J. L. O'Sullivan to Van Buren, May 27, 28, 1844, Van Buren Papers.

18 So Jordan argues, *loc. cit.*

19 Polk to Cave Johnson, May 13, 14 (two letters), 1844, *Tennessee Historical Magazine*, I (September 1915), 239-243.

20 For proceedings of May 29, see O'Sullivan to Van Buren, May 29, 1844, Van Buren Papers; B. F. Butler to Van Buren, May 31, 1844, in Lambert, *Presidential Politics*, 207-213; Pillow to Polk, May 29, 30, 1844, *Am. Hist. Rev.*, XI (July 1906), 841-843; Cave Johnson to Polk, May 29, 1844, Polk Papers; Pickens to H. W. Conner, May 29, 1844, Conner Papers; Washington *Spectator*, May 30, 1844.

21 Willie P. Mangum to P. H. Mangum, May 29, 1844, Mangum Papers; E. L. Morse, *Samuel F. B. Morse*, II, 226.

22 *Madisonian*, May 28, 29, 30, 1844.

23 Edward Stanwood, *History of the Presidency*, I, 199-200, 215-216.

24 Pickens to Conner, May 29, June [?], 1844, Conner Papers; ——— to Van Buren, May 29, 1844, Van Buren Papers; B. F. Butler to Van Buren, May 31, 1844, Lambert, *Presidential Politics*, 207-213; Cave Johnson to Polk, June 13, 1844, E. I. McCormac, *James K. Polk*, 255; Jackson to Blair, June 25, 29, 1844, Jackson's *Correspondence*, VI, 298-299; Laughlin to Polk, June 28, 1844, Polk Papers; Polk to Donelson, July 22, 1844, *Tennessee Historical Magazine*, III (March 1917), 57-58; N. O. Palmer to Van Buren, July 29, 1844, *North Carolina Historical Review*, XV (April 1938), 146-147; T. Fisk to Polk, Jan. 3, 1845, Polk Papers. The *Democratic Review* for June 1844, XIV, 559-564, carried an article, written before the convention, which was in effect a blunt

warning from the Northern to the Southern Democracy; a warning that unless the nominee (who the writer assumed would of course be Van Buren) was cordially supported by the South, tariff, abolitionism, and all, reprisals would be swift and sure. The language was unmistakably that of the stronger to the weaker side. The vote on the Texas treaty is in *Senate Journal,* 28th, 1st, 436-438.

[25] Polk to John M. Kane, June 19, 1844, *Niles,* LXVI, 295.

[26] *Madisonian,* July 25, 26, 27, 29, Aug. 2, 1844; Polk to Donelson, Aug. 3, 1844, Donelson Papers; to Jackson, Aug. 3, 1844, Jackson Papers; F. Byrdsall to Polk, July 25, 1844, Polk Papers; Poinsett to Van Buren, Aug. 28, 1844, Van Buren Papers; B. F. Butler to Donelson, Nov. 8, 1844, Donelson Papers; J. D. Hammond, *Life of Silas Wright,* 498-501.

[27] Walker to Polk, July 10, 1844, Lambert, *Presidential Politics,* 201-203; Polk to Donelson, July 23, 1844, *Tennessee Historical Magazine,* III (March 1917), 58-59.

[28] Jackson to Blair, July 26, 1844, Jackson's *Correspondence,* VI, 304-305; to Mason, Aug. 1, 1844, *ibid.,* 305-306; to Lewis, Aug. 1, 1844, *ibid.,* 306-308; Tyler to Jackson, Aug. 18, 1844, *ibid.,* 315; *Madisonian,* Aug. 20, 1844.

[29] Ingersoll's diary, June 3, 1844, Meigs, *Ingersoll,* 267-268.

[30] *National Intelligencer,* Aug. 19, 1844; Calhoun to Donelson, Aug. 23, 1844, Donelson Papers; Polk to Donelson, Aug. 27, 1844, *Tennessee Historical Magazine,* III (March 1917), 60-61.

[31] Washington *Globe,* Sept. 7, 1844; Hammond, *Wright,* 490-492; Smith, *Annexation of Texas,* 312; Donovan, *Barnburners,* 57-59.

[32] Harris probably assumed the editorship of the *Spectator* when Rhett gave it up in September. He bought the paper, in partnership with its nominal publisher, John Heart, in October, and began issuing semiweekly as the *Constitution* on the 18th of that month. The original intention was to acquire the *Madisonian* also, and merge the two, but this proved unfeasible. See Calhoun to Hunter, Sept. 27, 1844, *Hunter Correspondence,* 72. The *Constitution* became a daily with its issue of Dec. 27, 1844.

[33] Calhoun to J. A. Stuart, Oct. 21, 1844, *Correspondence,* 626; Washington *Constitution,* Nov. 1, 1844.

[34] Calhoun to J. R. Matthews, Oct. 14, 1844, Calhoun Papers, LC; Giddings to Oran Follett, Nov. 18, 1844, Historical and Philosophical Society of Ohio, *Quarterly Publications,* X, 20. See also G. M. Dallas to Polk, Sept. 30, 1844, Polk Papers, second series.

[35] Stanwood, *History of the Presidency,* I, 222-225; Edward Channing, *History of the United States,* V, 544. See also such contemporary reactions as Frelinghuysen to Clay, Nov. 9, 1844, Clay's *Works,* V, 495-496; Ambrose Spencer to Clay, Nov. 21, 1844, *ibid.,* 501-502.

CHAPTER XIV

[1] See J. N. Norwood, *The Schism in the Methodist Episcopal Church, 1844.*

[2] The story unfolds by way of letters in the Charleston *Courier,* July 18, 19, 24, 27, 1844. See also White, *Rhett,* 72-73.

[3] Richmond *Enquirer,* June 28, July 4, 1844; Charleston *Courier,* June 27, July 3, 10, 15, 17, 1844; Boucher, "Annexation of Texas and the Bluffton Move-

ment," *Mississippi Valley Historical Review*, VI (June 1919), 17-18; White, *Rhett*, 74 ff.

⁴ R. M. Saunders to Calhoun, June 24, 1844, Calhoun Papers, CC; Clay to Stephen Miller, July 1, 1844, Clay's *Works*, V, 490-491; Blair to Jackson, July 7, 1844, Jackson's *Correspondence*, VI, 299-302; anonymous to Calhoun, July 12, 1844, Calhoun Papers, CC.

⁵ See especially R. R. Russel, *Economic Aspects of Southern Sectionalism, 1840-1861*, 33-39, 68-70. Statistics are in *Report of the Secretary of the Treasury, 1854-1855*, 116.

⁶ Charleston *Mercury*, July 3, 4, 1844; Charleston *Courier*, July 18, 1844. Cf. H. W. Conner to Calhoun, July 24, 1844, Calhoun Papers, CC: "Mr. McDuffie told me when here that he had yielded the convictions of his own mind to the judgment & advice of others—meaning yourself I believe, & would direct his efforts no farther than to produce union amongst the Southern States."

⁷ Charleston *Mercury*, July 23, 26, 27, 1844; White, *Rhett*, 74ff.

⁸ Holmes to Hammond, July 23, 1844, Hammond Papers.

⁹ White, *Rhett*, 74-79; Boucher, "Annexation of Texas and the Bluffton Movement," *Mississippi Valley Historical Review*, VI (June 1919), 18-19. The files of both *Mercury* and *Courier* for the whole period are indispensable.

¹⁰ Charleston *Courier*, Aug. 1, 8, 12, 14, 21, 1844; Charleston *Mercury*, Aug. 20, 21, 1844; Bailey to Calhoun, July 30, 1844, *Correspondence II*, 241-242; Elmore to Calhoun, July 30, 1844, *ibid.*, 242-243; Calhoun to Burt, Aug. 7, 1844, Calhoun Papers, Duke; Conner to Calhoun, Aug. 8, 1844, Calhoun Papers, CC; Seddon to Hunter, Aug. 9, 1844, *Hunter Correspondence*, 66-67, 69-70; R. F. Simpson to Calhoun, Aug. 24, 1844, *Correspondence II*, 246-248; Hammond to M. C. M. Hammond, Aug. 25, 1844, Hammond Papers; Elmore to Calhoun, Aug. 26, 1844, *Correspondence*, 967-968; Poinsett to Van Buren, Aug. 28, 1844, Van Buren Papers; Rhett to Hunter, Aug. 30, 1844, *Hunter Correspondence*, 70-71; Boucher, *op. cit.*, 21.

¹¹ Pickens to Calhoun, Sept. 9, 1844, *Correspondence*, 968-971; Calhoun to F. Wharton, Sept. 17, 1844, *ibid.*, 616.

¹² Charleston *Mercury*, Sept. 11, 1844; Charleston *Courier*, Sept. 18, 1844; *Niles*, LXVII, 49-52; Boucher, *op. cit.*, 22-25.

¹³ W. H. Haywood, Jr., to Polk, Sept. 26, 1844, *N. C. Hist. Rev.*, XVI (July 1939), 347; McDuffie to Hammond, Sept. 22, 1844, Hammond Papers; Hamilton to Hammond, Oct. 4, 1844, *ibid.;* Charleston *Mercury*, Sept. 27, Oct. 1, 1844.

¹⁴ Calhoun to Hammond, Sept. 21, 1844, Hammond Papers; to Hunter, Sept. 27, 1844, *Hunter Correspondence*, 72; to Joseph W. Sessue, Sept. 27, 1844, Calhoun Papers, SCL; Petigru to T. Petigru, Sept. 30, 1844, Carson, *Petigru*, 239; Charleston *Mercury*, Oct. 1, 1844; Charleston *Courier*, Oct. 2, 1844; Hammond, *Diary*, Oct. 25, 1844, Hammond Papers; Stuart to Calhoun, Oct. 25, 1844, *Correspondence II*, 253-254; White, *Rhett*, 79-80; Boucher, *op. cit.*, 21-27; Wallace, *History of South Carolina*, II, 489-490.

¹⁵ Bailey to Calhoun, Nov. 6, 1844, Calhoun Papers, CC; Elmore to Calhoun, Nov. 18, 1844, *ibid.;* Hamilton to Hammond, Nov. 12, 17, 1844, Hammond Papers; Hammond, *Diary*, Nov. 17, 1844, *ibid.;* Charleston *Courier*, Nov. 8, 12, 1844.

¹⁶ Hammond, *Diary*, Nov. 24, 1844, Hammond Papers.

¹⁷ Charleston *Courier*, Nov. 28, 1844. The message is also in J. H. Hammond, *Selections from Letters and Speeches*, 79-104; and there are pertinent excerpts in *Niles*, LXVII, 227-228.

[18] Charleston *Courier,* Nov. 28, 1844.

[19] *Ibid.,* Nov. 30, 1844; Hammond, *Diary,* Nov. 26, 27, 28, 1844, Hammond Papers. Writing on June 15, 1847, to his close friend William Gilmore Simms, Hammond states: "You may be surprised to hear that Calhoun denies that he knew anything of Pickens' resolutions of 1844 before hand & did not altogether approve when he saw them. He intimated that he rather preferred the Sentiments of my message. Neither of these statements which he made to me do I believe." It is difficult to determine how much credence to give such a statement. Undoubtedly Calhoun would have denied advance knowledge of the resolutions. He could not have known of them, since he knew nothing of the content of the message to which they referred; but they certainly spoke his sentiments as of that date, and as certainly Pickens knew those sentiments. Hammond's message, on the other hand, took a tone that the Calhoun of 1844 would willingly have changed. It is true that by 1847 Calhoun was being driven farther in the direction Hammond had taken three years earlier; but it is also true that in 1847 Hammond was becoming increasingly bitter and irrationally critical toward his former patron. The most likely explanation is that Calhoun was thinking not of these resolutions, but of another set introduced by Pickens a few days later, of which, as we shall see presently, he did not approve.

[20] Hammond, *Diary,* Nov. 28, 1844, Hammond Papers; Pickens to Calhoun, Dec. 6, 1844 [misdated Nov. 6], *Correspondence,* 990; Charleston *Courier,* Nov. 29, 1844, *et seq.*

[21] Rhett to Hammond, Dec. 3, 1844 [misdated Nov. 3], Hammond Papers; Holmes to Hammond, Dec. 9, 1844, *ibid.;* Ker Boyce to Calhoun, Nov. 28, Dec. 13, 1844, Calhoun Papers, CC; Charleston *Courier,* Dec. 9, 1844.

[22] *House Journal,* 28th, 2nd, 9, 10-12; Holmes to Hammond, Dec. 9, 1844, Hammond Papers.

[23] Charleston *Courier,* Dec. 19, 1844.

[24] Charleston *Courier,* Dec. 21, 1844; Hammond, *Diary,* Dec. 22, 26, 1844, Hammond Papers.

[25] Charleston *Courier,* Dec. 7, 1844; *Niles,* LXVII, 226-227; Wallace, *History of South Carolina,* II, 496-498. A printed circular issued by the government of South Carolina for official distribution to other states contains all the documents. A copy sent by Hammond to Calhoun is in State Department, Miscellaneous Letters, in the National Archives.

[26] Hammond to Bailey, Dec. 5, 1844, Hammond Papers; Brooks to Hammond, Dec. 6, 1844, *ibid.;* Hammond, *Diary,* Dec. 5, 7, 1844, *ibid.* Also Adams, *Diary,* XII, 119; and "Mr. Hoar's Mission," *Southern Quarterly Review,* XII (April 1845), 455-478.

[27] McDuffie to Hammond, Dec. 12, 1844, Hammond Papers; D. J. McCord to Hammond, Dec. 12, 1844, *ibid.;* A. P. Aldrich to Hammond, Dec. 18, 1844, *ibid.;* Hammond to M. C. M. Hammond, Dec. 24, 1844, *ibid.;* Hammond to McDuffie, Dec. 27, 1844, *ibid.;* J. M. Walker to Hammond, Jan. 17, 1845, *ibid.;* Hammond, diary, Dec. 1844—Feb. 1845, *ibid.;* Boucher, *op. cit.,* 27-33.

CHAPTER XV

[1] *Cong. Globe,* 28th, 1st, 660-661, 673, 688; *Senate Executive Journal,* VI, 314.

[2] Calhoun to Howard, June 18, 1844, Manning, *Diplomatic Correspondence, Inter-American Affairs,* XII, 73-75; to Shannon, June 20, 1844, *ibid.,* VIII, 151-

155; B. E. Green to J. M. Bocanegra, May 23, 1844, *ibid.*, 586-587; Bocanegra to Green, May 30, 1844, *ibid.*, 587-591. Also Smith, *Annexation of Texas*, 295, 361-362; Sioussat, "Calhoun," 172.

[3] Howard to Calhoun, Aug. 3, 1844, Manning, *op. cit.*, XII, 359-360; Howard to Calhoun, Aug. 7, 1844, *ibid.*, 364, and enclosures.

[4] Smith, *Annexation of Texas*, 382-389.

[5] *Ibid.*, 389-392; Sioussat, "Calhoun," 165-168; A. Smith, *Reminiscences of the Texas Republic*, 64-65. The characterization of Houston is from James Hamilton to Calhoun, July 13, 1844, Calhoun Papers, CC. W. S. Murphy to Calhoun, Apr. 29, 1844, indicates that Houston and his government were highly pleased with the treaty; but M. P. Norton wrote the same day from the town of Houston, where he was postmaster, that the entire Texan Government was in fact hostile. *Correspondence*, 947-952.

[6] Lewis to Jackson, July 19, 1844, Jackson's *Correspondence*, VI, 302-303; McCormac, *Polk*, 270-271. Donelson to Calhoun, July 29, 1844, *Correspondence*, 964-965, indicates that Jackson did write a strong letter to Houston.

[7] Smith, *Annexation of Texas*, 399-403; Sioussat, "Calhoun," 170-171. The letter to King will be found in the usual sources, most conveniently in Calhoun's *Works*, V, 379-392.

[8] Howard to Calhoun, Aug. 7, 1844 (received Aug. 26), Manning, *op. cit.*, XII, 364.

[9] Calhoun to Howard, Sept. 10, 1844, *ibid.*, 78-79; to Shannon, Sept. 10, *ibid.*, VIII, 155-161.

[10] Raymond to Anson Jones, Sept. 13, 1844, Anson Jones, *Memoranda and Official Correspondence*, 382-383.

[11] Sioussat, "Calhoun," 173; Calhoun to Donelson, Sept. 17, 1844 [misdated Sept. 16], *Correspondence*, 614-615; and separate letter of instructions, Sept. 17, 1844, in Manning, *op. cit.*, XII, 80-81. Also Tyler to Jackson, Sept. 17, 1844, Jackson's *Correspondence*, VI, 319-320. Calhoun's first letter refers to receiving news of Howard's death "yesterday" in the mail, and Tyler's letter says the "mail of last night." This fixes the date as the 16th, since the 15th was a Sunday when there would have been no mail, and makes clear that Calhoun's first letter was misdated. He probably wrote it late at night, after his conference with the President.

[12] Houston to Jones, Sept. 24, 1844, Houston's *Writings*, IV, 371-372; A. Smith, *Reminiscences*, 61-65.

[13] Aberdeen to Pakenham, Mar. 4, 1844, *Oregon Historical Quarterly*, XXXIX (March 1938), 74-76; Everett to Nelson, Apr. 1, 1844, State Department, Letters Received, LII.

[14] Pakenham to Calhoun, July 22, 1844, Calhoun's *Works*, V, 419-420; Calhoun to Pakenham, Aug. 22, 1844, *ibid.*, 420-421; Calhoun to Mrs. Clemson, Aug. 29, 1844, Calhoun Papers, CC.

[15] The protocol and documents are in Calhoun's *Works*, V, 421-457, where Calhoun's statement of September 2 is misdated September 13, and his rejoinder of September 20 is misdated September 29, 1844.

[16] Shannon to Calhoun, Sept. 21, 1844, Manning, *op. cit.*, VIII, 640-642; Calhoun to Shannon, Sept. 10, 1844, *ibid.*, 155-161; Calhoun to Shannon, Sept. 11, 1844, State Department, Mexico, XV.

[17] The documents are in Manning, *op. cit.*, VIII, 644-698. See also Shannon to Calhoun, Oct. 29, Nov. 12, 1844, *Correspondence*, 980-982, 995; Duff Green

to Calhoun, Oct. 28, Nov. 12, 1844, *ibid.*, 975-980, 991-995; Donelson to Calhoun, Dec. 5, 1844, Manning, *op. cit.*, XII, 378-381.

[18] Richardson, *Messages and Papers of the Presidents*, 2187-2205; *Cong. Globe*, 28th, 2nd, 16-17, 19, 26; *Senate Document* 1; S. Penn, Jr., to Calhoun, Dec. 4, 1844, Calhoun Papers, CC; Cave Johnson to Polk, Dec. 12, 1844, Polk Papers.

[19] *House Document* 19, 28th, 2nd; Adams, *Diary*, XII, 127-128; *National Intelligencer*, Dec. 20, 21, 1844.

[20] Donelson to Calhoun, Nov. 11, 23, 24, 1844, Manning, *op. cit.*, XII, 371-378.

[21] Donelson to Calhoun, Dec. 5, 17, 1844, and enclosures, *ibid.*, 378-381, 387-389.

[22] Donelson to Calhoun, Dec. 24, 1844, *ibid.*, 389-391.

[23] *National Intelligencer*, Jan. 2, 4, 1845; *Madisonian*, Jan. 2, 1845; Charleston *Courier*, Jan. 7, 1845.

[24] *Cong. Globe*, 28th, 2nd, 84-88, 100-102, Appendix, 85-90; J. W. DuBose, *Life and Times of William Lowndes Yancey*, I, 140-145; Washington *Globe*, Jan. 7, 1845; *National Intelligencer*, Jan. 15, 1845; Charleston *Courier*, Jan. 15, 1845.

[25] *Cong. Globe*, 28th, 2nd, 107ff, *passim*.

[26] *Ibid.*, 191-194.

[27] Washington *Globe*, Jan. 25, 1845; W. Hunt to G. Dawson, Jan. 26, 1845, *Mass. Hist. Soc. Proc.*, LIII, 58; Burt to Hammond, Jan. 28, 1845, Hammond Papers.

[28] Mrs. Calhoun to James Edward Calhoun, Jr., Feb. 1, 1845, Calhoun Papers, SCL; Washington *Constitution*, Feb. 4, 1845; Charleston *Courier*, Feb. 5, 8, 25, 1845; Calhoun to James Edward Calhoun, Sr., Feb. 16, 1845, Calhoun Papers, CC; F. Wharton, Notes of Conversations with Calhoun, Feb. 18, 20, 1845, *Correspondence*, 644.

[29] Donovan, *Barnburners*, 65-67.

[30] *Senate Journal*, 28th, 2nd, 134; *Cong. Globe*, 244; Washington *Globe*, Feb. 5, 1845; *Madisonian*, Feb. 7, 1845; Charleston *Courier*, Feb. 11, 1845.

[31] *Cong. Globe*, 28th, 2nd, 271, 278ff.

[32] A. Smith, *Reminiscences*, 70-71; King to Calhoun, Feb. 27, 1845, State Department, France, XXX; *Hansard's Debates*, third series, LXXVII, 1325-1340; Washington *Constitution*, Apr. 10, 1845. For Calhoun's activities, see Calhoun to Donelson, May 23, 1845, *Correspondence*, 658-659; for Polk's, see Smith, *Annexation of Texas*, 348 n.

[33] *Cong. Globe*, 28th, 2nd, 359. See also Jordan, "Walker," *Mississippi Valley Historical Review*, XIX (December 1932), 371-372.

[34] Charleston *Courier*, Mar. 1, 1845; Charleston *Mercury*, Mar. 3, 1845; *National Intelligencer*, Mar. 10, 1845; Hammond, *Diary*, Mar. 9, 1845, Hammond Papers. See also Calhoun to Clemson, Feb. 26, 1845, *Correspondence*, 645.

[35] *Cong. Globe*, 28th, 2nd, 362-363; 371-372.

[36] Calhoun to Donelson, May 23, 1845, *Correspondence*, 658-659; to John Y. Mason, May 30, 1845, *ibid.*, 659-663; Tyler to Calhoun, Jan. 2, 1849, *ibid.*, 1187-1188; Tyler to William Wilkins, Nov. 27, 1848, and enclosure, Tyler, *Times of the Tylers*, II, 364-365.

[37] Tyler, *Times of the Tylers*, II, 364-365; Calhoun to Donelson, Mar. 3, 1845, Manning, *op. cit.*, XII, 83-85. For the pros and cons of Polk's possible commitment to choose the Benton version, see Smith, *Annexation of Texas*,

348*n*. The furious attack on the whole procedure by Blair in the *Globe* of March 4 seems to bear out Calhoun's fears. See also the reply of the *Madisonian*, Mar. 6, 1845. Blair and ex-Senator Tappan of Ohio (the same who violated the confidence of the Senate by giving the Pakenham letter to the New York *Evening Post*) revived the charges by way of a political attack on Polk in the *Post*, July 28, 1848, and Polk then wrote out his own recollections in his diary. See M. M. Quaife, ed., *The Diary of James K. Polk*, IV, 38-47, 49, 126-127.

³⁸ Polk to Calhoun, Mar. 6, 1845, State Department, Miscellaneous Letters; to Donelson, Mar. 7, 1845, *Tennessee Historical Magazine*, III (March 1917), 62; Tyler to Calhoun, Jan. 2, 1849, *Correspondence*, 1187-1188; Manning, *op. cit.*, XII, 85-88; Smith, *Annexation of Texas*, 353-355, 433.

³⁹ Unless otherwise noted, the story is drawn from Smith, *Annexation of Texas*, 432-469. The documents are in Manning, *Diplomatic Correspondence, Inter-American Affairs*, XII, 88-100, 392-460; and in Garrison, *Diplomatic Correspondence of the Republic of Texas*, II, 1170-1200, 1492-1505. Also Donelson to Calhoun, Apr. 24, 1845, *Correspondence*, 1029-1032.

⁴⁰ A. Smith, *Reminiscences*, 76-77.

⁴¹ Buchanan to Donelson, June 15, 1845, Manning, *op. cit.*, 94-97; Polk to Donelson, June 15, 1845, Donelson Papers.

CHAPTER XVI

¹ *Madisonian*, Feb. 14, 1845; Washington *Constitution*, Feb. 15, 1845; Charleston *Courier*, Feb. 18, 1845.

² Polk to Wright, Dec. 7, 1844, Polk Papers; Wright to Polk, Dec. 20, 1844, *ibid*. On the copy of Polk's letter, in his own distinctive hand, the postscript is crossed out, indicating its omission from the message as actually sent.

³ A. V. Brown to Polk, Dec. 14, 1844, Jan. 15, 1845, Polk Papers; J. Hamilton to Polk, Nov. 29, 1844, *ibid.*; A. B. Longstreet to Polk, Nov. 22, 28, 1844, *ibid*. See also Seddon to Hunter, Nov. 16, 1844, *Hunter Correspondence*, 72-74; Elmore to Calhoun, Nov. 18, 1844, Calhoun Papers, CC; W. Lumpkin to Calhoun, Nov. 18, 1844, *Correspondence II*, 264; W. R. King to Calhoun, Nov. 29, 1844, *ibid.*, 265-266; Calhoun to F. Wharton, Nov. 20, 1844, *Correspondence*, 630; J. S. Barbour to Calhoun, Nov. 21, 1844, *ibid.*, 997-998; Calhoun to Clemson, Dec. 13, 1844, *ibid.*, 633-634.

⁴ Polk to Van Buren, Jan. 4, 1845, Van Buren Papers; Cave Johnson to Polk, Jan. 5, 1845, Polk Papers; Charleston *Courier*, Jan. 17, 1845; Van Buren to Polk, Jan. 18, 1845, Van Buren Papers; Polk to Van Buren, Jan 30, 1845, *ibid*.

⁵ Calhoun to Hunter, Feb. 14, 1845, *Hunter Correspondence*, 75; to James Edward Calhoun, Feb. 16, 1845, Calhoun Papers, CC; F. Wharton, Notes of Conversations with Calhoun, Feb. 18, 20, 1845, *Correspondence*, 644-645.

⁶ Polk to Buchanan, Feb. 17, 1845, George Ticknor Curtis, *Life of James Buchanan*, I, 547-548; Buchanan to Polk, Feb. 18, 1845, *ibid.*, 548-549; Polk to Walker, Feb. 19, 1845 (draft), Polk Papers; Polk to Van Buren, Feb. 22, 25, 1845, Van Buren Papers; Van Buren to Polk, Feb. 27, 1845, *ibid.*; Butler to Polk, Feb. 27, 1845, *ibid*.

⁷ Polk to Van Buren, Mar. 1, 3, 1845, Van Buren Papers.

⁸ The conditions are succinctly stated in Polk to Walker, Feb. 19, 1845, Polk Papers.

[9] Calhoun to Clemson, Feb. 26, 1845, *Correspondence*, 645-646; to Polk, Feb. 27, 1845, Polk Papers; to Pickens, Mar. 1, 1845, Calhoun Papers, Duke; Burt to Hammond, Jan. 28, 1845, Hammond Papers; Calhoun to Mrs. Clemson, Mar. 11, 1845, *Correspondence*, 647-648; to Hunter, Mar. 26, 1845, *Hunter Correspondence*, 75-76. See also Maury, *Statesmen of America*, 180.

[10] Brown to Polk, undated but probably between Feb. 27 and Mar. 3, 1845, Polk Papers; Holmes's Eulogy in the *Carolina Tribute*, 31. Both interviews presumably took place before Polk's inauguration, or Calhoun would have added the President's Oregon policy as further ground for his refusal. See also Maury, *op. cit.*, 180, 183; and Elmore to Hammond, Mar. 24, 1845, Hammond Papers.

[11] Washington *Constitution*, Mar. 4, 1845; Washington *Globe*, Mar. 5, 1845; *National Intelligencer*, Mar. 5, 1845; Charleston *Courier*, Mar. 8, 1845; *Niles*, LXVIII, 1; Adams, *Diary*, XII, 178-179.

[12] Richardson, *Messages and Papers of the Presidents*, 2223-2232.

[13] Calhoun to James Edward Calhoun, Mar. 9, 1845, Calhoun Papers, CC; to Hunter, Mar. 26, 1845, *Hunter Correspondence*, 75-77; to H. W. Conner, May 2, 1845, Conner Papers. I have assumed that the Oregon question was discussed at the Feb. 16 meeting between Calhoun and Polk, since Calhoun says in his letter of May 6 to Pickens, *Correspondence*, 653-654, that he had endeavored to warn Polk of the danger "in my first interview." In the letter to Conner cited above he says it was before the inaugural address was prepared. The problem was much on his mind when he talked to Francis Wharton, Feb. 18, 20, 1845, *Correspondence*, 644-645, at which time he thought the negotiations were coming to a satisfactory conclusion.

[14] Van Buren to Bancroft, Mar. 7, 1845, *Mass. Hist. Soc. Proc.*, XLII, 440.

[15] *Madisonian*, Mar. 11, 1845; *Constitution*, Mar. 12, 1845; *National Intelligencer*, Mar. 14, 1845.

[16] Ritchie to T. H. Bayly, Dec. 28, 1844, Ambler, *Ritchie*, 247-249; Polk to Donelson, Mar. 28, 1845, *Tennessee Historical Magazine*, III (March 1917), 62-64.

[17] Duff Green to Calhoun, Mar. 26, 1845, *Correspondence II*, 288; Coryell to Calhoun, Apr. 6, 1845, *ibid.*, 291-292; Calhoun to Clemson, Apr. 25, 1845, *Correspondence*, 652-653. Polk's version is in his *Diary*, I, 356-359. The best secondary accounts are in Ambler, *Ritchie*, 246ff; and McCormac, *Polk*, 299ff.

[18] Coryell to Calhoun, Apr. 6, 1845, *Correspondence II*, 291-292; Harris to Calhoun, July 11, 1845, *Correspondence*, 1042.

[19] Calhoun to Clemson, Mar. 23, 1845, *Correspondence*, 650; to Hunter, Mar. 26, 1845, *Hunter Correspondence*, 75-77; J. S. Barbour to Polk, Mar. 22, 1845, Polk Papers, second series; Richmond *Enquirer*, Mar. 17, 1845; Charleston *Courier*, Mar. 17, Apr. 1, 1845; Charleston *Mercury*, Mar. 19, 1845; Pendleton *Messenger*, Mar. 21, 28, 1845.

[20] See, *e.g.*, Charleston *Courier*, Apr. 2, 1845; Buchanan to Calhoun, Apr. 9, 1845, *Correspondence II*, 292; Pendleton *Messenger*, Apr. 11, 18, 1845.

[21] Polk to Elmore, Apr. 8, 1845, Polk Papers; Buchanan to Calhoun, Apr. 9, 1845, *Correspondence II*, 292; Elmore to Polk, Apr. 15, 1845, Polk Papers; Elmore to Calhoun, Apr. 16, 1845, *Correspondence II*, 292-293; Polk to Pickens, Apr. 21, 1845, Polk Papers; Pickens to Polk, Apr. 28, 1845, *ibid.* The *Caledonia* had been held at Liverpool until the papers came out with accounts of the debates in Parliament on Apr. 4. She docked in Boston the evening of Apr. 21, and the news reached Washington sometime during the day on the 23rd. The Cabinet was immediately called, sitting until near midnight. Charleston *Courier*,

Apr. 28, May 2, 1845. See also *Hansard,* third series, LXXIX, 115-124, 178-201; and T. P. Martin, "Free Trade and the Oregon Question," *Facts and Factors in Economic History,* 483-484.

[22] Buchanan to Polk, May 3, 1845, Polk Papers, second series; Bancroft to Van Buren, May 5, 1845, *Mass. Hist. Soc. Proc.,* XLII, 441-442; Polk to B. F. Butler, May 5, 1845, Van Buren Papers; Butler to Van Buren, May 7, 1845, *ibid.;* Van Buren to Bancroft, May 12, 1845, *ibid.* The Bancroft and Van Buren letters are also in M. A. de W. Howe, *Life and Letters of George Bancroft,* I, 267-273. Calhoun's terms for accepting the British Mission were sent by Elmore to Duff Green, May 10, 1845, Green Papers, to be shown to Polk. They were that the Oregon settlement should be spelled out in instructions so detailed that the administration would have to assume full responsibility and fight for the treaty in the Senate; that there should be similarly precise instructions covering a commercial treaty; and that Calhoun should have full power to deal with fugitive slave cases. See also D. H. Lewis to Calhoun, May 9, 1845, *Correspondence II,* 293-294; Polk to Woodbury, May 19, 1845, Gist Blair Papers; Woodbury to Polk, May 26, 1845, Polk Papers; Polk to McLane, May 31, 1845, *ibid.;* McLane to Polk, June 12, 1845, *ibid.;* and for the Virginia election, Richmond *Enquirer,* Apr. 25, 1845, and R. G. Scott to Calhoun, Apr. 27, 1845, *Correspondence,* 1032.

[23] Washington *Union,* esp. May 13, 20, 27, June 14, 1845; Barbour to Calhoun, May 21, 1845, *Correspondence,* 1036-1038; Coryell to Calhoun, May 27, June 4, 6, 1845, Calhoun Papers, CC (May 27 in part in *Correspondence II,* 295); Duff Green to Calhoun, June 1, 1845, *Correspondence II,* 295-297; Calhoun to Clemson, June 7, 1845, *Correspondence,* 663-664.

[24] Lewis to Calhoun, May 9, 1845, *Correspondence II,* 293-294; Hamilton to Calhoun, May 18, 1845, Calhoun Papers, CC; Calhoun to [Lewis], May 16, 1845, *Hunter Correspondence,* 77-79. I have supplied the addressee, since the letter is clearly in answer to Lewis' of May 9.

[25] W. A. Harris to Calhoun, July 11, 1845, *Correspondence,* 1038-1043; Calhoun to Coryell, July 19, 1845, *ibid.,* 666-667; Ambler, *Ritchie,* 260-262.

[26] Charleston *Mercury,* Aug. 7, 1845; Hammond to Simms, July 14, 1845, Hammond Papers. Also D. J. McCord to Hammond, July 24, 1845, *ibid.;* and the files of the *Mercury* for June and July, 1845.

[27] W. A. Harris to Calhoun, Aug. 4, 1845, *Correspondence II,* 300-302; Calhoun to Clemson, Aug. 12, 1845, *Correspondence,* 669. For the New York situation see F. Byrdsall to Duff Green, Sept. 1, 1845, Polk Papers, second series; to Polk, Sept. 14, 1845, *ibid.;* A. D. Wilson to Polk, Sept. 15, 1845, *ibid.*

[28] Rhett to Calhoun, Sept. 18, 1845, *Correspondence,* 1049-1051; Crallé to Calhoun, Sept. 23, 1845, *ibid.,* 1051-1054. Also J. M. Walker to Hammond, Sept. 20, 1845, Hammond Papers.

[29] Charleston *Mercury,* Oct. 7, 1845; *Niles,* LXIX, 94-95.

[30] J. M. Walker to Hammond, Mar. 22, 1845, Hammond Papers; Bancroft to Van Buren, Jan. 22, 1845, *Mass. Hist. Soc. Proc.,* XLII, 434; Washington *Globe,* Feb. 11, 1845.

[31] Huger to Calhoun, Mar. 24, 1845, *Correspondence,* 1027-1029, and the Calhoun correspondence generally for March-October 1845.

[32] Barbour to Calhoun, June 26, Aug. 14, 1845, Calhoun Papers, CC. The portion quoted from the June 26 letter, all except the last sentence, is in *Correspondence II,* 297-298.

[33] Buchanan to Calhoun, Aug. 22, 1845, *Correspondence II*, 302; Calhoun to Pickens, Aug. 21, 1845, *South Carolina Historical and Genealogical Magazine*, VII (January 1906), 14-15; Pickens to Calhoun, Sept. 1, 1845, Calhoun Papers, CC.

[34] Calhoun to Burt, Sept. 17, 1845, American Historical Association, *Annual Report*, 1913, II, 163-164; Fisher to Calhoun, Sept. 2, 1845, Calhoun Papers, CC. Cf. Calhoun to Pickens, Sept. 23, 1845, *S. C. Hist. and Geneal. Mag.*, VII (January 1906), 16-19.

[35] James E. Walmsley, "The Return of John C. Calhoun to the Senate in 1845," American Historical Association, *Annual Report,* 1913, I, 161-165; Maury, *Statesmen of America,* 183; Wallace, *History of South Carolina,* II, 491. Calhoun to James Edward Calhoun, Jan. 16, 1846, *Correspondence,* 675-676, places his decision to return to the Senate wholly on the danger of war over Oregon.

[36] Holmes to Calhoun, Nov. 18, 1845, Calhoun Papers, CC; W. B. Lewis to Calhoun, Nov. 7, 1845, *ibid.*

CHAPTER XVII

[1] Richardson, *Messages and Papers of the Presidents,* 2235-2266.

[2] Calhoun to W. Lumpkin, Feb. 4, 1842, Calhoun Papers, Duke. For background see Wiltse, *Calhoun, Nationalist,* Chap. 10; and *Calhoun, Nullifier,* Chap. 23.

[3] *DeBow's Review,* I (January 1846), 9.

[4] *Southern Literary Messenger,* XI (October 1845), 577-602; Charleston *Courier,* Oct. 4, 9, 10, 11, 13, 14, 17, 18, 1845; Washington *Union,* Oct. 8, 1845. See also Louis B. Schmidt, "Internal Commerce and the Development of National Economy before 1860," *Journal of Political Economy,* XLVII (December 1939), 798-822; R. S. Cotterill, "Southern Railroads and Western Trade, 1840-1850," *Mississippi Valley Historical Review,* III (March 1917), 427-441; F. J. Turner, *Significance of Sections in American History,* 198-199.

[5] Washington *Union,* Sept. 20, 1845; Duff Green to Calhoun, Sept. 24, 1845, *Correspondence,* 1055; Polk, *Diary,* I, 38.

[6] Gadsden to Calhoun, Oct. 6, 7, 21, 24, 1845, Calhoun Papers, CC; Oct. 9, 1845, *Correspondence,* 1060-1062; Elmore to Calhoun, Oct. 10, 1845, *ibid.,* 1062-1063; Charleston *Courier,* Oct. 7, 23, 1845; Charleston *Mercury,* Oct. 25, 1845; Calhoun to Duff Green, Oct. 18, 1845, Green Papers.

[7] Calhoun to Clemson, Dec. 13, 1845, *Correspondence,* 674; Charleston *Courier,* Nov. 11, 13, 1845; Washington *Union,* Nov. 14, 1845; *Magazine of American History,* IX (January 1883), 66; D. G. Burnet, M. B. Lamar, *et al.,* to Calhoun, Oct. 31, 1845, Calhoun Papers, CC; W. B. Lewis to Calhoun, Nov. 7, 1845, *ibid.;* W. C. Anderson to Calhoun, Nov. 6, 1845, *Correspondence II,* 307-308.

[8] Memphis *Daily Eagle,* Nov. 13, 1845; Charleston *Courier,* Nov. 19, 1845. The *Courier's* story, dated aboard the *Maria* Nov. 10 and signed "Southron," was probably by J. D. B. De Bow, who was one of the South Carolina delegates. The same pseudonym had been signed to a series of articles in the *Courier* during October, dealing with the problems to be discussed at Memphis, and these were almost certainly De Bow's.

[9] The proceedings are reported in detail in the Memphis *Eagle,* Nov. 14, 15, 17, 18, 1845; and in more summary fashion in the Charleston *Courier,* Nov.

21, 24, 1845, and in *Niles,* LXIX, 196-197, 212-214. The best account is that of De Bow, *De Bow's Review,* I (January 1846), 7-21. See also Herbert Wender, *Southern Commercial Conventions,* 1837-1859, 49-69. The Memorial presented to Congress, Calhoun's *Works,* V, 293, specifies 583 representatives, "from the States of Pennsylvania, Virginia, North and South Carolina, Florida, Alabama, Louisiana, Texas, Mississippi, Tennessee, Arkansas, Missouri, Kentucky, Illinois, Indiana, Ohio, and Iowa." De Bow's list, however, included no delegates from Florida.

[10] This much of the program had been advocated since 1839 by Lieutenant Matthew Fontaine Maury of the United States Navy, writing intermittently in the *Southern Literary Messenger* under the pseudonym of "Harry Bluff." See especially his summation, "The Maritime Interests of the South and West," *Southern Quarterly Review,* IV (October 1843), 309-346. Calhoun's speech is in *Works,* VI, 273-284, and in abbreviated and somewhat inaccurate form in *Niles,* LXIX, 212-213.

[11] Memphis *Daily Eagle,* Nov. 17, 1845. Compare Varina Howell Davis, *Jefferson Davis,* I, 209-213. The Davises entertained Calhoun at Vicksburg on his way home.

[12] Charleston *Courier,* Nov. 27-Dec. 3, 1845, *passim;* Charleston *Mercury,* Nov. 29, Dec. 2, 3, 1845.

[13] See T. P. Martin, "Cotton and Wheat in Anglo-American Trade and Politics, 1846-1852," *Journal of Southern History,* I (August 1935), 306.

[14] *Southern Quarterly Review,* IX, 243-272. This issue, for January 1846, was unaccountably delayed in the printing, and was not actually distributed until the beginning of February, thus coinciding precisely with the presentation of the Memphis Memorial in Congress. See Charleston *Mercury,* Feb. 4, 1846; Charleston *Courier,* Feb. 9, 1846.

[15] Pickens to Calhoun, Apr. 7, 1846, Calhoun Papers, CC; Calhoun to Mrs. Clemson, June 11, 1846, *Correspondence,* 694-696, where the *Southern Quarterly Review* article is incorrectly identified in Jameson's footnote.

[16] Charleston *Mercury,* July 14, 1846; Calhoun to James Edward Calhoun, Aug. 8, Oct. 29, 1846, *Correspondence,* 703, 708-709; to Clemson, Aug. 8, 1846, *ibid.,* 704-705; Rhett to Elmore, Sept. 6, 1846, Elmore Papers. Rhett wrote an article upholding the Memphis doctrines in the October number of the *Southern Quarterly Review,* X, 377-417, though he had to refute a speech he had himself made in February to do it.

[17] Calhoun to James Edward Calhoun, Dec. 14, 1845, Jan. 16, 1846, *Correspondence,* 675, 676-677; *Senate Journal,* 29th, 1st, 39, 61, 88.

[18] *Senate Journal,* 29th, 1st, 131; *Cong. Globe,* 297; Calhoun to Lewis Shanks, Feb. 6, 1846, Calhoun Papers, SCL. A similar course was intended in the House, where Holmes moved on February 3 for a suspension of the rules to permit him to present the Memphis Memorial. The motion was lost, 72 to 78. Among Southern votes in the negative were R. M. T. Hunter, R. B. Rhett, R. F. Simpson, and W. L. Yancey. See *House Journal,* 29th, 1st, 342-343.

[19] *Senate Document,* 410, 29th, 1st; Calhoun's *Works,* V, 246-311; Calhoun to Mrs. Clemson, June 11, 1846, *Correspondence,* 694-696; to Clemson, June 11, 1846, *ibid.,* 697.

[20] *Cong. Globe,* 29th, 1st, 1028, 1084.

[21] *Senate Journal,* 29th, 1st, 7, 60, 132; *House Journal,* 180, 563; *Cong. Globe,* 530-531.

[22] *Senate Journal*, 29th, 1st, 46, 278, 336, 359, 380, 387, 392-393, 396; *Cong. Globe*, 1040-1041, 1057-1058; Charleston *Courier*, July 13, 1846.

[23] *Senate Journal*, 29th, 1st, 407; *Cong. Globe*, 1084.

[24] *House Journal*, 29th, 1st, 1096; *Cong. Globe*, 1094; Adams, *Diary*, XII, 269.

[25] *Senate Journal*, 29th, 1st, 476; *House Journal*, 1225-1228; Charleston *Courier*, Aug. 7, 1846. Polk's veto message is in Richardson, *Messages and Papers of the Presidents*, 2310-2316. See also Sargent, *Public Men*, II, 299-300.

CHAPTER XVIII

[1] T. P. Martin, "Free Trade and the Oregon Question," *Facts and Factors in Economic History*, 485. Buchanan to McLane, July 12, 1845, G. B. Moore, ed., *Works of James Buchanan*, VI, 186-194; to Pakenham, July 12, 1845, *ibid.*, 194-204; Pakenham to Buchanan, July 29, 1845, *ibid.*, 212-220; Buchanan to Pakenham, Aug. 30, 1845, *ibid.*, 231-254; Polk, *Diary*, I, 1-12.

[2] Pakenham to Aberdeen, Sept. 13, 1845 (two dispatches), Great Britain, Public Record Office, F. O. 5-428, photostats in LC, endorsed "received September 29"; Aberdeen to Pakenham, Oct. 3, 1845, *Selections from the Correspondence of George, Earl of Aberdeen*, 326-328; Peel to Aberdeen, Oct. 2, 1845, *ibid.*, 328-329.

[3] *Memoirs of Sir Robert Peel*, II, 140-222; Aberdeen to Pakenham, Oct. 23, Dec. 3, 1845, *Aberdeen Correspondence*, 405-406, 507-509. See also D. G. Barnes, *History of the English Corn Laws*, 272-282.

[4] New York *Herald*, Oct. 29, 1845; Washington *Union*, Oct. 31, Nov. 6, 1845; Buchanan to McLane, Oct. 28, 1845, Buchanan's *Works*, VI, 285-286; Sioussat, "James Buchanan," *American Secretaries of State and their Diplomacy*, V, 251-253; Polk, *Diary*, I, 62-64, 155.

[5] Charleston *Courier*, Nov. 6, 11, 1845; F. Olmsted to Hammond, Nov. 6, 1845, Hammond Papers; F. Byrdsall to Polk, Nov. 9, 1845, Polk Papers, second series; Polk, *Diary*, I, 94-95.

[6] *Senate Document* 2, 29th, 1st.

[7] Calhoun to James Edward Calhoun, Dec. 14, 1845, *Correspondence*, 675.

[8] Calhoun to Clemson, Dec. 13, postscript Dec. 26, 1845, Calhoun Papers, CC (in part in *Correspondence*, 674-675); *Senate Journal*, 29th, 1st, 57-58; *House Journal*, 137, 145-146; *Cong. Globe*, 75-76, 85, 86.

[9] Webster to F. Haven, Dec. 20 [misdated Dec. 26], 1845, Webster's *Writings*, XVI, 439; R. L. King to Calhoun, Dec. 10, 1845, *Correspondence II*, 310-311; Fernando Wood to Calhoun, Dec. 26, 1845, *Correspondence*, 1065-1067.

[10] Speech of Holmes in the House, June 28, 1848, *Cong. Globe*, 30th, 1st, Appendix, 806-807; Holmes to Calhoun, Oct. 6, 1848, Calhoun Papers, CC.

[11] Polk, *Diary*, I, 131-132.

[12] Charleston *Courier*, Jan. 3, 1846; Polk, *Diary*, I, 140-142; Pakenham to Aberdeen, Dec. 29, 1845 (Nos. 137 and 138), and private letter of same date, F. O. 5-430, photostats in LC; *Cong. Globe*, 29th, 1st, 96-97.

[13] *Cong. Globe*, 29th, 1st, 109-112.

[14] *Ibid.;* Charleston *Courier*, Jan. 3, 5, 1846; Pakenham to Aberdeen, Dec. 31, 1845 (No. 140), F. O. 5-430; Jan. 2, 1846 (No. 1), F. O. 5-446.

[15] Polk, *Diary*, I, 153-156.

[16] *Ibid.*, 158-162.

[17] Calhoun to Andrew Pickens Calhoun, Jan. 16, 1846, *Correspondence*, 677;

Cong. Globe, 29th, 1st, 182-183; Webster to N. Appleton, Jan 12, 1846, Webster's *Writings,* XVI, 439-440; Pakenham to Aberdeen, Jan. 13, 1846 (No. 4), F. O. 5-446; Charleston *Courier,* Jan. 16, 17, 1846; W. H. Seward to Mrs. Seward, Jan. 16, 1846, W. H. Seward, *Autobiography,* 775-776.

[18] Peel's *Memoirs,* II, 223-260; Frederick Merk, "British Party Politics and the Oregon Treaty," *Am. Hist. Rev.* XXXVII (July 1932), 667-669.

[19] Everett to Russell, Dec. 28, 1845, in *ibid.,* 656-657; Green to McGregor, Dec. 29, 1845, Green Papers.

[20] Merk, *op. cit.,* 658; *Hansard,* third series, LXXXIII, 152, 237 ff. It is doubtless correct, as Professor Merk argues in his "British Corn Crisis of 1845-46 and the Oregon Treaty," *Agricultural History,* VIII (July 1934), 95-123, that the crop failures of 1845 were not actually of crisis proportions; and that the repeal of the Corn Laws was more beneficial to the Baltic States than to America—meant, in fact, some actual loss to the United States. It is nevertheless true that the crop failures served as the excuse which enabled Peel to secure repeal of the Corn Laws; and it is also true that repeal had a direct bearing on the settlement of the Oregon boundary. Well-informed Americans were not misled as to the results to expect. At least Secretary Walker told British Minister Pakenham in September 1845 that repeal of the Corn Laws would leave American wheat growers in a less advantageous position than that which they then occupied, owing to the prevalent custom of shipping by way of Canada and enjoying thereby a colonial preference. See Pakenham to Aberdeen, Sept. 13, 1845, F. O. 5-428. The importance of Corn Law repeal, so far as the United States was concerned, lay in another direction. Tariff reform was "sold" to the American public in terms of the standard free-trade arguments, and the average voter, once he had come to accept the theory, could hardly be persuaded that it worked only one way. If Congress took off trade restrictions, Parliament would, in his eyes, have to do likewise. It was actually the reduction of duties, especially those on T-iron, by the United States that benefited the Western farmer most, but the whole question was still tied up in his mind with Corn Law repeal. He still believed that, once he had built his transportation lines, he could undersell Eastern Europe in the British market; and in due time he could, and did.

The other and perhaps more important bearing of Corn Law repeal on United States policy lay in its relation to internal politics in England. As Professor Merk has also pointed out, in his "British Party Politics and the Oregon Treaty," *Am. Hist. Rev.,* XXXVII (July 1932), 653-677, the Peel Ministry could not afford to go out of office leaving the Oregon boundary unsettled, and the Whigs did not wish to resume office with that question still hanging fire. It was clear to both sides, however, that once the Corn Laws were gone, Peel could not sustain himself and would have to leave office, whatever the immediate excuse might be. Stated in more simplified form, Sir Robert Peel set himself to get rid of the protective policy, following his own conversion to free trade some time between 1842 and 1845. The party over which he presided, however, was traditionally the party of protection. He needed, therefore, both a crisis situation and Whig help. He got both in the winter of 1845-1846, but would clearly lose in the aftermath the conservatives of his own party, while he could count on the Whigs no further than the immediate measure in which they were interested. He would, in a word, be defeated whenever the Whigs chose to vote against him.

The Whigs were as loath to assume power with a war threatening as the

Tories were to go into opposition with a potential war which could be blamed on them still looming in the Pacific Northwest. The Oregon boundary, therefore, was settled as were the Corn Laws—by a Tory Prime Minister with Whig backing; and the one followed the other. Had there been no potato blight, Peel could not have swung over enough conservatives to carry Corn Law repeal; had the Corn Laws not been repealed by his Ministry he would not have faced imminent defeat by a combination of Tory landlords and Whig merchants; and had he not expected momentarily to be thrust from power, it would not have been necessary to settle the Oregon question on any terms to get it settled at once. See also Henry Commager, "England and Oregon Treaty of 1846," *Oregon Historical Quarterly*, XXVIII (March 1927), 18-38. I agree with Professor Donald G. Barnes, *History of the English Corn Laws*, 282, that the Corn Laws would probably have been repealed even if the Walker tariff had not passed. The repeal measure did in fact pass Commons in February and the Lords in June, before the Walker bill had passed in either house of Congress. I do not believe, however, that the Walker bill would have gone through if the Corn Laws had not been repealed; and I think it possible that the Oregon Treaty would not have been ratified in the same contingency.

[21] Washington *Union*, Jan. 19, 26, 27, 1846; Charleston *Courier*, Jan. 23, 26, 29, 30, 1846; New York *Herald*, Jan. 24, 25, 26, 1846; telegram, Jan 19, 1846, Polk Papers, second series; Polk, *Diary*, I, 180-181.

[22] Louis McLane to Calhoun, Jan. 3, 1846, *Correspondence II*, 311-315. Also McLane to Calhoun, Jan. 2, 1846, Calhoun Papers, CC.

[23] Calhoun to H. W. Conner, Jan. 17, 1846, Conner Papers; to Hammond, Jan. 23, 1846, *Correspondence*, 678-679; to Clemson, Jan. 29, 1846, *ibid.*, 679-681; Webster to N. Appleton, Jan. 29, 1846, Webster's *Writings*, XVI, 441; Adams, *Diary*, XII, 231, 238; Giddings' speech in the House, Jan. 5, 1846, *Cong. Globe*, 29th, 1st, Appendix, 72-74; Charleston *Mercury*, Jan. 12, 1846; Charleston *Courier*, Jan. 21, 1846.

[24] *Cong. Globe*, 29th, 1st, 335-336, 339-350; Washington *Union*, Feb. 7, 9, 1846; Charleston *Courier*, Feb. 11, 13, 1846; Pakenham to Aberdeen, Feb. 10, 1846 (No. 14), F. O. 5-446, photostat in LC. A comparison of McLane's dispatch of Jan 3, 1846, as included in the President's message to the House, Feb. 7, *Cong. Globe*, 29th, 1st, 333, with the original in State Department, Dispatches, Great Britain, LVI, is an instructive lesson in political morality. Most of the omitted portions are in Hunter Miller, ed., *Treaties and other International Acts of the United States of America*, V, 54-55.

[25] *Cong. Globe*, 29th, 1st, 350-351; Charleston *Courier*, Feb. 17, 1846.

[26] See, *e.g.*, Charleston *Courier*, Feb. 21, 1846.

[27] Washington *Union*, Feb. 20, 23, 1846; Charleston *Courier*, Feb. 24, 25, 28, 1846; Polk, *Diary*, I, 241; Adams, *Diary*, XII, 248; *Niles*, LXIX, 385; Merk, "British Corn Crisis and the Oregon Treaty," *Agricultural History*, VIII (July 1934), 112.

[28] McLane to Buchanan, Feb. 3, 1846, State Department, Great Britain, Dispatches, LVI (in part in Miller, *Treaties*, V, 57-59); to Calhoun, Feb. 3, 1846, *Correspondence II*, 323-324.

[29] Polk, *Diary*, I, 246-253; McDuffie to Polk, Feb. 25, 1846, Polk Papers, second series; Pakenham to Aberdeen, Feb. 26, 1846, F. O. 5-446, photostat in LC; New York *Herald*, Feb. 27, 1846. Negotiations between Calhoun Demo-

crats and Whigs are detailed in Ellwood Fisher to Calhoun, Feb. 25, 1846, Calhoun Papers, CC.

[30] Buchanan to McLane, Feb. 26, 1846 (No. 23), Buchanan's *Works,* VI, 377-383; Buchanan to McLane, Feb. 26, 1846 (private), *ibid.,* 385-387.

[31] Pakenham to Aberdeen, Feb. 28, 1846 (No. 18), and enclosures, F. O. 5-446, photostat in LC.

[32] Washington *Union,* Mar. 12, 1846; Charleston *Courier,* Mar. 20, 1846; Charleston *Mercury,* Mar. 20, 1846.

[33] *Cong. Globe,* 29th, 1st, 502-506; Calhoun's *Works,* IV, 258-290.

[34] Charleston *Courier,* Mar. 21, 26, 1846; Charleston *Mercury,* Mar. 20, 23, 1846; Calhoun to Mrs. Clemson, Mar. 23, 1846, *Correspondence,* 684-685; to Clemson, Mar. 23, 1846, *ibid.,* 685-687; Duff Green to Calhoun, Mar. 18, 1846, *Correspondence II,* 333; Parke Godwin to Calhoun, Mar. 20, 1846, Calhoun Papers, CC; A. S. Doane, president, New York and Boston Magnetic Telegraph Association, to Calhoun, Mar. 21, 1846, *ibid.;* Edward Everett to Calhoun, Apr. 6, 1846, *Correspondence,* 1080-1081. Many similar letters will be found in the second volume of the Calhoun Correspondence, and in the Clemson College collection of papers.

[35] *Cong. Globe,* 29th, 1st, 680, 683; Washington *Union,* Mar. 20, 21, 23, Apr. 4, 16, 1846; Charleston *Courier,* Mar. 28, Apr. 7, 20, 1846; Charleston *Mercury,* Apr. 20, 1846.

[36] Washington *Union,* Feb. 14, 1846, names individuals from the customhouses of Boston, New York, Philadelphia, and Baltimore. See also *ibid.,* July 2, 1846; and speech of John M. Niles of Connecticut in the Senate, July 20, 1846, *Cong. Globe,* 29th, 1st, Appendix, 882.

[37] "Some Reflections of a Free Trader," *Democratic Review,* XVIII (February 1846), 136-140; Washington *Union,* Feb. 14, 1846. The *Southern Quarterly Review* added its mite in April with a collective review, probably by David J. McCord, of Polk's first annual message, Walker's Treasury Report, and Peel's January speech in the House of Commons, IX, 392-433; but these sentiments were nothing unusual for the *Southern Quarterly Review.*

[38] *House Journal,* 29th, 1st, 406, 410, 412, 413, 422; Washington *Union,* Feb. 19, 20, 21, 1846; R. J. Walker to Pakenham, Feb. 25, 1846, and enclosure, accompanying Pakenham to Aberdeen, Feb. 28, 1846 (No. 18), F. O. 5-446, photostat in LC.

[39] Washington *Union,* Mar. 27, 28, 1846; Charleston *Courier,* Apr. 4, 1846; McDuffie to Hammond, Apr. 10, 1846, Hammond Papers.

[40] Polk, *Diary,* I, 323-326.

[41] *House Journal,* 29th, 1st, 672-673; *Cong. Globe,* 670-671.

[42] Washington *Union,* Apr. 14, 1846, *et seq.,* esp. Apr. 25, May 6, May 28, June 15; Charleston *Mercury,* Apr. 29, May 12, June 3, 1846; Charleston *Courier,* June 5, 1846; Calhoun to Clemson, May 28, 1846, *Correspondence,* 692.

[43] Washington *Union,* June 15, 1846.

[44] Washington *Union,* Apr. 23, 24, 1846; Calhoun to Clemson, Apr. 25, *Correspondence,* 688-689; Polk, *Diary,* I, 350-353.

[45] McLane to Calhoun, May 18, 1846, *Correspondence,* 1081-1083; to Buchanan, May 3, 18, 1846 (Nos. 43 and 44), Miller, *Treaties,* V, 68-72; Aberdeen to Pakenham, May 18, 1846 (No. 19), F. O. 115-91, photostat in LC.

[46] Polk, *Diary,* I, 447-448, 451-455.

[47] *Ibid.,* 456-457, 461-463, 465-466, 467; *Senate Executive Journal,* VII, 84-89;

Calhoun to Mrs. Clemson, June 11, 1846, *Correspondence*, 694-696; to Clemson, June 11, 1846, *ibid.*, 697.

[48] *Cong. Globe*, 29th, 1st, 972, 979, 986; Charleston *Courier*, June 20, 1846; Polk, *Diary*, I, 471-472; *Senate Executive Journal*, VII, 90, 94-95. Text of the treaty is in Miller, *Treaties*, V, 3-5.

[49] Calhoun to James Edward Calhoun, July 2, 1846, *Correspondence*, 698; *Hansard*, third series, LXXXVII, 961, 1027-1032, 1040-1059; Miller, *Treaties*, V, 96-97. See also Calhoun to Clemson, May 12, 1846, *Correspondence*, 690; and Webster to Peter Harvey, May, 1846, Webster's *Writings*, XVI, 453.

[50] Buchanan to McLane, June 22, 1846, Buchanan's *Works*, VII, 17; Dix to Wright, July 10, 1846, Morgan Dix, *Memoirs of John A. Dix*, I, 202; Dix to Dr. G. C. Shattuck, Nov. 14, 1846, *Mass. Hist. Soc. Proc.*, L, 166. For an ingenious attempt to get Calhoun appointed to the British Mission see Sarah Mytton Maury to Buchanan, June 10, July 10, 1846, Curtis, *Buchanan*, I, 612, 614-615; and Polk, *Diary*, II, 6-10, 18-19.

[51] Charleston *Mercury*, June 30, 1846; Washington *Union*, June 20, July 2, 1846. See also Howell Cobb to his wife, June 14, 1846, *Toombs, Stephens, Cobb Correspondence*, 81-82.

[52] *Cong. Globe*, 29th, 1st, 976-1053, *passim;* Washington *Union*, July 3, 1846; Charleston *Courier*, July 7, 8, 1846; Charleston *Mercury*, July 8, 1846.

[53] Washington *Union*, July 3, 25, 1846.

[54] Calhoun to Clemson, July 11, 1846, *Correspondence*, 700-701. Gadsden wrote July 9 from Charleston that "the passage of the Tariff [in the House] has pleased, but not satisfied us," though he conceded it was probably the best that could be done. *Ibid.*, 1085-1086.

[55] *Cong. Globe*, 29th, 1st, 1081ff; Webster to N. Appleton, July 8, 1846, Webster's *Writings*, XVI, 456-457; Washington *Union*, July 15, 1846; Charleston *Courier*, July 17, 1846.

[56] Polk, *Diary*, II, 26, 29-30, 32-33. There are many examples in Calhoun's correspondence of the kind of pressure used by the manufacturers. See, *e.g.*, Abbott Lawrence to Calhoun, July 14, 1846, *Correspondence*, 1086-1087; Thompson & Co. to Calhoun, July 7, 1846, *Correspondence II*, 350-351; and the next several letters in this volume. Others are in the Calhoun Papers, CC.

[57] Polk, *Diary*, II, 33-35, 42-47.

[58] Washington *Union*, July 25, 1846; Charleston *Courier*, July 29, 1846; Charleston *Mercury*, July 29, 1846; Polk, *Diary*, 48-49.

[59] Polk, *Diary*, II, 25, 47-48. For a bitter reflection on Haywood from Calhoun's camp see Elmore to Calhoun, July 28, 1846, Calhoun Papers, CC.

[60] Webster to Fletcher Webster, July 29, 1846, Webster's *Writings*, XVI, 459-464.

[61] *Ibid.;* Polk, *Diary*, II, 51-52; *Cong. Globe*, 29th, 1st, 1141-1145. Why Clayton should have blocked Webster's ingenious device for defeating the bill is not clear, unless, as John M. Niles, protariff Democrat from Connecticut, insisted, Clayton really wanted the bill to pass in order to make political capital of it. See Niles to Van Buren, Aug. 8, 1846, Van Buren Papers. This letter is misfiled as of Aug. 8, 1844, and is entered in the calendar of the Van Buren Papers under the erroneous date.

[62] *Cong. Globe*, 29th, 1st, 1149-1158; Polk, *Diary*, II, 52-54; Webster to Fletcher Webster, *loc. cit.;* Washington *Union*, July 28, 1846; Charleston *Courier*,

July 31, Aug. 1, 1846; Calhoun to James Edward Calhoun, July 29, 1846, *Correspondence*, 701; to Clemson, July 30, 1846, *ibid.*, 702.

CHAPTER XIX

[1] Buchanan to Parrott, Mar. 28, 1845, Manning, *Diplomatic Correspondence, Inter-American Affairs*, VIII, 164-166; to Shannon, Mar. 29, 1845, *ibid.*, 166-167. There are numerous secondary accounts, including J. S. Reeves, *American Diplomacy under Tyler and Polk*, 268ff; J. H. Smith, *The War with Mexico*, I, 88; McCormac, *Polk*, 383-384; and Sioussat, "Buchanan," *American Secretaries of State*, V, 266-267. For a highly critical version of the whole affair see R. R. Stenberg, "The Failure of Polk's Mexican War Intrigue of 1845," *Pacific Historical Review*, IV (March 1935), 39-68.

[2] Parrott's dispatches are in Manning, *op. cit.*, 712-766, *passim*.

[3] Taylor to Donelson, July 20, 1845, Donelson Papers; Dallas to Polk, Aug. 25, 1845, Polk Papers, second series; Polk, *Diary*, I, 8-10, 12.

[4] Polk, *Diary*, I, 33-36, 91-94; Buchanan to Black, Sept. 17, 1845, Manning, *op. cit.*, 167-169; Parrott to Buchanan, Oct. 11, 1845, *ibid.*, 760-761; Black to Buchanan, Oct. 17, 1845, *ibid.*, 764-765.

[5] Polk, *Diary*, I, 83-84; Buchanan to Larkin, Oct. 17, 1845, Manning, *op. cit.*, 169-171. Larkin's dispatches are in the same volume. See esp. those of June 6, 1845 (received Sept. 16), and July 10 (received Oct. 11), 721-722, 735-736.

[6] Buchanan to Slidell, Nov. 10, Dec. 17, 1845, Manning, *op. cit.*, 172-182, 184-185; Polk, *Diary*, I, 93-94.

[7] Slidell to Buchanan, Nov. 19, Dec. 17, 1845, Manning, *op. cit.*, 774-775, 777-783; Black to Slidell, Dec. 15, 1845, *ibid.*, 778-779 note; Black to Buchanan, Dec. 18, 1845, *ibid.*, 783-784.

[8] The documents are in Manning, *op. cit.*, 777-810. See also Smith, *War with Mexico*, I, 96-100; and Reeves, *American Diplomacy under Tyler and Polk*, 282-283.

[9] Buchanan to Slidell, Jan. 20, 1846, Manning, *op. cit.*, 185-187; Polk, *Diary*, I, 164. Taylor's orders are in *House Document* 196, 29th, 1st.

[10] Polk, *Diary*, I, 171, 197; Calhoun to Clemson, Jan. 29, 1846, *Correspondence*, 680; Charleston *Courier*, Jan. 30, 1846; Buchanan to Slidell, Jan. 28, 1846, Manning, *op. cit.*, 187-189.

[11] Polk, *Diary*, I, 222-225, 227-230, 233.

[12] The documents are in Manning, *op. cit.*, 814-832.

[13] Buchanan to Slidell, Mar. 12, 1846, Manning, *op. cit.*, 189-192; Slidell to Buchanan, Apr. 2, 1846, *ibid.*, 837-839.

[14] Calhoun to Clemson, Mar. 23, 1846, *Correspondence*, 687; Polk, *Diary*, I, 310-311.

[15] *Ibid.*, 311-313, 317, 322.

[16] *Ibid.*, 325-328.

[17] *Ibid.*, 337-338.

[18] *Ibid.*, 354, 363; Black to Buchanan, Mar. 19, 1846, Manning, *op. cit.*, 832-833.

[19] Polk, *Diary*, I, 365, 375-380. Taylor's dispatches are in *House Document* 196, 29th, 1st. It was the General's message of April 6 that was received the 29th.

[20] Polk, *Diary*, I, 380, 381, 382, 384-385.

[21] *Ibid.*, 386-391; Washington *Union*, May 9, 1846; Charleston *Courier*, May 8, 14, 1846; Sioussat, "Buchanan," 276-277.

[22] Richardson, *Messages and Papers of the Presidents*, 2287-2293.

[23] *Cong. Globe*, 29th, 1st, 791-795; V. H. Davis, *Jefferson Davis*, I, 245; Joshua Giddings, *History of the Rebellion*, 251-253; Polk, *Diary*, I, 387-391.

[24] *Cong. Globe*, 29th, 1st, 783. The whole Senate debate for this day, May 11, 1846, is in *ibid.*, 782-788.

[25] Polk, *Diary*, I, 390-393.

[26] *Cong. Globe*, 29th, 1st, 795-804; Calhoun to A. P. Calhoun, May 14, 1846, *Correspondence*, 690-691; to Clemson, May 12, 1846, *ibid.*, 689-690.

[27] Holmes to Hammond, May 10, 1846, Hammond Papers; Calhoun to Conner, May 15, 1846, Conner Papers; Dix to Van Buren, May 16, 1846, Van Buren Papers. See also Calhoun to Wilson Lumpkin, Dec. 13, 1846, Calhoun Papers, Duke. The book on which Calhoun probably relied for his views on the Texas boundary was William Kennedy, *Texas: Its Geography, Natural History, and Topography* (New York, 1844), which was a reprint of a part of a work published in England in 1841. See reference in K. H. Fish to Calhoun, Mar. 7, 1846, Calhoun Papers, CC.

[28] Charleston *Mercury*, May 19, 1846; R. M. Saunders to Polk, May 14, 1846, Polk Papers, second series; Albon Chase to Howell Cobb, May 20, 1846, *Toombs, Stephens, Cobb Correspondence*, 78; W. H. Hull to Cobb, May 22, 1846, *ibid.*, 79; George Curtiss to Calhoun, May 26, 1846, *Correspondence II*, 347-348; Calhoun to Clemson, June 11, 1846, *Correspondence*, 697; Barbour to Calhoun, no date, 1846, Calhoun Papers, CC.

[29] Smith, *War with Mexico*, I, 196-203.

[30] Calhoun to Clemson, May 28, 1846, *Correspondence*, 691-692.

CHAPTER XX

[1] Polk, *Diary*, II, 50-51, 56-60, 70-73; Buchanan to D. H. Lewis, Aug. 7, 1846, Buchanan's *Works*, VII, 52-53; *Senate Executive Journal*, VII, 132-134, 136-137; Richardson, *Messages and Papers of the Presidents*, 2309-2310; *Cong. Globe*, 29th, 1st, 1211-1213.

[2] *Ibid.*, 1213-1218.

[3] *Ibid.*, 1220-1221; Polk, *Diary*, II, 74-78.

[4] Calhoun to Coryell, Nov. 7, 1846, *Correspondence*, 709-710; to ——, Nov. 7, 1846, *ibid.*, 710-711.

[5] The controversy may be followed in the files of the Charleston *Mercury* and Charleston *Courier* from mid-September 1846 until the meeting of the legislature in late November. Calhoun's letter, addressed to James L. Orr, William Sloan, A. Evins, and F. W. Symmes, appeared in the Pendleton *Messenger* (of which Symmes was editor) on Nov. 13, but was written before the end of October. "I declined coming out before the election," he wrote to his brother-in-law, "to avoid the imputation of improper interference." Calhoun to James Edward Calhoun, Oct. 29, 1846, *Correspondence*, 708. The letter is in *Works*, VI, 254-272.

[6] Charleston *Courier*, Dec. 4-15, *passim;* William Sloan to Calhoun, Dec. 12, 1846, Calhoun Papers, CC.

[7] Charleston *Courier*, Dec. 7, 10, 1846. The Hammond Papers for late Octo-

ber through mid-December contain much material on the factional struggle for McDuffie's seat. See also R. F. W. Allston to Mrs. Allston, Dec. 10, 1846, J. H. Easterby, *South Carolina Rice Plantation,* 97.

[8] Polk, *Diary,* II, 181-182, 198-199, 221-223, 231-233.

[9] *Ibid.,* 239-246, 261-263.

[10] Richardson, *Messages and Papers of the Presidents,* 2321-2356. For the election returns see *Niles,* LXXI, 121, 160; and Polk, *Diary,* II, 217-218.

[11] Calhoun to Wilson Lumpkin, Dec. 13, 1846, Calhoun Papers, Duke; Polk, *Diary,* II, 268-306, *passim;* Richardson, *op. cit.,* 2358.

[12] *Cong. Globe,* 29th, 2nd, 175-177, 184-187; Polk, *Diary,* II, 347; Calhoun to Duff Green, Apr. 17, 1847, *Correspondence,* 727-728.

[13] See, *e.g.,* Calhoun to Mrs. Clemson, Dec. 27, 1847, *Correspondence,* 715-716; and Wilson Lumpkin to Calhoun, Jan. 6, 1847, *ibid.,* 1103. See also Polk, *Diary,* II, 283-284.

[14] *Cong. Globe,* 29th, 2nd, 105, 114-115.

[15] Charleston *Courier,* Jan. 11, 1847; Charleston *Mercury,* Jan. 13, 1847; Polk, *Diary,* II, 304-306, 308-309; Calhoun to Conner, Jan. 14, 1847 [misdated 1846], Conner Papers; Crallé to Calhoun, Jan. 19, 1847, Calhoun Papers, CC; F. Byrdsall to Calhoun, Feb. 14, 1847, *Correspondence,* 1105. Compare Lumpkin to Calhoun, Jan. 6, 1847, written before the former Georgia Congressman could have heard of King's move, *ibid.,* 1103.

[16] *Cong. Globe,* 29th, 2nd, 178-180, and Appendix, 116-119; Charleston *Courier,* Jan. 18, 1847. For Calhoun's hand in it, see his remarks in the Senate, Feb. 19, 1847, *Works,* IV, 347.

[17] *Cong. Globe,* 29th, 2nd, 187, 188, and Appendix, 244-247. The Washington *Union* did not print the speech until Jan. 30. The Library of Congress copy is that sent to S. H. Laughlin, Tennessee friend and supporter of Polk, and across the top of the first page is written in Laughlin's hand: "Mr. Rhett's Admirable speech against restricting Slavery in New Territor[y]."

[18] Polk, *Diary,* II, 308-309, 334-335.

[19] Charleston *Mercury,* Jan. 16, 21, Feb. 5, 10, 1847; Pendleton *Messenger,* Jan. 22, 29, 1847.

[20] Calhoun to Conner, Jan. 14, 1847 [misdated 1846], Conner Papers; Burt to Conner, Feb. 1, 1847, *ibid.*

[21] Polk, *Diary,* II, 323-339, *passim; Cong. Globe,* 29th, 2nd, 204, 218; Buchanan's *Works,* 198-199.

[22] *Senate Journal,* 29th, 2nd, 166-183, *passim; House Journal,* 298-325, *passim; Cong. Globe,* 346-349, 376-377; Charleston *Courier,* Feb. 12, 15, 1847; Polk, *Diary,* II, 371-372; Washington *Union,* Feb. 8, 1847.

[23] *Cong. Globe,* 29th, 2nd, 356-359, and *Appendix,* 323-327; *Works,* IV, 303-327. Benton's garbled account, *View,* II, 693-694, and especially the implied charge that Calhoun was seeking more slave territory, is not consistent either with the journal and debates of the Senate or with Polk, *Diary,* II, 283-284.

[24] *Cong. Globe,* 29th, 2nd, 366-367.

[25] *Ibid.,* 392-400. For Calhoun's remarks see also *Works,* IV, 328-339.

[26] Charleston *Courier,* Feb. 16, 1847.

[27] *Cong. Globe,* 29th, 2nd, 406-417; Charleston *Courier,* Feb. 17, 22, 1847; Charleston *Mercury,* Feb. 22, 1847. See also Washington *Union,* Feb. 12, 13, 1847; and Polk, *Diary,* II, 375-379.

CHAPTER XXI

[1] *Cong. Globe*, 29th, 2nd, 425; Charleston *Mercury*, Feb. 20, 1847.

[2] *Cong. Globe*, 29th, 2nd, 453-455; *Works*, IV, 339-349.

[3] *Cong. Globe*, 29th, 2nd, 455-460, and Appendix, 218-223.

[4] Washington *Union*, Feb. 22, 1847; Charleston *Mercury*, Feb. 25, 1847; Charleston *Courier*, Feb. 27, Mar. 1, 1847.

[5] *Cong. Globe*, 29th, 2nd, 494-498.

[6] *Ibid.*, 498-501; *Works*, IV, 362-382; Charleston *Courier*, Mar. 1, 1847; Charleston *Mercury*, Mar. 4, 1847; Pendleton *Messenger*, Mar. 5, 1847; T. Fitman to Calhoun, Feb. 24, 1847, Calhoun Papers, CC.

[7] *Senate Journal*, 29th, 2nd, 252-253; Charleston *Courier*, Mar. 8, 1847. The passage with Allen is not included in *Cong. Globe*, 570-571, where only the most sketchy report appears. The reporters of that day, being employed by the various newspapers rather than by Congress itself, often did not cover night sessions at all, and when the calendar was crowded as it always was in the final days of the short session, the reports of the long day sittings are sometimes less than nominal. The *Union* had forecast this new line of attack on March 1, when Ritchie had severely criticized Calhoun's handling of the Oregon negotiation and had charged the former Secretary of State with having erroneously abandoned the United States' claim to the whole territory.

[8] Duff Green to Crallé, Mar. 5, 1847, Green Papers (in part in Southern History Association, *Publications*, VII, 424).

[9] Charleston *Mercury*, Mar. 5, 8, 10, 1847; Charleston *Courier*, Mar. 8, 9, 10, 1847; Calhoun to Clemson, Mar. 19, 1847, *Correspondence*, 720.

[10] Charleston *Mercury*, Mar. 10, 1847; Charleston *Courier*, Mar. 10, 1847; Calhoun to Duff Green, Mar. 9, 1847, *Correspondence*, 718-720. The text of the speech, summarized below, is in *Works*, IV, 382-396.

[11] Polk, *Diary*, II, 457-459; Washington *Union*, Mar. 15, 20, 27, 1847, and generally through April. See also the countering arguments in the Charleston *Mercury* over a similar period; and Benton's letter to the people of Oregon in the same paper for May 19. The address on the subject of slavery to which Polk makes reference in the passage cited was in fact the prospectus of a newspaper, which will be discussed later in this chapter.

[12] Polk, *Diary*, II, 429-478, *passim*.

[13] Washington *Union*, June 15, July 13, 14, 15, 16, Aug. 7, 1847; *Niles*, LXXII, 310, 332-333; *De Bow's Review*, IV, 122-127, 291-296; Allan Nevins, *Ordeal of the Union*, I, 38.

[14] See, *e.g.*, F. Byrdsall to Calhoun, July 29, 1847, *Correspondence II*, 389. See also the address to the convention by David Dudley Field, young Barnburner delegate, in the *Democratic Review*, XXI (September 1847), 189-202.

[15] Polk, *Diary*, III, 11, 52-54, 57-59, 75-79, 89-90.

[16] Elmore to Calhoun, Jan. 29, 1847, Calhoun Papers, CC; Duff Green to Calhoun, Mar. 4, 1847, *ibid.*; Green to Calhoun, Mar. 17, 1847, *Correspondence II*, 370-372; Green to ———, Mar. 22, 1847, Green Papers. A copy of the prospectus is in the Hammond Papers, with a covering note from Isaac W. Hayne, dated Mar. 31, 1847. An endorsement by Hammond, dated Apr. 5, reflects his old bitterness toward Calhoun, whose Presidential ambitions he will not further in this fashion.

[17] Elmore to Calhoun, Apr. 10, 1847, Calhoun Papers, CC; Conner to Calhoun, May 7, 1847, *Correspondence II,* 374-375; Calhoun to Conner, May 14, 1847, Conner Papers; I. W. Hayne to Hammond, May 29, 1847, Hammond Papers; Hammond to Hayne, June 4, 1847, *ibid.;* Conner to Calhoun, June 16, 1847, Calhoun Papers, CC.

[18] *Laws of Pennsylvania,* 1847, No. 159; C. J. Faulkner to Calhoun, July 15, 1847, *Correspondence II,* 385-387; *Niles,* LXXII, 177, 379; Charleston *Mercury,* July 27, 1847; Calhoun to Clemson, July 24, 1847, *Correspondence,* 735-736; Giddings to Oran Follett, July 26, 1847, Historical and Philosophical Society of Ohio, *Quarterly Publications,* X, 32. Officially the decision of the B & O directors against the Pittsburgh route was owing to difficulties of another sort, thrown in the way by the Pennsylvania legislature, which had just chartered the competing Pennsylvania Railroad. See Edward Hungerford, *Story of the Baltimore & Ohio Railroad,* I, 240-250. In either case, however, it is a sectional reaction on the part of a Maryland corporation to a sectional provocation from Pennsylvania.

[19] *Correspondence II,* 399-402. There are thirty-seven names signed to the original in the Calhoun Papers, CC, including besides Huger, R. W. Barnwell, Wade Hampton, and W. F. DeSaussure.

[20] A copy of the subscription form in the Calhoun Papers, CC, dated Aug. 8, 1847, has the names of 10 subscribers, pledging a total of $7,000, written in. These are Nathaniel Heyward, R. F. W. Allston, William Aiken, and Joshua I. Ward, $1,000 each; and D. E. Huger, P. W. Fraser, Daniel Heyward, L. L. Manning, W. H. Trescott [?], and M. C. Mordecai, $500 each.

[21] Joseph W. Lesesne to Calhoun, Aug. 21, 1847, *Correspondence II,* 391-393; Conner to Calhoun, Aug. 23, 1847, *Correspondence,* 1128-1129; I. W. Hayne to Pierre Soulé, Aug. 25, 1847, Hammond Papers; Calhoun to Conner, Aug. 25, 1847, Conner Papers; Elmore to Calhoun, Aug. 25, 1847, Calhoun Papers, CC; A. P. Aldrich to Hammond, Aug. 26, 30, 1847, Hammond Papers; Calhoun to Clemson, Sept. 6, 1847, *Correspondence,* 737; Conner to Calhoun, Sept. 7, Oct. 28, 1847, Calhoun Papers, CC; Hayne to Calhoun, Sept. 15, 1847, *ibid.*

[22] L. M. Keit to Calhoun, Oct. 1, 1847, *Correspondence II,* 402. Calhoun's suggestion was made in a letter reproduced without date or addressee but with caustic commentary in Benton, *View,* II, 698-700, where it constitutes one of Benton's "proofs" of the South Carolinian's alleged desire to destroy the Union because he could not be President of it. Both style and matter are distinctively Calhoun's, and the context fits so well the pattern of his correspondence at this time that there seems no reason to doubt its authenticity, even while rejecting Benton's deduction from it. It was in all probability addressed to Joseph W. Lesesne, leader of the Calhoun forces in Alabama's legislature, either the last week in August or the first week in September 1847. Benton states that the letter was addressed to a member of the Alabama Legislature, and it fits well the context of Lesesne's letters to Calhoun of Aug. 24 and Sept. 12, *Correspondence,* 1130-1131, 1133-1135. See also W. M. Meigs, *Life of John Caldwall Calhoun,* II, 405.

[23] Charleston *Courier,* Sept. 8, 13, 14, 29, Oct. 1, 20, 1847; Charleston *Mercury,* Sept. 9, 10, 13, Oct. 20, 1847; Washington *Union,* Sept. 14, 16, 30, Oct. 2, 4, 5, 6, 1847; Polk, *Diary,* III, 185-186; Calhoun to Clemson, Oct. 24, 1847, *Correspondence,* 737.

[24] Calhoun to Duff Green, Nov. 9, 1847, *Correspondence,* 740; Conner to Calhoun, Oct. 6, 1847, *Correspondence II,* 402-404; Fisher to Calhoun, Dec. 4,

1847, Calhoun Papers, CC (in part in *Correspondence,* 1145-1147); Charleston *Mercury,* Dec. 4, 1847.

CHAPTER XXII

[1] A typical comment came from Calhoun's son Patrick, now a Brevet Captain on the staff of the superannuated General Gaines. "Nothing is talked of here," wrote the young West Pointer from New York to his politically minded father, "but the recent victories gained by General Taylor in Mexico—they will surely make him President unless some unforseen misfortune should occur to mar his increasing popularity—Whigs and Democrats go for him here—that is the portion of the Democratic party which carries the election—Every labourer, foreigner & otherwise, you meet in the street throws up his hat and hurrahs for General Taylor—Military fame and glory is everything with the people and carries all before it." Patrick Calhoun to Calhoun, Apr. 5, 1847, Calhoun Papers, CC.

[2] Charleston *Courier,* Apr. 14, 1847; Polk, *Diary,* II, 470-471.

[3] Calhoun to Conner, May 14, 1847, Conner Papers. See also Calhoun to Clemson, May 6, July 24, 1847, *Correspondence,* 728-729, 735; Charleston *Mercury,* May 13, 1847; Pendleton *Messenger,* May 28, 1847.

[4] Conner to Calhoun, May 21, July 27, 1847, Calhoun Papers, CC; Hammond to Edmund Ruffin, June, 1847, Ruffin Papers; Hammond to Simms, June 15, 1847, Hammond Papers; Rhett to Calhoun, June 21, 1847, *Correspondence,* 1119-1121; Charleston *Courier,* July 20, 1847; Elmore to Calhoun, May 16, 1847, *Correspondence II,* 376; Orr to Calhoun, Aug. 9, 1847, *ibid.,* 390.

[5] Charleston *Courier,* June 14, 1847; J. W. A. Pettit to Calhoun, June 18, 1847, *Correspondence II,* 384; F. Byrdsall to Calhoun, July 19, 1847, *Correspondence,* 1121-1127; Salmon P. Chase to Preston King, July 15 [1847], *Diary and Correspondence of Salmon P. Chase,* 120-122; J. R. Giddings to Oran Follet, July 26, 1847, Historical and Philosophical Society of Ohio, *Quarterly Publications,* X, 30-33; E. D. Ellis to Calhoun, Aug. 18, 1847, Calhoun Papers, CC.

[6] Washington *Union,* Aug. 30, 1847; *Niles,* LXXIII, 6-9; Polk, *Diary,* III, 153; John A. Garraty, *Silas Wright,* 397-398.

[7] Buchanan to Charles Kessler, *et al.,* Aug. 25, 1847, Buchanan's *Works,* VII, 385-387; Polk, *Diary,* III, 142-143; Washington *Union,* Aug. 31, 1847.

[8] Washington *Union,* Sept. 3, 9, 11, 24, 1847; Rhett to Calhoun, Sept. 8, 1847, *Correspondence,* 1132-1133; S. P. Chase to Charles Sumner, Sept. 22, 1847, *Chase Correspondence,* 122-124; David Wilmot to Preston King, Sept. 25, 1847, Van Buren Papers; Wilmot to Van Buren, Oct. 6, 1847, *ibid.;* Charleston *Mercury,* Sept. 30, 1847.

[9] There are full reports in the New York *Herald,* Sept. 30-Oct. 6. 1847; and a useful commentary in the Charleston *Courier,* Oct. 9, 1847. A good secondary account is in Donovan, *Barnburners,* 93-97.

[10] Stewart Mitchell, *Horatio Seymour of New York,* 109, New York *Herald,* Oct. 6, 1847.

[11] Donovan, *op. cit.,* 95-96; New York *Herald,* Oct. 29, 1847.

[12] Washington *Union,* Oct. 30, Nov. 1, 3, 6, 1847; Charleston *Courier,* Nov. 2, 1847; F. Byrdsall to Calhoun, Nov. 12, 1847, *Correspondence II,* 409-410; Polk, *Diary,* III, 214-215.

[13] Benton to Polk, Nov. 21, 1847, Van Buren Papers; Polk, *Diary,* III, 228-

229. The possibility that Benton was indeed flirting with the Barnburners is given some weight by the fact that his letter to Polk here cited is to be found in the Van Buren Papers, in the hand of Senator Dix, who must have been allowed by Benton himself to take a copy for that purpose.

[14] Charleston *Courier*, Nov. 18, 1847. See also *ibid.*, Dec. 6, 1847; and Hone, *Diary*, 827-828.

[15] *House Journal*, 30th, 1st, 8-14; *Cong. Globe*, 2. Joshua Giddings, *History of the Rebellion*, 261, says that Winthrop was chosen by the refusal of two Southern Democrats, unnamed, to vote. The Charleston *Courier*, Jan. 1, 1848, gives the credit to Isaac Holmes, who did not vote on the third ballot. Neither of these accounts, however, is strictly correct. Holmes's withdrawal did not alter the number needed to elect. The other man who failed to vote, Tompkins, was not a Democrat but a Whig, though he was a Southerner and his action did reduce by one the majority needed. The fact remains, however, that Winthrop was actually chosen by the vote of Lewis C. Levin, who was to do the Whigs still greater service in the coming Presidential election.

[16] Polk, *Diary*, III, 236-239; Richardson, *Messages and Papers of the Presidents*, 2382-2414; Washington *Union*, Dec. 7, 1847; Charleston *Mercury*, Dec. 10, 11, 1847; Charleston *Courier*, Dec. 10, 11, 1847.

[17] *Cong. Globe*, 30th, 1st, 21.

[18] Calhoun to Conner, Dec. 16, 1847, Conner Papers; to Elmore, Dec. 22, 1847, Elmore Papers.

[19] *Cong. Globe*, 30th, 1st, 26.

[20] *Ibid.*, 53-56; Charleston *Courier*, Dec. 20, 1847; Cass to A. O. P. Nicholson, Dec. 24, 1847, in Washington *Union*, Dec. 30, 1847.

[21] Washington *Union*, Jan. 4, 1848; *National Intelligencer*, Jan. 5, 1848; Charleston *Courier*, Jan 10, 1848; Charleston *Mercury*, Jan. 10, 1848. The speech is in Calhoun's *Works*, IV, 396-424. See also Calhoun to A. P. Calhoun, Dec. 11, 1847, Calhoun Papers, Duke (in part in *Correspondence*, 741); and Calhoun to Mrs. Clemson, Dec. 26, 1847, *Correspondence*, 741-742.

[22] Calhoun elaborated some of the points made in this speech in one delivered Mar. 16 to 17, 1848, on the Ten-Regiment Bill, *Works*, IV, 425-450.

[23] Responses to Calhoun's speech are too numerous for individual citation. Most of them are in the Calhoun Papers, CC, with a fair sampling in *Correspondence II*, 423ff. See also A. P. Butler to Elmore, Jan. 5, 1848, Elmore Papers; J. B. Mowrer to John McLean, Jan. 10, 1848, McLean Papers; Calhoun to Clemson, Feb. 4, 1848, *Correspondence*, 742-743; to Mrs. Clemson, Feb. 20, 1848, *ibid.*, 743-744. The President's troubles are detailed in Polk, *Diary*, III, 266ff.

[24] *Cong. Globe*, 30th, 1st, 157-160, 350, 374, and Appendix, 86-89, 302-306; Calhoun to H. Gourdin, Jan. 8, 1848, Conner Papers; to A. P. Calhoun, Feb. 23, 1848, *Correspondence*, 744; J. S. Barbour to Calhoun, Feb. 4, 1848, Calhoun Papers, CC.

[25] Polk, *Diary*, III, 350-351, 356; Washington *Union*, Feb. 23, 25, Mar. 14, 1848; Charleston *Courier*, Feb. 18, 1848.

[26] Polk, *Diary*, III, 346-352; *Senate Executive Journal*, VII, 302-303.

[27] Miller, *Treaties*, V, 207-428, tells the whole story.

[28] Polk, *Diary*, III, 361, 363-367.

[29] *Ibid.*, 367-378; *Senate Executive Journal*, VII, 340; Washington *Union*, Mar. 10, June 9, 1848; Charleston *Courier*, Mar. 14, 20, 28, 31, Apr. 1, 1848.

[30] Calhoun to A. P. Calhoun, Feb. 23, 1848, Calhoun Papers, Duke.

CHAPTER XXIII

¹ William E. Dodd, *Cotton Kingdom*, 24, estimates that in 1850 a thousand families in the South divided an annual income of more than $50 million, leaving only some $60 million for distribution among the remaining 666,000 Southern families. For Calhoun's trenchant attack on the theory of government by the numerical majority, see especially his letter to the Hon. William Smith, July 1843, *Works*, VI, 209-239, where he comments on the questions at issue in the Dorr uprising.

² [Orestes Brownson], "Slavery and the Mexican War," *Brownson's Quarterly Review*, IV (July 1847), 334-367.

³ Hammond to Calhoun, Sept. 26, 1845, Calhoun Papers, CC; Calhoun to Hammond, Sept. 28, 1845, *Correspondence*, 672-673.

⁴ Joseph J. Gurney, *A Journey in North America*, 387-390.

⁵ See, *e.g.*, Nathan Towson to Calhoun, May 27, 1847, *Correspondence II*, 379. It should be noted that there were also Northern men who accepted the doctrine of slavery as a positive good, intellectuals for the most part, and men associated with the ruling class in their own section. See Fitzwilliam Byrdsall to Calhoun, Feb. 22, 1847, *ibid.*, 368-369; and Fernando Wood to Calhoun, July 23, 1847, *Correspondence*, 1127-1128.

⁶ In this connection an interesting study is W. Carsel, "Slaveholders' Indictment of Northern Wage Slavery," *Journal of Southern History*, VI (November 1940), 504-520.

⁷ See Charles W. Ramsdell, "The Natural Limits of Slavery Expansion," *Mississippi Valley Historical Review*, XVI (September 1929), 151-171; "The Wilmot Proviso," *Southern Quarterly Review*, XI (April 1847), 377-406; Wilson Lumpkin to Calhoun, Aug. 27, 1847, *Correspondence II*, 396; F. Byrdsall to Calhoun, Nov. 12, 1847, *ibid.*, 410. See also Calhoun's speech of June 27, 1848, *Works*, IV, 504-505.

⁸ Luther *v.* Borden, *et al.*, 48 U. S. 1-87. Chief Justice Taney, the erstwhile Jacksonian "liberal," delivered the opinion of the Court at the beginning of the January 1849 term, upholding the Circuit Court from which the case had come on appeal. He held, that is, that the case was not legal but political, and that the established government of Rhode Island had acted within its rights in confiscating the property of the plaintiff, who was in rebellion. Justices Catron, Daniel, and McKinley, all slaveholders, did not participate because they had been absent due to illness when the case was argued. Justice Levi Woodbury, who had sustained the Dorr rebellion as Senator from New Hampshire, sustained it still in a long, well-reasoned dissent. See also "The Rhode Island Question—Sovereignty of the People," *Democratic Review*, XXII, 193-199, which was the *Review's* leading article for March 1848.

⁹ *National Intelligencer*, Mar. 21, 1848; Calhoun to Clemson, Mar. 22, 1848, *Correspondence*, 746-747; Calhoun to James Edward Calhoun, Jr., Mar. 23, 1848, Calhoun Papers, Duke. For more detailed discussion, see C. M. Wiltse, "A Critical Southerner: John C. Calhoun on the Revolutions of 1848," *Journal of Southern History*, XV (August 1949), 299-310.

¹⁰ Calhoun to Mrs. Clemson, November 21, 1846, *Correspondence*, 712; to Clemson, Sept. 6, 1847, *ibid.*, 736.

¹¹ *Works*, IV, 416; Calhoun to Mrs. Clemson, Mar. 7, 1848, *Correspondence*, 744-745.

[12] *Cong. Globe*, 30th, 1st, 549, 568-569; Calhoun's *Works*, IV, 450-454.

[13] *Cong. Globe*, 30th, 1st, 569-570; Washington *Union*, Mar. 31, 1848.

[14] *Cong. Globe*, 30th, 1st, 579-80, 590-592; Richardson, *Messages and Papers of the Presidents*, 2429-2430; Polk, *Diary*, III, 415-417. The two who remained to reverse their position were A. P. Butler and Jefferson Davis. The Charleston *Courier's* Washington correspondent commented, by way of explaining Calhoun's absence, that "he seldom remains so late in the chamber as half past six, when the vote was taken. A setting [sic] of six or seven hours exhausts men of infirm health"; but the coincidental absence of eleven others, most if not all of them in sound health, cannot be so easily passed off. See Charleston *Courier*, Apr. 12, 1848; also Washington *Union*, Apr. 7, 1848.

[15] *Cong. Globe*, 30th, 1st, 603-604; Charleston *Courier*, Apr. 15, 18, 1848.

[16] Calhoun's correspondence on the subject is voluminous. See especially his letters to Clemson, Apr. 1, 13, May 13, 26, 1848, *Correspondence*, 747-748, 748-749, 754, 756-757; to James Edward Calhoun, Apr. 15, May 22, 1848, *ibid.*, 749-750, 755; to Mrs. Clemson, Apr. 28, June 23, 1848, *ibid.*, 752-753, 757-759; to A. J. Donelson, May 23, 1848, *Tennessee Historical Magazine*, III (December 1917), 262-263; to Baron von Gerolt, May 28, 1848, in Merle E. Curti, ed., "John C. Calhoun and the Unification of Germany," *Am. Hist. Rev.*, XL (April 1935), 477-478. Of particular interest also is Mrs. Clemson to Calhoun, Apr. 18, 1848, Calhoun Papers, CC. For other citations and for more detailed discussion, see Wiltse, *loc. cit.*

[17] *Cong. Globe*, 30th, 1st, 576-577.

[18] The story is pieced together from various sources, the best account being that in the *National Intelligencer*, Apr. 19, 1848. See also Polk, *Diary*, III, 428-429; Charleston *Courier*, Apr. 24, 1848; and Giddings, *History of the Rebellion*, 272-279.

[19] *Cong. Globe*, 30th, 1st, 641, 649-673; Polk, *Diary*, III, 429; *National Intelligencer*, Apr. 20, 21, 1848; *National Era*, Apr. 20, 27, 1848; Charleston *Courier*, Apr. 28, 1848; *Liberator*, May 19, 1848.

[20] *Cong. Globe*, 30th, 1st, Appendix, 500-510, has the whole debate.

[21] Conner to Calhoun, Apr. 30, 1848, Calhoun Papers, CC; Fisher to Calhoun, May 19, 1848, *ibid.*; Polk, *Diary*, III, 443 (May 4, 1848).

CHAPTER XXIV

[1] *Cong. Globe*, 30th, 1st, 865-866, 870-871.

[2] Polk, *Diary*, III, 501-503; *Cong. Globe*, 30th, 1st, 873-874.

[3] Polk, *Diary*, III, 503-505; *Cong. Globe*, 30th, 1st, 875-876.

[4] Charleston *Mercury*, July 1, 3, 1848; Charleston *Courier*, July 1, 1848. The speech is in *Cong. Globe*, 30th, 1st, Appendix, 868-873; and Calhoun's *Works*, IV, 479-512.

[5] Richardson, *Messages and Papers of the Presidents*, 2437-2443; *Cong. Globe*, 30th, 1st, 901-902.

[6] *Ibid.*, 927-928; Polk, *Diary*, IV, 9, 12-15.

[7] Charleston *Courier*, July 17, 1848.

[8] *Cong. Globe*, 30th, 1st, 932; Charleston *Courier*, July 17, 19, 1848. The members were voted upon, not by the whole Senate but by each section for itself. See Calhoun to Clemson, July 23, 1848, *Correspondence*, 760.

[9] Polk, *Diary*, IV, 17-22.

[10] *Ibid.*, 23-24; *Cong. Globe*, 30th, 1st, 950; Charleston *Courier*, July 22, 1848. The text of the bill as finally passed by the Senate takes 10 columns in the *Cong. Globe*, 1002-1005. Calhoun was inclined to take the major share of credit to himself. "The settlement," he wrote to Clemson a few days later, "is based on the principle of non interference, as laid down in my speech on the Oregon territorial bill. . . . It is regarded here, as a great triumph on my part." Calhoun to Clemson, July 23, 1848, *Correspondence*, 760.

[11] The entire debate is brought together in *Cong. Globe*, 30th, 1st, Appendix, 1139-1204, and there are full running accounts in the daily papers. I have used those in the Washington *Union*, July 19-27, 1848; and the Charleston *Courier*, July 24-31, 1848. See also Charleston *Mercury*, July 24, 1848.

[12] Bright's speech is not reported in the *Globe*. This version is from the Charleston *Mercury*, July 31, 1848.

[13] *Cong. Globe*, 30th, 1st, 1002; Polk, *Diary*, IV, 31.

[14] I have accepted Adams' account of the Missouri debate incident in the first volume of this work, *Calhoun, Nationalist*, 196. The hostile account referred to above is that of Gideon Welles, then a clerk in the Navy Department, as recorded in an undated entry preceding that for August 7, 1848, in his manuscript diary, Huntington Library. Welles' description of the scene is hard to reconcile with the reported version of what Calhoun actually said, which seems calm and courteous enough; but the Carolinian's manner was undoubtedly positive. It generally was, and he would probably have been influenced on this occasion by fatigue, and the fact that he was taken by surprise in what looked like a planned attack. The Senate had already been continuously in session for some eight hours or more when the episode occurred, in the hottest part of the summer, and on a man of 66 who was in precarious health the strain must have been considerable. On the other hand, it must be remembered that Gideon Welles was closely associated with Senator John M. Niles, who was identified with the Barnburners, and his personal feelings were strongly on the side Dix represented. It remained for Francis Preston Blair to insinuate in private, when Calhoun was on his deathbed and could not have repudiated it if he had heard it, that the written opinions referred to had been deliberately destroyed during Calhoun's tenure in the State Department. See Blair to Van Buren, March 26, 1850, Van Buren Papers.

[15] *Cong. Globe*, 30th, 1st, 1006-1007; Polk, *Diary*, IV, 33-35; Washington *Union*, July 29, Aug. 1, 2, 1848; Charleston *Courier*, Aug. 1, 2, 1848. See also F. Byrdsall to Calhoun, Aug. 31, 1848, *Correspondence*, 1180-1181.

[16] The vote is not recorded in the *Globe*, but will be found in *House Journal*, 30th, 1st, 1155.

[17] *Cong. Globe*, 30th, 1st, 1031, and Appendix, 1204-1209.

[18] *Ibid.*, 1048, 1060-1061.

[19] The speech was delivered without special preparation or advance warning, and it was two months or more before Calhoun found time to write it out from the hasty notes he made at the time. It is not surprising, therefore, that the speech in its printed form combines remarks made on August 10 with others on the same topic made two days later. The report in the *Cong. Globe*, 30th, 1st, 1060, 1074, is sketchy in the extreme, and the revised text does not appear at all in the appendix for the session. The speech was first published in the Pendleton *Messenger*, Oct. 29, 1848, and reprinted in Calhoun's *Works*, IV, 513-535, where it is misdated Aug. 12, 1849. See contemporary accounts in the

Charleston *Mercury,* Aug. 14, 1848; and Charleston *Courier,* Aug. 15, 16, 1848. Since the bulk of the speech clearly belongs in the context of Aug. 10, it is here treated as a unit in the discussion of that day's debate, with only a minimum of recurrence to it in connection with the later date.

[20] *Cong. Globe,* 30th, 1st, 1061; *Senate Journal,* 590. The form of the amendment was more precise than that of the earlier Polk-Bright version, reading as follows: "That the line of thirty-six degrees and thirty minutes of north latitude, known as the Missouri Compromise line, as defined by the eighth section of an act entitled 'An act to authorize the people of the Missouri Territory to form a constitution and State government, and for the admission of such State into the Union on an equal footing with the original States, and to prohibit slavery in certain Territories,' approved Mar. 6, 1820, be, and the same is hereby, declared to extend to the Pacific ocean; and the said eighth section, together with the compromise therein effected, is hereby revived, and declared to be in full force and binding, for the future organization of the Territories of the United States, in the same sense, and with the same understanding with which it was originally adopted."

[21] *Cong. Globe,* 30th, 1st, 1061.

[22] The whole debate is in *ibid.,* 1074-1078. There were many who felt that this was the crucial time—perhaps the last time a settlement would be possible. Compare John B. Lamar to Howell Cobb, July 12, 1848, *Toombs, Stephens, Cobb Correspondence,* 116.

[23] The *Congressional Globe* gives a most inadequate impression of a very hectic session indeed. The course of events may be pieced out, however, from the accounts in the Charleston *Courier,* Aug. 16, 18, 21, 23; and the Charleston *Mercury,* Aug. 18, 1848. The affair between Butler and Benton was with some difficulty patched up.

[24] Charleston *Mercury,* Aug. 21, 1848; Charleston *Courier,* Aug. 21, 1848.

[25] Calhoun to Conner, Oct. 18, 1848, Conner Papers. Cf. Calhoun to "a prominent Gentleman in Georgia," Oct. 16, 1848, in Charleston *Mercury,* May 2, 1860.

CHAPTER XXV

[1] New York *Herald,* Feb. 18, 19, 1848; Donovan, *Barnburners,* 98-99; S. P. Chase to Charles Sumner, Mar. 25, 1848, Chase *Correspondence,* 132.

[2] Burt to Conner, Mar. 29, 30, Apr. 8, 1848, Conner Papers; Calhoun to Conner, Apr. 4, 6, 1848, *ibid.*

[3] Z. Taylor to Capt. J. S. Allison, Apr. 22, 1848, Washington *Union,* May 3, 1848. For original text and discussion of the Allison letter see Holman Hamilton, *Zachary Taylor, Soldier in the White House,* Chap. 7. See also John Bell to W. B. Campbell, Apr. 13, 1848, *Tennessee Historical Magazine* III (June 1917), 210; Taylor to Clay, Apr. 30, 1848, Clay's *Works,* V, 557-560.

[4] W. L. Yancey to Levi Woodbury, Mar. 10, 1848, Woodbury Papers; Preston King to Gideon Welles, Mar. 16, 1848, Welles Papers; Burt to Conner, May 5, 1848, Conner Papers; Howell Cobb to J. C. Nolland, May 11, 1848, Woodbury Papers; Woodbury to Yancey, May 15, 1848, *ibid.;* Polk, *Diary,* III, 398-404, 421-422, 448-460; Charleston *Courier,* May 1, 4, 11, 15, 1848.

[5] Burt to Conner, May 5, 1848, Conner Papers. Calhoun's preference for Woodbury was no doubt personal in part, since the former New Hampshire

Senator had been his own running mate in the 1844 campaign. In part, however, it was on principle. In the January 1847 term of the Supreme Court, Associate Justice Woodbury had delivered the opinion of the Court upholding the fugitive slave law of 1793, in a case in which counsel for the losing side included William H. Seward and Salmon P. Chase. See Jones v. Van Zandt, 46 U. S. 215-232.

[6] Conner to Calhoun, Apr. 13, 1848, *Correspondence*, 1166-1167; Calhoun to Conner, Apr. 20, 1848, Conner Papers; Burke to Woodbury, Apr. 24, 1848, Woodbury Papers; Charleston *Mercury*, May 20, 1848; Burt to Conner, May 21, 1848, Conner Papers; Crallé to Calhoun, Mar. 19, June 3, 1848, Calhoun Papers, CC (June 3 in part in *Correspondence*, 1169-1172); D. H. Lewis to Crallé, May 11, 1848, Crallé Papers, LC (in part in Southern History Association, *Publications*, VII, 425). Also Polk, *Diary*, III, 458.

[7] Washington *Union*, May 4, 20, 1848; Charleston *Courier*, May 24, 26, 1848.

[8] The complete report of the proceedings is in the Washington *Union*, May 23-27, 1848. There is a competent summary in Stanwood, *History of the Presidency*, I, 232-237. For Commander's appearance in Washington, see Burt to Conner, May 21, 1848, Conner Papers. The reaction is in Burt to Conner, May 23, 1848, *ibid.;* and Calhoun to Conner, May 23, 1848, *ibid.* See also Charleston *Mercury*, May 26, 1848.

[9] Stanwood, *History of the Presidency*, I, 234-236.

[10] The Charleston *Mercury* of June 1, reprinting Yancey's speech from the *Union*, calls it "an able, faithful, and lucid exposition of the principles" of the South.

[11] Burt to Conner, May 27, 28, June 3, 1848, Conner Papers; Charleston *Mercury*, June 12, 1848. Cf. H. Bailey to Calhoun, June 2, 1848, *Correspondence II*, 438; R. F. W. Allston to Calhoun, June 3, 1848, Calhoun Papers, CC.

[12] Stanwood, *History of the Presidency*, I, 237-238, has a succinct account. The best study of this convention yet to appear is that of Holman Hamilton, *Zachary Taylor, Soldier in the White House*, Chap. 8.

[13] Conner to Calhoun, June 23, 1848, Conner Papers; Hammond to M. C. M. Hammond, June 12, 1848, Hammond Papers; James A. Seddon to Hunter, June 16, 1848, *Hunter Correspondence*, 90-91; Yancey to Calhoun, June 14, 1848, *Correspondence II*, 441; Yancey to Calhoun, June 21, 1848, *Correspondence*, 1177; J. A. Campbell to Calhoun, June 20, 1848, Calhoun Papers, CC. Hammond, it should be noted, was sure that the third-party movement was entirely Calhoun's doing, and that Calhoun himself was to be the candidate. See Hammond to Simms, June 20, 1848, Hammond Papers.

[14] Donovan, *Barnburners*, 103-104.

[15] *Ibid.*, 104-105; New York *Herald*, June 22-25, July 1, 1848. See also *Niles*, LXXIV, 8; and F. Byrdsall to Calhoun, June 25, 1848, *Correspondence II*, 444-445.

[16] Stanwood, *op. cit.*, I, 238; Chase to Sumner, June 20, 1848, Chase *Correspondence*, 137-138.

[17] Polk, *Diary*, III, 502; Washington *Union*, June 27-30, 1848.

[18] Calhoun to Mrs. Clemson, June 23, 1848, *Correspondence*, 758-759; A. B. Longstreet to Calhoun, July 4, 1848, Calhoun Papers, CC; Ellwood Fisher to Calhoun, July 21, 1848, *ibid.;* Crallé to Calhoun, July 23, 1848, *ibid.* (in part in *Correspondence II*, 459-460); Calhoun to Conner, July 9, 1848, Conner Papers; to Eustis Prescott, Jr., July 15, 1848, Calhoun Papers, SCL. See also

Correspondence II, 444ff; the Calhoun Papers, CC, generally through July and early August 1848; and the files of the Charleston papers for the same period.

[19] Polk, *Diary,* IV, 8-12.

[20] *Ibid.,* 36-37, 57-58.

[21] There are many accounts of the Free-Soil convention. I have followed O. C. Gardiner, *The Great Issue,* 137-151; the New York *Herald,* Aug. 9-13, 1848; the Washington *National Era,* Aug. 17, 1848; and the briefer notices in *Niles,* LXXIV, 109-110. There is a useful secondary version in Donovan, *Barnburners,* 105-107.

[22] Washington *Union,* Aug. 16, 1848.

[23] *Liberator,* Aug. 11, 18, 1848; Washington *Union,* Aug. 8, 1848; Polk, *Dairy,* IV, 67; Calhoun to Clemson, Aug. 11, 1848, *Correspondence,* 760-761; Hammond to M. C. M. Hammond, Aug. 13, 1848, Hammond Papers.

[24] Charleston *Mercury,* Aug. 21, 1848.

[25] *Ibid.,* Aug. 21, 22, 1848; Gadsden to Hammond, Aug. 19, 1848, Hammond Papers; J. M. Walker to Hammond, Aug. 22, 1848, *ibid.*

[26] Caleb Cushing to Calhoun, Aug. 26, 1848, *Correspondence,* 1181-1182; Calhoun to the Editor of the *Mercury,* Sept. 1, 1848, Charleston *Mercury,* Sept. 5, 1848. Cf. Calhoun to Wilson Lumpkin, Sept. 1, 1848, Calhoun Papers, LC (photostat); Pendleton *Messenger,* Sept. 1, 1848.

[27] See Hammond to Simms, Sept. 7, 1848, Hammond Papers; James Gadsden to Hammond, Sept. 15, 1848, *ibid.;* Waddy Thompson to Crittenden, Sept. 8, 1848, Crittenden Papers; Isaac Holmes to Crittenden, Sept. 24, 1848, *ibid.;* R. Toombs to Crittenden, Sept. 27, 1848, *Toombs, Stephens, Cobb Correspondence,* 128-129; B. Tucker to Hammond, Oct. 11, 1848, Hammond Papers.

[28] Washington *Union,* from mid-August through October 1848; Polk, *Diary,* IV, 114.

[29] Taylor to Allison, Sept. 4, 1848. The letter appeared first in the New Orleans *Picayune,* but was widely reprinted around the middle of September. It is also in *Niles,* LXXIV, 200-201.

[30] Calhoun to "a prominent Gentleman in Georgia," Oct. 16, 1848, in Charleston *Mercury,* May 2, 1860.

[31] For Van Buren's motives, see W. A. Butler, *Reminiscences of Forty Years,* 189-191; the same writer's *Martin Van Buren, Lawyer, Statesman and Man,* 33-34; and Mitchell, *Horatio Seymour,* 110-112. The quotations are from the prefatory note in C. C. Gardiner, *The Great Issue,* published by Bryant in 1848.

[32] Charleston *Mercury,* Oct. 12, 17, Nov. 8, 1848; Charleston *Courier,* Nov. 9, 1848.

[33] Stanwood, *History of the Presidency,* I, 243.

CHAPTER XXVI

[1] Polk, *Diary,* IV, 224; Washington *Union,* Dec. 13, 16, 1848, Jan. 4, 1849; Charleston *Courier,* Dec. 11, 1848; Channing, *History of the United States,* VI, 40ff.

[2] C. S. Boucher, "Secession and Cooperation Movements in South Carolina, 1848-1852," *Washington University Studies,* V, no. 2, 71-72.

[3] Charleston *Courier,* Nov. 30, 1848; Charleston *Mercury,* Dec. 7, 8, 11, 14, 1848; David Johnson to Calhoun, Oct. 18, 1848, *Correspondence II,* 480-482; C. G. Memminger to Calhoun, Dec. 9, 1848, *ibid.,* 486; telegram, W. B. Seabrook

to Calhoun, Jan. 13, 1849, Calhoun Papers, CC; P. M. Hamer, *Secession Movement in South Carolina, 1847-1852,* 28-29.

[4] *Cong. Globe,* 30th, 2nd, 1, 21; Charleston *Courier,* Dec. 6, 11, 1848; Polk, *Diary,* IV, 228, 232-233, 236-237.

[5] *Cong. Globe,* 30th, 2nd, 26; Charleston *Courier,* Dec. 16, 1848; Oliver Dyer, *Great Senators,* 147-149; Polk, *Diary,* IV, 233.

[6] *Cong. Globe,* 30th, 2nd, 46-49.

[7] *Ibid.,* 38-39, 52-56, 71; Polk, *Diary,* IV, 235-238; Washington *Union,* Dec. 14, 1848; Charleston *Courier,* Dec. 18, 22, 1848.

[8] *Cong. Globe,* 30th, 2nd, 83-84; Washington *Union,* Dec. 22, 1848.

[9] *Hunter Correspondence,* 104, where the undated resolution is placed with material for 1850. The signature of Benjamin Fitzpatrick, however, places it in the 2nd session of the 30th Congress, the only one he attended before 1853, and subsequent events place it before December 22, 1848. The failure to mention Gott's resolution seems to put it before December 21, but it would hardly have been relevant before the 14th, when the House Committee on Territories was instructed to bring in a bill excluding slavery from the Mexican cession. The signers, in the order of their names, were Davis, Calhoun, Downs, Hunter, Butler, Yulee, H. V. Johnson, Atchison, Rusk, King, Foote, Fitzpatrick, Westcott, and Sebastian.

[10] Polk, *Diary,* IV, 248-251; *House Journal,* 30th, 2nd, 142. Foote took the major responsibility in remarks made in the Senate Feb. 23, and in published correspondence six months later he stated categorically that Calhoun knew nothing of the proposed meeting until most of those who took part in it had been "summoned." See Foote to Wise, June 23, 1849, Washington *Union,* June 24, 1849.

[11] Official proceedings are in the Washington *Union,* Jan. 28, 1849. See also Charleston *Courier,* Dec. 25, 28, 1848; *Niles,* LXXV, 84, 100-101; Polk, *Diary,* IV, 252-253.

[12] The "official" proceedings cited above do not include debate. I have followed the reports of Calhoun's remarks given in *Niles,* LXXV, 45-46; and the Charleston *Mercury,* Dec. 30, 1848.

[13] Washington *Union,* Jan. 28, 1849; Charleston *Courier,* Jan. 1, 5, 8, 9, 10, 13, 1849. There were hostile critics, of course, most outspoken of them Benton. See his exaggerated account in the *View,* II, 733-736; cf. Crittenden to Clayton, Jan 7, 1849, Crittenden Papers.

[14] *Cong. Globe.,* 30th, 2nd, 210-216. Albert J. Beveridge, *Life of Abraham Lincoln,* I, 481-484, is in error in his conclusion that the Lincoln District of Columbia slave bill "was a moving cause" of Calhoun's Southern Address. The address, by this time, was already prepared and the causes already at least three weeks old. Lincoln's bill was in fact an evasion, for no one could believe after the excitement of April 1848 that the white male inhabitants of the District would accept such a measure.

[15] Charleston *Courier,* Jan. 17, 1849.

[16] Washington *Union,* Jan. 28, 1849; Charleston *Courier,* Jan. 17, 18, 1849.

[17] Polk, *Diary,* IV, 280-284; Charleston *Courier,* Jan. 18, 1849.

[18] The address in slightly modified form is in Calhoun's *Works,* VI, 290-313. It will be found in its original form in the Washington *Union,* Feb. 4, 1849, where the portions omitted before signature are enclosed in brackets. None of the alterations is material.

[19] Calhoun's original makes a possible exception for the states of Indiana and Illinois.

[20] Washington *Union*, Jan. 16, 17, 28, 1849; Charleston *Courier*, Jan. 18, 1849; J. S. Pendleton to Rives, Feb. 7, 1849, Rives Papers; Calhoun to James Edward Calhoun, Jr., Jan. 17, 1849, Calhoun Papers, Duke; statement of A. W. Venable, Calhoun's *Works*, VI, 285-288.

[21] Washington *Union*, Jan. 28, 1849; Metcalfe to Venable, Feb. 1, 1849, in *ibid.*, Feb. 4, 1849, and also Calhoun's *Works*, VI, 289; Toombs to Crittenden, Jan. 22, 1849, *Toombs, Stephens, Cobb Correspondence*, 141-142.

[22] Washington *Union*, Jan. 28, 1849.

[23] Calhoun to Clemson, Jan. 22, 1849, Calhoun Papers, CC; to Mrs. Clemson, Jan. 24, 1849, *Correspondence*, 761; Thomas Metcalfe to Crittenden, Jan. 23, 1849, Crittenden Papers; Mrs. Clemson to Calhoun, Jan. 27, 1849, Calhoun Papers, CC; Crallé to Calhoun, Feb. 2, 1849, *ibid.; National Intelligencer*, Jan. 20, 1849; Charleston *Courier*, Jan. 24, 25, 27, 1849; Venable's Eulogy in the *Carolina Tribute*, 36; Rhett's Oration, *ibid.*, 369.

[24] Washington *Union*, Jan. 28, 1849; Venable's statement, Calhoun's *Works*, VI, 285-288.

[25] The official record in the *Union*, Jan. 28, 1849, gives the vote on Berrien's draft as 27 to 34, and lists Calhoun among those voting in the negative. Metcalfe, who chaired the meeting, says positively, however, that Calhoun was too ill to attend, and gives the vote as 27 to 33. See Metcalfe to Crittenden, Jan. 23, 1849, Crittenden Papers. It is possible that Venable, the secretary, took the liberty of recording the vote he knew Calhoun would have given. There is a distinctly hostile reference to the meeting in Sam Houston to Henderson Yoakum, Jan. 31, 1849, Houston's *Writings*, V, 71; and there are contemporary newspaper accounts in the Washington *Union*, Jan. 24; and the Charleston *Courier*, Jan. 27. If the reporters were not officially admitted, they were at least not far out of earshot.

[26] *Niles*, LXXV, 73, 94; J. C. Sitterson, *Secession Movement in North Carolina*, 46.

[27] Charleston *Courier*, Jan. 29, 30, Feb. 7, 1849; Calhoun to Mrs. Clemson, Jan. 24, 1849, *Correspondence*, 761-762; to Conner, Feb. 2, 1849, Conner Papers. The signers are conveniently listed in Calhoun's *Works*, VI, 312-313.

[28] Washington *Union*, Jan. 28, 1849. The Address was widely reprinted, even appearing in the *National Era*, Feb. 1, 1849, and the *Liberator*, Feb. 2, 1849. Also in *Niles*, LXXV, 84-88, 101-104. For the Whig position see Toombs to Crittenden, Jan. 3, 22, 1849, *Toombs, Stephens, Cobb Correspondence*, 139-142; U. B. Phillips, "The Southern Whigs," *Turner Essays*, 222-223; U. B. Phillips, *Life of Robert Toombs*, 60.

[29] *Cong. Globe*, 30th, 2nd, 190-198, 254.

[30] Washington *Union*, esp. Jan. 18, 21, 28, Feb. 4, 8, 1849; Polk, *Diary*, IV, 282ff.

[31] *Cong. Globe*, 30th, 2nd, 340-342.

[32] *Ibid.*, 381.

[33] *Ibid.*, 319, 477-480; Toombs to Crittenden, Feb. 9, 1849, *Toombs, Stephens, Cobb Correspondence*, 147. Cf. Toombs to Crittenden, Jan. 22, 1849, Coleman, *Crittenden*, I, 335-336.

[34] See, *e.g.*, the embittered reaction of Howell Cobb, who wrote to his wife on Feb. 8, 1849, that the Douglas bill would pass but for Calhoun's opposition.

"It does not suit his purposes to get clear of it upon any reasonable terms. It constitutes his last hope of organizing a Southern party of which he shall be head & soul. God grant that we may be able to floor the old reprobate & thereby preserve the honor of the South, and secure the permanency of the Union. If it would please our Heavenly Father to take Calhoun & Benton *home* I should look upon it as a national blessing." *Georgia Historical Quarterly,* V, no. 2 (June 1921), 38.

[35] *Cong. Globe,* 30th, 2nd, 561-566, 573-574, and Appendix, 253-276, where the debate is reproduced as a whole; *Senate Journal,* 241-244, 262-264, 275-278; Polk, *Diary,* IV, 346-347; Charleston *Courier,* Feb. 28, 1849.

[36] *House Journal,* 30th, 2nd, 528, 539; *Cong. Globe,* 605-609. The procedure for getting rid of Preston's substitute was to add the Wilmot Proviso to it as an amendment, after which the substitute was defeated without a single vote in its favor.

[37] *Senate Journal,* 30th, 2nd, 314; Polk, *Diary,* IV, 346-347.

[38] Washington *Union,* Apr. 5, 6, 7, 1849.

[39] *Cong. Globe,* 30th, 2nd, 682-691, 695-696; *National Intelligencer,* Mar. 5, 1849; Charleston *Courier,* Mar. 8, 1849; W. R. King to J. W. Womack, Mar. 10, 1849, *Gulf States Historical Magazine,* II (September 1903), 125. See also Polk, *Diary,* IV, 364-369.

[40] *Cong. Globe,* 30th, 2nd, 669-680; Charleston *Mercury,* Feb. 17, 1849; Charleston *Courier,* Mar. 7, 1849; Jordan, "Walker," *Mississippi Valley Historical Review,* XIX (December 1932), 373-374. Polk tended to agree with Calhoun, but signed the bill because he saw no constitutional objection to it; *Diary,* IV, 371-372.

CHAPTER XXVII

[1] *National Intelligencer,* Mar. 6, 1849; Richardson, *Messages and Papers of the Presidents,* 2542-2544.

[2] Polk, *Diary,* IV, 375-376.

[3] Charleston *Courier,* Mar. 13, 1849; Calhoun to Donelson, Mar. 23, 1849, *Tennessee Historical Magazine,* III (December 1917), 265-266.

[4] Baker to Clayton, Mar. 20, 1849, Clayton Papers.

[5] Clayton to King, Apr. 3, 1849, *House Document* 17, 31st, 1st, 9-11.

[6] *House Document* 17, 31st, 1st, 748-752, 776-780. King's report is *House Document* 59, of the same session.

[7] For the Southern disillusionment with Taylor see especially the Clayton, Crittenden, and Hammond Papers from April on through the summer and fall of 1849.

[8] Toombs to Crittenden, Jan. 22, 1849, Coleman, *Crittenden,* I, 335-336; F. Byrdsall to Calhoun, Feb. 1, Mar. 16, 1849, *Correspondence II,* 496-497, 500; R. Wickliffe to Calhoun, Feb. 26, 1849, *ibid.,* 499; Pendleton *Messenger,* Apr. 20, 1849.

[9] Pendleton *Messenger,* Feb. 23, 1849; Charleston *Courier,* Feb. 28, Mar. 20, 1849; Calhoun to J. H. Means, Apr. 13, 1849, *Correspondence,* 764-766; Boucher, "Secession and Cooperation," 79-80; Hamer, *Secession Movement in South Carolina,* 31-33.

[10] For the proceedings see Charleston *Mercury,* May 15, 16, 1849. There is a condensed version in *Niles,* LXXV, 328-329; and brief secondary accounts

in Boucher, "Secession and Cooperation," 79-80; Hamer, *Secession Movement in South Carolina*, 33-35; and Kibler, *Perry*, 239-241.

11 Calhoun to J. H. Means, Apr. 13, 1849, *Correspondence*, 764-766.

12 W. D. Moseley, Governor of Florida, to Seabrook, May 18, 1849, Seabrook Papers; Elmore to Seabrook, May 30, 1849, *ibid.*

13 S. Treat to Calhoun, June 17, 1849, *Correspondence II*, 511-512; Henry Young to Calhoun, June 6, 1849, *ibid.*, 506-508; W. E. Smith, *The Francis Preston Blair Family in Politics*, I, 249ff.

14 The Missouri resolutions are in *Niles*, LXXV, 270; and there is a useful summary of Benton's speech in the same volume, 390-392, 397-399. The full text is in the *National Intelligencer*, June 20, 21, 1849. This speech and its Senate predecessors form the germ of the peculiarly distorted political history later enlarged on in the *View*. Cf. Sam Houston to his Constituents, Mar. 2, 1849, Houston's *Writings*, V, 78-88.

15 Foote to Calhoun, June 5, 1849, *Correspondence II*, 505-506; June 11, 1849, Calhoun Papers, CC. These contemporary letters of Foote's should be compared with his account as given in the Senate, Dec. 18, 1851, *Cong. Globe*, 32nd, 1st, Appendix, 50. He tells still a different version in his *War of the Rebellion*, 101-102, written in 1866 after he had had the dubious advantage of reading Benton's memoirs. See also S. Treat to Calhoun, June 17, 1849, *Correspondence II*, 511-512; and H. V. Johnson to Calhoun, June 28, 1849, *ibid.*, 512-513.

16 Washington *Union*, June 1, 24, 1849; Pendleton *Messenger*, June 29, July 6, 1849. Cf. Calhoun to A. P. Calhoun, June 23, 1849, *Correspondence*, 768-769.

17 Most convenient sources are probably the New York *Herald*, July 21, 1849; Charleston *Courier*, July 17, 1849; and Washington *Union*, July 22, 1849. It was also distributed in pamphlet form. Surprisingly, Crallé did not include it in his edition of Calhoun's *Works*, though he was one of those who commented most enthusiastically at the time. See Crallé to Calhoun, July 25, 1849, *Correspondence*, 1199-1202.

18 Charleston *Mercury*, July 18, 1849; H. V. Johnson to Calhoun, July 20, 1849, *Correspondence*, 1197-1199; S. K. Borland to Calhoun, Aug. 5, 1849, Calhoun Papers, CC; F. Byrdsall to Calhoun, July 23, 1849, *ibid.;* New York *Herald*, July 23, 1849.

19 H. Young to Calhoun, June 6, 1849, *Correspondence II*, 507; H. V. Johnson to Calhoun, July 20, 1849, *Correspondence*, 1198-1199; Johnson to Calhoun, Aug. 25, 1849 (second letter), *North Carolina Historical Review*, IV (April 1927), 196-197; New York *Herald*, July 31, 1849.

20 Bemis, *Diplomatic History*, 244-250, 313-314.

21 *Ibid.*, 314-315; Richardson, *Messages and Papers of the Presidents*, 2545-2546; Charleston *Mercury*, Aug. 16, 1849; Pendleton *Messenger*, Aug. 24, 1849; B. Tucker to Hammond, Aug. 20, 1849, Hammond Papers.

22 Mitchell, *Horatio Seymour*, 111-112; Arthur C. Cole, *Whig Party in the South*, 147; Byrdsall to Calhoun, Oct. 5, 1849, Calhoun Papers, CC; J. T. Trezevant to Calhoun, Oct. 15, 1849, *ibid.;* Crallé to Calhoun, Oct. 18, 1849, *ibid.;* Baltimore *Sun*, Oct. 5, 13, 1849; Charleston *Courier*, Oct. 16, 26, 1849, *et seq.;* Seward to Taylor, Nov. 10, 1849, Clayton Papers; Toombs to Crittenden, Apr. 25, 1850, Coleman, *Crittenden*, I, 364-366.

23 Bennett to Calhoun, June 9, 1849, Calhoun Papers, CC; Scoville to Hammond, Apr. 18, 1850, Hammond Papers; Scoville to Bennett, Apr. 30, 1850, in

the New York *Herald,* May 3, 1850, and Bennett's editorial comments in the same issue. Unfortunately, Scoville had a too-great fondness for drink, which he indulged after his departure from Fort Hill, and his effectiveness was impaired during the remainder of his Southern trip. His amiability and his genuine fondness for Calhoun made it easier to overlook his shortcomings, but he was and remained imprudent and unreliable. See Calhoun to A. P. Calhoun, Sept. 22, 1849, Calhoun Papers, Duke.

[24] Calhoun to Collins S. Tarpley, July 9, 1849, in *Cong. Globe,* 32nd, 1st, Appendix, 52. It was read into the record in December 1851 by Foote whose purpose then was to prove that Calhoun had inspired the Mississippi Convention and that his aim had been secession. It will be seen, however, that the letter parallels closely that of Apr. 13, to John H. Means, *Correspondence,* 764-766. The same ideas are also expressed in his letter to Andrew Calhoun, July 24, 1849, where he suggests that Alabama might call such a convention. He also suggested that the call might come from the legislatures of one or more Southern states, or from the Southern members of Congress when they met in December. *Ibid.,* 769. He was firmly set on a Southern convention, which was to state grievances and threaten secession if they were not redressed, but he still believed they would be if the alternative were clearly presented. He was not seeking a dissolution of the Union, but some way to avoid it. The Mississippi Convention was simply one of several possibilities, but happened to be the one that panned out.

[25] Calhoun to Foote, Aug. 3, 1849, in Charleston *Mercury,* June 4, 1851; Foote to Calhoun, Sept. 25, 1849, *Correspondence,* 1204-1205; A. Hutchinson to Calhoun, Oct. 5, 1849, *ibid.,* 1206-1207; Wallace to Seabrook, Oct. 20, Nov. 7, 1849, Seabrook Papers; Cleo Hearon, *Mississippi and the Compromise of 1850,* 51-68; Boucher, "Secession and Cooperation," 83-85; Jackson (Miss.) *Southron,* Oct. 5, 12, 1849.

[26] The Address is reprinted in the *National Intelligencer* for April 27, 1850, with comments that identify it as Sharkey's work.

[27] Calhoun to J. R. Matthews, Oct. 20, 1849, Calhoun Papers, LC. This letter is misdated "June 20, 1849," a slip undoubtedly arising from Calhoun's preoccupation with the "June next" date of the Nashville Convention, to which the letter refers. It follows the Mississippi Convention at a sufficient interval to have permitted Calhoun to receive the proceedings, and precedes the meeting of the Georgia Legislature on Nov. 5, to which Calhoun refers as imminent. Cf. Calhoun to A. P. Calhoun, Oct. 22, 1849, *Correspondence,* 772-773. See also Charleston *Courier,* Nov. 8, 27, 28, 1849, Charleston *Mercury,* Nov. 14, 15, 1849; Hammond to M. C. M. Hammond, Nov. 16, 1849, Hammond Papers; W. B. Johnston, editor of the *South Carolinian,* to Calhoun, Nov. 8, 1849, *Correspondence,* 1208-1210; Calhoun to Johnston, Nov. 16, 1849, in Columbia *South Carolinian,* May 25, 1850; H. V. Johnson to Calhoun, Nov. [?] 1849, *North Carolina Historical Review,* IV (April 1927), 198; Hamer, *Secession Movement,* 46. The Foote-Clingman correspondence is in the Washington *Union,* Nov. 21, 1849.

[28] Richard H. Shryock, *Georgia and the Union in 1850,* 217-219; Clarence P. Denman, *The Secession Movement in Alabama,* 19-20. Cf. Reuben Chapman to Calhoun, Oct. 19, 1849, *Correspondence,* 1207-1208.

[29] Charleston *Courier,* Nov. 28, 1849, *et seq.;* Hamer, *Secession Movement,* 43-45.

[30] Charleston *Courier,* Dec. 20, 1849; Wallace, *History of South Carolina,* II, 484; John A. Calhoun to Calhoun, Dec. 14, 1849, *Correspondence II,* 532-533.

[31] Charleston *Courier,* Dec. 12, 1849; Charleston *Mercury,* Dec. 13, 1849.

[32] H. T. Shanks, *Secession Movement in Virginia,* 29-30; Charleston *Courier,* Dec. 11, 1849.

CHAPTER XXVIII

[1] These points were made by various reviewers of the volumes. See especially the *Southern Quarterly Review,* IX (January 1846), 204-236; and *Brownson's Quarterly Review,* I (January 1844), 105-131.

[2] W. H. Roane to Van Buren, Sept. 11, 1843, Van Buren Papers.

[3] Calhoun to T. W. Gilmer, July 28, 1843, *William and Mary Quarterly,* XX (July 1911), 8; F. Wharton, Notes of Conversations with Calhoun, Feb. 18, 20, 1845, *Correspondence,* 644-645.

[4] Calhoun to C. J. Ingersoll, Apr. 12, 1845, *Correspondence,* 652; to Mrs. Clemson, May 22, 1845, *ibid.,* 657; F. Wharton to Calhoun, Apr. 19, 1845, Calhoun Papers, CC.

[5] *E.g.,* Charleston *Courier,* Mar. 26, 1847, quoting the Philadelphia *Inquirer.*

[6] Calhoun to James Edward Calhoun, Apr. 15, 1848, *Correspondence,* 749-751; to Mrs. Clemson, Apr. 28, 1848, *ibid.,* 752-753.

[7] A. B. Longstreet to Calhoun, July 4, 1848, Calhoun Papers, CC.

[8] Calhoun to Mrs. Clemson, June 15, 1849, *Correspondence,* 767-768; to A. P. Calhoun, July 24, 1849, *ibid.,* 769-770. Scoville indicates that at least one chapter of the *Discourse* was dictated to him that summer, and even has some colorful anecdotes to tell of the process. See his accounts in the Columbia (S. C.) *Transcript,* Aug. 6, 1851; and the New York *Herald,* Feb. 5, 1854. In the brief "advertisement" to the published volume, however, Richard K. Crallé, who performed the editorial task as a labor of love, says explicitly that "with the exception of a few pages" the entire manuscript of the *Discourse* was in Calhoun's own hand, "on loose sheets,—bearing evident marks of interrupted and hurried composition." Calhoun's references in letters later in 1849 also seem to indicate that his own hand guided the pen. See especially Calhoun to Mrs. Clemson, Oct. 14, Dec. 31, 1849, *Correspondence,* 772, 777.

[9] The first request from Harpers came through William Gilmore Simms, whose novels were also published by that firm. See Simms to Calhoun, May 21 [1849], Calhoun Papers, CC. Also Calhoun to A. P. Calhoun, July 24, Oct. 22, 1849, *Correspondence,* 769-770, 772; to Mrs. Clemson, Oct. 14, 1849, *ibid.,* 772. The Washington correspondent of the New York *Herald,* probably Scoville, went so far as to say in his dispatch of Dec. 30, 1849, that the work was "now in press." See the *Herald* for Jan. 3, 1850.

[10] Crallé to Calhoun, Feb. 27, July 25, Oct. 18, 1849, Calhoun Papers, CC; Calhoun to Mrs. Clemson, Dec. 31, 1849, Feb. 24, 1850, *Correspondence,* 777, 782; Charleston *Courier,* Nov. 30, 1850, Feb. 4, 7, Nov. 26, 1851. Needless, perhaps, to add that Crallé's projected biography of Calhoun was never written.

[11] In the remainder of this chapter I have drawn freely from a paper I read before the South Carolina Historical Association in 1948, published in the Association's *Proceedings* for that year under the title "Calhoun: An Interpretation." It was then understood that the paper, or parts of it, would ultimately

be fitted into the biography, on the second volume of which I was then at work. See also my "Calhoun and the Modern State," *Virginia Quarterly Review,* XIII (summer 1937), 398-408; "Calhoun's Democracy," *Journal of Politics,* III (May 1941), 210-223; and "From Compact to National State in American Political Thought," *Essays in Political Theory, Presented to George H. Sabine,* 153-178 (1948).

[12] See Wiltse, *Calhoun, Nationalist,* 381-383, for discussion of his early reading. Also Calhoun to A. D. Wallace, Dec. 17, 1840, *Correspondence,* 468-469; F. Byrdsall to Calhoun, Mar. 1, 1847, Calhoun Papers, CC; "A Few Thoughts on the Death of John C. Calhoun," *Southern Literary Messenger,* XVI (June 1850), 378; M. R. H. Garnett, "Calhoun on Government," *Southern Quarterly Review,* XXIII (April 1853), 347; C. C. Pinckney, "John C. Calhoun from a Southern Standpoint," *Lippincott's,* LXII (July 1898), 85; W. A. Cocke to Lyon G. Tyler, Mar. 3, 1886, *Tyler's Quarterly,* XX (January 1939), 145; James Edward Calhoun to Martha M. Calhoun, Apr. 16, 1850, Calhoun Papers, CC.

[13] Calhoun to Mrs. Clemson, May 22, 1845, *Correspondence,* 657; F. Wharton, Notes on Conversations with Calhoun, Feb. 18, 20, 1845, *ibid.,* 644-645.

[14] Calhoun to J. R. Matthews, Aug. 18, 1845, Calhoun Papers, LC; to James Edward Calhoun, May 29, Oct. 29, 1846, *Correspondence,* 692-693, 708-709; *Works,* VI, 254-272. The curious reader will find a similar but harsher and more bitter analysis of the effects of patronage in Polk, *Diary,* II, 314, and IV, 193-194, 274-275.

CHAPTER XXIX

[1] "A Visit to Fort Hill," New York *Herald,* July 26, 1849. This is the same document cited in *Calhoun, Nullifier* as reprinted in somewhat shortened form in the Anderson (S. C.) *Daily Mail,* Oct. 23, 1926, where it bore the title "John C. Calhoun's Home Life." I am now of the opinion that, although the writer conveys an impression that he is a relative stranger, the piece was actually written by Joseph A. Scoville. Internal evidence dates the visit as late June 1849, when we know Scoville was at Fort Hill; the presence of no other visitor is mentioned; the article was featured in the New York *Herald* by which paper Scoville was then employed. There are, moreover, some characteristic tricks of style that tend to give this article a place in the series of 40 or more that Scoville contributed to the *Herald* over various pseudonyms during the summer and fall of 1849.

[2] C. C. Pinckney, "John C. Calhoun from a Southern Standpoint," *Lippincott's Magazine,* LXII (July 1898), 87.

[3] See Chapter IX, sec. 6, above. Also Calhoun to Clemson, Apr. 25, 1845, Calhoun Papers, CC (in part in *Correspondence,* 652-653).

[4] Ker Boyce to Calhoun, Dec. 26, 1844, Calhoun Papers, CC; Elmore to Calhoun, Apr. 16, 1845, *ibid.;* Calhoun to Clemson, Apr. 25, July 26, 1845, *ibid.*

[5] Calhoun to Clemson, Apr. 25, June 7, 23, 1845. Calhoun Papers, CC (all partially reproduced in *Correspondence,* 653, 664, 665).

[6] Calhoun to Hammond, Aug. 2, 1845, *Correspondence,* 668-669; R. Beale to Calhoun, Aug. 31, 1845, Calhoun Papers, CC (in part in *Correspondence II,* 303); J. G. Bowman to Calhoun, Sept. 2, 13, 1845, Calhoun Papers, CC; Beale to Calhoun, Sept. 20, 1845, *Correspondence II,* 305-306; James Edward Calhoun, Jr., to Calhoun, Feb. 26, 1846, Calhoun Papers, CC.

[7] Calhoun to Clemson, Oct. 27, 1845, Calhoun Papers, CC.

[8] Calhoun to A. P. Calhoun, Jan. 16, 1846, Calhoun Papers, SCL (in part in *Correspondence*, 677); Calhoun to Clemson, Feb. 25, 1846, *Correspondence*, 682; to A. P. Calhoun, May 14, 1846, Calhoun Papers, SCL (in part in *Correspondence*, 690-691).

[9] Calhoun to A. P. Calhoun, May 20, June 3, July 15, 1846, Calhoun Papers, Duke.

[10] Calhoun to Clemson, Sept. 20, 1846, Calhoun Papers, CC (in part in *Correspondence*, 707); J. E. Bonneau to Calhoun, Nov. 6, 1846, Calhoun Papers, CC; Calhoun to Elmore, Dec. 10, 26, 1846, Elmore Papers.

[11] Calhoun to A. P. Calhoun, July 8, 1847, Calhoun Papers, Duke; Clemson to Calhoun, Oct. 14, 1847, Clemson Papers.

[12] Calhoun to Clemson, Mar. 22, May 26, 1848, Calhoun Papers, CC (both in part in *Correspondence*, 746, 757); to A. P. Calhoun, May 18, June 24, 1848, Calhoun Papers, Duke.

[13] Conner to Calhoun, June 28, 1848, Calhoun Papers, CC; Calhoun to A. P. Calhoun, Apr. 26, Sept. 13, Oct. 11, 1848, Calhoun Papers, Duke.

[14] Calhoun to A. P. Calhoun, Nov. 25, 1848, Calhoun Papers, Duke.

[15] Calhoun to Clemson, Apr. 25, Oct. 27, 1845, Apr. 25, 1846, Calhoun Papers, CC; Feb. 25, 1846, *Correspondence*, 682. (Apr. 25, 1845, and Apr. 25, 1846 in part in *ibid.*, 653, 689.)

[16] Calhoun to Clemson, Aug. 19, Oct 9, Nov. 6, 1846, Calhoun Papers, CC; to Mrs. Clemson, Nov. 21, 1846, *Correspondence*, 712-713.

[17] Calhoun to Clemson, Apr. 13, May 13, 1848, *Correspondence*, 749, 755; Clemson to Calhoun, Apr. 26, 1848, Clemson Papers (copy); Calhoun to Clemson, July 23, Aug. 11, 1848, Calhoun Papers, CC (both in part in *Correspondence*, 760); Calhoun to Mrs. Clemson, July 26, 30, 1848, Calhoun Papers, CC. See also Calhoun to A. P. Calhoun, Oct. 11, 1848, Calhoun Papers, Duke.

[18] H. St. G. Tucker to Calhoun, Nov. 21, 1844, Calhoun Papers, CC; James Edward Calhoun, Jr., to Calhoun, Nov. 27, 1844, *ibid.*; Mrs. Calhoun to James Edward Calhoun, Jr., Feb. 1, 1845, Calhoun Papers, SCL; C. P. McKennie to James Edward Calhoun, Jr., July 1, 1845, Calhoun Papers, CC. For James's resemblance to his father, see "A Visit to Fort Hill," New York *Herald*, July 26, 1849.

[19] Mrs. Calhoun to James Edward Calhoun, Jr., Feb. 1, 1845, Calhoun Papers, SCL; Calhoun to Mrs. Clemson, Mar. 11, 1845, Calhoun Papers, CC (in part in *Correspondence*, 648); to Clemson, Mar. 23, 1845, Calhoun Papers, CC (in part in *Correspondence*, 649-650); to James Edward Calhoun, Mar. 23, 1845, Calhoun Papers, CC; to Clemson, Apr. 8, 1845, *ibid.*; Gen. E. P. Gaines to Calhoun, July 2, 1845, *ibid.*

[20] Calhoun to James Edward Calhoun, Oct. 2, 1845, Calhoun Papers, CC.

[21] W. R. Colhoun to James Edward Calhoun, Jr., Dec. 10, 1845, Calhoun Papers, Duke; Calhoun to James Edward Calhoun, Sr., Dec. 14, 1845, Jan. 16, Apr. 1, 1846 (the two latter in part in *Correspondence*, 675-677, 688); May 29, July 2, 1846, *Correspondence*, 694, 699; James Edward Calhoun, Jr., to Calhoun, Feb. 26, 1846, Calhoun Papers, CC; Calhoun to James Edward Calhoun, Jr., June 29, 1846, Calhoun Papers, Duke.

[22] Mrs. Clemson to Patrick Calhoun, Apr. 11, 1846, Calhoun Papers, Duke; Calhoun to James Edward Calhoun, Jr., June 29, 1846, *ibid.*; to Mrs. Clemson, Dec. 27, 1846, *Correspondence*, 714-716.

[23] Calhoun to James Edward Calhoun, July 9, 1846, *Correspondence*, 702;

Sept. 15, Oct. 29, 1846, Calhoun Papers, CC (both in part in *Correspondence,* 706, 709).

[24] Calhoun to James Edward Calhoun, Oct. 29, 1846, Calhoun Papers, CC (in part in *Correspondence,* 709); Francis Lieber to Calhoun, Nov. 2, 1846, *ibid.;* Calhoun to James Edward Calhoun, Jr., Nov. 17, Dec. [n.d., rec'd Dec. 16], 1846, Jan. 16, 1847, Calhoun Papers, Duke; to Mrs. Clemson, Dec. 27, 1846, *Correspondence,* 714-715.

[25] Patrick Calhoun to Calhoun, Apr. 5, 1847, Calhoun Papers, CC.

[26] Calhoun to A. P. Calhoun, Dec. 11, 1847, Calhoun Papers, Duke (in part in *Correspondence,* 741).

[27] Lieber to Calhoun, Dec. 29, 1847, *Correspondence,* 1156; Calhoun to Mrs. Clemson, Feb. 20, 1848, Calhoun Papers, CC (in part in *Correspondence,* 743); Calhoun to Hon. G. W. Barton, Mar. 6, 1848, Calhoun Papers, SCL; to Mrs. Clemson, Mar. 7, 1848, Calhoun Papers, CC (in part in *Correspondence,* 745); to James Edward Calhoun, Jr., Mar. 23, 1848, Calhoun Papers, Duke.

[28] Calhoun to A. P. Calhoun, Apr. 26, Oct. 11, 1848, Calhoun Papers, Duke.

[29] Calhoun to Mrs. Clemson, July 30, 1848, Calhoun Papers, CC.

[30] Calhoun to A. P. Calhoun, Oct. 15, Nov. 25, 1848, Calhoun Papers, Duke.

[31] Polk, *Diary,* IV, 196-197; Calhoun to A. P. Calhoun, Nov. 25, 1848, Calhoun Papers, Duke.

[32] Calhoun to A. P. Calhoun, Dec. 15, 1848, Calhoun Papers, Duke.

[33] *Ibid.;* Pendleton *Messenger,* Dec. 15, 1848. See also W. C. Preston to Calhoun [1849], Calhoun Papers, CC.

[34] Calhoun to A. P. Calhoun, Dec. 15, 1848, Jan. 17, 1849, Calhoun Papers, Duke.

[35] Calhoun to James Edward Calhoun, Jr., Jan. 17, 1849, Calhoun Papers, Duke. For the record it should be noted that sometime after his father's death, James did go to California, settling in San Francisco where he died during the Civil War.

[36] Calhoun to Clemson, Jan. 22, 1849, Calhoun Papers, CC; to Mrs. Clemson, Jan. 24, 1849, *Correspondence,* 761; Venable's Eulogy, in the *Carolina Tribute,* 36.

[37] Mrs. Clemson to Calhoun, Jan. 27, 1849, Calhoun Papers, CC.

[38] Calhoun first mentions the possibility of this loan in April 1848, when he indicates that it depends on his prospective creditor, a Dr. Broyle[s], collecting from an estate. It is there that the sum of $18,000 is mentioned. A year later he reports the deposit of $4,980, which is part of the money he is getting from Broyle[s], with whom a Mr. Maxwell is now associated. See Calhoun to A. P. Calhoun, Apr. 26, 1848, Apr. 10, 1849, Calhoun Papers, Duke.

[39] Calhoun to Mrs. Clemson, Apr. 10, 1849, *Correspondence,* 763-764.

[40] Mrs. Clemson to Calhoun, Apr. 15, 1849, Calhoun Papers, CC.

[41] Mrs. Clemson to Calhoun, May 22, 1849, Calhoun Papers, CC.

[42] Calhoun to Mrs. Clemson, June 15, 1849, Calhoun Papers, CC (in part in *Correspondence,* 766-768).

[43] Calhoun to A. P. Calhoun, June 23, July 24, Oct 9, 1849, Calhoun Papers, Duke (the first two in part in *Correspondence,* 768, 769-770); to N. Whitner, Dec. 4, 1849, *ibid.;* to James Edward Calhoun, Jr., Jan. 11, 1850, *ibid.*

[44] Mrs. Clemson to Calhoun, Oct. 26, Dec. 22, 1849, Jan. 22, Feb. 18, Mar. 4, 1850, Calhoun Papers, CC.

[45] Calhoun to Clemson, Dec. 8, 1849, Calhoun Papers, CC (in part in *Correspondence,* 776); to H. W. Conner, Mar. 18, 1850, Conner Papers.

[46] Circular, Apr. 1, 1850, signed by Huger, Conner, and Gourdin, Conner Papers.

[47] Circular of Jan. 1, 1851, Conner Papers; Mrs. Calhoun to Floride Clemson, Aug. 11, 1850, Clemson Papers (copy).

[48] H. T. Cook, *Life and Legacy of David Rogerson Williams*, 278-279, citing articles by R. W. Simpson, Clemson's attorney. I have not seen the articles cited.

[49] Agreement between Andrew, Patrick, James Edward, and William Lowndes Calhoun, Aug. 30, 1850, Clemson Papers; Mrs. Calhoun to Mrs. Clemson, Oct. 1, 1850, *ibid.*

CHAPTER XXX

[1] Calhoun to A. P. Calhoun, Dec. 2, 1849, *Correspondence*, 774-775; Charleston *Courier*, Dec. 6, 1849; Cobb to his wife, Dec. 4, 1849, *Toombs, Stephens, Cobb Correspondence*, 177-178; Toombs to Crittenden, Apr. 25, 1850, Coleman, *Crittenden*, I, 365.

[2] Foote, *War of the Rebellion*, 116, is authority for the greetings. It is an authority dubious on many points, but for this one none at all would be needed. Calhoun and Webster unquestionably followed the time-honored custom of the Senate and made the first advance toward an older colleague who had been for some years absent.

[3] The whole proceeding will be found in *Cong. Globe*, 31st, 1st, 2-67, *passim;* and *House Journal*, 8-163. The best secondary account is in Holman Hamilton, *Zachary Taylor, Soldier in the White House*, Chapter 19. See also Avery Graven, *Coming of the Civil War*, 247-249.

[4] *Cong. Globe*, 31st, 1st, 18-24.

[5] *Ibid.*, 24-28; Charelston *Courier*, Dec. 17, 1849; Chase to Sumner, Dec. 14, 1849, *Chase Correspondence*, 188; Pendleton *Messenger*, Dec. 21, 1849.

[6] *Cong. Globe*, 31st, 1st, 61-67; Cobb to his wife, Dec. 20, 22, 1849, *Toombs, Stephens, Cobb Correspondence*, 178-180; Calhoun to Mrs. Clemson, Feb. 24, 1850, *Correspondence*, 783.

[7] Charleston *Courier*, Dec. 21, 1849; Chase to E. S. Hamlin, Dec. 17, 1849, *Chase Correspondence*, 189-192; *Cong. Globe*, 31st, 1st, 39-41, 44-45.

[8] Richardson, *Messages and Papers of the Presidents*, 2547-2562.

[9] Webster to F. Haven, Dec. 25, 1849, Webster's *Writings*, XVI, 527; Washington *Union*, Jan. 1, 1850; Charleston *Mercury*, Dec. 27, 28, 1849.

[10] Charleston *Courier*, Jan. 7, 12, 1850; Calhoun to Hammond, Jan. 4, 1850, *Correspondence*, 778-780; to A. P. Calhoun, Jan. 12, 1850, *ibid.*, 780; Berrien to Jenkins, Jan. 7, 1850, Berrien Papers; L. J. Glenn to Howell Cobb, Jan. 15, 1850, *Georgia Historical Quarterly*, V, No. 3 (September 1921), 36; H. V. Johnson to Calhoun, Jan. 19, 1850, *North Carolina Historical Review*, IV (April 1927), 200-201; *Cong. Globe*, 31st, 1st, 119-123, 133-137. Rhett to Crallé, Oct. 25, 1854, *Am. Hist. Rev.*, XIII (January 1908), 312, says Southern Senators signed a paper, drawn up by Calhoun, pledging themselves to defeat the admission of California in whatever manner their own majority should determine. There were undoubtedly discussions, and very possibly mutual pledges, but it is unlikely that there was anything more than that. Rhett himself was not a member of this Congress, and was probably recalling imperfectly the newspaper stories current at the time that Southern members of the House—not the Senate—

had pledged themselves to block all other business until the slavery question was settled. See, *e.g.*, New York *Tribune*, Feb. 25, 1850.

[11] *Cong. Globe*, 31st, 1st, 244-252.

[12] *Ibid.;* Charleston *Courier*, Feb. 2, 8, 1850; James M. Mason to Rives, Feb. 4, 1850, Rives Papers; B. Tucker to Hammond, Feb. 2, 8, 1850, Hammond Papers. It is instructive to note how sharply protagonists were divided, even on the meaning of the resolutions. "As to Mr. Clay and his sneaking compromises, I have not yet heard of any man who does not speak of them with disgust. I trust in God that his power to befool the South, and to barter away our rights for Northern support is gone forever." So wrote Beverley Tucker to Hammond, Feb. 8, 1850, Hammond Papers. But to Salmon P. Chase, writing on Feb. 2, 1850, to E. S. Hamlin, the very reverse appeared to be the case: "You have seen Clay's Compromise resolutions—sentiment for the north substance for the south—just like the Missouri Compromise—all that is in issue given up by the nonslaveholders—unsubstantial concessions of matters not in issue by the slaveholders." *Chase Correspondence*, 200-201.

[13] Senator A. P. Butler, when he announced his colleague's death in the Senate, said that Calhoun's own conviction had been for some time past that he had not long to live. See the *Carolina Tribute*, 1.

[14] However thankless the task, it is one of the biographer's functions to dispose of myth and legend where he can. One of the Calhoun legends is that told by Joseph A. Scoville ("Manhattan") in the London *Herald*, Sept. 1, 1863. Scoville was in Washington on New Year's Day 1850, and as he tells it almost 14 years later, Calhoun bade him go to the President's reception and see who was there. "I did so, and returned home about evening, and gave him a description of the throng, and of the officials, senators, and ministers who offered their adulation to power. After I had finished, I asked, 'who has been here to-day?' I shall never forget the curl of scorn on his lip as he replied, 'No one.' It needed no words. . . ." But the New York *Herald* of Jan. 4, 1850, prints the following dispatch from its Washington correspondent, dated Jan. 1, 1850: "Mr. Calhoun had quite a host of visitors to see him at his lodgings." The *Herald* kept more than one correspondent in the Capital at that date, but one of them—and almost certainly the author of that dispatch—was Joseph A. Scoville!

[15] The progress of Calhoun's illness is minutely detailed in the Washington correspondence of the Charleston *Courier*. See especially issues for Jan. 23, 25, 29, 30, 31, and Feb. 5, 1850. His return to the Senate is in *ibid.*, Feb. 23. See also Chase to Mrs. Chase, Feb. 18, 1850, Chase Papers.

[16] *Cong Globe*, 31st, 1st, Appendix, 115-127. Clay's speech appeared at once in the *National Intelligencer*, Feb 5, 7, 1850. See also Calhoun to Clemson, Feb. 6, 1850, *Correspondence*, 780-781.

[17] Thomas Ritchie, *Reminiscences of Clay and the Compromise*, reprinted from the Richmond *Enquirer*, Sept. 10, 1852.

[18] *Cong. Globe*, 31st, 1st, 319-323, 329-333, and Appendix, 202-211.

[19] Charleston *Courier*, Feb. 18, 1850; *Cong. Globe*, 31st, 1st, 355, 356, 365-369; Washington *Union*, Feb. 16, 1850.

[20] *Cong Globe*, 31st, 1st, 386, and Appendix, 165-176; Calhoun to Mrs. Clemson, Feb. 24, 1850, *Correspondence*, 782-783.

[21] *Cong. Globe*, 31st, 1st, 276. Most widely quoted of Southern fire-eaters at this time was Thomas L. Clingman. See his speech in the House, Jan. 22, 1850, in *ibid.*, 200-205.

[22] Charleston *Courier*, Feb. 25, Mar. 1, 1850; Washington *Union*, Feb. 21, 28, 1850; *Cong. Globe*, 31st, 1st, 416-421.

[23] Washington *Union*, Feb. 26, 1850; Charleston *Courier*, Mar. 2, 1850.

[24] Scoville recounts the circumstances in a letter addressed to Bennett, Apr. 30, 1850, in the New York *Herald*, May 3, 1850. In an editorial calling attention to and commenting on Scoville's letter, Bennett reproduces the note he received from Calhoun. The original manuscript of the speech in Scoville's hand, with corrections in Calhoun's own, is in the Library of Congress.

[25] *Cong. Globe*, 31st, 1st, 439; Charleston *Courier*, Mar. 4, 1850.

[26] New York *Herald*, Mar. 8, 1850. I have given general credence to the *Herald's* precise account of these and subsequent meetings between Calhoun and Webster, and their purposes, because of the preferred position Bennett's paper occupied with respect to Calhoun. Bennett himself had been in Washington only a few days earlier—possibly was there still; and Scoville was continued on the *Herald* pay roll almost as a personal aide to the South Carolinian. He was in constant attendance on the sick man, and was in better position than anyone else to know who called and how long he stayed. There is also the substantiating, though less precise, evidence of Jeremiah Clemens' recollections, as published in the *Herald*, Jan. 14, 1859; of Edward A. Pollard's "Personal Recollections of John C. Calhoun," in the New York *Citizen*, May 9, 1868; and of Peter Harvey's *Reminiscences of Webster*, 218-222, to cite only those references that seem most reliable. See also Webster to C. H. Warren, Mar. 1, 1850, Webster's *Writings*, XVI, 334.

[27] Scoville to Bennett, Apr. 30, 1850, New York *Herald*, May 3, 1850; Charleston *Courier*, Mar. 7, 1850.

[28] Descriptions of the scene are almost as various as they are numerous. I have followed the New York *Herald*, Mar. 5, 6, 1850; Charleston *Courier*, Mar. 9, 1850; and John Wentworth, *Congressional Reminiscences*, 22-23. See also V. H. Davis, *Jefferson Davis*, I, 457-458; and H. S. Foote, *Casket of Reminiscences*, 81. Sargent, *Men and Events*, II, 363, says Calhoun was supported by Butler and Mason, but the *Herald's* contemporary reference to Hamilton seems preferable. The speech is in *Cong. Globe*, 31st, 1st, 451-455; and *Works*, IV, 542-573.

[29] New York *Herald*, Mar. 6, 1850.

[30] *Cong. Globe*, 31st, 1st, 461-464; Calhoun's *Works*, IV, 574-578; New York *Herald*, Mar. 8, 9, 1850.

[31] *Cong. Globe*, 32nd, 1st, Appendix, 49-54.

[32] So Hammond, himself a skillful debater and thoroughly familiar with Calhoun's style, analyzed it. See Hammond's Oration in the *Carolina Tribute*, 317.

[33] Calhoun's *Works*, I, 391-392; Charleston *Courier*, Mar. 18, 1850.

[34] Calhoun's *Works*, IV, 572; Yulee to Calhoun, July 10, 1849, *Correspondence II*, 516; *Niles*, LIII, 357; Wiltse, *Calhoun, Nullifier*, 368-369; Charleston *Mercury*, Mar. 9, 1850; Charleston *Courier*, Mar. 18, 1850.

[35] Tyler, who thought Calhoun's speech "too ultra, and his ultimata impracticable" would himself propose an amendment to safeguard the South at the Peace Convention of 1861; and in the Congressional session of 1860-1861, Crittenden too would offer a "compromise" which had as its basis a constitutional amendment to guarantee the security of the South. See Tyler to Robert Tyler, Mar. 12, 1850, Tyler, *Times of the Tylers*, II, 481; and *ibid.*, 606. Also Coleman, *Crittenden*, II, 233-237. Calhoun would probably have accepted either of these

propositions although the authors of both condemned him in 1850 for demanding an amendment. He was simply far ahead of his contemporaries in his understanding of the true nature of the problem. See also Coit's Eulogy in the *Carolina Tribute*, 173; and Hammond's oration, *ibid.*, 319.

36 New York *Herald*, Mar. 8, 1850.

37 Charleston *Courier*, Mar. 11, 1850; Harvey, *Reminiscences of Webster*, 218-220; G. W. Julian, *Political Recollections*, 87-88.

38 *Cong. Globe*, 31st, 1st, 476-483. See also H. D. Foster, "Webster's Seventh of March Speech and the Secession Movement of 1850," *Am. Hist. Rev.*, XXVII (January 1922), 245-270.

39 Charleston *Mercury*, Mar. 11, 14, 1850; Washington *Union*, Mar. 8, 9, 1850; New York *Herald*, Mar. 8, 9, 1850; Charleston *Courier*, Mar. 15, 1850; *Liberator*, Mar. 15, 1850, *et seq.* Cf. Chase to Sumner, Mar. 7, 1850, Chase Papers.

40 *Cong. Globe*, 31st, 1st, 517-521.

41 Charleston *Mercury*, Mar. 19, 1850; Charleston *Courier*, Mar. 20, 1850; Chase to Sumner, Mar. 13 [misdated Mar. 15], 1850, *Chase Correspondence*, 203-204; George P. Fisher, "Webster and Calhoun in the Compromise Debate of 1850," *Scribner's Magazine*, XXXVII, 579-580.

CHAPTER XXXI

1 Charleston *Courier*, Mar. 16, 1850.

2 Calhoun to Conner, Mar. 18, 1850, Conner Papers; memorandum by James M. Mason in Virginia Mason, *Public Life of James M. Mason*, 72-73. Cf. notes of conversations, probably with Scoville, in the New York *Herald*, Apr. 11, 1850.

3 Blair to Van Buren, Mar. 24, 26, 1850, Van Buren Papers; C. S. Morehead to Crittenden, Mar. 30 [postscript of Mar. 31], 1850, Coleman, *Crittenden*, I, 363. Foote elaborates the notion that Calhoun was in favor of secession at this time in his *War of the Rebellion*, 19-20 (1866), where he manages to leave the impression that Calhoun had reconciled himself to disunion "several years" before his death. He says specifically that Calhoun told him early in 1850 he had drawn up a constitution for a new slaveholding republic. Foote did not see fit to mention it, however, in his speech in the Senate of December 18, 1851, although his purpose on that occasion was to show that Calhoun had been a disunionist. See *Cong. Globe*, 32nd, 1st, Appendix, 49-54. The record seems to indicate that Calhoun was not on terms of confidence with Foote at any time during that last session of Congress; and the official report of the two clashes in March, already noted in these pages, is hardly compatible with any such belief as that which the Mississippi Senator says, 16 years later, Calhoun then held. We may be sure that if Calhoun had prepared any such document as a constitution for a Southern confederacy, many people would have seen it before Foote did; so many, in fact, that we should certainly have heard of it from some more reliable quarter. See also contemporary criticism of Foote's account by Edward A. Pollard, "Personal Recollections of John C. Calhoun," New York *Citizen*, May 9, 1868. The draft of the resolutions referred to in the text is in *Correspondence*, 785-787.

4 These details are compounded primarily from the accounts of Scoville, Burt, and Hamilton. See J. Hamilton to Hammond, Mar. 31, 1850, Hammond Papers; Hamilton to W. B. Seabrook, Apr. 2, 1850, in Charleston *Courier*, Apr. 8, 1850;

Scoville to Hammond, Apr. 18, 1850, Hammond Papers; Scoville to J. G. Bennett, Apr. 30, 1850, in New York *Herald,* May 3, 1850; and A. Burt to Clemson, May 20, 1850 (copy), Clemson Papers. James L. Orr to Scoville, May 5, 1850, Calhoun Papers, SCL, confirms Scoville's account as given in the *Herald.* See also Jeremiah Clemens' account in the New York *Herald,* Jan. 14, 1859; and another version by Hamilton in a letter to the South Carolina Legislature, Nov. 13, 1857, in New York *Times,* Dec. 11, 1857.

[5] Burt to Clemson, *op. cit.,* says he sent for Floride without consulting Calhoun, who did not think it necessary. Calhoun knew by March 24, however, that she was coming, and expected her "the last of this week." See Lizzie Green to Margaret Green Calhoun, Mar. 25, 1850, Calhoun Papers, SCL. Also Scoville to Bennett, *op. cit.*

[6] The daily ups and downs of his disease were faithfully reported in the Charleston papers, with telegraphic notices every time there was a change either way. The Washington correspondent for the *Courier,* in that paper for Apr. 5, says Calhoun had known of his true condition for some time. The Washington *Union,* Apr. 2, 1850, agrees with Hamilton as to the nature of the disease. Calhoun's letter to Butler dated Mar. 27, 1850, Calhoun Papers, LC, informing his colleague of his desire to be heard in the Senate debate, does not indicate any sudden resurgence of powers. The letter is unquestionably misdated, belonging clearly to the context of a month earlier. It was on Feb. 28 that Butler requested permission of the Senate for Calhoun to speak on Mar. 4, undoubtedly in response to this note.

[7] The best contemporary account is Scoville's telegraphic dispatch in the New York *Herald,* Apr. 1, 1850; and the follow-up story by mail, in the same paper for Apr. 2. Both were widely reprinted. Venable tells substantially the same story in his eulogy in the House, *Cong. Globe,* 31st, 1st, 622.

[8] Charleston *Courier,* Apr. 1, 1850; Chase to Mrs. Chase, Mar. 31, 1850, Chase Papers; Morehead to Crittenden, Mar. 30 [postcript Mar. 31], 1850, Coleman, *Crittenden,* I, 363; Webster to J. P. Healy, Apr. 2, 1850, Webster's *Writings,* XVI, 537; Washington *Union,* Apr. 2, 1850; Benjamin Silliman's diary, Apr. 7, 1850, in G. P. Fisher, *Life of Benjamin Silliman,* II, 97-99; "John C. Calhoun," *Democratic Review,* XXVI (May 1850), 401; "Thoughts on the Death of John C. Calhoun," *Southern Literary Messenger,* XVI (June 1850), 377; Richard Rush, "Character of Calhoun," *Occasional Pieces,* 107-115. South Carolinians who did not conceal their relief at Calhoun's death included B. F. Perry, Waddy Thompson, J. L. Petigru, W. C. Preston, J. R. Poinsett, and Francis Lieber. See Kibler, *Perry,* 243-244.

[9] Senate proceedings are in *Cong. Globe,* 31st, 1st, 623-626, and are reprinted in J. P. Thomas, ed., *The Carolina Tribute to Calhoun,* 1-16.

[10] New York *Herald,* Apr. 3, 1850; Jefferson Davis to Mrs. George Robertson, *et al.,* Apr. 10, 1887, in *Calhoun Monument,* 118; Harvey, *Webster,* 231-232.

[11] Wentworth, *Congressional Reminiscences,* 23-24; Harvey, *Reminiscences of Webster,* 230-232. It was nevertheless Benton who, by virtue of his seniority, took the lead in making the arrangements for the occasion, and who asked Webster to speak. See Webster to Fletcher Webster, Mar. 31, 1850, Webster's *Writings,* XVIII, 363.

[12] *Cong. Globe,* 31st, 1st, 620-622; *Carolina Tribute,* 24-38. See also Howell Cobb to his wife, Apr. 2, 1850, *Georgia Historical Quarterly,* V, No. 3 (September 1921), 40-41.

[13] *Cong. Globe*, 31st, 1st, 626; *Carolina Tribute*, 15-20; Washington *Union*, Apr. 3, 1850; Charleston *Courier*, Apr. 8, 1850.

[14] *Carolina Tribute*, 39-53.

[15] *Carolina Tribute*, 65-82, 383-384; Mary Bates, *Private Life of Calhoun*, 27-29; Pendleton *Messenger*, Apr. 12, 19, 26, 1850.

[16] Judge E. W. Huntington to John McLean, June 15, 1850, McLean Papers.

[17] See, *e.g.*, Fisher, *Silliman*, II, 98-99; *Southern Literary Messenger*, XVI (May 1850), 302; *Cong. Globe*, 32nd, 1st, Appendix, 49-50; Plumer to Ticknor, Apr. 2, 1853, in Webster's *Writings*, XVII, 566.

[18] *Cong. Globe*, 36th, 2nd, 487; Amos Kendall, *Autobiography*, 628-639; J. A. Hamilton, *Reminiscences*, 444-450. Typical of the press comment is Anna E. Carroll, "Calhoun and his Nullification Doctrine," *Living Age*, LXX (Aug. 17, 1861), 444-446; and New York *Times*, Aug. 24, 1863. See also Blair to the New York Republicans, Apr. 26, 1856, New York *Evening Post*, May 2, 1856.

[19] See, *e.g.*, William H. Sparks, *Memories of Fifty Years*, 59-60; and H. S. Foote, *History of the Rebellion, passim*.

BIBLIOGRAPHY

Only the more important materials are listed. Newspapers are listed **only** where an extensive file of the paper was consulted.

MANUSCRIPTS

R. F. W. Allston Papers. South Carolina Historical Society.
John M. Berrien Papers. University of North Carolina.
Gist Blair Papers. Library of Congress.
John C. Calhoun Papers. Clemson College.
John C. Calhoun Papers. Duke University.
John C. Calhoun Papers. Library of Congress.
John C. Calhoun Papers. South Caroliniana Library.
Campbell-Preston Family Papers. Library of Congress.
Salmon P. Chase Papers. Library of Congress.
Henry Clay Papers. Library of Congress.
John M. Clayton Papers. Library of Congress.
Thomas G. Clemson Papers. Clemson College.
Henry W. Conner Papers. Charleston Library Society.
Richard K. Crallé Papers. Clemson College.
Richard K. Crallé Papers. Library of Congress.
John J. Crittenden Papers. Library of Congress.
Andrew J. Donelson Papers. Library of Congress.
Franklin H. Elmore Papers. Library of Congress.
Charles F. Fisher Papers. University of North Carolina.
Great Britain, Public Record Office, Foreign Office Papers. Photostats in **Library** of Congress.
Duff Green Papers. Library of Congress.
James H. Hammond Papers. Library of Congress.
William Henry Harrison Papers. Library of Congress.
Robert M. T. Hunter Papers. Clemson College.
George McDuffie Papers. Duke University.
George McDuffie Papers. South Caroliniana Library.
John McLean Papers. Library of Congress.
Virgil Maxcy Papers. Library of Congress.
Virgil Maxcy Papers, second series. Library of Congress.
James L. Petigru Papers. Library of Congress.
James K. Polk Papers. Library of Congress.
James K. Polk Papers, second series. Library of Congress.
William Cabell Rives Papers. Library of Congress.
Edmund Ruffin Papers. University of North Carolina.
Whitemarsh B. Seabrook Papers. Library of Congress.
State Department, Diplomatic Correspondence. National Archives.
State Department, Instructions. National Archives.
State Department, Miscellaneous Letters. National Archives.

556

Andrew Stevenson Papers. Library of Congress.
Waddy Thompson Papers. University of North Carolina.
John Tyler Papers. Library of Congress.
Martin Van Buren Papers. Library of Congress.
Daniel Webster Papers. Library of Congress.
Gideon Welles Papers. Library of Congress.
Levi Woodbury Papers. Library of Congress.

NEWSPAPERS

Charleston *Courier*.
Charleston *Mercury*.
The Liberator.
The Madisonian.
The National Era.
National Intelligencer.
New York *Herald*.
Niles' Weekly Register.
Pendleton *Messenger*.
Richmond *Enquirer*.
Washington *Constitution*.
Washington *Globe*.
Washington *Spectator*.
Washington *Union*.

BOOKS AND PERIODICALS

Aberdeen, George, Earl of. *Selections from the Correspondence of George, Earl of Aberdeen*. Privately printed, 1885.

Adams, Ephraim D. *British Interests and Activities in Texas, 1838-1846*. Baltimore, 1910.

Adams, John Quincy. *Memoirs of John Quincy Adams;* Charles Francis Adams, ed. 12 vols. Philadelphia, 1874-1877.

Alexander, Holmes Moss. *The American Talleyrand; the Career and Contemporaries of Martin Van Buren, Eighth President*. New York, 1935.

Ambler, Charles H. *Sectionalism in Virginia from 1776 to 1851*. Chicago, 1910.

Ambler, Charles H. *Thomas Ritchie; a Study in Virginia Politics*. Richmond, 1913.

Ambler, Charles H., ed. "Virginia and Texas, 1844," *Branch Historical Papers*, Vol. IV, No. 1, pp. 116-137.

Ambler, Charles H. "Virginia and the Presidential Succession, 1840-1844," *Essays in American History Dedicated to Frederick Jackson Turner*, pp. 165-202. New York, 1910.

American Almanac and Repository of Useful Knowledge, annual issues 1841-1851. Boston, 1841-1851.

Ames, Herman V. "John C. Calhoun and the Secession Movement of 1850," American Antiquarian Society, *Proceedings*, n.s., Vol. XXVIII (April 1918), pp. 19-50.

Appleton, Nathan. *Remarks on Currency and Banking; Having Reference to the Present Derangement of the Circulating Medium in the United States*. Boston, 1841.

Atchison, Theodore C. "David Atchison; a Study in American Politics," *Missouri Historical Review*, Vol. XXIV (July 1930), pp. 502-515.

Bailey, Thomas A. *A Diplomatic History of the American People.* 4th edition. New York, 1950.

Baker, Elizabeth Feaster. *Henry Wheaton, 1785-1848.* Philadelphia, 1937.

Bancroft, George. "Correspondence with Van Buren," Massachusetts Historical Society, *Proceedings,* Vol. XLII, pp. 381-442.

Barnes, Donald Grove. *A History of the English Corn Laws from 1660 to 1846.* London, 1930.

Barnes, Gilbert H. *The Anti-Slavery Impulse, 1830-1844.* New York, 1933.

Bates, Mary. *Private Life of John C. Calhoun.* Charleston, 1852.

Bell, John. "Letters of John Bell to William B. Campbell," *Tennessee Historical Magazine,* Vol. III (September 1917), pp. 201-227.

Bemis, Samuel Flagg. *A Diplomatic History of the United States.* 3rd edition. New York, 1950.

Benton, Thomas Hart. *Thirty Years' View.* New York, 1854-1856.

Beveridge, Albert J. *Life of Abraham Lincoln.* 2 vols. Boston, 1928.

Biddle, Nicholas. *The Correspondence of Nicholas Biddle dealing with National Affairs, 1807-1844;* Reginald C. McGrane, ed. Boston & New York, 1919.

Biographical Directory of the American Congress, 1774-1927. Washington, 1928.

Birney, James G. *Letters of James Gillespie Birney, 1831-1857;* Dwight L. Dumond, ed. 2 vols. New York, 1938.

Boucher, Chauncey S. "The Annexation of Texas and the Bluffton Movement in South Carolina," *Mississippi Valley Historical Review,* Vol. VI (June 1919), pp. 3-33.

Boucher, Chauncey S. "The Ante-Bellum Attitude of South Carolina towards Manufacturing and Agriculture," *Washington University Studies,* Vol. III (April 1916), pp. 243-270.

Boucher, Chauncey S. *"In Re* That Aggressive Slavocracy," *Mississippi Valley Historical Review,* Vol. VIII (June 1921), pp. 13-79.

Boucher, Chauncey S. "The Secession and Cooperation Movements in South Carolina, 1848 to 1852," *Washington University Studies,* Vol. V, No. 2 (April 1918), pp. 65-138.

Boucher, Chauncey S. "Sectionalism, Representation, and the Electoral Question in Ante-Bellum South Carolina," *Washington University Studies,* Vol. IV (October 1916), pp. 3-62.

Boynton, Lucien C. "Selections from the Journal of Lucien C. Boynton, 1835-1853"; Solon J. Buck, ed. American Antiquarian Society, *Proceedings,* n.s., Vol. XLIII (October 1933), pp. 329-380.

Bretz, Julian P. "Economic Background of the Liberty Party," *American Historical Review,* Vol. XXXIV (January 1929), pp. 250-264.

Brewster, Lawrence Fay. *Summer Migrations and Resorts of South Carolina Low-Country Planters.* Durham, N. C., 1947.

[Brownson, Orestes]. "Life and Speeches of John C. Calhoun," *Brownson's Quarterly Review,* Vol. I (January 1844), pp. 105-131.

[Brownson, Orestes]. "Mr. Calhoun and the Baltimore Convention," *Brownson's Quarterly Review,* Vol. I (April 1844), pp. 257-269.

Brownson, Orestes. *The Works of Orestes A. Brownson;* Henry F. Brownson, ed. Vols. XV-XVIII. Detroit, 1884-1905.

Bryan, Wilhelmus B. *A History of the National Capital.* 2 vols. New York, 1914-1916.

Buchanan, James. *Works of James Buchanan;* G. B. Moore, ed. 12 vols. Philadelphia, 1908-1911.

Buckingham, James Silks. *The Slave States of America.* 2 vols. London, 1842.

Butler, William Allen. *Martin Van Buren: Lawyer, Statesman and Man.* New York, 1862.

Butler, William Allen. *A Retrospect of Forty Years, 1825-1865;* Harriet Allen Butler, ed. New York, 1911.

Calhoun, John C. "A Few Thoughts on the Death of John C. Calhoun," *Southern Literary Messenger,* Vol. XVI (May 1850), pp. 376-379.

Calhoun, John C. "Calhoun as seen by his Political Friends"; F. W. Moore, ed. Southern History Association, *Publications,* Vol. VII (1903), pp. 159-169, 267-291, 353-361, 419-426.

Calhoun, John C. "Calhoun on Government," *Putnam's Monthly Magazine,* Vol. VII (January 1856), pp. 90-100.

Calhoun, John C. *The Calhoun Textbook.* New York, 1843.

Calhoun, John C. *The Carolina Tribute to Calhoun;* J. P. Thomas, ed. Columbia, S. C., 1857.

Calhoun, John C. *Correspondence Addressed to John C. Calhoun, 1837-1849;* Chauncey S. Boucher and Robert P. Brooks, eds. Annual Report of the American Historical Association, 1929. Washington, 1931.

Calhoun, John C. *Correspondence of John C. Calhoun;* J. Franklin Jameson, ed. Annual Report of the American Historical Association, 1899. Vol. II. Washington, 1900.

Calhoun, John C. "John Caldwell Calhoun," *American Review,* Vol. XII (August 1850), pp. 164-175.

Calhoun, John C. "John Caldwell Calhoun," *Southern Quarterly Review,* Vol. XVIII (November 1850), pp. 486-509.

Calhoun, John C. "John C. Calhoun," *Southern Literary Messenger,* Vol. XVI (May 1850), pp. 301-303.

Calhoun, John C. "John C. Calhoun," *United States Magazine and Democratic Review,* Vol. XXVI (May 1850), pp. 401-414.

Calhoun, John C. "John C. Calhoun of South Carolina," *United States Magazine and Democratic Review,* Vol. XII (January 1843), pp. 93-95.

Calhoun, John C. "Letters from Calhoun to F. W. Pickens," *South Carolina Historical and Genealogical Magazine,* Vol. VII (January 1906), pp. 12-19.

Calhoun, John C. *Life and Character of the Hon. John C. Calhoun, with illustrations: Containing notices of his father and uncles, and their brave conduct during our struggle for independence, in the American Revolutionary War.* New York, 1843.

Calhoun, John C. "Mr. Calhoun's Parliamentary Eloquence," *United States Magazine and Democratic Review,* Vol. XIV (February 1844), pp. 111-130.

Calhoun, John C. *Works of John C. Calhoun;* Richard K. Crallé, ed. New York, 1854-1857.

Calhoun, John C. "Works of Calhoun," *Southern Literary Messenger,* Vol. XX (June 1854), pp. 321-330.

Capers, Henry D. *The Life and Times of C. G. Memminger.* Richmond, 1893.

Carpenter, Frank G. "A Talk with a President's Son," *Lippincott's Monthly Magazine,* Vol. XLI (March 1888), pp. 416-421.

Carpenter, Jesse T. *The South as a Conscious Minority, 1789-1861; a Study in Political Thought.* New York, 1930.

Carsel, Wilfred. "The Slaveholders' Indictment of Northern Wage Slavery," *Journal of Southern History*, Vol. VI (November 1940), pp. 504-520.

Carson, James Petigru. *Life, Letters and Speeches of James Louis Petigru.* Washington, 1920.

Cash, W. J. *The Mind of the South.* New York, 1941.

Channing, Edward. *History of the United States.* Vols. V and VI. New York, 1937-1938.

Chase, Salmon P. *Diary and Correspondence of Salmon P. Chase.* Annual Report of the American Historical Association, 1902. Vol. II. Washington, 1903.

Chitwood, Oliver Perry. *John Tyler, Champion of the Old South.* New York, 1939.

Christman, Henry. *Tin Horns and Calico.* New York, 1945.

Claiborne, J. F. H. *Life and Correspondence of John A. Quitman.* 2 vols. New York, 1860.

Clapham, J. H. *An Economic History of Modern Britain.* Vol. I. Cambridge, 1926.

Clark, Bennett Champ. *John Quincy Adams, "Old Man Eloquent."* Boston, 1932.

Clark, R. C. "British and American Tariff Policies and their Influence on the Oregon Boundary Treaty," American Historical Association, Pacific Coast Branch, *Proceedings*, 1926, pp. 32-49.

Clark, Victor A. *History of Manufactures in the United States.* 3 vols. New York, 1929.

Clay, Henry. *The Works of Henry Clay;* Calvin Colton, ed. 10 vols. New York & London, 1904.

Cleaves, Freeman. *Old Tippecanoe: William Henry Harrison and his Time.* New York & London, 1939.

Cobb, Howell. "Howell Cobb Papers"; Robert P. Brooks, ed. *Georgia Historical Quarterly*, Vol. V, No. 1 (March 1921), pp. 50-61; No. 2 (June 1921), pp. 29-52; No. 3 (September 1921), pp. 35-55.

Coit, Margaret L. *John C. Calhoun, American Portrait.* Boston, 1950.

Cole, Arthur Charles. *The Whig Party in the South.* Washington, 1913.

Coleman, Mrs. Chapman. *The Life of John J. Crittenden, with Selections from his Correspondence and Speeches.* 2 vols. Philadelphia, 1871.

Commager, Henry. "England and Oregon Treaty of 1846," *Oregon Historical Quarterly*, XXVIII (March 1927), pp. 18-38.

Condon, William H. *Life of James Shields.* Chicago, 1900.

Congressional Globe. Twenty-sixth Congress, First Session, to Thirty-first Congress, First Session. Vols. 8-19. Washington, 1840-1850.

Corey, Albert B. *The Crisis of 1830-1842 in Canadian-American Relations.* New Haven, 1941.

Cotterill, R. S. "Southern Railroads and Western Trade, 1840-1850," *Mississippi Valley Historical Review*, Vol. III (March 1917), pp. 427-441.

Cotterill, R. S. "The Telegraph in the South, 1845-1850," *South Atlantic Quarterly*, Vol. XV (April 1917), pp. 149-154.

Craven, Avery. *The Coming of the Civil War.* New York, 1942.

Craven, Avery. "Poor Whites and Negroes in the Antebellum South," *Journal of Negro History*, Vol. XV (January 1930), pp. 14-25.

Current, Richard Nelson. "John C. Calhoun, Philosopher of Reaction," *Antioch Review*, Vol. III (Summer 1943), pp. 223-234.

Curry, J. L. M. *Principles, Utterances and Acts of John C. Calhoun, promotive of the True Union of the States.* Chicago, 1898.

Curtis, George Ticknor. *Life of James Buchanan.* 2 vols. New York, 1883.

Curtis, George Ticknor. *Life of Daniel Webster.* 2 vols. New York, 1870.

Darling, Arthur B. *Political Changes in Massachusetts, 1824-48; a Study of Liberal Movements in Politics.* New Haven, 1925.

Davis, Jefferson. "Life and Character of the Hon. John Caldwell Calhoun," *North American Review,* Vol. CXLV (September 1887), pp. 246-260.

Davis, Varina Howell. *Jefferson Davis, Ex-President of the Confederate States of America: A Memoir.* 2 vols. New York, 1890.

Denman, Clarence P. *The Secession Movement in Alabama.* Montgomery, Ala., 1933.

Dickens, Charles. *American Notes.* Paris, 1842.

Dictionary of American Biography. 20 vols. New York, 1928-1936.

Dix, Morgan, comp. *Memoirs of John Adams Dix.* 2 vols. New York, 1883.

Dixon, James. *Personal Narrative of a Tour through a Part of the United States and Canada.* New York, 1849.

Dodd, Dorothy. "The Secession Movement in Florida," *Florida Historical Quarterly,* Vol. XII (July, October 1933), pp. 3-24, 45-66.

Dodd, William E. *The Cotton Kingdom.* New Haven, 1919.

Dodd, William E. *Statesmen of the Old South.* New York, 1911.

Donovan, Herbert D. A. *The Barnburners.* New York, 1925.

Dorfman, Joseph. *The Economic Mind in American Civilization.* Vol. II. New York, 1946.

DuBose, John W. *William Lowndes Yancey.* 2 vols. Birmingham, Ala., 1892.

Dumond, Dwight L. *The Antislavery Origins of the Civil War in the United States.* Ann Arbor, 1939.

Duniway, Clyde A. "Daniel Webster," *American Secretaries of State and their Diplomacy,* Vol. V, pp. 3-64. New York, 1928.

Dyer, Brainard. *Zachary Taylor.* Baton Rouge, 1946.

Dyer, Brainard. "Zachary Taylor and the Election of 1848," *Pacific Historical Review,* Vol. IX (June 1940), pp. 173-182.

Dyer, Oliver. *Great Senators of the United States Forty Years Ago, 1848-1849.* New York, 1889.

Easterby, J. Harold. *The South Carolina Rice Plantation.* Chicago, 1945.

Eaton, Clement. *Freedom of Thought in the Old South.* Durham, N. C., 1940.

Ellet, Mrs. Elizabeth F. *Court Circles of the Republic.* Hartford, 1869.

Elliott, Charles Winslow. *Winfield Scott: The Soldier and the Man.* New York, 1937.

Ewing, Thomas. "Diary of Thomas Ewing, August and September, 1841," *American Historical Review,* Vol. XVIII (October 1912), pp. 97-112.

Fisher, Ellwood. *The North and the South.* Cincinnati, 1849.

Fisher, George Park. *Life of Benjamin Silliman.* 2 vols. New York, 1866.

Fisher, George Park. "Webster and Calhoun in the Compromise Debate of 1850," *Scribner's Magazine,* Vol. XXXVII (May 1905), pp. 578-586.

Flippin, Percy Scott. *Herschel V. Johnson of Georgia, State Rights Unionist.* Richmond, 1931.

Follett, Oran. "Selections from the Follett Papers"; L. Belle Hamlin, ed. *Historical and Philosophical Society of Ohio, Quarterly Publications,* Vols. IX-XI, *passim.*

Foote, Henry Stuart. *Casket of Reminiscences.* Washington, 1874.

Foote, Henry Stuart. *War of the Rebellion.* New York, 1866.

Franklin, John Hope. *From Slavery to Freedom.* New York, 1947.

Fuess, Claude Moore. *Daniel Webster.* 2 vols. Boston, 1930.

Fuess, Claude Moore. *Life of Caleb Cushing.* 2 vols. New York, 1923.

Fuller, John D. P. "Slavery Propaganda during the Mexican War," *Southwestern Historical Quarterly,* Vol. XXXVIII (April 1935), pp. 235-245.

Gardiner, Oliver C. *The Great Issue.* New York, 1848.

Garnett, M. R. H. "Calhoun on Government," *Southern Quarterly Review,* Vol. XXIII (April 1853), pp. 333-379.

Garraty, John Arthur. *Silas Wright.* New York, 1949.

Giddings, Joshua R. *History of the Rebellion: Its Authors and Causes.* New York, 1864.

Godwin, Parke. *Democracy, Constructive and Pacific.* New York, 1844.

Godwin, Parke. *A Popular View of the Doctrines of Charles Fourier.* New York, 1844.

Going, Charles Buxton. *David Wilmot, Free Soiler.* New York, 1924.

Gordon, Armistead C. *William Fitzhugh Gordon, a Virginian of the Old School.* New York & Washington, 1909.

Green, Benjamin E. "Calhoun—Nullification Explained," Southern Historical Society, *Papers,* Vol. XIV (1886), pp. 226-241.

Green, Duff. *Facts and Suggestions, Biographical, Historical, Financial and Political.* New York, 1866.

Green, Edwin L. *George McDuffie.* Columbia, S. C., 1936.

Green, Fletcher M. "Duff Green: Industrial Promoter," *Journal of Southern History,* Vol. II (February 1936), pp. 29-42.

Greene, William. "Selections from the William Greene Papers"; L. Belle Hamlin, ed. Historical and Philosophical Society of Ohio, *Quarterly Publications,* Vols. XIII-XIV, *passim.*

Gregg, William. *Essays on Domestic Industry.* Graniteville, S. C., 1941.

Gurney, Joseph John. *A Journey in North America.* Norwich, Eng., 1841.

Hamer, Philip May. *The Secession Movement in South Carolina, 1847-1852.* Philadelphia, 1918.

Hamilton, Holman. *Zachary Taylor.* 2 vols. Indianapolis & New York, 1941-1951.

Hamilton, James A. *Reminiscences of James A. Hamilton.* New York, 1869.

Hamilton, James G. de Roulhac. *Party Politics in North Carolina, 1835-1860.* Chapel Hill, 1916.

Hammond, Jabez D. *Life and Times of Silas Wright, Late Governor of the State of New York.* Syracuse, N. Y., 1848.

Hammond, James Henry. *Selections from Letters and Speeches.* New York, 1866.

Hansard's Parliamentary Debates. 3rd series, vols. 60-88. London, 1842-1846.

Harvey, Peter. *Reminiscences and Anecdotes of Daniel Webster.* Boston, 1882.

Hearon, Cleo. *Mississippi and the Compromise of 1850.* Oxford, Miss., 1913.

Hofstadter, Richard. *The American Political Tradition and the Men Who Made It.* New York, 1948.

Hollis, Christopher. *The American Heresy.* New York, 1930.

Holmes, Alester Garden. "John C. Calhoun," *Southern Magazine,* Vol. II, No. 10 (1936).

Holmes, Alester Garden, and George R. Sherrill. *Thomas G. Clemson: His Life and Work.* Richmond, 1937.

Holst, Herman von. *John C. Calhoun.* Boston, 1882.

Hone, Philip. *Diary of Philip Hone, 1828-1851;* Allan Nevins, ed. New York, 1936.

Houston, Sam. *The Writings of Sam Houston, 1813-1863;* Amelia W. Williams and Eugene C. Barker, eds. Vols. III-V. Austin, 1938-1943.

Howe, M. A. de Wolfe. *Life and Letters of George Bancroft.* 2 vols. New York, 1908.

Hunt, Gaillard. *John C. Calhoun.* Philadelphia, 1908.

Hunter, Martha T. *A Memoir of Robert M. T. Hunter.* Washington, 1903.

Hunter, Robert M. T. *Correspondence of Robert M. T. Hunter, 1826-1876;* C. H. Ambler, ed. Annual Report of the American Historical Association, 1916. Vol. II. Washington, 1918.

[Hunter, Robert M. T.]. *Life of John C. Calhoun.* New York, 1843.

Ingersoll, Ernest. "The Calhoun Summer Home," *Scribner's Monthly,* Vol. XXI (April 1881), pp. 892-895.

Jackson, Andrew. *Correspondence of Andrew Jackson;* J. S. Bassett, ed. Vol. VI. Washington, 1935.

Jenkins, John S. *Life of John Caldwell Calhoun.* Auburn & Buffalo, 1850.

Jenkins, William S. *Pro-Slavery Thought in the Old South.* Chapel Hill, 1935.

Johnson, Herschel V. "Herschel V. Johnson Correspondence"; Percy S. Flippin, ed. *North Carolina Historical Review,* Vol. IV (April 1927), pp. 182-201.

Jones, Anson. *Memoranda and Official Correspondence.* New York, 1859.

Jordan, H. Donaldson. "A Politician of Expansion: Robert J. Walker," *Mississippi Valley Historical Review,* Vol. XIX (December 1932), pp. 362-381.

Journal of the Executive Proceedings of the Senate of the United States. Vols. 5-8. Washington, 1887.

Journal of the House of Representatives of the United States. 26th-31st Congresses. Washington, 1840-1850.

Journal of the Senate of the United States. 26th-31st Congresses. Washington, 1839[1840]-1850.

Julian, George W. *Political Recollections.* Chicago, 1884.

Kendall, Amos. *Autobiography of Amos Kendall;* William Stickney, ed. Boston, 1872.

Kibler, Lillian Adele. *Benjamin F. Perry, South Carolina Unionist.* Durham, N. C.

Lambert, Oscar Doane. *Presidential Politics in the United States, 1841-1844.* Durham, N. C., 1936.

Lloyd, Arthur Young. *The Slavery Controversy, 1831-1860.* Chapel Hill, 1939.

Longstreet, Augustus B. "Review of Ex-Gov. Perry's Sketch of J. C. Calhoun," *XIX Century,* Vol. II (January 1870), pp. 618-623.

Lowndes [pseud.]. Letters of Lowndes, addressed to the Hon. John C. Calhoun. Philadelphia, 1843.

Lunt, George. *The Origin of the Late War.* New York, 1866.

Lyell, Charles. *Travels in North America.* 2 vols. London, 1845.

Lyman, S. P. *Life and Memorials of Daniel Webster.* New York, 1853.

Lynch, Denis Tilden. *An Epoch and a Man; Martin Van Buren and His Times.* New York, 1929.

McCormac, E. I. *James K. Polk.* Berkeley, Calif., 1922.

McGrane, Reginald C. *Foreign Bondholders and American State Debts.* New York, 1935.

Mackay, Alexander. *The Western World; or Travels in the United States in 1846-47.* 3 vols. London, 1849.

McLaughlin, Andrew C. *Constitutional History of the United States.* New York, 1935.

McLaughlin, Andrew C. *Lewis Cass.* New York, 1899.

Manning, William R., ed. *Diplomatic Correspondence of the United States, Canadian Relations.* Vol. III. Washington, 1943.

Manning, William R., ed. *Diplomatic Correspondence of the United States, Inter-American Affairs, 1831-1860.* Vols. VII, VIII, XII. Washington, 1940-1945.

Martin, Thomas P. "Conflicting Cotton Interests at Home and Abroad, 1848-1857," *Journal of Southern History,* Vol. VII (May 1941), pp. 173-194.

Martin, Thomas P. "Cotton and Wheat in Anglo-American Trade and Politics, 1846-1852," *Journal of Southern History,* Vol. I (August 1935), pp. 293-319.

Martin, Thomas P. "Free Trade and the Oregon Question, 1842-1846," *Facts and Factors in Economic History,* 470-491. Cambridge, Mass., 1932.

Martin, Thomas P. "Some International Aspects of the Anti-Slavery Movement, 1818-1823," *Journal of Economic and Business History,* Vol. I (November 1928), pp. 137-148.

Martin, Thomas P. "The Upper Mississippi Valley in Anglo-American Anti-Slavery and Free Trade Relations: 1837-1842," *Mississippi Valley Historical Review,* Vol. XV (September 1928), pp. 204-220.

Mason, Virginia, ed. *Public Life and Diplomatic Correspondence of James M. Mason.* Roanoke, Va., 1903.

Maury, Sarah Mytton. *Statesmen of America in 1846.* Philadelphia, 1847.

[Maxcy, Virgil]. *Democratic National Convention.* New York, 1843.

Meigs, William Montgomery. *Life of Charles J. Ingersoll.* Philadelphia, 1897.

Meigs, William Montgomery. *Life of John Caldwell Calhoun.* 2 vols. New York, 1917.

Meigs, William Montgomery. *The Life of Thomas Hart Benton.* Philadelphia, 1904.

Merk, Frederick. "The British Corn Crisis of 1845-46 and the Oregon Treaty," *Agricultural History,* Vol. VIII (July 1934), pp. 95-123.

Merk, Frederick. "British Party Politics and the Oregon Treaty," *American Historical Review,* Vol. XXXVII (July 1932), pp. 653-677.

Merritt, Elizabeth. *James Henry Hammond, 1807-1864.* Baltimore, 1923.

Messages and Papers of the Presidents; J. D. Richardson, comp. 20 vols. New York, 1897-1927.

Miller, [David] Hunter, ed. *Treaties and other International Acts of the United States of America.* Vol. V. Washington, 1931.

Mitchell, Stewart. *Horatio Seymour of New York.* Cambridge, Mass., 1938.

Mowry, Arthur May. *The Dorr War.* Providence, R. I., 1901.

Nevins, Allan. *Frémont, Pathmarker of the West.* New York, 1939.

Nevins, Allan. *Ordeal of the Union.* 2 vols. New York, 1947.

Nichols, Roy Franklin. *Franklin Pierce, Young Hickory of the Granite Hills.* Philadelphia & London, 1931.

Norwood, John Nelson. *The Schism in the Methodist Episcopal Church, 1844.* Alfred, N. Y., 1923.

O'Neall, John Belton. *Biographical Sketches of the Bench and Bar of South Carolina.* 2 vols. Charleston, 1859.

Parton, James. "John C. Calhoun," *Famous Americans of Recent Times,* pp. 113-171. Boston, 1883.

Peel, Sir Robert. *Memoirs of Sir Robert Peel.* 2 vols. London, 1856-1858.

Pendleton, Louis. *Alexander H. Stephens.* Philadelphia, 1908.

Perry, Benjamin F. *Letters of Gov. Benjamin Franklin Perry to his Wife.* Second series. Greenville, S. C., 1890.

Perry, Benjamin F. *Reminiscences of Public Men.* Philadelphia, 1883.

Perry, Benjamin F. *Reminiscences of Public Men, with Speeches and Addresses.* Second series. Greenville, S. C., 1889.

Persinger, Clark E. "The 'Bargain of 1844' as the Origin of the Wilmot Proviso," Annual Report of the American Historical Association, 1911. Vol. I, pp. 187-195. Washington, 1913.

Phillips, Ulrich B., ed. *Correspondence of Robert Toombs, Alexander H. Stephens, and Howell Cobb.* Annual Report of the American Historical Association, 1911. Vol. II. Washington, 1913.

Phillips, Ulrich B. *The Course of the South to Secession;* E. Merton Coulter, ed. New York, 1939.

Phillips, Ulrich B. *Georgia and State Rights.* Annual Report of the American Historical Association, 1901. Vol. II. Washington, 1902.

Phillips, Ulrich B. *A History of Transportation in the Eastern Cotton Belt.* New York, 1908.

Phillips, Ulrich B. *Life and Labor in the Old South.* Boston, 1929.

Phillips, Ulrich B. *Life of Robert Toombs.* New York, 1913.

Phillips, Ulrich B. "The Southern Whigs, 1834-1854," *Essays in American History Dedicated to Frederick Jackson Turner,* 203-216. New York, 1910.

Pinckney, Charles Cotesworth. "John C. Calhoun, from a Southern Stand-Point," *Lippincott's Monthly Magazine,* Vol. LXII (July 1898), pp. 81-90.

Pinckney, Gustavus M. *Life of John C. Calhoun.* Charleston, 1903.

Poage, George Rawlings. *Henry Clay and the Whig Party.* Chapel Hill, 1936.

Polk, James K. *The Diary of James K. Polk, during his Presidency, 1845-1849;* M. M. Quaife, ed. Chicago, 1910.

Polk, James K. "Letters to Andrew J. Donelson, 1843-1848"; St. G. L. Sioussat, ed. *Tennessee Historical Magazine,* Vol. III (March 1917), pp. 51-73.

Polk, James K. "Letters to Cave Johnson, 1833-48"; St. G. L. Sioussat, ed. *Tennessee Historical Magazine,* Vol. I (September 1915), pp. 209-256.

Polk, James K. "Letters of Gideon Pillow to James K. Polk, 1844"; J. S. Reeves, ed. *American Historical Review,* Vol. XI (July 1906), pp. 832-843.

Polk, James K. "Unpublished Letters from North Carolinians to Polk"; Elizabeth G. McPherson, ed. *North Carolina Historical Review,* Vol. XVI (1939) and XVII (1940), *passim.*

Poore, Ben Perley. *Perley's Reminiscences of Sixty Years in the National Metropolis.* 2 vols. Philadelphia, 1886.

Prescott, William Hickling. *Correspondence of William Hickling Prescott, 1833-1847;* Roger Wolcott, ed. Boston, 1925.

Proctor, John Claggett, ed. *Washington, Past and Present; a History.* 4 vols. New York, 1930.

Ramsdell, Charles W. "The Natural Limits of Slavery Expansion," *Mississippi Valley Historical Review,* Vol. XVI (September 1929), pp. 151-171.

Reeves, Jesse Slidell. *American Diplomacy under Tyler and Polk*. Baltimore, 1907.

Rezneck, Samuel. "The Social History of an American Depression, 1837-43," *American Historical Review*, Vol. XL (July 1935), pp. 662-687.

Rhea, Linda. *Hugh Swinton Legaré, a Charleston Intellectual*. Chapel Hill, 1934.

Ritchie, Thomas. *Reminiscences of Henry Clay and the Compromise*. Richmond, 1852.

Ritchie, Thomas. "Ritchie Letters," *John P. Branch Historical Papers*, Vol. III, pp. 354-357; Vol. IV, pp. 372-418.

Ruffin, Edmund. "Edmund Ruffin's Visit to John Tyler," *William and Mary Quarterly*, Vol. XIV (January 1906), pp. 193-211.

Russel, Robert R. *Economic Aspects of Southern Sectionalism, 1840-1861*. Urbana, Ill., 1922.

Russel, Robert R. "A Revaluation of the Period before the Civil War: Railroads," *Mississippi Valley Historical Review*, Vol. XV (December 1928), pp. 341-354.

Sargent, Nathan. *Public Men and Events from the Commencement of Mr. Monroe's Administration, in 1817, to the Close of Mr. Fillmore's Administration, in 1853*. 2 vols. Philadelphia, 1875.

Schafer, Joseph. "The British Attitude toward the Oregon Question, 1815-1846," *American Historical Review*, Vol. XVI (January 1911), pp. 273-299.

Schafer, Joseph, ed. "Documents Relative to Warre and Vavasour's Military Reconoisance in Oregon, 1845-46," *Oregon Historical Quarterly*, Vol. X (March 1909), 1-99.

Schafer, Joseph. "Oregon Pioneers and American Diplomacy," *Essays in American History Dedicated to Frederick Jackson Turner*, pp. 35-55. New York, 1910.

Schaper, William A. *Sectionalism and Representation in South Carolina*. Annual Report of the American Historical Association, 1900. Vol. I, pp. 237-463. Washington, 1901.

Schlesinger, Arthur M., Jr. *The Age of Jackson*. New York, 1945.

[Scoville, Joseph A. ?]. "A Visit to Fort Hill," New York *Herald*, July 26, 1849.

Sears, Louis Martin. *John Slidell*. Durham, N. C., 1925.

Seaton, Josephine. *William Winston Seaton of the "National Intelligencer."* Boston, 1871.

Seward, William H. *Autobiography of William H. Seward . . . with a Memoir . . . and Selections from His Letters;* Frederick W. Seward, ed. New York, 1877.

Shanks, Henry Thomas. *The Secession Movement in Virginia, 1847-1861*. Richmond, 1934.

Shryock, Richard H. *Georgia and the Union in 1850*. Durham, N. C., 1926.

Simms, Henry Harrison. *Life of Robert M. T. Hunter*. Richmond, 1935.

Simpson, Richard Wright. *History of Old Pendleton District*. Anderson, S. C., 1913.

Sioussat, St. George L., ed. "The Accident on Board the U. S. S. Princeton, February 28, 1844: A Contemporary News-Letter," *Pennsylvania History*, Vol. IV (July 1937), pp. 161-189.

Sioussat, St. George L., ed. "Duff Green's 'England and the United States,' with an Introductory Study of American Opposition to the Quintuple Treaty of 1841," American Antiquarian Society, *Proceedings*, n.s., Vol. XL (October 1930), pp. 175-276.

Sioussat, St. George L. "James Buchanan," *American Secretaries of State and Their Diplomacy*, Vol. V, pp. 237-336.

Sioussat, St. George L. "John Caldwell Calhoun," *American Secretaries of State and Their Diplomacy*, Vol. V, 127-233.

Sitterson, J. Carlyle. *The Secession Movement in North Carolina*. Chapel Hill, 1939.

Sloan, Dave M. *Fogy Days, and Now; or, The World Has Changed*. Atlanta, 1891.

Smith, Ashbel. *Reminiscences of the Texas Republic*. Galveston, 1876.

Smith, Justin H. *The Annexation of Texas*. Corrected edition. New York, 1941.

Smith, Justin H. *The War with Mexico*. 2 vols. New York, 1919.

Smith, William E. *The Francis Preston Blair Family in Politics*. 2 vols. New York, 1933.

Smith, William L. G. *Fifty Years of Public Life: The Life and Times of Lewis Cass*. New York, 1856.

Soulsby, Hugh G. *The Right of Search and the Slave Trade in Anglo-American Relations, 1814-1862*. Baltimore, 1933.

Stanwood, Edward. *American Tariff Controversies in the Nineteenth Century*. 2 vols. Boston & New York, 1903.

Stanwood, Edward. *A History of the Presidency*. 2 vols. Boston & New York, 1930.

Steiner, Bernard C. *Life of Reverdy Johnson*. Baltimore, 1914.

Stenberg, Richard R. "The Failure of Polk's Mexican War Intrigue of 1845," *Pacific Historical Review*, Vol. IV (March 1935), pp. 39-68.

Stephenson, Nathaniel W. "Calhoun and the Divine Right of the Majority," *Lectures on Typical Americans and Their Problems*. Scripps College Papers, No. 3. Claremont, Calif., 1930.

Story, William W. *Life and Letters of Joseph Story*. 2 vols. Boston, 1851.

Sturge, Joseph. *A Visit to the United States in 1841*. Boston, 1842.

Styron, Arthur. *The Cast-iron Man; John C. Calhoun and American Democracy*. New York & Toronto, 1935.

Swisher, Carl Brent. *Roger B. Taney*. New York, 1935.

Sydnor, Charles S. *Development of Southern Sectionalism, 1819-1848*. Baton Rouge, 1948.

Texas. *Diplomatic Correspondence of the Republic of Texas;* George P. Garrison, ed. Annual Reports of the American Historical Association, 1907, vol. II; 1908, vol. II. Washington, 1908, 1909.

Ticknor, George. *Life, Letters and Journals of George Ticknor;* Anna Ticknor and G. S. Hillard, eds. 2 vols. Boston, 1876.

Torrence, George P. "Selections from the Torrence Papers"; Isaac J. Cox, ed. Historical and Philosophical Society of Ohio, *Quarterly Publications*, Vols. I-VI, *passim*.

Trent, William Peterfield. *Southern Statesmen of the Old Regime*. New York, 1897.

Turner, Frederick Jackson. *The Significance of Sections in American History*. New York, 1932.

Turner, Frederick Jackson. *The United States, 1830-1850*. New York, 1935.

Tyler, Julia Gardiner. "Letters from Tyler Trunks," *Tyler's Quarterly Historical and Genealogical Magazine,* Vol. XVIII (July, October, 1936, January 1937), pp. 8-31, 88-97, 141-163.

Tyler, Lyon Gardiner. *The Letters and Times of the Tylers.* 3 vols. Richmond, 1884-1896.

Van Buren, Martin. "Unpublished Letters from North Carolinians to Van Buren"; Elizabeth G. McPherson, ed. *North Carolina Historical Review,* Vol. XV (1938), *passim.*

Van Deusen, Glyndon G. *The Life of Henry Clay.* Boston, 1937.

Van Deusen, John G. *The Ante-Bellum Southern Commercial Conventions.* Durham, N. C., 1926.

Van Deusen, John G. *Economic Bases of Disunion in South Carolina.* New York, 1928.

Wallace, David Duncan. *History of South Carolina.* 4 vols. New York, 1934.

Walmsley, James Elliott. "The Return of John C. Calhoun to the Senate in 1845," Annual Report of the American Historical Association, 1913. Vol. I, pp. 161-165.

Webster, Daniel. "Letters to Thomas B. Curtis, 1844-1851," Massachusetts Historical Society, *Proceedings,* Vol. XLV, pp. 159-165.

Webster, Daniel. "Correspondence with John Tyler," *Tyler's Quarterly Historical and Genealogical Magazine,* Vol. VIII (July 1926), pp. 16-29.

Webster, Daniel. *The Writings and Speeches of Daniel Webster;* National Edition. 18 vols. Boston, 1903.

Weed, Thurlow. *Autobiography of Thurlow Weed;* Harriet A. Weed, ed. Boston, 1883.

Weisenburger, Francis P. *The Life of John McLean; a Politician on the United States Supreme Court.* Columbus, O., 1837.

Weld, Theodore D. *Letters of Theodore Dwight Weld, Angelina Grimké Weld, and Sarah Grimké, 1822-1844;* Gilbert H. Barnes and Dwight L. Dumond, eds. 2 vols. New York, 1934.

Wender, Herbert. *Southern Commercial Conventions, 1837-1859.* Baltimore, 1930.

Wentworth, John. *Congressional Reminiscences.* Chicago, 1882.

White, Laura A. *Robert Barnwell Rhett: Father of Secession.* New York, 1931.

Williams, Eric. *Capitalism and Slavery.* Chapel Hill, 1944.

Willis, Nathaniel P. *Hurrygraphs; or, Sketches of Scenery, Celebrities and Society, taken from Life.* London, 1851.

Wiltse, Charles M. "Calhoun: An Interpretation." South Carolina Historical Association, *Proceedings,* 1948, pp. 26-38.

Wiltse, Charles M. "Calhoun and the Modern State," *Virginia Quarterly Review,* Vol. XIII (Summer 1937), pp. 396-408.

Wiltse, Charles M. "Calhoun's Democracy," *Journal of Politics,* Vol. III (May 1941), pp. 210-223.

Wiltse, Charles M. "A Critical Southerner: John C. Calhoun on the Revolutions of 1848," *Journal of Southern History,* Vol. XV (August 1949), pp. 299-310.

Wiltse, Charles M. "From Compact to National State in American Political Thought," *Essays in Political Theory Presented to George H. Sabine,* pp. 153-178. Ithaca, N. Y., 1948.

Wise, Barton H. *Life of Henry A. Wise of Virginia.* New York, 1899.

Wise, Henry A. *Seven Decades of the Union.* Philadelphia, 1872.

Woodford, Frank B. *Lewis Cass, the Last Jeffersonian.* New Brunswick, N. J., 1950.

Woodley, Thomas F. *Thaddeus Stevens.* New York, 1937.

Yancey, William Lowndes. Address on the Life and Character of John C. Calhoun. Montgomery, Ala., 1850.

PERSONAL ACKNOWLEDGMENTS

THIS third and final volume of the life of Calhoun has been completed only with the generous assistance of many individuals and institutions. For financial aid over a two-year period I am indebted to the John Simon Guggenheim Memorial Foundation. Much of the research and all of the actual writing has been done at the Library of Congress, and I wish to acknowledge especially the numerous contributions made by the staffs of the Manuscript Division, the Stack and Reader Division, and the Newspaper Reference Room. To the Library of Clemson College, where the largest collection of Calhoun papers is housed, my obligation is also great. Another major source of material was the South Caroliniana Library at the University of South Carolina whose able director, Professor Robert L. Meriwether, has answered my queries in person and by mail over a period of years with unfailing zeal and good humor. To a lesser but still substantial extent I am indebted to librarians and scholars at Duke University, the University of North Carolina, the Charleston Library Society, the South Carolina Historical Society, and the College of Charleston. To the National Archives I am under obligation both for the privilege of examining the State Department records and for many of the illustrations in this volume.

The entire manuscript has been read and criticized with cordial severity by Mr. Holman Hamilton of Fort Wayne, Indiana, whose own long sojourn in the same period as biographer of Zachary Taylor has given him a special competence for the task. I can only say that the book is much better than it would have been without Mr. Hamilton's friendly stricture. Chapters V and XXIII, dealing with aspects of the slavery controversy, have been read in manuscript by Professor John Hope Franklin of Howard University; and Chapter XXIII, because it deals in part with events in Europe, has also been read by Professor Jerome Blum of Princeton University. Chapters IV and XIV, dealing primarily with South Carolina politics, and Chapters IX and XXIX, concerned mainly with Calhoun's personal and family affairs, have been read by Professor A. G. Holmes of Clemson College. Professor Robert S. Lambert of Clemson reviewed the chapters dealing with the Presidential campaign of 1844. Chapters V and XVIII, which include much in the way of economic history as well as Anglo-American relations, have been read by Professor Thomas P. Martin of the University of Indiana. I am indebted to Professor Merle Curti of the University of Wisconsin for a careful reading of Chapter XXVIII, which is devoted to Calhoun's political theory. To each of these critics my thanks are due for helpful suggestions, and especially for saving me from errors I might otherwise have made. Needless to say, however, no one of them may be held responsible in any way for the interpretations and judgments in the volume.

The end papers are again the work of Miss Frances Shattuck of Washington, as is the map accompanying Chapter IX. Miss Shattuck also gave a general editorial review to the entire manuscript, which was typed by Mr. David B. Washington. For skillful assistance with the index I am indebted to Miss Kelly T. Tooks. Credits for the pictures are included in the List of Illustrations at the front of the volume.

INDEX

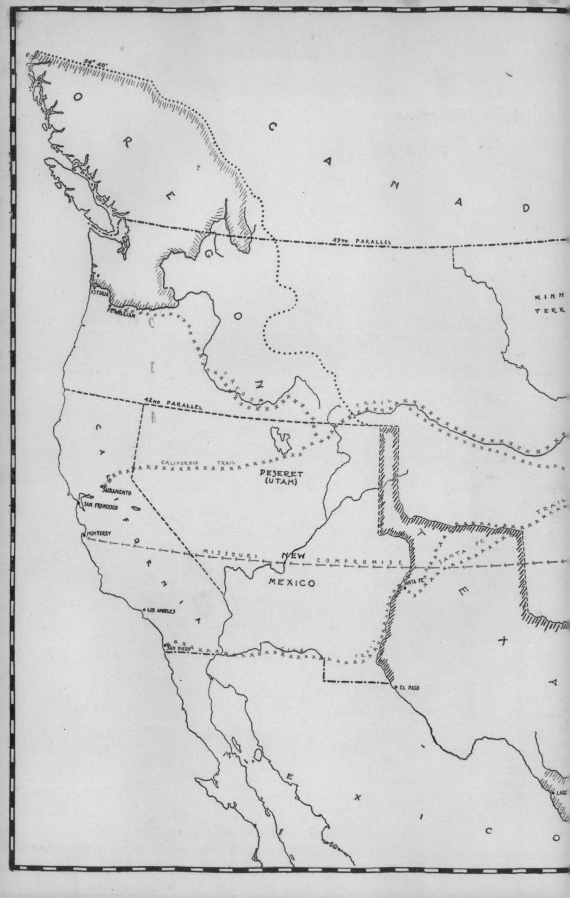